# Financial Market Analysis

## Second Edition

*David Blake*

JOHN WILEY & SONS, LTD

Chichester · New York · Weinheim · Brisbane · Singapore · Toronto

Email (for orders and customer service enquiries): cs-books@wiley.co.uk
Visit our Home Page on www.wileyeurope.com or www.wiley.com

First edition published 1990 by McGraw-Hill Publishing Company

Reprinted with corrections July 2001 and September 2002, December 2003, April 2004
January 2005, April 2006

Reprinted May 2007

*Other Wiley Editorial Offices*

John Wiley & Sons Inc., 111 River Street, Hoboken, NJ 07030, USA

Jossey-Bass, 989 Market Street, San Francisco, CA 94103-1741, USA

Wiley-VCH Verlag GmbH, Boschstr. 12, D-69469 Weinheim, Germany

John Wiley & Sons Australia Ltd, 33 Park Road, Milton, Queensland 4064, Australia

John Wiley & Sons (Asia) Pte Ltd, 2 Clementi Loop #02-01, Jin Xing Distripark, Singapore
129809

John Wiley & Sons Canada Ltd, 22 Worcester Road, Etobicoke, Ontario, Canada M9W 1L1

*British Library Cataloguing in Publication Data*

A catalogue record for this book is available from the British Library

ISBN-13: 978-0-471-87728-8 (P/B)

Printed and bound in Great Britain by Antony Rowe Ltd, Chippenham, Wiltshire
This book is printed on acid-free paper responsibly manufactured from sustainable forestry
in which at least two trees are planted for each one used for paper production.

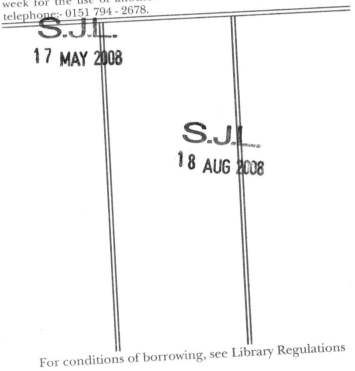
Financial M

*'To a little tiger.'*

# Contents

# Preface

This book deals with the following issues:

- the structure of financial markets with special reference to the UK;

- the analysis and valuation of securities traded in financial markets;

- the use of securities in constructing portfolios, in managing portfolios and in contributing to portfolio performance;

- the causes of failure in financial markets;

- recent developments in the analysis of financial markets.

The aim is to provide readers with a good understanding of the practice of analyzing financial markets from within the framework of modern finance theory. Modern finance theory offers certain predictions about how an efficiently organized financial system operates, and we will examine the practice of financial market analysis in the light of these predictions. For example, we will examine how securities such as bonds and shares ought to be analyzed and evaluated in the light of modern finance theory. Similarly, we will examine how securities ought to be structured in portfolios and how these portfolios ought to be managed in the light of modern finance theory. We can then compare the theory with the real world of security analysis and evaluation, and the theory with the real world of portfolio structuring and management, in order to determine how well practice corresponds with the theory, or, alternatively, how difficult the theory is to implement in practice.

This book was originally written for an advanced undergraduate course in financial market analysis at City University Business School. I felt that what was badly needed was a text that provided a comprehensive and up-to-date treatment of the analysis of financial markets, using numerous practical illustrations from the UK financial markets. The text should be sufficiently rigorous and should pay due attention to modern finance theory and its implications, without being a text on the principles of finance, of which there are many good examples. It should also provide sufficient illustrations of the various financial instruments and how they are used, but without being merely a handbook for professionals.

The nearest existing texts did not, in my view, meet these objectives. In particular, they paid inadequate attention (or worse, no attention at all) to the following issues:

- new types of investment product (e.g., synthetic securities, swaps, exotic options);

- different portfolio management strategies (e.g., passive/active management, bond *v.* equity *v.* treasury portfolio management);

- speculation and arbitrage strategies;

- hedging strategies;

- financial market failure;

- recent advances in financial market analysis (e.g., value-at-risk analysis, speculative bubbles, volatility clustering, asymmetry and spillovers, chaos and neural networks).

This text has chapters on all these topics.

While initially conceived as a text suitable for advanced undergraduates in UK universities, the resulting book is relevant to a much wider constituency. In particular, it is of relevance to postgraduates (both MSc and MBA), and it provides a useful source of reference to professionals in the financial markets. The text has subsequently been taught as an option on the M.Sc. (Economics) course at Birkbeck College and as part of the graduate induction programme of a number of major European investment banks. In addition, given the generality of approach, the book will be useful to both students and professionals worldwide.

The text does not require a strong quantitative background, although readers with no such background may find some sections hard going. Four useful books covering this area are T. Watsham and K. Parramore's *Quantitative Methods in Finance* (Thompson Business Press, London), J. Curwin and R. Slater's *Quantitative Methods for Business Decisions* (Van Nostrand Reinhold, London), S. Glaister's *Mathematical Methods for Economists* (Blackwell, Oxford) and G. Bancroft and G. O'Sullivan's *Maths and Statistics for Accounting and Business Studies* (McGraw-Hill, Maidenhead).

At the end of each chapter there is a set of exercises, most of which can be addressed using the material from the preceding chapter. Solutions to the exercises involving calculations are available to *bona fide* instructors free of charge from the publishers.

D.B.

# Acknowledgements

I am deeply indebted to the following for their help in preparing this edition of *Financial Market Analysis*: Sue Kirkbride for her superb efforts in typing the entire manuscript, Mina Moskeri for preparing the figures, Peter Cassidy for advice on the accounting section of Chapter 6, Michael Thompson for advice on publishing, Sarah Cheriton for checking the proofs, and Malcolm Hyatt for reading over and suggesting improvements to the manuscript and for typesetting the book.

# Abbreviations

| | |
|---|---|
| ACT | Advance corporation tax |
| ADR | American depository receipt |
| AIM | Alternative Investment Market |
| ALM | Asset-liability management |
| ANNA | Association of National Numbering Agencies |
| API | Application programming interface |
| APR | Annual percentage rate |
| APT | Arbitrage pricing theory (or Automated pit trading) |
| ARCH | Autoregressive conditional heteroscedasticity |
| ARCH-M | ARCH-in-mean |
| AUT | Authorized unit trust |
| ATOM | Automated trade order matching |
| BBAISR | British Bankers' Association interest settlement rate |
| BBS | Board of Banking Supervision |
| BECS | Bearer eurodollar collateralized security |
| BFI | Bank financial intermediary |
| BPV | Basis point value |
| BTF | Basis trade facility (or Block trading facility) |
| CAD | Capital Adequacy Directive |
| CAPM | Capital asset pricing model |
| CBOE | Chicago Board Options Exchange |
| CBOT | Chicago Board of Trade |
| CCA | Current cost accounting |
| CD | Certificate of deposit |
| CFX | Credit for Export PLC |
| CGT | Capital gains tax |
| CME | Chicago Mercantile Exchange |
| CML | Capital market line |
| CMO | Central Moneymarkets Office (or Collateralized mortgage obligation) |
| CP | Commercial paper |
| CPS | Clearing processing system |
| CRSP | Center for Research in Security Prices |
| CTD | Cheapest to deliver |
| DBV | Delivery by value |
| DGARCH | Dummy GARCH |
| DHR | Duration hedge ratio |

| | |
|---|---|
| DIE | Designated investment exchange |
| DM | Discounted margin (or Deutschmark) |
| DMO | Debt Management Office |
| DOT | Designated order turnaround |
| DTB | Deutscheterminbörse |
| DVP | Delivery-versus-payment |
| EASDAQ | European Association of Securities Dealers Automated Quotations |
| EBF | European Bankers' Federation |
| ECB | European Central Bank |
| ECHO | Exchange Clearing House |
| ECP | Eurocommercial paper |
| ECU | European currency unit |
| EDSP | Exchange delivery settlement price |
| EFA | European Financial Area |
| EFTPOS | Electronic funds transfer at the point of sale |
| EGARCH | Exponential GARCH |
| EMCF | European Monetary Co-operation Fund |
| EMH | Efficient markets hypothesis |
| EMI | European Monetary Institute |
| EMQS | Exchange minimum quote size |
| EMS | European Monetary System |
| EMU | Economic and monetary union |
| EPM | Efficient portfolio management |
| EPS | Earnings per share |
| ERB | Excess return to beta |
| ERM | Exchange rate mechanism (of the EMS) |
| ESCB | European System of Central Banks |
| ESCP | Eurosterling commercial paper |
| ESI | Electronic Share Information |
| EU | European Union |
| EURIBOR | European (EBF) interbank offered rate |
| FIFO | First in, first out |
| FLEX | Flexible exchange option |
| FOF | Futures and options fund |
| FOTRA | Free of tax to residents abroad |
| FRA | Forward rate agreement |
| FRN | Floating-rate note |
| FRS | Financial Reporting Standard |
| FSA | Financial Services Act 1986 (or Financial Services Authority) |
| FTSE | FTSE International (originally Financial Times – Stock Exchange) |
| GARCH | Generalized autoregressive conditional heteroscedasticity |
| GC | General collateral |
| GDP | Gross domestic product |
| GDR | Global depository receipt |
| GEMM | Gilt-edged market maker |
| GEMMA | Gilt Edged Market Makers Association |
| GFOF | Geared futures and options fund |
| GMRA | Global master repurchase agreement |

| | |
|---|---|
| GNMA | Government National Mortgage Association |
| GROI | Guaranteed return-on-investment |
| GSO | Gilts Settlements Office |
| ICCH | International Commodities Clearing House |
| IDB | Inter-dealer broker |
| IEM | International equity market |
| IIMR | Institute of Investment Management and Research |
| IMAS | Integrated Monitoring and Surveillance System |
| IMRO | Investment Managers Regulatory Organization |
| IOSCO | International Organization of Securities Commissions |
| IRG | Interest rate guarantee |
| ISD | Investment Services Directive |
| ISDA | International Swaps and Derivatives Association |
| ISIN | International security identification number |
| ISMA | International Securities Market Association |
| ISV | Independent software vendors |
| LBO | Leveraged buy-out |
| LCH | London Clearing House |
| LDA | Liability-driven asset |
| LDFRA | Long-dated FRA |
| LDPA | Liability-driven performance attribution |
| LIBID | London interbank bid rate |
| LIBOR | London interbank offered rate |
| LICOM | London Interbank Currency Options Market |
| LIFFE | London International Financial Futures and Options Exchange |
| LIFO | Last in, first out |
| LIMID | London interbank mid rate |
| LOTS | LIFFE order transit system |
| LSE | London Stock Exchange |
| LSM | Listed Securities Market |
| LTOM | London Traded Options Market |
| M&A | Mergers and acquisitions |
| MBB | Mortgage-backed bond |
| MBO | Management buy-out |
| MCF | Multiple component facility |
| MCT | Mainstream corporation tax |
| MD | Modified duration |
| MECS | Marketable eurodollar collateralized security |
| MLP | Multilayer perceptron |
| MMD | Money market deposit |
| MMQS | Market maker quote size |
| MPL | Maximum publication level |
| MRS | Marginal rate of substitution |
| MRT | Marginal rate of transformation |
| MSCI | Morgan Stanley Capital International |
| NASDAQ | National Association of Securities Dealers Automated Quotations |
| NBFI | Non-bank financial intermediary |
| NDO | National Debt Office |

| NERB | Net excess return to beta |
|------|---------------------------|
| NIF | Note issuance facility |
| NILO | National Investment and Loans Office |
| NMS | Normal market size |
| NSSR | National Savings Stock Register |
| NYSE | New York Stock Exchange |
| OECD | Organisation for Economic Co-operation and Development |
| OEIC | Open-ended investment company |
| OPR | Options position ratio |
| OTC | Over-the-counter |
| PDS | Price distribution system |
| PE | Price-earnings ratio |
| PIA | Personal Investment Authority |
| PIBs | Permanent income-bearing shares |
| PINC | Property income certificate |
| PIP | Protected index participation |
| P/L | Profit and loss |
| PLC | Public limited company |
| PLOB | Public limit order board |
| POS | Public offers of securities |
| POTAM | Panel on Takeovers and Mergers |
| PPP | Purchasing power parity |
| PSA | Public Securities Association |
| PSBR | Public sector borrowing requirement |
| PSDR | Public sector debt repayment |
| PSE | Philadelphia Stock Exchange |
| QET | Quote extension time |
| QM | Quoted margin |
| RCH | Recognized clearing house |
| RFQ | Request for quotes |
| RIE | Recognized investment exchange |
| RPB | Recognized professional body |
| RPI | Retail price index |
| RRT | Request response time |
| R/S | Rescaled range analysis |
| RUF | Revolving underwriting facility |
| SAA | Strategic asset allocation |
| SAFE | Synthetic agreement for forward exchange |
| SAR | Substantial acquisition rule |
| SAPCO | Single asset property company |
| SCP | Sterling commercial paper |
| SEAQ | Stock Exchange Automated Quotations |
| SEAQ-I | SEAQ International |
| SEATS | Stock Exchange Alternative Trading Service |
| SEDOL | Stock Exchange Daily Official List |
| SEMB | Stock exchange money broker |
| SETS | Stock Exchange Electronic Trading Service |
| SFA | Securities and Futures Authority |

| | |
|---|---|
| SIB | Securities and Investments Board |
| SIMEX | Singapore International Monetary Exchange |
| SLOB | Secured lease bond |
| SML | Security market line |
| SOEF | Small order execution facility |
| SOFFEX | Swiss Options and Financial Futures Exchange |
| SPAN | Standard portfolio analysis of risk |
| SPOT | Single property ownership trust |
| SPUT | Single property unit trust |
| SRO | Self-regulatory organization |
| STAGS | Sterling transferable accruing government security |
| STF | Spread trading facility |
| SUPSI | Specific unpublished price-sensitive information |
| TAA | Tactical asset allocation |
| TIBOR | Tokyo interbank offered rate |
| TB | Treasury bill |
| TFE | Tokyo Futures Exchange |
| TOPIC | Teletext Output Price Information by Computer |
| TRS | Trade registration system |
| TRUF | Transferable revolving underwriting facility |
| UCITS | Undertakings for collective investments in transferable securities |
| USM | Unlisted Securities Market |
| VaR | Value-at-risk |
| WDA | Writing-down allowance |
| WDV | Written-down value |
| WPA | Worked principal agreement |
| YTM | Yield to maturity |
| ZEBRAS | Zero-coupon eurosterling bearer or registered accruing security |
| Z-TIBOR | Zenginkyo Tokyo interbank offered rate |

# Part I

# INTRODUCTION TO FINANCIAL MARKETS

The first part of the book is designed to introduce readers to the financial system of an advanced market economy. We shall consider the composition of the financial system with special reference to the UK. In particular, we shall examine the participants, securities, markets, trading arrangements and regulations that collectively constitute a modern financial system. We shall also examine how financial markets determine the discount rates that are used to value the securities that are traded in them, and also review the financial arithmetic used to determine security values.

# Chapter 1

# The Financial System

Every advanced financial system is composed of *participants*, *securities*, *markets*, *trading arrangements* and *regulations*. In this chapter, we examine each of these components in turn, concentrating in particular on the financial system in the UK (sometimes known as the 'City'). We conclude by placing the current UK financial system in a temporal context.

## 1.1  Participants

There are three main classes of participant in an advanced financial system: *end-users*, *financial intermediaries* (general and specialist) and *market-makers*.

### 1.1.1  End-users of the financial system

The following identity holds at all times:

$$
\begin{aligned}
\text{Saving} - \text{Investment} \quad &\equiv \quad \text{Increase in financial assets} - \text{Increase in financial liabilities} \\
&= \quad \text{Net acquisition of financial assets} \\
&= \quad \text{Net financial surplus/deficit.}
\end{aligned}
$$

For the economy as a whole this identity is zero, but for sectors in financial surplus the identity is positive, while for sectors in financial deficit it is negative. Typically in the UK (although not always), the household and overseas sectors will be in financial surplus and will therefore be net lenders to the financial markets, and the industrial, commercial and government sectors will be in financial deficit and will therefore be net borrowers from the financial markets. So there are two types of end-user of the financial system: *primary lenders* and *ultimate borrowers*.

The ultimate objective of an individual in the household sector, say, is to maximize the expected welfare or utility of his lifetime consumption stream. If the individual is currently not spending all his income on consumption, he will want to find a temporary repository for his current savings until they are required to finance future expenditure. This will involve the purchase of financial assets.

For a given ultimate objective, the individual's proximate objective is to allocate his surplus funds across different assets in such a way as to maximize the expected utility of the characteristics of the portfolio of assets that he holds, taking into account any *aversion to risk*, *preference for liquidity*, etc. The unpredictability of the future consumption profile, the uncertainty attached to the returns from the asset holdings (especially in real terms, taking into account the effects of inflation) and the cost of liquidating assets in terms of both transaction costs and capital value uncertainty (especially before assets have matured), all tend to combine to induce the individual to select the maturity profile of the asset portfolio to match as closely as possible the maturity profile of planned consumption.

This suggests that the optimal portfolio of an individual in the household sector is likely to be one that is held short, i.e., one that is easily liquidated at low cost. The more uncertain the future consumption plan, the more uncertain the portfolio returns, the greater the costs of liquidating assets and the lower the confidence in the solvency of the ultimate borrower, the more liquid will be the optimal portfolio. In the extreme case, only the most liquid asset will be held, and this may not necessarily be a financial asset; for example, during the German hyperinflation after the First World War, cigarettes were more liquid than cash.

Without loss of generality, we can say that the preferred position for an individual in financial surplus is to 'lend short'.

The ultimate objective of a firm, on the other hand, is to maximize the expected utility of its profit stream. If we assume that the firm has a *neutral attitude to risk*, this can be shown to be equivalent to maximizing the long-term value of the firm. In order to do this, the firm will need to invest in real plant and equipment. It does this for two reasons. First, it will have to replace worn out or obsolete equipment: this it must do simply to maximize profits and the value of the firm at a given level of output. This is called *replacement investment*. Second, the firm can generate further profits from expanding the level of its activity. This requires investing in additional plant and equipment, a process known as *net investment*. *Gross investment* is the sum of replacement investment and net investment, and it has to be financed in advance of the revenues generated by using the plant and equipment. In addition, there is considerable uncertainty attached to these future revenues. In the extreme case, demand patterns might change and the expected revenues might not materialize at all. So long-term investment involves substantial risk.

There are a number of ways of financing long-term investment:

1  It can be financed out of the retained earnings from the existing activities of the firm.

2  It can be financed by taking out bank loans or by issuing long-term marketable corporate bonds.

3  It can be financed by issuing new equity or share capital, a method that extends the ownership of the firm because the new shareholders become part-owners in it, having the right to participate in future decision-making and to receive a stream of dividends from its earnings.

So we may summarize the firm's position as follows. Despite a pool of retained earnings, the firm is typically in deficit and wishes to finance that deficit on a long-term basis; that is, it wants to be in a position to 'borrow long'.

One of the fundamental problems in finance therefore is to match the preferences of the surplus sector to 'lend short' with those of the deficit sector to 'borrow long'. Hicks (1939) called this the 'constitutional weakness' of unintermediated financial markets. How can this constitutional weakness be resolved? Can it, for example, be resolved by the price mechanism? If there is direct trading between the household sector and the industrial and commercial sector, why does the yield on long-term securities not rise sufficiently to induce the individual in the household sector out of his *preferred habitat*, and why does the yield on short-term securities not fall sufficiently to induce the firm out of its preferred habitat? The probable answer is that the yields at the long end would be so high that there would be very little long-term investment, while the yields at the short end would be so low that there would be very little short-term saving. It was this constitutional weakness that led to the development of the second major class of participant in the financial markets, *financial intermediaries*.

## 1.1.2 General financial intermediaries

The simplest role of a financial intermediary is the pure *agency* or *brokerage* role, that is, acting as an *agency-broker* for a primary lender or an ultimate borrower in the purchase or sale of a security. In return, the intermediary will receive a fee from the party for whom he is acting as agent. Financial intermediaries can also act on their own account by buying and selling securities for a profit. Such intermediaries are known as *broker-dealers*.

However, the general role of financial intermediaries is considerably more important than this, because they are in a position effectively to resolve the constitutional weakness implicit in direct trading between individuals. Rather than simply on-lending funds that have been deposited with them (i.e., rather than just redistributing liquidity), they create a completely new financial security by issuing a type of liability that the surplus sector prefers to hold as an asset (i.e. the *intermediate security*) and holding as an asset the type of liability that the deficit sector wishes to issue (i.e. the *primary security*). This means that they issue short-term liabilities and hold long-term assets, so that the liability side of their balance sheet is much more liquid than the asset side. But this balance sheet mismatch does not imply a high risk of insolvency, because financial intermediaries maintain sufficient liquidity to meet their maturing liabilities. This is because they make use of economies in the scale of their operations to give themselves sufficient liquidity to meet anticipated liquidations and sufficient illiquidity to fulfil their obligations as providers of long-term investment finance. The ultimate borrower is able to get the required investment funding on long-term guarantee, and the primary lender is able to get both liquidity and reduced risk on his lending. In return for this extra security, the lender will be prepared to accept a lower rate of interest, so that the borrower gets his finance at lower cost than otherwise.

The most important activity engaged in by financial intermediaries is that of *asset transformation*. The intermediary has to transform the extremely risky liabilities of ultimate borrowers into safe assets for primary lenders; it has to transform liabilities with long-term maturities into assets that can be readily liquidated, and it has to transform the high costs involved in direct trading between end-users into the low costs associated with intermediation.

**Transformation of risk.** Financial intermediaries are able to reduce risk through risk spreading and risk pooling. The type of risk that financial intermediaries are able to reduce in this way is known as *specific risk*.

One example of specific risk is the risk of a borrower being unable to pay the interest or repay the principal when it is due. (This is also known as *default* or *credit risk*.) The financial intermediary therefore has to assess the risk on each loan that it makes. This is a question of information collection, and it involves the problem of *asymmetric information* sets. A borrower has more information about himself in terms of his ability to repay loans than does any lender. This is the familiar problem of *adverse selection*: the lender has difficulty in distinguishing good-quality debt from bad-quality debt. This is to the disadvantage of borrowers as well as lenders, because bad-quality debtors may drive out good-quality debtors. The problem is especially important for new or small firms about which there is little or no publicly available information. The large scale of operations of a financial intermediary compared with that of an individual lender enables the intermediary to be much more efficient in gathering information than the individual acting on his own. Once the risk class of the potential borrower and of the prospective investment project have been assessed, an appropriate risk-loading factor can be incorporated into the interest charge for the loan. The intermediary can then control for overall risk by *risk spreading*, that is, by spreading any risky investment across a sufficiently large number of lenders and having adequate capital and reserves to cover the actual defaults that will almost certainly occur from a given set of loans: a classic example is the *syndicated loan*. In this way, financial intermediaries are able to transform high-risk assets (borrowers' loans) into low-risk liabilities (lenders' savings).

Another example of specific risk is the uncertainty attached to the income stream derived from an investment project, since the value of the equity investment will rise if the underlying capital stock is used productively and will decline or even vanish if it is used unproductively. (This risk is sometimes called *equity risk*.) It is possible to reduce this type of risk by diversification or *risk pooling*, that is, by constructing portfolios of assets that exploit any offsetting risks between the returns on assets in the portfolio and thereby reducing overall risk. But a sufficiently well-diversified portfolio contains a relatively large number of assets, and this, together with the high transaction costs involved in trading in assets, makes it difficult for individual savers to obtain an adequate pooling of assets at an acceptable cost.

The large scale of financial intermediaries, on the other hand, allows them to exploit fully the benefits from risk pooling. In addition, the unit costs of operating at this level are much lower for the financial intermediary than for the individual because marginal transaction costs decline with the volume of transactions and any fixed costs are spread over a wider total volume of transactions. A classic example of risk pooling is a unit trust or mutual fund.

However, not all risk can be diversified away, either by spreading or by pooling. There will always be some risk that has to be borne, however effective financial intermediaries are in transforming it. This irreducible risk is known as *market risk*, and will be discussed at some length later in the text.

**Transformation of maturities and provision of liquidity.** The second important role of financial intermediaries is the transformation of maturities and the provision of liquidity. An important key to the success of financial intermediaries is the ability to hold assets that are less liquid (e.g. because of greater maturity) than the liabilities that they issue and yet to remain solvent. If, in addition, intermediaries are willing to act as principals in the sense of guaranteeing to repurchase immediately any of the liabilities that their lenders wish to sell, then this is equivalent to guaranteeing complete liquidity. By structuring the maturity profile of their asset portfolios satisfactorily, intermediaries can ensure that they are able to meet any likely claim on their liabilities.

This success depends to a great extent on the large scale of operations of financial intermediaries, which allows them both to estimate fairly accurately what proportion of their liabilities is likely to be liquidated over a particular period and to be in a position to replace the liquidated funds with new sources of funds. Both of these activities can be more easily carried out by a large-scale organization than a small-scale one. For example, the economies of scale of financial intermediaries considerably widen the opportunity set of these intermediaries for tapping different markets compared with the options available to individuals: this is the case of economies leading to asymmetric opportunity sets. An unscrupulous borrower would be less willing to defraud a large financial intermediary than a single individual when both might very well be equally ignorant of his true intent. This is not a question of differential information or of differential costs: it is a question of differential opportunities.

The additional liquidity provided by the maturity-transforming activities of financial intermediaries means that lenders are prepared, in return, to accept lower interest rates, and so borrowers, in turn, are charged lower interest.

**Transformation of transaction costs.** The third important role of financial intermediaries is to reduce the transaction costs associated with trading in securities between borrowers and lenders, and again the scale of operations of financial intermediaries helps to make this possible. Examples of the different ways in which intermediaries reduce costs include:

1  The provision of convenient and safe locations for borrowers and lenders to transact, which reduces search costs.

2  The provision of standardized forms of securities, which reduces the information costs from examining a wide range of financial instruments and offers convenience of denomination to borrowers.

3  The conducting of activities on a large scale and the specialization in different markets, which reduces operating costs and allows intermediaries to acquire expertise which can be passed on to their clients (for example, marginal and therefore average brokerage costs decline as the volume of transactions increases).

4  The creation of tax-efficient financial instruments, which help to reduce capital gains, income or inheritance tax costs.

These cost reductions can be passed on in the form of lower transaction-cost loading factors in interest charges, and so can narrow the difference between borrowing and lending rates.

**Types of general financial intermediary.** There are two main types of general financial intermediary: *bank financial intermediaries* (BFIs) and *non-bank financial intermediaries* (NBFIs). There are two main types of BFI: retail (or high street) banks and investment (or wholesale or merchant) banks.

*Retail banks* deal mainly with households and small businesses. They issue deposits to members of the household and company sectors in surplus and make loans to members of those sectors that are in deficit. They are also involved in providing money transmission services. They are obliged to observe a cash ratio (a ratio of cash to deposits) which gives them sufficient liquidity to meet any likely level of withdrawals from their deposit accounts without having to recall loans. From experience, the banks know that, over a given period, the net flow of withdrawals will be a very small percentage of deposits and will vary within a very narrow range. Therefore, as long as they keep sufficient liquid reserves, they will be able to meet these withdrawals. The remainder of the deposits are then available for loans.

Depositors gain because the BFIs take away the risk of default from borrowers and guarantee a virtually costless withdrawal scheme and a stable return on deposits. Borrowers gain because the banks take away the risk of early recall of loans, guarantee the amount and term of loans and associated repayments, and offer a stable interest cost (which may be fixed for fixed-term loans or variable for overdrafts).  The banks gain because they make their profit from *intermediation*, that is, from the difference between borrowing and lending rates.  In return, they accept the risk of default and must maintain a reserve of funds to meet the defaults that arise, although the banks also use credit assessment techniques to develop a specialist knowledge of their potential borrowers in order to minimize default risk.

Retail banks both in the UK and elsewhere have to abide by a common set of *capital adequacy standards* which were established by the Basle Committee of Central Bank Regulators (part of the Bank for International Settlements) in 1987 and came fully into operation in 1993.  These standards specify a minimum ratio of bank capital to risk-weighted assets.  Some of the assets held by a bank such as cash and gold bullion are zero risk-weighted and so the banks do not have to provide capital to support these assets.  Other assets are 100% risk-weighted and the full book value of these assets is included in the capital adequacy calculation; examples are loans to non-bank customers and loans to banks and public sector entities outside the OECD (Organisation for Economic Co-operation and Development).  Lying between these extremes are 10% risk-weighted assets (e.g. holdings of fixed-interest securities issues by OECD governments with maturities under a year), 20% risk-weighted assets (e.g. holdings of fixed-interest securities issued by OECD governments with maturities over a year and loans to banks and public sector entities located in the OECD), and 50% risk-weighted assets (e.g. residential mortgages).  Also included in the calculation are the net short open foreign exchange position of banks and off-balance sheet items such as standby letters of credit and forward asset purchases.  Once the risk-weighted assets have been added up, the banks must have capital equal to at least 8 per cent of the value of the total risk-weighted assets.  The capital is divided into two types, *Tier 1* or *core* capital and *Tier 2* or *supplementary* capital.  Tier 1 capital comprises permanent shareholders' capital, in the form of either equity or perpetual non-cumulative preference shares.  Tier 2 capital comprises subordinated debt instruments, provisions and revaluation reserves (which covers the revaluation of the bank's own fixed assets, mainly its premises).  Tier 1 capital cannot be less than 4 per cent of total risk-weighted assets.  It is possible for banks to convert Tier 2 capital into Tier 1 capital.  For example, in February 1989, National Westminster Bank made a scrip issue to shareholders capitalising £600m of property revaluation reserves.  The effect was to raise Tier 1 capital from 5.5 per cent to 6.2 per cent, with the total capital ratio standing at 9.2 per cent.

*Investment banks* deal mainly with large corporations, institutional investors, governments and local authorities.  Despite being called 'banks', they do not generally take deposits from the public.  Instead they act as agents for their customers.  A typical investment bank performs the following functions: corporate finance, asset management, export finance, international investment advice, agency broking and market-making.  The bank can also act as an agent of another, possibly overseas bank: this function is known as *correspondent banking*.  Accounts kept by one bank with a correspondent bank are called *nostro accounts*.

The first function of an investment bank is that of corporate finance.  This involves advising on, arranging (this function is known as *origination*) and underwriting the finances for the investment programmes of its corporate clients.  The bank's activities can range from providing corporate loans, through arranging the initial flotation on a stock exchange, to issuing a bond to finance a corporate takeover (this latter activity is generally undertaken by the mergers and acquisitions or M&A team).  Corporate loans are provided by the *commercial banking* (sometimes called the *merchant banking*) division of the bank.  These can be in the form of corporate credits, syndicated loans (where a large-scale loan is provided by a syndicate of banks), structured finance (sometimes called project finance, where the interest payments on the loan are linked to the cash flows from a large scale project, such as the

Channel Tunnel, where these cash flows are delayed until the project comes on stream) and large-scale, specialist loans (such as those involved with property, aviation or shipping finance). This division also provides other credit-related services such as leasing, factoring, forfaiting, and even sovereign debt reschedulings. It will also operate the global credit policy of the bank, including credit monitoring and administration, and counterparty and country risk analysis. In contrast, securitized products (such as bonds and shares) are arranged by the *corporate banking* (sometimes also called the *investment banking*) division of the bank. The finance is drawn mainly from institutional investors (such as pension funds). The bond or equity issue is underwritten by the bank, so that any shortfall in funds raised has to be met from the bank's own resources. Investment banks are also involved in asset management. This can range from managing the short-term cash flows of their corporate clients (known as *treasury management*) through to the management of long-term bond and equity portfolios for their institutional and private clients (in the latter case this is known as *private banking*); in many cases they are also responsible for the safe custody of these securities (this is known as *global custody*).

In addition to giving advice and arranging finance for their domestic customers, investment banks provide advice to international clients and arrange export finance (including letters of credit). Finally, and much more recently (since the Big Bang in October 1986), investment banks have begun to engage in agency broking and security market-making. They have divisions that are involved in the purchase and sale of securities for clients, and divisions that are engaged in market-making in those securities. (Market-making will be discussed later.) The main activities here are the issuing, trading and distribution of financial products.

An investment bank not only provides services to clients, it also operates on its own account. The main examples of this are proprietary trading and equity banking. With *proprietary trading*, the bank uses its own capital to make money from the movements in the prices of financial products; a typical example is the bank's forex trading, whereby the bank attempts to make money from movements in foreign exchange rates. With *equity banking*, the bank itself makes a direct equity investment in a new company, as opposed to arranging a loan or issuing equity which is purchased by, say, a pension fund; the bank hopes to make an adequate return on this investment over the medium term.

The bank must also be concerned about both its own short-term liquidity and long-term solvency. It will therefore have a liquidity control committee that controls and monitors liquidity and all positions with respect to currencies, interest rates and maturities, and an asset and liability management committee for the whole bank whose objective is to maximize the bank's net interest income and return on capital. Related to this there will be a credit committee (which monitors on-going credit exposures, ensures credit policy standards are met and maintained, and reviews problem loans and co-ordinates appropriate action) and a risk management committee (which monitors all business areas where market risks arise and regularly reviews risk limits).

The main categories of NBFI are finance houses, building societies, insurance companies (both general and life), pension funds, unit trusts, investment trusts and open-ended investment companies (OEICs). This constitutes an important group of institutional investors in Britain (and their investment interests are collectively represented by the Institutional Shareholders' Committee which was set up in the 1970s). They developed for various different and diverse historical reasons, but they can be divided into five broad classes:

1 NBFIs to finance the short-term durable expenditure of members of the household sector, e.g. *finance houses* which finance hire purchase agreements.

2 NBFIs to finance long-term durable expenditure of the members of the household sector, e.g. *building societies* to finance house purchase.

3 NBFIs to finance the long-term contingent claims and retirement pensions of the household sector, e.g. *life assurance companies* and *pension funds*.

4 NBFIs to finance general contingent claims, e.g. *general insurance companies*.

5 NBFIs to facilitate the risk spreading and risk pooling of the savings of the members of the household sector in surplus, e.g. *unit* and *investment trusts* and *open-ended investment companies*.

In each case, there is a mutual benefit enjoyed by both the surplus and deficit sectors. For example, with finance houses, members of the household sector receive their durable goods immediately and are able to pay for them smoothly over time, while members of the company sector face a high demand for their goods and services which is not subject to credit constraints.

In every case, the success of NBFIs at intermediation depends closely on the underlying success of the risky activities undertaken by the company sector, i.e. on the underlying performance of the real economy. For example, the market value of Britain's housing stock is generally about three times the market value of British industry (as measured by the market capitalization of the London Stock Exchange); and part of the success of building societies lies in the fact that the household's liability, the mortgage commitment, is denominated in nominal terms, while the household's asset, the house, grows in real terms, and hence the house-owning members of the household sector experience an increase in their real marketable wealth. But this can be sustained only if British industry is able to generate the increasing level of real incomes necessary to finance new mortgages at the appropriate level. If British industry and hence real incomes collapsed or even just declined, then the market value of houses would fall and households would then hold fixed nominal debts on declining real assets. This would tend to have the effect of reinforcing the decline in industry, either by reducing household mobility, thereby adding to industrial inefficiency, or by forcing households to declare themselves bankrupt if they did have to sell their houses in order to move. In a similar way, the ability of assurance companies and pension funds to guarantee future annuities, such as pensions, depends crucially on the ability of industry to grow in a sustained and stable manner. And again, the benefits from the risk-reducing activities of unit trusts are of little use if there are no anticipated gains to be made from the risky activities of British industry, but only anticipated losses.

Finally, it is important to note that the historical distinction between BFIs and NBFIs is disappearing over time. As a result of technological innovation, increasing competitive pressures and government legislation (such as the 1986 Building Societies Act and the 1987 Banking Act), the traditionally separate areas of activity of banks and non-banks are rapidly disappearing, so that banks, for example, have become involved in housing finance, while building societies have become involved in money transmission services. The outcome is likely to be the emergence of a general or *universal banking system*, in which a single banking group provides the complete range of financial intermediation services.

### 1.1.3 Specialist financial intermediaries

Specialist financial intermediaries are also involved in such activities as the transformation of risk and the provision of liquidity. But their participation in the markets tends to be more active and more short-term than is the case with general intermediaries. They may also act as principals on their own account rather than as brokers for others. The specialists cover the activities of arbitrage, hedging and speculation.

*Arbitrageurs* are specialist financial intermediaries who act to ensure both that the prices of securities do not get out of line with their *fair* or *fundamental values*, and that the prices of identical
securities traded in different market-places do not get out of line with each other. We can consider
some examples of the two cases.

An equity arbitrageur will constantly check the market price of a share against its fair price based
on a fundamental analysis of the firm and its prospects. In an efficient market without transaction
costs, the market price of a share would never get out of line with its fair price. But in the real world,
the market price will wander around the fair price but within a band (called an *arbitrage band*; see
Figure 1.1). The width of the arbitrage band will depend on the level of transaction costs; the higher

**Figure 1.1** Arbitrage bands: the case of a single market

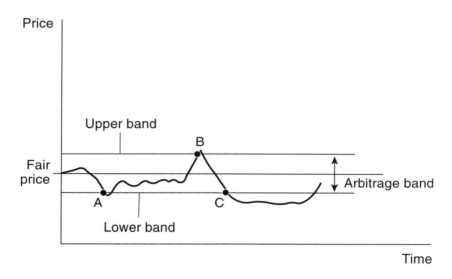

the transaction costs, the wider the band. As soon as the share price wanders outside the band, it
becomes profitable for the arbitrageur to act. If the market price falls below the lower band (as just
past A in Figure 1.1), it becomes profitable for the arbitrageur to buy the share in large volumes
because the share is underpriced compared with its theoretical value. The arbitrageur then waits for
the market price to correct itself by rising sufficiently to lie again within the arbitrage band, at which
time he sells out and takes his profit. If the market price rises above the upper band (as just past B in
Figure 1.1), it becomes profitable for the arbitrageur to sell shares and wait for the market price to fall
before repurchasing them. If the arbitrageur does not actually own the shares, the same result can be
achieved by short-selling the shares (examined in section 1.4.3 below) or by buying put options on the
share (examined in Chapter 9). In all cases, the arbitrageur is not interested in the absolute *level* of the
share price; he is interested only in the *difference* between the market price and the fair price.

Arbitrageurs behave in a similar way when dealing with identical securities traded in different
markets, e.g. foreign exchange traded in New York and London. What is important in this case is
the difference in price between the two markets. Again, there will be arbitrage bands, as shown in
Figure 1.2. If the price in market 1 falls too far compared with the price in market 2 (as just past A
in Figure 1.2), it becomes profitable for the arbitrageur to buy the security in market 1 and sell it in

**Figure 1.2** Arbitrage bands: the case of two markets

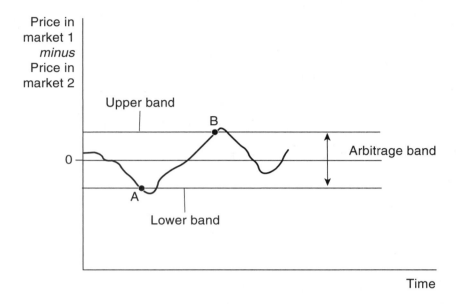

market 2. If the price in market 1 rises too far compared with the price in market 2 (as just past B in Figure 1.2), the arbitrageur buys in market 2 and sells in market 1.

The second case is an example of *pure* or *riskless arbitrage*, because the security purchased in the cheaper market can be immediately resold in the dearer market. However, the first case involves considerable risk. This is because it is possible for an inefficiency in the market to persist for some time. This is shown to the right of C in Figure 1.1. The arbitrageur might have bought at C with borrowed funds and the position might then have to be held for some time before the market inefficiency is removed.

*Hedgers* are specialist financial intermediaries who wish to lay off risks that they currently face or expect to face in the future. The following are examples of the kinds of risk that hedgers might wish to lay off: they might hold long positions in a cash market portfolio of shares and wish to lay off the risk of share prices falling; they might have debts at market-related rates of interest and wish to lay off the risk that interest rates rise; they might be expecting to receive funds denominated in US dollars in three months' time and wish to lay off the risk that the dollar falls relative to sterling; they might be expecting to make payments in yen in six months' time and wish to lay off the risk that sterling falls against the yen. The list is endless.

Many end-users of the financial system who hold stable long-term portfolios of securities may also be active short-term hedgers and so could be classified as both end-users and hedgers. Hedging itself is also included as a form of financial intermediation because hedgers can be actively engaged in intermediating between different financial markets, as we shall now see.

How do hedgers in practice lay off the risk that they face? The principal means of doing this is by using the market for *derivative securities*, such as futures and options (as opposed to the *spot* market for *cash securities*). Take, for example, the case of a portfolio of securities with the risk that share prices might suddenly fall. The position could be hedged by selling stock index futures contracts (examined in Chapter 8) or by buying stock index put options (examined in chapter 9), in other words by taking out a kind of *portfolio insurance*. Any fall in the value of the cash portfolio could be exactly offset by increases in the value of the futures or options position, thereby effectively locking in the value of the cash portfolio at a predetermined level. The interest rate payable on loans could be locked in by selling interest rate futures contracts or interest rate call options. In a similar way, exchange rate futures and options could be used to hedge long or short currency exposures.

While it is possible to use futures and options to create a 'perfect' hedge and so perfectly protect the cash position from adverse changes in spot security prices, the hedge will give good protection only if the change in spot prices is small. If there are substantial changes in spot prices, the hedge would have to be regularly rebalanced. In this case hedgers will be frequently intermediating between cash, futures and options markets.

*Speculators* or *traders* are specialist financial intermediaries who attempt to make profits by taking a view on where markets are moving. They are not interested in the current level of prices, only in predicting where prices are about to move next. If speculators are expecting the prices of certain securities to rise, they will take long (unhedged or uncovered) positions in those securities. If they are expecting prices to fall, they will take short (unhedged or uncovered) positions. Because transaction costs in cash markets are sometimes higher than in the markets for derivatives, speculators often prefer to take positions in futures and options markets rather than in cash markets.

Speculation is therefore a gamble as to where the markets are moving. If speculators are successful, they can make quick profits. If they are unsuccessful, they can make equally quick losses. To be successful overall, speculators must be able to 'follow the money': that is, they must know both when to 'run their profits' and 'cut their losses'.

Because much speculative activity is conducted with borrowed funds, speculators tend to hold positions in the markets for only very short periods of time. For example, speculators do not generally like holding overnight positions in case adverse news materializes when the markets are closed. Speculators can be in and out of markets several times a day, usually for periods of no more than an hour or so. Sometimes the time periods are much less than this, even as short as a few minutes. For example, there is some evidence from financial futures markets that speculators on average make money if they take futures positions for three minutes or less, and on average lose money if they take positions for longer than three minutes.

Nevertheless, despite being directly comparable with gambling, speculation is very important for the efficient running of financial markets. This is because the most important side benefit from the activities of speculators is the provision of liquidity to the market. If there is a continuous flow of both buy orders and sell orders from speculators while the market is open, then the market will be highly liquid. This, in turn, requires that there is a heterogeneity of view among speculators, with a good balance between speculators believing prices are going to rise and those believing prices are going to fall. Occasionally, however, the balance of view lies in one direction only, with the majority of speculators believing that prices will fall, say. In this case, the liquidity of the market is one-sided: it remains very easy to buy securities but very difficult to sell them. This is what happened on Black Monday (19 October 1987), for example.

However, under most market conditions, where there is a heterogeneity of view among speculators, they will provide good two-way liquidity to the market. This is essential for an efficient market and for the activities of other market participants such as hedgers, and long-term investors and fund-raisers. If market liquidity is poor, arbitrageurs will not be able to create an efficient market, hedgers will not be able to lay off risks, and long-term investors and fund-raisers will not be able to use the capital markets to achieve their objectives.

The second most important side benefit from the activities of speculators is the provision of insurance to hedgers. Hedgers wish to lay off risks from the long or short cash market positions that they hold. In order to this, a hedger has to find someone else who is willing to take the opposite position to himself. This role is undertaken by the speculator, provided he is compensated for doing so. In this way, speculators can be induced to provide *insurance* to hedgers.

### 1.1.4   Market-makers

*Market-makers* (or *dealers*) also intermediate between the end-users of the financial system, but unlike general financial intermediaries, they do not act as agents for the end-users. Instead they act as principals, buying and selling securities for their own account. To do this efficiently, they must hold an inventory of securities on their books, which grows when they purchase securities and declines when they sell them. They are rewarded for their activities in one of two ways. The first way is through the *bid-offer spread*, the difference between the *bid price* at which they will buy a security and the higher *offer price* at which they will sell the security. The second way is through taking a position (or speculation). If they believe that prices will rise in the near future, they will increase their inventory holdings; while if they expect prices to fall, they will reduce or even eliminate their inventory holdings.

## 1.2   Securities

The second component of the financial system is *securities* (sometimes called *investment products*). Every financial transaction creates a security which is simultaneously a financial asset (to the holder) and a financial liability (to the issuer). A security is a claim against real resources either in the form of an income stream or in the form of physical capital or assets. It should never be forgotten that, however bizarre and exotic financial securities can be, the entire financial system is and always will be derivative to the real economy. A substantial part of this book is concerned with describing and valuing different types of securities, so this section will discuss securities briefly and in very general terms.

Securities can be classified in the following ways. They can be classified according to:

1  Their issuer.

2  Their currency of denomination.

3  Their ownership and participation rights.

4  The collateral pledged against them.

5  Their term to maturity.

6  Their income payments.

7  The predictability of their capital value.

8  Their degree of liquidity.

9  Their degree of reversibility.

10  Their tax treatment.

11  Whether they are derivatives of another security.

12  Whether they involve composite securities.

Securities can be classified according to who issues them because this helps to determine the degree of risk attached to them. Two otherwise identical bonds will differ because one was issued by the government while the other was issued by a private corporation. The government bond (also known as a *gilt-edged bond* or simply a *gilt* has virtually no risk of default, whereas the corporate bond has some risk of default.

Securities can also be classified according to their currency of denomination. For example, most bonds traded in the UK will be denominated in sterling. Sterling-denominated bonds issued by a domestic resident are known as *domestic bonds*, while sterling-denominated bonds issued by a foreign issuer are known as *foreign bonds* or *bulldog bonds*. But many bonds traded in the UK are denominated in currencies other than sterling, such as US dollars or Japanese yen: such bonds are known as *eurobonds*.[1]

Securities can also be classified according to whether they are equity or debt, i.e. according to their ownership and participation rights. Equity-type securities (such as *common stock*) involve rights of both ownership and participation. That is, the holders of common stock own the underlying physical assets of the corporation and also have the right to participate in both the profits and the decision-making of the company. (In practice, they delegate their decision-making powers to a management group.) Debt-type securities (e.g. *corporate bonds*) do not involve rights of ownership or participation. Holders of such securities are merely creditors of the firm. If the firm defaults on its contractual obligations to the debt-holders, they can appoint an administrator under the terms of the Insolvency Act 1986 to look after their interests. An exception here is *income bonds*, where failure to pay interest does not in general lead to insolvency. Some securities have rights of ownership but not participation; certain classes of equity (i.e. non-voting shares) fall into this category, but the most important example is preference shares. *Preference shares* have some of the characteristics of equity and some of the characteristics of debt; while classified as equity in terms of ownership, they are classified as debt in terms of participation in profits and decision-making. This is because the obligation of firms to preference shareholders is fixed, although, because they are also treated as owners, they are unable to have the firm declared insolvent if it does not meet those obligations.

Securities are also classified according to the collateral that is pledged against them. This is particularly important for debt securities because it helps to determine the riskiness of the debt. The most secure form of debt and therefore the least risky is *debentures*: these are secured against specific assets of the firm. The least secure and therefore the most risky form of debt is *unsecured loan stock*: holders of this rank with other unsecured creditors in the event of default. In turn, particular categories

---

[1]Following the introduction in January 1999 of the *euro* as the currency for countries participating in European monetary union, there has been some confusion over terminology. The securities that were known as 'eurobonds' are now frequently referred to as 'international bonds' in listings of prices in the financial press. The term 'eurobond' remains, though, in informal use. Similarly, 'eurocurrency' interest rates are now formally known as 'international currency rates' although the CME, for instance, still lists a 'eurodollar' short-term interest rate futures contract (see Chapter 8). In the absence of a new terminology that is universally accepted, we will continue to use such terms as 'eurobonds', 'eurocurrencies' and 'euromarkets' as traditionally defined.

of debt can be subordinated or unsubordinated. For example, subordinated debentures rank below unsubordinated debentures in the event of default.

Some securities have fixed maturity or redemption dates, some have variable maturity dates, while others have no maturity dates at all. A 3-month Treasury bill is an example of a short-term security with a fixed maturity date. At the end of the period, the holder receives the face value of the bill, namely £100. A government bond with a single redemption date is an example of a long-term security with a fixed maturity date (e.g. Exchequer 10.5 per cent 2005 matures in the year 2005, at which time, the holder receives the face value of the bond, also £100). Some securities have variable maturity dates, either because they are callable or because they are puttable. A *callable bond* is one that can be redeemed at the option of the issuer; e.g. Exchequer 12 per cent 2013–17 can be redeemed by the government on any one of the coupon payments dates between 2013 and 2017. Similarly, if the bond has a purchase fund or sinking fund attached to it, a fraction of the bonds will be retired each year before maturity, e.g. by lottery. A *puttable bond* is one that can be redeemed at the option of the holder. A *convertible bond* is an example of this because it can be converted at the option of the holder either into another bond or into common stock and so the original convertible will have variable redemption dates. Some securities have no maturity dates at all. Examples of this are current and deposit accounts, perpetual floating rate notes and irredeemable bonds (e.g. 2.5 per cent Consols), preference shares and equity. Current and deposit accounts can, of course, be closed, in which case the security as such disappears; but if they are not closed, they will survive indefinitely. The other examples will also survive indefinitely unless they are terminated through insolvency, for example.

Securities can be classified according to their income payments. Some securities pay income monthly (certain deposit accounts), quarterly (certain deposit accounts and one government bond, i.e. 2.5 per cent Consols), semi-annually (all other government and local authority bonds, bulldogs, most corporate bonds, preference shares and equity) or annually (certificates of deposit, eurobonds). Some securities never make explicit income payments at all. The reward from owning them accrues entirely in the form of capital appreciation; they therefore sell at a discount to their face value (Treasury bills, commercial bills, commercial paper, bankers acceptances, zero-coupon bonds). Some securities make fixed income payments (e.g. fixed-coupon bonds, income bonds, preference shares), while for others (e.g. deposit accounts, variable-rate gilts, index-linked gilts, equity), the payments vary for one reason or another. With deposits and variable-rate gilts, the interest payments are linked to current market interest rates; with index-linked gilts, the interest payments are linked to the retail price index; while with equity, the dividends depend on such factors as the firm's profitability, retained earnings and its current investment programme.

The predictability of capital value provides another way of classifying securities. This depends partly on whether or not the security is marketable. For non-marketable securities such as deposits, the value of the principal is always completely certain, at least in nominal terms. For some marketable securities, the capital value is perfectly predictable only at certain times. For example, with government bonds having a single redemption date, the capital value is known with certainty only on the maturity date. At other times, the capital value is uncertain, although the known terminal value of such bonds helps to place bounds on the possible range of capital values prior to maturity. A similar situation arises with Treasury bills; other things being equal, the value of a Treasury bill will rise between issue and redemption in a reasonably predictable way to reflect the accrued interest on the bill. For other securities, the capital value can never be perfectly predicted at any future date; the best example here is equity. Also, it is difficult, if not impossible, to place bounds on the capital values of such securities: equity has no theoretical finite upper bound to its value.

The degree of liquidity and reversibility are measures of the marketability of different securities.

*Liquidity* is measured by the time and/or cost of converting a security into cash. A perfectly liquid security can be converted into cash instantaneously and at zero cost. Only cash itself has this property (by definition). Even securities that are regarded as very close substitutes for cash, such as current accounts, are less than perfectly liquid; it takes time to go to the bank to cash a cheque and there is also some cost (often implicit) to cashing a cheque. Time and cost are, of course, substitutes that can be traded off against one another. For example, a deposit account requiring seven days' notice of withdrawal can be liquidated either instantly but at the cost of losing seven days' interest, or at no cost, if seven days' notice is given. All other securities (apart from cash) are therefore less than perfectly liquid. For example, to convert bonds or shares into cash involves time (although with the technology currently available the time required to liquidate securities has been reduced to an absolute minimum) and cost in the form of brokerage commissions.

*Reversibility*, on the other hand, is measured by the bid-offer spread. If a security is perfectly reversible, it is possible (in the absence of brokerage commissions) to move from cash into that security and immediately back into cash without any loss of value. Only cash and other non-marketable securities such as deposits are perfectly reversible. All marketable securities are imperfectly reversible, because the market-maker's spread has to be paid when the security is traded.

So liquidity and reversibility are different but related aspects of the *marketability* of securities. A market involves both brokers and market-makers. The size of the broker's commission defines the degree of liquidity of a security, while the size of the market-maker's spread defines the degree of reversibility of a security. A security is highly marketable if it is both highly liquid and highly reversible. A security is regarded as non-marketable if it is illiquid or irreversible. For example, the pension fund assets of a non-retired worker are non-marketable because they are both completely illiquid and irreversible: there is no price at which they can be converted back into cash before retirement. But note that deposit accounts, despite being very liquid and perfectly reversible, are also non-marketable: they cannot be sold to another individual.

The tax treatment of securities is another important way of classifying securities. Of course, the incidence of taxation falls on individuals and corporations rather than on the securities themselves. The payment of tax therefore depends on the circumstances of those individuals and corporations. In general terms, income from securities attracts income or corporation tax, while realized capital gains attract capital gains tax. But there are many exceptions to this, as the following examples show. Tax-exempt organizations such as charities do not have to pay income tax or capital gains tax on their investments. Gilt-edged securities are not liable for capital gains tax. Individuals or corporations who trade rather than invest in securities are liable for income or corporation tax on all the proceeds of their trading whether these are in the form of income or capital gains. The proceeds on discount instruments such as Treasury bills or commercial paper attract income tax even though no explicit interest is paid. Some securities, e.g. gilts, are free of tax to residents abroad (FOTRA). The income on many other securities is liable to withholding tax rather than income or corporation tax if the owner is an overseas resident; such tax is generally offsettable against the domestic income or corporation tax liabilities of such individuals or corporations.

In general, then, the income from securities is taxed at the highest marginal rate of income tax or corporation tax payable by the individual or corporation. In most cases, income tax at the basic rate (22 per cent from April 2000) is deducted at source and the holder of the security is provided with a tax credit indicating the amount of tax deducted. The tax is reclaimable by individuals and organizations not liable for tax, except in the case of bank and building society deposit accounts and UK equities. Higher-rate tax (currently 40 per cent) may also have to be paid. With some types of securities (e.g.

National Savings accounts and accounts held off-shore in places like the Channel Islands), interest is paid gross and UK residents are liable for basic and higher rate tax.

Since the Budget of March 1988, realized capital gains have been taxed at the same rate as income, currently 22 per cent (basic rate) and 40 per cent (higher rate) for individuals, and 20 per cent (smaller companies rate) and 30 per cent (standard rate) for corporations. However (for individuals though not for corporations), the first £7100 of realized capital gains in any one year is free of tax.

The tax treatment of securities has the following main effects on the willingness to hold different types of securities. Tax-exempt organizations, like charities, are completely indifferent to income or capital gains, other things being equal. Therefore they would be as willing to hold high-coupon (i.e. high-income) bonds, for example, as low-coupon (i.e. low-income) bonds, other things being equal. Individuals and corporations liable for tax have a preference, other things being equal, for capital gains rather than income. This is because, even though income and capital gains are taxed at the same marginal rate, capital gains tax can be deferred until the capital gains are actually realized, and, for individuals at least, some of the capital gains each year are tax-free.

Finally in this section, we will consider derivative securities and composite securities. A *derivative security* is one that delivers another security at some future date. This future delivery can be either obligatory or contingent. Examples here are financial futures and financial options contracts. A *financial futures contract* delivers a cash instrument (or sometimes even cash) at some date in the future at a price that is determined today. With a futures contract, future delivery of the instrument is obligatory unless the futures position is closed out with an offsetting transaction. A *financial option contract* also delivers a cash instrument at some date in the future at a price that is determined today. But with an option, delivery is at the option of the holder of the contract and is not obligatory; in short, an option is a contingent claim. Futures and options are known as derivative instruments because their values are derived from the values of the underlying cash instrument.

A *composite security* is one that is a mixture of two (or more) different securities. Examples here are convertible bonds, swaps and synthetic securities. A *convertible bond* is one that converts at some future date into equity at the option of the holder. A convertible bond is therefore a mixture of a bond and an option on equity. A *swap contract* (or a *contract for differences*) is, for example, a mixture of a fixed-rate security and a floating-rate security, or a mixture of two current securities and a forward exchange rate contract. A *synthetic* long put option on a security can be constructed from a short position in a cash instrument and a long position in a call option.

## 1.3   Markets

### 1.3.1   The classification of financial markets

The third component of a financial system is the markets in which securities are traded. An organized financial market is a place where, or a system through which, securities are created and transferred.

Financial markets can be classified in a number of ways:

1  Physical *v.* over-the-counter markets.

2  Continuous *v.* call markets.

3 Money *v.* capital markets.

4 Primary *v.* secondary markets.

5 Stock *v.* flow markets.

A financial market does not have to have a *physical* location. Indeed, since the Big Bang in October 1986, most securities in Britain have not traded in a physical market. Shares, bonds and money market instruments are traded *over-the-counter* using a system of computer screens and telephones. Only financial futures and financial options are still traded in a physical market, namely at LIFFE (the London International Financial Futures and Options Exchange).

Most markets operate on a *continuous* basis during opening hours, implying that trading can take place at any time that the markets are open. Examples here are the markets for shares, bonds and money market instruments. However, some markets trade at specific times during opening hours. Such markets are known as *call* markets because the securities are 'called' for trading. There has to be sufficient time between calls to allow offers to buy and sell securities to accumulate and so make trading worthwhile. Examples here are the pit trading of some financial futures and financial options and certain precious metals such as gold.

Markets can also be classified according to the maturity of the securities traded in them. A major distinction is usually drawn between money markets and capital markets. *Money markets* deal in securities with less than one year to maturity, whereas *capital markets* deal in securities with more than one year to maturity. Examples of money market instruments are Treasury bills, commercial bills, commercial paper, bankers acceptances and negotiable certificates of deposit. Examples of capital market instruments are bonds with more than a year to maturity and shares.

An important distinction can also be drawn between primary and secondary markets. The *primary market* is the new issues market. When an investment bank brings a new company to flotation, its shares are issued on the primary market (as an *initial public offer*). If this company subsequently decides to gear up by issuing bonds, these are also floated on the primary market. Similarly, if a company decides to expand using either equity finance or bond finance, the additional shares or bonds are floated on the primary market (known as a *secondary public offer*). The most difficult problem facing an investment bank involved in a new issue is deciding on the offer price of the issue. If the offer price is too low and there is an excess demand for the new shares or bonds, then the issuing company will be annoyed because it could have raised additional revenue from the issue. But if the offer price is too high and there is insufficient demand for the new shares or bonds, then the investment bank as underwriter will be involved in often considerable losses. The important point about the primary market is that the initial price of the security is set rather than determined by the market, unless the security is issued through a tender offer or by auction.

The *secondary market* is the market in which existing securities are subsequently traded. There are two main reasons why individuals transact in the secondary market: *information-motivated* reasons and *liquidity-motivated* reasons. Information-motivated investors believe that they have superior information about a particular security than other market participants. This information leads them to believe that the security is not being correctly priced by the market. If the information consists of good news, this suggests that the security is currently underpriced, and investors with access to such information will want to buy the security. On the other hand, if the information consists of bad news, the security will be currently overpriced, and such investors will want to sell their holdings of the security. Liquidity-motivated investors, on the other hand, transact in the secondary market because they are currently in a position of either excess or insufficient liquidity. Investors with surplus cash holdings (e.g. as a result of an inheritance) will buy securities, whereas investors with insufficient cash (e.g. to purchase a car) will sell securities.

The prices of securities in the secondary market are determined by the market-makers in those securities. Precisely how those prices are determined can be seen once we have discussed the final way in which securities markets can be classified, namely as stock or flow markets. This classification leads us directly to the concept of *equilibrium*. Once a security has been issued, it exists in the market-place until it matures and is redeemed. Although a security can be sold, it can be sold only to someone who is willing to buy it. Clearly, it is impossible for *everyone* to sell their holdings of a particular security. Therefore there is a market for the entire stock of a particular security, and there is also a market for the flow purchases and sales of that security over time. These are shown in Figure 1.3. The left-hand diagram, which shows the *stock market*, indicates a fixed stock supply and a downward-

**Figure 1.3** The stock and flow markets for a security

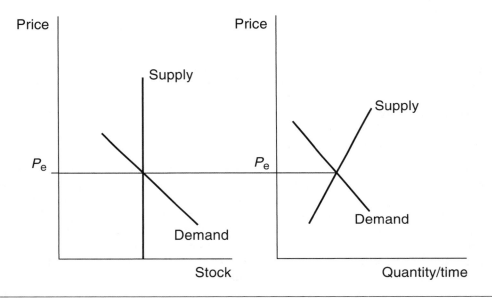

sloping stock demand with respect to the price of the security. The lower the price of the security, the higher the stock demand. The right-hand diagram shows the *flow market* per unit of time. If the time period is a day, for example, the diagram indicates a downward-sloping daily demand curve and an upward-sloping daily supply curve for the security. Equilibrium in the stock market is defined as the situation in which the entire stock supply of the security is voluntarily held. This occurs when the stock market price of the security is $P_e$. Equilibrium in the flow market is defined as the situation in which the flow supply of the security on the market equals the flow demand. This occurs when the flow market price of the security is $P_e$. Overall equilibrium occurs when both the stock and flow markets are simultaneously in equilibrium. This occurs when the stock and flow market equilibrium prices are identical. Out of equilibrium, prices will adjust to clear both markets.

Figure 1.4 shows the *equilibrium price*, but this price is never actually observed in the market-place. What is observed are *transaction* (or *trade*) *prices*, and these take into account the bid-offer

**Figure 1.4** The bid-offer spread

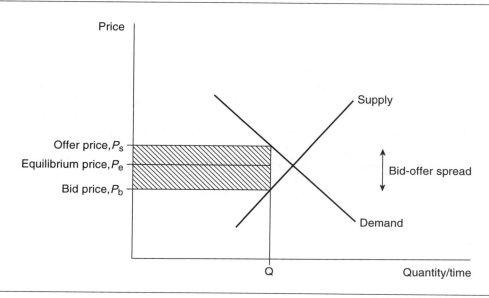

spread of the market-makers. The transaction price at which a market-maker buys securities is the *bid price* and the transaction price at which he sells security is the *offer price*. The difference between the two is the *bid-offer spread*. If there is more than one market-maker, then the difference between the highest bid price and the lowest offer price is known as the market bid-offer spread or the *touch*. The equilibrium price lies within the touch, as Figure 1.4 shows for the flow market. When the market maker makes a sale at the offer price, he will often say that he has been *lifted* (or *taken* or *lost*); in contrast, when he makes a purchase at the bid price, he will often say that he has been *hit*.

What determines the bid-offer spread? This can be answered once we have examined the role of a market-maker. In an organized financial market, the role of a recognized market-maker is to provide continuous and effective two-way prices (i.e., both bid and offer prices) in all market conditions. In short, the market-maker has the responsibility of keeping an orderly market. To do this effectively, he must hold an inventory of securities to smooth out price fluctuations. The market-maker must be compensated for holding these inventories, and the bid-offer spread is the way in which the market-maker receives his compensation. The bid-offer spread will be determined to compensate the market-maker for the cost of and risk to the capital that he has tied up in the inventory of securities. The total compensation to all the market-makers is given by the shaded area in Figure 1.4, i.e. $(P_S - P_B)Q$.

The costs and risks of market-making depend on such characteristics of the market as its *breadth*, *depth* and *resilience*. They also depend on the ratio of information-motivated investors to liquidity-motivated investors.

A market for a particular security is said to have *breadth* if it has a substantial volume of both buy and sell orders at the equilibrium price, i.e. if it has a good two-way flow of orders. Markets with few buyers and sellers are called *thin* markets. A security will be regarded as highly liquid if the market for that security has substantial breadth. Market-makers in a broad market will operate with lower bid-offer spreads than those in a thin market, because broad markets provide a bigger volume of business and are also less risky.

A market for a security is said to have *depth* if it has a continuous flow of buy and sell orders at prices above and below the equilibrium price. This means that both the flow demand curve and the flow supply curve must be continuous at prices above and below the equilibrium price. It also means that both the demand curve and the supply curve must be highly elastic (i.e. quite flat) at prices around the equilibrium price. If these conditions hold, then only small changes in the price of the security will be required to restore equilibrium should a sudden imbalance between buy and sell orders arise. In short, price changes will be continuous in deep markets. In *shallow* markets, on the other hand, the flow demand and supply curves are either discontinuous or highly inelastic (steep). In such markets price changes will be both highly variable and discontinuous (i.e. they will jump around a great deal). Price changes will be smaller in deep markets than in shallow markets. Therefore there is less risk of market-makers incurring losses on their inventories as a result of sudden large adverse price movements in deep markets compared with shallow markets. As a result, market-makers' spreads will be lower in deep markets than in shallow markets. A security will be regarded as highly reversible if the market for that security has substantial depth. Figure 1.5 shows a broad, deep market, while Figure 1.6 shows a thin, shallow market.

**Figure 1.5** A broad, deep market

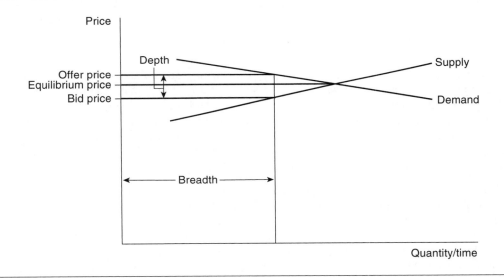

A market is said to be *resilient* if the flow of buy and sell orders does not dry up whenever the price changes. If price changes do not reduce the flow of orders, then the market-makers will not be faced with an inventory of unsaleable securities, and as a result they will be willing to charge lower spreads.

So we can see that the bid-offer spread will be lower the broader the market, the deeper the market, and the more resilient the market.

But the bid-offer spread will be higher, the larger the ratio of information-motivated investors to liquidity-motivated investors. It is clear from Figure 1.4 that the market-maker will always make money if the equilibrium price for the security lies between the bid and offer prices. This is because he buys at below the equilibrium price and sells at above the equilibrium price. Since most liquidity-motivated investors are willing to accept these terms, the market-maker, on average, makes money from liquidity-motivated investors. Similarly, he will on average make money out of badly

**Figure 1.6** A thin, shallow market

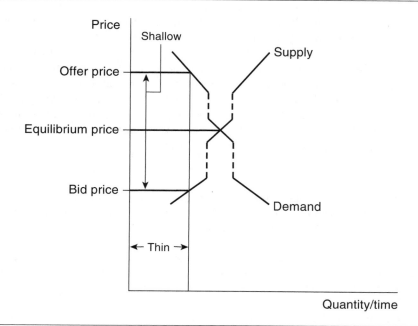

informed information-motivated investors. However, he will on average lose money to well-informed information-motivated investors. Such investors will want to buy the security if they believe that the true equilibrium price is above the offer price and will want to sell the security if they believe that the true equilibrium price is below the bid price. They hope that the market will soon adjust so that they can take their profits. So the larger the ratio of information-motivated to liquidity-motivated investors, the bigger risk of losses to the market-maker and therefore the wider the spread.

The market-maker therefore always has an incentive to ensure that the equilibrium price of the security never lies outside his bid and offer prices. He can do this by having a wide bid-offer spread. But if this is set too wide, he will be uncompetitive and will lose business. An alternative way of protecting himself, especially in a volatile market, is to limit the size of each transaction. Rather than quoting bid and offer prices that are good for up to 10,000 shares, for example, the market-maker's quote might be good only for 1000 shares. Market-makers therefore make a very important contribution towards what is known as *price discovery* or *efficient price formation*. This is the process by which the equilibrium prices of securities become known to investors in general; and it follows because market-makers have every incentive to ensure that the equilibrium price lies within the market bid-offer spread.

### 1.3.2 Financial markets in the UK

We conclude this section with a discussion of the three most important cash securities markets in the UK: the money market, the bond market and the share (or equity) market. The markets in derivative securities (e.g. options and futures) are explained later (see Chapters 8 and 9).

**The money market.**    The money market trades money market securities such as Treasury bills and commercial bills. The main components of the money market are the discount market (which trades Treasury bills and commercial bills eligible for rediscount at the Bank of England, the inter-bank market (which trades the temporary surpluses and deficits of the banking system), the certificate of deposit market (which trades certificates of deposit), the local authority market (which trades local authority bills), and the inter-company market (which trades the temporary surpluses and deficits of the company sector). The settlement period for money market securities is one day: this means that the securities must be delivered to the buyer by the seller on the next business day following the transaction. This is known as *cash settlement*. However, it is now also possible to have same-day settlement if required. The settlement process for money market instruments is conducted through the Central Moneymarkets Office (CMO) which was established in 1990.

**The bond market.**    The bond market trades UK government and government-guaranteed bonds (or gilts), corporate bonds (debentures and loan stock), foreign bonds and eurobonds. The dealing and settlement procedures differ for different types of bond.

The most important bond market in the UK is the *gilts* or *gilt-edged market*, so-called because originally the bond certificates were edged in gilt. This market began in 1694 when the government of William III raised £1 million to finance a war against France. This event signalled the start of the UK National Debt and also the beginning of the Bank of England, since the financiers who raised the £1 million were, in return, granted a royal charter to set up a bank, which became known as the Bank of England. The Bank of England is the *central bank* of the UK.

Until 1998, the Bank of England had responsibility both for issuing new gilts and for the financial regulation of the gilts market (i.e., ensuring investor protection and the capital adequacy of market-makers). Since 1998, the institutional framework underlying the gilts market has been as follows. The primary (or new issues) market in gilts is controlled by the Debt Management Office (DMO), an executive agency of HM Treasury established in 1998, which acts as the government's agent in managing the *public sector borrowing requirement* (PSBR) (if a borrowing requirement exists) and the *national debt*, as well as actively managing the net cash flows of the government (this activity is called *exchequer cash management*). The Treasury informs the DMO of the size of any borrowing requirement, but the DMO decides on all other aspects of the issue, such as maturity and coupon, taking into account its remit to minimize the cost of financing government borrowing. The DMO is also involved in refinancing the National Debt, i.e., in issuing new gilts to replace maturing gilts.[2] The responsibility for the financial regulation of the gilts market lies with the Financial Services Authority (see section 1.5 below). Dealing in gilts is the responsibility of the London Stock Exchange (LSE), while the clearing and settlement process in the gilts market is conducted through the Gilts Settlements Office (GSO) (see also section 1.4.4 below). Finally, the Bank of England is responsible for keeping the register of gilt owners.[3] The aim is to provide a highly liquid market in government debt securities, with high standards of investor protection and an efficient trading system. We will now examine, in

---

[2]The DMO is separate from the National Debt Office (NDO), which manages several statutory funds, including the National Loans Fund, the National Insurance Fund and the National Savings Bank. The NDO, along with the Public Works Loan Board (which lends to local authorities), is part of the National Investment and Loans Office (NILO) of the Treasury.

[3]The Bank of England is also responsible for the *open market operations* (i.e., the buying and selling of Treasury bills and eligible commercial bills) needed to maintain interest rates at a level consistent with the government's monetary policy objective of controlling inflation; this is a completely separate activity from that of actively managing the government's net cash flows in order to reduce the government's debt servicing costs, an activity conducted by the DMO. The Bank also manages the government's foreign currency borrowing programme which is used to finance the government's foreign currency reserves.

turn, the primary and secondary markets in gilts; the operational structure of the gilts market in its current form was established at the time of the Big Bang in October 1986 (see section 1.6.1 below).

There are two main methods of issuing gilts in the UK: tender and auction. Most gilts are offered for sale by *tender*. A tender issue will be announced at 3.30pm on a Friday and will take place the following Wednesday or Thursday. Tenders can involve both conventional and index-linked gilts and typically will involve a substantial amount of stock (i.e. £750–£1000 million nominal). Any member of the public can submit an application for stock (specifying a price and an amount of stock demanded at that price), although most tender offers will usually end up in the portfolios of large institutional investors such as pension funds and insurance companies. Most tender offers are fully paid, although some are partly paid and so allow investors to spread their payments over time. All tender issues are allocated at a single price (called the *allotment price*): equal to the lowest price at which tenders are accepted (which must be at or above the *minimum tender price* of the offer). All bids submitted at prices above the tender price are allotted in full. Bids submitted at the tender price will be allocated stock on a pro rata basis, until the entire amount of stock is allocated. If at the minimum tender price, not all of the stock available has been allotted, then the DMO retains the unallotted stock as a *tap stock*, to sell into the secondary market as conditions dictate. Some gilts issues are specifically intended to be tap stocks. The gilt is issued in *tranches* (or *tranchettes*, if less than £100 million nominal is issued at a particular time). The existing stock is known as the *parent stock* and the tranche is said to be fully *fungible* with the parent stock. Gilts designed for specialist investors (e.g. low-coupon deep-discount gilts designed for higher-rate taxpayers, or index-linked gilts designed for pension funds) are also often issued in tranches. Particularly actively traded bonds (usually a recently issued tranche or tranchette) are known as *runners*.

The second and most recent method of issuing gilts is via *auction*, a system widely used in the US Treasury bond market. The first gilts auction took place on 13 May 1987 and involved £1 billion of 8% Treasury Loan Stock 1992. The DMO announces that an auction will take place some weeks ahead. Details of the issue (size, e.g. £750 million, and maturity, e.g. ten years) are confirmed seven days before the auction. Dealings can take place prior to the auction. (This is known as *when issued* or *grey market* trading.) Irrevocable bids (a maximum of three per applicant) for the stock together with same-day funds must be submitted to the DMO by 10am on the day of the auction. Gilt-edged market-makers are expected to bid competitively for the stock (but, unlike in the USA, are not obliged to bid). Successful bidders at an auction (in contrast with successful bidders for a tender issue) are allotted stock at the price that they bid and not at a single allotment price. The difference between the average price and the lowest accepted price is called the *tail*. The DMO is also willing to accept non-competitive bids for amounts between £1,000 and £100,000. These bids will be allotted in full at the average allotment price. Settlement of grey market deals takes place on the day following the auction.

In January 1989, *reverse auctions* were introduced. As a result of the government running a budget surplus at the time, the public sector borrowing requirement (PSBR) turned into the *public sector debt repayment* (PSDR). At first this was achieved by the direct repurchase of gilts from the market. But now it is achieved by reverse auction, whereby the DMO bids directly for the gilts held by institutional investors.

At the centre of the secondary market in gilts is a set of approved *gilt-edged market-makers* (GEMMs). The role of GEMMs is to make a market in the full range of gilts. They have an obligation to provide continuous and effective two-way prices on demand and in any trading conditions to other member firms of the LSE (i.e. broker-dealers, but excluding other GEMMs) and to outside investors known directly to them. GEMMs can, but are not required to, display their prices on SEAQ (the *Stock Exchange Automated Quotations* system which is carried by TOPIC, an electronic informa-tion transmission service). GEMMs are required to report their position risks to the DMO on a daily basis. The DMO can require GEMMs to reduce their risk exposure or to increase their capital basis. The DMO is also keen to ensure that the gilts market is highly liquid. It helps this process by ensuring that there is a significant issue of bonds at particular maturities, namely 5, 10 and 15 years. Such bonds are known as *benchmark* or *reference* bonds. It does this by issuing new bonds at these maturities or by adding to existing issues. Such bonds are attractive to investors and this is indicated by the fact that they typically trade at higher prices and lower yields than bonds with neighbouring maturities.

GEMMs have exclusive access to *inter-dealer brokers* (IDBs). The role of inter-dealer brokers is to allow GEMMs to unwind long or short positions that arise as a result of their market-making activities and to do this anonymously so that their *book* is not exposed. So, for example, a GEMM that finds that it has an excessive holding of a particular gilt can sell the excess holding to another GEMM which would like to take more of this particular gilt on to its books. It will do this using the services of an IDB, and neither GEMM will be able to identify the counterparty. The IDBs will display anonymously the GEMMs' bids and offers and then seek to match bids with offers. IDBs are not permitted to take positions for their own account; they merely earn commission from the GEMM on whose behalf they are acting. It is vitally important for the liquidity of the market that anonymity is preserved. Therefore IDBs must be established as completely independent entities.

The liquidity of the gilts market was further enhanced by the introduction of a *repurchase* or *repo market* in 1996. A gilt repo or repurchase market enables investors to sell gilts for cash (that is, borrow funds) and then repurchase them at a later date on prearranged terms. The implied rate of interest on the loan is known as the *repo rate* and this is slightly higher than the yield on a Treasury bill of the same term. The most common type of repo is the *overnight repo*; a repo lasting more than one business day is known as a *term repo*. The agreement is fully collateralized since, if the borrowing counterparty fails to repay the loan, the lender is able to retain ownership of the gilts (see also sections 1.4.3 and 5.10). When the gilt repo market started in January 1996, about £100bn of the £230bn of gilts then outstanding were made available for repo trading by being placed by wholesale market participants, such as commercial and investment banks, building societies, insurance companies and pension funds in Central Gilts Office Star accounts. Large banks quote two-way prices on terms extending out to a year. The GEMMs use repos not only to meet their market making obligations, but also in both their matched and mismatched book trading (e.g., a GEMM borrows a gilt in the repo market, in the expectation of a price rise, and when this occurs relends it at a more favourable repo rate).

The government expects the introduction of the repo market to lead to a more efficient gilts market with closer links between it and the money markets; it also expects gilt yields to fall as liquidity improves, thereby reducing the cost of servicing the National Debt. As in other money markets, the repo rate has become the benchmark UK interest rate, replacing both the commercial banks' base lending rate and the discount rate on Treasury bills. One consequence of the introduction of the gilts repo market was the ending of the role of *stock exchange money brokers* (SEMBs) in the gilts market. The SEMBs used to provide a link between GEMMs and institutional investors, enabling the former to cover short positions by borrowing stock on a temporary basis from the latter. This role is no longer required since the GEMMs can use the repo market directly and SEMBs have either merged with banks, or have reverted to stand-alone *money brokers*, arranging stock lending agreements in other securities such as equities or currencies.

As in the money market, the settlement period in the gilts market is one day, so that the relevant gilts must be delivered against a sale the following business day. It is this short settlement period that makes IDBs and repurchase agreements so important. However, with the permission of the LSE, it is possible to have delayed settlement (known as *forward settlement*) of up to 14 days after a trade, so long as both parties agree. This allows, for example, for delays in currency conversion, the transit of requisite documentation or the realization of proceeds from a related sale of a security. Settlement between market-makers and other members of the CGO is made by *book entry transfer* rather than by the physical transfer of gilt certificates. The method used is known as *delivery-versus-payment* (DVP) and involves an automated stock transfer and assured payment service, whereby positive acceptance of the stock by the buyer and a guarantee from the buyer's settlement bank to make payment occur simultaneously. In return, the settlement banks take a floating charge over the stock in case the member defaults. Small investors can buy and sell gilts through the National Savings Stock Register (NSSR) which is administered by the Department of National Savings.

A recent innovation in the gilts market was the introduction of *gilt stripping* in 1997. Gilt stripping involves the separation of a bond into its two constituent components, the coupon payments (also called the *annuity component*) and the par value (also called the *zero coupon component*). These two components are then traded separately, enabling investors to buy just the income component of the gilt, say. Capital gains on gilt strips as well as coupon payments are subject to income tax (for individuals) or corporation tax (for companies), although capital losses can be offset against other taxable income. The introduction of gilt repoing and stripping, by making the gilts market more attractive to investors, should help to reduce government borrowing costs: institutional investors such as pension funds are likely to be the major investors in the zero coupon component of the strip since these match their longer-term liabilities, whilst the annuity component will be most highly valued by those wanting regular income, such as pensioners.

The UK *corporate bond market* trades on the LSE the debentures and loan stocks of UK-based corporations. It is much smaller than the gilts market and relatively much smaller than the corporate bond markets in other financial systems (e.g. the USA) because of the tendency of UK corporations to raise debt finance through the banking system rather than through the markets. Market-makers register to trade in particular bonds. Unlike GEMMs who have to trade in all government bonds, market-makers in this sector do not have to trade in all corporate bonds outstanding. As a result many corporate bonds are not very liquid. The settlement system used is the same as that used for domestic equities (see below).

The *foreign bond market* (both governmental and corporate) operates in a very similar way to the UK corporate bond market. For example, the Kingdom of Sweden might issue a bond in sterling, and it will be traded just like the sterling bond of a UK company.

The *eurobond market* is rather different from the markets considered above. Eurobonds are bonds whose capital and interest payments are generally denominated in a currency different from that of the country in which the bond is issued; the issuer can be of any nationality. The eurobond market was established in the early 1960s in response to what was regarded as over-regulation in domestic bond markets, especially that in the USA. It remains a largely unregulated market, with transactions between participants being a question of honour, there being no arbitration procedure in the event of dispute. The eurobond market in the UK has the status of a Designated Investment Exchange (see below) and is organized by the International Securities Market Association (ISMA), comprising international banks and brokers.

Some eurobonds are quoted on the official stock exchanges in London, Zurich and Luxembourg. However, eurobonds do not have to be listed on an official exchange, and most trading in eurobonds is conducted over-the-counter by telephone between market-makers (mainly international banks and especially the lead managers involved in the original issue) and brokers acting on behalf of investors.

Market-makers' price quotes are carried by Reuters and other electronic information services. Settlement and delivery take place three calendar days following the dealing date, although by mutual agreement it is possible to have *urgent settlement* which is two business days following the dealing date. Clearing is usually done through systems known as *Cedel* (based in Luxembourg) and *Euroclear* (based in Brussels).

Besides the gilt repo market, London has bond repo markets in the major European currencies, in particular the Deutschmark and the euro. A number of factors have encouraged this development, in particular, the rapid growth in new issues of bonds by a number of governments and the introduction of standardized documentation, namely, the PSA/ISMA Global Master Repurchase Agreement. Confidence in the security of repos has been enhanced by the introduction of the *tri-party repo*, where a repo bank manages a standard two-party agreement by ensuring adequate collateral, daily marking to market and the payment of margin (see chapter 8). In addition, regulations make it unprofitable to undertake repos in many of the domestic European markets. For example, most Deutschmark repos are booked in London because of minimum reserve requirements set by the Bundesbank which require any liability (including repos) taken from either a non-bank customer or a foreign bank by a German bank to be secured by a non-interest bearing deposit at the Bundesbank. To avoid this penalty, Germany banks trade repos in London through their London subsidiaries.

**The share market.**  In the UK, the principal body responsible for the *domestic equity market* is the London Stock Exchange which oversees the Listed Securities Market and the Alternative Investment Market. Outside the direct control of the Stock Exchange is the over-the-counter (OTC) share market, the venture capital market and a number of screen-based electronic trading systems.

The *Listed Securities Market* is the main market of the LSE. It began in 1773. The idea of owning shares in a joint-stock company goes back to the seventeenth century, when companies such as 'The Mysterie and Companie of the Merchant Adventurers for the Discoverie of Regions, Dominions, Islands and Places unknowen' (later shortened to the Muscovy Company) began trading. Merchants would take shares in a particular venture and divide up the company and the profits at the end of the voyage. Soon it was realized that it was not necessary to break up the company after each venture as long as the original investors could get their money back by selling their shares to new investors. An informal market in shares was established in the coffee houses around the Royal Exchange in London. In 1773 one of them, New Jonathan's, became 'the Stock Exchange' and was the first building in the world to carry this name.

The primary market in listed securities is controlled by the LSE. Only *public limited companies* (i.e. companies with 'PLC' after their name, having a minimum share capital of £50,000, at least two directors and a trading certificate issued by the Registrar of Companies) can apply for listing. *Private limited companies* (i.e. companies with 'Limited' or 'Ltd' after their name) cannot be listed on the listed market. *Listed securities* are the securities (i.e. shares and bonds) of listed companies that have been admitted to the *Official List* of the LSE and whose prices are quoted on the LSE via SEAQ.

The requirements for listing are contained in the LSE's Yellow Book (officially, *The Admission of Securities for Listing*). The main conditions that have to be met are as follows. The minimum market value of an initial listing in shares is £700,000, while that in bonds is £200,000, although in practice, as a result of transaction costs, it is unusual to find firms being listed on the main market with a market capitalization below £10 million. The firm must have at least a three-year trading record (with accounts properly filed at Companies House). At least 25 per cent of the shares must be available for the public to acquire, and the shares must be freely transferable. The company must pay an initial fee to the LSE based on the size of the issue and then an annual fee based on market capitalization. Directors of the company have a continuing obligation to provide for the disclosure of information which is necessary both to protect the investor and to maintain an orderly market.

The issuing company will have to appoint a member firm of the LSE to act as its sponsor. The sponsor will typically be a large investment bank, which will then be responsible for all matters concerning listing, including the publication of the *prospectus* detailing the nature of the firm, its activities and directors, and the announcement of the issue in the national press. In particular, the sponsor must ensure that the board of directors of the company has the expertise necessary to run a listed company or must decide whether the board needs to be augmented by the appointment of non-executive directors.

Once approval for listing has been given, the company has to decide on the method of issue. The most common method is an *offer for subscription* for the securities of a company, made by or on behalf of the company direct to the public. The issue will generally be underwritten by an investment bank or insurance company. The offer for subscription can be either at a fixed price or by tender. In the case of a fixed-price offer, the company sets the price and investors apply for shares at that price. If the offer is oversubscribed, the company has to scale down applications. If the offer is undersubscribed, the underwriter has to buy from the company the unallotted shares. With a tender offer, investors are required to state both the number of shares that they wish to buy and the price that they are prepared to pay, subject to a minimum tender price specified by the company. When the applications have been received, the company determines an allotment price and issues shares at the allotment price to investors who applied for shares at or above this price.

There are other issue methods, but they are generally used when a company wishes to increase the number of shares issued, rather than as the method of initial issue. These include: (1) *offers for sale* (either at a fixed price or by tender) where an issuing house buys the whole issue and then offers it for sale to the general public; (2) *placings* or *selective marketings* to specific investors (the LSE usually only gives approval for these when significant public demand for the securities is not expected; in the case of initial listing, no more than £15 million worth of shares can be issued by selective marketing); (3) *introductions* (requiring only an abridged announcement in the national press; these are another concessionary method of issue, suitable when the existing shares of the company are widely held and hence already very marketable, or when the shares are already listed on another stock exchange); (4) *rights issues* (offers to existing shareholders to subscribe for new shares in proportion to their existing holdings, thereby recognizing the pre-emptive rights of shareholders as laid down in the Companies Act 1985; made in the form of a *renounceable letter* that can be sold if the shareholder does not wish to exercise his rights); and (5) *open offers* (also offers to existing shareholders to subscribe for shares although not necessarily in proportion to their existing shareholdings, and not in renounceable form). A final method of issuing shares is known as a *capitalization issue* (also known as a *scrip* or *bonus issue*). This is simply the issue of new shares to current shareholders in proportion to their existing holdings because the company wishes to make a transfer from the retained earnings account to the capital account. The shares are issued free of charge and so no new money is raised.

The share prices of Britain's companies are collected together in share price indices of various kinds. The most important of these is the *FTSE 100 Index* which is an index of the share prices of Britain's largest 100 companies by market capitalisation and which is compiled by the *Financial Times*, the Institute and the Faculty of Actuaries, and the LSE; it covers about 74 per cent by value of all UK shares. The *FTSE 250* is an index of the share prices of the next largest 250 companies by capitalisation below the constituent companies of the FTSE 100 Index; it covers about 18 per cent by value of all UK shares. The *FTSE 350 Index* combines the constituents of the FTSE 100 and FTSE 250 indices, and covers 92 per cent of the total stock market by value. The *FTSE Small Cap Index* is an index of the share prices of 450 small companies, and covers 6 per cent of the stock market by value. The *FTSE Fledgling Index* deals with very small companies with market capitalizations below £50m and covers 1.5 per cent of the market. The *FT-A All Share Index* covers 800 shares prices from large and small companies across the economy.

The secondary market in listed shares is conducted using one of two different trading systems: an electronic order-book system and a more traditional market-making system. We will consider each of these systems in turn.

Since October 1997, the shares of the largest companies operating in the UK (namely those comprising the FTSE 100 index as well as companies on the FTSE reserve list which, for example, contains companies for which LIFFE offers traded options) have been traded using an *order-book* (or *order-driven*) *system* called *SETS* (the *Stock Exchange Electronic Trading Service*) which automatically matches orders placed electronically by potential buyers and sellers. The motivation for this innovation was increased competition from other exchanges in Europe and elsewhere which were offering greater efficiency, greater transparency and lower costs, by automating the execution of trades, publishing immediately the transaction prices and by narrowing the spread between buy and sell prices. Greater transparency is achieved because there is no opportunity for *iceberg orders*, i.e. limit orders which disclose only part of the order the investor wishes to trade. It also gives investors greater choice by allowing them to trade immediately at the best available price or by placing an order on the book so as to influence the way in which the price changes.

The electronic order book is available for public inspection, but only member firms of the LSE can directly input buy or sell orders. An investor who wishes to trade contacts their broker by telephone and stipulates the number of shares and the price at which they are willing to either buy or sell. The broker enters the details in the order book and these will be displayed anonymously on the order book screen. The order book works by automatically matching buy and sell orders at the same price and then executing the orders to create trades.

To illustrate, an order book screen might look like this for a particular share:

| BUY | | SELL | |
|---|---|---|---|
| *Volume* | *Price* | *Price* | *Volume* |
| 10000 | 235 | 237 | 8000 |
| 11000 | 234 | 238 | 10000 |
| 9500 | 232 | 241 | 4500 |

If another investor now wished to sell 4,000 shares at 238p, the 'sell volume' at this price would rise from 10,000 shares to 14,000 shares. If the investor wishes to sell immediately at the best possible price, he could do so at 235p and the 'buy volume' at 235p would fall to 6,000. Once an order has been executed, the trade is reported to the exchange which then informs the two member firms involved. Only the two member firms get to know each other's identity; this information is not reported to the market as a whole and, similarly, the identities of the two principals to the trade remain anonymous.

Large block trades (those greater than eight times NMS, see below) operate on the basis of a *worked principal agreement* (WPA) (also known less formally as an *upstairs trading facility*), whereby 80 per cent of a trade can be unwound before details of the trade are published.

The order book is open from 9:00 to 16:30. Between 8:30 and 9:00, there is an 'orientation' period, during which orders can be added or removed in readiness for the market opening. Between 16:30 and 17:00, there is a 'housekeeping' period, allowing unexecuted orders to be removed if investors wish.

All prices reported (including current, opening, closing, high and low) are based on the relevant transaction prices rather than on the more traditional mid prices (between the bid and offer prices). In fact, conventional bid and offer prices do not exist with an order book system, since there are no market-maker quotes. The spread is simply the difference between the lowest price for a sell order and the highest price for a buy order at any one time. The opening price is either the price at which the first trade takes place or the *uncrossing price*, the price chosen by the exchange which allows as many of the orders left from the previous day to execute. The official closing price is the last trade price before the 16:30 close. In a volatile market, if the price of a share changes during the day by more than 10 per cent of its opening price, the order book will be suspended for 10 minutes.

The *market-making* (or *quote-driven*) *system* is conducted through SEAQ. Market-makers in listed securities are obliged to make firm bid and offer prices in the shares that they are registered to make a market in. They must display on SEAQ firm two-way prices in not less than a minimum specified quantity of shares, known as a *minimum quote size*, as laid down by the LSE. (The minimum quote size in a particular share is equal to the normal market size for that share as explained below.) The highest quoted bid price and the lowest quoted offer price are displayed in the *yellow strip* on SEAQ. Once a trade has taken place, it must be reported immediately to the exchange. In return for these obligations, registered market-makers are accorded certain privileges. For example, only registered market-makers can input prices into SEAQ. In addition, market-makers are allowed to hold short positions in the shares in which they are registered. They do this by borrowing shares from authorized lending institutions using the services of money brokers. Inter-dealer brokers (IDBs) also exist in the equity market to help market-makers unwind their positions.

Since 1991, listed shares quoted on SEAQ have been classified according to *normal market size* (NMS) *bands*. There are twelve bands ranging from 500 to 200,000, where each band size indicates the average number of institutional-sized trades (defined as a deal of 10,000 shares) made in that share during the previous year. The twelve NMS bands are shown in Table 1.1.

**Table 1.1** The NMS bands

| NMS band | Range of institutional-sized trades per year | Number of SEAQ shares |
|---|---|---|
| 500 | 0 – 667 | 960 |
| 1,000 | 668 – 1,333 | 321 |
| 2,000 | 1,334 – 2,400 | 214 |
| 3,000 | 2,401 – 3,750 | 159 |
| 4,000 | 3,751 – 6,667 | 158 |
| 5,000 | 6,668 – 12,000 | 135 |
| 10,000 | 12,001 – 18,000 | 61 |
| 25,000 | 18,001 – 33,000 | 74 |
| 50,000 | 33,001 – 60,000 | 53 |
| 75,000 | 60,001 – 93,000 | 12 |
| 100,000 | 93,001 – 160,000 | 9 |
| 200,000 | more than 160,000 | 2 |
| | | 2,158 |

The average number of institutional-sized trades (of 10,000 shares) in a particular share is calculated as follows:

$$\frac{\text{Value of turnover in previous 12 months}}{\text{Closing mid-price on last day of quarter} \times 10,000}.$$

As an example, consider Abbey National ordinary 10p shares. Suppose that the value of the turnover in these shares during the previous 12 months was £1,071.36m and that the closing mid-price was £2.31. Then the average number of institutional-sized trades during the previous 12 months was:

$$\frac{1,071,360,000}{2.31 \cdot 10,000} = 46,379.$$

Since this is in the range 33,001 to 60,000, the NMS band for Abbey National shares is 50,000.

The NMS bands are important for a number of reasons. Most significantly, the NMS band indicates the degree of liquidity of the share: the higher the band, the greater the liquidity. Second, the bands indicate the minimum quote size for a particular share. Third, the bands are used for *trade reporting* purposes. All shares in NMS bands 2,000 and above have immediate trade publication (i.e. within 3 minutes) on SEAQ for all trades up to six times the size of the NMS band (this is known as the *maximum publication level* (MPL)). Trades between 6 and 75 times the size of the NMS band have to be reported with a maximum delay of 60 minutes. *Block trades* greater than 75 times NMS have to be reported after three days or once 90 per cent of the trade has been offset (whichever is sooner). There is no trade publication on SEAQ for bargains of value below £1,000 or for shares in bands 500 and 1,000. These are fairly illiquid shares and the publication of trades in these shares appears the next business day in the Stock Exchange's *Daily Official List*. However all trades that do not involve market-makers assuming risk (e.g. agency cross trades between brokers and riskless principal trades including those between market makers) are published immediately on SEAQ. Similarly, the trades in shares of companies subject to a takeover bid are published immediately.

Once a share has moved to SETS, it will remain there. But international experience indicates that order-book systems work best with very liquid shares. The LSE does not believe that SETS would be suitable for shares outside the FTSE350 index. So the quote-driven system using SEAQ will remain in place for such shares.

Listed shares (and also corporate bonds) are cleared and settled using the LSE's CREST electronic (i.e. paperless or 'dematerialized') settlement system (see also section 1.4.4 below). CREST began operating in July 1996 and replaced the exchange's 200-year old, fortnightly, paper-based account settlement system known as TALISMAN. CREST operates a *rolling settlement* system known as T+5 whereby settlement (the exchange of cash for share certificates) takes place five business days after the transaction date (e.g. on the next Monday for a trade taking place on a Monday etc.). The tight five-day schedule for delivering share certificates means that an increasing number of active investors hold their certificates in a *nominee account*, although this is at the price of transferring nominal (although not beneficial) ownership of the shares to the company operating the nominee account (typically a broker). Only one copy of the annual report is sent to the broker running the nominal account, unless investors become *designated nominees* in which case additional copies of the annual report are sent to brokers who then pass them on to these investors. There has also been an increased use of deposit accounts held with brokers (and linked to a nominee account), together with an increased use of margin accounts (see Section 1.4.2 below). An alternative to nominee accounts is *sponsored membership* of CREST. This enables shareholders to retain their names on the company register and to receive annual reports and accounts, invitations to annual meetings and other shareholder information and benefits (such as discounts when buying company products), directly from the company. The shareholder is sponsored by an intermediary (typically a broker or a solicitor) who can charge for this service. There is a nominee company compensation scheme, but this does not cover sponsored membership. Eventually the T+5 rolling settlement system will be reduced to T+3.

The *Alternative Investment Market* (AIM) was established by the LSE in June 1995 to trade the shares of companies that are not suitable for a listing on the listed market. These include *small-cap companies* (young, fast-growing companies with currently low stock market capitalizations), management buy-outs and buy-ins, companies with shares that are closely-held (i.e. companies owned by a few people, typically members of the same family, whose shares are traded only infrequently) and Enterprise Investment Scheme companies. AIM also trades the bonds of such companies as well as the shares and bonds of foreign companies not incorporated in the UK. AIM replaced the Unlisted Securities Market or Second Market (which operated between 1980 and 1996), the Third Market (which operated between 1987 and 1990), and an earlier LSE market known as the section 4.2 market.

Any company wishing for an AIM listing needs to find an approved sponsor called a *nominated adviser*, one of whose responsibilities is to ensure that the company's prospectus complies with the *public offers of securities* (POS) regulations. AIM is regulated by the LSE's Supervision and Surveillance Department, but the nominated adviser is responsible for ensuring that AIM companies meet all the regulatory standards. For example, the prospectus must provide details of the company, the directors' business background, substantial shareholdings, relevant financial results and a risk warning. But there is no requirement for any minimum percentage of the share capital to be made publicly available, nor is a minimum trading period required. Continuing obligations will be similar to those for companies with a full listing. For example, interim figures and audited accounts plus any price-sensitive information must be disclosed to the LSE. The exchange will assess the performance of nominated advisers and their registration can be withdrawn if they have behaved in a way that impairs the 'integrity and reputation of AIM'. On the other hand, if a nominated adviser resigns, the company's shares will be suspended until it gets another one; if it fails to find a new adviser within a month, its trading facilities will be cancelled. There are some important tax advantages available to AIM companies that are not available to listed market companies. For example, there is income tax relief for losses made on subscribed shares, capital gains tax gift and reinvestment relief, and 100 per cent business property relief from inheritance tax if more than one quarter of a company's equity is inherited (50 per cent relief if less than one quarter is inherited).

AIM uses a trading system called SEATS PLUS (the *Stock Exchange Alternative Trading Service*) to deal with the problem of illiquidity in small company shares. Prior to this, if at least two market-makers could not be found to make competitive prices in a particular share, investors had to use a *bulletin board*, a system of order-book trading between brokers conducted on a *matched bargain basis*. This meant that an investor could not sell his shareholding until another investor was willing to buy it: there was no market-maker who was willing to take the risk of buying the shares from the first investor and wait until the second investor came along to buy the shares from him. A bulletin board system clearly indicates the lack of liquidity in what are called *thinly-traded shares*. SEATS PLUS is a screen-based trading system that allows a single market-maker to trade in such shares. The market-maker quotes bid and offer prices and the broker who wishes to deal in a particular share has to indicate to the market-maker whether he is a potential buyer or a potential seller and has to give the market-maker first refusal on the deal (in contrast, brokers using SEAQ do not have to indicate whether they are buyers or sellers). If the market-maker decides to go ahead with the deal, it is executed at the quoted bid or offer price. The size of the deal has to be reported immediately, but information concerning the price only has to be reported on a five-day rolling settlement basis. If a second market-maker chose to trade in the share, then the share would be transferred to the SEAQ trading system. The bulletin board will be retained for a small number of around 100 companies whose shares are so tightly held that few ever change hands or for new companies wanting to use the status of a public quotation to enhance their prospects of raising funds. The LSE hopes that SEATS PLUS, by improving the liquidity of the shares of small companies, will make small company shares more attractive to institutional investors who invest almost exclusively in the shares of the top 350 companies. Nevertheless, spreads tend to be much wider on AIM than on the main market. They can vary between 2 per cent and 20 per cent compared with about 5 per cent for small companies quoted on the main market.

There are a number of other markets trading domestic equities that are not operated by the LSE.

The *OTC* (over-the-counter) *market* (which began in 1971) is for new companies which do not have a sufficiently long track record to warrant listing on one of the LSE's markets. Most business is carried out by telephone buyers and sellers on a commission basis, although some act as market-makers by directly buying from and selling to investors.

The *venture capital market* (which began to take off in the mid-1970s) provides development or redevelopment capital for unquoted speculative companies which have extremely high risks attached to them but from which higher returns are expected. A venture capital investment is generally illiquid and is realizable only when the company is sold or begins to have its shares traded on the OTC market or one of the LSE markets. The entire investment can be lost if the company fails, as frequently happens. The venture capital market has been used for start-up or greenfield investments, expansion by high growth companies, refinancing, rescue of unprofitable companies through capital injection, and management buy-outs. The most common features of a venture capital investment are: that the investment is through equity participation or with an option to convert to equity; it is of medium term (five to ten years); and there is generally active involvement by the investor with the management of the company.

Recently a number of electronic trading systems have been developed and these compete directly with the LSE in the trading of domestic securities. The most important is *Tradepoint Financial Networks PLC* (or simply Tradepoint) which began operating in 1995 and provides a screen-based, order-matching market in domestic securities for banks and institutional investors, thereby saving on market-makers' spreads. Tradepoint uses Windows software and users such as fund managers and stockbrokers enter the shares they wish to buy or sell together with the volume and price at which they wish to deal. If there are other orders outstanding at that price, the new order is aggregated with these and takes a place at the back of the queue. The user's screen will signal the order in the 'my bids' or 'my offers' column. When a counterparty comes in willing to deal at the price displayed, the trade takes place automatically and the screen records this at the top. If the counterparty wishes to buy fewer shares than the total number on offer, the order goes to the first seller in the queue at that price. If the counterparty wishes to buy more shares than the total on offer, the unfilled part of the order remains on the screen and will be executed as soon as any new shares are offered for sale at that price. Users who change their bid and offer prices during the day have to go to the back of the queue. All orders that are not executed by the end of the business day are cancelled. There is continuous matching of buy and sell orders in liquid shares, but Tradepoint holds periodic auctions for less liquid shares. The trades are settled via the London Clearing House (which also settles deals on the derivatives exchanges in London), but Tradepoint has also been designed to use the LSE's CREST settlement system. Other examples are *Instinet*, a subsidiary of Reuters, which also operates an order-matching market in a limited number of shares via a bulletin board, *Ofex* which was developed by market-maker JP Jenkins, and ESI (*Electronic Share Information*) which uses the Internet, thereby enabling investors to deal in shares using their home computers, with the deals channelled through Charles Schwab (formerly Share-Link), an execution-only broker and member firm of the LSE: ESI supplies current bid and offer prices, the last trade price and the volume of shares changing hands.

*International equities* are the shares issued and traded in the domestic markets of overseas countries. They are purchased and sold using the services of local dealers and brokers. As an alternative to directly accessing the various domestic markets overseas, large investors wishing to invest internationally can use the *international equity market* (IEM) in blue-chip shares. The first genuine example of an international placing of a British company's equity was 25 million shares of Britoil in July 1985. Before that, in November 1984, 90 million British Telecom shares were sold in Switzerland as part of the Swiss tranche of the initial public offering, but this was really part of a placing exercise in different domestic overseas markets.

Having begun in 1983, the international equity market is exactly twenty years younger than the eurobond market and shares many of its characteristics. In particular, the same investment banks that are involved in the eurobond market are using similar resources and techniques to issue and distribute equities. They are involved in the underwriting and placing of the primary issue of equity as well as acting as brokers and even market-makers in the secondary market.

The key advantage of an organized international equity market to international investors is ease and speed of communications. Information concerning shares in companies in different countries can be communicated to international investors much more rapidly using the centralized resources of the investment banks than by using local brokers alone.

One advantage to corporations of an international issue compared with a conventional domestic issue is the saving on costs. By circumventing the need for roadshows, pathfinder prospectuses, stock exchange listing fees and meetings with fund managers and investment analysts in different cities, substantial savings can be made. In addition, there can be time savings in the selling period of up to two months compared with the traditional approach. Another advantage is the access to funds that are not available when the issue is confined to domestic investors. Also, by using international equity issues, companies can bypass some of the restrictive rules and regulations (e.g. with regard to disclosure requirements) of domestic stock exchanges and regulatory authorities.

One of the main constraints on the development of the international secondary market for equities is the absence of an efficient clearing and settlement system. The time taken to settle transactions between different financial centres during the initial phase of the international equity market has been excessive. A similar problem affected the eurobond market in the 1960s. The solution was the introduction of the two clearing systems, Euroclear and Cedel. The same solution has been introduced by both of these systems for international equities, mostly in bearer-form although in some countries (e.g. Sweden) only registered-form equity can be traded. In total, more than 600 equities worldwide have a significant international market.

Another feature of the international equity market is the consequential foreign exchange transactions. An international investor may purchase, say, 10,000 ICI shares in London in sterling and resell half of them in Frankfurt in Deutschmarks and the other half in New York in dollars. Euroclear and Cedel offer such international investors the opportunity of dealing in different markets in a single base currency.

In a further attempt to head off another innovation outside its control, the LSE introduced in 1986 *SEAQ International* (or SEAQ-I) a price quotations system used by more than forty market-makers for trading international equities. Within the European time zone, SEAQ International provides real-time dealing prices for all the main international regions. For example, it covers the 'Big Board' stocks listed on the New York Stock Exchange, such as AT&T, Coca Cola, Exxon, General Motors and IBM, and allows investors to execute orders six hours before the New York Market opens. It also covers the markets in Australia, Canada, Hong Kong, Japan, Scandinavia, South Africa and other emerging markets, with most of the shares quoted in domestic currencies.

SEAQ-I ceased trading European equities in January 1996 because of increasing competition from continental stock exchanges which modernized their rules and their operating systems in an attempt to win back trade in their own domestic shares from London, e.g. they are now more willing to engage in block trades. In October 1995, NatWest Securities, one of the UK's leading market makers, announced that it intended to conduct more of its business on continental exchanges than on SEAQ-I: 'Although London remains the most active trading centre in the world for European equities, we believe our clients can benefit significantly from the growing sophistication and transparency of local dealing systems in Europe ... where we are finding greater efficiency in both cost and execution.' Under EU rules, which came into effect in January 1996, NatWest Securities has applied for *remote membership* of the exchanges in Paris, Madrid and Frankfurt. In 1997, the *FTSE Eurotop 300* index of the shares of Europe's largest 300 companies was launched.

In 1989, the *London Securities and Derivatives Exchange* (or OMLX, an acronym that reflects its original name of Options Market London) began to trade the securities and derivatives of certain Swedish and German companies and equity indices. In 1996, EASDAQ (the *European Association of Securities Dealers Automated Quotations*) began to trade the shares of European smaller companies.

In 1996, all the quote-driven electronic trading systems operated by the LSE, namely SEAQ, SEATS PLUS and SEAQ-I, were integrated into a single trading platform called SEQUENCE, with the aim of executing transactions more rapidly and cheaply. The *London Market Information Link*, introduced in 1994, has reduced the waiting time for information by 15 seconds.

The shares of UK corporations are also traded in overseas markets. For example, in the USA they are traded in the form of *American depository receipts* (ADRs). The UK shares are held by the UK branches of US banks which issue ADRs against them. The ADRs are then traded on the major markets or the OTC market. The original shares do not have to be listed on the relevant US market. ADRs are negotiable bearer securities which are denominated in US dollars. The holders of ADRs are entitled to receive dividends which are payable in US dollars by the custodian bank, subject to a withholding tax of 15 per cent. The holders of ADRs also have voting rights and can request the underlying shares at any time. The attractiveness of ADRs lies in the fact that they are bearer securities and so the holder avoids having to register as the beneficial owner of the UK shares. ADRs are now being replaced by GDRs (*global depository receipts*). Depository receipts in London are traded on SEAQ-I.

## 1.4   Trading arrangements

In this section, we consider some of the trading arrangements that are common to organized financial markets. This covers such issues as the kinds of orders received by brokers, the kinds of accounts kept by investors, and the kinds of stock borrowing agreements made by investors. We also examine the clearing and settlement of trades, as well as official intervention in markets.

## 1.4.1 Types of order

There are various types of order that an investor can give to his broker:

1 *Market* (or *at best*) *order.* The most common type of order is the market order, which is an instruction to buy or sell a particular security immediately at the best possible price (i.e. to buy at the lowest offer price available and sell at the highest bid price).

2 *Stop order.* This is an instruction to buy or sell a particular security as soon as the price passes a particular level. A *buy stop order* for 1000 shares at £2.50 is an instruction to purchase 1000 shares as soon as the share price rises above £2.50. There is no guarantee that the trade will take place at £2.50 and it might be that the order is executed at £2.52. Similarly, a *sell stop order* (also called a *stop-loss order*) on the same terms might be executed at £2.47 rather than £2.50.

3 *Limit order.* This is an instruction to buy or sell a particular security only up to a stated limit price. If the limit price is exceeded, the order will not be executed. For example, a *buy limit order* for 1000 shares at £2.50 is an instruction to purchase 1000 shares if the price is at or below £2.50. The order will not be executed if, by the time it reaches the market, the share price has risen above £2.50.

4 *Stop limit order.* This is a combination of the last two orders. For example, the instruction to 'sell 1000 shares at £2.50 stop, £2.47 limit' will be executed if the share price falls below £2.50 but does not fall below £2.47.

5 *Day order.* This is an order (of the type 2, 3 or 4) that is cancelled if it is not executed on the day the instruction is received.

6 *Open order* (or *Good-till-cancelled order*). This is an order that remains in effect until it is either executed or cancelled.

7 *Fill-or-kill order.* This is an order that is cancelled if it cannot be executed immediately.

8 *Round lot order.* This is an order to buy or sell a security in the standard trading unit for a given stock exchange. For example, on the LSE a round lot for shares is 1000 shares. Similarly, a single LSE share option is for 1000 shares.

9 *Odd lot order.* This is any order for other than a round lot.

## 1.4.2 Types of account

There are two main types of account that an investor can keep with his broker:

1 *Cash account.* This is the most common type of account kept by an investor with his broker. It is exactly like a standard bank account: deposits (in the form of cash and revenue from the sale of securities) must exceed withdrawals (in the form of cash and security purchases).

2 *Margin account.* A margin account is like a bank account with an overdraft limit. It allows investors to buy securities with credit supplied by the broker. The securities are kept with the broker as collateral. The broker charges interest on this loan, at a rate that is related to current money market interest rates. Trading on margin is a means of leverage or gearing that magnifies the percentage gain or loss from a given change in security prices.

The following example illustrates how a margin account works. Suppose initially that an investor buys 1000 shares at £2.00 for cash and sells them after a year for £2.50. His initial cash outflow is £2000 and his cash inflow after a year is £2500. The return on his investment is:

$$\text{Rate of return} \quad = \quad \frac{\text{Net cash inflow}}{\text{Initial cash outflow}}$$

$$= \quad \frac{£2500 - £2000}{£2000} \quad = \quad 25\%.$$

Now suppose instead that the investor purchased the shares on margin subject to an *initial margin requirement* of, say, 75 per cent. This means that he has to put up 75 per cent of the cash himself but can borrow the other 25 per cent at, say, 10 per cent. His initial cash outflow is therefore only £1500 although the shares still cost £2000 to buy. At the end of the year, he again sells the shares for £2500 but the net cash inflow is reduced by the £50 interest he has to pay to the broker. The rate of return on investment is:

$$\text{Rate of return} \quad = \quad \frac{\text{Net cash inflow}}{\text{Initial cash outflow}}$$

$$= \quad \frac{£2500 - £2000 - £50}{£1500} \quad = \quad 30\%.$$

So with margining, the rate of return has been magnified from 25 to 30 per cent.

Suppose, however, that the share price had fallen to £1.50 rather than risen to £2.50. The value of the shares at the end of the year would have been £1500, a loss of £500. The cash investor would have made a loss of 25 per cent (i.e. $[£1500 - £2000]/£2000$). But the marginal investor, who still has to pay interest on the borrowed funds, would have made a loss of 37 per cent (i.e. $[£1500 - £2000 - £50]/£1500$). So with margining, the rate of loss has been magnified from 25 to 37 per cent.

Even worse, the marginal investor suffering adverse price movements may also be faced with a *margin call*. This will occur when the *percentage margin* falls below the *maintenance margin* level, which is set at, say, 70 per cent. Initially the percentage margin was 75 per cent (equal to the initial margin):

$$\text{Initial percentage margin} \quad = \quad \frac{\text{Initial value of investor's equity}}{\text{Initial value of investor's equity} + \text{Value of loan}}$$

$$= \quad \frac{£1500}{£1500 + £500} \quad = \quad 75\%.$$

If the maintenance margin is 70 per cent, then the value of the investor's equity (and the value of the shares) can fall by £333 before a margin call is made, since:

$$\text{Value of investor's equity at time of margin call} \quad = \quad \frac{0.7(\text{Value of loan})}{1 - 0.7}$$

$$= \quad 2.33 \cdot (£500) \quad = \quad £1167,$$

and the initial value of the investor's equity was £1500 ($£333 = £1500 - £1167$). Now a fall in the value of the shares by £333 is equivalent to a fall of 17 per cent (i.e. $£333/£2000$). But by the year end, the value of the shares had fallen by 25 per cent or £500. In order to meet the maintenance margin, the investor would have had to deposit a total of £167 (i.e. $£500 - £333$) with the broker by the end of the year. However, the effect of the margin call is to reduce the loss from 37 to 33 per cent (i.e. $[£1500 - £2000 - £50]/[£1500 + £167]$). The procedure of paying maintenance margin is known as *marking to market*.

### 1.4.3 Stock borrowing agreements

Trading on margin is equivalent to borrowing cash. But there are other trading arrangements that are equivalent to borrowing securities. The most important ones are *short sale agreements* and *repurchase agreements*.

**Short sale agreements.** If an investor expects security prices to rise, he undertakes a marginal purchase of securities. However, if he believes security prices are going to fall, he makes a *short sale*. Short selling involves the sale of a security that is not currently owned by the seller. Initially, the security is borrowed from the short-seller's broker (e.g. from an inventory of securities held as collateral for the margined purchases of other investors) and delivered to the buyer. But at the end of the agreement with the broker, the security has to be repaid to the broker. This is achieved by the short-seller buying the security in the open market and handing it over to the broker.

It follows from this arrangement that the short-seller gains if the security price falls and loses if the security price rises. There is no limit to the potential loss from a short sale, because the security's price can increase without limit. (It can only ever fall to zero.) This makes short selling a very risky activity. It can also be risky for the lender of the security because the short-seller can default on his obligations and not repay the loan. The broker as security lender can protect himself from default through the requirement of the short-seller to make both initial margin and maintenance margin payments. For example, 50 per cent of the proceeds of the short sale may have to be deposited as initial margin. If the security price subsequently rises, maintenance margin payments have to be made. On the other hand, if the security price subsequently falls, cash can be withdrawn by the short-seller. In other words, the margin account is marked to market.

It is difficult if not impossible to provide a sensible way of calculating the rate of return on a short sale. This is because the short seller does not have to put up any capital to support the transaction. Strictly speaking, therefore, the rate of return on a short sale is always plus or minus infinity. However, many people base the rate of return on the value of the initial proceeds, as the following example illustrates.

Suppose that 1000 shares are sold short for £2.00 each. This raises £2000. At the end of the year the shares are standing at £1.50, so that the short-seller has to pay only £1500 for the 1000 shares he has to return to the broker. Suppose also that the £2000 raised could be invested at 10 per cent, generating £200 over the year. However, the short-seller will have to pay the dividend (called a *manufactured dividend*) on the shares borrowed which we take to be payable at 8 per cent, costing £160. The total gain from the transaction is £540 (i.e. £2000 − £1500 + £200 − £160). The rate of return is:

$$\text{Rate of return} = \frac{\text{Net cash inflow}}{\text{Proceeds from short sale}}$$

$$= \frac{£540}{£2000} = 27\%.$$

If instead the share price had risen to £2.50, then the total loss from the transaction is £460 (i.e. £2000 − £2500 + £200 − £160). This implies a rate of return of:

$$\text{Rate of return} = \frac{\text{Net cash inflow}}{\text{Proceeds from short sale}}$$

$$= -\frac{£460}{£2000} = -23\%.$$

Finally, it is important to note that for most investors there are limits to the extent that they can engage in short selling. These are designed to protect the market from a downward slide in prices that substantial short selling activity could generate. The fewest restrictions on short selling are those faced by market-makers themselves.

**Repurchase agreements.**  A *repurchase agreement* (or *repo*) is also an arrangement for borrowing securities but, unlike a short sale, the payments under the transaction are determined at the beginning of the deal. The buyer of a repo buys the security for a fixed term on the understanding that the seller of the repo will repurchase the security at the end of the term at a price that is either set at the beginning of the agreement or determined according to an agreed formula.

We can consider an example of an overnight repo. The buyer of a repo agrees to buy a government bond overnight. The seller agrees to repurchase the bond the following day at a price that includes overnight interest rates. The seller gets the use of cash for one day (i.e. borrows cash against the bond as collateral) and the buyer invests cash overnight in the government bond (i.e. effectively borrows the bond). The opposite transaction to a repo is a *reverse* (or a *reverse repo* or even a *resale*).

Suppose that the seller of the repo is a GEMM who has just agreed to buy £5 million of a government bond but does not have the funds to pay for it, while the buyer of the repo is an investor with surplus cash who wishes to earn the overnight *repo rate* of 8 per cent, say. The interest received by the repo buyer is calculated as follows:

$$\text{Interest} \quad = \quad \text{Principal} \times \text{Repo rate} \times \frac{\text{Repo term}}{365}$$

$$= \quad 5,000,000 \cdot 0.08 \cdot \frac{1}{365} \quad = \quad £1095.89.$$

This interest is paid indirectly as follows. The repo seller sells the bonds on one day for £4,998,904.11 (i.e. £5,000,000 − £1,095.89) and buys them back the next day for £5,000,000.

Repos are attractive for two main reasons. First, bond holders can generate extra yield by repoing out their bonds to dealers for short periods. Second, investors with surplus cash can undertake very secure collateralised investments when they lend dealers cash against bonds. The repo market began in the US in the 1980s as a means for investment banks to finance both their long bond positions and to cover their short positions by respectively lending and borrowing bonds. Since 1992, a common international repo contract has been traded. As we saw above, the Bank of England began a repo market in gilts in 1996 (this is explained in more detail in section 5.11).

## 1.4.4   Clearing and settlement of trades

An important aspect of the secondary market is the clearing and settlement of trades between sellers and buyers of securities. These are sometimes called *back office* functions to contrast with the *front office* activities of trading and sales.

*Clearing* covers all the activities prior to settlement such as trade comparison and matching, trade netting, securities messages and numbering, and securities lending. The first part of the clearing process is trade comparison and matching which involves confirmation between the counterparties that a deal has been done and that the details of the deal have been agreed on both sides. The next step is the netting of trades. During the course of a trading day an investor might sell 100 shares in a particular company and later that day buy back 80 shares in the same company; at the end of the day only 20 shares would have to be delivered since only 20 shares net have been sold. Security messaging and numbering involves informing the relevant clearing system that a transaction in an identified security is about to take place, that delivery or receipt of securities has taken place, or that such a transaction has been cancelled. This is particularly important for international securities transactions (say involving Cedel or Euroclear) where two different countries' clearing systems will be involved (and possibly a third country's as well if the securities involved are domiciled in a third country). Related to this is the correct identification of the shares and bonds being sold. UK securities used to have identification names listed in the UK Stock Exchange Daily Official List (SEDOL). But these have been replaced by an ISIN (International Security Identification Number) operated by ANNA (Association of National Numbering Agencies). The final aspect of clearing is securities lending which occurs at the point where settlement is about to take place and there are either insufficient or surplus securities available (this could be due to human error or a deliberate strategy by a market maker). At this point securities may have to be borrowed to complete the deal, while surplus securities might be lent or repoed.

*Settlement* deals with the actual transfer of ownership of securities in exchange for cash and the confirmation that this has taken place and as the saying goes 'if it does not settle, it is not a trade'. There are risks even at this stage because it is possible for one of the counterparties to go bankrupt just after receiving securities but before delivering cash. This is known as *settlement risk* and becomes an increasing possibility as real-time settlement systems are introduced. In the case of gilts, the settlement of repos is facilitated by a system offered by the Gilts Settlements Office known as *delivery by value* (DBV). Registered members of the GSO wishing to borrow money against gilt collateral can have stock in their GSO account automatically pledged overnight against an assured payment from the lender's bank. The gilts are returned to the account the next business day and the money is automatically returned to the bank. The stock lender usually requires collateral in the form of DBVs (i.e. gilts in the GSO) or certificates of deposit. He also requires a fee for the loan as well as any income payments that become due on the stock lent.

### 1.4.5 Official intervention in markets

Occasionally the authorities intervene in the operation of financial markets, especially when they believe that the actions of speculators have created a disorderly market. There are many examples of *official intervention* in the gilt-edged, money and foreign exchange markets. For example, in the gilts market, the government aims to maximize investors' desires to hold gilt-edged stock in the long run. This objective is more likely to be achieved if there are not sudden falls in gilt prices from one day to the next. The Bank of England therefore sometimes buys gilts from market-makers in a falling market in order to smooth out price falls. It also sells gilts onto the market to smooth out sharp price rises caused by the activities of short-term speculators who are likely to sell out suddenly, causing a collapse in gilt prices. However, it is possible for the actions of the authorities to be counter-productive, i.e. to be destabilizing rather than stabilizing. This is because of the activities of speculators who attempt to exploit the predictable behaviour of the authorities.

In a rising market, speculators will be tempted to join the bandwagon and make their short-term profits, while always being prepared to sell out at the first piece of bad news. Such selling when it occurs depresses prices and shakes the confidence of long-term investors who might then be tempted to sell stock themselves. Similarly in a falling market, speculators will wish to make profits by taking short positions but must always be ready to cover their short positions at the first sign of good news. There will generally be more speculative activity if speculators are confident that the authorities will act to smooth out price reversals, because this helps to prevent speculators getting their fingers burned. So the price smoothing activities of the authorities might counter-productively encourage speculation.

It is arguable that it would be better if there was no official intervention and if markets were left alone to stabilize themselves. This could be achieved through the *technical adjustments* of market-makers. For example in a rapidly rising market, market-makers are likely to find themselves short of stock to deliver against sales that they have made. They sometimes respond to this by sharply marking prices down. This has the effect of shaking out speculators who have long positions and who fear further price falls. The market-makers are therefore able to get the stock they need. But another effect is to help stabilize the market, because, once price rises resume, they do so in a more stable market with fewer speculators, and hence in a market that is more resistant to any further bad news. But the risk to market-makers is that the fall in prices not only does not frighten off speculators, it actually encourages long-term investors to buy more securities. Market-makers have to make a careful assessment about how the situation will develop and they will not implement a technical adjustment until they feel that speculators' holdings are substantial.

Technical adjustments also occur in falling markets. Institutional investors tend not to buy long-term securities in falling markets. Instead they will save up surplus funds until prices begin to rise again. However if large numbers of institutional investors all begin to buy securities at the same time then this can create a disorderly market. Market-makers attempt to prevent demand penting up in this way by initiating a series of sharp upward technical adjustments in prices to encourage institutional investors to buy.

It has been argued that to reduce the impact of speculators, the authorities should do the opposite of what they actually do at this time. Rather than sell gilts when the market stops falling, the Bank should execute a *bear squeeze* against speculators by buying gilts. If speculators waited until this stage before closing their short positions, they would find not only that they had difficulty in acquiring the stock to do so but that what stock was available was available only at high prices. In order to avoid being squeezed speculators would have to close their short positions before prices stopped falling and this would help to stabilize the market.

Depending on how it is implemented, official intervention can therefore be either stabilizing or destabilizing.

## 1.5  Regulation

In this section,[4] we examine the set of regulations that confront the financial system. Everyone who operates in a financial system (in particular, financial intermediaries and market-makers) faces a particular regulatory environment. This environment can differ from one financial system to another. We will examine the set of regulations operating in the UK.

Figure 1.7 shows the hierarchical structure of regulatory control in the UK. The *Financial Services Act 1986*, the *Bank of England Act 1998*, and the *Financial Services and Markets Act 2000* are the key to the whole system of regulatory control. These Acts give overall responsibility for regulating the financial system to HM Treasury, although there are other organizations engaged in regulation which do not report directly to the Treasury. An example is the *Panel on Takeovers and Mergers*. This is a non-statutory body established by the City itself. It operates two sets of rules: the *City*

---

[4]This section draws heavily on *Financial Services Authority: An Outline* (1997).

**Figure 1.7** Regulatory control of the UK financial system

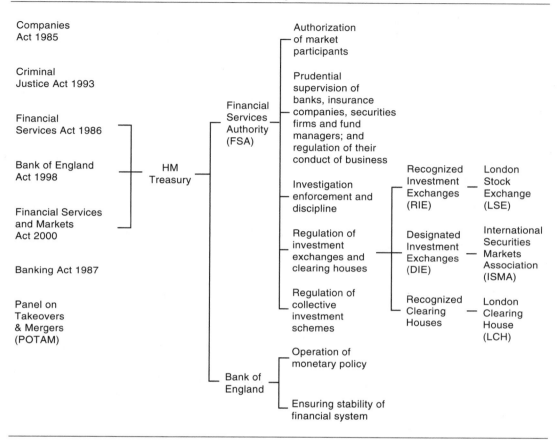

*Code on Takeovers and Mergers*, and the *Rules on Substantial Acquisition of Shares*. While the rules are non-statutory, they generally work because rule-breakers can be *cold-shouldered* by everyone else operating in the City.

The Treasury has overall responsibility for the institutional structure of regulation and for the legislation that governs it. However, it has delegated operational matters to the *Financial Services Authority* (FSA) and the *Bank of England*.

The FSA has five statutory objectives:

1 To sustain confidence in the UK financial sector and markets.

2 To protect consumers by ensuring that firms are competent and financially sound and to give their customers confidence in their integrity, while recognizing consumers' own responsibility for their financial decisions.

3 To promote improvement in public understanding of the benefits and risks associated with financial products.

4  To monitor, detect and prevent financial crime.

5  To pursue these objectives in a way which:

    a) is efficient and economic and ensures that costs and restrictions on firms are proportionate to the benefits of regulation;

    b) facilitates innovation in financial services;

    c) takes account of the international nature of financial regulation and financial services businesses.

The FSA has three principal aims:

1  *To protect consumers of financial services.* The FSA will:

    a) set, promote, monitor and enforce high standards of integrity, financial soundness, fair dealing and competence for those it regulates, in order to protect and secure fair treatment for investors, depositors and policyholders;

    b) aim to ensure that consumers receive clear and adequate information about services, products and risks;

    c) acknowledge customers' responsibility for their own decisions, while aiming to ensure that they are not exposed to risks that they should not reasonably be expected to assume.

2  *To promote clean and orderly markets.* The FSA will:

    a) promote fairness, transparency and orderly conduct in financial markets, looking in the first instance to the markets and market participants to set and enforce high standards in this area;

    b) take action where such standards are inadequate or are ineffectively enforced.

3  *To maintain confidence in the financial system.* The FSA will:

    a) set, promote, monitor and enforce high standards of financial soundness and probity for financial services businesses, in order to contribute to the soundness of the financial system as a whole and to promote consumers' and financial institutions' confidence in its strength and integrity;

    b) aim to ensure, in co-operation with the Bank of England, that the failure of individual financial institutions does not undermine the overall stability and soundness of the financial system.

The FSA will pursue these aims and objectives in an efficient way and will seek to ensure that the costs of regulation are proportionate to the benefits. To achieve this, the FSA exercises the following functions:

1  *The authorization of market participants*

*Authorized persons* must meet specified standards of integrity, financial soundness and competence in order to operate in the financial services industry. Authorized persons have to demonstrate through examinations and other means that they are *fit and proper* persons to engage in investment business. One way of achieving this is to pass the examination for *securities repre-sentative* set by the Securities Institute. It is a criminal offence to carry on investment business without being either authorized or exempted. *Exempted persons* do not require authorization to carry on investment business and include the Bank of England, recognized investment exchanges and recognized clearing houses. Persons carrying on investment business without being authorized or exempted can be fined or imprisoned; any contracts that they make cannot be enforced but can be enforced against them if the investor wishes; and a restitution order can be made against them so that they can be obliged to return any profits that they make or meet any losses caused by investors.

In recent years, the City has begun to emphasize the importance of professional training. The FSA has established the Securities Industry Diploma through the Securities Institute, and the Society of Financial Advisers requires its members to pass examinations set by the Chartered Insurance Institute. It is also possible to become an associate of the Institute of Investment Management and Research (IIMR) by obtaining the Institute's Investment Management Certificate.

2 *The prudential supervision of banks, life companies, securities firms and fund managers, and regulation of their conduct of business*

The FSA is responsible for implementing a co-ordinated supervisory programme for every bank, life company, securities firm and fund manager. This involves an understanding, in respect of each such organization, of: its business strategy; its management capabilities and policies; its systems and controls; the adequacy of its resources, both human and financial; and the economic environment in which it operates, in the UK and overseas.

The FSA also makes rules governing the carrying on of investment business. These cover:

a) the *conduct of business*: an investment adviser (e.g. a broker or an investment bank) must *know his client*, give him the *best advice* for his circumstances, ensure *best execution* (buying and selling for the client on the best terms available), ensure the client understands any *risk* involved in a proposed transaction, *disclose* any interest his company may have in the transaction, inform the client of the size of any fee or commission from arranging the transaction, keep good records, and establish barriers to passing on information gained in confidence (the so-called Chinese Walls rule);

b) *unsolicited calls*: for example, the selling of investment products following an unsolicited call (i.e. *cold calling*) is closely regulated and customers are permitted to cancel some types of deals after unsolicited calls;

c) *clients' money*: for example, a client's money must be kept in a separate account from that of the firm acting for the client.

The rules are collected together in a *rule book* which is given to every member of staff when they join a company. The rule book provides for an *arbitration procedure* in the case of customer complaints and a *compensation scheme* to compensate depositors, investors and policyholders in the event of default or fraud. The FSA monitors financial service companies by means of *compliance visits* to ensure that they comply with the rules. Firms appoint *compliance officers* to ensure their actions are compatible with the rules. The rule book allows for the disciplining and expulsion of members who break the rules.

3 *Investigation, enforcement and discipline*

In order to exercise effectively its regulatory authority, the FSA needs to have powers of investigation, enforcement and discipline over the individuals, firms and markets that it regulates.

Under the Banking Act 1987 it also has intervention powers in relation to the banking system. This means that it has powers to prevent unauthorized investment business and illegal deposit-taking.

There is increasing use of both information technology and international co-operation in the investigation process. For example, in 1993, the Surveillance Department of the LSE introduced a computer system to help identify cases of illegal share dealings. It is called IMAS, the *Integrated Monitoring and Surveillance System*, and uses different sources of electronic financial information to detect unusual market situations (known as *alerts*), such as unusually large transactions, sharp price changes, unorthodox price quotes by market-makers or apparent breaches of the rules on the reporting of transactions. Graphs showing the transactions made by different brokers on behalf of clients can be superimposed on charts depicting prices and volumes, enabling investigators to pick out suspicious trades within a few minutes of them occurring. The US equivalent is called *Stockwatch*. About 1,000 unusual share price movements are examined daily. There is also increasing cooperation with regulators in other countries, via the *International Organization of Securities Commissions* (IOSCO) and *Inter-Market Surveillance*. Inter-Market Surveillance is an international group of exchanges and regulators which has agreed to pool information. This is because of the increasing number of suspicious trades that are made by shell companies in offshore financial centres such as Jersey and the Cayman Islands.

There have been other measures to tighten up the regulatory control of the financial markets. For example, in 1994, the *Market Conduct Regulators Group* was established to ensure that regulators operate in a coherent manner and become more effective in detecting financial market abuses. Its aim is to offer 'explicit standards of market integrity and investor protection'. The argument is that a unified system of surveillance is needed for all markets where UK equities, say, are traded (including derivative markets), so that abuse can be detected and punished.

4  *The regulation of investment exchanges and clearing houses*

A *recognized investment exchange* (RIE) is one that is recognized as being engaged in the dealing or arrangement of deals in authorized UK securities. The main RIEs of the UK are: the London Stock Exchange, Tradepoint, the London International Financial Futures and Options Exchange (LIFFE), and the London Securities and Derivatives Exchange (OMLX).

A *designated investment exchange* (DIE) is one that is engaged in the dealing or arrangement of deals in international securities but without being subject to UK regulation. An example of a DIE is the International Securities Market Association (ISMA), which organizes a market in international bonds (mainly eurobonds) from London

A *recognized clearing house* (RCH) is one that is recognized as being engaged in the business of the clearing and settlement of deals in authorized UK securities, in other words in the transfer of ownership of securities between counterparties. The largest clearing house in the UK is the *London Clearing House* (LCH) which clears trades on the London International Financial Futures and Options Exchange, the London Metal Exchange, the International Petroleum Exchange and Tradepoint. The next largest is the *Exchange Clearing House* (ECHO) which clears (via multilateral netting) foreign exchange trades between banks.

The FSA supervises the above exchanges and clearing houses as well as the over-the-counter market.

5  *Regulation of collective investment schemes*

The FSA will regulate collective investment schemes (i.e., unit trusts, investment trusts and open-ended investment companies). In particular, the FSA will authorize and recognize new schemes and approve changes to existing schemes.

The Bank of England has been given responsibility for the operation of monetary policy and for ensuring the stability of the financial system as a whole. This involves:

1 The stability of the monetary system. The Bank monitors this, as part of its monetary policy functions. It acts daily in the markets, to deal with day-to-day fluctuations in liquidity (see section 1.4.5 above).

2 The financial system infrastructure, in particular payments systems at home and abroad. As the bankers' bank, the Bank stands at the heart of the system. The Bank advises the Chancellor on any major problem inherent in the payments systems. The Bank is also closely involved in developing and improving the infrastructure, and strengthening the system to help reduce systemic risks.

3 The broad overview of the system as a whole. The Bank is responsible for monetary stability, and, through its involvement in the payments system, it may be the first to identify potential problems. The Bank advises on the implications for financial stability of developments in the domestic and international markets and payments systems; and it assesses the impact on monetary conditions of events in the financial sector.

4 Being able, in exceptional circumstances, to undertake official financial operations, in order to limit the risk of problems in or affecting particular institutions spreading to other parts of the financial system.

5 The efficiency and effectiveness of the financial sector, with particular regard to international competitiveness.

The FSA and the Bank of England also share certain responsibilities for regulation. For example, they are both represented on the Basle Supervisors' Committee and the European Central Bank Banking Supervisors' Sub-Committee. They have also agreed the following chairing of domestic market committees:

1 Sterling Markets Joint Standing Committee: the FSA;

2 Foreign Exchange Joint Standing Committee: the Bank;

3 Derivatives Joint Standing Committee: the FSA;

4 Stocklending and Repo Committee: the Bank.

On an historical note, the Financial Services Authority was created in 1997 and replaced the Securities and Investments Board (SIB) which was established by the Financial Services Act 1986. As a result of the Bank of England Act 1998, responsibility for supervising banks, listed money market institutions and related clearing houses was transferred from the Supervision and Surveillance Division of the Bank of England to the FSA. The Bank of England retained responsibility for the operation of monetary policy and for ensuring financial stability. As a result of the Financial Services and Markets Act 2000, the FSA acquired the regulatory and registration functions of:

Building Societies Commission (BSC)      Building societies

Friendly Societies Commission (FSC)      Friendly societies

Insurance Directorate (ID) of the            Insurance
Department of Trade and Industry

Investment Management Regulatory         Investment management
Organisation (IMRO)

Personal Investment Authority (PIA)       Retail investment business

Registry of Friendly Societies (RFS)       Credit unions' supervision
                                                              (and the registration and
                                                              public records of building
                                                              societies, friendly societies,
                                                              industrial and provident
                                                              societies and other mutual
                                                              societies)

Securities and Futures Authority (SFA)    Securities and derivatives
                                                              business

Securities and Investments Board (SIB)    Investment business
                                                              (including responsibility
                                                              for supervising exchanges
                                                              and clearing houses)

Recognized Professional Bodies (RPBs)   Accountants, solicitors and
                                                              actuaries for example.

The analysis so far has dealt with the regulation of market participants. But there are also regulations covering the behaviour of end-users of the financial system. These are specified in the Companies Act 1985 and the Criminal Justice Act 1993.

The *Companies Act 1985* specifies the obligations that various people have in disclosing their interests in the shares of companies. This is particularly important in the case of takeover bids. For example, directors must disclose to their company all share dealings in their company within five days. Similarly, shareholders with more than 5 per cent of total shareholdings must disclose to the company any transaction involving 1 percentage point or more shareholdings within five days, while shareholders with more than 15 percent of total shareholdings must report any transaction involving 1 percentage point or more shareholdings within one day. (The latter case is governed by the Rules on Substantial Acquisition of Shares of the Panel on Takeovers and Mergers.)

The *Criminal Justice Act 1993* prohibits the use of confidential inside information. An *insider* is a person *knowingly connected with a company* (e.g. a director of, employee of or an adviser to the company). Such a person may have access to *specific unpublished price-sensitive information* (SUPSI) (e.g. about the possibility of a takeover bid). It is a criminal offence for an insider to deal in securities on a *regulated market* or through a *professional intermediary* on the basis of SUPSI, or for an *unconnected person* to deal in securities on the basis of SUPSI acquired from an insider with both the insider and unconnected person culpable (unless the unconnected person acquired that information in his capacity as a market-maker), or even for inside information to be disclosed to an unconnected person, other than in the usual performance of employment. The Act covers dealings in shares, bonds and derivatives of these, such as futures and options, but excludes inside information about the state of the economy in general. The maximum penalty for insider dealing is seven years' imprisonment or an unlimited fine or both. Responsibility for policy on insider dealing and market manipulation lies with the Treasury. Responsibility for the statutory investigation of alleged insider dealing and market manipulation lies with the FSA, while responsibility for prosecution lies with the Serious Fraud Office and the Crown Prosecution Service.

## 1.6 The financial system in a temporal context

In this final section of the chapter we will place the UK financial system in a temporal context. In particular, we will discuss the recent past and examine prospects for the near future.

### 1.6.1 The recent past: the Big Bang of October 1986

On Monday 27 October 1986, the City of London experienced what has become known as the *Big Bang*. It represented just one part of the biggest revolution taking place in the UK financial system in more than two centuries. The Big Bang itself had two dimensions: a regulatory dimension and a technological dimension. Both were intended to unleash a wave of competition and therefore to increase choice in a way that has not been known hitherto.

For the previous two hundred years the Stock Exchange in London had operated along the lines of a cosy though honourable gentleman's club. It had been owned by its own members, and in order to avoid too much competition it operated a system of minimum fixed brokerage commissions on all stock transactions. But to protect the investor, it also operated as a single-capacity system, whereby the activities of the stockjobbers (the principals or dealers who make a market in each stock) and the stockbrokers (the agents who act in the best interests of the client by buying from or selling to the jobber offering the best prices) were kept entirely separate, thereby avoiding any potential conflict of interest. Under the new deregulated environment following the Big Bang, it was possible for the LSE to be owned by non-member firms. So, for example, Barclays Bank took over a member firm (the stockbroker de Zoete and Bevan) and a stockjobber (Wedd Durlacher) to create the new investment bank Barclays de Zoete Wedd (or BZW). Out went the system of fixed commissions: since Big Bang all commissions have been fully negotiable. Finally, the single-capacity system has been replaced by a dual-capacity system in which firms can act both as agents and principals, i.e. broker-dealers: they can therefore deal in a particular stock as well as advising clients to trade in the same stock.

The technological dimension to the Big Bang was the new method by which the LSE dealt in stocks. Before 27 October trading took place on the floor of the exchange, and brokers would physically approach the jobbers to find the best prices for their clients. The jobbers would quote two prices, a bid price and an offer price, and the difference (or spread) would be the jobbers' reward for making a market. In turn, the broker would charge the client a commission which depended on the size of the transaction. Since 27 October 1986 the trading system has been computerized. The market-makers announce their bid and offer prices through SEAQ and these prices are transmitted to the brokers through TOPIC. The brokers simply sit in their offices in front of their TOPIC screens and select the best prices for their clients.

The Big Bang was just one part of the financial revolution taking place in the UK. Again, there were two main dimensions to the changes taking place outside the LSE.

First, the structure of all British financial institutions has been changing rapidly. This is due partly to the government's wish to increase competition and choice and partly to technology. For example, in the 1980s there was a huge increase in competition between banks and building societies (the latter traditionally lending money solely for the purpose of house purchase). This increased competition was formalized in the Building Societies Act 1986. The banks became involved in lending for house purchase and also in estate agency work. Now building societies are able to offer current accounts, make unsecured loans, engage in estate agency work and conveyancing, sell unit trusts and personal pension plans, and raise funds through the wholesale money markets. Similarly, insurance companies began to give advice on a wider range of financial products such as mortgages and pensions. The major financial institutions were beginning to provide a common set of financial services and the differences between them were disappearing. Technological developments have also had an important influence on these changes. Indeed, it is arguable that it is technological developments that have made the changes possible. The rate of technological progress is such that we could soon be entering the *cashless society*. If the use of EFTPOS (electronic funds transfer at point of sale) becomes widespread, then cash could be rendered unnecessary.

Second, the government decided to increase the degree of investor protection through the Financial Services Act 1986. It was the failure in 1983 of Norton Warburg, a licensed dealer in securities, that led to the Gower Report recommending a new system of investor protection based on the principle of self-regulation rather than government control. The aim was to cover all investment products and services (e.g. life assurance services and commodities) and not just those traded on the LSE.

The London Big Bang is only one of a number of Big Bangs that have taken place in the world's financial centres in recent years, beginning with New York in May 1975. The Japanese Big Bang took place in April 1998. So why did the Big Bang take place in London in 1986?

One of the most important underlying causes of all the Big Bangs has been the *internationalization of finance* following the dramatic changes in the world economy since the beginning of the 1970s. After the ending of the Bretton Woods agreement on fixed exchange rates in 1971, the world has seen a huge increase in exchange rate variability. This led to the introduction of a new range of exchange rate hedging instruments, such as options, futures and swaps. Similarly, since the oil price shock of 1973, there has been a huge increase in interest rate variability which has resulted in a new range of interest rate hedging instruments, again mainly options, futures and swaps. The Third World debt crisis (which began with Mexico nearly defaulting on its debt service payments in August 1982) dramatically changed the way in which the major banks operate their balance sheets. With the development of the unregulated eurobond markets, big borrowers have been bypassing the banking system and going directly to the international markets to raise capital. This has resulted in a movement away from syndicated bank lending (which had become relatively unprofitable and, in the light of the debt crisis, had weakened banks' balance sheets) towards the earnings of commission fee income from selling corporate debt on the eurobond markets using a new range of securitized instruments such as NIFs (note issuance facilities) and RUFs (revolving underwriting facilities). This has led to the *securitization* of parts of the banks' balance sheets, thus making them much more liquid. Another aspect of the internationalization of finance has been the relaxation of exchange controls, which has permitted institutional investors such as pension funds and insurance companies to invest up to a quarter of their portfolios across national frontiers. There has also been a movement of banks across national boundaries. For example, there are about 500 foreign banks in London, 260 in New York and 80 in Tokyo. A parochial and inward-looking stock exchange could not hope to survive in a world of such rapid change.

Another cause of the Big Bang was the loss of business to US and Japanese securities houses. London broking firms had been losing market share in both UK and overseas markets because the London firms were too small and LSE commissions were too large relative to those on the New York Stock Exchange (NYSE). British shares had been trading on the NYSE in the form of ADRs with lower transaction costs than in London; so London was losing market share even in British stock traded on the LSE.

Third, there has been the development of risk products such as options, futures, swaps and over-the-counter securities, which have traded outside the LSE. So the LSE was losing market share to other domestic markets.

Finally, the development of computer technology has made possible international dealing in securities 24 hours a day between Tokyo, London and New York. When the London market opens, the trading books are handed over by Tokyo, and when the New York market opens they are handed over by London. The net result is the interdependence (or *globalization*) of the world's three major financial centres, although the move towards globalization was slowed down as a result of the crash in October 1987.

The explanation for the Big Bang occurring in London is now clear. The capital base of the old member-firms of the LSE was far too small to compete effectively on the world stage. This explains the change in the LSE membership rules to allow UK and foreign banks to purchase member-firms. The abolition of fixed minimum commissions was necessary to prevent the LSE losing any more market share to other domestic and the international markets. The brokerage commissions are now set by negotiation and must be competitive with New York, Tokyo and, increasingly, financial centres on the European continent. With the ending of minimum commissions, the single-capacity separation of stockbroker and stockjobber was no longer feasible and had to be replaced by the dual-capacity system of combined dealers and brokers. With the potential conflicts of interest that might arise in the new dual-capacity world, a new system of investor protection was necessary, with a new set of supervisory bodies with powers to inflict penalties if the rules were not observed. Finally, with the huge increase in the number of competing players in the market-place, the old system of posting up bid and offer prices on the floor of the Stock Exchange was no longer feasible, and a new system of publishing prices on the SEAQ system became necessary.

## 1.6.2 The near future

**The consequences of the Big Bang.** Before examining the prospects for the UK financial system in the near future, and in particular the likely consequences of the Big Bang, it is interesting to examine what happened on the NYSE when it had its Big Bang in May 1975. Between 1975 and 1980, commission rates fell by 50 per cent on large transactions; the volume of trading activity taking place outside the NYSE in the Third Market (which is not subject to NYSE rules) fell sharply; there was a substantial increase in concentration among broker-dealers as the number of firms engaged in the market-place fell from 422 to 389 and the share of business of the top 25 firms rose from 53 to 61 per cent; there was an increase in *discount broking* (that is, a straight broking service without any investment advice); and because of the reduction in commissions, there was an increase in trading volume on the NYSE leading to an increase in profitability and employment.

The few years after the Big Bang in London were extremely challenging ones both for the individual players and for the system as a whole.

In terms of the individual players, it was likely that the problems would be more acute for the new British investment banks than for the foreign ones. The British investment banks were cobbled together in a few months in 1986 from three completely separate entities: merchant banks, stockbrokers and stockjobbers. Historically, there had been enormous cultural differences between these three groups. The stockjobbers, for example, were akin to street traders, used to making instant decisions. The merchant bankers, on the other hand, were the aristocrats of the City, used to spending three hours over lunch and taking much time and much discussion in committee before making decisions. Then suddenly these different groups were thrown together in the same organization and given very little time to integrate properly.

The London capital market has now become extremely competitive and the British investment banks did not have much experience at market-making in very competitive conditions. For example, the London gilts market initially became considerably more competitive than the US Treasury bond market. In London there were initially 27 market-makers, whereas in the USA there are 37 market-makers serving a market ten times larger. There was clear excess capacity in the gilts market and the number of market-makers fell to below 20. It is also questionable whether the UK firms have a sufficiently large capital base to support risk-taking in all market conditions. The UK investment house Mercury Asset Management had a market capitalization of $0.9 billion in 1986, but Salomon Brothers, the US investment house, had a market capitalization of $5.6 billion and the Japanese company, Nomura, the world's largest investment bank, had a market capitalization of $27.8 billion. The UK banks have been dwarfed by these overseas giants invading their hitherto sacred territory. MAM was eventually bought out by Merill Lynch in 1997.

Take, for example, Salomon Brothers, the largest and most profitable underwriter of new bond and equity issues in New York. Following Big Bang, it was trading skill that replaced fixed commissions as the key to success and profitability in the City of London. And Salomons brought its hustling Wall Street methods to London in order to win over market share. Immediately, they flexed their muscles by arranging the first *bought deal* in the UK. In mid-October 1986 they raised £30 million for the Granada takeover of Lasky by buying-in the entire stock and selling it out again to institutional clients within two hours for a profit of £200,000 (and in less time than a traditional City lunch!). On an average day in New York in 1986, Salomons would trade $18 billion of stock and might end a day's trading with more than $40 billion of stock on its own book. Salomons is a world leader in market skills: they are extremely price-competitive and will take on huge blocks of stock for only tiny margins; half their profits come from trading on their own account; they are very innovative, and are continually designing new types of corporate bonds (for example, in late 1986 they issued a bond for Eastman Kodak which was denominated in Australian dollars but was convertible to US dollars); and they are experienced at 24-hours-a-day trading. An even bigger giant is Nomura, which has grown to be the world's largest financial institution as a result of the insatiable desire of the Japanese to save. Nomura is Number One in Japan and intends to become Number One in the world by expanding at the rate of 40 per cent per year.

With rivals of this kind entering the London markets, the British dealing and broking firms were justifiably feeling very nervous. Their degree of nervousness was doubled when they heard that big institutional investors such as the Prudential Insurance Company intended to use the brokers and dealers offering the best deals, regardless of past loyalties. With this kind of post-Big Bang environment in the City, it is felt that the smaller broker will not be able to compete in market-making, agency broking or the international markets. Unless they are able to tap the private client market or the smaller independent fund management groups, they are not likely to survive.

However, not all the overseas banks which came to London during the 1980s were successful. For example, Citibank bought up UK brokers Scrimgeour Kemp Gee and Vickers da Costa and formed the investment bank Citicorp Scrimgeour Vickers. Immediately there were cultural conflicts between the US owners and British brokers. In addition, Citibank made the disastrous purchase of the old Billingsgate fish market building on the banks of the Thames. The architect Richard Rogers was commissioned to spend millions of pounds converting the building into a trading floor for CSV. When the work was completed, the basement cold storage system (which has been used for the previous 200 years to keep the market's fish frozen) was switched off and, as the ice melted, the whole building, which in effect was built on a huge block of ice, began to sink into the Thames. Despite millions more pounds being spent to rectify this problem, CSV was never able to use the building and had to be located elsewhere. More disasters followed and in 1990 CSV closed with net losses to Citibank of £330m. Similarly, the US bank Security Pacific bought UK brokers Hoare Govett in 1982 and formed Security Pacific Hoare Govett. Again there were cultural conflicts and in 1987 the bank lost millions of pounds underwriting the British Petroleum privatisation issue which came to the market just after the October stock market crash. In 1990, SPHG was closed with a net loss to Security Pacific of £200m.

It was not only US banks which made disastrous acquisitions in London. Some British companies also made mistakes. For example, merchant bank Morgan Grenfell wished to expand into equity broking, so it purchased Pember and Boyle and formed Morgan Grenfell Securities. But Pember and Boyle were gilts brokers and had no expertise in equity broking and the whole enterprise failed with Morgan Grenfell Securities closing down in December 1988 with net losses of £90m. Morgan Grenfell was later taken over by Deutsche Bank. In fact, European investment banks have on the whole been much more successful in their acquisitions of UK merchant banks than have US investment banks. The year 1995 saw the effective end of the independent British merchant bank. One of the oldest British banks, Baring, was taken over by the Dutch group ING (International Netherlands Group), after its Singapore subsidiary lost £800m on Nikkei futures contracts. Warburgs was bought out by Swiss Bank Corporation and Kleinwort Benson was purchased by Dresdner Bank.

There are also problems for the system as a whole. One of the most important questions raised is over the effectiveness of the system of investor protection. What occurred in 1986 was a deregulation of financial markets but an increased supervision of players. But the supervision was in the form of self-regulation, and self-regulation works best with homogeneous groups of people with common objectives and restrictions on entry to maintain standards. If it is not possible to restrict entry, then self-regulation will not be effective. In addition, if competition keeps profits margins small, then there is an increased risk of fraud. This is exactly what happened in the early 1980s in the Lloyds of London reinsurance market, another self-regulated market. Unless the policing of the deregulated market place is adequate, the potential conflicts of interest that result from dual-capacity trading will turn into real conflicts of interest and fraud will result. The system of self-regulation was also highly fragmented without clear lines of responsibility. The effects of this were shown most clearly by the personal pensions misselling scandal in the late 1980s and early 1990s which the system of investor protection through decentralized self-regulation failed to prevent. This scandal was the primary reason behind the introduction of an integrated system of financial regulation beginning with the establishment of the Financial Services Authority in 1997.

Another problem for the system is the new computer technology that is needed to run it. So much of the dealing and settlement is now done using computers that if the computer systems crash and there is a failure to deliver either stock or payments, the costs could be enormous. To illustrate the problem, in November 1985 the Bank of New York's computer broke down for two days and so much money was drawn out of the bank that it had to borrow $22 billion from the Federal Reserve. The interest cost of this two-day loan was almost $8 million. There was a similar failure of Super-DOT, the computerized Designated Order Turnaround list-processing system, which automatically executes small orders on the NYSE, on Black Monday, 19 October 1987. The problems that the Stock Exchange itself had during the first few days of post-Big Bang trading, with the TOPIC service failing intermittently, shows that similar problems with the computer technology could arise in the UK. So while computer technology has been the most important single factor in the rapid expansion of the financial system both domestically and globally, there always remains the danger of systems crashes.

What are the likely long-term effects of the Big Bang? For the City of London itself, the long-term effects are likely to be similar to those that arose in New York after its Big Bang, namely a reduction in commissions and spreads on large trades and an increase in the volume of activity; there will also be an increase in concentration as competition reduces the numbers of both brokers and dealers. For large institutional investors and large corporate borrowers, the Big Bang is likely to be regarded as a success. The increase in competition in trading the stock of large companies is likely to benefit both groups. The reduction in commissions and spreads will help to lower the cost of raising capital for large companies, and the increase in liquidity will help large investors switch their portfolios more easily. These groups are also sufficiently large and influential in the market place that they do not require a system of investor protection. But small- and medium-sized firms or small investors may not fare so well. This is because the increase in competition in market-making and broking is not uniform across all companies' stocks. Smaller company stocks have actually been less well traded after Big Bang than before. This in turn will tend to raise the cost of capital to these firms and make their stock less liquid in the market-place and therefore less attractive to investors. Small investors have found that they have to pay more for broking services since the broking firms were more interested in competing for large investors. Also, the smaller investor may be more in need of investor protection than before.

The Big Bang was one large step towards reducing restrictive practices in the LSE. But many restrictive practices still remain and will increasingly be challenged either by the authorities or by competitive rivals such as Tradepoint. For example, in the mid-1990s the Office of Fair Trading issued two reports (*Trade Publication Rules of the London Stock Exchange*, November 1994, and *Rules of the London Stock Exchange relating to Market Making*, March 1995) that argued that, despite the changes since Big Bang, market making on the LSE remained uncompetitive. This was because the current system was *quote-driven* with market makers having exclusive use of SEAQ to post the prices at which they are willing to trade and also having exclusive access to the prices quoted by inter-dealer brokers. Furthermore, market makers were able to delay the reporting of large blocks of shares and the prices at which such deals were done by 90 minutes. The OFT reports regarded these as excessive privileges for market makers.

The reports noted that only one other major market in the world (namely NASDAQ, the *National Association of Securities Dealers Automated Quotations*, in the US) was quote-driven. All the other major markets (including those in New York, Tokyo and continental Europe) are *order-driven*. This means that customers post buy and sell orders for securities in the *public order book* and the exchange matches buy and sell orders for a share at the same price without the need for a market maker as such. It is considerably more expensive to deal using quote-driven systems compared with order-driven systems. For example, in 1995 the average bid-offer spread for the most popular shares traded in London was 1.4 per cent, while on the New York Stock Exchange and the Paris Bourse, it was only 0.32 per cent and 0.30 per cent respectively. Associated with an order-driven trading system is a *post-trade reporting system* in the form of a *last trade tape* or *ticker tape* which shows the transaction prices at which the last trade took place. Investors therefore know the actual price of the last trade which contrasts with a quote-driven trading system where investors know the indicative bid and offer prices at which the next trade might take place. With the order-driven system, investors can either place a market order to be executed at the last trade price or place a limit order which will be executed if the limit price is reached. Of particular concern are the shares of small companies which are difficult to trade using a quote-driven system. Proponents argue that order-matching is the only way to generate *liquidity* in the shares of small companies.

The delayed reporting of block trades by 90 minutes was criticized because it reduces the *transparency* of the market in terms of promoting *efficient price formation* and in ensuring that investors are treated fairly and equitably. This is because delayed publication might give an unfair advantage to both market makers and the institutions that place the trades at the expense of less well-informed market participants. Market makers argue that they need the time to break up a block of shares into smaller packages which can then be unloaded on to the market. If they do not have this breathing space, they argue, they might be left with unsaleable stock which increases the risk to market making and may eventually lead to a reduction in liquidity if market makers are, as a consequence, driven out of the industry. But small-scale investors who buy these small packages of shares might regret having bought them had they known that a block trade had just occurred. This is because they might have inferred that the reason the block trade was taking place was because the seller was aware of some adverse news concerning the company. So there appears to be a trade off between transparency and liquidity: greater transparency may well come at the cost of reduced liquidity.

Also during the early 1990s, there were rumours about market abuses, many of them taking place outside the direct control of the LSE. For example, much of the market manipulation and insider dealing in company shares was believed to be taking place through ADRs. One notable illustration of this was the share dealings carried out by Robert Maxwell prior to his death in 1991, most of which took place via ADRs. Similarly, the Guinness share support operation at the time of its takeover of Distillers was conducted using ADRs. Another type of market abuse involves short selling. Unscrupulous investors attempted to use short selling as a mechanism for driving down the issue price of shares in Wellcome and the third British Telecom privatization offer.

The Securities and Investments Board or SIB (the chief UK financial services regulator between 1986 and its replacement by the Financial Services Authority in 1997) responded to all these criticisms and complaints, as well as to the development of competitive rivals to the LSE, by issuing a set of proposals concerning market maker privileges and obligations on the LSE (*Regulation of the United Kingdom Equity Markets*, June 1995). The SIB argued that 'the primary objective of regulation of the UK equity markets is to enable investors to use these markets with confidence. Regulation seeks to achieve this by providing investors with an appropriate level of protection in the form of fair and clean markets, but without being so burdensome as to reduce the overall volume of trading... Investors will generally have confidence in the market process if they believe they can: deal satisfactorily, at an acceptable cost, in a market that is fair and is not misled, manipulated or abused; and rely on the integrity of the trading process overall, and in particular on the operation of trading and settlement systems' (p.15). This regulatory objective, the SIB argued, should be implemented via a number of guiding principles, such as: *market freedom*, investor protection should not impede market evolution and competition; and *cost-effectiveness*, by supporting the integrity of the trading process, regulation should minimize the cost to investors when things go wrong, and by increasing the confidence of investors, regulation should reduce the cost of raising new capital. The SIB argued that success in achieving these objectives can be measured in three main ways: *fairness* in terms of market users having *equitable access to trading opportunities* on the basis of having *sufficient information* and with the *opportunity to exercise choice* in the light of their differing preferences and priorities, in terms of, say, immediate execution as against execution at acceptable prices; *freedom from abuse* in the sense that market users have confidence that the markets that they trade in are 'clean'; and *efficient price formation* which is vital for determining the fair value of securities and for achieving best execution for clients. In turn, efficient price formation relies on the transparency of dealings and the free flow of information.

In the light of these objectives, the SIB and the LSE negotiated a new deal which came into effect at the beginning of 1996 and which makes trades much more transparent. Trades up to six times normal market size and all trades between market-makers have their details published immediately (i.e. within three minutes). Details of trades between six and 75 times normal market size have to be published within 60 minutes (rather than 90 minutes as formerly). The disclosure of block trades larger than this can be delayed for up to three days or until the market-maker has unwound 90 per cent of the position. The SIB estimated that under the new rules 75 per cent of trades by value are disclosed immediately and a further 20 per cent of trades by value are disclosed within one hour.

The LSE's order-driven share dealing system called SETS began in October 1997. But there was substantial opposition to this development from market-makers who would lose the privileges they enjoyed under the traditional quote-driven system (such as delays in reporting details and avoidance of stamp duty). Indeed their hostility was such that they forced the resignation of the LSE's chief executive in January 1996. However, there was equal support for the move from the Institutional Fund Managers Association, representing institutional investors such as pension and insurance fund managers, who would benefit from lower dealing costs and greater liquidity. They had threatened to move their business away from London to other European centres operating order-driven systems, pointing out that SEAQ-I was now defunct in European stocks. There was also support from the Association of Private Client Stockbrokers and Investment Managers.

Another practice that developed after Big Bang is the *soft commission arrangement* or *softing*. This is an arrangement whereby stockbrokers offer research and information services to institutional clients in return for guaranteed business to trade in securities. Since brokers do not charge explicitly for these services, the subsequent payment for them is said to be in *soft money*. The practice started because the increase in competition following Big Bang drove commissions down to the levels charged by the most cost-efficient brokers. After this, brokers could only compete on service not on price. But investment banks with both broking and market-making arms could use their economies of scale to offer better softing deals than independent brokers. This is because the broking arm of the bank could cover their costs through a cross-subsidy from the market-making arm. They could negotiate keener prices (higher sale prices and lower purchase prices) than was available to outside brokers who were forced to deal at the official prices quoted by the market-maker on SEAQ. By keeping the difference between the official and negotiated prices, the broking arm could pay for the services that the independent broker could not afford to provide. The independent brokers argued that this was unfair competition and complained to the SIB. The SIB published a report in 1991 (*Soft Commissions — Recent Developments*) which recognized the problem but stated that it was impossible to prevent this happening. The integrated investment banks were only taking advantage of their greater economies of scale. But the long-run outcome is likely to be reduced numbers of independent brokers as they become absorbed by the large investment banks.

**Developments in Europe.** Within a European context, two important factors are affecting or are about to affect the UK financial system in a substantial way. These are the creation of the *European Financial Area* (EFA) and the introduction of *Economic and Monetary Union* (EMU) within the European Union (EU).

The European Financial Area formally came into effect on 1 January 1993 with the intention of establishing an integrated European financial system. This was part of the process of creating the *single European market* in goods and services by the end of 1992, a process that in the UK context was sanctioned by the 1986 *Single European Act*. The objective was to remove all barriers to entry in the provision of goods and services between member states of the EU, and, in the particular context of financial services, the liberalization of capital movements between member states and a common regulatory framework for financial services. By 1 July 1990, all capital controls had been removed by all member states.

Banking was one of the first financial service industries to begin the process of harmonization within the EU. The First Banking Directive of 1977 established minimum legal requirements for the authorization of credit institutions in member states. The Second Banking Directive which came into force in 1993 established minimum prudential standards to enable a credit institution authorized in one member state to offer core banking services in other member states under a single licence or *passport*. Core banking services include: deposit taking; lending (e.g. consumer credit, mortgage finance, trade finance); financial leasing; money transmission services; credit cards and travellers' cheques; guarantees and commitments; trading in money market instruments, foreign exchange, financial futures and options, and securities; participation in share issues; corporate finance advice; money broking; portfolio management and advice; and custodial services. A similar process occurred with insurance. Under a series of Life Insurance Directives (beginning in 1979) and Non-life Insurance Directives (beginning in 1973) insurance companies headquartered within the EU can, under the single passport scheme, offer services anywhere in the EU.

In 1996, the European Union's Investment Services Directive (ISD) and Capital Adequacy Directive (CAD) came into force. The objective behind these directives was to create a single market in financial services across Europe and to provide a passport for non-bank financial firms wanting to offer services in other member states. Home country authorization became a sufficient criterion for being able to operate cross-border, given, in addition, the acquisition of the passport. However, this greater freedom to operate cross-border was tempered by the simultaneous implementation of stringent capital adequacy requirements. Minimum levels of *initial capital*, in three tiers, were defined for firms wishing to trade under the provisions of these directives. Firms authorized to act as principals and to take positions on their own account were required to have initial capital of 730,000 ECUs (about £600,000) and also to hold additional capital equal to three months' fixed overhead costs. Firms acting as an agent or a fund manager and holding clients' money or securities were required to have initial capital of 125,000 ECUs (about £100,000). Firms acting as agents but are not authorised to hold clients' money were exempted from the initial capital requirement unless they deal in derivatives, such as options and warrants, in which case they were required to maintain 50,000 ECUs (about £40,000). However, the British government negotiated certain exemptions which resulted in 90 per cent of British independent financial advisers not having to meet the initial capital requirements of the CAD. Nevertheless, the British government has imposed its own minimum capital requirement of £10,000 irrespective of the size of the firm, as a means of cutting down on fraud.

The initial capital requirements have been criticized on the grounds that they are likely to reduce rather than enhance competition. Some have even argued that capital adequacy requirements for investment advisors who act only as agents are completely unnecessary; rather capital requirements are needed only for those organisations, such as banks, insurance companies and market makers, that act as principals, taking positions on their own account. There was a danger of over-regulation for a number of reasons. While large well-established companies can easily meet the capital requirements, dynamic new firms might be prevented from entering the industry. All firms have to meet the new requirements even if they do not intend to operate cross-border. Furthermore, business might shift to less regulated centres outside Europe. On top of this, banks had licences to do business throughout Europe, three years prior to the introduction of the passport and this has given them a head start over investment businesses.

The move towards mutual recognition began before 1996. For example, in October 1989, UCITS (or *undertakings for collective investments in transferable securities*) were introduced on an EU-wide basis. UCITS are unit trusts that are eligible for marketing and selling between member states. UCITS must be 90 per cent invested in transferable securities, such as shares and bonds, and they cannot invest directly in property, precious metals or options. They are limited to a 5 per cent investment in any single security, and 10 per cent in futures contracts. UCITS can invest through any recognized stock exchange in the world and they pay dividends gross to all investors. They can be bought and sold in any EU country that has introduced regulations that are compatible with the EU directive on investor protection. UCITS are subject to the marketing rules of the country in which they are being sold, not the country of origin. But they are not covered by any compensation scheme, even when sold in the UK.

There is no comparable EU directive on futures and options funds and developments have taken place on a piecemeal basis. In the UK, the Financial Services (Regulated Schemes) Regulations came into effect in 1991. These permitted managed futures and options funds to be marketed to the general public as authorized unit trust schemes. There are two types: *futures and options funds* (FOFs) and *geared futures and options funds* (GFOFs). FOFs are permitted to invest in transferable securities, derivatives (exchange-traded futures and options and certain over-the-counter options), cash, units in certain collective investment schemes, gold (up to 10 per cent of the value of the fund) and forward transactions in currencies or gold; investment in derivatives must be fully covered by the assets of the scheme (including permitted borrowing up to 10 per cent of the value of the assets). GFOFs can invest in the same assets as FOFs but in addition are allowed to invest up to 20 per cent of their assets in initial outlay (i.e. initial margin payments and premiums paid on options and warrants) and are not required to maintain sufficient assets to cover their full exposure; in other words, they are permitted to gear-up their investment exposure, but they are not permitted to cover this through borrowing.

The proposals for Economic and Monetary Union were contained in the *Delors Report* of June 1989 and form another aspect of the movement towards European integration. The Delors Reports envisaged a three-stage plan for EMU.

*Stage 1*, which began on 1 July 1990, further consolidated moves towards the single European market. It involved:

1 The complete removal of physical, technical and fiscal barriers;

2 The strengthening of competition policy and the reduction of state subsidies to industry;

3 The reform of structural funds, which offer regional aid, and the doubling of their resources;

4 Closer co-ordination of economic and monetary policies;

5 The deregulation of financial markets;

6 All EU currencies joining the *exchange rate mechanism* (ERM) of the *European Monetary System* (EMS).

The EMS began operating in March 1979. It has four components. The first component is the *exchange rate mechanism*. The ERM requires each participant to maintain its currency within specific bands around a central rate of exchange against other currencies in the mechanism. The band limits are changed periodically and have varied from 2.25 per cent on either side of the central rates to 15 per cent. Central banks are obliged to maintain their currencies within these limits. They can do so either by changing interest rates or by intervening in the foreign exchange markets when their currencies reach the band limits. If market pressures become too great and the policies required to retain exchange rates within band limits become unsustainable, then a realignment of central rates may be required. This is likely to occur if a member state runs a substantial trade surplus or deficit, or if there are widely differing inflation rates between member states. There were eleven central rate realignments between March 1979 and January 1987. Of the twelve member states of the EU at the beginning of Stage 1 of EMU, nine were members of the ERM (Germany, France, Italy, the Netherlands, Denmark, Belgium, Luxembourg, Ireland and Spain) and three were not (the UK, Greece and Portugal).

The UK joined the ERM on 8 October 1990 with a central rate of 2.95 DM per £ and with band limits of 6 per cent on either side of the central rate. The other currencies in the ERM had band limits of only 2.25 per cent, with the exception of the peseta which shared sterling's 6 per cent range. The Portuguese escudo joined the ERM in April 1992.

The second component of the EMS is the *European Currency Unit* (ECU). The ECU is calculated with reference to fixed quantities (or a basket) of EU currencies. The quantities are reset periodically. In September 1989, the ECU was reset to contain:

|  |  |  |  |
|---:|---|---:|---|
| 3.301 | Belgian francs | 0.008552 | Irish pounds |
| 0.1976 | Danish krone | 151.8 | Italian lire |
| 0.6242 | Deutschmark | 0.13 | Luxembourg francs |
| 0.2198 | Dutch guilder | 1.393 | Portuguese escudos |
| 1.332 | French francs | 0.08784 | Pounds sterling |
| 1.44 | Greek drachmas | 6.885 | Spanish pesetas |

The market value of the ECU is therefore equal to the weighted sum of the market values of the twelve EU currencies. The ECU is used in all official EU transactions, and is increasingly being used in transactions between large corporations within the EU. In October 1988, the UK government introduced Treasury bills denominated in ECUs.

The third component of the EMS is the *European Monetary Co-operation Fund* (EMCF). The EMCF is run by the governors of all the central banks in the EU. Its purpose is to create a fund of 'official' ECUs that can be used in transactions between the central banks, such as the settling of debts arising from operating the ERM. The EMCF operates by issuing ECUs to central banks in exchange for deposits from them equal to 20 per cent of their gold and dollar reserves. The reserves remain with the central banks who retain any interest earned on them.

The final component of the EMS is the *Very Short-term Financing Facility*. This allows funds to be borrowed by one central bank in the currency of another central bank to finance an intervention under the ERM. The funds have to be repaid after a short period.

*Stage 2* of the Delors plan is a transition stage. It established a *European System of Central Banks* (ESCB) through the mechanism of a *European Monetary Institute* (EMI) which would begin to take decisions on a common monetary policy, independent of political control. At this stage, central banks would begin pooling their reserves.

*Stage 3* involves a move to irrevocably fixed exchange rates, binding constraints on national budgets, and the EU acting as a single entity in international policy measures. The EMI would take over responsibility for the formulation and implementation of monetary policy. The EMI would also determine currency market interventions in respect of non-EU currencies and manage all official reserves. Finally a single EU currency (to be called the *euro*) would be established and the EMI would be replaced by a single *European Central Bank* (ECB).

The Delors Report was not accepted in full by all EU member states. All that was agreed was the starting date for Stage 1, namely 1 July 1990, and the condition that Stage 2 would not start until Stage 1 had been fully implemented. Nevertheless the report did establish a provisional timetable for the three stages: Stage 1 was to be completed by 31 December 1993, Stage 2 was scheduled to last between 1 January 1994 and 31 December 1996, and Stage 3 was scheduled to last between 1 January 1997 and 1 January 1999. Stage 2 did begin with the establishment of the EMI, but the other aspects of Stage 2, a common monetary policy and the pooling of reserves, did not materialize by the provisional completion date of 31 December 1996.

The most notable critic of the report has been the UK government. While not ruling out the principle of economic and monetary union as a long term objective, the UK government preferred an evolutionary and less bureaucratic approach, one that respected both parliamentary accountability and the diversity of member states. The government argued that Stage 1 involved profound changes that had to be implemented and analyzed before further developments took place. This was especially important, given the likely increase in membership of the EU following the revolutions in Eastern Europe in 1989.

The UK government accepted most of Stage 1 of the Delors Report because it promoted a single market with free movement of people, goods, services and capital, and equal access to capital and financial services for all citizens and companies. But the government wanted Stage 1 to be followed by a system: that increased the influence of markets and competition; that promoted price stability through a system of competing currencies, with citizens preferring to transact in the more stable currencies; that kept national control over economic policy making; and that involved no major constitutoinal changes. Stages 2 and 3 of the Delors plan involved the establishment of a new layer of bureaucratic institutions and laid down rigid rules that were potentially anti-competitive. For example, there was no guarantee that the European Central Bank would deliver successful counter-inflationary policies. The Delors plan for regional aid involved compensating poorer EU member states for moving towards EMU. The government felt that this form of intervention was inefficient. It preferred the use of market forces to enable countries with lower costs to prosper under the single market. The UK government's position was that it would begin to participate in EMU and, in particular, in the ERM, when the UK inflation rate had been reduced to EU levels, when there was full capital liberalization in the EU, and when adequate progress had been made towards completing the single market.

The UK government's concerns about both the form and speed of implementation of EMU were not shared by other member states. In 1991 the Delors Report was formalized in the Maastricht Treaty. The Maastricht Treaty leads to the following:

1  Single currency by 1999 for EU member states meeting a set of convergence criteria (the UK opted out of this).

2  Independent European Central Bank to manage the single currency.

3 Gradual convergence of EU economies, especially in respect of interest and exchange rates, government expenditure and national debt in the run up to the single currency.

4 A Stability Pact to ensure convergence is maintained after the single currency is introduced; this will place severe limitations on the fiscal policies of national governments adopting the euro.

5 Cohesion Fund established by the richer countries to help the poorer ones (Spain, Portugal, Greece and Ireland) improve their economies.

6 More social legislation (known as the Social Chapter) governing the work-place (the UK opted out of this initially, although the Social Chapter was accepted by the newly-elected Labour Government in 1997).

7 Greater inter-governmental cooperation in foreign policy and defence, but individual member states will retain power of veto in foreign affairs except in narrow fields of non-military action; a common defence policy and a joint army are ultimate objectives.

8 Greater inter-governmental cooperation in justice, crime and immigration affairs.

9 European citizenship, with full voting rights in country of residence.

10 Emphasis on 'subsidiarity', with decision-making at national level except in areas where EU-wide decisions can be justified.

11 New EU powers in environmental and consumer protection and setting up cross-border transport, energy and telecommunications networks in culture, education and training, and research.

12 European Parliament given greater powers to confirm the appointment of the President of the Commission, to amend or veto legislation, audit EU expenditure and investigate maladministration.

The *convergence criteria* specified in the Maastricht Treaty for membership of the single European currency by 1 January 1999 are as follows. Each member state must satisfy the following conditions:

1 Average inflation rate less than 1.5 per cent above the average of the lowest three member states during the preceding year.

2 Exchange rate within the narrow band of the ERM ($\pm 2.25$ per cent) for two years.

3 Average long-term interest rate less than 2 per cent above the average of the lowest three member states during the preceding year.

4 Budget deficit (PSBR) less than 3 per cent of GDP.

5 National debt less than 60 per cent of GDP.

6 Have passed legislation guaranteeing the political independence of the central bank.

Even if the five financial criteria are satisfied, a member state could not participate in the single European currency unless its central bank was politically independent and that legislation had been passed to ensure this.

The European Central Bank, which came into effect in 1998, has four main characteristics:

1  Its principal objective is the maintenance of price stability; however this has been defined, not as zero inflation, but as an inflation rate in any member state no higher than 1.5 per cent above the average of the lowest three member states (the central bank is also able to support the general economic policies and objectives of the EU, but without prejudice to the objective of price stability).

2  It is independent of political interference.

3  It has full responsibility for monetary policy across Europe.

4  It has powers to ensure that governments do not finance their budget deficits by printing money (i.e. that budget deficits are not monetized, since this tends to be inflationary).

The preference amongst the majority of member states to move towards full monetary union sooner rather than later was influenced by the recognition that the EMS was not likely to be sustainable in the long run as a result of the liberalization of capital controls within the EU after July 1990. With complete freedom of capital movements (i.e. perfect capital mobility), it is not possible for countries to maintain interest rate differentials in order to support their currencies; and exchange rate realignments are not readily permitted in the ERM. Until July 1990, countries that maintained capital controls were able to support their currencies by restricting capital outflows. With no controls, countries that had higher inflation rates than other ERM countries would find it difficult to devalue (since ERM rules do not allow this), and therefore would lose competitiveness. They would tend to experience persistent trade deficits compared with other ERM members. These trade imbalances would have put considerable pressure on countries to revert back to the early pattern of the EMS, when realignments within the ERM were fairly frequent.

The argument therefore was that, since capital controls had been removed, the EMS would come under increasing strain if inflation differentials persisted. Given that most countries did not want to leave the ERM, since this might damage the credibility of their counter-inflationary policies, further monetary integration was seen as the only option. Full monetary integration, where all countries agreed to have a single currency, by definition, implies irrevocably-fixed exchange rates, so, by design, there could be no realignments. In other words, monetary union would have the same effect as occurs in a single country with different regions all using the same currency (such as the USA). Monetary union of this form also implies a single monetary policy for all countries conducted by a single central bank.

A further impetus for EMU came from the single market in goods and services. Since the end of 1992, all trade barriers have been removed and workers and companies can now move freely between member states. Associated with these trends towards freedom of movement for factors of production (mainly labour and capital), it was argued by many member states that the existence of national currencies imposed unnecessary costs on transactions in Europe. It has been estimated that the cost of transacting in multiple currencies amounts to 4 per cent of Europe's GDP per year. So it would be much cheaper to conduct transactions in a common medium of exchange, i.e. in a single European currency.

The pressure for choosing the fast track towards EMU was further increased, at least in continental Europe, by the crises that occurred in the ERM in 1992 and 1993.

For nearly five years from January 1987 to September 1992 there were no realignments of exchange rates within the ERM. Many commentators regarded this period as evidence that, after a somewhat turbulent beginning, the EMS was able finally to offer its members a stable regime of fixed exchange rates. However, in September 1992 there was a crisis in the ERM involving speculative attacks on sterling, the Italian lira, the Spanish peseta, the Portuguese escudo, the Irish punt and the French franc. The crisis resulted in:

1 Sterling's and the lira's membership of the ERM being suspended.

2 The peseta being devalued within the ERM.

3 Spain, Portugal and Ireland reintroducing exchange controls.

4 The attack on the franc being defeated only as a consequence of massive support from the German central bank (the Bundesbank).

The UK had for nearly four years been in the deepest recession since the 1930s. Despite this, the Conservative government, in power since 1979, won an historic fourth consecutive victory in a General Election in April 1992. However, the group most affected by the recession was its own electoral supporters. These were the businesses and home-owners who were being hurt by high borrowing costs necessitated by the UK having to match the high real interest rates that Germany required to attract the funds needed to finance the costs of German reunification. The government had used up most of its goodwill in persuading the electorate that a Conservative victory at the election would reinforce the credibility of the government's counter-inflation policy and, as a result, the financial markets would reward the UK with lower nominal and hence real interest rates.

However, the lowering of interest rates did not arrive in the aftermath of the Conservative election victory. There was only further, gloomy news confirming more bankruptcies, more home repossessions, more redundancies, and a bigger current account deficit. All this pointed to a deepening of the recession rather than to recovery. Every sign indicated that if the government could not cut interest rates at home to encourage investment and hence boost domestic demand, then it would have desperately liked to reduce the exchange rate to boost export demand. This was despite protestations to the contrary. However, membership of the ERM prevented sterling from falling below 2.7780 DM per £ (the 6 per cent limit below the central parity of 2.95 DM per £).

It was well established that the UK had entered the ERM in October 1990 at too high an exchange rate against the Deutschmark. During the spring and autumn of 1990, John Major, then Chancellor of the Exchequer, had talked up the value of sterling from 2.70 DM to 2.95 DM per £ with promises of ERM membership, while keeping interest rates at 15 per cent. When sterling joined at a central rate of 2.95 DM per £ on 8 October 1990, interest rates were cut to 14 per cent, with expectations of further falls as the counter-inflationary disciplines of the ERM came into effect.

But the other members of the ERM had not been consulted either about the UK's intention to join or about the entry rate. The Germans certainly thought that the central rate was too high, making UK exports uncompetitive. They had also just embarked on the process of German reunification, following the collapse of the Soviet empire in Eastern Europe. The high costs of financing this were going to keep German interest rates high and were correspondingly going to keep UK interest rates high, whatever the need for lower interest rates in the UK.

In the event, sterling traded above the central rate for only five weeks of its 23-month membership of the ERM. The government was boxed in with very little room for manoeuvre. With sterling almost always trading below its central parity, nominal interest rates could not be cut as frequently as the government wished. Nominal interest rates were however reduced from 14 per cent to 10 per cent between October 1990 and June 1992. But the UK inflation rate had fallen at a faster rate during this period, so the real interest rate was actually rising during this period and there was no sign that the recession was ending.

The catalyst to the September crisis was the Danish rejection of the Maastricht Treaty in a referendum on 2 June 1992. The train leading to European monetary and political union was derailed, if only temporarily, by what was regarded as an inner-core member of the ERM. The train was gradually put back on the tracks over the summer as the Maastricht Treaty was ratified by other member states, but its speed was not as great as before.

It was becoming clear over the summer that the Italian government budget deficit was out of control and that, as a result, Italy would find it increasingly difficult to maintain its exchange rate parity within the ERM. Also, over the summer, the financial markets came to the view that the UK recession was so deep that the government would not raise interest rates whatever happened to the value of sterling.

As sterling began to slide, the Prime Minister, the Chancellor, and the Governor of the Bank of England, as well as the EU finance ministers, all attempted to talk back up the value of sterling. But the markets began to sense that there was no clout behind the rhetoric, especially when sterling fell below the 75 per cent divergence indicator, the point at which intervention to defend the exchange rate is mandatory, and the Bank still did not intervene. The Bank believed that investors would not sell sterling as it approached its ERM floor because they knew that it was 'impossible' for sterling to fall below the floor.

But the markets became convinced that the government would not take the only measure that was necessary to lift sterling off the floor, namely raise interest rates. Even a £7.25bn loan, announced on 3 September, was designed to defend sterling without having to trigger a rise in interest rates.

The speculators also knew that they had up to £600bn of 'hot money' to sell short against sterling and the Chancellor had only £7.25bn to defend it. In addition, the government did not begin the defence of the pound until, in the words of the City commentator, 'it was on the goal-line'.

The attack came on 16 September 1992 (a date which has gone down in UK financial history as 'Black Wednesday'), three days after Italy had devalued within the ERM, and so three days after the markets had realized that the move to an 'irrevocable fixed exchange rate' had been put slightly in question! Currency dealers, acting on behalf of their clients, began selling massive quantities of sterling and the Bank of England was forced to buy it. They sold short; they sold forward; they did everything to drive down the price of sterling below the ERM floor, knowing that if they succeeded in doing this they could close their positions and make huge profits.

As the Bank's reserves ran out, the Chancellor was forced to raise interest rates. They were raised an unprecedented two times during the day from 10 per cent to 12 per cent, and then to 15 per cent. But it was too little and it was too late. Sterling eventually fell by 3.2 per cent against the Deutschmark during the day.

In order to fully protect investors in sterling assets from a fall of this size during a single day, overnight interest rates would have had to have risen to about 1200 per cent (i.e. 3.2 per cent × 365 days per year). The actual rise in interest rates, as with the £7.25bn loan, was wholly inadequate to protect sterling within the ERM. At 7.30pm on 'Black Wednesday', sterling was forced to make a humiliating withdrawal from the ERM. The Prime Minister was said to be 'devastated'. The total profits made by speculators on this single day were estimated to be at least £1bn.

The government immediately began to blame the Bundesbank and, in particular, its president, Professor Helmut Schlesinger, for helping to undermine sterling's position in the ERM. The government listed five occasions on which senior officials of the Bundesbank had used language that had undermined sterling and the ERM: on August 25 and 28, and September 10, 15 and 16. For example, on 15 September, news agencies reported sources in the Bundesbank as suggesting that a sterling devaluation could not be ruled out, and on 'Black Wednesday' itself, Schlesinger was quoted as saying that Europe's financial problems were unresolved in spite of Italy's devaluation within the ERM the previous Sunday. Following the Bundesbank's successful intervention on 23 September to save the franc, the government also blamed the Bundesbank for not doing enough to save sterling.

The Bundesbank rejected all these criticisms. Specifically, it denied that it had favoured the franc over sterling, by revealing that it had spent DM 44bn (£17.3bn) defending the pound and the lira, most of it on sterling. The Bundesbank also said that it could not be blamed for anonymous statements and rumours in the markets or for inaccurate reproduction of its statements by news agencies.

At the end of July 1993 there was a second crisis which almost destroyed what remained of the ERM. In June 1993, France foolishly challenged German monetary leadership of the EMS by lowering its key short-term interest rate below that of Germany during an argument with Germany over the conduct of monetary policy shortly after the Balladur government took power in France. Within weeks, the speculators began to attack the French franc in an attempt to drive it out of the ERM just as they had done with sterling ten months before. However, rather than suspend the franc's membership of the ERM, as happened with sterling in September 1992, or change the central rates, as happened eleven times between March 1979 and January 1987, the remaining ERM members decided to widen the band limits to 15 per cent for all currencies in the ERM except for the guilder and the Deutschmark which remained within the 2.25 per cent band (i.e. for the French franc, Belgian franc, peseta, Danish krone, escudo and Irish punt).

From the UK government's viewpoint, an important underlying cause of these crises was the excessive haste to economic and monetary union implied by the timetable laid out in the Delors Report and the Maastricht Treaty. Everything had to be completed by the year 1999. The ERM, which had been conceived as a system of fixed but adjustable exchange rates and which the UK joined to give credibility to its counter-inflation policy, suddenly became the first stage of EMU and, therefore, became a test of commitment to EMU with its requirement for irrevocably fixed exchange rates followed by a single currency. The flexibility of the ERM was immediately taken away. The UK was expected to move rapidly to the narrow ±2.25 per cent bands of the mechanism as a prelude to the irrevocable fixing of exchange rates. Any thought of realignment of the ERM was ruled out of order, and any country that did realign would have lost its credibility in the financial markets, however much its domestic economy needed a realignment. Supporters of EMU argued that if a country did devalue, the markets would not believe any assurances it gave that it would not devalue again and hence would demand higher interest rates to protect investors from the risk of further devaluations.

However, from the viewpoint of most of the other member states of the EU, these crises, far from deterring them, had the effect of renewing their determination to proceed to full monetary union and a single currency at the earliest opportunity. Only with a single currency, backed by the vast resources of the Bundesbank, could the speculators be defeated. In fact, after July 1993, it was not the speculators that worried most supporters of EMU. It was whether Germany could be compensated politically (in terms of being given the political leadership of Europe as well as a permanent seat on the UN Security Council) for giving up the Deutschmark in favour of the euro.

That EMU would come was not in much doubt, although it was clear that not all members of the EU would join at the same time. There was even a timetable for joining laid down in the Maastricht Treaty. By May 1998, the Council of Ministers of Economics and Finance had to determine which countries satisfied the convergence criteria for admission to the euro, which was scheduled to be introduced on 1 January 1999. National debts had to be redenominated in euros by 1 July 2002. Even countries that did not satisfy the convergence criteria to the letter could still join if they had made sufficient progress towards meeting them, especially those criteria dealing with deficits and debt. The budget deficit to GDP ratio could exceed 3 per cent if it 'has declined substantially and continuously and reached a level that comes close to the reference value' or if 'the excess over the reference level is only exceptional and temporary'. The debt to GDP ratio could exceed 60 per cent if it is 'sufficiently diminishing and approaching the reference value at a satisfactory pace' (quoted from Maastrich Treaty, Articles 109j and 104c respectively). It turned out that 14 out of 15 countries (the exception was Greece) had budget deficits below 3 per cent of GDP, but very few countries had budget deficits below 60 per cent of GDP (and none if their unfunded state pension liabilities were officially included in measures of national debt). Only 11 of the 14 eligible countries opted to adopt the euro in May 1998: Germany, France, Italy, Holland, Belgium, Luxembourg, Spain, Austria, Portugal, Finland and Ireland. The UK, Sweden and Denmark opted to stay out of the first round of membership.

The British government decided that the UK would not adopt the euro as part of the first wave on 1 January 1999. However in October 1997, it set five economic tests for membership of EMU:

1 *Cyclical convergence.* Are business cycles and economic structures compatible so we can live comfortably with euro interest rates on a permanent basis?

2 *Flexibility.* If problems emerge, is there sufficient flexibility to deal with them?

3 *Investment.* Would joining EMU create better conditions for firms making long-term decisions to invest in Britain?

4 *Financial services.* What impact would EMU have on the competitive position of the UK's financial services industry, particularly the City's wholesale markets?

5 *Employment and growth.* In summary, will joining EMU promote higher growth, stability and a lasting increase in jobs?

These developments in Europe are in one way or another likely to have a dramatic effect on the City of London as the dominant financial centre in the European time zone. If the EFA is a success and if EMU goes ahead with UK participation and is also a success, there will be a big increase in competition in financial services between member states, there will be price (or at least inflation rate) stability, and exchange rate volatility will be a thing of the past. The single market will permit UK firms to market their products in other EU countries, but will also allow non-UK companies to market their products in the UK. For example, UCITS may well prove an attractive alternative to traditional unit trusts, since the management fees are about half those of unit trusts. But it is also possible that local loyalties might remain. The single market is likely to increase corporate finance activities such as mergers and acquisitions. But again the companies involved might prefer to take local advice on the matter. All this suggests a decentralization in the provision of financial services with strong regional financial centres developing.

Different parts of the UK financial system have responded in different ways to the pending increase in competition. In April 1990, the UK and German stock exchanges announced plans for increased co-operation through the *Federation of European Stock Exchanges*; in 1992 the Federation started *Eurolist*, a cross-border price-quotation and dealing system. Also in 1992 the London Traded Options Market (LTOM) and the London International Financial Futures Exchange merged to form the London

International Financial Futures and Options Exchange (LIFFE), following the growing threat from the MATIF in Paris and the DTB in Frankfurt. In 1998, the DTB merged with the Swiss options and futures exchange, SOFFEX, to form *Eurex*. In 1999, LIFFE introduced an automated trading system to compete against the one operating at Eurex.

However, two aspects of the new regime might actually reduce competition. The first is the capital adequacy requirements which, because of their relatively high fixed capital requirements, are likely to reduce the entry of small firms into the industry. The second is the problem of designing an acceptable investor protection framework that reduces investors' fears of investing in strange, foreign products.

While the UK financial system has been subjected to substantial interest rate and exchange rate volatility for the past 20 years, this might all change. If sterling enters the ERM or is replaced by the euro, many of the financial futures and options contracts currently trading may become obsolete. They will be replaced by new contracts, such as *credit derivatives*, denominated in euros. Further there is the prospect of the loss of monetary independence by the Bank of England. If monetary and fiscal policies are to be controlled by Europe rather than national governments, then the prospect of the ending of the UK gilts market becomes a possibility.

If the UK does not participate in EMU, then the outcome for the City depends on the success of EMU. If EMU turns out to be a bureaucratic nightmare with high costs of compliance, high reserve requirements and other restrictive policies, European banks might move to London and the City's relative importance in Europe might well increase. If EMU works and the euro replaces the currencies of continental Europe, a huge market in euro-denominated securities might develop in Frankfurt, eventually swamping the sterling-denominated markets in London and marginalizing London as a financial centre. Time will tell.

# Appendix: The City Research Project 1991–95

In 1991 the Corporation of London, the local authority responsible for the City of London, initiated a study to examine the City's competitive position in financial services in the light of the European single market which came into effect in 1992. The study, entitled the City Research Project, was conducted by the London Business School.

The aims of the project were to: collect and collate a full range of data pertaining to the City's financial services; describe and analyze the activities in the City and the sources of its competitive advantage; and to initiate a debate about London's future by highlighting possible directions for change. Of particular concern was whether London's predominance as the premier financial centre in the European time zone would survive the competitive pressures from other centres such as Frankfurt, Paris and Amsterdam, and whether there was any risk that the UK's financial sector would go the same way as much of the rest of British industry in the post-war period. The main conclusion of the study are as follows.

Of the world's three major financial centres (London, New York and Tokyo), London is the most important internationally. The other two are much larger, but this is due to the size of their domestic business. London is the global leader in foreign exchange trading, international bank lending to non-residents, marine and aviation insurance, international bond underwriting and trading, cross-border fund management, metals futures trading and shipbroking. The City employs some 150,000 people and makes a contribution of £10-15bn a year to the UK's GDP. The financial sector of the UK as a whole is responsible for 20 per cent of the UK's GDP. There has also been rapid growth since the beginning of the 1980s, largely as a result of the introduction of new products such as swaps, financial futures, and the underwriting of international equities and commercial paper. London has, however, lost market share in some of the more mature markets such as bank lending and general insurance.

There are several sources of London's competitive advantage. Historically, London has benefited from what is known as first mover advantage. Being Europe's first significant financial centre, London achieved a critical mass in a whole range of activities that other centres were not able to reach. As Stanislas Yassukovich, the Chairman of the Governing Board of the City Research Project, said in the Final Report: 'The sharing of common services, access to pools of skills, speed of dissemination of information and risk are all forces which lead to the clustering of practitioners. Thus externalities are created, such that each firm derives extra benefit from the proximity of other firms. These externalities protect the incumbent producer so that it is possible for no one city to have an inherent advantage over another, but once services have concentrated in one centre, there is no incentive for anyone to leave' (p.x).

Currently, London has four principal competitive advantages: strategic assets, relationship structures, reputation and innovation. Strategic assets include favourable regulatory, tax and legal structures, although it is possible to duplicate these elsewhere. But the most important strategic asset is a large pool of skilled personnel whose competitive advantage is constantly enhanced by the transferable skills acquired as a result of the shared experience of being located in the same city. New financial centres have difficulties in achieving the critical mass necessary for this to happen. Certain ancillary services, such as accounting, actuarial, legal, printing, telecommunications and information, computing and technical support services, are strategic assets which are difficult to introduce at low cost into small centres. Relationship structures, in particular the nature of personal contacts, are important for establishing trust and reducing the likelihood of corrupt practices. These, in turn, help to secure and enhance reputation, and reputation, in turn, helps to attract both new business and the best entrepreneurs and innovators. In this way a virtuous circle develops as innovation helps to preserve the primacy of the first mover.

While these competitive advantages are not easy to replicate elsewhere, there have certainly been challenges to the City's position. The report concludes that London will not face a serious threat from continental financial centres, despite the fact that Paris and Frankfurt have done much to attract business away from London. There are three reasons for this. London's position depends chiefly on the world-wide growth in demand for financial services, rather than on what is happening in the rest of Europe, and this demand depends on global economic growth and the global regulatory framework. Much of the activity in different financial centres is complementary rather than competitive, e.g., the origination of business is best conducted in dispersed financial centres, but the trading of the securities subsequently issued is best conducted in a single financial centre in order to maximize liquidity, so the greater the origination the better it is for the principal trading centre. Competitive threats to London are more likely to come not from monolithic financial centres but from niche centres, e.g. Dublin, Jersey and Luxembourg in offshore fund management, Bermuda in insurance, and Piraeus in shipbroking. The report also dismisses the threat from regional centres such as Hong Kong and Singapore; while the growth in Hong Kong and Singapore as financial centres certainly reflects the increasing economic importance of the Pacific Rim, this does not necessarily imply that they will take business away from London.

However, the Report does conclude that London, while not facing serious external threats, does face a number of significant internal threats to its competitive advantage. These relate to the co-ordination of policy and to the physical and institutional infrastructure.

The Report argues that policy-making in a number of important areas, such as promotion, education and training, establishing protocols and reacting to crises, is fragmented. For example, promotion is undertaken by the Corporation of London, British Invisibles, London First Centre and the many trade associations. But there is both wasteful duplication and significant gaps: no organisation is responsible for promoting inward investment by financial institutions or increasing the total volume of business in London. The Report calls for improved policy coordination in these areas. In particular, it recommends that there should be mergers between related trade associations and that the merged associations should be made more effective through the employment of full-time professional staff. These associations have an important role in helping to keep the regulatory framework supportive and up to date. The report also criticises the UK's implementation of EU directives which, because of the precise drafting requirements of English law, is less flexible than is the case in other member states. Because EU legislation, once implemented, is difficult to change, this could place severe constraints on the dynamism of London's financial system.

In terms of physical infrastructure, the Report argues that this is a major responsibility of the government. London's roads are heavily congested, its underground system is antiquated and unreliable, the co-ordination of transport policy in London is fragmented, long-term investment planning is hampered by short-term expediency over government spending, and the planning process itself is slow and ineffective compared with the rest of Europe. The Report argues that the private sector financing of transport projects in Central London is not really feasible, but that individuals and businesses which are based in the City and will benefit from improved transport will have to finance the expenditure in one way or another. Fare increases will not provide all the required finance, but the report suggests two radical solutions: road pricing could provide both funds and more efficient road use, and a property tax on the businesses in Central London that would benefit most from improvements in the transport system.

Historically, the City of London has had a more international outlook than the other major financial centres, New York and Tokyo, and the institutional infrastructure within which the City operates reflects this: the stable and pragmatic political, regulatory and legal systems have all helped to promote London's international reputation. The location of financial services is very sensitive to the tax and regulatory regimes of different financial centres and to any changes in these regimes. The classic example is the euromarkets which started when the US imposed the Interest Equalisation Tax in the early 1960s. The Report warns that London could lose its competitive advantage either if the tax and regulatory regime in the UK were to be made more onerous or if deregulation in other financial centres continued. The Report suggests some regulatory principles that should be adopted in the UK (p.xxii):

1 The purpose of regulation is to alleviate market failures, which are typically connected with a) systemic risk, b) fraud, or c) lack of information. The purpose should not be to protect investors from risks which the market can reasonably assess.

2 If the regulatory system is unable to provide investor protection, there should be compensation, but this should always include a deductible to ensure that the investor is subject to the principle of *caveat emptor*.

3 The focus of regulation should be primarily on retail markets; wholesale investors should as far as possible be exposed to the principle of *caveat emptor*.

4 Where possible, regulation should employ market, rather than administrative solutions to market failure.

5 The efficiency of the regulatory structure is likely to be improved by the Securities and Investments Board focusing as far as possible on standard-setting rather than detailed rule-making. The Report acknowledges that there is a widespread view that the regulatory system in the UK imposes high costs of compliance yet has failed to provide satisfactory investor protection. However there were no direct measures of these costs. The Report provides some measures which indicate that the direct costs of regulating the securities industry are similar to those in the US and France. But the indirect costs of compliance on firms were up to three times the size of the direct costs, so that the total cost of financial service regulation amounted to 3-4 per cent of net operating expenses. The Report argues that it is important that regulation provides 'value-for-money'. These ideas appear to have been taken into account in the design of the Financial Services Authority which replaced the SIB in 1997.

The Report also warns of the dangers of the politicization of regulation within an EU context. There were four main concerns (p.xxiii):

1 Harmonization of regulation is likely to result in rules which are less well-suited to individual markets or institutions.

2 Harmonization may make regulation more remote from practitioner expertise.

3 International agreements are hard to reach, so that there is likely to be reluctance to adapt them as shortcomings are revealed and markets change.

4 Regulation becomes politicized, so that rules are the outcome of a bargaining process. One consequence is that financial services shift out of the EU to more hospitable centres.

The Report argues that the UK tax system causes a number of distortions in respect of financial transactions, e.g. the differences between taxable and accounting income, the division between income and capital gains, and the treatment of foreign exchange gains and losses and off-balance sheet items such as options. Rapid financial innovation is likely to lead to tax anomalies, but the Report argues there should be a speedy resolution to these, possibly through the use of outside experts in the tax reform process. Uncertainty over taxation issues places any financial centre at a strong competitive disadvantage. The taxation of personal income is also an important matter, because it affects the remuneration of expatriate staff employed by overseas financial institutions. The Report notes that in recent years, many of the tax reliefs for expatriate staff have been phased out, so that any increase in income tax rates would reduce the attractiveness of overseas institutions locating in London.

Finally, the Report considers the consequences of Economic and Monetary Union within the EU. EMU and the introduction of a single currency would lead to the closing of a number of markets and the expansion of others. Intra-European foreign currency dealing would disappear as would the national money and bond markets. These would be replaced with the market for the euro and the euro-denominated money and bond contracts of the regional governments of the EU. The Report notes that the effect on London would depend on whether the UK joined EMU. If the UK joined, London and the Bank of England might have the same dominant role as New York and the New York Federal Reserve Bank does in the US. If the UK stayed outside EMU and those that joined faced excessive reserve requirements and other restrictive policies, European banks might relocate in London. On the other hand, EMU might succeed and a strong liquid euro money and bond market might develop in Frankfurt. The Report does not predict which of these outcomes will materialise, but it does end by proposing a number of ways in which the Bank of England might harmonise its operating procedures with those of other central banks and also increase the liquidity of the UK money markets. These include: widening the range of instruments with which the Bank of England deals by replacing outright bill purchases in its money-market operations with repurchase agreements, enabling the Bank to lend cash against an extended set of eligible securities, such as government bonds, as collateral; widening the set of institutions with which it deals by establishing an open gilt repo system, thereby eliminating the special privileges of the discount houses (these two proposals were adopted in 1996); paying Treasury receipts into secured accounts with commercial banks rather than the Exchequer accounts at the Bank. The Report notes that current practices have led to recent very high volatility in the overnight interest rate, ranging from 4.5 per cent to 20 per cent. The proposed changes would increase the depth and liquidity of the money market, make money-market shortages more predictable and reduce the volatility of the overnight rate.

## The City Research Project Reports

*Interim Report: Executive Summary*, July 1992

*Final Report*, March 1995

## The City Research Project Subject Reports

   I S. Glaister and A. Travers (London School of Economics), *Meeting the Transport Needs of the City*, March 1993.

  II J.R. Franks and S.M. Schaefer (London Business School), *The Costs and Effectiveness of the UK Financial Regulatory System*, March 1993.

 III C. Higson and J. Elliott, *Implications of Surplus ACT for the Location of Financial Services*, Spring 1993.

 IV B. Khan and J. Ireland, *Use of Technology for Competitive Advantage: A Study of Screen v Floor Trading*, September 1993.

  V J. Ireland and T. Ryan (London Business School), *Equity Settlement in London: Its Importance to London as a Financial Centre*, September 1993.

 VI R.A. Brealey and M. Soria (London Business School), *Revenues from the City's Financial Services*, December 1993.

 VII N. Schnadt (London School of Economics), *The Domestic Money Markets of the UK, France, Germany & the US; European Monetary Union and the Sterling Money Market (Papers I and II)*, January 1994.

VIII E. Dimson and P. Marsh (London Business School), *The Debate on International Capital Requirements*, February 1994.

 IX J. Kay, R. Laslett, and N. Duffy (London Economics), *The Competitive Advantage of the Fund Management Industry in the City of London*, February 1994.

X J. Kay (London Economics), *The Competitive Advantage of the Shipping Industry in the City of London*, September 1994.

XI R.A. Brealey and E. Kaplanis (London Business School), *The Growth and Structure of International Banking*, July 1994.

XII H.B. Rose (London Business School), *International Banking Developments and London's Position as an International Banking Centre*, July 1994.

XIII H.B. Rose (London Business School), *The Role of London as an International Financial Centre: A Narrative History*, July 1994.

XIV J.R. Franks and S.M. Schaefer (London Business School), *Custodianship and the Protection of Client Property*, July 1994.

XV S. Szymanski (Imperial College), *The City Labour Market*, September 1994.

XVI R. Goddee (London Business School), *A Review of Professional and Managerial Skills*, September 1994.

XVII J. Raybould (Kings College), *London's Futures Exchanges*, November 1994.

XVIII J. Ireland (London Business School), *The Importance of Telecommunications to London as an International Financial Centre*, September 1994.

XIX J. Kay (London Economics), *The Competitive Advantage of Law and Accountancy in the City of London*, September 1994.

XX Jones Lang Wootton, *Property Occupation Trends by the Financial Services Sector in London*, November 1994.

XXI C. Higson (London Business School), *The Effectiveness of the Tax Reform Process in the UK*, to be published.

XXII O. Hart and J. Moore (Harvard University and London School of Economics), *The Governance of Exchanges: Members' Cooperatives versus Outside Ownership*, to be published.

XXIII J. Ireland (London Business School) and R. Wilkinson, *The Promotion of the City and the Coordination of Policy*, to be published.

XXIV J. Kay and others (London Economics), *Distinctive Capabilities in the London Market for General Insurance*, to be published.

XXV A.J. Neuberger (London Business School), *Structure of Financial Markets*, December 1994.

XXVI J.R. Franks, S.M. Schaefer and M. Staunton (London Business School), *Costs of Regulatory Compliance for Financial Firms*, to be published.

**The City Research Project Special Report**

*London's Contribution to the UK Economy.*

These reports were published by The Corporation of London, Guildhall, London EC2P 2EJ.

## Selected references

Bain, A.D. (1992), *The Economics of the Financial System,* Martin Robertson, Oxford.

Chapman, C. (1988), *How the Stock Markets Work*, Hutchinson, London.

Coopers and Lybrand (1991), *The Financial Jungle: A Guide to Financial Instruments,* Coopers and Lybrand, London.

Delors, J. (1989), *Report on Economic and Monetary Union in the European Community*, Commission of the European Community, Brussels.

*Financial Services Authority: An Outline* (1997), Financial Services Authority, London.

Francis, J.C. (1991), *Investments*, McGraw-Hill, Singapore. (Chapters 2 and 3.)

*Guidance Notes for SETS* (1997), London Stock Exchange, London.

Hallwood, C. and MacDonald, R. (1994), *International Money and Finance*, Blackwell, Oxford.

Her Majesty's Treasury (1989), *An Evolutionary Approach to Economic and Monetary Union*, HM Treasury, London.

Her Majesty's Treasury (1997), *The Future of UK Government Debt and Cash Management*, HM Treasury, London.

Hicks, J. (1939), *Value and Capital*, Oxford University Press, Oxford.

*Order Book Trading* (1997), London Stock Exchange, London.

Scott-Quinn, B. and Walmsley, J. (1993), *Towards a Single European Securities Trading Market*, International Securities Market Association, Zurich.

Sharpe, W.F., Alexander, G. and Bailey, J. (1995), *Investments*, Prentice-Hall, Englewood Cliffs, NJ. (Chapters 1–3.)

Wilson, H. (1980), *Report of the Committee to Review the Functioning of Financial Institutions*, HMSO, London.

See also the following publications:

*Financial Stability Review* (Bank of England and Financial Services Authority);

*Interchange: Quarterly Journal of the Stock Exchange*;

*Euromoney*;

*Intermarket: The Magazine of Financial Risk Management*;

*Risk*;

*Quality of Markets Quarterly Review*;

*Securities Institute Information Brochure.*

**Exercises**

1  Who are the main participants in the financial system?

2  What are the main functions of financial intermediaries?

3  What are the main types of financial intermediary?

4  What are the principal differences between retail and investment banks?

5  What are the main ways of classifying securities?

6  How would you measure the marketability of a particular security?

7  Why are futures and options known as derivative instruments?

8  Why is a convertible bond a composite security?

9  What is the difference between money markets and capital markets?

10  What is the difference between primary and secondary markets?

11  What are the main reasons for trading in secondary markets?

12  What is the difference between transaction prices and equilibrium prices?

13  What is the bid-offer spread? What is the touch?

14  What is the role of a market-maker?

15  Explain the difference between quote-driven and order-driven trading systems.

16  Explain the difference between a broad, deep market and a thin, shallow market?

17  What factors are likely to determine the size of the bid-offer spread?

18  How can a market-maker protect himself in a volatile market?

19  Explain the terms 'market order', 'stop order', 'limit order', 'stop limit order'. Give examples.

20  What is the difference between a cash account and a margin account? Illustrate using an example.

21  What is the difference between a short sale agreement and a repurchase agreement? Illustrate using an example.

22  What role do regulations play in a financial system?

23  Explain the role of the Financial Services Authority.

24  What are conduct of business rules?

25  What is the difference between a recognized investment exchange and a designated investment exchange?

26  What is specific unpublished price-sensitive information? Why is it important?

27 Compare and contrast the different roles played by GEMMs, IDBs and repurchase agreements in the UK gilts market.

28 Compare and contrast the different methods of issuing:

a) gilts in the UK;

b) shares in the UK.

29 What is the 'when issued' market?

30 Compare and contrast the different markets trading shares in the UK.

31 How are international securities traded in the UK?

32 What are American depository receipts?

33 What was 'Big Bang'? What are the likely consequences of 'Big Bang'?

34 How successful will Economic and Monetary Union be within Europe?

# Chapter 2

# The market determination of discount rates

Market-determined discount rates are used to discount the cash flows from securities and hence to determine the market values of securities. Discounting is examined in more detail in the next chapter. In this chapter we examine how the market determines discount rates.

## 2.1 The price of time and risk

When an individual undertakes an investment in a security, he is forgoing a certain sum of money today (which could otherwise be devoted to consumption) for a generally uncertain sum of money in the future (which again could be devoted to consumption at that time). In short, investment is the sacrifice of certain current consumption for generally uncertain future consumption. The individual will want to be compensated both for the time that his money is tied up in the investment and for the risk that is involved during that time. The issuer of the security must be prepared to compensate the investor for the time and risk involved, otherwise no one will be willing to buy the security. An individual investor can be compensated either by receiving income from his investment (interest from deposits, coupons from bonds, dividends from shares, rent from property, etc.) or through an increase in the capital value of the investment. We will simply call the overall rate of return on the investment (whether income or capital gain) the rate of interest on the investment. In simple terms, therefore, we can think of the rate of interest as the price of *time* and *risk*.

The next step is to break down the rate of interest into its various components. We will show in the following sections that the nominal interest rate can be decomposed as follows:

$$
\begin{aligned}
\text{Nominal interest rate} \quad = \quad & \text{Expected real interest rate} \\
& + \text{Expected inflation rate} \\
& + \text{Expected liquidity premium} \\
& + \text{Expected risk premium.} \qquad (2.1)
\end{aligned}
$$

The first three components are time components of the interest rate, while the fourth is the risk component. Also, because the nominal interest rate is the interest rate that is expected to hold over a future period (say the next year), we will assume that individuals are interested in the *expected* values of the components over that period. And because in an *efficient market* (which will be discussed in detail in Chapter 11) the nominal interest rate will equal the *expected* nominal interest rate, we have the nominal interest rate on the left-hand side of equation (2.1). (This is known as the *expectations hypothesis*.)

## 2.2 The expected real interest rate

In a world that lasts for two periods (which are, say, a year apart), has no inflation and no risk, the expected real interest rate is the rate of interest that equates the supply of funds from those willing to lend between the two periods with the demand for funds from those wishing to borrow between the two periods. But what determines why some individuals are borrowers while others are lenders?

The answer lies in the different rates of *time preference* held by different individuals. An individual's time preference measures the *willingness* of the individual to forgo consumption in the first period in return for additional consumption in the second period. If the individual's rate of time preference is 10 per cent, this means that, in order to induce the individual to give up £1 worth of consumption today, he must be compensated by being given £1.10 worth of consumption in a year's time. Alternatively, we can say that the individual is *indifferent* between £1 worth of consumption today and £1.10 worth of consumption in a year's time. Other things being equal, individuals with high rates of time preference prefer current consumption to future consumption and may well borrow to support that current consumption; while individuals with low rates of time preference prefer future consumption to present consumption and may be willing to lend today in order to generate funds to finance that future consumption.

If the rate of time preference measures the willingness of individuals to transfer resources over time, the rate of interest measures their *ability* to do so. If the rate of interest is 12 per cent, then anyone who lends £1 for one year will receive £1.12 in a year's time, while anyone who borrows £1 for one year will have to repay £1.12 in a year's time.

If the interest rate is too low, there will be more people willing to borrow than to lend, while if the interest rate is too high, more people will want to lend than to borrow. The equilibrium rate of interest will exactly balance the supply of funds for lending with the demand for funds for borrowing. This can be seen from Figure 2.1.

Figure 2.1 depicts the behaviour of two individuals A and B over two time periods. Individual A receives income of $Y_1^A$ in period 1 and $Y_2^A$ in period 2. He has an *indifference curve* denoted $I^A$. This measures the rate at which the individual is willing to trade off consumption in period 1 for consumption in period 2 and remain as well off after the trade as before. In other words, $I^A$ is a locus indicating constant utility or satisfaction between different consumption bundles in period 1 and period 2. The slope of $I^A$ at any point measures A's marginal rate of time preference. The convex shape of $I^A$ results from the fact that, as A's period 1 consumption is reduced, he has to be compensated with additional period 2 consumption at *an increasing rate* to preserve his utility level. In other words, the marginal rate of time preference increases as period 1 consumption is reduced and decreases as period 1 consumption is increased. Individual B, on the other hand, has income $Y_1^B$ and $Y_2^B$ in the two periods and indifference curve $I^B$.

**Figure 2.1** The determination of the real rate of interest

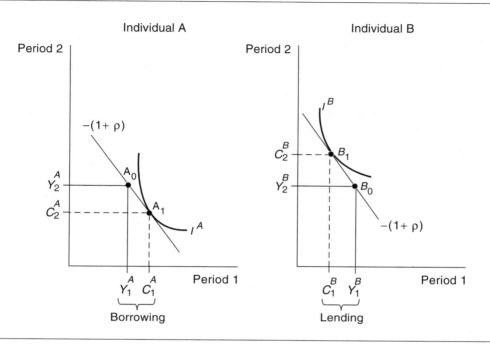

Without borrowing and lending, A would be confined to consuming $Y_1^A$ in period 1 and $Y_2^A$ in period 2; i.e. he would be confined to point $A_0$ in Figure 2.1. Similarly, B would be confined to $B_0$. But suppose that borrowing and lending are permitted at the same rate of interest $\rho$. The two individuals can then borrow and lend along the straight line in Figure 2.1 with slope denoted by $-(1+\rho)$. Movements to the right of the individuals' initial position ($A_0$ or $B_0$) represent borrowing, while movements to the left represent lending. The optimal position for each individual occurs at the point where his marginal rate of time preference (the rate at which he is willing to substitute consumption between periods) just equals the rate of interest (the rate at which he is able to substitute consumption between periods). This occurs at the point of tangency between the indifference curve and the borrowing-lending line, i.e. at $A_1$ for A and at $B_1$ for B. Given the borrowing-lending line, $A_1$ offers the highest possible level of utility or satisfaction achievable by A (and in particular is higher than the utility level at $A_0$, i.e. is on a higher indifference curve than the one passing through $A_0$), while $B_1$ gives the highest possible utility level achievable by B (and again is higher than the utility level at $B_0$).

Finally, we can see how the equilibrium rate is determined. Suppose that the market for borrowing and lending consists only of individual A and individual B (or, to make it slightly more general, only of individuals either identical to A or identical to B). The equilibrium interest rate will therefore be the rate that balances the amount of borrowing ($C_1^A - Y_1^A$), from individuals like A who wish to borrow, with the amount of lending ($Y_1^B - C_1^B$), from individuals like B who wish to lend. If the interest rate is too high (i.e. if the borrowing-lending line is 'too steep'), there will be an excess of lending over borrowing which will tend to drive the interest rate down. If the interest rate is too low (i.e. if the borrowing-lending line is 'too flat'), there will be an excess of borrowing over lending which will tend to drive the interest rate up. Figure 2.1 shows the equilibrium rate as $\rho$ which exactly balances borrowing and lending.

## 2.3    The expected inflation rate

The equilibrium interest rate $\rho$ is the interest rate that we would expect to observe in the absence of inflation, risk and a liquidity premium.

If there is inflation in the economy, lenders will be expected to be compensated for that inflation. If they do not take inflation into account in deciding whether or not to lend, this will please borrowers who will be repaying the loan in depreciated currency. This would be equivalent to a free transfer of real resources from lenders to borrowers. Such behaviour is clearly irrational (lenders would be said to be suffering from *money illusion*), and we will assume that lenders are not irrational.

If prices are expected to rise by 6 per cent between two periods a year apart, lenders will want to get at least £1.06 back for every £1 lent just in order to be able to buy the same bundle of goods that they could have bought in period 1. They will want more than this, of course, because they also want to be compensated for lending their money for a year. Suppose the equilibrium real interest rate is 4 per cent. The amount repayable on a loan of £1 in period 2 will be £1.1024:

$$
\begin{aligned}
\text{Loan repayment amount} \;&=\; £1 \cdot (1 + \text{Real interest rate}) \cdot \frac{\text{Price level in period 2}}{\text{Price level in period 1}} \\[2mm]
&=\; £1 \cdot (1.04) \cdot \frac{£1.06}{£1} \\[2mm]
&=\; £(1.04)(1.06) \\[2mm]
&=\; £1.1024 \,.
\end{aligned}
\tag{2.2}
$$

This suggests that the *nominal* rate of interest is 10.24 per cent.

In general, the nominal interest rate is determined from the following equation (known as the *Fisher equation* for the nominal interest rate, after Irving Fisher (1930) who invented it):

$$
\begin{aligned}
1 + \text{Nominal interest rate} \;&=\; (1 + \text{Real interest rate}) \cdot \frac{\text{Price level in period 2}}{\text{Price level in period 1}} \\[2mm]
&=\; (1 + \text{Real interest rate}) \cdot (1 + \text{Inflation rate}) \,,
\end{aligned}
\tag{2.3}
$$

or in symbols:

$$
\begin{aligned}
1 + r \;&=\; (1 + \rho)(1 + \pi) \\
&=\; 1 + \rho + \pi + (\rho)(\pi) \,,
\end{aligned}
\tag{2.4}
$$

where:

$$
\begin{aligned}
r \;&=\; \text{nominal interest rate;} \\
\rho \;&=\; \text{real interest rate;} \\
\pi \;&=\; \frac{\text{Price level in period 2}}{\text{Price level in period 1}} - 1 \\
&=\; \text{expected inflation rate.}
\end{aligned}
$$

In (2.4) the cross product $(\rho)(\pi)$ is usually quite small and therefore often ignored. A simplified version of the Fisher equation is therefore:

$$
r \;=\; \rho + \pi \,.
\tag{2.5}
$$

## 2.4 The expected liquidity premium

So far we have examined the determination of the nominal interest rate in a two-period model (with no risk). However, many loans extend beyond two periods, and we have to take into account the effect of the duration of the loan on the nominal rate.

The relationship between the maturity of the loan and the rate of interest is known as the *yield curve* (or the *term structure of interest rates*). Figure 2.2 gives a typical example of a yield curve. As can be seen, the interest rate generally increases with the term to maturity. This is true even if the real interest rate ($\rho$) and the inflation rate ($\pi$) are not expected to change over time. The upward-sloping yield curve must therefore be related to the duration of the loan. Figure 2.3 decomposes the yield curve under the assumption that the real rate and expected inflation are constant over time. The third component is a *liquidity premium* (also called a *term premium* or *horizon premium*) that is positive and increases with the term to maturity. What is the liquidity premium, and why does it increase with maturity?

---

**Figure 2.2** A typical yield curve

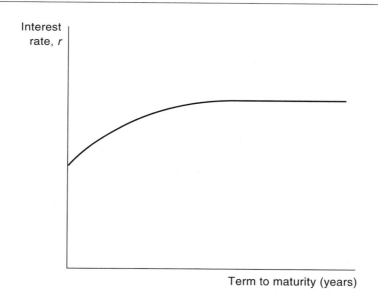

---

Most lenders prefer to lend for short periods; i.e. they prefer to invest in short-term securities. This is because short-term securities are generally more liquid than long-term securities; they can be more easily converted to cash without the risk of losing capital value. Investors will therefore be willing to accept lower yields on short-term securities. Most borrowers, on the other hand, prefer to borrow for long periods; i.e. they prefer to issue long-term securities. This is because short-term borrowing has to be rolled over and there is the risk that this can be done only on unfavourable terms to the borrower. Borrowers will therefore be willing to pay higher yields on long-term securities to avoid this *reinvestment risk* (or *rollover risk*).

The preferences of both borrowers and lenders will therefore combine to give the upward-sloping yield curve in Figure 2.3. In order to induce lenders away from their preferred habitat of lending short, they have to be offered a liquidity premium to hold long-term securities; and it will be a premium that

**Figure 2.3** Decomposing the yield curve; $\rho$, $\pi$ and $l$

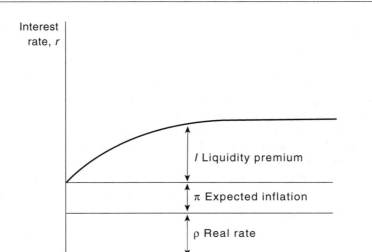

borrowing firms will be willing to pay to guarantee long-term funding. The liquidity premium is likely to increase with term to maturity but at a decreasing rate, so that the yield curve initially rises steeply but then flattens out. This is because the premium required to induce an investor to invest for five years rather than one year will be quite high; but, having induced an investor to invest for 20 years, the additional premium required to get him to invest for 25 years will not be so high. This follows because the discounted value of the additional five years' cash flows involved will not be high. In other words, given how heavily the distant future is discounted, an investor will not differentiate greatly between a 20-year and a 25-year security.

The liquidity premium will still be positive and increasing even if the security is perfectly marketable (although it may not be as high as with imperfectly marketable securities). This is because, even though an investor can sell the security immediately for cash, he still has to sell it to someone who must either hold it for the remainder of its term or in turn sell it on to yet another investor. Since each subsequent investor will require a liquidity premium appropriate for the remaining duration of the security, so will the current investor.

If the liquidity premium is denoted $l$, the nominal rate of interest becomes:

$$r \;=\; \rho + \pi + l. \tag{2.6}$$

## 2.5　The expected risk premium

The final component of the rate of interest is the risk premium. So far we have considered a world without risk. But there are two important types of risk that must be taken into account when investors are deciding which different securities to invest in. These are specific risk and market risk.

*Specific risk* (or *variant risk* or *idiosyncratic risk* or *unsystematic risk* or *diversifiable risk*) is the risk that the issuer of a particular security will become insolvent and default on his obligations. Specific risk itself has four components: management risk, business (or operating) risk, financial risk, and collateral risk.

*Management risk* is the risk that the managers running the firm that issued the security are incompetent and will make decisions that will lead the company into insolvency. Management risk is likely to be high in new firms with untried and untested managers.

*Business risk* arises from the asset side of the firm's balance sheet. It is the risk that the firm will not generate sufficient sales revenue to finance the fixed costs of its operations. Firms can choose to operate with different production technologies. Firms with a labour-intensive production technology use little fixed capital and therefore have low fixed operating costs in relation to total costs; i.e. they have low *operating leverage*. Firms with a capital-intensive choice of technique use a large amount of fixed capital and correspondingly have high fixed operating costs in relation to total costs; i.e. they have high operating leverage. High operating leverage has the effect of magnifying profits if sales revenue is high but magnifying losses if sales revenue is low. So the combination of sales revenue variability and operating leverage constitute the firm's business risk. The lower a firm's sales revenue variability, the higher the quality of the firm's earnings. Clearly, if sales revenue is highly volatile, the firm can reduce business risk by using lower operating leverage.

*Financial risk* arises from the liability side of the firm's balance sheet. It is the risk that the firm will not generate sufficient sales revenue to finance the fixed-charge liabilities (such as fixed-interest debt) on its balance sheet. The ratio of debt to equity in the balance sheet is known as *financial leverage* (or *gearing*). Firms can choose to finance their assets with different degrees of financial leverage. They can choose a high proportion of fixed-interest debt relative to equity, i.e. can have high financial leverage; or they can choose a low proportion of debt and have low financial leverage. High financial leverage has the effect of magnifying profits if sales revenue is high but magnifying losses if sales revenue is low. So the combination of sales revenue variability and financial leverage constitutes the firm's financial risk. If sales revenue is highly volatile, the firm can reduce financial risk with lower financial leverage. Similarly, if the firm cannot avoid operating with high operating leverage, it can help to reduce the overall risk of default by using low financial leverage.

The previous three components of specific risk affect the overall riskiness of the firm. Any one of them, if sufficiently extreme, can lead the firm into insolvency. But investors in the firm do not have equal claims on the underlying assets of the firm in the event of insolvency and therefore do not face equal risks. Some investors have weaker claims than others because they have poorer collateral. Such investors face higher *collateral risk*. The investors with the strongest claim on assets are those holding secured debt, such as debenture holders and mortgage lenders. Next in priority come general or unsecured creditors, such as those holding junior or subordinated bonds. After that come preferred stockholders, while common stockholders come last in the ranking of priorities.

Specific risk certainly exists. But if it is independent of (that is, uncorrelated with) other things that are happening in the economy, then it can be reduced if not eliminated entirely through low-cost *diversification*. Diversification involves holding portfolios of securities whose specific risks are uncorrelated with each other. We will see in Chapter 13 precisely how diversification reduces specific risk. But the important point to note now is that, if default risk can be diversified away at low cost, then in equilibrium the market will not pay a default risk premium. In other words, we can say that diversifiable risk will not be priced in an efficient market.

Some risk, however, simply cannot be diversified away. The world is a very risky place and that risk has to be borne by someone. Such risk exists because much of what happens in a company depends not just on the internal management decisions of the company, but also on wider market conditions, about which management can do virtually nothing. A substantial part of the earnings generated by the company will be correlated with market conditions, which are themselves correlated with the state of the economy as represented by the fairly regular pattern of boom and slump of the business cycle.

Since most firms' earnings are positively correlated with the business cycle, this limits the effectiveness of diversification. As we shall see in Chapter 13, effective risk diversification involves taking on offsetting risks. If most risks are positively correlated, then the complete elimination of risk through diversification cannot be achieved. The risk attached to earnings (and therefore to securities dependent on those earnings) that results from the dependence of earnings on market conditions, and which cannot be eliminated through diversification, is called *market risk* (or *covariant risk* or *systematic risk* or *undiversifiable risk*). In extreme cases market risk can lead to insolvency. But in most cases the effect of market risk is to cause fluctuations in the capital values of the securities issued by firms. Market risk has different effects on the values of shares and bonds and it is important to isolate the differences.

---

**Figure 2.4** Decomposing the yield curve; $\rho$, $\pi$, $l$ and $\sigma$

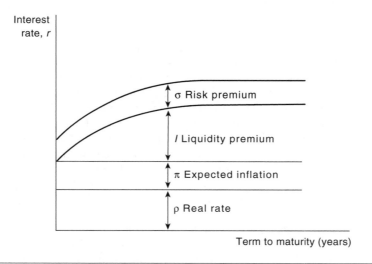

---

The main way in which market risk affects share values is through fluctuations in earnings. The relative volatility of a particular firm's earnings compared with those of the market average is called the firm's *beta*. If the firm has a beta of unity, this means that its earnings fluctuate in line with the market average. A beta less than unity implies that the firm's earnings are less volatile than the market average. A beta greater than unity implies that the firm's earnings are more volatile than the market average. Clearly, the larger a firm's beta, the larger the market risk of its shares.

The main way in which market risk affects bond values is through fluctuations in the general level of interest rates. The coupon payments on bonds are contractually fixed and so cannot be varied in the same way that dividends can. But the general level of interest rates fluctuates with the business cycle, and bond values fluctuate inversely with interest rates, as we shall see in Chapter 5 which deals with bond valuation. The fluctuation of bond values as interest rates change is known as *interest rate risk*. The extent by which the price of a bond changes in response to a given change in interest rates is known as *duration*: the greater the response, the greater the duration. Clearly, the larger a bond's duration, the larger its market risk. With deposit type securities whose terms and capital values are fixed, the main risk is *reinvestment risk*, the risk of having to redeposit at the end of the term at a lower interest rate. With such securities, the greater the fluctuations in general interest rates, the greater the reinvestment risk.

Whatever the source of market risk, the important point to note is that the effect of market risk is to add a *market risk premium* to the required interest rate. If the market risk premium is denoted $\sigma$, the nominal interest rate becomes:

$$r \;=\; \rho + \pi + l + \sigma. \tag{2.7}$$

This is shown in Figure 2.4.

## 2.6 Interest rates and discount rates

We have seen how the market determines the nominal rate of interest on different securities. It depends on the expected real rate, the expected inflation rate, and the appropriate expected liquidity and risk premia. But this market-determined interest rate is, in market equilibrium, precisely equivalent to the discount rate that is required to discount the cash flows on securities of the same duration and risk and so determine the market values of those securities. In other words, discounting a security's cash flow using the market equilibrium discount rate gives the equilibrium value for the security. At this value, the cash flows from the security imply a rate of return or interest rate on the security equal to the discount rate. This means that in equilibrium the discount rate is equivalent to the required rate of return on the security. These issues will be covered in more detail in the next chapter dealing with financial arithmetic and in the chapters in Part II of the book dealing with the valuation of securities.

**Selected references**

Fisher, I. (1930), *Theory of Interest*, Macmillan, New York.

Francis, J.C. (1991), *Investments*, McGraw-Hill, New York. (Chapters 12 and 14.)

Weston, J.F. and Copeland, T.E. (1992), *Managerial Finance*, Dryden Press, Chicago. (Chapter 6.)

**Exercises**

1  In what sense is the market interest rate the price of time and risk?

2  What are the main components of the market rate of interest?

3  What does the rate of time preference measure?

4  Why do some people wish to borrow at the current rate of interest while other people wish to lend?

5  Explain the Fisher equation.

6  Why do lenders expect to be compensated for expected inflation?

7  What is the yield curve?

8  Why is the liquidity premium positive? Why does it increase with the term to maturity?

9  What are the main components of specific risk?

10  What is the difference between specific risk and market risk?

11  Explain the similarities and differences between the way in which market risk affects shares, bonds and money market securities.

# Chapter 3

# Financial arithmetic

This chapter covers some of the most important aspects of financial arithmetic that will be required in later chapters. It covers such issues as simple interest, compound interest, future values, present values, internal rates of return and time-weighted rates of return; and it uses as interest rates the appropriate market-determined discount rates derived in the last chapter.

## 3.1 Future values: single payments

The *future value* of a sum of money (the *principal*) invested at a given annual rate of interest will depend on:

1 whether interest is paid only on the principal (this is known as *simple interest*), or, in addition, on the interest that accrues (this is known as *compound interest*);

2 (in the case of compound interest) the frequency with which interest is paid (e.g. annually, semi-annually, quarterly, monthly, daily, continuously).

### 3.1.1 Simple interest

With simple interest, the future value is determined by:

$$F = P(1+rT), \tag{3.1}$$

where:

$$
\begin{aligned}
P &= \text{principal amount;} \\
F &= \text{future value (or end-of-period value or terminal value);} \\
r &= \text{rate of interest (annual);} \\
T &= \text{number of years.}
\end{aligned}
$$

For example, if $P = £1000$, $r = 0.1$ (10 per cent) and $T = 2$ years, then:

$$
\begin{aligned}
F &= 1000[1 + (0.1)(2)] \\
&= £1200.00.
\end{aligned}
$$

### 3.1.2 Compound interest: annual compounding

With compound interest, the future value (also known now as the *compound value*) is determined by:

$$
F = P(1+r)^T. \tag{3.2}
$$

In this case, interest is earned on the interest that accrues. This can be seen by looking at the case when $T = 2$ years. After one year, the principal will have increased to $P(1+r)$, the same as in the simple interest case. But in the second year interest is earned on the accrued interest, so that at the end of the second year the principal will have increased to:

$$
\begin{aligned}
F &= P(1+r)(1+r) \\
&= P(1+r)^2.
\end{aligned}
$$

Using the information in the last example, the compound value after two years is:

$$
\begin{aligned}
F &= 1000(1+0.1)^2 \\
&= £1210.00,
\end{aligned}
$$

which is £10 greater than with simple interest.

### 3.1.3 Compound interest: more frequent compounding

Sometimes compounding takes place more frequently than once a year. For example, if compounding takes place semi-annually, then an interest payment (equal to half the annual interest payment) will be made at the end of six months and that interest payment will itself earn interest for the next six months. After two years, four interest payments will have been made.

In general, if compounding takes place $m$ times per year, then at the end of $T$ years, $mT$ interest payments will have been made and the future value of the principal will be:

$$
F = P\left(1 + \frac{r}{m}\right)^{mT}. \tag{3.3}
$$

For example, with semi-annual compounding, the future value of £1000 at the end of two years when the interest rate is 10 per cent is:

$$
\begin{aligned}
F &= P\left(1 + \frac{r}{2}\right)^{2T} \\
&= 1000\left(1 + \frac{0.1}{2}\right)^{(2)(2)} \\
&= £1215.51.
\end{aligned}
$$

We can examine the effect of the frequency of compounding by examining the annualized interest rate factors,

$$\text{Interest rate factor} = \left(1 + \frac{r}{m}\right)^m.$$

Assuming that $r = 0.1$ (10 per cent):

| *Compounding frequency* | *Interest rate factor* | | |
|---|---|---|---|
| Annual | $(1 + r)$ | = | 1.100000 |
| Semi-annual | $\left(1 + \frac{r}{2}\right)^2$ | = | 1.102500 |
| Quarterly | $\left(1 + \frac{r}{4}\right)^4$ | = | 1.103813 |
| Monthly | $\left(1 + \frac{r}{12}\right)^{12}$ | = | 1.104713 |
| Daily | $\left(1 + \frac{r}{365}\right)^{365}$ | = | 1.105156 |

Clearly, the more frequent the compounding, the greater the interest rate factor.

The limit to this process occurs when interest is compounded continuously. This limit is derived as follows. Equation (3.3) can be rewritten:

$$\begin{aligned}
F &= P\left[\left(1 + \frac{r}{m}\right)^{m/r}\right]^{rT} \\
&= P\left[\left(1 + \frac{1}{m/r}\right)^{m/r}\right]^{rT} \\
&= P\left[\left(1 + \frac{1}{n}\right)^{n}\right]^{rT},
\end{aligned}$$
(3.4)

where $n = m/r$. As $m$ and hence $n$ approach infinity (and compounding becomes continuous), the expression in square brackets in (3.4) tends to the value known as $e$:

$$e = \lim_{n\to\infty} \left(1 + \frac{1}{n}\right)^n = 2.71828.$$

Substituting this into (3.4) gives:

$$F = Pe^{rT}$$
(3.5)

in the case of continuous compounding.

In (3.5), $e^{rT}$ is known as the *exponential function* of $rT$. It provides the continuously-compounded interest rate factor. If $r = 0.1$ (10 per cent) and $T = 1$ year, then:

$$e^r = (2.71828)^{0.1} = 1.105171.$$

This is the limit to the process of more frequent compounding.

To illustrate continuous compounding, the future value of £1000 at the end of two years when the interest rate is 10 per cent is:

$$\begin{aligned}
F &= 1000e^{(0.1)(2)} \\
&= £1221.40.
\end{aligned}$$

### 3.1.4 Flat and effective rates of interest

The *flat rate* of interest is the interest rate that is quoted on a deposit, loan, etc. But the *effective rate* of interest (sometimes called the *annual percentage rate* or APR) will be greater than the flat rate if compounding takes place more than once a year. The effective rate *re* is the compounded interest rate:

$$re = \left(1 + \frac{r}{m}\right)^m - 1. \tag{3.6}$$

For example, if the flat rate of interest is 10 per cent and compounding takes place 12 times per year, then the effective interest rate is:

$$
\begin{aligned}
re &= \left(1 + \frac{0.1}{12}\right)^{12} - 1 \\
&= 0.1047 \quad \text{(i.e. 10.47\%)}.
\end{aligned}
$$

## 3.2 Present values: single payments

If an amount $F$ is to be received in $T$ years' time, the *present value* of that amount is the sum of money $P$ which, if invested today, would generate the compound amount $F$ in $T$ years' time. The process of finding present values is known as *discounting* and is the exact inverse of the process of finding future values.

### 3.2.1 Present value: annual discounting

With annual discounting, a sum of money $F$ to be received in $T$ years' time has a present value of:

$$
\begin{aligned}
P &= \frac{F}{(1+r)^T} \\
&= F(1+r)^{-T}.
\end{aligned} \tag{3.7}
$$

This is found by dividing both sides of (3.2) by $(1+r)^T$.

For example, the present value of £1000 to be received in five years' time when the interest rate is 10 per cent is:

$$
\begin{aligned}
P &= 1000(1+0.1)^{-5} \\
&= \pounds 620.92.
\end{aligned}
$$

This is because £620.92 invested for five years at 10 per cent generates £1000. The rate of interest $r$ involved in this calculation is known as the *discount rate* and the term $(1+r)^{-T}$ is known as the $T$-year *discount factor*, $D_T$:

$$D_T = (1+r)^{-T}. \tag{3.8}$$

Hence (3.7) can be written in the equivalent form:

$$P = F \cdot D_T. \tag{3.9}$$

The five-year discount factor when the discount rate is 10 per cent is:

$$D_5 = (1+0.1)^{-5}$$
$$= 0.62092.$$

## 3.2.2 Present values: more frequent discounting

If discounting takes place $m$ times per year, then we can use (3.3) to derive the appropriate present value formula:

$$P = F\left(1+\frac{r}{m}\right)^{-mT}. \tag{3.10}$$

For example, with semi-annual discounting, the present value of £1000 to be received in five years' time when $r = 0.1$ (10 per cent) is:

$$P = 1000\left(1+\frac{0.1}{2}\right)^{-(2)(5)}$$
$$= £613.91.$$

The more frequent the discounting, the lower the present value. In the limiting case of continuous discounting, we can use (3.5) to derive the appropriate present value formula:

$$P = Fe^{-rT}. \tag{3.11}$$

Using (3.11), the present value of the £1000 to be received in five years' time is:

$$P = 1000e^{-(0.1)(5)}$$
$$= £606.53.$$

## 3.3 Future values: multiple payments

So far, we have considered the future value of a single payment. But we can also calculate the future value of a stream of payments. Initially we will assume that the stream of payments is an irregular one. Then we will consider the simpler case of a regular stream of payments.

### 3.3.1 Irregular payments

To calculate the future value of an irregular stream of payments, the appropriate future value formula is applied to each individual payment and the resulting individual future values are then summed. The formula for this is:

$$F = \sum_{t=1}^{T} d_t(1+r)^{T-t}, \tag{3.12}$$

where $d_t$ = payment in year $t$ (assuming payment is made at end of year). Since interest does not accrue until the end of each year, the first payment will accrue interest for $(T-1)$ years, the second payment for $(T-2)$ years and so on.

To illustrate, the future value of the following stream of annual payments, $d_1 = £1000$, $d_2 = £1100$, $d_3 = £1200$, when the interest rate is 10 per cent is:

$$
\begin{aligned}
F &= 1000(1.1)^{3-1} + 1100(1.1)^{3-2} + 1200(1.1)^{3-3} \\[2mm]
&= 1210 + 1210 + 1200 \\[2mm]
&= £3620.00 .
\end{aligned}
$$

### 3.3.2  Regular payments: annual payments with annual compounding

A regular stream of payments (for a given number of years) is called an *annuity*. (If the payments are made at the end of the year, as we are assuming here, the annuity is known as an *immediate annuity* or an *annuity in arrears*; if the payments are made at the beginning of the year, the annuity is known as an *annuity due* or an *annuity in advance*; if the annuity commences further than a year ahead, it is called a *deferred annuity*.) With an annuity, the payments $d_t$ in (3.12) are identical and can be denoted as $d$. This allows the formula (3.12) to be simplified, as we shall now see. If $d_t = d$ for all $t$, then (3.12) becomes:

$$
F = d \sum_{t=1}^{T} (1+r)^{T-t} . \tag{3.13}
$$

If we multiply both sides of (3.13) by $(1+r)$ and subtract the result from (3.13), we get:

$$
\begin{aligned}
F - (1+r)F &= d \left[ \sum_{t=1}^{T} (1+r)^{T-t} - \sum_{t=1}^{T} (1+r)^{T-t+1} \right] , \tag{3.14} \\[2mm]
&= -d[(1+r)^T - 1]
\end{aligned}
$$

which, on rearranging, yields:

$$
F = d \left[ \frac{(1+r)^T - 1}{r} \right] . \tag{3.15}
$$

To illustrate this formula, we can calculate the future value of a three-year annuity, paying £1000 per year for three years, when the interest rate is 10 per cent:

$$
\begin{aligned}
F &= 1000 \left[ \frac{(1.1)^3 - 1}{0.1} \right] \\[2mm]
&= £3310.00 .
\end{aligned}
$$

As another example of the use of (3.15), we can calculate the size of an annuity necessary to accumulate a particular sum of money at a particular future date when the interest rate is known. An example of this would be the establishment of a *sinking fund* to provide for the retirement of a bond at some future date. Another example would be the establishment of a pension fund of a particular size at some future date; the pension fund could then be used to provide a pension annuity to retired workers. The required size of the annuity is given by rearranging (3.15):

$$d = F\left[\frac{r}{(1+r)^T - 1}\right]. \tag{3.16}$$

Suppose that a pension fund of £100,000 is required in 20 years' time. What should the annual pension contribution be if the rate of interest is 10 per cent? Using (3.16):

$$d = 100,000\left[\frac{0.1}{(1.1)^{20} - 1}\right]$$

$$= £1745.96.$$

### 3.3.3 Regular payments: annual payments with more frequent compounding

If compounding takes place $m$ times per year, then (3.13) becomes:

$$F = d\sum_{t=1}^{T}\left(1+\frac{r}{m}\right)^{m(T-t)}. \tag{3.17}$$

If we multiply both sides of (3.17) by $[1+(r/m)]^m$ and subtract the result from (3.17), we get:

$$F - [1+(r/m)]^m F = d\left\{\sum_{t=1}^{T}[1+(r/m)]^{m(T-t)} - \sum_{t=1}^{T}[1+(r/m)]^{m(T-t)+m}\right\}$$

$$= -d\left\{[1+(r/m)]^{mT} - 1\right\}, \tag{3.18}$$

which, on rearranging, yields:

$$F = d\left\{\frac{[1+(r/m)]^{mT} - 1}{[1+(r/m)]^m - 1}\right\}. \tag{3.19}$$

Therefore a three-year annuity paying £1000 per year for three years compounded quarterly when the interest rate is 10 per cent has a future value of:

$$F = 1000\left[\frac{(1.025)^{12} - 1}{(1.025)^4 - 1}\right]$$

$$= £3322.22.$$

In the limiting case of continuous compounding, (3.19) tends to:

$$F = d\left(\frac{e^{rT} - 1}{e^r - 1}\right). \tag{3.20}$$

Using the previous example of a three-year annuity of £1000 compounded continuously at 10 per cent, we derive the following future value for the annuity:

$$F \;=\; 1000\left(\frac{e^{(0.1)(3)}-1}{e^{0.1}-1}\right)$$

$$\;=\; £3326.57\,.$$

### 3.3.4   Regular payments: more frequent payments with more frequent compounding

If there are $m$ payments per year which are compounded $m$ times per year, then (3.13) becomes:

$$F \;=\; \frac{d}{m}\sum_{t=1}^{mT}\left(1+\frac{r}{m}\right)^{mT-t}. \tag{3.21}$$

If we multiply both sides of (3.21) by $[1+(r/m)]$ and subtract the result from (3.21), we get:

$$F-[1+(r/m)]F \;=\; -\frac{d}{m}\left\{[1+(r/m)]^{mT}-1\right\}, \tag{3.22}$$

which on rearranging yields:

$$F \;=\; d\left\{\frac{[1+(r/m)]^{mT}-1}{r}\right\}. \tag{3.23}$$

In the limiting case of continuous payments with continuous compounding, (3.23) becomes:

$$F \;=\; d\left(\frac{e^{rT}-1}{r}\right). \tag{3.24}$$

## 3.4   Present values: multiple payments

In a similar way, we can calculate the present value of a stream of future payments. Again, the solution depends on whether the future payments are regular or irregular.

### 3.4.1   Irregular payments

To calculate the present value of an irregular stream of payments, the appropriate present value formula is applied to each individual payment and the resulting individual present values are then summed. The formula for this is:

$$P \;=\; \sum_{t=1}^{T}d_{t}(1+r)^{-t}, \tag{3.25}$$

where $d_t$ = payment in year $t$ (payment made at end of year).

To illustrate, the present value of the following stream of annual payments, $d_1 = £1000$, $d_2 = £1100$, $d_3 = £1200$, when the interest rate is 10 per cent is:

$$
\begin{aligned}
P &= 1000(1.1)^{-1} + 1100(1.1)^{-2} + 1200(1.1)^{-3} \\
&= 909.09 + 909.09 + 901.58 \\
&= £2719.76.
\end{aligned}
$$

## 3.4.2 Regular payments: annual payments with annual discounting

The present value of an annuity is found very simply by finding the present value of (3.15):

$$
\begin{aligned}
P &= \frac{F}{(1+r)^T} \\
&= d\left[\frac{(1+r)^T - 1}{r}\right]\left[\frac{1}{(1+r)^T}\right] \\
&= d\left[\frac{1-(1+r)^{-T}}{r}\right].
\end{aligned}
\tag{3.26}
$$

To illustrate this formula, we can calculate the present value of a three-year annuity, paying £1000 per year for three years when the interest rate is 10 per cent:

$$
\begin{aligned}
P &= 1000\left[\frac{1-(1.1)^{-3}}{0.1}\right] \\
&= £2486.85.
\end{aligned}
$$

## 3.4.3 Regular payments: annual payments with more frequent discounting

The present value of an annuity with discounting $m$ times per year is given by the present value of (3.19):

$$
\begin{aligned}
P &= \frac{F}{[1+(r/m)]^{mT}} \\
&= d\left\{\frac{1-[1+(r/m)]^{-mT}}{[1+(r/m)]^{m} - 1}\right\}.
\end{aligned}
\tag{3.27}
$$

In the limiting case of continuous discounting, (3.27) tends to:

$$
P = d\left(\frac{1-e^{-rT}}{e^{r} - 1}\right).
\tag{3.28}
$$

### 3.4.4 Regular payments: more frequent payments with more frequent discounting

If there are $m$ payments per year which are discounted $m$ times, then the present value of these payments is given by the present value of (3.23):

$$P = \frac{F}{[1+(r/m)]^{mT}}$$

$$= d\left\{\frac{1-[1+(r/m)]^{-mT}}{r}\right\}. \tag{3.29}$$

In the limiting case of continuous payments with continuous discounting, (3.29) becomes:

$$P = d\left(\frac{1-e^{-rT}}{r}\right). \tag{3.30}$$

**Table 3.1** Repayment of a mortgage loan

| Month | (1) Payment | (2) Interest [0.1/12]·(4) | (3) Repayment of principal (1) − (2) | (4) End-of-month balance (4) − (3) |
|-------|-------------|---------------------------|--------------------------------------|------------------------------------|
|       | (£)         | (£)                       | (£)                                  | (£)                                |
| 0     | —           | —                         | —                                    | 100,000.00                         |
| 1     | 908.70      | 833.33                    | 75.37                                | 99,924.63                          |
| 2     | 908.70      | 832.71                    | 75.99                                | 99,848.64                          |
| 3     | 908.70      | 832.07                    | 76.63                                | 99,772.01                          |
| 4     | 908.70      | 831.43                    | 77.27                                | 99,694.74                          |
| ⋮     | ⋮           | ⋮                         | ⋮                                    | ⋮                                  |
| 299   | 908.70      | ·                         | ·                                    | 901.19                             |
| 300   | 908.70      | 7.51                      | 901.19                               | 0.00                               |
| **Totals:** | 272,610.00 | 172,610.00           | 100,000.00                           |                                    |

As an example of (3.29), we can calculate the size of an annuity necessary to pay off a loan made at the beginning of the period. An example of this would be a *mortgage loan* or a *repayment mortgage*. Suppose that a £100,000 mortgage is to be paid off in equal monthly instalments over 25 years. The rate of interest is expected to remain constant at 10 per cent. The monthly payments are determined using (3.29):

$$d^* = \frac{d}{12} = \frac{P}{12}\left\{\frac{r}{1-[1+(r/12)]^{-(12)(T)}}\right\}. \tag{3.31}$$

Using the information in the example, we get:

$$d^* = \frac{100,000}{12} \left\{ \frac{0.1}{1 - [1 + (0.1/12)]^{-(12)(25)}} \right\}$$

$$= £908.70$$

as the required monthly payment. This monthly payment involves an interest rate component and a repayment of principal component as Table 3.1 shows.

Since the monthly payment involves both a principal and an interest rate component, a repayment mortgage is an example of an *amortized loan*, which simply means that the monthly payment involves a repayment of principal. (This compares with a *straight* or *bullet loan*, in which none of the principal is repaid until the end of the loan; a mortgage of this kind is known as an *endowment mortgage*.)

**Table 3.2** The burden of a mortgage loan as a proportion (percentage) of income

| Year | Inflation rate | | |
|---|---|---|---|
| | *5%* | *10%* | *15%* |
| 0 | 27 | 38 | 50 |
| 5 | 21 | 24 | 25 |
| 10 | 17 | 15 | 12 |
| 15 | 13 | 9 | 6 |
| 20 | 10 | 6 | 3 |
| 25 | 8 | 4 | 2 |
| *Monthly repayment (£)*: | 908.70 | 1280.83 | 1678.45 |

We can also use the repayment mortgage just discussed to calculate the *burden* of the mortgage (i.e. the level of repayments in relation to the size of an individual's income) at different levels of inflation. Suppose that the individual who took out this mortgage had an annual salary ($Y$) of £40,000 (or £3,333.33 per month). Suppose also that the inflation rate is 5 per cent and expected to remain at this rate over the next 25 years. Using (3.31), the burden of the mortgage is given by:

$$\frac{d^*}{Y} = \frac{908.70}{3333.33} = 0.27,$$

i.e., 27 per cent of the monthly income goes in mortgage repayments. However, if the individual's salary grows at the same rate as the inflation rate (5 per cent per year) then the burden falls over time, since the mortgage repayment itself does not change. The first column of Table 3.2 shows how the burden falls to 8 per cent of salary by the 25th year of the loan. Suppose, however, that the inflation rate increases to 10 per cent, but the real rate of interest on the loan does not change. This implies from the Fisher equation (see chapter 2) that the nominal interest rate rises to 15 per cent, preserving the real rate at 5 per cent. Using (3.31), the monthly repayments rise to £1280.83, implying a burden of 38 per cent of the starting salary. But because the individual's salary is increasing at 10 per cent per year the burden falls more rapidly over time compared with an inflation rate of 5 per cent. By the end of the term, the burden is only 4 per cent (see second column of the table). If the inflation rate rises to 15 per cent and the nominal interest rate rises to 20 per cent, the real rate is still 5 per cent, but the monthly repayment is £1678.45 or 50 per cent of starting salary. The burden declines even more rapidly over time, falling to only 2 per cent by the end of the term (see third column of the table). So as can be seen very clearly from Table 3.2, the burden of an amortized loan is more heavily concentrated in the early years of the loan, the higher the inflation rate, but also declines much more rapidly as the loan matures. This phenomenon is known as the *front-end loading* of inflation.

### 3.4.5   Perpetuities

An annuity that continues indefinitely is called a *perpetuity*. The future value of a perpetuity is obviously infinite, but its present value is easy to determine using (3.26), recognizing that as $T$ tends to infinity the term $(1+r)^{-T}$ tends to zero. This leads to:

$$P \;=\; \frac{d}{r} \tag{3.32}$$

as the present value of a perpetuity.

An example of a perpetuity is an irredeemable bond, such as a 2.5 per cent Consols, which pays £1.25 per £100 nominal every six months. On a coupon payment date when there is no accrued interest, the price of the bond when the rate of interest is 10 per cent is:

$$
\begin{aligned}
P \;&=\; \frac{d/2}{r/2} \\[2mm]
&=\; \frac{1.25}{0.05} \\[2mm]
&=\; £25.00 \,.
\end{aligned}
$$

## 3.5   Rates of return

So far we have assumed that the rate of interest or the rate of return is given. But sometimes we do not know the rate of interest or the rate of return on an investment and it has to be calculated. There are several different ways of calculating such rates.

### 3.5.1   Single-period rate of return

The simplest way of measuring a rate of return is to do so over a single period. If, for instance, we buy a security today for $P_0$ and sell it after a period for $P_1$, then the return on holding that security from $t = 0$ to $t = 1$ is given by:

$$
\begin{aligned}
r \;&=\; \frac{P_1 - P_0}{P_0} \\[2mm]
&=\; \frac{P_1}{P_0} - 1 \,.
\end{aligned}
\tag{3.33}
$$

For example, if an investor buys a security for £100 and sells it one week later for £110, his return over the week is:

$$r = \frac{110}{100} - 1 = 0.1 \quad (\text{i.e. } 10\%).$$

The ratio $P_1/P_0$ in (3.33) is known as the *price relative*. In many applications, the rate of return over a single period is calculated as a continuously-compounded rate of return, often known as the *log price relative*. This is given by:

$$r = \ln\left(\frac{P_1}{P_0}\right). \tag{3.34}$$

If, for instance, an investor held a portfolio of shares comprising the FTSE 100 index, then the change in the level of that index over a period could be used to measure his return from holding the portfolio. Also, since the level of the index is continuously changing, it might seem reasonable to measure the return in terms of the log price relative. So, if the index is at 6141 ($P_0$) at the close of business on one day and falls to 5833 ($P_1$) by the close of business the next day then, from (3.34), his return on the portfolio for that 24-hour period is:

$$r = \ln\left(\frac{5833}{6141}\right) \approx -0.051 \quad (\text{i.e. } -5.1\%).$$

## 3.5.2   Internal rate of return or money-weighted rate of return

One of the most common ways of measuring the return on an investment is the *internal rate of return* or the *money-weighted rate of return* (sometimes called the *yield to maturity*).

This is simple to calculate with single payments. Since $F = P(1+r)^T$, the annual internal rate of return on an investment of $P$ paying $F$ in $T$ years' time is the solution to:

$$(1+r)^T = F/P,$$

that is:

$$r = (F/P)^{1/T} - 1. \tag{3.35}$$

For example, the annual internal rate of return on an investment costing £1000 today and returning £1500 in three years' time is:

$$r = (1500/1000)^{1/3} - 1$$
$$= 0.1447 \quad (\text{i.e. } 14.47\%).$$

With compounding taking place more frequently than once per year, the annual rate of return is the solution to:

$$\left(1 + \frac{r}{m}\right)^{mT} = F/P;$$

that is:

$$r = m[(F/P)^{1/mT} - 1]. \tag{3.36}$$

Using the last example but with quarterly compounding, the annual internal rate of return is:

$$r = 4[(1500/1000)^{1/(4 \cdot 3)} - 1]$$
$$= 0.1375 \quad \text{(i.e. 13.75\%)}.$$

The more frequent the compounding, the lower the internal rate of return.

With continuous compounding, the internal rate of return is the solution to:

$$e^{rT} = F/P. \tag{3.37}$$

In general, if $x^b = y$ then $b$ is called the *logarithm* of $y$ to the base $x$, i.e. $b = \log_x(y)$. In the case of (3.37), we have:

$$rT = \log_e(F/P); \tag{3.38}$$

i.e. $rT$ is the logarithm of $(F/P)$ to the base $e$. Logarithms to the base $e$ are known as *natural logarithms* and are denoted by $b = \ln(y)$. Therefore (3.38) becomes:

$$r = \frac{1}{T} \ln(F/P). \tag{3.39}$$

Using the last example, but with continuous compounding, the annual internal rate of return is:

$$r = \frac{1}{3} \ln(1500/1000)$$
$$= 0.1352 \quad \text{(i.e. 13.52\%)}.$$

With multiple payments, an analytical solution for the internal rate of return does not generally exist. In general, the solution $r$ to either:

$$F = \sum_{t=1}^{T} d_t(1+r)^{T-t} \tag{3.40}$$

or:

$$P = \sum_{t=1}^{T} d_t(1+r)^{-t} \tag{3.41}$$

has to be found numerically, i.e. by trial and error. This is true even if the payments are regular, as with an annuity.

Take, for example, the formula for the present value of an annuity:

$$P = d\left[\frac{1-(1+r)^{-T}}{r}\right]. \tag{3.42}$$

Suppose we know that a three-year annuity of £1000 has a present value of £2465.12 and we want to find the internal rate of return. We begin with an estimate of the internal rate of return, say, $r = 0.1$ (10 per cent). At $r = 0.1$ we find that $P = £2486.85$ which is greater than £2465.12. This implies that our estimate of $r$ is too low. We should try a larger value for $r$, say $r = 0.11$ (11 per cent). At $r = 0.11$, we find that $P = £2443.71$ which is less than £2465.12. The correct value of $r$ must therefore lie between

10 and 11 per cent. Suppose that we try $r = 0.105$ (10.5 per cent). At this value of $r$ we find that $P = £2465.12$ as required, so that the internal rate of return is 10.5 per cent. This method is known as interval bisection; a simpler iterative method is given in the appendix.

Only in the case of a perpetuity is the internal rate of return easy to calculate. From (3.32), we see that the internal rate of return is simply:

$$r = \frac{d}{P}. \tag{3.43}$$

If the present value of a perpetuity of £5 per year is £41.67, then the internal rate of return is:

$$r = \frac{5}{41.67}$$

$$= 0.12 \quad \text{(i.e. 12\%)}.$$

### 3.5.3 Time-weighted rate of return or geometric mean rate of return

The *time-weighted rate of return* or the *geometric mean rate of return* takes into account the value of earlier payments at the time that the next payment in the series arises. If $P$ is the initial value of an investment, $F$ is the final value, $d_t$ is the payment received by the investment in year $t$ and $V_t$ is the value of the investment when the payment is received, then the time-weighted rate of return is calculated as follows:

$$(1+r)^T = \left(\frac{V_1}{P}\right)\left(\frac{V_2}{V_1+d_1}\right)\left(\frac{V_3}{V_2+d_2}\right)\cdots\left(\frac{F}{V_{T-1}+d_{T-1}}\right). \tag{3.44}$$

But $(V_1/P) = (1+r_1)$, one *plus* the return on the investment in the first period, $[V_2/(V_1+d_1)] = (1+r_2)$, one *plus* the return on the investment in the second period, etc., so that this equation can be rewritten:

$$(1+r)^T = (1+r_1)(1+r_2)\cdots(1+r_T), \tag{3.45}$$

or, solving for $r$:

$$r = [(1+r_1)(1+r_2)\cdots(1+r_T)]^{1/T} - 1. \tag{3.46}$$

From (3.46), it is clear that the time-weighted rate of return is the geometric mean of the individual period returns.

To illustrate, consider the case of an investment beginning with £100, attracting £50 at the end of year 1 (when the value of the investment was £110), and at the end of year 2 the value of the investment was £225. The time-weighted rate of return is calculated as:

$$r = \left[\left(\frac{110}{100}\right)\left(\frac{225}{110+50}\right)\right]^{1/2} - 1$$

$$= [(1.10)(1.406)]^{1/2} - 1$$

$$= [1.5469]^{1/2} - 1$$

$$= 0.2437 \quad (24.37\%).$$

The comparable money-weighted rate of return is given by the solution to the following calculation:

$$225 \; = \; 100(1+r)^2 + 50(1+r),$$

implying a money-weighted rate of return of 27.07 per cent.

## Appendix: A simple iterative method for calculating internal rates of return

Suppose an investor pays a price $P$ to receive $N$ future payments $d_1, \ldots, d_N$ (which must all be positive) at times $\tau_1, \ldots, \tau_N$ (which can be regularly or irregularly spaced apart). We wish to find the internal rate of return $r^*$ on this investment. Define:

$$f(r) \; = \; \sum_{i=1}^{N} d_i e^{-r\tau_i}.$$

If $\bar{r}$ is the solution to the equation

$$f(\bar{r}) \; = \; P,$$

then the internal rate of return is defined by $r^* = e^{\bar{r}} - 1$.

Beginning with an arbitrary value $r_0$, we can calculate $r_1, r_2, \ldots$ using the recursive formula:

$$r_{j+1} \; = \; \frac{\ln(P/d)}{\ln(f(r_j/d))} r_j, \quad j = 0, 1, \ldots$$

where $d = d_1 + \ldots + d_N$ is the undiscounted sum of the future payments. Gerber (1995) shows that $r_j$ converges to $\bar{r}$ in only a few iterations. Given $\bar{r}$, we can readily derive the internal rate of return $r^*$.

To illustrate, an initial investment of £1,500 generates the following cash inflows:

| Time (years) | Cash payments (£) |
|:---:|:---:|
| 0.5 | 200 |
| 1.0 | 200 |
| 1.5 | 200 |
| 2.0 | 1250 |

Suppose that the initial guess for the internal rate of return is $r_0 = 0.3$ (i.e. 30 per cent). The first iteration gives $r_1 = 0.1285129$ and the second iteration gives $r_2 = 0.1265200$. Thereafter, convergence is very rapid to the final solution $\bar{r} = 0.1264781$, from which we can derive the internal rate of return $r^* = 0.1348$, i.e. 13.48%.

## Selected references

Adams, A., Bloomfield, D., Booth, P. and England, P. (1993), *Investment Mathematics and Statistics*, Graham and Trotman, London.

Batchelor, R. (1985), *Financial Arithmetic*, City University Business School, London.

Gerber, H. (1995) *Life Insurance Mathematics*, Springer, Zurich.

McCutcheon, J. and Scott, W. (1986), *An Introduction to the Mathematics of Finance*, Butterworth-Heinemann, Oxford.

Weston, J.F. and Copeland, T.E. (1992), *Managerial Finance*, Dryden Press, Chicago. (Chapter 5.)

## Exercises

1 The rate of interest is 8 per cent. What will £100 be worth in three years' time using

   a) simple interest?

   b) annual compound interest?

2 If the interest rate is 12 per cent, calculate the interest rate factors when the compounding frequencies are as follows:

   a) annual;

   b) semi-annual;

   c) quarterly;

   d) monthly;

   e) daily;

   f) continuous.

3 If the flat rate of interest is 14 per cent and compounding takes place monthly, what is the effective rate of interest?

4 What is the present value of £100 to be received in 10 years' time when the interest rate is 12 per cent and

   a) annual discounting is used?

   b) semi-annual discounting is used?

5 You have bought a bond paying coupons semi-annually on the day following a coupon payment. The coupon payments on the bond are £12.50 per £100 nominal, and the bond matures in five years' time. What is the compound value of the coupons at the end of five years if they can be invested at 10 per cent?

6 A worker is planning to retire in 40 years' time with a pension fund valued at £250,000. What is the annual pension contribution if the rate of return on investments is a) 5 per cent? b) 10 per cent? c) 15 per cent?

7 You have just bought a bond paying coupons semi-annually on the day following a coupon payment. The coupon payments on the bond are £12.50 per £100 nominal and the bond matures at par (£100) in five years' time. The interest rate is 10 per cent.

a) What is the present value of the par value of the bond?

b) What is the present value of the coupon payments on the bond?

c) How much should you have paid for the bond?

8 A mortgage of £250,000 is to be paid off in equal monthly instalments over 25 years. The interest rate is expected to remain constant at 10.75 per cent. What are the monthly repayments?

9 A five-year annuity of £500 has a present value of £1847.95. What is the money-weighted rate of return on the annuity?

10 You are given the following information about an individual's investment in a unit trust:

| Year | Value of investment (£) | Net cash flow (£) |
|------|-------------------------|-------------------|
| 0    | 1000                    | 0                 |
| 1    | 1150                    | 50                |
| 2    | 1300                    | −100              |
| 3    | 1500                    | 60                |
| 4    | 1400                    | −20               |
| 5    | 1600                    | 0                 |

What is the time-weighted rate of return on the investment?

11 You are advising a 70-year-old client with savings of £50,000 and no other income. The client wishes to consume the same amount each year for ten years with a zero savings balance at the end. How much can be withdrawn each year if the interest rate on the savings deposit is 7 per cent and the first withdrawal does not take place for a year?

# Part II

# THE ANALYSIS AND VALUATION
# OF SECURITIES

The second part of this book deals with the analysis and valuation of securities, ranging from cash market securities such as CDs, bills, bonds, shares and foreign currency, through derivative securities such as futures and options, to synthetic securities such as swaps. It is essential for the efficiency of a modern financial system to analyze all the securities traded in it, since only then is it possible to determine whether securities are fairly priced or whether they are underpriced or overpriced and hence give rise to profitable trading possibilities.

# Chapter 4

# Money market securities

Money market securities are securities with maturities of less than a year. This contrasts with capital market securities, which have maturities in excess of one year. There are two main classes of money market security: those that are quoted on a *yield basis* and those that are quoted on a *discount basis*. The UK money markets assume a 365-day year in contrast with the US and euro markets which assume a 360-day year. This is important for calculating interest payments. All three money markets count the actual number of days between payments. These day count methods are known respectively as actual/365 or actual/360; in the latter case, a one-year money market instrument will have accrued interest at the rate 365/360. The *settlement day* or *value day* for money market securities in the UK is the first business day following purchase.

One of the most important sets of reference interest rates is that determined in the *London Inter-bank Market*. This market determines the rate at which one bank can temporarily deposit its surplus funds with another bank. This rate is called LIBID, the *London inter-bank bid rate* and is the rate at which one bank will bid for funds (accept deposits) from another bank. The interbank market also determines the rate at which one bank can temporarily borrow funds from another bank to meet, say, an unexpected large withdrawal of deposits or a sudden and urgent request for a loan from a customer. This rate is called LIBOR, the *London inter-bank offered rate* and is the rate at which one bank will offer to lend funds to another bank. LIBID and LIBOR are quoted in a number of major currencies (e.g. sterling, dollars, yen, euros, etc.) and for a number of different terms ranging from overnight to one year.

Interest rates are always quoted on an annual basis even though the term might be for less than one year. For example in the case of sterling, we might observe the following:

|  | *LIBID*<br>*(% per annum)* | *LIBOR*<br>*(% per annum)* |
|---|---|---|
| Overnight | 8.1250 | 8.8750 |
| One week | 9.1875 | 9.4375 |
| One month | 9.3750 | 9.5000 |
| Three months | 9.6250 | 9.7500 |
| Six months | 10.0000 | 10.3125 |
| One year | 10.5000 | 10.3750 |

This means, for example, that a bank can place funds on deposit for six months with another bank for an equivalent annual interest rate of 10 per cent, while it can borrow funds for one week from another bank for an equivalent annual interest rate of 9.4375 per cent.

LIBID and LIBOR are known as *reference interest rates* because many other interest rates are set with reference to the bid and offer rates quoted in the London Inter-bank Market. While London is the most important, there are now other inter-bank interest rates quoted, such as NYBOR (New York), EURIBOR (euro zone), TIBOR (Tokyo), SIBOR (Singapore) and HIBOR (Hong Kong).

## 4.1 Securities quoted on a yield basis

The most important examples of money market securities that are quoted on a yield basis are money market deposits and negotiable certificates of deposit. Such instruments are always issued at par.

### 4.1.1 Money market deposits

*Money market deposits* (MMDs) are fixed-interest, fixed-term deposits of up to one year with banks. The deposits can be for the following terms: overnight, 1 week, or 1, 2, 3, 4, 5, 6, 9 or 12 months. They are not negotiable so cannot be liquidated before maturity. The interest rates on the deposits are fixed for the term and are related to LIBID of the same term. For example, the 1-month deposit rate could be 1-month LIBID *less* 0.125 per cent. The interest and capital are paid in one lump sum on the maturity day. Therefore the amount of interest due at the end of the period is calculated according to the formula for simple interest:

$$R \ = \ M \cdot d \cdot (N/365), \tag{4.1}$$

where:

$$
\begin{aligned}
R &= \text{amount of interest;} \\
M &= \text{face or par value of deposit;} \\
d &= \text{interest rate on deposit (as a proportion);} \\
N &= \text{number of days between deposit and maturity.}
\end{aligned}
$$

The maturity value of the deposit $(F)$ is therefore $F = M + R$.

**Example 4.1 (Money market deposit)** *A money market deposit is opened on 15 January and matures on 15 February:*

$$
\begin{aligned}
M &= £1,000,000 \\
d &= 9.25\% \quad \text{(1 month, annualized)} \\
N &= 31 \text{ days} \\
R &= £1,000,000 \cdot 0.0925 \cdot (31/365) \\
&= £7,856.16.
\end{aligned}
$$

*On 15 February, the depositor would get back £1,007,856.16. The effective rate of interest (re) on the deposit is given by:*

$$re = \left[1 + d\left(\frac{N}{365}\right)\right]^{365/N} - 1$$

$$= \left[1 + 0.0925\left(\frac{31}{365}\right)\right]^{365/31} - 1$$

$$= 0.0965 \quad (9.65\%).$$

We can use money market deposits to demonstrate the problem of *reinvestment risk*, the risk of renewing the deposit at a lower rate in a subsequent period. Suppose that on 15 January, the 1-month and 2-month rates were the same at 9.25 per cent; i.e., the yield curve was flat over this range and expected to remain flat, so that the 1-month rate starting in one month's time is also expected to be 9.25 per cent. In this case it would always be advantageous to invest for one month at a time rather than for two months at one go. This is because in the first case the interest earned at the end of the first month can be reinvested in the second month; in the second case, the whole interest does not accrue until the end of the second month and so is not available for reinvestment until then.

In the first case, the maturity value of the deposit at the end of two months is:

$$F = M \cdot \left[1 + {}_0d_1\left(\frac{N_1}{365}\right)\right] \cdot \left[1 + {}_1d_2\left(\frac{N_2}{365}\right)\right]$$

$$= £1,000,000 \cdot \left[1 + 0.0925\left(\frac{31}{365}\right)\right] \cdot \left[1 + 0.0925\left(\frac{28}{365}\right)\right]$$

$$= £1,015,007.80,$$

where ${}_0d_1$ is the current 1-month rate, ${}_1d_2$ is the 1-month rate beginning in one month's time, and $N_1$ and $N_2$ are the number of days in the months of January and February. In the second case, the maturity value of the deposit at the end of two months is:

$$F = M \cdot \left[1 + {}_0d_2\left(\frac{N_1 + N_2}{365}\right)\right]$$

$$= £1,000,000 \cdot \left[1 + 0.0925\left(\frac{59}{365}\right)\right]$$

$$= £1,014,952.06,$$

where ${}_0d_2$ is the current 2-month interest rate.

The reinvestment return is £55.74 but the reinvestment risk is that on 15 February the 1-month rate will have fallen from the 9.25 per cent expected to, say, 8.75 per cent. The value of the deposit at the end of two months would have fallen from £1,015,007.80 to £1,014,621.23, which represents a loss of £386.57.

## 4.1.2 Negotiable certificates of deposit

*Negotiable certificates of deposit* (CDs) are receipts from banks for deposits that have been made with them. The deposits themselves carry a fixed interest rate related to LIBID and have a fixed term to maturity, so cannot be withdrawn before maturity. But the certificates or receipts on those deposits can be traded in a secondary market; i.e. they are negotiable. CDs are therefore very similar to negotiable money market deposits, although the yields are about 0.25 per cent below the equivalent period deposit rates because of the added benefit of liquidity. The maturities of CDs are generally between one and three months, although some CDs have maturities in excess of one year (e.g. five years). Interest is paid at maturity except for CDs lasting longer than a year, in which case interest is paid annually. While most CDs are fixed-rate, some have variable interest rates. For example, a 6-month CD could have a 30-day rollover; this means that the interest rate on the CD is related to 6-month LIBID and is fixed for 30 days, and will change every 30 days if LIBID has changed.

The interest on a fixed-rate CD is calculated exactly as in (4.1) above, where $d$ is called the *coupon rate* on the CD. However, $d$ does not necessarily represent the yield on the CD, because the price of the CD is not fixed since the CD is traded in a secondary market.

If the current market price of the CD including accrued interest is $P$ and the current yield is $r$, we can calculate the yield given the price using:

$$r \;=\; \left\{ \frac{M}{P} \cdot \left[ 1 + d \left( \frac{N_{im}}{365} \right) \right] - 1 \right\} \cdot \left( \frac{365}{N_{sm}} \right), \tag{4.2}$$

or the price given the yield using:

$$P \;=\; M \cdot \left[ 1 + d \left( \frac{N_{im}}{365} \right) \right] \Big/ \left[ 1 + r \left( \frac{N_{sm}}{365} \right) \right]$$
$$\;=\; F \Big/ \left[ 1 + r \left( \frac{N_{sm}}{365} \right) \right], \tag{4.3}$$

where:

$$
\begin{aligned}
M \;&=\; \text{face value of the CD;} \\
F \;&=\; \text{maturity value of the CD;} \\
N_{im} \;&=\; \text{number of days between issue and maturity;} \\
N_{sm} \;&=\; \text{number of days between settlement and maturity;} \\
N_{is} \;&=\; \text{number of days between issue and settlement.}
\end{aligned}
$$

Equation (4.3) calculates the current market price by discounting the maturity value $F$ at a yield $r$ with $N_{sm}$ days to maturity.

**Example 4.2 (Certificates of deposit)** *The three illustrations that follow show various aspects of calculations involving certificates of deposit.*

*1  £1m CD issued at par on 15 April with a coupon of 10 per cent with 91 days to maturity (matures on 15 July):*

$$
\begin{aligned}
M \;&=\; P \;=\; \text{£1,000,000;} \qquad d \;=\; \text{10\% (3-month, annualized);} \\
N_{im} \;&=\; N_{sm} \;=\; \text{91 days.}
\end{aligned}
$$

*The initial yield is:*

$$
\begin{aligned}
r \;&=\; \left\{ \frac{\text{£1,000,000}}{\text{£1,000,000}} \cdot \left[ 1 + 0.10 \left( \frac{91}{365} \right) \right] - 1 \right\} \cdot \left( \frac{365}{91} \right) \\
&=\; 0.10 \quad (10.00\%).
\end{aligned}
$$

**2** *£1m CD issued at par with a coupon of 8 per cent with 91 days to maturity, currently priced at £1,005,000 with 61 days remaining:*

$$
\begin{aligned}
M &= £1,000,000; & P &= £1,005,000; & d &= 8\% \ (\text{3-month, annualized}); \\
N_{im} &= 91 \text{ days}; & N_{sm} &= 61 \text{ days}.
\end{aligned}
$$

*The current yield is:*

$$
\begin{aligned}
r &= \left\{ \frac{£1,000,000}{£1,005,000} \cdot \left[ 1 + 0.08 \left( \frac{91}{365} \right) \right] - 1 \right\} \cdot \left( \frac{365}{61} \right) \\
&= 0.089 \quad (8.90\%).
\end{aligned}
$$

**3** *£1m CD issued at par with coupon of 8 per cent with 91 days to maturity, currently yielding 9 per cent with 61 days remaining:*

$$
M = £1,000,000; \quad r = 9\%; \quad N_{im} = 91 \text{ days}; \quad N_{sm} = 61 \text{ days}.
$$

*The current price is:*

$$
\begin{aligned}
P &= £1,000,000 \cdot \left[ 1 + 0.08 \left( \frac{91}{365} \right) \right] \Big/ \left[ 1 + 0.09 \left( \frac{61}{365} \right) \right] \\
&= £1,004,831.44.
\end{aligned}
$$

*The effective rate of interest re on a CD yielding 9 per cent with 61 days to maturity is:*

$$
\begin{aligned}
re &= \left[ 1 + r \left( \frac{N_{sm}}{365} \right) \right]^{365/N_{sm}} - 1 \\
&= \left[ 1 + 0.09 \left( \frac{61}{365} \right) \right]^{365/61} - 1 \\
&= 0.0934 \quad (9.34\%).
\end{aligned}
$$

It is possible to decompose the current market price $P$ into accrued interest and principal using the formula:

$$
\text{Accrued interest} = M \cdot d \cdot (N_{is}/365). \tag{4.4}
$$

Using (4.4):

$$
\text{Principal} = P - \text{Accrued interest}. \tag{4.5}
$$

The principal in the last example above is therefore:

$$
\begin{aligned}
\text{Principal} &= £1,004,831.44 - £1,000,000 \cdot 0.08 \cdot (30/365) \\
&= £1,004,831.44 - £6,575.34 \\
&= £998,256.10.
\end{aligned}
$$

The increase in money market interest rates from 8 to 9 per cent has had the effect of reducing the principal (i.e. the *clean price* of the CD without accrued interest) below the par value of £1 million.

The reason for the fall in the clean price of the CD is simple. Money market interest rates have risen from 8 to 9 per cent in the course of one month. A newly issued CD with a maturity of, say, two months will therefore have to yield 9 per cent if an investor is going to hold it. Since it is issued at par, this CD will therefore have a coupon rate of 9 per cent. As an alternative, the investor might consider investing in the CD just considered. It was originally issued with a three-month maturity but now has two months left. It is therefore identical to the two-month CD apart from the lower coupon rate of 8 per cent. In order to be actively traded in the secondary market, this CD must also yield 9 per cent. Since the coupon rate cannot be changed, the CD will yield 9 per cent only if the clean price falls to £998,256.10. Since the accrued interest of £6,575.34 is guaranteed, the market price which includes accrued interest will be £1,004,831.44.

Finally, we can calculate the *holding period yield* on a CD. We will consider the general case of a CD purchased after issue and sold before maturity. The holding period yield, *rh*, is given by:

$$rh = \left\{ \left[ 1 + r_p \left( \frac{N_{pm}}{365} \right) \right] \Big/ \left[ 1 + r_s \left( \frac{N_{sm}}{365} \right) \right] - 1 \right\} \cdot \left( \frac{365}{N_{pm} - N_{sm}} \right), \qquad (4.6)$$

where:

$$r_p = \text{yield on the CD at purchase;}$$
$$r_s = \text{yield on the CD at sale;}$$
$$N_{pm} = \text{number of days between purchase and maturity;}$$
$$N_{sm} = \text{number of days between sale and maturity.}$$

To illustrate the holding period return, consider an investor who purchases a 91-day CD (with a coupon of 10 per cent) with 50 days to maturity at a yield of 10 per cent and sells 30 days later at a yield of 10 per cent. Therefore, $r_p = r_s = 10$ per cent, $N_{pm} = 50$ days, and $N_{sm} = 20$ days, so that:

$$
\begin{aligned}
rh &= \left\{ \left[ 1 + 0.10 \left( \frac{50}{365} \right) \right] \Big/ \left[ 1 + 0.10 \left( \frac{20}{365} \right) \right] - 1 \right\} \cdot \left( \frac{365}{50 - 20} \right) \\
&= 0.0995 \quad (9.95\%).
\end{aligned}
$$

So even though the yield has not changed from 10 per cent over the period, the holding period return is less than 10 per cent. This is the result of compounding: the CD is priced to include accrued interest, but the interest is not paid until maturity.

## 4.2 Securities quoted on a discount basis

Treasury bills, bills of exchange, bankers' acceptances and commercial paper are the most important examples of money market securities that are quoted on a discount basis, i.e. that are sold on the basis of a discount to par.

*Treasury bills* (TBs) are short-term UK government IOUs of three or six months' duration. If a three-month TB is issued on 10 January, it will mature on 10 April. On maturity, the holder receives the par value of the bill by presenting it to the Bank of England. The proceeds are paid from the National Loans Fund. TBs are allocated to one of four bands depending on their remaining days to maturity: band 1 for bills with between 2 and 14 days to maturity, band 2 between 15 and 33 days to maturity, band 3 between 34 and 63 days and band 4 between 64 and 91 days. A computerized book-entry transfer system for TBs is operated by the *Central Moneymarkets Office* (CMO) at the Bank of England, although TBs are in general bearer securities. Most TBs are denominated in sterling, but in October 1988, *ECU-denominated TBs* were introduced, being sold by monthly tender, in maturities of 1, 3 or 6 months on an actual/360 basis. However they do not contribute directly to financing the public sector borrowing requirement; rather the proceeds are added to the government's foreign exchange reserves.

*Bills of exchange* (or *trade bills* or *commercial bills*) are similar to Treasury bills but are issued by private companies against the sale of goods. They are used to finance trade in the short term.

*Bankers' acceptances* are written promises issued by borrowers to banks to repay borrowed funds. The lending bank lends funds and in return accepts the bankers acceptance. The acceptance is negotiable and can be sold in a secondary market. The investor who buys the acceptance can collect the loan on the day that repayment is due. If the borrower should default, the investor has legal recourse to the bank that made the first acceptance.

*Commercial paper (CP)* refers to unsecured promissory notes issued by large corporations with maturities of between one day and a year. The notes are not backed by any collateral; rather, they rely on the high credit rating of the issuing corporation. Such corporations also tend to maintain credit lines with their banks sufficient to repay all their outstanding commercial paper. CP is therefore a quickly and easily arranged alternative to a bank loan. The *sterling commercial paper* (SCP) market began in April 1986. Corporations qualify for access to this market if they have a stock exchange listing and net assets exceeding £50 million.

All these securities are sold at a discount to their par value. On maturity, the investor receives the par value. Explicit interest is not paid on discount instruments. However, interest is reflected implicitly in the difference between the discounted issue price and the par value received at maturity. So while interest is received in the form of a capital value change, this is treated as income for tax purposes and not as capital gains.

Securities that are sold at a discount, pay no interest explicitly, and mature at par are known as *pure discount* securities. If we know the yield on these securities, then we can calculate their price at issue by using the simple present value formula:

$$P = M \bigg/ \left[ 1 + r \left( \frac{N_{sm}}{365} \right) \right]. \tag{4.7}$$

This can be illustrated using TBs. A 91-day £100 TB issued with a yield of 10.26 per cent would therefore have an issue price of:

$$P = £100 \bigg/ \left[ 1 + 0.1026 \left( \frac{91}{365} \right) \right]$$
$$= £97.51.$$

However, convention has it that TBs are not quoted on the basis of a yield, rather, they are quoted on the basis of a *discount rate*; and the issue price of TBs is not calculated as in (4.7); instead, it is determined as the difference between the face value and the *discount*.

Given the discount rate, $d$, the discount is found as follows:

$$\text{Discount} = M \cdot d \cdot (N_{sm}/365). \tag{4.8}$$

From this we can find the issue price as:

$$P = M - \text{Discount}$$
$$= M \cdot \left[1 - d\left(\frac{N_{sm}}{365}\right)\right]. \tag{4.9}$$

If we know that the discount rate on a 91-day £100 TB is 10 per cent, then we can calculate the issue price as:

$$P = £100 \cdot \left[1 - 0.10\left(\frac{91}{365}\right)\right]$$
$$= £97.51,$$

implying a discount of £2.49.

The *equivalent yield*, $r$, on the TB is given by:

$$r = \frac{\text{Discount}}{P} \cdot \frac{365}{N_{sm}}$$
$$= \frac{d}{1 - d(N_{sm}/365)}. \tag{4.10}$$

For the TB given here:

$$r = \frac{0.10}{1 - 0.10(91/365)}$$
$$= 0.1026 \quad (10.26\%).$$

The alternative way of pricing the TB is to substitute this yield into the present value formula (4.7) to give exactly the same issue price (£97.51) as that using the discount rate formula (4.9).

The important point to note is that with all discount securities the yield is always greater than the discount rate; i.e., from (4.10), $r > d$. This follows precisely because the securities trade at a discount: the return of £2.49 is achieved with an investment of only £97.51, not £100; the yield is based on £97.51, whereas the discount is based on £100. The difference is greater, the higher the rate of discount and the longer the time to maturity. For example, a 10 per cent discount rate implies yields of 10.08 per cent (over 30 days), 10.52 per cent (over 182 days) and 11.11 per cent (over 365 days).

The yield on pure discount securities such as TBs can also be compared with that on coupon-paying bonds. To do this we need to calculate the *bond equivalent yield* (or *coupon equivalent yield*), $rb$. This allows for the fact that a coupon security will pay interest before it matures whereas a discount security will not. The bond equivalent yield is the coupon of a bond which when trading at par would give the same yield as a discount security.

For a discount security with less than six months to maturity, the bond equivalent yield is the same as the simple equivalent yield (4.10) because the bond will make only one coupon payment during the six-month period (on the maturity date).

However, for a discount security with more than six months (182 days) to maturity, the bond equivalent yield has to take into account the fact that the corresponding bond makes two coupon payments and that interest is earned by investing the first coupon. Let $rb$ be the coupon rate and also the yield that a bond must have in order for the bond that has an issue price $P$ (the same as the discount security) to have a value $M$ at maturity (again the same as the discount security). The maturity value $M$ will have four components (where we assume $N_{sm} > 182$ days).

1 The first coupon payment, which consists of the interest accrued from the settlement date to the first payment date:

$$P \cdot rb \cdot \left( \frac{N_{sm} - (365/2)}{365} \right);$$

2 The interest earned by reinvesting the first coupon payment at the rate $rb$ for half a year:

$$P \cdot rb \cdot \left( \frac{N_{sm} - (365/2)}{365} \right) \cdot \frac{1}{2} rb;$$

3 The return of principal:

$$P;$$

4 The final coupon payment:

$$P \cdot \frac{1}{2} rb.$$

Adding these components together gives:

$$M \;=\; P \cdot \left[ 1 + \frac{1}{2} rb + \left( 1 + \frac{1}{2} rb \right) \left( \frac{N_{sm} - (365/2)}{365} \right) rb \right].$$

Rearranging this equation gives:

$$rb \;=\; \frac{-2H + 2\left\{ H^2 + (2H - 1)[(M/P) - 1] \right\}^{1/2}}{2H - 1}, \tag{4.11}$$

where:

$$H \;=\; N_{sm}/365.$$

To illustrate, consider a discount security with 246 days to maturity with a discount rate of 9.43 per cent. The purchase price will be:

$$P \;=\; £100 \cdot \left[ 1 - 0.0943 \left( \frac{246}{365} \right) \right]$$

$$=\; £93.65,$$

and the maturity value will be $M = £100$. The bond equivalent yield (using $H = 246/365 = 0.674$) will be:

$$rb \;=\; \frac{-2(0.674) + 2\left\{ (0.674)^2 + [2(0.674) - 1][(100/93.65) - 1] \right\}^{1/2}}{2(0.674) - 1}$$

$$=\; 0.0993 \quad (9.93\%).$$

The simple equivalent yield is, from (4.10):

$$r \;=\; \frac{0.0943}{1 - 0.0943(246/365)}$$

$$=\; 0.1007 \quad (10.07\%).$$

As can be seen, the bond equivalent yield is always less than the simple equivalent yield because with the bond, the first coupon payment can be reinvested, whereas this possibility is not available for a discount security, which therefore has to have a higher yield to compensate.

Finally, we can calculate the holding period yield on a discount security such as a TB. We again consider the general case of a TB purchased after issue and sold before maturity. The holding-period yield, $rh$, is given by:

$$rh = \left\{ \left[ 1 - d_s \left( \frac{N_{sm}}{365} \right) \right] \Big/ \left[ 1 - d_p \left( \frac{N_{pm}}{365} \right) \right] - 1 \right\} \cdot \left( \frac{365}{N_{pm} - N_{sm}} \right) \qquad (4.12)$$

where:

$$
\begin{aligned}
d_p &= \text{rate of discount at purchase;} \\
d_s &= \text{rate of discount at sale;} \\
N_{pm} &= \text{number of days between purchase and maturity;} \\
N_{sm} &= \text{number of days between sale and maturity.}
\end{aligned}
$$

To illustrate, consider an investor who purchases a 91-day bill 10 days after issue at a rate of discount of 10 per cent and sells it 7 days later at the same rate of discount. Therefore $d_p = d_s = 10$ per cent, $N_{pm} = 81$ days and $N_{sm} = 74$ days, so that:

$$
\begin{aligned}
rh &= \left\{ \left[ 1 - 0.10 \left( \frac{74}{365} \right) \right] \Big/ \left[ 1 - 0.10 \left( \frac{81}{365} \right) \right] - 1 \right\} \cdot \left( \frac{365}{81 - 74} \right) \\
&= 0.1023 \quad (10.23\%).
\end{aligned}
$$

So even though the discount rate has not changed from 10 per cent, the holding-period return is greater than the 10 per cent discount rate, although it is less than the 10.26 per cent yield to maturity calculated using (4.10). The first result follows from the fact that the investment in the TB is less than £100. The second result follows from the fact that the TB is priced to include accrued interest but the interest is not paid till maturity.

## 4.3   Recent innovations

We end this chapter with a brief discussion of some recent innovations in the money market.

A *note issuance facility* (NIF), first introduced in 1981, is a medium-term commitment between a borrowing corporate and a bank, whereby the corporate can issue commercial paper (the 'note') in its own name but the issue is effectively underwritten by the bank. The bank stands committed either to purchase any paper that the corporate is unable to sell on a rollover date or, alternatively, to provide standby credit. The bank therefore has an incentive to ensure that the paper is widely distributed among investors. If the borrower happens to be another bank, then the notes are usually certificates of deposit. The NIF commitment generally lasts for between five and seven years, with the commercial paper issued on a revolving basis, typically with maturities of three or six months. One advantage of a NIF is that the underwriting commitment remains off-balance-sheet until it is called upon, although there is an annual commitment fee payable on the unused portion of the facility. Another advantage of a NIF is that the borrower gets the advantage of guaranteed long-term floating-rate funding, yet borrows only the amount necessary to finance his short-term needs. The NIF can be triggered under the following circumstances: demand in the commercial paper market has temporarily dried up, say, as the result of the failure of other borrowers or changes in regulatory conditions; or, the corporate is having financial problems (although the bank can protect itself with a 'material adverse change' clause).

In the euromarkets, *euronotes* are issued with maturities of three or six months under NIFs underwritten by banks; this contrasts with *eurocommercial paper* (ECP) and *eurosterling commercial paper* (ESCP), which have maturities of between one day and a year, but are not underwritten by banks. The main currency of issue of ECP is US dollars but about half the issues are swapped into the main European currencies such as Swiss francs, French francs and Deutschmarks, giving investors fully-hedged short-term investments in these currencies. The second main currency of issue is the euro.

A *multiple component facility* (or MCF), first used in 1984, allows the borrower to raise funds in a number of different forms, each of which is associated with a NIF. The different forms can include short-term advances, *swingline credits* (which allow borrowers to draw same-day funds to cover delays in issuing notes) and bankers acceptances. Thus an MCF is a multiple NIF, allowing the borrower to draw funds by whichever means is cheapest or most convenient at the time.

*Revolving underwriting facilities* (RUFs) are NIFs that have become common in the euromarkets. RUFs can take two forms: either a single bank acts as a *placing agent* and arranges for a group of banks to underwrite an issue on a revolving basis; or a group of banks act as a *tender panel* for the placement of the notes. The role of tender panels is to bid for the notes issued by the corporate and to use their placing power to transfer them to investors. An extension of a RUF is a *transferable underwriting facility* (TRUF) which permits underwriters to transfer their commitments to other banks.

## Selected references

Fage, P. (1986), *Yield Calculations*, Credit Suisse First Boston, London. (Chapter 3.)

Stigum, M. (1981), *Money Market Calculations*, Dow Jones-Irwin, Homewood, Ill.

Stigum, M. (1990), *The Money Market*, Irwin, Burr Ridge, Ill.

Stigum, N. and Fabozzi, F.J. (1987), *Bond and Money Market Instruments*, Dow Jones-Irwin, Homewood, Ill. (Chapters 2, 3, 4.)

Vittas, D. (1986), 'The New Market Menagerie', *The Banker*, June, 16–27.

## Exercises

1 On 10 May you open a 2-month money market deposit paying 8.75 per cent with £5,000,000. What is the maturity value of the deposit?

2 What is reinvestment risk? Provide an illustration of reinvestment risk.

3 A £1,000,000 certificate of deposit was issued at par with a coupon of 9.5 per cent and 91 days to maturity. It is currently priced at £1,005,500 with 65 days to maturity. What is the current yield on the CD?

4  A £1,000,000 certificate of deposit was issued at par with a coupon of 10.5 per cent and 91 days to maturity. It is currently yielding 11.5 per cent with 30 days to maturity. What is the current price of the CD?

5  You buy a 91-day CD (with a coupon of 9 per cent) with 60 days to maturity and a yield of 9.5 per cent. Later you sell the CD when there are 10 days to maturity and the yield is 10 per cent. What is your holding period return?

6  Calculate the issue price of a 91-day Treasury bill with a par value of £10,000 and a discount rate of 9 per cent. What is the yield at issue?

7  The yield at issue on 60-day commercial paper is 8.878 per cent. What was the discount rate?

8  Why does the yield on a discount security exceed the discount rate?

9  Why does the yield on a discount security generally exceed the bond equivalent yield?

10  What is the yield on a euro-money market instrument paying 10 per cent if it is held for a full year?

# Chapter 5

# Bonds

Bonds are capital market securities and as such have maturities in excess of one year, unlike money market securities discussed in the last chapter which have maturities of less than a year. Bonds also have more intricate cash flow patterns than money market securities, which typically involve just a single payment at maturity. This makes bonds more difficult to price than money market instruments. It also makes these prices more responsive to changes in the general level of interest rates than is the case with money market instruments. Further, the day count basis in the bond market sometimes differs from that in the corresponding money market: the UK uses an actual/actual day count in the bond market but an actual/365 day count in the money markets. Most of the world's bond markets now use the actual/actual day count.

In this chapter we consider the following issues: different types of bond, the fair pricing of bonds, different yield measures, different yield curves (or term structures of interest rates), various theories underlying the yield curve, fitting the yield curve, and different measures of the interest rate risk, e.g. duration and convexity. We conclude with a discussion of floating-rate notes. The analysis of convertible bonds and bonds with warrants is deferred until Chapter 9.

## 5.1   Types of bond

There are many different types of bond that can be issued. The most common type is the *straight* (or *plain vanilla* or *bullet*) *bond*. This is a bond paying a regular (usually semi-annual), fixed coupon over a fixed period to maturity or redemption, with the return of principal (i.e. the par or nominal value of the bond) on the maturity date. All other bonds will be variations on this. The frequency of coupon payments can differ between bonds; for example, some bonds pay coupons quarterly, others pay annual coupons. The coupon payment terms can also differ between bonds. For example, some bonds might not pay coupons at all (such bonds are called *zero-coupon* bonds, and they sell at a deep discount to their par values since all the reward from holding the bond comes in the form of capital gain rather than income); some bonds make coupon payments that change over time, e.g. because they are linked to current market interest rates (*variable rate bonds* or *floating rate notes*) or to an index such as the retail price index (*index-linked bonds*); and some bonds make coupon payments only if the income generated by the issuing firm is sufficient (such bonds are known as *income bonds*; unlike other bond-holders, an income bond-holder cannot put the firm into liquidation if a coupon payment is not paid).

The redemption terms can also differ between bonds: some bonds have a single redemption date, while others have a range of possible redemption dates (such bonds are known as *double-dated bonds*), and sometimes the actual date of redemption is chosen by the issuer (*callable bonds*) and sometimes by the holder (*puttable bonds*); some bonds have no redemption date at all, so that interest on them will be paid indefinitely (such bonds are known variously as *irredeemables*, *perpetuals* or *consols*). Some bonds have option features attached to them: callable and puttable bonds are examples of this, as are *convertible bonds* (bonds that can be converted into other types of bond or into equity) and bonds with warrants attached to them.

Bonds can also be differentiated according to their issuer. Most bonds in the UK are issued by the British government in order to finance and manage the National Debt (such bonds are known as *gilts*). Most of these bonds will be in registered form, but the government also issues *bearer bonds* which are denoted as loan stock. Then there are bonds that are issued by UK public authorities, especially local authorities. Such bonds are secured on the revenues of the local authorities and are generally not guaranteed by the government. The duration of local authority bonds is typically between one and five years, although most are for one year and are known as *yearling bonds*.

Private companies also issue bonds, known as *corporate bonds*. There are several classes of corporate bond. *Debentures* are the most secured form of corporate debt (unlike in the USA, where debentures are unsecured corporate obligations). They are secured by either a *fixed* or a *floating charge* against the assets of the company. *Fixed-charge debentures* specify certain specific assets that are chargeable as security and which the company is not permitted to dispose of; in the event of default these assets are sold and the proceeds used to repay the debenture-holders. *Floating-charge debentures* are secured by a general charge on all the assets of the company. The company is able to dispose freely of assets until a default crystallizes the floating charge, at which time the charge fixes on the assets of the company that are not secured by a fixed charge. Fixed-charge debentures rank above floating-charge debentures in the event of default, but only floating-charge debenture-holders can ask for a company to be declared insolvent under the 1986 Insolvency Act. Each class of secured bond can also be categorized as either *senior* or *junior*, with senior bonds ranking above junior bonds in the event of default. *Unsecured loan stocks* are corporate bonds that are not secured by either a fixed or a floating charge. In the event of liquidation, loan stockholders rank beneath debenture-holders and preferential creditors (such as the Inland Revenue). *Guaranteed loan stocks* are corporate bonds that are not secured by a fixed or a floating charge, but are guaranteed by a third party, typically the parent-company of the issuer.

*Mezzanine debt* lies 'in the middle' between equity and senior secured debt. It is generally secured, at least in Europe, but ranks behind senior loans. Its main use has been to finance management buy-outs and it can be structured to take account of such factors as low initial cash flows from the bought-out business. Mezzanine finance is provided by both banks and venture capitalists, with banks sometimes calling it 'stretch lending'. Since June 1991, building societies have issued *permanent income bearing shares* (Pibs) which despite their name are bond- rather than share-type securities. They have a fixed semi-annual coupon, no redemption date and no voting rights; they are sold in units of £1,000 of nominal value on the stock exchange. More recently, floating rate Pibs have been issued.

Bonds can also be distinguished by the currency of denomination. Bonds issued in the UK in sterling by domestic issuers or foreign issuers are known as *domestic* and *foreign* (or *bulldog*) *bonds* respectively. The coupons on domestic bonds are generally paid net of UK basic rate income tax, whereas the coupons on bulldogs do not generally have tax deducted.

Bonds issued and/or traded in the UK in a currency other than sterling are known as *eurobonds*. The first eurobond was issued by SG Warburg in 1963 for the Italian motorway company Autostrada with a coupon of 5.5 per cent redeemable between 1972 and 1978 with an issue size of $15 million. *Eurosterling bonds* were first issued in 1972; they have all the characteristics of eurobonds rather than those of domestic or bulldog bonds, and the main issuers have been UK building societies, seeking long-term funds to finance their home loans. The main currencies of issue of eurobonds are US dollars, euros and Japanese yen. They are generally issued by banks, multinational companies, international agencies (such as the World Bank) and sovereign governments, and are generally unsecured. New issues are underwritten and placed with investors by a syndicate of international banks led by a *lead manager bank* (such as Credit Suisse First Boston or Deutsche Bank); the lead manager's fee is called the *praecipium*. The size of a eurobond issue usually lies between $50 and $100 million with a maturity of about six or seven years. Eurobonds are principally in bearer form, transferable by delivery with no record of holder, thereby preserving anonymity. The bond certificates have detachable coupon claim tokens, and coupon payments are generally paid annually free of UK income tax and withholding tax. Eurobonds are usually listed on the London or Luxembourg stock markets. Some eurobonds have a *lock-up period* of 90 days before they can be sold through the secondary markets to domestic investors. Recently the UK government has issued eurobonds. In February 1991, the government issued ECU2.75bn of a 10-year *ECU-denominated bond*. In January 1992, the government issued a three-year *ECU Treasury note*, with the intention of having quarterly tenders in such issues. There have also been issues in US dollars and Deutschmarks: e.g. $4bn floating rate note which matured in September 1996, DM 5.5bn 7.125% eurobond which matured in October 1997 and $3bn 7.5% eurobond which matured in December 2002.

The eurobond market has been the most innovative of all bond markets in designing new types of bond, both in terms of coupon payments and redemption proceeds. For example, there are *dual currency bonds*, where the coupon payments are in one currency and the redemption proceeds are in another; *currency change bonds*, where coupons are first paid in one currency and then in another; *deferred coupon bonds*, where there is a delay in the payment of the first coupon; *multiple-coupon bonds*, where the coupon payments change over the life of the bond (although in a predetermined manner), *fixed-then-floating bonds*, where the coupons change from being fixed-rate to floating-rate, *floating-then-zero bonds*, where the bonds change from being *floating-rate* coupon bonds to zero-coupon bonds; *missing coupon bonds*, where a coupon payment is missed whenever a dividend payment on the issuing corporation's shares are missed; *refractable bonds* with both call and put options attached; and *bull and bear bonds* where the principal on redemption depends on how a stock market index has performed up to redemption, with a bull tranche where the principal increases with an increase in the index and a bear tranche where the principal increases with a decrease in the index.

Finally, bonds can be classified according to their default risk and event risk. UK government bonds have a negligible risk of default, whereas the unsecured loan stock of private corporations has a much higher risk of default. The *default risk* (or *credit risk*) on a bond is usually assessed in the form of a *credit rating*. There are two main services providing credit ratings: Moody's and Standard & Poor's. These are shown in Table 5.1. Associated with a bond's credit rating will be a default risk premium: the lower the credit rating, the greater the risk of default and the higher the default risk premium. Table 5.2 shows some typical default risk premia (in excess of that on AAA bonds) on corporate bonds with different credit ratings. Non-investment grade bonds are sometimes known as *junk bonds* (or *high-yielding bonds*). Junk bonds have been used, mainly in the USA, to finance *leveraged buy-outs* (LBOs) and *management buy-outs* (MBOs).

There is another type of risk affecting corporate bonds that has recently come to prominence and this is known as *event risk* (or *restructuring risk*). Event risk is the risk of an unanticipated and dramatic fall in the credit quality of different classes of bonds following a leveraged buyout, takeover

**Table 5.1** Credit ratings on bonds

| *Moody's* | | | *Standard & Poor's* |
|---|---|---|---|
| | | **Investment grade** | |
| Smallest degree of risk — gilt-edged | Aaa | AAA | Highest rating: capacity to pay interest and repay capital extremely strong |
| High quality | Aa | AA | Strong capacity to service debt |
| Upper-medium grade: elements suggest possible future weakness | A | A | Strong capacity to service debt but susceptible to adverse changes in circumstances or economic conditions |
| Adequate security at present but may be unreliable over time; has speculative characteristics | Baa | BBB | Adequate capacity to service debt over time but adverse conditions likely to weaken capacity to service debt |
| | | **Non-investment grade** | |
| Speculative: uncertain future | Ba | BB | Lowest degree of speculation |
| No desirable investment characteristics | B | B | Speculative |
| Poor standing: in default or in danger of going into default | Caa | CCC | Speculative |
| Highly speculative | Ca | CC | Highly speculative |
| Lowest rated: poor prospect of ever attaining investment grade | C | C | No interest is being paid |
| | | D | In default |
| *Grades B to Aa can be modified by 1, 2 or 3* | | | *Grades B to AAA can be modified by '+' or '−'* |

or other restructuring of a corporation's balance sheet. Event risk results from the potential conflict of interest between different claimants on the firm's assets, that is, different classes of bondholder and shareholder. It is possible for corporate restructuring (following, say, a hostile takeover or leveraged buyout) to benefit one class of claimants and to harm another class. The latter class of claimants, generally bondholders, will suffer a fall in the market value of their claims. Shareholders can protect themselves from hostile takeovers and leveraged buyouts by not agreeing to sell their shareholdings at a discount. Bondholders have begun demanding event risk protection or greater security in the form of asset-backing.

Event risk protection has generally taken the form of either protective covenants or a put-at-par option, which is exercisable if specific designated events occur that lead to a deterioration of credit quality rating to non-investment grade level. In the euromarkets, there appears to be a difference in preferences between eurosterling and eurodollar bondholders. Eurosterling bondholders tend to prefer protective covenants that prevent a deterioration in credit quality, whereas eurodollar bondholders prefer the put-at-par option.

The alternative to event risk protection is to secure the bonds against the firm's assets. The most important examples of asset-backed securities in the UK are fixed- or floating-charge debentures, *first mortgage debentures*, and *sterling mortgage-backed floating-rate notes*; in the US, the best-known examples are *secured lease bonds* (SLOBs) and *collateralized mortgage obligations* (CMOs). Additionally, bondholders might demand *credit enhancement* in the form of an insurance contract, letters

**Table 5.2** Default risk premia on bonds

| Bond rating | Redemption yield (%) | Default risk premium (%) |
|---|---|---|
| AAA | 12.34 | — |
| AA | 12.50 | 0.16 |
| A | 12.70 | 0.36 |
| BBB | 13.41 | 1.07 |

of credit, recourse to the issuer, subordination of a second tranche which absorbs losses first, over-collateralization or a reserve fund.

So prevalent has event risk become, that, in July 1989, Standard and Poor's introduced event risk rankings, ranging from E-1 (strong) to E-5 (insignificant). The most common ranking is E-3 which means 'some protection against event risk: protection may not be provided against some anticipated events, or the effectiveness of protective provisions is questionable, or the benefits of protection are modest'.

Finally, we note that bonds in the UK are quoted in decimals. Prior to 1998, they were quoted in thirty-seconds of a pound (£1/32).

## 5.2 The fair pricing of bonds

A *straight bond* is a security that promises to pay a fixed interest or coupon payment every half-year, together with the return of principal or par value of the bond at maturity. For example, 8.75 per cent Treasury Loan Stock 1997 was issued on 9 March 1987 and made 20 coupon payments of £4.375 on 1 September and 1 March each year together with a final payment of £104.375 on 1 September 1997.

The *fair price* of such a bond is given by the discounted present value of the cash flow stream, using the market-determined discount rate for a bond of this maturity and risk class (and also using *semi-annual* discounting):

$$
\begin{aligned}
P_0 &= \frac{d/2}{(1+\frac{r}{2})} + \frac{d/2}{(1+\frac{r}{2})^2} + \cdots + \frac{d/2}{(1+\frac{r}{2})^{2T-1}} + \frac{d/2}{(1+\frac{r}{2})^{2T}} + \frac{B}{(1+\frac{r}{2})^{2T}} \\
&= \sum_{t=1}^{2T} \frac{d/2}{(1+\frac{r}{2})^t} + \frac{B}{(1+\frac{r}{2})^{2T}} \\
&= \frac{d}{r}\left[1 - \frac{1}{(1+\frac{r}{2})^{2T}}\right] + \frac{B}{(1+\frac{r}{2})^{2T}},
\end{aligned}
\tag{5.1}
$$

where:

$P_0$ = fair price of the bond;
$d$ = annual fixed coupon payment;
$B$ = par value of the bond;
$T$ = number of *complete* years to maturity;
$r$ = market-determined discount rate or required rate of return on a bond with this risk class and maturity (as a proportion).

The formula in (5.1) calculates the fair price on a coupon payment date, so that there is no accrued interest incorporated into the price. It also assumes that there is an even number of coupon payment dates remaining before maturity. If there is an *odd* number of coupon payment dates before maturity, the formula in (5.1) becomes:

$$P_0 \;=\; \frac{d}{r}\left[1-\frac{1}{(1+\frac{r}{2})^{2T+1}}\right]+\frac{B}{(1+\frac{r}{2})^{2T+1}}.\tag{5.2}$$

**Example 5.1 (Fair pricing of a bond)** *Treasury Loan Stock 8.75 per cent 1997:*

$$d \;=\; £8.75 \text{ per } £100 \text{ nominal};$$
$$B \;=\; £100;$$
$$T \;=\; 9 \text{ years (i.e. the date of the calculation is 1 September 1988)};$$
$$r \;=\; 9.54 \text{ per cent.}$$

*The fair price of this bond is:*

$$\begin{aligned}
P_0 &=\; \frac{£8.75}{0.0954}\left\{1-\frac{1}{\left[1+\frac{1}{2}(0.0954)\right]^{18}}\right\}+\frac{£100}{\left[1+\frac{1}{2}(0.0954)\right]^{18}}\\
&=\; £52.07+£43.23\\
&=\; £95.30.
\end{aligned}$$

*The fair price is composed of the sum of the present value of the stream of coupon payments (£52.07) and the present value of the return of principal (£43.23).*

The fair price of a perpetual or irredeemable bond (or consol) is given from (5.1) or (5.2) by setting $T=\infty$:

$$P_0 \;=\; \frac{d}{r}.\tag{5.3}$$

## 5.3   Clean and dirty bond prices

In the UK bond markets (since 10 February 1986), the price that is quoted is the *clean price*. This is the price disregarding accrued interest. However, the price that is actually paid for the bond in the market is the *dirty price* (also called *gross price* or *full price*), which is the clean price *plus* net accrued interest. In other words, the net accrued interest must be added to the quoted price to get the total price.

Accrued interest compensates the seller of the bond for giving up all of the next coupon payment even though he will have held the bond for part of the period since the last coupon payment. This is illustrated in Figure 5.1. The clean price is constant for the whole period. But the dirty price moves up and down like saw-teeth. On the coupon payment date $(C)$, the clean and dirty prices are the same and accrued interest is zero. Between the coupon payment date and the next *ex dividend* date $(X)$, the bond is traded *cum dividend*, so that the buyer gets the next coupon payment. The seller is compensated for not receiving the next coupon payment by receiving accrued interest instead. This is positive and increases up to the next *ex dividend* date, at which point the dirty price falls by the present value of the amount of the coupon payment. The dirty price is now below the clean price, reflecting the fact that

**Figure 5.1** Clean and dirty bond prices

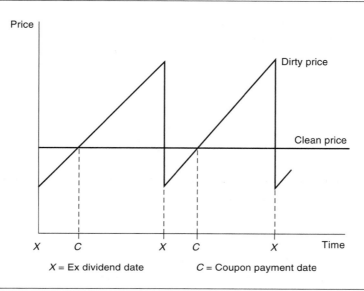

X = Ex dividend date    C = Coupon payment date

accrued interest is negative. This is because after the *ex dividend* date, the bond is traded *ex dividend*; the seller not the buyer receives the coupon and the buyer has to be compensated in terms of a lower price for holding the bond but not receiving the next coupon payment. The interest accruing between *X* and *C* takes the net accrued interest back to zero on the coupon payment date.

The net interest accrued since the last *ex dividend* date is determined as follows:

$$AI = d \cdot \left( \frac{N_{xt} - N_{xc}}{365} \right), \tag{5.4}$$

where:

$AI$ = net accrued interest;
$N_{xc}$ = number of days between the *ex dividend* date and the coupon payment date (7 days for UK government bonds);
$N_{xt}$ = number of days between the *ex dividend* date and the date for which the calculation is being made.

If AI is positive (which occurs between *C* and *X*), AI is known as *gross accrued interest*; if AI is negative (which occurs between *X* and *C*), AI is known as *rebate interest*.

## 5.4 Yield measures on bonds

Bonds are generally traded on the basis of their prices, but because of the complicated patterns of cash flows that different bonds can have, they are usually not compared in terms of prices; instead they are generally compared in terms of yields. There are many different types of yield measure.

### 5.4.1   Current yield

The simplest measure of the yield on a bond is the *current yield* (or *flat yield*, *interest yield*, *income yield* or *running yield*). This is defined as:

$$rc = \frac{d}{P},$$                                                    (5.5)

where:

$$rc = \text{current yield};$$
$$P = \text{clean price}.$$

For example, if the clean price of the bond is £95.30 and the coupon is £8.75, then the current yield is:

$$rc = \frac{8.75}{95.30}$$

$$= 0.0918 \quad (9.18\%).$$

A more accurate measure of the current yield would be to use the dirty price (rather than the clean price), since this is the price actually paid for the bond. However, the consequence of doing this is that the current yield would then exhibit a saw-tooth pattern as shown in Figure 5.2.

---

**Figure 5.2** Clean and dirty current yields

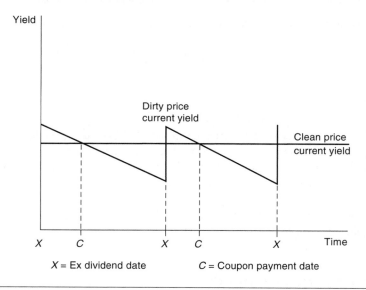

---

The current yield is used to estimate the cost of or profit from holding a bond. For example, if other short-term interest rates are higher than the current yield, the bond is said to involve a *running cost*. This is also known as *negative carry* or *negative funding*.

The main problem with current yield is that it does not take into account capital gains or losses resulting from the differences between the current price of the bond and its maturity value. Suppose that the bond just discussed will be redeemed in a year's time for £100. The overall return is then given by:

$$\left( \frac{100 + 8.75 - 95.30}{95.30} \right) \cdot 100 \quad = \quad 14.11\%,$$

which exceeds the current yield by 4.93 per cent. The current yield is therefore only really useful when there is a long time to maturity, in which case the capital gain or loss element will be small.

## 5.4.2 Simple yield to maturity

The *simple yield to maturity rms* attempts to rectify the shortcomings of the current yield measure by taking into account capital gains or losses. The assumption made is that the capital gain or loss occurs evenly over the remaining life of the bond. The resulting formula is:

$$rms \quad = \quad \frac{d}{P} + \frac{100 - P}{T \cdot P}, \tag{5.6}$$

where:

$$
\begin{aligned}
rms \quad &= \quad \text{simple yield to maturity;} \\
P \quad &= \quad \text{clean price;} \\
T \quad &= \quad \text{number of years to maturity.}
\end{aligned}
$$

For the bond just discussed, and assuming $T = 9$ years:

$$
\begin{aligned}
rms \quad &= \quad \frac{8.75}{95.30} + \frac{100 - 95.30}{9 \cdot 95.30} \\
&= \quad 0.0918 + 0.0055 \\
&= \quad 0.0973 \quad (9.73\%).
\end{aligned}
$$

The main problem with the simple yield to maturity is that it does not take into account compound interest. As the dividends are paid they can be reinvested, and hence interest can be earned. This increases the overall return from holding the bond.

## 5.4.3 Yield to maturity

The *yield to maturity* (or *redemption yield*) is the most frequently used measure of the return from holding a bond. It takes into account the pattern of dividend payments, the bond's term to maturity, and the capital gain or loss arising over the remaining life of the bond. From (5.1), these are three of the most important components determining a bond's price. The yield to maturity is equivalent to the *money-weighted rate of return* or the *internal rate of return* on the bond.

The yield to maturity ($rm$) is calculated by solving the following equation:

$$P_d = \left[\frac{1}{(1+\frac{rm}{2})^{N_{tc}/182.5}}\right] \cdot \left[\frac{d}{2} + \frac{d/2}{(1+\frac{rm}{2})} + \cdots + \frac{d/2}{(1+\frac{rm}{2})^{S-1}} + \frac{B}{(1+\frac{rm}{2})^{S-1}}\right]$$

$$= \left[\frac{1}{(1+\frac{rm}{2})^{N_{tc}/182.5}}\right] \cdot \left[\sum_{t=0}^{S-1}\frac{d/2}{(1+\frac{rm}{2})^t} + \frac{B}{(1+\frac{rm}{2})^{S-1}}\right]$$

$$= \left[\frac{1}{(1+\frac{rm}{2})^{N_{tc}/182.5}}\right] \cdot \left\{\frac{d}{rm}\left[\left(1+\frac{rm}{2}\right) - \frac{1}{(1+\frac{rm}{2})^{S-1}}\right] + \frac{B}{(1+\frac{rm}{2})^{S-1}}\right\}, \qquad (5.7)$$

where:

$$
\begin{aligned}
P_d = P + AI &= \text{dirty bond price (clean price \textit{plus} accrued interest);}\\
rm &= \text{yield to maturity;}\\
N_{tc} &= \text{number of days between current date and next coupon}\\
&\quad\text{payment date;}\\
S &= \text{number of coupon payments before redemption; if } T\\
&\quad\text{is the number of \textit{complete} years before redemption,}\\
&\quad\text{then } S = 2T \text{ if there is an even number of coupon pay-}\\
&\quad\text{ments before redemption, and } S = 2T + 1 \text{ if there is an}\\
&\quad\text{odd number of coupon payments before redemption.}
\end{aligned}
$$

Equation (5.7) uses $rm$ to discount the bond's cash flows back to the date of the next coupon payment and then discounts the present value at that date back to date $t$. The $rm$ will be the yield to maturity if the value so achieved equals the dirty price of the bond at date $t$. In other words, $rm$ is the *internal rate of return* that equates the present value of the discounted cash flows on the bond to the current dirty price of the bond (if date $t$ is the current date). The solution for $rm$ cannot be found analytically and has to be found through numerical iteration using a computer or a programmable calculator.

**Example 5.2 (Yield to maturity)** *A bond has a dirty price of £96.50, an annual coupon payment of £8.75, and there is exactly one year before maturity. Therefore (5.7) becomes:*

$$96.50 = \frac{4.375}{(1+\frac{rm}{2})} + \frac{104.375}{(1+\frac{rm}{2})^2}.$$

*Since this is a quadratic equation there will be two solutions, only one of which gives a positive rm. The positive solution is rm = 12.58 per cent.*

As an example of an iterative solution method, suppose that we start with a trial value for $rm$ of $r_1 = 12$ per cent and plug this into the right-hand side of the above equation. This gives a value for the right-hand side of:

$$RHS_1 = 97.02,$$

which is higher than the left-hand side ($LHS = 96.50$); the trial value for $rm$ was too low. Suppose next that we try $r_2 = 13$ per cent and plug into the right-hand side of the equation. This gives:

$$RHS_2 = 96.13,$$

which is lower than $LHS$. Because $RHS_1$ and $RHS_2$ lie on either side of $LHS$, we know that the correct $rm$ lies between 12 and 13 per cent. Using the formula for linear interpolation:

$$rm = r_1 + (r_2 - r_1) \cdot \frac{RHS_1 - LHS}{RHS_1 - RHS_2}, \qquad (5.8)$$

our linear approximation for $rm$ is $rm = 12.58$ per cent, the same as the exact solution. (A more general iterative solution technique was outlined in the appendix to Chapter 3.)

The *net yield to maturity* (or *net redemption yield*) is the yield to maturity that results from multiplying $d$ in (5.7) by (1 - marginal tax rate). The net redemption yield is lower than the gross redemption yield.

So far, we have calculated the yield to maturity on the basis of semi-annual discounting of semi-annual coupon payments. This is appropriate for most UK bonds. But eurobonds make annual payments, and the appropriate method of calculating the yield to maturity is to use annual discounting. However, the two yields to maturity are not then comparable directly. We could make the eurobond directly comparable with the UK bond by using semi-annual discounting of the eurobond's annual coupon payments. Alternatively, we could make the UK bond comparable with the eurobond by using annual discounting of the UK bond's semi-annual coupon payments.

The above four possibilities are listed below (assuming the calculation takes place on a coupon payment date so that $AI = 0$):

1 Semi-annual discounting of semi-annual payments:

$$P_d = \frac{d/2}{(1 + \frac{rm}{2})} + \frac{d/2}{(1 + \frac{rm}{2})^2} + \frac{d/2}{(1 + \frac{rm}{2})^3} + \cdots + \frac{B + (d/2)}{(1 + \frac{rm}{2})^{2T}}. \qquad (5.9)$$

2 Annual discounting of annual payments:

$$P_d = \frac{d}{(1 + rm)} + \frac{d}{(1 + rm)^2} + \frac{d}{(1 + rm)^3} + \cdots + \frac{B + d}{(1 + rm)^T}. \qquad (5.10)$$

3 Semi-annual discounting of annual payments:

$$P_d = \frac{d}{(1 + \frac{rm}{2})^2} + \frac{d}{(1 + \frac{rm}{2})^4} + \frac{d}{(1 + \frac{rm}{2})^6} + \cdots + \frac{B + d}{(1 + \frac{rm}{2})^{2T}}. \qquad (5.11)$$

4 Annual discounting of semi-annual payments:

$$P_d = \frac{d/2}{(1 + rm)^{1/2}} + \frac{d/2}{(1 + rm)} + \frac{d/2}{(1 + rm)^{3/2}} + \cdots + \frac{B + (d/2)}{(1 + \frac{rm}{2})^T}. \qquad (5.12)$$

Using the last example of a bond with a dirty price of £96.50, coupon payments of £8.75 per annum and a year to maturity, we get the following yields to maturity:

| Discounting | Payments | Yield to maturity (%) |
| --- | --- | --- |
| Semi-annual | Semi-annual | 12.58 |
| Annual | Annual | 12.70 |
| Semi-annual | Annual | 12.32 |
| Annual | Semi-annual | 12.98 |

The patterns that emerge from this table are that: (1) the *higher* the frequency of discounting, the *lower* the yield; and (2) the *higher* the frequency of payments, the *higher* the yield.

It is possible to convert between annually and semi-annually compounded yields using the following formulae:

$$\left.\begin{array}{rcl} rm_a &=& \left[\left(1+\frac{rm_s}{2}\right)^2 - 1\right] \\[2ex] rm_s &=& \left[(1+rm_a)^{1/2} - 1\right] \cdot 2 \end{array}\right\}, \tag{5.13}$$

or between annually and quarterly compounded yields using the following formulae:

$$\left.\begin{array}{rcl} rm_a &=& \left[\left(1+\frac{rm_q}{4}\right)^4 - 1\right] \\[2ex] rm_q &=& \left[(1+rm_a)^{1/4} - 1\right] \cdot 4 \end{array}\right\}, \tag{5.14}$$

where $rm_q$, $rm_s$ and $rm_a$ are respectively the quarterly, semi-annually and annually compounded yields to maturity.

For example, a semi-annual yield of 12.58 per cent implies an annual yield of

$$\begin{aligned} rm_a &=& \left(1+\frac{0.1258}{2}\right)^2 - 1 \\ &=& 0.1298 \quad (12.98\%), \end{aligned}$$

while an annual yield of 12.98 per cent implies a quarterly yield of

$$\begin{aligned} rm_q &=& \left[(1+0.1298)^{1/4} - 1\right] \cdot 4 \\ &=& 0.1239 \quad (12.39\%). \end{aligned}$$

While the yield to maturity is the single most commonly used measure of yield, it nevertheless has several disadvantages. The most important of these is that it will almost certainly not equal the actual return from holding the bond even if the bond is held to maturity. This is because implicit in the calculation of the yield to maturity as the internal rate of return is the assumption that each coupon payment as it arises is reinvested at the internal rate of return. This is demonstrated by multiplying both sides of (5.9) by $(1+rm/2)^{2T}$:

$$P_d\left(1+\frac{rm}{2}\right)^{2T} = \frac{d}{2}\cdot\left(1+\frac{rm}{2}\right)^{2T-1} + \frac{d}{2}\cdot\left(1+\frac{rm}{2}\right)^{2T-2} + \cdots + \frac{d}{2} + B. \tag{5.15}$$

The LHS gives the value of the investment in the bond on the maturity date, compounding at the yield to maturity. The RHS gives the terminal value of the returns from holding the bond. The first coupon payment is reinvested for $(2T-1)$ half-years at the yield to maturity, the second coupon payment is reinvested for $(2T-2)$ half-years at the yield to maturity, and so on. This is valid only if the rate of interest is constant for all future time periods, that is, if the yield curve (which will be discussed in the next section) is flat. But a flat yield curve implies that the yields to maturity of all bonds should be identical. This is clearly false.

Another disadvantage of yield to maturity is that investors do not typically hold bonds to maturity. They would be much more interested in holding period returns, which depend on the bond's price when it is sold (in relation to the purchase price) and on the coupons received during the holding period.

### 5.4.4 Holding-period yield

The *holding-period yield* (sometimes called the *reinvestment yield*) is the average yield realized during the holding period, taking into account changes in the *rollover rate* (the interest rate at which coupon payments can be reinvested). The risk that the rollover rate is less than yield to maturity is known as *reinvestment risk* (or *rollover risk*).

The holding-period yield, $rh$ (assuming that the bond is bought on a coupon payment date, so that $AI = 0$, and sold an even number of coupon payment dates later, so that $T$ is an integer), is calculated using:

$$P_d\left(1+\frac{rh}{2}\right)^{2T} = \frac{d}{2}\cdot\left(1+\frac{r_1}{2}\right)^{2T-1}+\frac{d}{2}\cdot\left(1+\frac{r_2}{2}\right)^{2T-2}+\cdots+\frac{d}{2}+P_1 \qquad (5.16)$$

or

$$rh = \left\{\left[\frac{\frac{d}{2}\cdot\left(1+\frac{r_1}{2}\right)^{2T-1}+\cdots+\frac{d}{2}+P_1}{P_d}\right]^{1/2T}-1\right\}\cdot 2, \qquad (5.17)$$

where $r_i$ is the rollover rate of interest earned by the $i$th coupon payment and $P_1$ is the price at which the bond was sold.

**Example 5.3 (Holding period yield)** *A bond is purchased on a coupon payment date for £96.50 and sold exactly two years later for £97.125. The annual coupon payment is £8.75 and the rollover rates for the first three coupon payments are 10.00, 10.25, and 10.40 per cent respectively. Using (5.17), the holding-period yield is:*

$$rh = \left\{\left[\frac{F+101.50}{96.50}\right]^{1/4}-1\right\}\cdot 2$$
$$= 0.0942 \quad (9.42\%),$$

*where:*

$$F = 4.375\cdot\left[\left(1+\frac{0.10}{2}\right)^3+\left(1+\frac{0.1025}{2}\right)^2+\left(1+\frac{0.1040}{2}\right)\right].$$

### 5.4.5 Yield to par

The *yield to par* (or *par yield*) is the yield on bonds trading at or near their par values (i.e. between about £99 and £101). The yield to par is therefore equal to the coupon rate for such bonds.

### 5.4.6 Yield to call and yield to put

*Callable bonds* are bonds that can be called at the option of the issuer. Such a bond is likely to be called when the market rate of interest is lower than the coupon rate on the bond. This will occur when the bond is trading above the call price. Suppose that a bond is issued with 10 years to maturity and is callable after 5 years with the following call schedule:

**Call schedule**

| Years to maturity | Call price (£) |
|---|---|
| 5 | 104 |
| 4 | 103 |
| 3 | 102 |
| 2 | 101 |
| 1 | 100 |

The *yield to first call* is the yield to maturity assuming that the bond is redeemed on the first call date. It can be calculated using (5.7) with $B = £104$. Similarly, the *yield to next call* is the yield to maturity assuming the bond is called on the next available call date.

The *operative life* of a callable bond is the bond's expected life. This depends on both the current price of the bond and the call schedule. If the bond is currently trading below par, its operative life is likely to be the number of years to maturity. If the current price is above par, the operative life of the bond will depend on the date on which the call price falls below the current price. For example, if the current price is £103, the bond is not likely to be called until three years before maturity. In this case, the operative life is three years less the number of years to maturity. Similarly, the *operative yield* is either the yield to maturity or the yield to relevant call depending on whether the bond is trading above or below par.

The *yield to put* is calculated in a similar manner as the yield to call. But the put is exercised at the option of the investor, and he will exercise it only if this strategy maximizes the value of the bond. Therefore a bond with a put option will always trade on the basis of the yield to maturity or the yield to put, whichever is greater.

### 5.4.7   Yield to average life and yield to equivalent life

Some bonds have a sinking fund or purchase fund attached to them. For such bonds a proportion of the issue is redeemed before maturity, either randomly on the basis of the bond serial numbers or through direct purchase in the market. A redemption schedule specifies the dates, the proportions and (in the case of random drawings) the values of the redemption payments.

The *average life* of a bond is defined as the weighted average time to redemption using relative redemption cash flows as weights:

$$\text{Average life} \quad = \quad \frac{\sum\limits_{t=1}^{T} \theta_t \cdot B_t \cdot t}{\sum\limits_{t=1}^{T} \theta_t \cdot B_t}, \tag{5.18}$$

where:

$$\theta_t \quad = \quad \text{proportion of bonds outstanding redeemed in year } t;$$
$$B_t \quad = \quad \text{redemption price of bonds redeemed in year } t;$$
$$T \quad = \quad \text{number of years to maturity.}$$

**Example 5.4 (Average life of a bond)** *A £50m 8 per cent bond (with annual coupon payments) issued with five years to maturity has the following redemption schedule:*

| Year (t) | Amount redeemed (£m) | Proportion redeemed ($\theta_t$) | Redemption price ($B_t$) | $\theta_t \cdot B_t \cdot t$ | $\theta_t \cdot B_t$ |
|---|---|---|---|---|---|
| 1 | 0 | 0.0 | — | 0.0 | 0.0 |
| 2 | 0 | 0.0 | — | 0.0 | 0.0 |
| 3 | 10 | 0.2 | 102 | 61.2 | 20.4 |
| 4 | 10 | 0.2 | 101 | 80.8 | 20.2 |
| 5 | 30 | 0.6 | 100 | 300.0 | 60.0 |
| **Totals:** | 50 | 1.0 | | | |

*From (5.18), the average life is given by:*

$$Average\ life \ = \ \frac{0+0+61.2+80.8+300.0}{0+0+20.4+20.2+60.0}$$

$$= \ 4.39\ years.$$

*After three years, £10m of the bonds have been redeemed, leaving 25 per cent (i.e. 10/40) of the remaining bonds to be redeemed in the following year and 75 per cent (i.e. 30/40) of the remaining bonds to be redeemed in the final year. The average remaining life of the bond is:*

$$Average\ life \ = \ \frac{(0.25 \cdot 101 \cdot 1)+(0.75 \cdot 100 \cdot 2)}{(0.25 \cdot 101)+(0.75 \cdot 100)}$$

$$= \ 1.75\ years.$$

The *yield to average life* is simply the yield to maturity under the assumption that the entire bond matures on the date corresponding to the average life at the average redemption price. The *average redemption price* is given by:

$$Average\ redemption\ price \ = \ \sum_{t=1}^{T} \theta_t \cdot B_t. \tag{5.19}$$

For the bond in the last example, after three years, the average redemption price is £100.25. If at this time the bond was trading at £99.25, the yield to average life (*ral*) is found by solving:

$$99.25 \ = \ \frac{8}{(1+ral)} + \frac{8+100.25}{(1+ral)^{1.75}},$$

to give *ral* = 9.77 per cent. The yield to maturity in this case is 8.42 per cent. This is below the yield to average life. The reason is that the bond is trading below par and the redemption schedule has the effect of shortening the period over which the capital gain arises, thereby enhancing yield.

An alternative to making yield calculations based on average life is to make them based on equivalent life. The *equivalent life* of a bond is defined as the weighted average redemption date using the *present values* of relative redemption cash flows as weights. The equivalent life therefore takes into account the fact that the redemption payments are received at different times:

$$Equivalent\ life \ = \ \frac{\sum_{t=1}^{T} \theta_t \cdot PVB_t \cdot t}{\sum_{t=1}^{T} \theta_t \cdot PVB_t}, \tag{5.20}$$

where $\theta_t$ and $T$ are defined as in (5.18) and where $PVB_t$ is the present value of the redemption price of bonds redeemed in year $t$. The discount factor used to calculate the present values of the redemption prices of the bonds is the yield to equivalent life, so we have to calculate the yield to equivalent life before we can calculate the equivalent life itself.

The *yield to equivalent life* (*rel*) is found by solving the following equation (assuming annual coupon payments and beginning on a coupon payment date so that $AI = 0$):

$$P_d \quad = \quad \frac{d + (\theta_1 \cdot B_1)}{(1+rel)} + \frac{d + (\theta_2 \cdot B_2)}{(1+rel)^2} + \cdots + \frac{d + (\theta_T \cdot B_T)}{(1+rel)^T}. \tag{5.21}$$

To illustrate, we can take the last example of the five-year bond which is purchased after three years. Equation (5.21) becomes:

$$99.25 \quad = \quad \frac{8 + (0.25 \cdot 101)}{(1+rel)} + \frac{8 + (0.75 \cdot 100)}{(1+rel)^2},$$

which solves to give $rel = 9.72$ per cent (cf. $ral = 9.77$ per cent). The corresponding equivalent life of the bond is found using (5.20):

$$\text{Equivalent life} \quad = \quad \frac{[0.25 \cdot (101/1.0972) \cdot 1] + \{0.75 \cdot [100/(1.0972)^2] \cdot 2\}}{[0.25 \cdot (101/1.0972)] + \{0.75 \cdot [100/(1.0972)^2]\}}$$

$$= \quad 1.73 \text{ years (cf. average life = 1.75 years).}$$

Both the equivalent life and the equivalent life yield are less than the corresponding average life and average life yield. This is always true and follows from using the present values of redemption cash flows rather than actual values, a procedure that gives greater weight to earlier cash flows.

As with callable bonds, the operative life and operative yield of a bond with a sinking fund depends on both the current price of the bond and the redemption schedule. If the bond is trading below par, the issuer is likely to repurchase the bond in the market. In this case, the operative yield is the yield to maturity. If, however, the bond is trading above the redemption price, the issuer is likely to draw bonds for redemption. In this case the operative yield is the yield to equivalent life.

## 5.4.8   Index-linked yields

With *index-linked* or *indexed* bonds, the coupon and principal are linked to a particular index, such as the retail price index (RPI), a commodity price index (e.g. oil) or a stock market index. In order to determine the yield on such bonds, it is necessary to make forecasts of the relevant index.

As an example, we will use the case of index-linked government bonds which were first introduced in the UK in March 1981. These bonds are linked to the RPI and are therefore designed to give a constant *real* yield. Initially only pension funds could invest in them, because pension funds had index-linked pensions to deliver to their pensioners. However, since March 1982 any investor can hold index-linked gilts. Most of the index-linked stocks that have been issued have annual coupon payments of 2 or 2.5 per cent; this is designed to reflect the fact that the long-run real rate of return on the UK capital stock is about 2.5 per cent.

Both the coupon and the principal on index-linked gilts are scaled up by the ratio of two values of the RPI. The denominator of this ratio is known as the *base RPI* and is the value of the RPI eight months prior to the month of the issue of the bond. The numerator is the value of the RPI eight months prior to the month of the relevant coupon or principal payment.

The semi-annual coupon payment is:

$$\text{Coupon payment} \quad = \quad \pounds(d/2) \cdot \frac{RPI_{m-8}}{RPI_b}, \tag{5.22}$$

and the principal repayment is:

$$\text{Principal repayment} \quad = \quad \pounds 100 \cdot \frac{RPI_{M-8}}{RPI_b}, \tag{5.23}$$

where $\pounds d$ is the *real* annual coupon payment and where:

$RPI_b$ = value of RPI eight months prior to month of issue of the gilt (i.e. base RPI);
$RPI_{m-8}$ = value of RPI eight months prior to the month in which the coupon is paid;
$RPI_{M-8}$ = value of RPI eight months prior to the month in which the bond matures.

The eight-month lag in the RPI is explained as follows. It is necessary to know each coupon payment six months before it is paid in order to determine the interest accruing between coupon payments. The two additional months are explained by the one-month's delay in publishing the RPI (e.g. June's RPI is not published until July) and an allowance of one month to make the relevant calculations.

It is also important to take into account any rebasing of the RPI. The two relevant bases are January 1974 = 100.0 and January 1987 = 100.0, the latter representing a rebasing from the 1974-base value of 394.5.

**Example 5.5 (Index-linked coupon and principal payments)** *Index-linked Treasury 2% 1988 was issued in March 1982 and matured on 30 March 1988. The base RPI was 297.1 (i.e. RPI for July 1981); the RPI for July 1987 was 101.8. Thus we can calculate the money value of the final coupon payment and principal repayment on 30 March 1988 as follows:*

$$\text{Coupon payment} \quad = \quad \pounds\left(\frac{2}{2}\right) \cdot \frac{394.5}{297.1} \cdot \frac{101.8}{100.0} \quad = \quad \pounds 1.3517,$$

$$\text{Principal repayment} \quad = \quad \pounds 100 \cdot \frac{394.5}{297.1} \cdot \frac{101.8}{100.0} \quad = \quad \pounds 135.1737.$$

*The interest accruing during the last coupon period (30 September 1987 - 30 March 1988) can be calculated once we know the final coupon payment, using:*

$$\pounds 1.3517 \cdot \frac{\text{No. of days accrued}}{(365/2)}.$$

There are two kinds of index-linked yields to maturity: the money (or nominal) yield, and the real yield.

The money yield requires forecasts of all future cash flows from the bond. This in turn requires forecasts of all the relevant future RPIs. The commonest way of doing this is to take the latest available RPI and to assume a constant inflation rate thereafter.

The forecast for the first relevant RPI is determined from:

$$RPI_1 = RPI_0 \cdot (1+\pi)^{m/12}, \tag{5.24}$$

where:

$$
\begin{aligned}
RPI_0 &= \text{latest available RPI;}\\
\pi &= \text{forecast of annual inflation rate;}\\
m &= \text{number of months between } RPI_0 \text{ and } RPI_1.
\end{aligned}
$$

Suppose, for example, that the bond pays coupons every March and September. The relevant months for forecasting the RPI are eight months prior to March and September, namely July and January. If the latest available RPI is for October, then we are attempting to make a forecast for the RPI the following January, in which case $m = 3$. The forecast for each subsequent relevant RPI is found using:

$$RPI_{j+1} = RPI_1 \cdot (1+\pi)^{j/2}, \tag{5.25}$$

where $j$ is the number of semi-annual forecasts after $RPI_1$ (which was the forecast for the RPI in January).

For example, if the October RPI is 102.8, and an annual inflation rate of 4.5 per cent is expected, then the forecast for the RPI for the following January is:

$$
\begin{aligned}
RPI_1 &= 102.8 \cdot (1.045)^{3/12}\\
&= 103.9,
\end{aligned}
$$

and for the January following that, it is:

$$
\begin{aligned}
RPI_3 &= 103.9 \cdot (1.045)\\
&= 108.6.
\end{aligned}
$$

The *money yield* ($rm$) is calculated by solving the following equation (assuming that the calculation is made on a coupon payment date so that $AI = 0$):

$$P_d = \frac{\frac{d}{2} \cdot \frac{RPI_1}{RPI_b}}{\left(1+\frac{rm}{2}\right)} + \frac{\frac{d}{2} \cdot \frac{RPI_2}{RPI_b}}{\left(1+\frac{rm}{2}\right)^2} + \cdots + \frac{\left(\frac{d}{2}+B\right) \cdot \frac{RPI_S}{RPI_b}}{\left(1+\frac{rm}{2}\right)^S}, \tag{5.26}$$

where $S$ is the number of coupon payments before redemption.

The *real yield* ($\rho m$) is related to the money yield through the *Fisher equation*:

$$\left(1+\frac{\rho m}{2}\right) = \left(1+\frac{rm}{2}\right) \Big/ (1+\pi)^{1/2}. \tag{5.27}$$

For example, if the money yield is 7 per cent, and the forecast inflation rate is 4.5 per cent, then the real yield is found from (5.27) as:

$$
\begin{aligned}
\rho m &= \left[\frac{\left(1+\frac{0.07}{2}\right)}{(1+0.045)^{1/2}} - 1\right] \cdot 2\\
&\approx 0.025 \quad (2.5 \text{ per cent}).
\end{aligned}
$$

Using (5.27), equation (5.26) can be rearranged as follows:

$$
\begin{aligned}
P_d &= \frac{RPI_a}{RPI_b} \cdot \left[ \frac{\frac{d}{2} \cdot (1+\pi)^{1/2}}{\left(1 + \frac{rm}{2}\right)} + \frac{\frac{d}{2} \cdot (1+\pi)}{\left(1 + \frac{rm}{2}\right)^2} + \cdots + \frac{\left(\frac{d}{2} + B\right) \cdot (1+\pi)^{S/2}}{\left(1 + \frac{rm}{2}\right)^S} \right] \\
&= \frac{RPI_a}{RPI_b} \cdot \left[ \frac{\frac{d}{2}}{\left(1 + \frac{\rho m}{2}\right)} + \cdots + \frac{\frac{d}{2} + B}{\left(1 + \frac{1}{2}\rho m\right)^S} \right],
\end{aligned}
\tag{5.28}
$$

where $RPI_a = RPI_1/(1+\pi)^{1/2}$ and $RPI_a/RPI_b$ is (one *plus*) the inflation rate between the date of the bond's issue and the date of the above calculation.

Equation (5.26) shows that the money yield is the appropriate discount rate for discounting money or nominal cash flows. Equation (5.28) shows that the real yield is the appropriate discount rate for discounting real cash flows.

Despite being linked to the RPI, index-linked gilts do not in practice offer a guaranteed real return. This is because of the eight-month lag in indexation, which means that the bond is not inflation-protected for the last eight months of its life. Any inflation occurring during that period will reduce the real value of the redemption payment and hence the real yield.

Finally, we can ask how an index-linked gilt can be compared with a conventional gilt. The best way is to calculate the *break-even inflation rate*. This is the inflation rate that makes the money yield on an index-linked gilt equal to the yield to maturity on a conventional gilt of the same maturity. Suppose that the yield to maturity on a conventional gilt is 8.3 per cent and that the real return on an index-linked gilt is 2.5 per cent; then using (5.27) we have a break-even inflation rate of:

$$
\begin{aligned}
\pi &= \left( \frac{1 + \frac{0.083}{2}}{1 + \frac{0.025}{2}} \right)^2 - 1 \\
&= 0.0581 \quad (5.81\%).
\end{aligned}
$$

If the expected rate of inflation is higher than the break-even rate of inflation, investors will prefer the index-linked bond, and vice versa.

## 5.5   Yield curves

In the last section we considered a variety of yield measures associated with individual bonds. In this section we shall examine the relationship between some of those yield measures and bonds which have different maturities but are otherwise similar. The relationship between a particular yield measure and a bond's maturity is called the *yield curve* (or *term structure of interest rates*) for that particular yield measure. To construct a yield curve correctly, only bonds from a homogeneous group should be included: for example, only bonds from the same risk class or with the same degree of liquidity. We would therefore not expect a yield curve to be constructed using both government and corporate bonds, since these would be from different risk classes. In this section we consider the following types of yield curve: the yield to maturity yield curve, the coupon yield curve, the par yield curve, the spot yield curve, the forward yield curve, the annuity yield curve and the rolling yield curve.

### 5.5.1   The yield to maturity yield curve

The most familiar yield curve is the *yield to maturity* (YTM) *yield curve*. This is a plot of the yield to maturity (derived from (5.7) above) against term to maturity for a group of homogeneous bonds. Three typical examples are given in Figure 5.3.

There are several problems with the YTM yield curve. Implicit in the definition of YTM is the assumption that coupon payments are reinvested at the YTM. As market rates of interest vary over time, it becomes difficult to achieve this, a feature known as *reinvestment risk*. The only type of bond devoid of reinvestment risk is a zero-coupon or pure discount bond. Another problem is that the YTM yield curve does not distinguish between the different payment patterns of low-coupon bonds and high-coupon bonds with the same maturity. With the latter, the payments are concentrated in the early years of their lives, while with the former, they are concentrated in the later years. Yet this is not taken into account in the YTM curve, which assumes a flat payments pattern. In other words, the cash payments on the bond are not discounted at the appropriate interest rate. For reasons such as these, bond analysts have devised a number of other types of yield curve.

### 5.5.2   The coupon yield curve

The *coupon yield curve* is a plot of the yield to maturity against term to maturity for a group of bonds with the same coupon. A typical set of coupon yield curves is presented in Figure 5.4, indicating that high-coupon bonds trade at a discount (have higher yields) relative to low-coupon bonds, because of reinvestment risk and tax reasons. There is a chance that interest rates will fall during the life of the bond and this reduces the reinvestment return from reinvesting the coupon payments (which is a greater risk for high coupon compared with low coupon bonds) and high-rate tax payers prefer to have a return in the form of capital gains rather than coupon income, since capital gains tax can be deferred (whereas income tax cannot). It is clear that yield can vary quite considerably with coupon for the same term to maturity, and with term to maturity for different coupons. In other words, different coupon curves not only have significantly different levels, but may also have significantly different shapes. Therefore the kinds of distortion that can arise in the YTM curve if no allowance is made for coupon are obvious.

As an alternative to the two-dimensional representation depicted in Figure 5.4, we can construct a three-dimensional *yield plane* of coupon against yield to maturity against term to maturity (see Figure 5.5).

### 5.5.3   The par yield curve

The *par yield curve* is a plot of the yield to maturity against term to maturity for bonds priced at par. The par yield is therefore equal to the coupon rate for bonds priced at or near par (since the YTM for bonds priced at par is equal to the coupon rate). The par yield curve is used to determine the required coupon on a new bond that is to be issued at par.

Suppose that the current par yields on bonds that will mature in one, two and three years' time are given respectively by 10, 10.25 and 10.75 per cent. This suggests, for example, that a new two-year bond issued at par would have to have a coupon of £10.25 per cent and that, from (5.10), for a three-year bond with annual coupons trading at par the following equality holds:

$$100 \; = \; \frac{10.75}{1.1075} + \frac{10.75}{(1.1075)^2} + \frac{110.75}{(1.1075)^3},$$

demonstrating that the YTM and the coupon are identical when a bond is trading at par.

**Figure 5.3** Yield to maturity yield curves

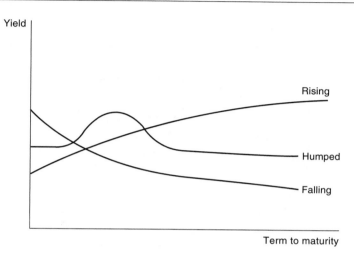

**Figure 5.4** Coupon yield curves

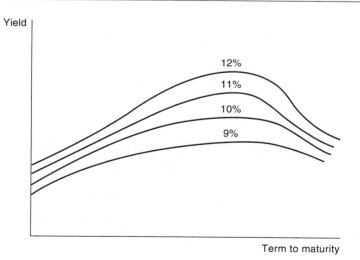

**Figure 5.5** Yield plane

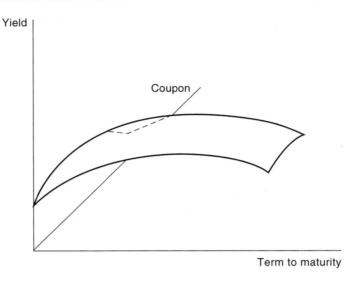

### 5.5.4   The spot (or zero-coupon) yield curve

The *spot* (or *zero-coupon*) *yield curve* is a plot of spot yields (or zero-coupon yields) against term to maturity.

Spot yields satisfy the following equation (assuming annual coupons and the calculation made on a coupon payment date so that $AI = 0$):

$$P_d = \sum_{t=1}^{T} \frac{d}{(1+rs_t)^t} + \frac{B}{(1+rs_T)^T}$$

$$= \sum_{t=1}^{T} d \cdot D_t + B \cdot D_T, \tag{5.29}$$

where:

$$rs_t = \text{the spot or zero-coupon yield on a bond with } t \text{ years to maturity;}$$
$$D_t = 1/(1+rs_t)^t = \text{the corresponding } discount\ factor.$$

In (5.29), $rs_1$ is the current one-year spot yield, $rs_2$, the current two-year spot yield, and so on.

The spot yield for a particular term to maturity is the same as the yield on a zero-coupon bond of the same maturity (hence the alternative name). The spot yields can be derived from the par yields as follows.

The derivation is based on the interpretation of a bond as a composition of an annuity (which provides the coupon stream) and a zero-coupon bond (which provides the principal repayment) represented by (using (5.29) with $P_d = B = 100$ and $d = rp_T$):

$$100 = 100 \cdot rp_T \cdot \sum_{t=1}^{T} D_t + 100 \cdot D_T$$
$$= 100 \cdot rp_T \cdot A_T + 100 \cdot D_T, \tag{5.30}$$

where $rp_T$ is the par yield for a term to maturity of $T$ years, where the discount factor $D_T$ is the fair price of a zero-coupon bond with par value of £1 and a term to maturity of $T$ years, and where:

$$A_T = \sum_{t=1}^{T} D_t = A_{T-1} + D_T \tag{5.31}$$

is the fair price of an annuity of £1 per year for $T$ years (with $A_0 = 0$ by convention). Substituting (5.31) into (5.30) and rearranging gives the expression:

$$D_T = \frac{1 - rp_T \cdot A_{T-1}}{1 + rp_T} \tag{5.32}$$

for the $T$-year discount factor.

For one-year, two-year and three-year par yields given by 10, 10.25 and 10.75 per cent respectively, we get the following solutions for the discount factors:

$$D_1 = \frac{1}{1 + 0.10} = 0.9091,$$

$$D_2 = \frac{1 - (0.1025)(0.9091)}{1 + 0.1025} = 0.8225,$$

$$D_3 = \frac{1 - (0.1075)(0.9091 + 0.8225)}{1 + 0.1075} = 0.7349.$$

It is easy to verify that these are the correct discount factors. Substituting them back into (5.30), we get respectively for the one-year, two-year and three-year par value bonds:

$$100 = 110 \cdot 0.9091,$$
$$100 = 10.25 \cdot 0.9091 + 110.25 \cdot 0.8225,$$
$$100 = 10.75 \cdot 0.9091 + 10.75 \cdot 0.8225 + 110.75 \cdot 0.7349.$$

Now that we have found the correct discount factors, it is easy to calculate the spot yields. From equation (5.29):

$$D_1 = \frac{1}{(1 + rs_1)} = 0.9091, \quad \text{implying } rs_1 = 10.0\%,$$

$$D_2 = \frac{1}{(1 + rs_2)^2} = 0.8225, \quad \text{implying } rs_2 = 10.26\%,$$

$$D_3 = \frac{1}{(1 + rs_3)^3} = 0.7349, \quad \text{implying } rs_3 = 10.81\%.$$

An alternative procedure for calculating the spot yields is to equate equations (5.29) and (5.30) for each $T$ and solve for the unknown spot yield $rs_T$. For example, when $T = 2$ (and given that $rp_1 = rs_1 = 10$ per cent and $rp_2 = 10.25$ per cent), we have:

$$\frac{10.25}{1.1025} + \frac{110.25}{(1.1025)^2} = 100 = \frac{10.25}{(1.10)} + \frac{110.25}{(1 + rs_2)^2},$$

which solves for $rs_2 = 10.26$ per cent. Similarly for $T = 3$ (and given that $rp_3 = 10.75$ per cent), we have:

$$\frac{10.75}{(1.1075)} + \frac{10.75}{(1.1075)^2} + \frac{110.75}{(1.1075)^3} = 100 = \frac{10.75}{(1.10)} + \frac{10.75}{(1.1026)^2} + \frac{110.75}{(1 + rs_3)^3},$$

which solves for $rs_3 = 10.81$ per cent.

In (5.29) we are discounting the $t$-year cash flow (coupon payment and/or principal repayment) by the corresponding $t$-year spot yield. In other words, $rs_t$ is the *time-weighted rate of return* on a $t$-year bond. Thus the spot yield curve is the correct method for pricing or valuing any cash flow (whether regular or irregular) because it uses the appropriate discount factors. This contrasts with the YTM procedure, shown in (5.10), in which *all* cash flows are discounted by the *same* yield to maturity.

### 5.5.5   The forward yield curve

The *forward* (or *forward-forward*) *yield curve* is a plot of forward yields against term to maturity. Forward yields satisfy:

$$
\begin{aligned}
P_d &= \frac{d}{(1 + {}_0rf_1)} + \frac{d}{(1 + {}_0rf_1)(1 + {}_1rf_2)} + \cdots + \frac{B}{(1 + {}_0rf_1)\ldots(1 + {}_{T-1}rf_T)} \\
&= \sum_{t=1}^{T} \frac{d}{\prod_{i=1}^{t}(1 + {}_{i-1}rf_i)} + \frac{B}{\prod_{i=1}^{T}(1 + {}_{i-1}rf_i)},
\end{aligned}
\tag{5.33}
$$

where:

$$ {}_{i-1}rf_t = \text{implicit forward rate (or forward-forward rate) on a one-year} $$
$$ \text{bond maturing in year } i. $$

Comparing (5.29) and (5.33), we can see that the spot yield is the *geometric mean* of the forward yields:

$$(1 + rs_t)^t = (1 + {}_0rf_1)(1 + {}_1rf_2)\ldots(1 + {}_{t-1}rf_t). \tag{5.34}$$

This implies that:

$$
\begin{aligned}
(1 + {}_{t-1}rf_t) &= (1 + rs_t)^t/(1 + rs_{t-1})^{t-1} \\
&= D_{t-1}/D_t.
\end{aligned}
\tag{5.35}
$$

For the spot yields given above, we can derive the implied forward yields from (5.35): ${}_0rf_1 = 10$ per cent, ${}_1rf_2 = 10.53$ per cent and ${}_2rf_3 = 11.92$ per cent. This means, for example, that, given the current spot yields, the market is expecting the yield on a one-year bond maturing in three years' time to be 11.92 per cent.

The relationship between the par yields, spot yields and forward yields is given in the following table:

| Year | Par yield (%) | Spot yield (%) | Forward yield (%) |
|------|---------------|----------------|-------------------|
| 1 | 10.00 | 10.00 | 10.00 |
| 2 | 10.25 | 10.26 | 10.53 |
| 3 | 10.75 | 10.81 | 11.92 |

This relationship is also shown in Figure 5.6 (in the case of rising yield curves) and Figure 5.7 (in the case of falling yield curves).

The relationship between par yields and spot yields can be shown using the following example. Suppose that a two-year bond with cash flows of £10.25 at the end of year 1 and £110.25 at the end of year 2 is trading at par (i.e. has a par yield of 10.25 per cent). To be regarded as equivalent to this, a pure discount bond (making a lump sum payment at the end of year 2 with no year 1 payment) would require a rate of return of 10.26 per cent (the spot yield), i.e., for the same investment of £100, the maturity value would have to be:

$$£100 \cdot (1.1026)^2 \quad = \quad £121.57.$$

As another example, if we know the spot yields, then we can calculate the coupon required on a new bond if it is to be issued at par using:

$$100 \quad = \quad \frac{d}{(1.10)} + \frac{d}{(1.1026)^2} + \frac{d+100}{(1.1081)^3}.$$

This gives $d = £10.75$, the same as the three-year par yield.

The relationship between spot yields and forward yields is shown in (5.34). If the spot yield is the *average return*, then the forward yield can be interpreted as the *marginal return*. If the marginal return between years 2 and 3 increases from 10.53 to 11.92 per cent, then the average return increases from 10.26 per cent to

$$\left[(1.1026)^2(1.1192)\right]^{1/3} - 1 \quad = \quad 0.1081 \quad (10.81\%).$$

The relationship between forward yields and par yields can be explained as follows. Suppose a three-year bond pays coupons equal to the corresponding forward rates; such a bond is similar to a floating rate note (see section 5.9 below) in the sense that the current forward rates are the market's best expectation of what the future spot rates will be. This bond will trade at par, since (discounting using spot rates):

$$100 \quad = \quad \frac{10.00}{(1.10)} + \frac{10.53}{(1.1026)^2} + \frac{111.92}{(1.1081)^3}.$$

A corresponding fixed-income bond which also trades at par will pay a fixed annual coupon equal to the three-year par yield, since (again discounting using spot yields):

$$100 \quad = \quad \frac{10.75}{(1.10)} + \frac{10.75}{(1.1026)^2} + \frac{110.75}{(1.1081)^3}.$$

**Figure 5.6** Rising par, spot and forward yield curves

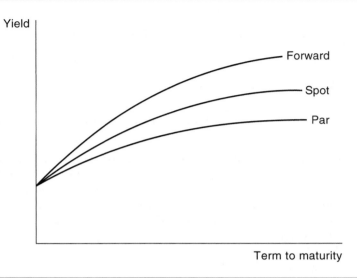

**Figure 5.7** Falling par, spot and forward yield curves

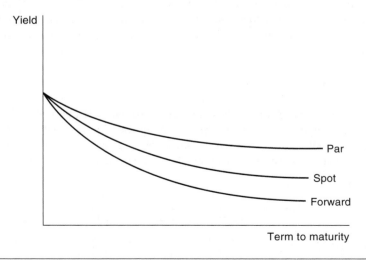

So the par yield is the constant yield corresponding to a given set of forward yields. This relationship between forward yields and par yields is used as the basis for deriving another type of yield curve, namely the *swap yield curve* (see section 10.3.1 below).

**Example 5.6 (Forward-forward interest rate calculation)** *Suppose that it is April 1 and a company needs a loan of £10m for three months in three months' time (i.e. between July 1 and October 1). The company is concerned that short term interest rates are going to rise in the near future. The company could borrow now for six months and invest the proceeds for three months until July 1 when the £10m is needed. Suppose that on April 1, the three month deposit rate is 8 per cent and the six month loan rate is 9 per cent. The company needs £10m in three months' time, so on April 1 it borrows:*

$$\frac{£10,000,000}{1+\left(0.08 \cdot \frac{3}{12}\right)} \quad = \quad £9,803,921.57,$$

*and invests this sum for three months at 8 per cent. On July 1, the company receives the £10m which it is able to use for three months. On October 1, the original loan matures and the company must repay the loan with interest at 9 per cent:*

$$£9,803,921.57 \cdot \left(1+0.09 \cdot \frac{6}{12}\right) \quad = \quad £10,245,098.04.$$

*This is equivalent to paying interest of £245,098.04 on a loan of £10,000,000 for three months between July 1 and October 1. The interest rate equivalent of this is:*

$$\frac{£245,098.04}{£10,000,000} \cdot \frac{12}{3} \quad = \quad 0.098 \quad (9.80\%).$$

This is the forward-forward interest rate for a three month period beginning in three months' time. The borrowing and lending strategy used to derive this interest rate is known as a *money market hedge* and can be used if it is believed that 3 month spot interest rates in three months' time will exceed 9.80 per cent.

The forward-forward interest rate can be calculated directly using the formula:

$$_s rf_\ell \quad = \quad \frac{(r_\ell \cdot N_\ell) - (r_s \cdot N_s)}{(N_\ell - N_s)\left[1 + r_s(N_\ell - N_s)/365\right]}, \tag{5.36}$$

where:

$$
\begin{aligned}
r_s &= \text{interest rate over the short period;} \\
r_\ell &= \text{interest rate over the long period;} \\
N_s &= \text{number of days in short period;} \\
N_\ell &= \text{number of days in long period.}
\end{aligned}
$$

Using the data in the example we have:

$$_3 rf_6 \quad = \quad \frac{(0.09 \cdot 183) - (0.08 \cdot 91)}{(183 - 91)[1 + 0.08(183 - 91)/365]}$$

$$= \quad 0.098 \quad (9.80\%).$$

### 5.5.6   The annuity yield curve

The *annuity yield curve* is a plot of annuity yields against term to maturity.

An *annuity yield* is the implied yield on an annuity where the annuity is valued using spot yields. In (5.30) above, we decomposed a bond into an annuity and a pure discount bond. We used the spot yield to price the discount bond component. Now we are concerned with the pure annuity (or pure coupon) component.

The value of the annuity component of a bond is given by:

$$
\begin{aligned}
A_T^* &= \sum_{t=1}^{T} \frac{d}{(1+rs_t)^t} \\
&= \sum_{t=1}^{T} d \cdot D_t \\
&= d \cdot A_T,
\end{aligned}
\tag{5.37}
$$

where $rs_t$ and $D_t$ are defined in (5.29) and $A_T$ is defined in (5.31). But $A_T$, the fair price of an annuity of £1 per year for $T$ years, is given by the standard formula:

$$
A_T = \frac{1}{ra_T} \cdot \left[ 1 - \frac{1}{(1+ra_T)^T} \right],
\tag{5.38}
$$

where $ra_T$ is the annuity yield on a $T$-year annuity.

Suppose that we have a three-year bond with annual coupon payments of £10.75. The value of the annuity component is given by (5.37):

$$
\begin{aligned}
A_3^* &= \frac{10.75}{(1.10)} + \frac{10.75}{(1.1026)^2} + \frac{10.75}{(1.1081)^2} \\
&= £26.51.
\end{aligned}
$$

This implies that $A_3 = £2.47$ (i.e. £26.51/£10.75). Solving for $ra_3$ in (5.38) or using standard present value of an annuity tables gives a three-year annuity yield of $ra_3 = 10.48$ per cent.

The relationship between the spot and annuity yield curves is shown in Figure 5.8. With an upward-sloping spot yield curve, the annuity yield is below the end-of-period spot yield ($10.48 < 10.81$); with a falling spot yield curve, the annuity yield curve lies above it.

### 5.5.7   Rolling yield curve

The *rolling yield curve* is a plot of rolling yields against term to maturity (see Figure 5.9).

The one-year *rolling yield* is the yield on a bond when the holding period is one year but the prices of bonds are assumed to remain constant during the year. For example, an investor could buy a ten-year bond, hold it for one year and receive the coupon, and then sell it for the current price of a nine-year bond with the same coupon. The rate of return on this investment would be the one-year rolling yield for a term to maturity of ten years.

**Figure 5.8** Spot and annuity yield curves

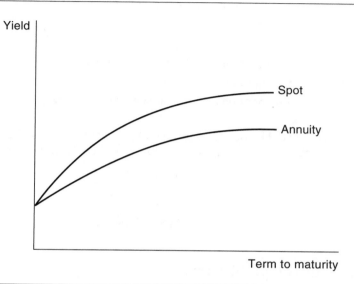

**Figure 5.9** Rolling yield curve (one-year horizon)

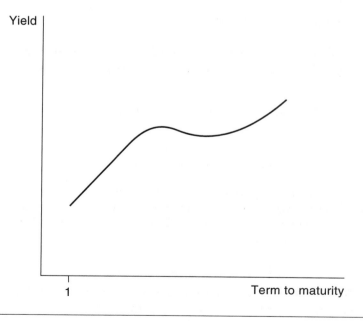

The one-year rolling yield is given by:

$$rr_T \quad = \quad \frac{d + P_{T-1}}{P_T} - 1,$$  (5.39)

where:

$$
\begin{aligned}
rr_T &= \quad \text{one-year rolling yield on a } T\text{-year bond;} \\
P_T &= \quad \text{dirty price on a } T\text{-year bond;} \\
P_{T-1} &= \quad \text{dirty price on a } T-1\text{-year bond with the same coupon } (d).
\end{aligned}
$$

For example, suppose that the price of a ten-year 10 per cent bond is £107.25 and the price of a nine-year 10 per cent bond is £106.75. The one-year rolling yield on a ten-year bond is:

$$rr_{10} \quad = \quad \frac{10.0 + 106.75}{107.25} - 1$$

$$= \quad 0.0886 \quad (8.86\%).$$

## 5.6    Theories of the yield curve

In this section, we consider some theories underlying the yield curve or the term of structure of interest rates.  As shown in Figure 5.3, the yield curve can be rising, falling or humped, and there are three main theories to explain this.

### 5.6.1    The expectations hypothesis

The *expectations hypothesis* argues that the long-term interest rate is a geometric average of expected future short-term rates.  This was the theory that was used to derive the forward yield curve in (5.33) and (5.34) above:

$$(1 + rs_T)^T \quad = \quad (1 + rs_1)(1 + {}_1rf_2)\ldots(1 + {}_{T-1}rf_T),$$  (5.40)

or:

$$(1 + rs_T)^T \quad = \quad (1 + rs_{T-1})^{T-1}(1 + {}_{T-1}rf_T),$$  (5.41)

where $rs_T$ is the spot yield on a $T$-year bond and ${}_{T-1}rf_T$ is the implied one-year forward yield $T-1$ years ahead. For example, if the current one-year rate is $rs_1 = 6.5$ per cent and the market is expecting the one-year rate in a year's time to be ${}_1rf_2 = 7.5$ per cent, then the market is expecting a £100 investment in two one-year bonds to yield:

$$£100 \cdot (1.065)(1.075) \quad = \quad £114.49$$

after two years.  To be equivalent to this, an investment in a two-year bond has to yield the same amount, implying that the current two-year rate is $rs_2 = 7$ per cent, since:

$$£100 \cdot (1.07)^2 \quad = \quad £114.49.$$

A rising yield curve is explained by investors expecting future short-term interest rates to rise, i.e. $_1rf_2 > rs_2$. A falling yield curve is explained by investors expecting short-term rates to be lower in the future. A humped yield curve is explained by investors expecting short-term interest rates to rise and long-term rates to fall. The main component of these expectations is expected inflation (see Chapter 2). If investors are expecting inflationary pressures in the future, the yield curve will be rising, while if they are anticipating disinflationary pressures, the yield curve will be falling.

The expectations hypothesis is discussed in more detail in Chapter 8.

## 5.6.2   The liquidity preference theory

When the inflation rate is expected to remain constant over time, the normal position of the yield curve is to be upward-sloping. The expectations hypothesis by itself is insufficient to explain this, since under constant inflationary expectations, the expectations hypothesis predicts a flat yield curve. A rising yield curve can be explained by the *liquidity preference theory*.

A rising yield curve results from investors' preferences to stay liquid. Since borrowers prefer to borrow long and lenders prefer to lend short, investors have to be compensated by a liquidity premium to forgo liquidity, and this increases with term to maturity. A humped yield curve is explained by the combination of a descending yield curve plus an upward-sloping liquidity preference curve (see Figure 5.10).

**Figure 5.10** Liquidity preference theory of the yield curve

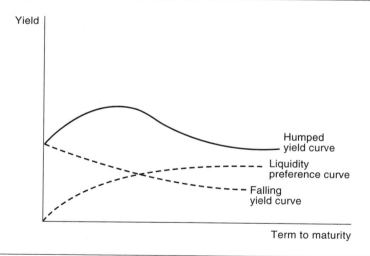

The expectations hypothesis assumes that forward yields are equal to expected future spot yields; in other words:

$$_{t-1}rf_t = E(_{t-1}rs_t),\qquad(5.42)$$

where $E(\ )$ is the conditional expectations operator for the current period. This assumption implies that the forward yield is an unbiased predictor of the future spot yield. The liquidity preference theory, on the other hand, recognizes the possibility that the forward yield may contain some element of liquidity premium which declines over time as the period approaches, so that:

$$_{t-1}rf_t \quad > \quad E(_{t-1}rs_t). \tag{5.43}$$

It is also possible of course for there to be uncertainty attached to the forward yield, which could lead to the reverse inequality in (5.43) holding.

### 5.6.3   The segmentation or preferred habitat theory

This theory argues that the bond market is segmented by maturity range and that there are no spillover effects between each market segment. The yield curve is therefore determined by supply and demand conditions in each market segment without reference to conditions in other segments. For example, banks are active in demanding bonds with short maturities, pension funds are active in demanding bonds with long maturities, while few institutional investors are greatly interested in medium-maturity bonds. Such behaviour would lead to high prices (low yields) at both the short and long ends and low prices (high yields) in the middle of the maturity structure. This provides an alternative explanation for the humped yield curve.

Another factor influencing the shape and level of the yield curve is government policy, especially in respect of public sector borrowing, debt management and open-market operations. The public sector borrowing requirement can affect the level of the yield curve: an increase in the requirement can lead to an increase in yields at all maturities. Open-market operations (the purchase and sale of money market securities by the Bank of England) can have a number of effects: in the short term it can have the effect of tilting the yield curve both upwards and downwards; in the longer term, by leading to changes in the money supply, it can influence inflationary expectations which in turn can affect the level of the yield curve. Debt management policy can influence the shape of the yield curve. Most government debt as it matures is rolled over, but the maturity of the replacement debt can have a significant influence on the yield curve in the form of humps in the market segment in which the debt is placed (since to be attractive to investors the debt must be placed at a relatively low price and a relatively high yield).

## 5.7   Fitting the yield curve

The term structure itself is a series of points on a graph of yield against maturity. The yield curve is a smooth curve through those points. There are several methods of fitting this curve.

### 5.7.1   Polynomial curve fitting

One of the simplest approaches is to fit a single polynomial in time. For example, an $N$-order polynomial could be used:

$$rm_i \quad = \quad \alpha + \beta_1 T_i + \beta_2 T_i^2 + \cdots + \beta_N T_i^N + u_i, \tag{5.44}$$

where:

$$
\begin{aligned}
rm_i &= \text{yield to maturity on } i\text{th bond;} \\
T_i &= \text{term to maturity on } i\text{th bond;} \\
\alpha, \beta_i &= \text{coefficients of the polynomial;} \\
u_i &= \text{residual error on the } i\text{th bond.}
\end{aligned}
$$

The coefficients of the polynomial are determined by minimizing the sum of squared residual errors, $\sum_i^M u_i^2$ for $M$ bonds used, as shown in Figure 5.11. The resulting curve depends on the order of

**Figure 5.11** Polynomial curve fitting

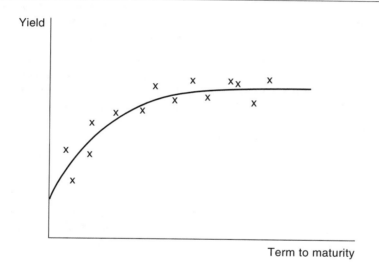

the polynomial $N$. If $N$ is too high, the curve will not be sufficiently smooth. (Indeed, if $N = M - 1$, the curve will go through every point and will be over-fitted). If $N$ is too low, the curve will be under-fitted.

A more sophisticated approach fits different polynomials over different but overlapping terms to maturity. The fitted curves are then spliced together to produce a single smooth curve (called a spline-curve) over the entire range.

## 5.7.2 Regression analysis

An alternative approach is to use regression analysis, with bond prices as the dependent variable and coupon payments and principal as the independent variables:

$$
P_{di} = \beta_1 d_{1i} + \beta_2 d_{2i} + \cdots + \beta_T (d_{Ti} + 100) + u_i, \tag{5.45}
$$

where:

$$P_{di} = \text{dirty price of } i\text{th bond;}$$
$$d_{ji} = \text{coupon on } i\text{th bond in period } j;$$
$$\beta_j = \text{coefficients of the regression equation;}$$
$$u_i = \text{residual error on the } i\text{th bond.}$$

It is clear from (5.29) that the coefficients in (5.45) are estimates of the discount factors:

$$\beta_j = D_j = \frac{1}{(1+rs_j)^j}, \tag{5.46}$$

and hence can be used to generate the spot yield curve.

The problem with (5.45), of course, from the point of view of estimation, is that the coupon payment dates differ for different bonds and that there are more coupon payment dates than the number of bonds available, so that (5.45) as it stands cannot in fact be estimated.

The solution is to divide the entire maturity spectrum into grid dates (denoted $d^*_{ji}$) and to allocate coupon payments between two grid dates in a way that preserves either the present value of the bond's cash flows or the duration of the bond (duration is defined in the next section). This is illustrated in Figure 5.12, which allows for more grid dates at the short end of the maturity spectrum relative to the

**Figure 5.12** Grid dates in years for regression analysis

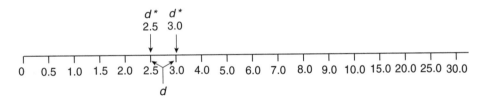

long end because of the greater difficulty of fitting the yield curve at the short end. The regression equation that is estimated is:

$$P_{di} = \beta_1 d^*_{1i} + \beta_2 d^*_{2i} + \cdots + \beta_T(d^*_{Ti} + 100) + u_i. \tag{5.47}$$

### 5.7.3   Matrix modelling

*Matrix modelling* (or *matrix pricing* or *pricing by analogy*) extends the multiple regression model (5.47) by taking into account other factors that can influence bond prices apart from term to maturity. It is known as matrix modelling because it assumes that the price of a bond is made up from each component of relative value taken separately. Besides term to maturity, the other components of relative value that have been added to (5.47) are as follows.

1 *Coupon as measured by current yield* — since high-coupon bonds trade at a discount relative to low-coupon bonds, we would expect the coefficient on current yield to be negative.

2 *Liquidity* as measured by *bid-offer spread, volume at issue, annual percentage turnover* or *number of market-makers* in the bond — the coefficient on the liquidity measure would be positive if liquidity and bond marketability were valued characteristics. If, however, liquidity were regarded as a scarce commodity, then the bond price would fall as the degree of liquidity rose, in which case the coefficient on the liquidity measure would be negative.

3 *Default risk* in the form of *sector risk* (e.g. UK government *v.* World Bank, bank sector *v.* oil sector), *quality risk* (e.g. AAA rating *v.* AA rating), etc. — default risk will be measured by the price spread on the two bonds being compared. The coefficient on the default risk measure is expected to be negative, so that higher default risk reduces prices and increases yields.

4 *Call effect* — this is always to the disadvantage of the bond-holder and will have a negative effect on price.

5 *Sinking fund* or *purchase fund effect* — this also has a negative effect on price.

6 *Convertibility* — this is an attractive feature and has a positive effect on price.

7 *Warrant attachments* — this is also an attractive feature and has a positive effect on price.

The last four features involve an implied option, and this option has to be priced. The pricing of options is discussed in Chapter 9.

Once we have price adjustment factors for a given set of bonds, we can use them to price different bonds with different amounts of the factors embodied in them. The price adjustments can also be converted into yield adjustments or yield spreads to give, for example, the difference in yield between bonds with and without a particular sector characteristic.

To illustrate this pricing by analogy, we will compare a low-coupon UK government bond with a high-coupon UK bank corporate bond with the same maturity:

|  | *Price (£)* | *Yield to maturity (%)* |
|---|---|---|
| **UK government bond** | 87.25 | 9.93 |
| Adjustments: |  |  |
| Coupon effect | −2.16 | +0.46 |
| Liquidity effect | −1.07 | +0.21 |
| Sector effect | −1.51 | +0.32 |
| Quality effect | −0.87 | +0.15 |
| **UK bank corporate bond** | 81.64 | 11.07 |

Taking into account all the adjustments, we can see that the bank bond ought to be trading at £5.61 lower than or at a yield to maturity of 1.14 per cent higher than the comparable government bond. If the bank bond is trading at a discount to the government bond of more than £5.61 (YTM of more than 1.14 per cent), then the bank bond is cheap relative to the government bond. Alternatively, the matrix pricing model can be used to determine the fair price of a newly issued bond.

## 5.8   Interest rate risk

Having discussed various ways of measuring the returns on bonds, the next step is to discuss different ways of measuring the risk from holding bonds. We have discussed earlier (Chapter 2) inflation risk, which is common to all bonds, and specific risk in the form of either business risk or financial risk, which depends on the industry or corporation that issues the bond. The required yield on a bond will have loadings for all these kinds of risk, and the greater the risk, the greater the risk loading. However, there is another type of risk that is common to all types of fixed-interest securities and which has an important effect on bond values. This is *interest rate risk*, the risk that bond prices will fall if market interest rates rise. Interest rate risk is the main form of market risk for bonds paying fixed coupons. There are a number of measures of interest rate risk that we will consider: duration, convexity and dispersion.

### 5.8.1   Duration

The measure of interest rate risk typically used by bond analysts is called *duration*, which was invented by Macaulay (1938). Duration is defined as the weighted average maturity of a bond using the relative discounted cash flows in each period as weights. If we assume annual coupons (see Chua (1984)), then:

$$
\begin{aligned}
D &= \frac{d}{P_d} \cdot \sum_{t=1}^{T} \frac{t}{(1+rm)^t} + \frac{B}{P_d} \cdot \frac{T}{(1+rm)^T} \\[2mm]
&= \frac{d}{P_d} \cdot \left[ \frac{(1+rm)^{T+1} - (1+rm) - (rm)T}{(rm)^2(1+rm)^T} \right] + \frac{B}{P_d} \cdot \frac{T}{(1+rm)^T} \,,
\end{aligned}
\tag{5.48}
$$

where:

$$
\begin{aligned}
D &= \text{duration (measured in years);} \\
d &= \text{annual coupon;} \\
B &= \text{par value of bond;} \\
P_d &= \text{dirty price of bond;} \\
t &= \text{time in years to } t\text{th cash flow;} \\
T &= \text{time in years to maturity;} \\
rm &= \text{yield to maturity.}
\end{aligned}
$$

In (5.48), $d/(1+rm)^t$ is the discounted value of the $t$th cash flow and so $d/P_d(1+rm)^t$ is the relative discounted value of the $t$th cash flow; similarly with the terminal value.

**Example 5.7 (Duration)** *A 10 per cent annual coupon bond is trading at par with three years to maturity, so $P_d = B = £100$, $d = £10$, $rm = 10\%$, $T = 3$ years. Therefore duration is given by:*

$$
\begin{aligned}
D &= \frac{10}{100} \cdot \left[ \frac{1}{(1.1)} + \frac{2}{(1.1)^2} + \frac{3}{(1.1)^3} \right] + \frac{100}{100} \cdot \left[ \frac{3}{(1.1)^3} \right] \\[2mm]
&= \frac{10}{100} \cdot \left[ \frac{(1.1)^4 - (1.1) - (0.1)(3)}{(0.1)^2(1.1)^3} \right] + \frac{100}{100} \cdot \left[ \frac{3}{(1.1)^3} \right] \\[2mm]
&= 2.74 \; years,
\end{aligned}
$$

*which implies that the average time taken to receive the cash flows on this bond is 2.74 years (see Figure 5.13).*

---

**Figure 5.13** Duration as the weighted average maturity of a bond

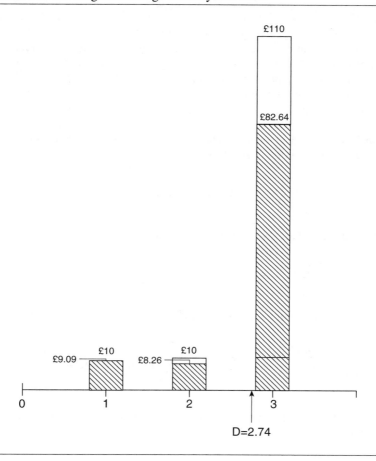

---

We can examine some of the properties of duration. Duration is always less than (or equal to) maturity. This is because some weight is given to the cash flows in the early years of the bond's life and this helps to bring forward the average time at which cash flows are received. In the above example, the coupon element contributes 0.5 years to duration, while the principal element contributes 2.24 years. Duration also varies with coupon, yield and maturity.

For a zero-coupon bond, duration equals the term to maturity. This is obvious from the definition of a zero-coupon bond and also from (5.48) given that $d = 0$ and $P_d = B/(1 + rm)^T$. For a perpetual bond, duration is given by:

$$D = \frac{1 + rc}{rc} = \frac{1}{rc} + 1, \tag{5.49}$$

where, from (5.5), $rc = (d/P_d)$ is the current yield. This follows from (5.48) as $T \to \infty$, recognizing, from (5.5) and (5.7), that for a perpetual bond $rm = rc$.

Equation (5.49) provides the limiting value to duration. For bonds trading at or above par (so that $rm \leq rc$), duration increases with maturity and approaches this limit from below. For bonds trading at a discount to par (so that $rm > rc$), duration increases to a maximum at around 20 years and then declines towards the limit given by (5.49). So in general, duration increases with maturity (see Figure 5.14).

Duration increases as coupon and yield decrease as shown in Figure 5.15. As the coupon falls, more of the relative weight of the cash flows is transferred to the maturity date and this causes duration to rise. Because the coupon on index-linked gilts is much lower than on conventional gilts, this means that the duration of index-linked gilts will be much higher than for conventional gilts with the same maturity. As yield increases, the present values of all future cash flows fall, but the present values of the more distant cash flows fall relatively more than those of the nearer cash flows. This has the effect of increasing the relative weight given to nearer cash flows and hence of reducing duration.

That duration is a measure of interest rate risk is demonstrated as follows. The present value equation for an annual coupon bond is given by:

$$P_d = \sum_{t=1}^{T} \frac{d}{(1+rm)^t} + \frac{B}{(1+rm)^T}. \tag{5.50}$$

Differentiating this equation with respect to $(1+rm)$ gives:

$$\frac{\Delta P_d}{\Delta(1+rm)} = -d \cdot \sum_{t=1}^{T} \frac{t}{(1+rm)^{t+1}} - B \cdot \frac{T}{(1+rm)^{T+1}}, \tag{5.51}$$

where $\Delta$ means 'a small change in'. Multiplying both sides of (5.51) by $(1+rm)/P_d$ gives:

$$\frac{\Delta P_d/P_d}{\Delta(1+rm)/(1+rm)} = -\frac{d}{P_d} \cdot \sum_{t=1}^{T} \frac{t}{(1+rm)^t} - \frac{B}{P_d} \cdot \frac{T}{(1+rm)^T}$$

$$= -D. \tag{5.52}$$

The LHS of (5.52) is the elasticity of the bond price with respect to (one *plus*) the yield to maturity, $\varepsilon[P_d, (1+rm)]$, where:

$$\varepsilon[P_d, (1+rm)] = \frac{\Delta \ln P_d}{\Delta \ln(1+rm)}$$

$$= \frac{\Delta P_d/P_d}{\Delta(1+rm)/(1+rm)}. \tag{5.53}$$

The RHS of (5.52) is (the negative of) duration. So duration measures the interest rate elasticity of the bond price, and is therefore a measure of interest rate risk. The lower the duration, the less responsive is the bond's value to interest rate fluctuations.

Figure 5.16 shows the present-value profile for a bond. There is a negative-sloping and convex relationship between (the natural logarithm of) the price of the bond and (the natural logarithm of) one *plus* the yield to maturity. The slope of the present-value profile at the current bond price and yield to maturity is equal to the (negative of the) duration of the bond. The flatter the present-value profile, the lower the duration and the lower the interest rate risk.

**Figure 5.14** Duration against maturity

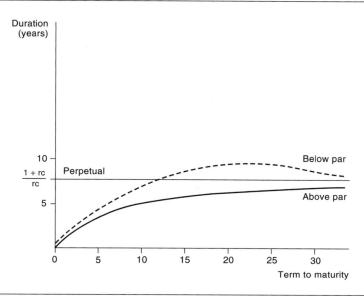

**Figure 5.15** Duration against coupon and yield

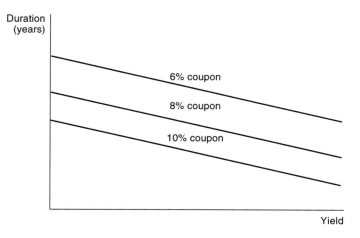

**Figure 5.16** Present-value profile and duration

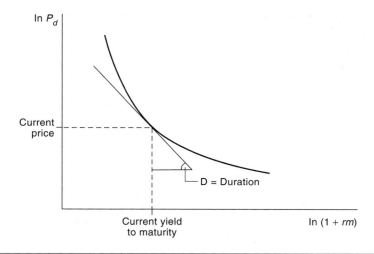

**Example 5.8 (First-order interest rate risk)** *A 10 per cent annual coupon bond is trading at par with a duration of 2.74 years. If yields rise from 10 to 10.5 per cent, then the price of the bond will fall by:*

$$\Delta P_d \quad = \quad -D \cdot \frac{\Delta(rm)}{1+rm} \cdot P_d$$

$$= \quad -2.74 \cdot \frac{0.005}{1.1} \cdot 100$$

$$= \quad -£1.25$$

*to £98.75.*

The UK markets use a concept called *modified duration* (also known as *volatility*), which is related to duration as follows:

$$MD \quad = \quad \frac{D}{1+rm}, \tag{5.54}$$

where $MD$ = modified duration in years. This means that the following relationship holds between modified duration and bond prices:

$$\Delta P_d \quad = \quad -MD \cdot \Delta rm \cdot P_d. \tag{5.55}$$

For example, if $D = 2.74$ years and yields are 10 per cent then:

$$MD \quad = \quad \frac{2.74}{1.1}$$

$$= \quad 2.49 \text{ years.}$$

Market practitioners also use a concept called *basis point value* (BPV) (which is sometimes referred to as *risk*). It is related to modified duration as follows:

$$BPV = \frac{MD \cdot Pd}{10000}. \tag{5.56}$$

While modified duration gives the percentage change in the price of a bond, BPV gives the money change in the price of a bond in response to a one basis point change in yield: from (5.55) it is clear that:

$$BPV = -\frac{\Delta P_d}{\Delta rm} \cdot \frac{1}{10000}.$$

Some practitioners in the financial markets (an example is Bloomberg, suppliers of on-line financial information) calculate duration and modified duration using numerical approximations to the first-order derivative given in (5.52). For example, modified duration can be calculated using the following expression:

$$MD = \frac{10^4}{2} \cdot \left( \frac{|\Delta P_d'|}{P_d} + \frac{|\Delta P_d''|}{P_d} \right), \tag{5.57}$$

where:

$|\Delta P_d'|$ = absolute value of the change in dirty price if yield increases by 1 basis point $(0.01\%)$;

$|\Delta P_d''|$ = absolute value of the change in dirty price if yield falls by 1 basis point $(0.01\%)$.

The scaling factor $10^4$ is explained by the fact that the price difference is calculated on the basis of a $100^{th}$ of 1 per cent change in yield, whereas the price level is based on 100 per cent of par value.

To illustrate this we can use the same bond as in the above example of duration. If the yield increases from 10.00 to 10.01 per cent then, using (5.1), the price of the bond will fall to:

$$P_d' = \frac{10}{(0.1001)} \cdot \left[ 1 - \frac{1}{(1.1001)^3} \right] + \frac{100}{(1.1001)^3}$$

$$= 99.9751359$$

or by $\Delta P_d' = -0.0248641$. If the yield falls to 9.99 per cent, the price of the bond will rise to:

$$P_d'' = \frac{10}{(0.0999)} \cdot \left[ 1 - \frac{1}{(1.0999)^3} \right] + \frac{100}{(1.0999)^3}$$

$$= 100.0248729$$

or by $\Delta P_d'' = 0.0248729$. Therefore:

$$MD = \frac{10^4}{2} \cdot \left( \frac{0.0248641}{100} + \frac{0.02489729}{100} \right)$$

$$= 2.49.$$

## 5.8.2  Convexity

Duration can be regarded as a first-order measure of interest rate risk: it measures the *slope* of the present-value profile. *Convexity*, on the other hand, can be regarded as a second-order measure of interest rate risk: it measures the *curvature* of the present-value profile.

A second-order Taylor's expansion of the present value equation (5.50) gives:

$$
\begin{aligned}
\frac{\Delta P_d}{P_d} &= \frac{1}{P_d} \cdot \frac{\Delta P_d}{\Delta rm} \cdot (\Delta rm) + \frac{1}{2 P_d} \cdot \frac{\Delta^2 P_d}{\Delta rm^2} \cdot (\Delta rm)^2 \\
&= -MD \cdot (\Delta rm) + \frac{C}{2} \cdot (\Delta rm)^2,
\end{aligned}
\tag{5.58}
$$

where:

$$
\begin{aligned}
MD &= \text{modified duration;} \\
C &= \text{convexity.}
\end{aligned}
$$

Convexity is the rate at which price variation to yield changes with respect to yield and, as is clear from (5.58), it is found by taking the second derivative of equation (5.50) with respect to $rm$ and dividing the result by $P_d$. Blake and Orszag (1996) show that this expression for convexity can be simplified as follows:

$$
\begin{aligned}
C &= \frac{1}{P_d} \cdot \frac{\Delta^2 P_d}{\Delta rm^2} \\
&= \frac{d}{P_d} \cdot \sum_{t=1}^{T} \frac{t(t+1)}{(1+rm)^{t+2}} + \frac{B}{P_d} \cdot \frac{T(T+1)}{(1+rm)^{T+2}} \\
&= -\frac{d}{P_d} \cdot \left\{ \frac{(T+1)(T+2)\left(\frac{1}{1+rm}\right)^{T+2}}{rm} + \frac{2 \cdot \left[ (T+2)\left(\frac{1}{1+rm}\right)^{T+2} - \left(\frac{1}{1+rm}\right) \right]}{rm^2} \right. \\
&\quad \left. + \frac{2 \cdot \left[ \left(\frac{1}{1+rm}\right)^{T+2} - \left(\frac{1}{1+rm}\right) \right]}{rm^3} \right\} + \frac{B}{P_d} \cdot \frac{T(T+1)}{(1+rm)^{T+2}}.
\end{aligned}
\tag{5.59}
$$

Convexity can also be approximated by the following expression for the numerical second-order derivative:

$$
C = 10^8 \left( \frac{\Delta P_d'}{P_d} + \frac{\Delta P_d''}{P_d} \right),
\tag{5.60}
$$

where:

$$
\begin{aligned}
\Delta P_d' &= \text{change in dirty bond price if yield increases by 1 basis point} \\
&\quad (0.01\%); \\
\Delta P_d'' &= \text{change in dirty bond price if yield decreases by 1 basis point} \\
&\quad (0.01\%).
\end{aligned}
$$

**Example 5.9 (Convexity)** *A 10 per cent annual coupon bond is trading at par with three years to maturity, so $P_d = B = £100$, $d = £10$, $rm = 10\%$, $T = 3$ years. Therefore, using the second line of (5.59), convexity is given by:*

$$C = \frac{10}{100} \cdot \left[ \frac{2}{(1.1)^3} + \frac{6}{(1.1)^4} + \frac{12}{(1.1)^5} \right] + \frac{100}{100} \cdot \frac{12}{(1.1)^5}$$

$$= 8.76.$$

*We get the same answer if we use the numerical approximation to the second-order derivative (5.60). We know that if the yield increases from 10.00 to 10.01 per cent, the price of the bond will fall by $\Delta P_d' = -0.0248641$, while if the yield falls to 9.99 per cent, the price of the bond will rise by $\Delta P_d'' = 0.0248729$. Therefore:*

$$C = 10^8 \left( \frac{-0.0248641}{100} + \frac{0.0248729}{100} \right)$$

$$= 8.76.$$

It can be shown that convexity increases with the square of maturity. It decreases with both coupon and yield. Index-linked bonds are more convex than conventional bonds.

That convexity is a second-order measure of interest rate risk is demonstrated in Figure 5.17. This shows the present-value profiles for two bonds A and B, trading at the same price and yield to

---

**Figure 5.17** Present-value profile and duration

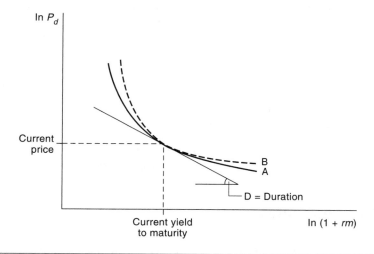

---

maturity, and having the same duration. Bond B however is more convex than bond A. B is clearly more desirable than A since B will out-perform A whatever happens to market interest rates. If yields rise, the price of B falls by less than the price of A, while if yields fall, the price of B rises by more than that of A. High convexity is therefore a desirable property for bonds to have.

When convexity is high, the first-order approximation for interest rate risk, (5.52) or (5.53), will become increasingly less accurate as the change in yield becomes large. This is clear from Figure 5.17. Duration is a linear approximation to the present-value profile. For small changes in yield, the linear approximation will be reasonably good. But for large jumps in yield, the linear approximation will become very poor if convexity is high. It will overestimate the risk (i.e. overestimate the price adjustment) when convexity is positive and underestimate risk and price adjustment when convexity is negative (which is the case, for example, with callable bonds near par). So for large jumps in yield, the quadratic approximation to the present-value profile given by (5.58) is preferred.

**Example 5.10 (Second-order interest rate risk)** *A 10 per cent annual coupon bond is trading at par with a modified duration of 2.49 and convexity of 8.76. If yields rise from 10 to 12 per cent, the price of the bond will fall by:*

$$
\begin{aligned}
\Delta P_d &= -MD \cdot (\Delta rm) \cdot P_d + \frac{C}{2} \cdot (\Delta rm)^2 \cdot P_d \\
&= -(2.49) \cdot (0.02) \cdot 100 + \frac{8.76}{2} \cdot (0.02)^2 \cdot 100 \\
&= -4.98 + 0.18 \\
&= -£4.80
\end{aligned}
$$

*to £95.20. The first-order approximation overestimates the fall by £0.18.*

### 5.8.3   Dispersion

The final measure of interest rate risk that we will consider is called *dispersion*. It measures the variance in the timing of the bond's cash flows around its duration date, using the cash flows' present values as weights:

$$
M^2 = \frac{d}{P_d} \cdot \sum_{t=1}^{T} \frac{t^2}{(1+rm)^t} + \frac{B}{P_d} \cdot \frac{T^2}{(1+rm)^T} - D^2, \tag{5.61}
$$

where $M^2 =$ dispersion. When cash flows are widely dispersed, $M^2$ will be a large number.

Duration, convexity and dispersion are all related as follows:

$$
C = \frac{M^2 + D^2 + D}{(1+rm)^2}. \tag{5.62}
$$

## 5.9   Floating rate notes

So far, we have considered bonds with coupons that are fixed in nominal terms (conventional bonds) or real terms (index-linked bonds). In this section we discuss *floating rate notes* (FRNs). FRNs are capital market securities, generally issued at par, in which the coupon payments are variable and depend on market rates of interest. The UK government has issued FRNs under the name of *variable-rate gilts*. With variable-rate gilts, interest was paid semi-annually at 0.5 per cent above the average weekly 3-month Treasury bill rate between the preceding ex-dividend dates.

With more general FRNs, the *reference interest rate* is one of the London interbank rates, either LIBOR (offered rate), LIBID (bid rate) or LIMID (mid rate) plus a *quoted margin*. The interest rate is fixed for a three- or six-month period and is reset using a set of reference banks at 11 am two business days before the new rate is implemented. For example, the reference interest rate might be six months LIBOR plus a quoted margin of 0.25 per cent. There might be four reference banks with the following LIBOR rates on the reference day:

|         | *Rate (%)* |
|---------|------------|
| Bank A  | 7.5        |
| Bank B  | 7.5625     |
| Bank C  | 7.5        |
| Bank D  | 7.5625     |
| *Average* | 7.53125  |

Adding the quoted margin to the average gives a coupon for the next six months of 7.78125 per cent.

Accrued interest is based on the actual number of days in a six-month period and the actual number of days in a year. This means that, in the above example, for every £100 nominal bond, interest accrues at the daily rate of £0.0213184.

Features that have been attached to FRNs include *floors* (the coupon cannot fall below a minimum rate), *caps* (the coupon cannot rise above a maximum rate), *droplocks* (if the coupon falls below a certain minimum the FRN converts to a fixed-rate instrument for the remainder of its life), *convertibility* (into a fixed-rate instrument at the option of the issuer or investor), *callability*, and a *sinking* or *purchase fund*. Some FRNs have been perpetual. *Perpetual* FRNs were popular with banks during 1986 because the regulatory authorities permitted them to be a source of bank primary capital; i.e., they ranked *pari passu* with equity capital. But the Brazilian debt crisis in December 1986 led to a collapse in the perpetual FRN market. There are also *mismatch* FRNs where there is a difference between the coupon payment period and the term of the reference interest rate, e.g. coupons paid every six months but based on the average of the one-month interest rates over the previous six months (this contrasts with a standard FRN which would use the six-month interest rate in the case of six-monthly coupons).

On the *coupon reset date*, the FRN should be priced exactly at par. At other times, the FRN should be priced very close to par because of the manner in which the coupon is reset. If market rates rise between coupon reset periods, the FRN will be trading slightly below par, while if market rates fall they will be trading slightly above. This makes FRNs very similar in behaviour (although not in maturity) to money market securities traded on a yield basis. European investors have traditionally taken this view of FRNs and have regarded them as close substitutes for money market securities. US investors, on the other hand, simply treat them as alternatives to conventional bonds. These two different approaches have led to two different ways of evaluating FRNs: the margin method and the yield to maturity spread method.

The *margin method* calculates the difference between the return on an FRN and that on an equivalent money market security. There are two variations on this: simple margin and discounted margin.

The simple margin method has the virtue of avoiding any forecasting of future interest rates and coupon values. *Simple margin* is defined as the average return on the FRN throughout its life compared with the reference rate of interest. It has two components: a *quoted margin* above (although sometimes below) the reference rate, and a capital gain or loss element which is calculated under the assumption that the difference between the current price of the FRN and the maturity value is spread evenly over the remaining life of the FRN. Thus we get:

$$\text{Simple margin} \quad = \quad \frac{B - P_d}{(100 \cdot T)} + QM, \tag{5.63}$$

where:

$$
\begin{aligned}
P_d &= P + AI = \text{dirty price of FRN;} \\
B &= \text{par value of FRN;} \\
T &= \text{number of years from settlement date to maturity of FRN;} \\
QM &= \text{quoted margin.}
\end{aligned}
$$

If this is positive, the FRN offers a higher yield than the corresponding money market security.

**Example 5.11 (Simple margin)** *An FRN with a par value of £100, a quoted margin of 0.25 per cent over six-month LIBOR, is currently trading with a clean price of £99. At the previous setting, LIBOR was 7.78125 per cent. There are 10 days of accrued interest, 170 days until the next coupon payment and 10 years from the next coupon payment to maturity. This means that:*

$$
\begin{aligned}
P_d &= 99 + \frac{10}{365} \cdot 7.78125 \\[2mm]
&= £99.213,
\end{aligned}
$$

*and*

$$
\begin{aligned}
T &= 10 + \frac{170}{365} \\[2mm]
&= 10.466.
\end{aligned}
$$

*Therefore:*

$$
\begin{aligned}
\text{Simple margin} &= \frac{100 - 99.213}{100 \cdot 10.466} + 0.0025 \\[2mm]
&= 0.00325 \quad (0.325\%).
\end{aligned}
$$

Sometimes the simple margin formula is adjusted to take account of any change in the reference interest rate since the last coupon reset date. This is done by defining an adjusted price, either:

$$AP_d = P_d + (rr + QM) \cdot \frac{N_{sc}}{365} \cdot 100 - \frac{d}{2} \cdot 100, \tag{5.64}$$

or:

$$AP_d = P_d + (rr + QM) \cdot \frac{N_{sc}}{365} \cdot P_d - \frac{d}{2} \cdot 100, \tag{5.65}$$

where:

$$
\begin{aligned}
AP_d \quad &= \quad \text{adjusted dirty price of FRN;} \\
rr \quad &= \quad \text{current value of reference interest rate (e.g. LIBOR);} \\
d/2 \quad &= \quad \text{next coupon payment (i.e. } d = \text{reference interest rate on last} \\
& \qquad \text{coupon reset date } plus \; QM); \\
N_{sc} \quad &= \quad \text{number of days between settlement and next coupon pay-} \\
& \qquad \text{ment date.}
\end{aligned}
$$

Equation (5.64) ignores the current yield effect: all payments are assumed to be received on the basis of par, and this understates the value of the coupon for FRNs trading below par and overstates the value when they are trading above par. Equation (5.65) takes the current yield effect into account. The adjusted price $AP_d$ replaces the current price $P_d$ in (5.63) to give an *adjusted simple margin*.

The simple margin method has the disadvantage of amortizing the discount or premium on the FRN in a straight line over the remaining life of the bond rather than at a constantly compounded rate. The discounted margin method uses the latter approach. The distinction between simple margin and discounted margin is precisely the same as that between simple yield to maturity and yield to maturity (cf. (5.6) and (5.7)). However, the discounted margin method has the disadvantage of needing a forecast of the reference interest rate over the remaining life of the bond.

The *discounted margin* (DM) is the solution to the following equation:

$$
P_d \quad = \quad \left[ \frac{1}{\left(1 + \frac{rr+DM}{2}\right)^{N_{tc}/182.5}} \right] \cdot \left\{ \frac{d}{2} + \sum_{t=1}^{S-1} \frac{(rr^* + QM) \cdot \frac{100}{2}}{\left(1 + \frac{rr^*+DM}{2}\right)^t} + \frac{B}{\left(1 + \frac{rr^*+DM}{2}\right)^{S-1}} \right\}, \tag{5.66}
$$

where:

$$
\begin{aligned}
DM \quad &= \quad \text{discounted margin;} \\
rr \quad &= \quad \text{current value of reference interest rate;} \\
rr^* \quad &= \quad \text{assumed (or forecast) value of reference interest rate over} \\
& \qquad \text{remaining life of bond;} \\
QM \quad &= \quad \text{quoted margin;} \\
d/2 \quad &= \quad \text{next coupon payment (i.e. } d = \text{reference interest rate on last} \\
& \qquad \text{coupon reset date } plus \; QM); \\
N_{tc} \quad &= \quad \text{number of days between current date and next coupon pay-} \\
& \qquad \text{ment date;} \\
S \quad &= \quad \text{number of coupon payments before redemption.}
\end{aligned}
$$

For perpetual FRNs, (5.66) becomes:

$$
P_d \quad = \quad \left[ \frac{1}{\left(1 + \frac{rr+DM}{2}\right)^{N_{tc}/182.5}} \right] \cdot \left[ \frac{d}{2} + \frac{(rr^* + DM) \cdot 100}{rr + DM} \right], \tag{5.67}
$$

and, on a coupon payment date:

$$
\begin{aligned}
DM \quad &= \quad \frac{rr^* + QM}{P} \cdot 100 - rr^* \tag{5.68} \\
&= \quad QM,
\end{aligned}
$$

if, as is expected on a coupon payment date, $P = 100$.

The *yield to maturity spread method* of evaluating FRNs is designed to allow direct comparison between FRNs and fixed-rate bonds. The yield to maturity on the FRN ($rmf$) is calculated using (5.66) with both ($rr + DM$) and ($rr^* + DM$) replaced with $rmf$. The yield to maturity on a reference bond ($rmb$) is calculated using (5.7). The *yield to maturity spread* is defined as:

$$\text{Yield to maturity spread} \quad = \quad rmf - rmb. \tag{5.69}$$

If this is positive, the FRN offers a higher yield than the reference bond.

There are also *reverse FRNs* where the coupon rises if the reference interest rate falls, e.g., the coupon might be determined as '12 per cent minus LIBOR'. A company might issue such an FRN if it believed that short term interest rates were going to rise over the life of the FRN.

It is possible for an FRN to have a *negative* duration measure. To illustrate, consider the case of a one-year FRN where the reference interest rate is LIBOR and the coupon is LIBOR minus 5%. In this case the price of the FRN is given by:

$$P_d \quad = \quad \frac{100(rr - 0.05) + 100}{1 + rr}. \tag{5.70}$$

Differentiating (5.70) with respect to $rr$ gives:

$$\frac{\Delta P_d}{\Delta rr} \quad = \quad \frac{100(1 + rr) - [100(rr - 0.05) + 100]}{(1 + rr)^2}. \tag{5.71}$$

Recognizing that $\Delta P_d / \Delta(1 + rr) = \Delta P_d / \Delta rr$, we can use (5.52) to get a measure of duration for this FRN:

$$
\begin{aligned}
D \quad &= \quad \frac{-\Delta P_d / P_d}{\Delta(1 + rr)/(1 + rr)} \\
&= \quad \frac{-0.05}{1 + (rr - 0.05)},
\end{aligned}
$$

which is negative. In other words, an increase in interest rates increases the price of this FRN. For example, if LIBOR is 5 per cent, then a 10 per cent increase in LIBOR to 5.5 per cent will raise the price of the FRN from £95.24 to £95.26 using (5.54) and (5.55).

## 5.10   Recent innovations: the gilt repurchase market

A *sale and repurchase agreement* (more commonly known as a *repurchase agreement* or just as a *repo*) is a legally binding agreement between two counterparties whereby one counterparty (known as the *repo seller, repoer, security seller* or *cash taker*) sells a security to the other counterparty (known as the *repo buyer, security buyer* or *cash giver*) in return for cash, while simultaneously agreeing to repurchase an equivalent security from the other counterparty at an agreed repurchase price on an agreed future termination date. From the viewpoint of the first counterparty, the transaction is a *repo*, i.e. the selling (or 'repoing out') of the security in exchange for cash. From the viewpoint of the second counterparty, the transaction is known as a *reverse repo*, i.e. the borrowing (or 'reversing in') of the security in exchange for cash. When there is a third-party custodian bank taking responsibility for monitoring all movements of cash and securities, the repo is known as a *tri-party repo*.

The agreed repurchase price equals the original dirty price *plus* an amount which reflects the cost of borrowing secured funds at the *repo rate*. Most repos are marked to market through the exchange of both an initial margin payment (called a *haircut*) and variation margin payments to ensure that the market value of the purchased securities plus the aggregate net margin payments always equals the agreed repurchase price.

The UK gilt repurchase market began in January 1996. Its introduction ended a number of privileges held by certain participants in the UK gilts market up to that time. Prior to 1996, only gilt-edged market makers (GEMMs) and discount houses could short gilts in the cash market; gilt owners could only lend them via stock exchange money brokers (SEMBs); and GEMMs could borrow only from SEMBs to fund their long positions. The government wished to end these restrictive practices, to improve the liquidity of the gilts market, and to increase the demand to hold gilts from international investors. Under the new arrangements: investors can borrow or lend gilts either directly or via an intermediary; they can use repos to fund gilt purchases, to earn additional income from existing gilt holdings or to invest surplus funds on a secured basis at about LIMEAN (London inter-bank mean rate) for the same term; and the tax treatment of gilts in respect of income and capital gains, and in respect of the domicile of the investor (i.e. whether a domestic or overseas resident) has been harmonized.

There is a standardized contract for all UK gilt repos called the *Gilt Repo Legal Agreement* which is based on the *Global Master Repurchase Agreement* (GMRA) designed by the US Public Securities Association (PSA) and the International Securities Markets Association (ISMA). The contract provides for the following: absolute transfer of title of the gilts sold and subsequently repurchased; daily marking-to-market of positions by means of initial margin and variation margin payments; substitution between forms of collateral; events of default and the consequential rights and obligations of the counterparties; and close out netting provisions. The *close out netting provisions* come into effect when there is by one of the counterparties: failure to pay on time the purchase price, any required margin or any *manufactured dividends* (i.e. the dividends payable by the counterparty who has shorted the gilt to the counterparty lending the gilt; the official dividends from the government will be paid to the investor who has purchased the gilt); an act of insolvency; false representation; and failure to perform obligations under the agreement. Except in the case of insolvency (where default is automatic), the non-defaulting counterparty has the discretion of deciding whether any of these events constitute an event of default leading to the termination of the contract, in which case a *default notice* must be served. The effect of the close out netting provisions is to pool all trades under the agreement into a single trade, with a net balance payable on the following business day by the counterparty owing the larger amount.

There is also a *gilt repo code of best practice*. This ensures that prior to trading: the trading arrangements are effective in terms of record keeping, credit control systems, and systems to account for margin payments and tax; counterparties have agreed documentation; and credit assessment of counterparties has taken place. When trading does take place, the code of practice recommends that: the transactions take place under the terms of the Gilt Repo Legal Agreement; the transactions are marked to market on a daily basis; and any collateral should be held by an independent third party.

The margin payments made under a repo transaction must be such that the value of the collateral pledged must at least equal the value of the obligations that it collateralizes. The margin payments can be in the form of cash or securities at the option of the receiving counterparty; if securities are delivered, they must have a maturity date matching that of the repo. The initial margin is expressed in the form of a *margin ratio*, defined as the ratio of the market price of securities pledged as collateral to the purchase price. For example, if the repoer of a gilt receives initial margin of 3 per cent, this implies a margin ratio of 1.03 (or 103%) from the repoer's viewpoint and a margin ratio of 0.971 (or 97.1%, i.e. 1/1.03) from the cash provider's viewpoint. The repoer receives £103 in cash for every £100 of bonds repoed. The initial margin is included in the initial purchase price in the form of a *haircut*, i.e. as a premium over the market value of the gilts being repoed. In this example, the security seller received the initial margin, but depending on the relative bargaining strengths of the counterparties, it is possible for the initial margin to go to the cash given, paid in the form of a discount on the market value of the gilts being repoed.

Variation margin is also payable on a portfolio basis, i.e. after netting all trades between counterparties. When the value of purchased securities (including any initial margin) moves outside a specified band in relation to the repurchase price, a variation margin payment must be made and if made in the form of a gilt, must be of the same type as the gilt underlying the transaction. For example, if bonds valued at £100 fall in price to £98, the repoer must make a variation margin payment of £2 to the cash giver.

There are three types of collateral that can be used in repos:

1 *General collateral* (GC). General collateral is characterized by having no 'special' value, i.e. there are no unusual demand conditions attached to it at the time it is being used. It is treated as being a substitute for a secured money market deposit. The quotes on GC are related to inter-bank rates of the same term. However, not all gilts are acceptable as GC, e.g. those with ex-dividend dates, or payment dates on partly-paid gilts, or conversion options on convertibles exercisable during the term of the repo.

2 *Specials*. A gilt becomes *special* if, for some reason, demand is high, say, because GEMMs are short of it and are facing difficulties in acquiring sufficient amounts to fulfil their obligations. In this case, the gilt is considered to be a substitute for securities lending and is treated as a capital market instrument.

3 *Delivery by value* (DBV). This is a transaction which allows a GSO (Gilts Settlements Office) member to borrow or lend cash overnight against gilt collateral. At 3.00pm, the GSO delivers gilts valued at GSO reference prices (which equal GEMMA (Gilt-Edged Market Makers Association) closing prices to two rather than five decimal points) and the same securities are returned the next business day at 9.30am.

As stated above, the rate of interest on a repurchase agreement is known as the *repo rate*. A repo quote of 7.50 - 7.40 means a bid (from a repo buyer) to buy collateral (gilts) in exchange for cash at a rate of 7.50 per cent per year (i.e. cash is given (lent) at 7.50 per cent) and an offer (from a repo seller) to sell collateral in exchange for cash at a rate of 7.40 per cent per year (i.e. cash is taken (borrowed) at 7.40 per cent). Money market conventions are used: the day count is actual/365 and there is no compounding. Note that the repo bid rate is higher than the repo offer rate, because the rate refers to the collateral rather than to cash (the corresponding repo bid price for the collateral is therefore lower than the corresponding repo offer price as expected).

Most gilts trade at the *general collateral* (GC) *repo rate* which means that there is no unusual demand to borrow these bonds. The level of the GC repo rate depends on the general level of demand by GEMMS to fund their long positions: an increase in the demand to borrow funds will tend to increase the GC repo rate. However, if a gilt is *trading on special* (or in the *specials market*), this means that the demand from GEMMs to acquire it is so great that the gilt owner can borrow cash via the repo market at a *special repo rate* which is well below the GC repo rate. The higher the demand for the gilt, the lower the special repo rate, i.e. the lower the rate at which the gilt seller is prepared to pay to borrow funds.

Gilt repos are settled by book entry transfer at the GSO. The settlement procedure used is known as *delivery versus payment* (DVP) which guarantees the simultaneous transfer of gilts and cash. Most repos are short term: about 40 per cent are for less than a week (most of which are *overnight repos* and these are frequently rolled over from one day to the next) and 85 per cent are for less than 90 days (repos that are not overnight repos are known as *term repos*). However there is increasing interest in repos with longer terms related to the expiry dates on the LIFFE long gilt futures contract. *Open repos* are transacted for an open-ended period but can be terminated by either counterparty at any time, subject to an agreed notice period.

The accounting convention for UK repos is the Financial Reporting Standard (FRS) 5, 'Reporting the Substance of Transactions' (April 1994). This treats the repo as a *financing mechanism* rather than an outright sale. As a consequence, there is *continued recognition* of the gilt on the balance sheet of the original owner, on the grounds that not all the risks and rewards associated with beneficial ownership of the asset are transferred and the market value of the gilt is readily determined. From the buyer's point of view: the gilts are not recorded on the balance sheet and any change in their market value does not lead to a profit or loss; and the cash remains an asset which is recorded on the balance sheet as 'securities purchased under agreement to resell' with interest accruing over the term of the agreement. From the seller's point of view: the gilts remain on the balance sheet as 'securities sold under repo'; the cash is recorded as a 'liability' and the interest payable on the cash is treated as a charge on an accruals basis. The most important feature of a repo is the obligation of the original owner to reacquire the gilt at the agreed repurchase price. The original owner therefore faces all the risks and rewards on the gilt. Whatever happens to the market price of the gilt during the life of the repo, the original owner (the repo seller) is obliged to pay the repurchase price to reacquire the gilt. The repurchase price equals the original purchase price *plus* the repo rate *plus* any coupon (not the market price of the bond at the time of repurchase).

The tax treatment of gilts changed in April 1996 following the introduction of the gilt repo market. The new rules apply to UK and overseas companies, but not to individuals, partnerships, overseas mutual funds and unauthorized unit trusts. Corporate holders of gilts can receive gross dividend payments on their gilts (i.e. without deduction of income tax or withholding tax), so long as the gilts are held in a Star account at the GSO. For UK corporate investors, both the income and capital gains are taxed on a quarterly basis, but with relief on capital losses. For individuals, partnerships and trusts, the coupon payments are taxed at source, with no tax on capital gains and no relief on capital losses. In respect of repurchase agreements, the buyer can manufacture gross dividend payments to reimburse the seller when the repo covers a coupon payment date. The rate of return on the cash side of the repo is taxable as income.

There are three main types of repo: the classic, the sell/buy-back and securities lending. The *classic* (or *US-style*) *repo* comprises two-thirds of the market in repos. It has the following structure. The sale and subsequent repurchase of the security are treated as two components of the same transaction. During the term of the transaction, full legal title is transferred from the seller to the buyer. However, the seller retains the right to receive the coupon on the official coupon payment date; the coupon is a manufactured dividend supplied by the buyer. On the termination date of the agreement, the seller is obliged to buy back the equivalent security (namely certificates with different serial numbers of the same underlying issue).

We can illustrate the classic repo as follows. Suppose the owner of Treasury 9 per cent 2012 sells £10m nominal for one month (30 days) at a repo rate of 7.50%. Suppose that the clean price is £105.25

and that there is 146 days of accrued interest totalling £3.60, so that the dirty price is £108.85. The value of the gilts sold is therefore £10,885,000.00. The repurchase price one month later is:

$$£10,885,000 \left[1 + 0.075 \left(\frac{30}{365}\right)\right] \quad = \quad £10,952,099.32,$$

and the repo interest amount is:

$$£10,952,099.32 - £10,885,000.00 \quad = \quad £67,099.32.$$

There is no allowance for accrued interest during the 30 day period.

The *sell/buy-back* is an agreement between two counterparties to sell a security at its spot price with a second separate agreement to repurchase it on a future date at a forward price based on an agreed repo rate. The return on the cash lent (i.e. the implied repo rate) is paid not as interest, but in the form of a price differential between the sale and repurchase components of the agreement. Any official coupon paid during the term goes to the buyer, but the amount of the coupon will be incorporated into the forward price; accrued interest is also included in the forward price. A sell/buy-back therefore differs from a classic repo because the two components of the repo are regarded as separate transactions. As a consequence, it is slightly riskier than a classic repo since there is no marking to market of collateral between the sale and repurchase dates. Using the same example as above, the sale would take place at £10,885,000.00 and the buy-back would take place at £10,952,099.32 and this would imply a repo rate of:

$$\frac{£10,952,099.32 - £10,885,000.00}{£10,885,000.00} \cdot \frac{365}{30} \quad = \quad 7.50\%.$$

The buy-back took place at a forward price of £109.52 with 176 days of accrued interest of £4.34 and repo interest of £0.67, implying a clean price of £104.51.

The sell/buy-back is easy to arrange, since there is no formal documentation. However, it is likely to become less popular as a consequence of the introduction of the EU Capital Adequacy Directive in 1996. Prior to 1996, banks and securities houses had to have capital to support their repo activities equal to the full value of the reverse repos in their repo book. Under CAD, so long as formal documentation is used covering both components of the repo, capital is required only to cover the cash margin. So for repos that are also marked to market on a daily basis (i.e. for classic repos) the counterparty risk is negligible and negligible capital needs to be applied to cover such repos. Since sell/buy-backs are neither documented formally nor marked to market, the relatively high capital requirements needed to use sell/buy-backs is likely to diminish interest in using them.

*Securities lending* involves the temporary exchange of two securities (one of which is generally a bond) with the same nominal value. The transaction takes place under a stock lending agreement, which in the UK is known as the *Gilt-Edged Stock Lending Agreement*. The bond lender is entitled to receive the accruing coupon interest. The transaction is recorded on the balance sheet as a 'contingent liability' and so does not alter the balance sheet. The fee on the agreement is paid monthly or as a single lump sum at the end of the agreement. To illustrate, we can consider the case of the owner of Treasury 9% 2012 lending £10m nominal of it for one month (30 days) for a fee of 60 basis points in exchange for £10m nominal of Treasury 8% 2021 as collateral. At the end of 30 days, the two bonds are re-exchanged and the original owner of the Treasury 9% 2012 gilt receives a stock lending fee of:

$$£10,000,000 \cdot 0.006 \cdot \frac{30}{365} \quad = \quad £4,931.51.$$

Having described the main types of repo, we can now consider how they are used in practice. The original purpose of repos was to reduce borrowing costs. Before the introduction of repos, institutions in need of funds could either borrow on an unsecured basis from a bank at up to 20bp above LIBOR or issue a commercial bill or commercial paper. The introduction of a repo market allowed such institutions to borrow funds using their gilt holdings as collateral at only 5bp above LIBOR. So funding costs could be reduced without any effect on the balance sheet.

Repos can also be used to finance long positions in gilts without the need to borrow funds. For example, an investor can purchase a gilt and immediately repo it out against cash at a repo rate typically between LIMEAN and LIBOR. The cash is used to pay for the gilt.

Repos can be used to establish short positions in gilts. This is done if an investor believes gilt prices are about to decline. Suppose the investor believes that the Treasury 9% 2012 is likely to fall in value over the next month (30 days). To take advantage of this anticipated price fall, the investor can establish a short position in the gilt as follows: he borrows (reverses in) the gilt in the repo market in exchange for lending cash to the original gilt owner at the repo rate; he sells the gilt in the cash market and places the proceeds on deposit for one month; and in one month's time when the repo agreement matures, he buys back the gilt in the cash market and hands it over to the original owner in return for the principal and interest on the cash loan. The short seller makes a profit if the repurchase price after one month is below the original sale price.

For example, suppose that £10m nominal of Treasury 9% 2012 is borrowed against cash for one month in the repo market at a repo rate of 7.50%. The gilt which has a dirty price of £108.85 is then sold and this raises £10,885,000.00. This sum is placed on deposit for one month at LIBID, 7.40%, say (LIBID is generally below the GC repo rate which typically lies between LIMEAN and LIBOR). After 30 days the deposit is worth:

$$£10,885,000\left[1+0.074\left(\frac{30}{365}\right)\right] \; = \; £10,951,204.66,$$

implying an interest amount of:

$$£10,951,204.66 - £10,885,000.00 \; = \; £66,204.66.$$

Suppose, also after 30 days, the dirty price of the bond has fallen to £107.21 and £10 million nominal is repurchased at a cost of £10,721,000.00. These bonds are immediately returned to the original owner who pays a repurchase price under the repo agreement of:

$$£10,885,000\left[1+0.075\left(\frac{30}{365}\right)\right] \; = \; £10,952,099.32,$$

giving the short seller a profit of:

$$£10,952,099.32 - £10,721,000.00 \; = \; £231,099.32.$$

For an initial cash investment of £10,885,000.00, the short seller made £231,099.32 from the sale and repurchase of the bond *plus* £66,204.55 from placing the proceeds of the short sale on deposit for one month. This gives a total return on the short sale of:

$$\frac{231,099.32 + 66,204.66}{10,885,000.00} \; = \; 2.73\%$$

over one month or 33.23% per annum.

Another use of repos is to lend specials. Specials are in such high demand that the repo rate (i.e. the borrowing rate on cash) is below LIBID (i.e. the deposit rate on cash). For example, if the one-month offered repo rate on a special is 7.25% while one-month LIBID is 7.75%, then the owner of the special can repo it out against cash at 7.25% and place the proceeds on deposit at 7.75%, earning a pure yield pickup of 50bp.

## Selected references

Allen, S. and Kleinstein, A. (1991), *Valuing Fixed-Income Investments and Derivative Securities*, New York Institute of Finance, New York.

Belchamber, C. (1988), *The UK Government Bond Market*, Credit Suisse First Boston, London. (Chapters on 'Analysis — Conventional Gilts'; 'Analysis — Index Linked Gilts'.)

Bierwag, G.O. (1987), *Duration Analysis*, Ballinger, Cambridge, Mass.

Blake, D. and Orszag, J.M. (1996), 'A Closed-form Formula for Calculating Bond Convexity', *Journal of Fixed Income*, 6, 88–91.

*British Government Securities* (1993), Bank of England, London.

Chua, J. (1984), 'A Closed-form Formula for Calculating Bond Duration', *Financial Analysts Journal*, 40, 76–78.

Dattatreya, R. (ed.)(1991), *Fixed Income Analytics*, McGraw Hill, London.

Douglas, L.G. (1988), *Yield Curve Analysis*, New York Institute of Finance, New York.

European Bond Commission (1989), *The European Bond Markets*, Probus, Chicago.

Fabozzi, F. (1988), *Fixed Income Mathematics*, Probus, Chicago.

Fabozzi, F. (ed.)(1991), *Handbook of Fixed Income Securities*, Business One Irwin, Homewood, Ill.

Fabozzi, F. (1997), *Fixed Income Securities*, FJF Publishing, New Hope, Penn.

Fabozzi, F.J. and Fabozzi, T.D. (1989), *Bond Markets, Analysis and Strategies*, Prentice Hall, Englewood Cliffs, NJ.

Fage, P. (1986), *Yield Calculations*, Credit Suisse First Boston, London. (Chapters 4 and 5.)

Fisher, I. (1930), *Theory of Interest*, Macmillan, New York.

Francis, J.C. (1991), *Investments*, McGraw-Hill, Singapore. (Chapters 12, 13 and 14.)

Frost, A.J. and Hager, D.P. (1990), *Debt Securities*, Heinemann, Oxford.

Gallant, P. (1988), *The Eurobond Market*, Woodhead-Faulkner, Cambridge.

Macaulay, F.R. (1938), *Some Theoretical Problems Suggested by the Movement of Interest Rates, Bond Yields and Stock Prices in the US since 1856*, National Bureau of Economic Research, New York.

Mason, R. (1986), *Innovations in the Structure of International Securities*, Credit Suisse First Boston, London.

Phillips, P. (1987), *Inside the New Gilt-Edged Market*, Woodhead-Faulkner, Cambridge.

Phillips, P. (1996), *Merrill Lynch Guide to the Gilt-Edged and Sterling Bond Markets*, Book Guild, Sussex.

Pitman, T. and Lund, T. (1990), 'Responding to Event Risk', *Relative Value and Credit*, Credit Suisse First Boston, London, January, 43–47.

Rutterford, J. (1993), *Introduction to Stock Exchange Investment*, Macmillan, London. (Chapters 3 and 4.)

Societe Generale Gilts (1996), *The Gilt Repo Market*, Societe Generale Gilts Ltd, London.

Sharpe, W.F., Alexander, G. and Bailey, J. (1995), *Investments*, Prentice-Hall, Englewood Cliffs, NJ. (Chapters 14 and 15.)

## Exercises

1  A UK government bond with a coupon of 7.5 per cent will be redeemed at par on 15 May 1999. What is the price of the bond on 16 May 1990 if the yield to maturity is 9 per cent?

2  What is the dirty price of a bond? How is it calculated?

3  Consider a UK government bond with a 9.25 per cent coupon. The bond is trading at £95.50 per £100 nominal. How much will an investor have to pay for the bond if he buys it:

    a)    3 days following the *ex dividend* date?

    b)    7 days following the *ex dividend* date?

    c)    100 days following the *ex dividend* date?

4  A bond with a coupon of 12 per cent and three years to maturity is trading at £102.25. What is:

    a)    the current yield?

    b)    the simple yield to maturity?

5  If the semi-annual yield to maturity on a bond is 12.38 per cent, what is:

    a)    the equivalent annual yield to maturity?

    b)    the equivalent quarterly yield to maturity?

6  What are the main disadvantages of the yield to maturity as a measure of the return from holding a bond?

7  The yield on a UK government bond is 11.5 per cent while the yield on a eurobond is 11.75 per cent. Which bond is offering the better return?

8 What is the 'break-even inflation rate'? How is it used in bond markets?

9 You are given the following information about the retail price index in the UK:

|  | 1998 | 1999 |
|---|---|---|
| January | 131.2 | 139.9 |
| February | 131.9 | 141.3 |
| March | 132.5 | 141.9 |
| April | 133.0 | 143.1 |
| May | 134.6 | 144.7 |
| June | 135.1 | 146.1 |
| July | 135.5 | 147.8 |
| August | 136.0 | 150.1 |
| September | 136.9 | 153.2 |
| October | 137.8 | 155.6 |
| November | 138.0 | 158.1 |
| December | 138.9 | 159.6 |

If an index-linked bond with a coupon of 2.5 per cent was issued on 15 October 1998, calculate the first three coupon payments.

10 The yield to maturity on a conventional gilt is 9.78 per cent and the real yield on an index-linked gilt is 2.5 per cent. What is the break-even inflation rate? If the expected rate of inflation is 10 per cent, which gilt is the better buy?

11 What is the par yield curve? How might the par yield curve for UK government bonds be useful to an investment bank seeking a eurobond mandate?

12 a)  You are given the following par yields:

| Term (years) | 1 | 2 | 3 |
|---|---|---|---|
| Par yield (%) | 9 | 9.125 | 9.25 |

Calculate the corresponding spot yields and forward yields.

Comment on the relationship between the three yield curves.

b)  To what purpose are par yields, spot yields and forward yields put?

13 Using the following information about three government bonds with the same maturity date (in 10 years' time), calculate the spot yield for year 10 (assuming annual coupon payments):

| Bond | Price (£) | Coupon (%) |
|---|---|---|
| A | 62.875 | 5 |
| B | 71.5625 | 7 |
| C | 101.50 | 12 |

14  You are given the following set of government bond prices, where the bonds pay coupons annually:

| *Term (years)* | 1 | 2 | 3 |
|---|---|---|---|
| *Coupon (%)* | 9 | 9.5 | 9.75 |
| *Price* | 99.25 | 100.125 | 99.0625 |

Calculate the issue price of a new two-year bond with a 10 per cent coupon.

15  A bond is priced at £80 per £100 nominal. It has a duration of 12 years and the current yield to maturity is 10 per cent. By how much will the price change if the yield to maturity falls to 9.5 per cent?

16  Discuss the main theories explaining the shape of the yield curve.

17  What is 'duration'? Why is it a measure of interest rate risk?

18  Prove that the duration of a perpetual bond is equal to one *plus* the inverse of the current yield on the bond.

19  What does the convexity of a bond measure?

20  It is 12 April 1990. A 12 per cent annual coupon bond will mature on 11 April 2000. The bond is currently priced at £98.50 per £100 nominal with a yield to maturity of 12.50 per cent. What is the duration of the bond?

21  What is the rolling yield on a bond?

22  What are the differences between a sterling bond and a eurosterling bond?

23  a)  Convert a 10 per cent yield on a eurobond to a euro-money market basis.

    b)  Convert a 10 per cent yield on a euro-money market instrument to a eurobond basis.

24  Suppose that Treasury 10 per cent 2010 is trading on special in the repo market with a repo rate of 8.30 for a 14 day term. The bond is trading at a clean price of £104.25 and there is 77 days of accrued interest. One month LIBID is 8.625 per cent. The owner of £50 million nominal repos the bond for two weeks and invests the proceeds at 12.5 basis points below LIBID. What is the net cash profit on the repo?

25  Suppose that Treasury 8 per cent 2006 is trading at a clean price of £102.9375 with 122 days of accrued interest. An investor with £100m nominal of this bond wishes to borrow US dollars for one month (31 days) against his holding of the bond and is offered a USD repo rate of 5.70%. What is the cost of the repo in US dollars if the exchange rate is $1.55 per £?

26  An investor with £100m in cash could invest this sum with a bank offering a deposit rate for 31 days of 4.875 per cent. However, the investor is concerned about the credit risk of the bank. Instead he could take out a collateralized cash investment by means of a reverse repo as follows. A repo bank offers £100m nominal of Treasury 4.75 per cent in exchange for £100m cash for 31 days at a repo rate of 4.75%. The bond has 50 days of accrued interest. Calculate:

    a)  the clean price of the bond if £100m nominal exactly collateralizes the cash investment,

    b)  the cash return to the investor on the reverse repo at the end of 31 days, and

    c)  the interest forgone by not placing the funds in the bank deposit.

27 A trader plans to sell short £40m nominal of Treasury 9 per cent 2012. The bond has a clean price of £102.9375 and there are 33 days of accrued interest. The trader can borrow funds at 12 per cent and lend funds at 6 per cent. The bond is trading on special in the repo market with a repo rate of 4 per cent. Suppose that the trader short sells the bond, covering his position by means of an open reverse repo with a pension fund. Suppose that the position is closed after 60 days with the bond trading at a clean price of £100.375. Calculate:

a)   the cost to the trader of covering his short position, and

b)   the net profit or loss to the trader.

# Chapter 6

# Shares

In comparison with bonds, the evaluation of shares is something of a nightmare. With bonds, the coupon payments are contractual and known with certainty (or at least, the promised payments on fixed-interest bonds are), the maturity date is known with certainty (at least for bonds with a fixed maturity date), the maturity value is known with certainty, and the appropriate discount rate is relatively easy to calculate, given the ease of comparability with similar bonds. All this renders the valuation and analysis of bonds relatively easy. In contrast, the valuation and analysis of shares is much more complicated. This is because: (1) the future earnings of and dividend payments on shares are unknown and have to be forecast; (2) there is no maturity date and hence no maturity value; and (3) shares are the riskiest investments to hold, having the *residual* claim on the firm's assets and the net income generated by these assets, so that the appropriate discount rate is very difficult to calculate. If bond analysis is a science, then share analysis is very much an art.

The process of valuing shares is known as *investment analysis* in the UK, while in the USA it is known as *financial analysis* or *securities analysis*. The most common valuation method used by investment analysts is called *fundamental analysis*. This approach examines the fundamental behaviour of the firm and also the economy in which the firm operates. It makes a detailed analysis of the firm's earnings and dividend policy, beginning with an analysis of the firm's financial structure.

In this chapter we start by examining the types of share issued by a firm. We then examine in detail the firm's financial structure, and look at two methods of valuing shares, one based on expected dividends and the other on expected earnings. We go on to examine the firm's dividend policy and how this affects the value of shares. The ability of the firm to pay dividends will depend on its ability to generate earnings, so we next analyze the sources of the firm's earnings growth. Finally we examine the value of the firm as a whole. Most firms finance their assets using leverage, i.e. a combination of share and bond finance. So the value of the firm depends not only on the value of the shares and the bonds issued by the firm, but may also depend on the combination of shares and bonds, i.e. on the degree of leverage.

## 6.1 Types of share in the firm

There are several types of share that can be issued by the firm as specified in the *memorandum* and *articles of association*. The most important type is *ordinary shares* (also called *common stock* or *equity*). Ordinary shareholders have voting privileges, the right to receive dividends, and subscription privileges in the event of new shares being issued. When a firm is first established, a certain number of shares will be *authorized*. They will have a *par value*, which in the UK is typically 10p, 25p, 50p or £1. Some or all of the authorized shares will be issued to shareholders (and are called *issued shares* or *called-up shares*), with an issue price which can be at or exceed the par value but cannot be less than the par value.

Any shares that are authorized but not issued are called *unissued shares*. All the issued shares will remain *outstanding*, unless they are repurchased by the firm. Firms in the UK have been able to repurchase their shares since the 1981 Companies Act, provided that shareholders are willing to sell and that the firm is left with some issue of share capital following the repurchase. If a firm repurchases its own shares these shares are cancelled. Thus a firm could have the following equity structure:

|  | *Number* | *£* |
|---|---|---|
| Issued and outstanding shares | | |
|    (or called-up capital) of 25p each | 800,000 | 200,000 |
| Unissued shares | 200,000 | 50,000 |
| Total authorized shares | 1,000,000 | 250,000 |

The par value of a share has no real significance, except in the event of insolvency. (The par value represents the nominal claim of shareholders if insolvency occurs.) What is important, however, is the *market value* of the share, and it is the determination of the fair market price of the share that occupies most of this chapter.

The other important class of shares is *preferred shares* (or *preference shares*). These have many of the characteristics of bonds, since the dividend payment is fixed (as opposed to ordinary shares where the dividend is variable) and valuation is normally based on a yield calculation. However for company law and for tax purposes, preference shares are regarded as share capital. Preferred shares do not guarantee the dividend payment, and a preferred dividend need not be paid if the firm's earnings are insufficient to fund it. If this situation arises, however, preferred shareholders do not have the right to have the firm declared insolvent, unlike bondholders. It is this fact that makes preference shareholders legal owners of the firm and explains why preference shares are included with ordinary shares in the analysis of the firm: if preferred shareholders do not receive dividends, then neither will ordinary shareholders.

There are several types of preferred shares. With *cumulative preferred shares*, all unpaid dividend payments cumulate and are paid when earnings are sufficient, unlike standard preferred shares, where a dividend is lost if it is not paid in any year. *Participating preferred shareholders* have the right to participate in a further share of the profits in addition to their fixed rate of dividend. For example, a 6% participating preference share may also entitle the shareholder to an additional dividend of up to, say, 4% on an equal basis with the ordinary shareholders but with an overall maximum, for the participating preference shareholder, of 10%. Certain preference shares may also give the right to have the shares converted to ordinary shares if the dividend is passed for a given number of years. There are also *redeemable preferred*, *convertible preferred* and *callable preferred* shares. The most common form of preferred share is a *cumulative, non-participating and irredeemable preferred share*.

## 6.2 The financial structure of the firm

It is important to understand the financial structure of the firm before we look at share pricing. This is because shareholders are residual claimants to the value of the firm. Bondholders, on the other hand, have a prior claim on the firm. They have a contractual relationship with the firm, and so long as the contract is honoured they have no additional claim. They will therefore be interested in the firm only insofar as its activities and financial structure influence the risk class of the bonds. Shareholders, however, own the firm and generally appoint managers (directors) to run it, and, as residual claimants, they will want to ensure that the value of the firm is maximized. Therefore they will be much more interested in the firm and its structure, particularly its long-term structure.

In order to analyze the effect of the firm's financial structure on the value of its shares, we have to examine the firm's financial statements: its income statement, statement of retained earnings, cash flow statement and its balance sheet.

### 6.2.1 The income statement and statement of retained earnings

The *income statement* (or *profit and loss account*) of the firm is illustrated in Table 6.1, which also shows the *statement of retained earnings*. While all firms have income and retained earnings statements

**Table 6.1** Income statement — Year to 31st December 20xx

|   |   | *£m* |
|---|---|---|
|   | Operating revenue | 680 |
| — | Operating costs (including depreciation) | (499) |
| = | Operating (trading) profit | 181 |
| — | Interest payable on bonds and loans | (104) |
| = | Profit before tax | 77 |
| — | Corporation tax | (24) |
| = | Profit after tax (earnings) | 53 |
| — | Dividends:    preference shares | (6) |
|   |                    ordinary shares | (21) |
| = | Retained earnings for year | 26 |
|   | Earnings per share[a] | 23.5p |

[a]Earnings per share are based on profits after tax available for ordinary shares of £47m (£53m – £6m) and 200m ordinary shares in issue.

similar to these, it is possible for two identical firms with identical cash flows to end up with different reported earnings because they use different accounting conventions, different accounting bases or have different accounting years. In the UK, companies use the *accruals convention* (revenue and expenditure are recorded as they occur, not when cash is received or paid). Similarly, non-cash fixed costs, such as depreciation, could be treated differently. Finally, the corporation tax liability could differ between the two firms, not just as a result of the above differences, but because one firm has income from abroad, whereas the other does not, or because they have different dividend policies. We can examine the effects of inflation, depreciation and tax in more detail.

## 6.2.2   Inflation accounting

Inflation affects the income statement in several ways including the method by which inventories are valued in the production process. A manufacturing firm buys inventories of raw materials which are used to produce finished goods which are subsequently sold. Because of the time lags in the production process, the cost of replacing inventories may well have risen by the time that the raw materials are used to make finished goods and then sold.

Sales revenues will be recorded at the actual prices at the time of sale. But how should expenditures on inventories be recorded? Should they be recorded at the original historical cost, or should they be recorded at the current replacement cost? The first method is known as FIFO (first in, first out) while the second method is known as LIFO (last in, first out). To illustrate the different methods, consider two firms (A and B) which have identical production processes and identical sales. They buy their inventories of raw materials at the same times and the same prices. The first batch of 50 units costs £10 per unit and the second batch of 50 identical units costs £14 per unit because of inflation. However, firm A uses FIFO while firm B uses LIFO. The income statements of the two firms are as follows:

|  | *Firm A*<br>*(FIFO)*<br>*(£)* | *Firm B*<br>*(LIFO)*<br>*(£)* |
|---|---|---|
| Revenue (50 units at £40) | 2000 | 2000 |
| Expenditure on inventory: |  |  |
| (50 units at £10) | (500) | – |
| (50 units at £14) | – | (700) |
| Other expenditure | (500) | (500) |
| Reported earnings | 1000 | 800 |

So firm A reports earnings of £1000, while firm B has earnings of only £800. Which is the better measure of costs? While FIFO corresponds most closely to the way in which firms actually use their inventories (i.e. the oldest stock is used up first) and corresponds to the actual cost paid for inventories, it ignores the fact that to replace the inventories now costs a great deal more. And since the firm's value depends on future cash flows, LIFO is the better measure for valuing inventories (in terms of the income statement). In other words, using FIFO overstates firm A's earnings. However the relevant Statement of Standard Accounting Practice for the UK recommends FIFO, and LIFO is not generally acceptable to the UK tax authorities.

## 6.2.3   Depreciation

Depreciation is the way in which the deterioration in the capital assets (i.e. plant, equipment, buildings) owned by the firm is taken into account in the income statement. If a firm is to be successful, it will have to generate sufficient income to cover the cost not only of financing a capital asset but of replacing it when it is worn out. Ideally, depreciation should be measured at market value (i.e. as the difference between the current second-hand market value of the asset and its second-hand market value in the previous year). However, since the market value of second-hand assets is difficult to determine, depreciation is recorded at book value (i.e. as the difference between the book values of the asset in consecutive years). This accords also with the accounting convention based on historic costs. In practice, a mechanical formula is used to measure depreciation.

The simplest one is the *straight-line* method, in which depreciation is recorded as a constant proportion of the original cost of the asset over its anticipated working life; for example, the depreciation on an asset costing £400 and expected to last five years will be £80 per year or 20 per cent of the original value of the asset. All other methods involve what is known as *accelerated depreciation*, because, with these methods, the depreciation is greater in the early years than in the later years. One example of this is the *declining balance* method, in which depreciation is recorded as a constant proportion of the depreciated book value (or *written-down value*) over the anticipated life of the asset. For example, if the *writing-down rate* (i.e., rate of depreciation) is 40 per cent, the depreciation on an asset costing £400 with a five-year life is determined as follows:

| Year | Book value B/F (£) | Depreciation at 40% (£) | Book value C/F (£) |
|------|------|------|------|
| 1 | 400 | 160 | 240 |
| 2 | 240 | 96 | 144 |
| 3 | 144 | 58 | 86 |
| 4 | 86 | 34 | 52 |
| 5 | 52 | 21 | 31 |

*Notes:*

1 Depreciation calculated to nearest £.

2 Depreciation for year 6 onwards would be on the same basis if the asset is still in use.

3 If the asset is scrapped at the end of five years, its book value of £31 will be written off.

4 If a firm chooses the declining balance method, it will generally choose a writing-down rate that is twice the corresponding straight-line rate: in this example $2 \times 20$ per cent.

## 6.2.4 Corporation tax and corporate capital gains tax

Corporation tax is the tax paid by all companies in the UK if they have sufficient taxable earnings. (Trading losses can be brought forward to offset taxable earnings in future years.) The rate of tax is currently 30% for large companies and 20% for small companies.

Another feature of the tax system is the *capital allowances* that can be used to offset tax liabilities. The system of capital allowances is the system of depreciation permitted by the Inland Revenue in arriving at taxable earnings. But it may not be the same as the system of depreciation used by firms in arriving at their reported earnings. The income statement in Table 6.1 is usually drawn up using depreciation to give reported earnings. In the corporation tax computation, depreciation (and any other disallowed expense such as entertaining) is added back and the resultant total is reduced by the capital allowances to give taxable earnings. In other words, taxable earnings equals reported earnings *plus* depreciation *minus* capital allowances.

The capital allowances differ for different classes of capital assets. For example, with industrial buildings the *writing-down allowance* is determined by the straight-line method (at the rate of 4 per cent per year over 25 years). But with office buildings there is no allowance at all. With plant and equipment, the capital allowance is determined using the 25 per cent declining balance method (over 8 years); i.e. the writing-down allowance is 25 per cent of the *written-down value*, as illustrated in section 6.2.3 above.

If the capital asset is sold before the end of its useful life, there may be a gain or a loss relative to its written-down value. A gain is taxed as a *balancing charge*, while a loss gives rise to a *balancing allowance* that can be used to reduce taxable earnings. This ensures that the sum of capital allowances is equal to the real depreciation incurred. This is the case if the firm treats its capital assets separately. However, most firms have their capital assets collected in a *pool*. In this case, the cost of a new asset is added to the accumulated written-down values of the firm's existing assets and the writing-down allowances are determined by the aggregate of written-down values. With *pooling*, the proceeds from the sale of an asset are deducted from the written-down value of the pool and there is no balancing allowance. However, if the sale proceeds exceed the value of the pool, the balance of the pool is reduced to zero and a balancing charge arises on the excess.

**Table 6.2** The difference between pooling and no pooling of capital assets

| Year | | Firm A (No pooling) | | | Firm B (Pooling) |
| --- | --- | --- | --- | --- | --- |
| | | Asset Y (£) | Asset Z (£) | Asset Y + Asset Z (£) | Asset (Y + Z) (£) |
| 1 | Purchase of Y | 100 | – | 100 | 100 |
| | WDA[a] (25%) | 25 | – | 25 | 25 |
| | WDV[b] | 75 | – | 75 | 75 |
| 2 | Purchase of Z | | 100 | 100 | 100 |
| | Pooled WDV | – | – | – | 175 |
| | WDA (25%) | 19 | 25 | 44 | 44 |
| | WDV | 56 | 75 | 131 | 131 |
| 3 | Sale of Y | 30 | – | 30 | 30 |
| | Pooled WDV | – | – | – | 101 |
| | Balancing allowance[c] | 26 | – | 26 | – |
| | WDA (25%) | – | 19 | 19 | 25 |
| | WDV | – | 56 | 56 | 76 |
| 4 | Sale of Z | – | 80 | 80 | 80 |
| | Pooled WDV | – | – | – | – |
| | Balancing charge[d] | – | 24 | 24 | 4 |

[a]WDA = writing-down allowance
[b]WDV = written-down value
[c]Balancing allowance = WDV (year 2) − sale of Y = 56 − 30
[d]Balancing charge = sale of Z − WDV (year 3) = 80 − 56

The difference between pooling and no pooling is illustrated in Table 6.2 for two firms (A and B), both of which purchase the same two capital assets (Y and Z) over consecutive years, but where firm B pools the assets, firm A does not. Before disposal of an asset, pooling makes no difference to the written-down values of the assets compared with no pooling. However, differences arise when the assets are sold in years 3 and 4. Firm A has a balancing allowance in year 3 of £26 and so has its corporation tax reduced by £8, i.e. £26×30% in that year, but ends up with a balancing charge of £24 in year 4 and so has an additional tax liability of £7, i.e. £24×30% in year 4. Firm B, on the other hand, has no balancing allowance in year 3 and has an additional corporation tax liability of £1, i.e. £4×30% in year 4. So two identical firms can end up with different reported earnings purely as a result of the way in which they elect to treat their capital assets.

From Table 6.1, it can be seen that interest payments on bonds and loans are an allowable deduction from earnings before tax but that dividends on both preferred shares and ordinary shares are not. This means that the net cost of raising bond finance is lower than the net cost of raising finance via a share issue. If a firm raises £1 million from issuing a bond with a coupon of 10 per cent, it makes annual interest payments of £100,000 at a net cost to itself of £70,000 per annum, i.e. £100,000(1 − 0.30). However, the net cost of £1 million raised from selling preferred shares with a 10 per cent dividend is £100,000 per annum. The implications of this are discussed in greater details in section 6.6. If, on the other hand, the firm holds shares in another company resident in the UK and itself receives dividends on those shares (this is called *franked investment income*), the dividends are exempt from further corporation tax because they have been paid out of earnings on which tax has already been paid. In contrast, when a dividend is paid to an individual shareholder, it is paid subject to a withholding tax of 20 per cent. The shareholder receives a tax credit of 20 per cent and if he is a basic rate tax payer, he has no further tax liability. If he is a higher rate tax payer, however, he has to pay an additional 20 per cent of the grossed up dividend, i.e. $[100/(100 − 20)] \times$ net dividend.

**Table 6.3** The effect of overseas earnings on the domestic tax liability

|  | Firm A<br>(Overseas tax rate 25%)<br>(£,000) | Firm B<br>(Overseas tax rate 50%)<br>(£,000) |
|---|---|---|
| Overseas earnings (gross) | 100 | 100 |
| Overseas tax: |  |  |
| $\quad 100 \times 25\%$ | 25 | – |
| $\quad 100 \times 50\%$ | – | 50 |
| Overseas earnings (net of overseas tax) | 75 | 50 |
| UK corporation tax: |  |  |
| $\quad 100 \times 30\%$ | 30 | 30 |
| Overseas tax credit: |  |  |
| $\quad 100 \times 25\%^a$ | 25 | – |
| $\quad 100 \times 30\%^b$ | – | 30 |
| Net UK corporation tax | 5 | 0 |
| Overseas earnings (net of UK corporation tax) | 70 | 50 |

[a] $25\% = \min\{25\%, 30\%\}$
[b] $30\% = \min\{50\%, 30\%\}$

If a firm has earnings from overseas, it will generally have to pay overseas taxation on them. If a double taxation relief agreement exists between the UK and the overseas country, relief is given in the form of a tax credit on the overseas earnings calculated on the lower of the UK and overseas corporate tax rates. For example, suppose that two firms have earnings abroad of £100,000 before tax. Firm A faces an overseas tax rate of 25 per cent whereas firm B faces an overseas tax rate of 50 per cent. The UK corporation tax for the two companies is determined in Table 6.3. So even though both firms have identical gross overseas earnings, they end up with different net overseas earnings as a result of the combination of different overseas tax rates and the system of double tax relief.

Corporation tax is not the only tax that a firm might be liable to pay. It might also have a capital gains tax (CGT) liability if it sells a capital asset, such as a building, in excess of its original purchase price (adjusted for depreciation and maintenance costs). (Note that a capital gain differs from a balancing charge which gives rise to a corporation tax liability.)

### 6.2.5  The effect of accounting conventions on reported earnings

We have seen that the reported earnings of two otherwise identical firms can differ as a result of different accounting conventions. And since, as we shall see, reported earnings form the basis of share valuation, such differences make it extremely difficult for the investment analyst to estimate the fair price of shares. We will illustrate the problem using a number of summary measures of the state of the firm typically used by analysts. These summary measures are earnings per share, the price-earnings ratio and the dividend yield.

*Earnings per share* (EPS) is defined as:

$$\text{Earnings per share} \quad = \quad \frac{\text{Earnings available for ordinary shareholders}}{\text{Ordinary shares in issue}} . \qquad (6.1)$$

The earnings available for ordinary shareholders are the profit after tax, minority interests and preference dividends. Ordinary shares in issue is the weighted average (on a time basis) of the number of shares outstanding, taking into account any issues (or repurchases) of ordinary shares in the financial year.

The *price-earnings* (PE) *ratio* is defined as:

$$\text{Price-earnings ratio} \quad = \quad \frac{\text{Price per share}}{\text{Earnings per share}} . \qquad (6.2)$$

It measures the number of years taken for a shareholder to recover his initial investment (assuming that all earnings are distributed); and, alternatively, it measures the price an investor has to pay to buy an income stream of £1 per annum in the company.

The *net dividend yield* is defined as:

$$
\begin{aligned}
\text{Net dividend yield} \quad &= \quad \frac{\text{Dividends per share}}{\text{Price per share}} \\
&= \quad \frac{\text{Reported earnings per share} - \text{Retained earnings per share}}{\text{Price per share}} . \qquad (6.3)
\end{aligned}
$$

This is the *net* dividend yield because the firm has already paid corporation tax on its earnings. But other securities such as government bonds have their yields quoted before income tax. To make comparisons with other securities, the dividend yield on shares is generally quoted gross. The net dividend yield is grossed up as follows:

$$\text{Gross dividend yield} \quad = \quad \text{Net dividend yield} \cdot \frac{100}{100 - T_p} , \qquad (6.4)$$

where $T_p$ = withholding tax rate (i.e. 20 per cent). The formula for the gross dividend yield is valid for preference shares as well as ordinary shares.

We will now consider two identical firms with identical operations and cash flows but employing different accounting conventions. The combined income and retained earnings statement of the two firms is depicted in Table 6.4. Both firms have identical cash flows and the markets, recognizing this, have given them the same share price. However A has a much higher PE and a much lower yield than B.

**Table 6.4** The effect of different accounting conventions

| | Firm A (£,000) | Firm B (£,000) |
|---|---|---|
| Revenue from operations | 10000 | 10000 |
| Expenditure on operations[a] | (6000) | (5600) |
| Cash fixed costs | (1000) | (1000) |
| Depreciation[b] | (1400) | (1000) |
| Interest payments on bonds | (800) | (800) |
| Accounting earnings | 800 | 1600 |
| Taxable earnings[c] | 1000 | 1400 |
| Corporation tax (30%) | (300) | (420) |
| Reported earnings[d] | 500 | 1180 |
| Dividends[e] | (250) | (900) |
| Retained earnings | 250 | 280 |
| Number of shares outstanding (m) | 10 | 10 |
| Share price (p) | 80 | 80 |
| Earnings per share (p)[f] | 5.00 | 11.80 |
| Price-earnings ratio[g] | 16.00 | 6.80 |
| Net dividend yield (%)[h] | 3.13 | 11.25 |
| Gross dividend yield (%)[i] | 3.91 | 14.06 |

[a]Firm A uses LIFO for stock valuation but firm B uses FIFO.
[b]Firm A uses accelerated depreciation (declining balance) whereas firm B uses straight-line depreciation.
  The capital allowances for tax purposes, for both firms, amount to £1,200,000.
[c]Taxable earnings = accounting earnings *plus* depreciation *minus* capital allowances.
  For firm A we have 800+1400−1200; for firm B we have 1600+1000−1200.
[d]Accounting earnings *less* corporation tax.
[e]A pays out 50% of reported earnings as dividend; B has a fixed dividend payout.
[f]Firm A: 500/10000=5.0p. Firm B: 1180/10000=11.8p.
[g]Firm A: 80/5.0=16.0. Firm B: 80/11.8=6.8.
[h]Firm A: 250/10000=2.50p; 2.50p/80p=3.13%. Firm B: 900/10000=9p; 9p/80p=11.25%.
[i]Firm A: 3.13%×100/80=3.91%. Firm B: 11.25%×100/80=14.06%.

What does an investment analyst make of all this? It is clear that both earnings per share and PE ratios can be dubious quantities, yet investment analysts make extensive use of both in attempting to estimate the true values of firms and in making comparisons between firms. However, it is clear that two identical firms with identical operations and cash flows should have identical values, whatever accounting conventions the two firms use. In the above example, the analysts and the market are doing their jobs properly, because both firms have the same share price of 80p and hence do indeed have the same value.

## 6.2.6   The balance sheet

Having examined the income and retained earnings statements of the firm, the final way to look at the firm's financial structure is to examine its balance sheet. A typical balance sheet is presented in Table 6.5.

A balance sheet can be drawn up in three different ways. It can be drawn up on the basis of *historic-cost book values*, *current-cost book values* or *market values*. The balance sheet that would be most useful to an investment analyst would be the market value balance sheet. This is the balance sheet in which assets and liabilities are recorded at their current market values. If the firm has its long-term liabilities traded on a stock exchange, the market values of the liabilities are relatively easy to determine. The market values of current liabilities will be close to their book values, and the market values of the long-term liabilities can simply be taken from a publicly available source such as the *Financial Times*. The firm's net worth is simply the difference between the market value of the ordinary shares and the book value of the ordinary shares (which equals par value *plus* premium value *plus* accumulated retained earnings). The market values of the assets, on the other hand, is much more difficult to determine because there is not an efficient market in second-hand assets. What for example is the market value for a three-year-old mainframe computer, or a seven-year-old fork-lift truck? However, most firms in the UK do not have their securities traded on the stock exchange, and so the market value balance sheet is never formally presented.

The next most useful balance sheet is the one based on current-cost book values. This is the balance sheet in which both inventories and long-term assets are valued at current replacement cost. For example, with inventories, this means that the FIFO valuation method is the best method to use. This method is the opposite to that which is most appropriate for the income statement. Using LIFO in the income statement implies that the older units remain in the inventory. These will therefore be valued effectively at historic cost when the balance sheet is drawn up.

In the UK very few firms present accounts on a current cost accounting (CCA) basis although a Statement of Standard Accounting Practice (SSAP16) was issued in 1980. However, this was suspended in 1985 and withdrawn in 1988, although a few companies still use all or part of it (e.g. the valuation of inventory at replacement cost).

Most firms in the UK still present their balance sheets based on historic-cost book values, the least useful method from the viewpoint of investment analysis. With this balance sheet, both assets and liabilities are recorded at their original (i.e. historical) costs, and again the book value of net worth is represented by the share capital and reserves.

To illustrate the difference between the historic-cost and the current-cost balance sheets, we will consider the two firms A and B in section 6.2.2 which used FIFO and LIFO to value their inventories in the production process. Firm A used FIFO and reported earnings of £1000, whereas firm B used LIFO and reported earnings of £800. The assets as shown by the balance sheet could be as shown in Table 6.6. Firm B's assets are undervalued compared with firm A's. The overall effect of the distortions to both the income statement and balance sheet is to give firm A a return on assets of 17.5 per cent and firm B a return on assets of 14.5 per cent, even though both firms are identical in every way except for the inventory valuation method used.

So it is clear that the financial statements of the firm, which are the only publicly available sources of financial information about the firm, are fraught with problems from beginning to end. This is what makes the job of the share analyst much more difficult than that of the bond analyst, because it makes a fair comparison between two firms extremely difficult.

**Table 6.5** Balance sheet — Year to 31st December 20xx

|  | £m | £m |
|---|---|---|
| Fixed assets (property, plant, etc.)[a] |  | 760 |
| Long-term investments |  | 105 |
|  |  | 865 |
| Current assets |  |  |
|     Stock (inventory) | 480 |  |
|     Debtors (accounts receivable) | 690 |  |
|     Cash | 20 |  |
|  | 1190 |  |
| Liabilities due within one year |  |  |
|     Creditors (accounts payable) | (460) |  |
|     Short-term loans & overdraft | (270) |  |
|     Corporation tax | (110) |  |
|     Dividend (proposed) | (90) |  |
|  | (930) |  |
| Net current assets |  | 260 |
| Total assets less current liabilities |  | 1125 |
| Liabilities due after more than one year |  |  |
|     Creditors | (30) |  |
|     Long-term loans | (425) | (455) |
| Net assets |  | 670 |
| Share capital |  |  |
|     Ordinary shares in issue |  | 200 |
|     Preference shares |  | 40 |
|  |  | 240 |
| Reserves |  |  |
|     Retained earnings | 260 |  |
|     Share premium[b] | 170 | 430 |
| Shareholders' funds (net worth) |  | 670 |

[a]The fixed assets are shown at original cost *less* accumulated depreciation.

[b]The share premium account is the value of the premium on share issues above par: e.g. if £1 million of 25p shares are issued at 60p each, raising £600,000, then £250,000 is share capital and £350,000 is share premium.

**Table 6.6** FIFO *v.* LIFO

|  | Firm A (FIFO) (£) | Firm B (LIFO) (£) |
|---|---|---|
| *Assets* | | |
| Inventory | | |
| (50 units at £10)[a] | — | 500 |
| (50 units at £14)[b] | 700 | — |
| Other current and long-term assets *less* liabilities | 5000 | 5000 |
| Net assets | 5700 | 5500 |
| | | |
| Return on assets (Reported earnings/net assets) | 17.5% | 14.5% |

[a]Firm B uses LIFO for the balance sheet and so has used up 50 'new' units of raw materials in production, with 50 'old' units remaining as inventory and valued at £10 per unit.
[b]Firm A uses FIFO for the balance sheet and so has used up 50 'old' units of raw materials in production, with 50 'new' units remaining as inventory and valued at £14 per unit.

## 6.3  The fair pricing of shares

The primary objective of fundamental analysis is to find the fair price of a share. This can then be compared with the market price of the share to determine whether it is underpriced or overpriced. There are two commonly used approaches to finding this fair price, one based on *expected dividends* and one based on *expected earnings*.

### 6.3.1  Valuation based on expected dividends

Suppose that a firm pays dividends once a year. In reality, they usually make two dividend payments per year, an interim and a final dividend. Suppose also that an investor intends to buy the share, hold it for one year and then sell it at the end of the year. He expects to receive a dividend at the end of the year as well as the price for the share at that time. In order to make this return, he will be prepared to pay the following fair price for the share today:

$$P_0 = \frac{E(d_1)}{1+r} + \frac{E(P_1)}{1+r},\tag{6.5}$$

where:

$$
\begin{aligned}
P_0 &= \text{fair price of the share;} \\
E(d_1) &= \text{expected annual dividend per share at the end of year 1;} \\
E(P_1) &= \text{expected price of the share at the end of year 1;} \\
E(\ ) &= \text{expectations operator based on all current information (the} \\
&\quad\ \text{average across all market participants);} \\
r &= \text{market-determined discount rate or cost of capital or required} \\
&\quad\ \text{rate of return on a firm with this risk class.}
\end{aligned}
$$

In (6.5), the return on the shareholding comprises an income element ($d_1$) and a capital gain element ($P_1 - P_0$). Clearly, if the return is constant, then the higher the income element, the lower the capital gain and vice versa.

It must also be the case that:

$$E(P_1) = \frac{E(d_2)}{1+r} + \frac{E(P_2)}{1+r}. \tag{6.6}$$

By substituting (6.6) into (6.5) we get:

$$P_0 = \frac{E(d_1)}{(1+r)} + \frac{E(d_2)}{(1+r)^2} + \frac{E(P_2)}{(1+r)^2}. \tag{6.7}$$

By substituting equations like (6.6) for $E(P_2)$, $E(P_3)$, etc., into (6.7), we get:

$$P_0 = \sum_{t=1}^{T} \frac{E(d_t)}{(1+r)^t} + \frac{E(P_T)}{(1+r)^T}, \tag{6.8}$$

where $d_t$ is the dividend per share in year $t$. As $T \to \infty$, (6.8) becomes:

$$P_0 = \sum_{t=1}^{\infty} \frac{E(d_t)}{(1+r)^t}, \tag{6.9}$$

since we assume that the second term on the right-hand side of (6.8) vanishes as $T \to \infty$, which will occur if $E(P_\infty)$ is finite (i.e., we rule out *speculative bubbles*, see section 18.2).

For preferred shares where the preferred dividend is known, (6.9) becomes:

$$P_0 = \frac{d}{r}, \tag{6.10}$$

which is identical to the formula for valuing perpetual bonds given in (5.3).

The model in (6.9) is known as the *dividend discount model* of share valuation. This model is the one that is most readily comparable with the model of bond valuation developed in the last chapter. The holder of the share or bond receives a stream of (expected) payments that are discounted at an appropriate discount rate over the remaining life of the security. However, for exact comparability between bonds and shares, both coupons and dividends must be on a net-of-tax basis since this is what recipients actually receive. Dividends are automatically calculated net of tax, but coupons are calculated gross and have to be adjusted.

There are several problems with (6.9) as it stands, however. First, it assumes that the market-determined discount rate is constant for all future time periods. We know from our study of bonds, however, that the appropriate discount rate for cash flows in different periods is the spot or zero-coupon rate. Using spot rates, (6.9) becomes:

$$P_0 = \sum_{t=1}^{\infty} \frac{E(d_t)}{(1+rs_t)^t}, \tag{6.11}$$

where $rs_t$ is the spot rate on a $t$-year risk-free zero-coupon bond *plus* a risk premium for the firm. However, for simplicity, we will disregard this refinement for the remainder of the chapter and assume that the discount rate is constant. A second problem is that (6.9) is an infinite sum which might diverge. However, we will shortly use an economic rationality argument to rule out divergence in (6.9) and hence to rule out an infinite share price. A third and more serious problem with (6.9) is that it is not operational because it involves expectations of dividend payments into the infinite future. To render the model operational, we need a theory of dividends.

But before discussing dividend policy, we will examine an alternative theory of share valuation, namely that based on expected earnings.

## 6.3.2   Valuation based on expected earnings

A second commonly used share valuation model is based on the expected earnings of the firm. The stream of expected earnings is discounted in precisely the same way as the stream of expected dividends using the same discount rate (because the discount rate applies to the risk class of the activities of the entire firm). However, a firm's *reported earnings* (also called *accounting income*) are usually larger than the firm's dividends, which would seem to suggest that the value of the firm based on earnings will be higher than the value based on dividends. Yet it must be the case that the two valuation methods lead to the *same* fair price, otherwise there is an inconsistency. To avoid any inconsistency, it is *economic earnings* (also called *economic income* or *permanent income*) and not *reported earnings* that is the appropriate measure of earnings for share valuation.

*Economic income* is simply the maximum amount of real income that can be consumed out of real wealth during a given period without impairing the ability of that stock of real wealth to deliver real income and hence real consumption in the future. Since a share is a financial claim on the firm's real wealth in the form of its physical assets, the *economic earnings* of a share are defined as the maximum amount of real resources that can be withdrawn from the share and used for real consumption without impairing the ability of the share to deliver real consumption in the future.

Reported earnings can be converted into economic earnings using the *cash flow statement* given in Table 6.7. Note that this is a *net* cash flow statement; a *gross* statement would add depreciation to the sources column and replace net investment with gross investment in the uses column.

**Table 6.7** Cash flow statement

| | *Sources* | | *Uses* |
|---|---|---|---|
| | Reported earnings | | Dividends |
| + | New external funds | + | Net investment |
| | | | |
| = | Total sources | = | Total uses |

The cash flow statement can be written in per-share form as the following identity:

$$y_t + f_t \quad \equiv \quad d_t + x_t, \tag{6.12}$$

where:

$$
\begin{aligned}
y_t &= \text{reported earnings per share in year } t; \\
f_t &= \text{new external funds per share in year } t; \\
d_t &= \text{dividends per share in year } t; \\
x_t &= \text{net investment per share in year } t.
\end{aligned}
$$

It is clear from (6.12) that, if the firm is able to raise new external funds (i.e., if $f_t \neq 0$), then the investment decision ($x_t$) can be determined independently of the funding decision ($f_t$). Only if all new investment in the firm has to be financed from retained earnings is it possible for an increase in dividends to reduce net investment and thereby reduce the ability of the firm to deliver real income in the future. If the firm has to reinvest some of its earnings to survive, then those retained earnings are not true economic income that could be consumed by the shareholder without reducing the share's consumption-generating power in the future.

This leads to the following definition of economic earnings per share:

$$\text{Economic earnings per share} \quad = \quad y_t + f_t - x_t, \tag{6.13}$$

subject to the restriction:

$$\sum_{t=1}^{\infty} \frac{f_t}{(1+r)^t} \quad = \quad 0, \tag{6.14}$$

which implies that the present value of new external funds must sum to zero over the life of the firm, i.e., the firm must eventually pay back any borrowings, otherwise the firm would not effectively have a budget constraint.

Economic earnings are therefore equal to reported earnings *plus* new external funds *less* net investment. The fair value of the share using economic earnings is given by:

$$
\begin{aligned}
P_0 &= \sum_{t=1}^{\infty} \frac{E(y_t + f_t - x_t)}{(1+r)^t} \\
&= \sum_{t=1}^{\infty} \frac{E(y_t - x_t)}{(1+r)^t},
\end{aligned} \tag{6.15}
$$

using (6.14).

Equations (6.9) and (6.15) will give exactly the same value for the share price. This is because, from (6.12) and (6.13), dividends and economic earnings are identical. The explanation for this is simple. Suppose that dividends (and therefore economic earnings) are constant for all future periods. In this case (6.9) becomes:

$$P_0 \quad = \quad \frac{d}{r}, \tag{6.16}$$

or:

$$d \quad = \quad r \cdot P_0. \tag{6.17}$$

Equation (6.17) implies that dividends are a constant proportion of share wealth ($P_0$) and are set at exactly the level necessary to enable that share wealth to deliver the same dividend in all future periods.

But this is precisely what economic income is. It is the amount that can be consumed out of wealth and leave sufficient wealth to deliver a constant economic income in all future periods. This is why economic income is sometimes called permanent income, and it is also why economic earnings and dividends are equivalent. If dividends were higher than $d$ in (6.17) because net investment was too low, then this would be equivalent to capital consumption and the future income-generating capacity of the share would be reduced.

So, if earnings are defined correctly, there is absolutely no distinction between the dividend valuation model and the earnings valuation model.

## 6.4  Dividend policy

Equation (6.12) appears to indicate that, as long as the firm can raise new external funds (i.e. $f_t \neq 0$), the dividend policy chosen by a firm will not affect the value of the firm. In other words, dividend policy appears to be irrelevant (see, e.g., Miller and Modigliani (1961)).

But even theoretically, there are problems with this proposition. Suppose that a firm decided never to pay dividends, preferring instead to reward shareholders entirely through capital gains. What would be the price of the share in this case? By putting $d_t = 0$ into (6.9), we get $P_0 = 0$. In other words, a non-dividend-paying share is worthless. The reason is simple. The entire value of the share is concentrated at $T = \infty$, but the present value of this is zero, in exactly the same way that the present value of a perpetual zero-coupon bond is zero. In other words, the value of a share comes from its ability to pay dividends, because it is dividends that finance consumption. Even if a share does not pay dividends temporarily, it must eventually pay dividends to have any value.

In practice also, the dividend policy chosen by the firm is important. Most firms appear to have a *target payout ratio* of dividends to long-run reported earnings. Earnings can fluctuate quite widely from one year to the next, but if long-run earnings are calculated as a moving average of short-run earnings, this will be a much more stable measure. For example, long-run earnings per share ($\bar{y}_t$) could be calculated as a three-year moving average:

$$\bar{y}_t \;\; = \;\; \frac{1}{3} \cdot \sum_{s=0}^{2} y_{t-s}. \tag{6.18}$$

Given this measure, dividends per share are determined by:

$$d_t \;\; = \;\; \bar{\theta}\bar{y}_t, \tag{6.19}$$

where $\bar{\theta}$ is the target dividend payout ratio.

Why is the paying of dividends so important, when there are so many advantages to not paying them? From the shareholder's point of view, dividends are taxed at a higher rate than capital gains (even though the marginal rates are identical). From the firm's point of view, retained earnings are generally regarded as a cheaper source of funds than new external funds, given the costs of raising external finance. There are three main explanations for the payments of dividends.

The first explanation involves the *principal-agent problem* (see Rozeff (1982)). In theory, shareholders *own* the firm but appoint managers to *run* the firm in their best interests. Thus, the shareholders are *principals* and the managers are *agents*. But there is a potential conflict of interest in this relationship. The managers might behave in a way that benefits themselves and does not maximize shareholders' wealth. Because of this possibility, shareholders will have to incur monitoring costs or agency costs to ensure that managers behave properly. These costs are reduced when new external funds are raised, because the firm is placed under greater financial scrutiny at this time. But flotation costs are higher, the more frequently new external funds are raised. The payment of dividends therefore represents a trade-off between agency costs and flotation costs. The higher the level of dividends, the more frequently new external funds have to be raised and the higher the average flotation costs, but the lower the average agency costs. The optimal dividend will minimize the sum of the two sets of costs (see Figure 6.1).

**Figure 6.1** Optimal dividend policy

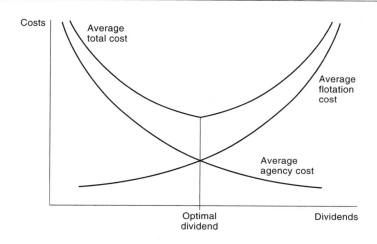

The second explanation involves *signalling* (see Ross (1977)). With this explanation, dividend announcements are regarded as important information signals to the market. Managers have more inside information about the state of the firm than shareholders and other outsiders. Clearly, managers with good information about the firm will want to transmit that information to the market, while managers with bad information might want to conceal it and might also be tempted to transmit false 'good' information to the market. An announcement that a firm is increasing its dividends is a good signal because it suggests that the managers believe that future earnings will be sufficient to sustain the higher level of dividends. But is this a true 'good' signal or a false 'good' signal? For dividend announcements to be treated unambiguously as good signals, managers must be given the correct incentive to transmit a true signal even if the information is bad. In other words, managers' salaries have to be made *incentive-compatible*, so that the penalty for sending a false 'good' signal is always greater than the penalty for sending a true 'bad' signal. In addition, the signal has to be correlated with observable future events (e.g., a 'bad' signal has to be correlated with future insolvency, while a 'good' signal has to be correlated with future survival), and the cost of sending a false 'good' signal has to be greater than the cost of sending a 'true' bad signal for the firm as well as the manager. That is, if an unsuccessful firm attempts to send a false 'good' signal by announcing an increase in dividends, this increases the risk of insolvency even more than would be the case if the firm sent a true 'bad' signal by not announcing a dividend increase or even by announcing a dividend reduction. If these conditions hold, then dividends and dividend changes have important signalling effects.

The third explanation for paying dividends involves the *tax clientele effect*, described by Miller and Modigliani (1961). Dividends can be used to influence the class of shareholder attracted to a particular firm. Shareholders with high tax rates will be attracted to firms paying low dividends, while shareholders with low or zero tax rates will be attracted to firms paying high dividends. If firms prefer a certain class of investor, they can use their dividend policy to achieve this.

So we can conclude this section by arguing that, for one reason or another, dividends are important and that a dividend policy of the kind indicated by (6.19) is one that many firms are likely to pursue. The next question is: given that dividends depend on earnings, what determines earnings? We answer this question in the next section.

## 6.5 Earnings analysis

Earnings analysis is concerned with forecasting the future earnings patterns of firms.

### 6.5.1 Constant or normal growth models

We begin with the dividend discount model:

$$P_0 = \sum_{t=1}^{\infty} \frac{E(d_t)}{(1+r)^t}, \tag{6.20}$$

and assume that there is a desired payout ratio of dividends to long-run earnings:

$$d_t = \bar{\theta}\bar{y}_t. \tag{6.21}$$

If $\bar{\theta}$ is constant over time, then the expectations or forecasts about future dividends in (6.20) are really expectations or forecasts about future earnings in (6.21), and in particular about the growth rate of those earnings over time.

The simplest models assume that earnings grow at a constant rate of $g$ per year. This means that the relationship between $y_t$, earnings in year $t$, and $y_0$, earnings in the current year, is given by:

$$y_t = y_0(1+g)^t, \tag{6.22}$$

while the relationship between dividends in year $t$ and earnings in year $t$ is given by:

$$\begin{aligned} d_t &= \theta y_t \\ &= \theta y_0(1+g)^t \\ &= d_0(1+g)^t, \end{aligned} \tag{6.23}$$

where:

$$\begin{aligned} \theta &= \text{actual dividend payout ratio } (d_t/y_t) \\ &= \frac{1}{3} \cdot \left[ 1 + \frac{1}{(1+g)} + \frac{1}{(1+g)^2} \right] \cdot \bar{\theta} \end{aligned}$$

if a three-year moving average of current earnings is used to determine long-run earnings.

Substituting the last line of (6.23) into (6.20) gives:

$$P_0 = \sum_{t=1}^{\infty} d_0 \frac{(1+g)^t}{(1+r)^t}. \tag{6.24}$$

The infinite sum in (6.24) will diverge unless $r > g$. We will assume that the sum converges and define:

$$(1+h) \equiv \frac{(1+g)}{(1+r)} < 1. \tag{6.25}$$

Using the compound sum formula, we get:

$$\sum_{t=1}^{T}(1+h)^t = (1+h)\left[\frac{(1+h)^T - 1}{h}\right]. \tag{6.26}$$

The limit of this as $T \to \infty$ is, using (6.25):

$$\begin{aligned}
\sum_{t=1}^{\infty}(1+h)^t &= -\frac{(1+h)}{g} \\
&= \frac{1+g}{r-g}.
\end{aligned} \tag{6.27}$$

Substituting (6.27) into (6.24) gives:

$$\begin{aligned}
P_0 &= \frac{d_0(1+g)}{r-g} \\
&= \frac{d_1}{r-g}.
\end{aligned} \tag{6.28}$$

Equation (6.28) is known as the *Gordon growth model* after Gordon (1962). The fair price of the share is found by discounting next period's forecast dividend by $(r - g)$, the difference between the discount rate and the growth rate.

We know that $r$ must exceed $g$, otherwise the share price would be infinite. But what guarantees that $r$ exceeds $g$? Suppose the opposite were true and $g$ exceeded $r$ for a particular firm. This would mean that the firm's growth rate exceeded its cost of capital. This is a very attractive position to be in and the firm would begin to expand very quickly, using more and more investment capital. But sooner or later the firm's demand for investment capital would become so large that this demand could not be met at a fixed cost of capital and $r$ would begin to rise. At the same time, the fact that initially $g$ exceeded $r$ would attract other competitors into the industry. But the expansion of output by both the firm and its competitors would sooner or later exhaust demand at existing prices. Prices and profitability would fall and the growth rate would begin to fall. Eventually, with $r$ rising and $g$ falling, $r$ would exceed $g$, which is the only sustainable long-run equilibrium position.

Equation (6.28) can be rearranged to yield:

$$r = \frac{d_1}{P_0} + g. \tag{6.29}$$

This shows that, in equilibrium, the required or expected rate of return is equal to the dividend yield *plus* the growth rate (i.e., the cost of capital equals the return on capital). If the payout ratio $\theta$ is constant, then earnings, dividends and the share price all grow at the same rate $g$, so $g$ in (6.29) is also equal to the rate of capital gains. The importance of (6.29) is to show that the return from holding a share is the sum of the dividend yield and the rate of capital gains. In the absence of differential income and capital gains taxes, transaction costs, etc., shareholders will be indifferent as to whether they receive their return in the form of dividends or capital gains. A lower dividend yield can be compensated for with higher capital gains and vice versa.

It is also instructive to examine the sources of earnings growth, $g$. On the assumption that net investment, $x_t$ is financed entirely from retained earnings, net investment is determined as follows:

$$x_t = (1-\theta)y_t, \tag{6.30}$$

where $(1-\theta)$ is the *retention ratio* (i.e. one *minus* the payout ratio). If the investment generates a return $\rho$ per year, this will add $\rho x_t$ to the earnings generated in the previous year. Hence:

$$\begin{aligned} y_{t+1} &= y_t + \rho x_t \\ &= y_t[1+\rho(1-\theta)] \\ &= y_t(1+g) \end{aligned} \tag{6.31}$$

by definition. Therefore:

$$g = \rho(1-\theta), \tag{6.32}$$

i.e., the growth rate is the product of the return on the investment and the retention ratio. The higher the retention ratio (i.e. the lower the dividend payout ratio), the higher the growth rate and vice versa.

Substituting (6.32) into (6.28) provides an alternative formula for the fair share price:

$$P_0 = \frac{d_1}{r-\rho(1-\theta)}. \tag{6.33}$$

If, instead, we chose to express the fair share price formula in terms of earnings rather than dividends, we would get, using the second line of (6.23), (6.28) and (6.32):

$$\begin{aligned} P_0 &= \frac{\theta y_1}{r-g} \\ &= \frac{\theta y_1}{r-\rho(1-\theta)}. \end{aligned} \tag{6.34}$$

Yet another formulation expresses the fair share price not in the form of a price level but in the form of the *price-earnings ratio* (PE). From (6.34), this version yields:

$$\begin{aligned} PE_0 &\equiv \frac{P_0}{y_1} = \frac{\theta}{r-g} \\ &= \frac{\theta}{r-\rho(1-\theta)}, \end{aligned} \tag{6.35}$$

where $PE_0 \equiv P_0/y_1 =$ fair price-earnings ratio. (Note that published PE ratios use last year's earnings per share, not an estimate of next year's earnings per share.) If we know the firm's PE ratio and its earnings per share (EPS), then we can recover the fair share price very simply using:

$$P_0 = PE_0 \cdot y_1. \tag{6.36}$$

This implies that a share should sell for $PE_0$ *times* its earnings per share if it is fairly priced.

In long-run equilibrium, we would expect the real return on a firm's investments to equal its cost of capital, i.e. $r = \rho$. This is the case in which the firm has reached maturity and has no more supernormal projects to invest in (see below). In this case (6.35) becomes:

$$PE_0 \;=\; \frac{1}{r},\tag{6.37}$$

i.e., the PE is the inverse of the discount rate. Similarly, the earnings yield will equal the discount rate or cost of capital:

$$r \;=\; \frac{1}{PE_0} \;=\; \frac{1}{P_0/y_1} \;=\; \frac{y_1}{P_0}.\tag{6.38}$$

## 6.5.2 Differential growth models

No firm grows at a constant rate throughout its life, so while the earnings model in the last subsection gives simple and convenient formulae for the share price, it is not very realistic. A slightly more realistic approach recognizes that firms have life-cycles and that during different stages in their life-cycles they grow at different rates.

One of the simplest differential growth models assumes that a firm has two stages: a *growth stage* and a *mature stage*. Typically, a new firm is established to exploit an attractive set of investment opportunities. The first stage in its life-cycle is therefore a period of very fast or *supernormal growth*. Sooner or later, however, these investment opportunities are fully exploited and the firm enters the second and final stage in its life-cycle, namely one of constant or *normal growth*. A slightly more sophisticated version of the model allows for a third stage in a firm's life-cycle, namely a *declining stage* (this is easy to incorporate in the following framework and is illustrated in the example below).

If there are $T$ years of supernormal growth at the rate $g_s$ after which the growth rate reverts to a normal $g$, then, using the dividend discount model, the fair share price is determined by:

$$P_0 \;=\; \sum_{t=1}^{T} d_0 \cdot \frac{(1+g_s)^t}{(1+r)^t} + \frac{1}{(1+r)^T} \cdot \frac{d_{T+1}}{r-g}.\tag{6.39}$$

The first part of the right-hand side of (6.39) is the present value of dividends during the supernormal growth stage, while the second part is the present value of the share in year $T$ (at the end of the supernormal growth phase and assuming constant growth thereafter), which is then discounted back to the present.

At this stage it will be instructive to consider the effects of different growth assumptions on a firm's share price, its dividend yield, its PE ratio and its total rate of return.

**Example 6.1 (The dividend discount model under different growth assumptions)** *We will review four different firms in the same risk class and therefore having the same required discount rate ($r = 15\%$), and the same initial dividend and earnings ($d_0 = £1$, $y_0 = £2$), but with four different growth assumptions:*

1  *declining firm: constant growth rate g = −5% p.a.*

2  *no growth firm: constant growth rate g = 0% p.a.*

3  *normal growth firm: constant growth rate g = 7% p.a.*

4  *supernormal growth firm: supernormal growth for 10 years at the rate $g_s$ = 25% p.a., followed by constant growth at the rate g = 7% p.a.*

*All firms are entirely equity-financed and have the same balance sheets. Assuming that there are 100,000 shares outstanding:*

| Assets (£) | | Liabilities (£) | |
|---|---|---|---|
| Total assets | 800,000.00 | Shareholders' equity | 800,000.00 |
| Total assets per share | 8.00 | Equity per share | 8.00 |

*For the first three firms we can use the Gordon growth model (6.28), while for the last firm we use the supernormal growth model (6.39).*

### 1  Declining firm

*Price (6.28):*

$$P_0 \;=\; \frac{d_0(1+g)}{r-g} \;=\; \frac{1 \cdot (1-0.05)}{0.15+0.05} \;=\; £4.75\,.$$

*Market-to-book ratio (see balance sheet):*

$$\frac{\text{Fair price per share}}{\text{Book price per share}} \;=\; \frac{4.75}{8.00} \;=\; 0.59\,.$$

*Dividend yield (6.3). Note that next year's dividend appears in the numerator, not the current dividend:*

$$\frac{d_1}{P_0} \;=\; \frac{1 \cdot (1-0.05)}{4.75} \;=\; 20\%\,.$$

*PE ratio (6.35):*

$$PE_0 \;=\; \frac{P_0}{y_1} \;=\; \frac{4.75}{2 \cdot (1-0.05)} \;=\; 2.5\,.$$

*Total rate of return (6.29):*

$$\frac{d_1}{P_0} + g \;=\; 20\% - 5\% \;=\; 15\%\,.$$

### 2  No growth firm

*Price:*

$$P_0 \;=\; \frac{d_0}{r} \;=\; \frac{1}{0.15} \;=\; £6.67\,.$$

*Market-to-book ratio:*

$$\frac{\textit{Fair price per share}}{\textit{Book price per share}} = \frac{6.67}{8.00} = 0.83 \, .$$

*Dividend yield:*

$$\frac{d_1}{P_0} = \frac{1}{6.67} = 15\% \, .$$

*PE ratio:*

$$PE_0 = \frac{P_0}{y_1} = \frac{6.67}{2} = 3.33 \, .$$

*Total rate of return:*

$$\frac{d_1}{P_0} + g = 15\% + 0\% = 15\% \, .$$

### 3 Normal growth firm

*Price:*

$$P_0 = \frac{d_0(1+g)}{r-g} = \frac{1 \cdot (1+0.07)}{(0.15-0.07)} = \pounds 13.38 \, .$$

*Market-to-book ratio:*

$$\frac{\textit{Fair price per share}}{\textit{Book price per share}} = \frac{13.38}{8.00} = 1.67 \, .$$

*Dividend yield:*

$$\frac{d_1}{P_0} = \frac{1 \cdot (1+0.07)}{13.38} = 8\% \, .$$

*PE ratio:*

$$PE_0 = \frac{P_0}{y_1} = \frac{13.38}{2 \cdot (1+0.07)} = 6.25 \, .$$

*Total rate of return:*

$$\frac{d_1}{P_0} + g = 8\% + 7\% = 15\% \, .$$

### 4 Supernormal growth firm

*Price,* (6.39) *using* (6.26) *with:*

$$(1+h) = \frac{(1+g_s)}{(1+r)} = \frac{1.25}{1.15} = 1.087 \, ,$$

$$P_0 = d_0(1+h) \cdot \left[\frac{(1+h)^T - 1}{h}\right] + \frac{1}{(1+r)^T} \cdot \frac{d_0(1+g_s)^T(1+g)}{(r-g)}$$

$$= 1 \cdot (1.087) \cdot \left[\frac{(1.087)^{10} - 1}{0.087}\right] + \frac{1}{(1.15)^{10}} \cdot \frac{1 \cdot (1.25)^{10}(1.07)}{(0.15 - 0.07)}$$

$$= 16.28 + 0.2472 \cdot 124.56$$

$$= 16.28 + 30.79 = £47.07.$$

*Market-to-book ratio:*

$$\frac{\textit{Fair price per share}}{\textit{Book price per share}} = \frac{47.07}{8.00} = 5.88.$$

*Dividend yield:*

$$\frac{d_1}{P_0} = \frac{1 \cdot (1 + 0.25)}{47.07} = 2.66\%.$$

*PE ratio:*

$$PE_0 = \frac{P_0}{y_1} = \frac{47.07}{2 \cdot (1 + 0.25)} = 18.83.$$

*Total rate of return:*

$$\frac{d_1}{P_0} + \bar{g} = 2.66\% + 12.34\% = 15\%,$$

*where $\bar{g}$ is the average growth rate and can be calculated approximately as follows:*

$$\bar{g} = (1+g_s)^\gamma(1+g)^{1-\gamma} - 1$$

$$= (1.25)^{0.3459}(1.07)^{0.6541} - 1$$

$$\approx 12.34\%,$$

*where:*

$$\gamma = \textit{relative contribution to price from growth stage} = 16.28/47.07;$$
$$1-\gamma = \textit{relative contribution to price from mature stage} = 30.79/47.07.$$

*These results can be summarized in the following table:*

| | Price | Market-to-book ratio | PE ratio | Dividend yield | Capital gain | Total rate of return |
|---|---|---|---|---|---|---|
| | (£) | | | (%) | (%) | (%) |
| *Declining firm* | *4.75* | *0.59* | *2.50* | *20.00* | *−5.00* | *15.00* |
| *No growth firm* | *6.67* | *0.83* | *3.33* | *15.00* | *0.00* | *15.00* |
| *Normal growth firm* | *13.38* | *1.67* | *6.25* | *8.00* | *7.00* | *15.00* |
| *Supernormal growth firm* | *47.07* | *5.88* | *18.83* | *2.66* | *12.34* | *15.00* |

*The first point to note is that, whatever their growth rates, all firms generate the same total rate of return on assets of 15 per cent, and that this is the same as the cost of capital or discount rate. This is the case because all firms are in the same risk class and because in equilibrium the rate of return on assets must equal the cost of capital. However, the composition of the rate of return differs for different firms. For example, the declining firm needs an annual dividend yield of 20 per cent to compensate for the capital loss of 5 per cent per annum, whereas the supernormal growth firm has a dividend yield of only 2.66 per cent, but this is compensated for by an average annual growth in the share price of 12.34 per cent. Similarly, the declining firm has a share price of only £4.75 and sells at a multiple to earnings of only 2.50, whereas the supernormal growth firm has a share price of £47.07 and sells at a multiple to earnings of nearly 19. Another measure of the effect of differential growth is the market-to-book ratio. This measures the ratio of the fair price of the share to the book price taken from the balance sheet. It increases with the growth rate. Static or declining firms are likely to be valued at less than the book value of their assets, while rapidly growing firms can be priced at many times the book value of their assets, reflecting the fact that growth adds value to the initial investment outlay. But despite this, all firms generate the same return on assets, as we have seen.*

### 6.5.3   Forecasting earnings

So far we have simply assumed a particular growth rate for the firm's earnings over future periods. But in practice, the growth rate in earnings is extremely difficult to determine and has to be forecast. There are two main ways of forecasting earnings: the bottom-up approach and the top-down approach.

In the *bottom-up* approach, investment analysts produce earnings forecasts on the basis of detailed research into the firm's activities. The analyst might start with a base-line figure $g_0$ which is determined from (6.32) as:

$$
\begin{aligned}
g_0 \;=\; & \text{5-year average return on investments} \\
& \times \text{5-year average retention ratio.}
\end{aligned}
\tag{6.40}
$$

This base-line figure is then modified in the light of the analyst's detailed research to give growth forecasts over the next two years, say, $g_1$ and $g_2$.

In the *top-down* approach, the effects of the wider macroeconomy on the firm's earnings are taken into account. This requires forecasts of the growth in GDP (gross domestic product) as well as forecasts of the share of dividends in GDP. If there is a stable relationship between the firm's earnings and GDP (where the relationship is estimated using regression techniques, for example), then the firm's earnings can be forecast given the forecasts of GDP. Alternatively, the firm's dividends could be forecast given forecasts of the share of dividends in GDP, assuming that a stable relationship exists between the firm's dividends, the share of dividends in GDP and GDP growth. Again, suppose that this analysis provides us with earnings growth forecasts over the next two years of $g_1$ and $g_2$.

Both the bottom-up and top-down methods used by analysts usually provide growth forecasts only for two years ahead. Beyond two years, neither method produces forecasts in which analysts have much confidence. They therefore tend to assume that after two years the firm (if it is not a supernormal growth firm) simply grows in line with GDP, on the grounds that, in the long run, the share of dividends or earnings in GDP does not trend in any significant way. Since the long-run real growth rate in GDP in the UK is between 2.5 and 3 per cent, and if we additionally assume that the long-run inflation rate is 5 per cent, then a realistic estimate of the long-run nominal growth rate in earnings is around 8 per cent per annum.

**Example 6.2 (Dividend discount model with different forecasts)** *To illustrate, consider a firm with earnings of £2 per share and a stable payout ratio of 50 per cent. Its required return on equity capital is 15 per cent. Suppose investment analysts have come up with the following forecasts for earnings growth:*

| Year | Growth rate | Bottom-up method (%) | Top-down method (%) |
|------|-------------|----------------------|---------------------|
| 1    | $g_1$       | 5                    | 10                  |
| 2    | $g_2$       | 6                    | 9                   |
| 3–∞  | $g$         | 8                    | 8                   |

*The dividend discount model in this case is:*

$$P_0 \;=\; \frac{d_0 \cdot (1+g_1)}{1+r} + \frac{d_0 \cdot (1+g_1)(1+g_2)}{(1+r)^2} + \frac{d_0 \cdot (1+g_1)(1+g_2)(1+g)}{(r-g)(1+r)^2}.$$

*Using the bottom-up earnings forecasts, we get:*

$$
\begin{aligned}
P_0 \;&=\; \frac{1 \cdot (1.05)}{1.15} + \frac{1 \cdot (1.05)(1.06)}{(1.15)^2} + \frac{1 \cdot (1.05)(1.06)(1.08)}{(0.15 - 0.08)(1.15)^2} \\
&=\; 0.9130 + 0.8416 + 12.9845 \;=\; £14.74.
\end{aligned}
$$

*Using the more optimistic top-down earnings forecasts, we get:*

$$
\begin{aligned}
P_0 \;&=\; \frac{1 \cdot (1.10)}{1.15} + \frac{1 \cdot (1.10)(1.09)}{(1.15)^2} + \frac{1 \cdot (1.10)(1.09)(1.08)}{(0.15 - 0.08)(1.15)^2} \\
&=\; 0.9565 + 0.9066 + 13.9878 \;=\; £15.85.
\end{aligned}
$$

*If the actual share price is £15.20, it is clear how investment advisers can give conflicting buy and sell recommendations!*

## 6.6   The value of the firm: the effect of leverage

So far we have examined different ways of valuing a single share in the firm. We end this chapter with a brief consideration of how to value the entire firm.

If the firm is entirely financed by ordinary shares, i.e. if the firm is *unlevered* (or *ungeared*), the fair value of the firm is simply the product of the fair price of the share and the number of shares outstanding:

$$V_U \;=\; V_{SU} \;=\; P_0 \cdot N_0, \tag{6.41}$$

where:

$$P_0 \;=\; \text{fair price of the share;}$$
$$V_U \;=\; \text{fair value of an unlevered firm;}$$
$$V_{SU} \;=\; \text{fair value of the shares in an unlevered firm;}$$
$$N_0 \;=\; \text{number of shares outstanding.}$$

If the firm pays out all its reported earnings as dividends and so has zero growth, the value of the firm will be, using (6.28) with $g = 0$:

$$
\begin{aligned}
V_U \;&=\; \frac{d_0 \cdot N_0}{r_U} \\[6pt]
&=\; \frac{y_0 \cdot N_0}{r_U} \\[6pt]
&=\; \frac{Y_0(1 - T_c) \cdot N_0}{r_U} \\[6pt]
&=\; \frac{\bar{Y}(1 - T_c)}{r_U},
\end{aligned}
\tag{6.42}
$$

where:

$$Y_0 \;=\; \text{earnings per share before interest and tax;}$$
$$T_c \;=\; \text{rate of corporation tax;}$$
$$\bar{Y} \;=\; Y_0 N_0 = \text{earnings of the firm before interest and tax;}$$
$$r_U \;=\; \text{cost of capital (required rate of return) for an unlevered firm.}$$

This, in turn, means that the cost of (equity) capital for an unlevered firm is given by:

$$
r_U \;=\; \frac{\bar{Y}(1 - T_c)}{V_U}.
\tag{6.43}
$$

If the firm is financed by both equity and debt, i.e. if the firm is *levered* (or *geared*), then the fair value of the firm is the sum of the fair value of the shares and the fair value of the bonds:

$$
V_L \;=\; V_{SL} + V_B,
\tag{6.44}
$$

where:

$$V_L \;=\; \text{fair value of a levered firm;}$$
$$V_{SL} \;=\; \text{fair value of the shares in a levered firm;}$$
$$V_B \;=\; \text{fair value of the bonds.}$$

In fact, to be completely accurate, the fair value of the firm is the sum of the fair values of the individual liabilities listed in Table 6.5. But why do we value a firm in terms of its liabilities rather than its assets? It is certainly true that the value of the firm is equal to the sum of its assets. However, because the market value of the liabilities is more easily determined than the market value of the assets, we generally prefer to estimate value on the basis of liabilities, not assets.

What is the connection between the value of the levered firm and the value of the unlevered firm? In other words, what is the effect of leverage on the value of the shareholders' wealth?

To answer these questions, we will examine two firms with identical cash flows and therefore identical risks. The first (firm A) is a levered firm and the second (firm B) is an unlevered firm which decides to take on some leverage by issuing a bond. Suppose that there is only one type of bond available. It is a perpetual bond with coupon $d$ and a required rate of return $r_B$. The fair value of this bond is:

$$V_B = \frac{d}{r_B}, \tag{6.45}$$

so that:

$$r_B V_B = d. \tag{6.46}$$

The value of shares in firm A is $V_{SL}$ and the return to shareholders, assuming that all earnings are distributed, is:

$$\text{Return to shareholders in firm A} = (\bar{Y} - r_B V_B)(1 - T_c), \tag{6.47}$$

which is earnings before tax but after debt interest has been deducted as an allowable expense *less* corporation tax. Note that the calculation of debt interest uses (6.46). Firm B is an unlevered firm with shares valued at $V_{SU}$ and with reported earnings of $\bar{Y}(1 - T_c)$. The firm decides to repurchase some of its shares in the market with the proceeds from the issue of a bond with the face value $(1 - T_c)V_B$; in other words, it substitutes debt for equity on its balance sheet. Because the firm is incorporated, the interest it pays on the bond is tax-deductible. Having issued the bonds, the value of the shares must be:

$$V_{SU} - (1 - T_c)V_B.$$

The return to shareholders, assuming that all earnings are distributed, is:

$$\begin{aligned}\text{Return to shareholders in firm B} &= \bar{Y}(1 - T_c) - (1 - T_c)r_B V_B \\ &= (\bar{Y} - r_B V_B)(1 - T_c). \end{aligned} \tag{6.48}$$

Because the return to shareholders and the risks in the two firms are identical, the value of the shares in the two firms must also be identical; i.e.:

$$V_{SL} = V_{SU} - (1 - T_c)V_B, \tag{6.49}$$

which, on rearranging, becomes:

$$V_{SL} + V_B = V_{SU} + T_c V_B; \tag{6.50}$$

or, using (6.44) and the fact that $V_U = V_{SU}$, we get:

$$V_L = V_U + T_c V_B. \tag{6.51}$$

The value of the levered firm therefore exceeds the value of the unlevered by an amount $T_c V_B$, which is known as the *gain from leverage* (or the *tax shield*). The gain from leverage arises because the interest payments on bonds are tax-deductible whereas the dividend payments on shares are not. From (6.51), it is clear that the value of the shareholders' wealth increases by $T_c V_B$; i.e., the entire gain from leverage accrues to shareholders (see Modigliani and Miller (1958)).

We can also calculate the cost of equity in a leveraged firm, $r_{SL}$. In equilibrium, the cost of equity capital will equal the return on equity capital; i.e., using (6.47):

$$r_{SL} = \frac{\text{Return to shareholders in levered firm}}{\text{Value of shares in levered firm}}$$

$$= \frac{\bar{Y}(1-T_c) - r_B(1-T_c)V_B}{V_{SL}};$$

using (6.42):

$$= \frac{r_U V_U - r_B(1-T_c)V_B}{V_{SL}};$$

using (6.51):

$$= \frac{r_U V_L - r_U T_c V_B - r_B(1-T_c)V_B}{V_{SL}};$$

and, using (6.44):

$$= \frac{r_U(V_{SL}+V_B) - r_U T_c V_B - r_B(1-T_c)V_B}{V_{SL}}$$

$$= r_U + (r_U - r_B)(1-T_c)(V_B/V_{SL}). \tag{6.52}$$

The cost of equity capital in a levered firm is equal to the cost of equity capital in an unlevered firm *plus* the post-tax difference between the cost of equity capital in an unlevered firm and the cost of debt, weighted by the *leverage ratio* $(V_B/V_{SL})$. The cost of equity capital increases with the leverage ratio because of the greater risk of not being able to meet the fixed-interest payments on the bonds.

The *weighted average cost of capital* (WACC) for a levered firm is the weighted average of the post-tax costs of equity and debt using the proportions of equity and debt in the balance sheet as weights:

$$r_L = r_B(1-T_c) \cdot \frac{V_B}{V_L} + r_{SL} \cdot \frac{V_{SL}}{V_L}. \tag{6.53}$$

Using (6.53), we can derive the value of the levered firm as follows:

$$V_L = \frac{\bar{Y}(1-T_c)}{r_L}, \tag{6.54}$$

where as before $\bar{Y}$ is earnings before interest and tax.

The value of the levered firm, $V_L$ given by (6.51), and the cost of equity capital in the levered firm given by (6.52) were first derived by Modigliani and Miller (1958).

**Example 6.3 (The valuation of the firm)** *Firm A is levered with the following balance sheet:*

| *Assets* (*£,000*) | | *Liabilities* (*£,000*) |
|---|---|---|
| | *Bonds* | *300* |
| | *Shareholders' equity* | *500* |
| *Total assets* 800 | *Total liabilities* | *800* |

*Firm B is unlevered with the following balance sheet:*

| *Assets* (*£,000*) | | *Liabilities* (*£,000*) |
|---|---|---|
| *Total assets* 800 | *Shareholders' equity* | *800* |

*The two firms' income statements are as follows:*

| | *Firm A* (*£,000*) | *Firm B* (*£,000*) |
|---|---|---|
| *Earnings before interest and tax* | 200.00 | 200.00 |
| *Interest on bonds (at 10%)* | (30.00) | |
| *Taxable earnings* | 170.00 | 200.00 |
| *Corporation tax (at 35%)* | (59.50) | (70.00) |
| *Reported earnings* | 110.50 | 130.00 |
| *Dividends (100% payout)* | 110.50 | 130.00 |

*We have the following additional information:*

| | | |
|---|---|---|
| *Required return on equity in unlevered firm* $(r_U)$ | = | 15% |
| *Required return on bonds* $(r_B)$ | = | 10% |
| *Corporation tax rate* $(T_c)$ | = | 35%. |

*Note that, because the required return on the bonds is the same as the coupon on the bonds, the bonds are selling at par so that* $V_B = £300,000$.

*Given this information, we can calculate the value of the unlevered firm B using (6.42):*

$$\text{Value of firm B} \quad = \quad V_U \quad = \quad \frac{\bar{Y}(1 - T_c)}{r_U}$$

$$= \quad \frac{130,000}{0.15} \quad = \quad £866,667.$$

*This is also equal to the value of the equity in the unlevered firm.*

*Using (6.51), the value of firm A is given by:*

$$\text{Value of firm } A = V_L = V_U + T_c V_B$$
$$= 866,667 + (0.35)(300,000)$$
$$= 866,667 + 105,000 = \text{£}971,667.$$

*So the value of firm A exceeds that of firm B by £105,000, the amount of the tax shield.*

*The value of the equity in firm A is determined from (6.44) as follows:*

$$\text{Value of firm } A \text{ equity} = V_{SL} = V_L - V_B$$
$$= \text{£}971,667 - \text{£}300,000 = \text{£}671,667.$$

*The cost of equity in firm A is, using (6.52):*

$$\text{Cost of firm } A \text{ equity} = r_{SL}$$
$$= r_U + (r_U - r_B)(1 - T_c) \cdot \frac{V_B}{V_{SL}}$$
$$= 15 + (15 - 10)(0.65) \cdot \frac{300,000}{671,667}$$
$$= 16.45\%,$$

*while its weighted average cost of capital is:*

$$\text{Weighted average cost of firm } A \text{ capital} = r_L$$
$$= r_B(1 - T_c) \cdot \frac{V_B}{V_L} + r_{SL} \cdot \frac{V_{SL}}{V_L}$$
$$= 10(0.65) \cdot \frac{300,000}{971,667} + 16.45 \cdot \frac{671,667}{971,667}$$
$$= 13.37907\%.$$

*An alternative way to value the levered firm is to use (6.54):*

$$V_L = \frac{\bar{Y}(1 - T_c)}{r_L}$$
$$= \frac{130,000}{0.1337907} = \text{£}971,667.$$

**Selected references**

Francis, J.C. (1991) *Investments*, McGraw-Hill, Singapore. (Chapters 15–18.)

Gordon, M.J. (1962) *The Investment, Financing and Valuation of the Corporation*, Irwin, Homewood, Ill.

Malkiel, B.G. (1996) *A Random Walk Down Wall Street*, W.W. Norton, New York. (Chapters 1–4.)

Miller, M.H., and Modigliani, F. (1961) 'Dividend Policy, Growth and the Valuation of Shares', *Journal of Business*, 34, 411–33.

Modigliani, F. and Miller, M.H. (1958) 'The Cost of Capital, Corporation Finance and the Theory of Investment', *American Economic Review*, 48, 261–97.

Ross, S. (1977) 'The Determination of Financial Structure: The Incentive-Signalling Approach', *Bell Journal of Economics*, Spring, 23–40.

Rozeff, M. (1982) 'Growth, Beta and Agency Costs as Determinants of Dividend Payout Ratios', *Journal of Financial Research*, 5, 249–59.

Rutterford, J. (1993) *Introduction to Stock Exchange Investment*, Macmillan, London. (Chapter 5.)

Sharpe, W.F., Alexander, G., and Bailey, J. (1995) *Investments*, Prentice-Hall, Englewood Cliffs, NJ. (Chapters 17–19.)

Weston, J.F., and Copeland, T.E. (1992) *Managerial Finance*, Dryden Press, Chicago.

Weston, J.F., and Copeland, T.E. (1988) *Managerial Finance*, UK edition, Cassell, London. (Chapter 4.)

**Exercises**

1  Can share valuation models help us determine whether or not dividend policy affects share prices?

2  Examine the relevance of PE ratios for the fundamental analysis of shares.

3  What are the main problems facing investment analysts when they analyze company reports?

4  Distinguish between 'accounting earnings' and 'economic earnings'. Which concept is more useful for share evaluation? Why?

5  Describe and critically appraise the dividend discount model.

6  Why do firms pay dividends?

7  Describe and critically appraise the Gordon growth model.

8  Why in long-run equilibrium will a company's cost of capital exceed its growth rate? What ensures this result?

9  In equilibrium, a firm's cost of capital equals the sum of its dividend yield and growth rate. Why?

10  Analyze the sources of a company's earnings growth.

11  Why, in equilibrium, will all firms in the same risk class generate the same rate of return on assets regardless of their growth rates?

12  You are given the following information about four firms:

| Firm | Growth rate (%) |
|------|-----------------|
| A | −3 |
| B | 0 |
| C | 5 |
| D | 15 |

If the rate of return on assets is 17 per cent for all firms, what does this imply about the dividend yields of the four firms?

13  Compare and contrast the 'top-down' and 'bottom-up' approaches to forecasting corporate earnings.

14  You are told by your investment adviser that ABC PLC is expected to earn 50p per share next year, 60p per share the following year and that thereafter earnings are expected to grow by 8 per cent per year. The dividend payout is 60 per cent and the required rate of return on ABC shares is 15 per cent. If the current share price is £4.00, would you expect your adviser to make a buy, hold or sell recommendation? If transaction costs are 25p per share, would you follow his advice?

15  A firm has just paid a dividend of 40p. The firm's earnings and dividends have grown in the past at the rate of 10 per cent per year and are expected to grow at the same rate indefinitely into the future. If the current share price is £8.80, what is the equilibrium rate of return on an investment in the shares of this firm?

16  The shares in DEF PLC are trading at 80p. The last dividend paid was 8p and the required return on shares in this risk class is 17 per cent. What is the expected future growth rate in dividends?

17  How much does the Gordon growth model tell us about the determinants of the price-earnings ratio?

# Chapter 7

# Foreign currency

An investor can invest in either domestic securities or foreign securities if there are no foreign exchange control restrictions preventing him from doing so. In order to invest abroad he first has to acquire foreign currency (i.e. foreign exchange), which can then be used to purchase overseas bonds and shares. UK residents have been able to invest freely abroad since October 1979 when foreign exchange control restrictions were fully lifted. However, since the early 1970s exchange rates have been floating instead of fixed; this means that, if the investor ultimately intends to liquidate the investment and repatriate the proceeds, he must take into account not only the risk associated with investing in overseas securities markets, but also the exchange rate risk: the risk of adverse movements in the exchange rate.

In this chapter, we cover the market for foreign currency, exchange rate risk, and the fair pricing of foreign currency.

## 7.1 The foreign exchange market

Foreign currency is not traded in a physical market-place. Rather, the market for foreign currency in London is composed of a number of international banks linked by electronic information screens such as Reuters. In total there are about 300 participants (including 50 large international banks) in the foreign currency market. The banks operate as principals (operating their own accounts) and as agents for their own customers. They therefore earn both dealing spreads and commission. The market also contains around 10–12 foreign exchange brokers who link buyers and sellers of foreign currency. The largest volume of business is in US dollars and Deutschmarks. There is both a spot market and a forward market in most currencies. London accounts for one third of all foreign currency transactions which, in 1998, averaged $1,500 billion per day. The clearing system for foreign currencies is called ECHO. The normal settlement period for spot transactions is two business days (excluding public holidays in the countries of both currencies) although it is possible to have one day settlement (this is known as a *before spot* or *over tomorrow* transaction). There is a risk that one counterparty to the transaction fails to deliver the currency in due time. This is known as *settlement risk*. (In the case where the failure to deliver is due to bankruptcy, the risk is sometimes called *del credere risk*; in the case where the bankruptcy occurs in one time zone after one currency has been received in that time zone but before the other currency has been delivered in a later time zone, the risk is known as *Herstatt risk*.)

A currency whose issuing central bank permits holders to exchange it unrestrictedly into the currency of another country is said to be *freely convertible*. If the central bank imposes certain restrictions on convertibility the currency is said to be *partially convertible*. Sterling, for example, has been freely convertible since 1979, but the South African rand, until recently, was only partially convertible. There used to be a two-tier foreign exchange market in South Africa with one market trading a 'commercial' rand and the other trading a 'financial' rand. Funds involving current transactions (in goods and services) were freely convertible using the commercial rand, while those involving capital transactions were only partially convertible using the more expensive financial rand.

Following the introduction of the euro (see footnote on page 17), exchange rates for the EMU member states continue to be quoted and related futures contracts (see Chapter 8) remain available. As the euro gains acceptance this situation is likely to change and, following the proposed introduction of euro notes and coin in January 2002, the currencies of the EMU member states will disappear altogether.

The euro replaced the European currency unit (Ecu) on a 1:1 basis and the existing currencies of the EMU member states were locked into the euro at the rates given in Table 7.1.

**Table 7.1** Euro locking rates for EMU member states

| Country | Currency | €1 equals | Country | Currency | €1 equals |
|---|---|---|---|---|---|
| Austria | *schilling* | 13.7603 | Italy | *lire* | 1936.27 |
| Belgium | *franc* | 40.3399 | Luxembourg | *franc* | 40.3399 |
| Finland | *markka* | 5.94573 | Netherlands | *guilder* | 2.20371 |
| France | *franc* | 6.55957 | Portugal | *escudo* | 200.482 |
| Germany | *Deutschmark* | 1.95583 | Spain | *peseta* | 166.386 |
| Ireland | *punt* | 0.78756 | | | |

**Note:** some values have been rounded.

### 7.1.1   Spot foreign exchange transactions

In terms of quoting the spot price of foreign currency, most countries use *direct quotation* which expresses the number of units of the domestic currency that can be exchanged for one unit of a foreign currency, e.g., £0.625 per \$ or DM1.39 per \$. Sometimes, however, *indirect quotation* is used and this method expresses the number of units of a foreign currency that can be exchanged for one unit of domestic currency, e.g., \$1.60 per £ or \$0.72 per DM. Sterling is, by convention, quoted using this latter method. Whichever method is used, the foreign currency involved is usually the US dollar, so that with direct quotation, we get the domestic currency price of the dollar, while with indirect quotation, we get the dollar price of domestic currency.

For example, we might observe the following spot rates quoted, allowing for the foreign exchange (forex) dealer's spread:

|  | **Buying rate** (bid) | **Selling rate** (offer) | **Mid rate** |
|---|---|---|---|
| DM/$ | 1.3880 (dollars) | 1.3885 (dollars) | 1.38825 |
| ¥/$ | 88.3300 (dollars) | 88.3800 (dollars) | 88.35500 |
| $/£ | 1.5958 (sterling) | 1.5963 (sterling) | 1.59605 |

The Deutschmark and Japanese yen are quoted direct, whereas sterling is quoted indirect. In the case of the D-mark quote of 1.3880–1.3885, for instance, the first rate is the buying rate for dollars and the selling rate for D-marks (from the viewpoint of the quote giver), while the second rate is the selling rate for dollars and the buying rate for D-marks (again from the viewpoint of the quote giver). In contrast, in the case of the sterling quote of 1.5958–1.5963, the first rate is the buying rate for pounds and the selling rate for dollars (from the viewpoint of the quote giver), while the second rate is the selling rate for pounds and the buying rate for dollars (again from the viewpoint of the quote giver).

In practice, forex dealers do not quote the full rate, just the last two decimal places: in the case of sterling, 58–63. In foreign exchange terminology, 0.0001 of the currency is called a *pip*, so what is being quoted is 58 to 63 pips. With a bank engaged in foreign exchange dealing, such a quote would be good for up to about $5m or equivalent.

A *spot foreign exchange transaction* between two banks might take place as follows. One bank (known as the *calling bank*) phones another bank engaged in foreign exchange dealing (and known as the *quoting bank*) and asks for the sterling rate. On being quoted 58–63, the calling bank might say: 'at 63 we buy £2,000,000'. The dealer shouts out to the other dealers 'we lose £2,000,000 at 63' and then fills out a purchase voucher as follows:

---

| | |
|---|---|
| *Sold to:* | Bank ABC, London |
| *Amount:* | £2,000,000 |
| | at rate of:    1.5963 |
| | value date:    today's date + 2 business days |
| *To be paid to:* | Deutsche Bank, Frankfurt |
| *Proceeds:* | $3,192,600 |
| *To be taken from:* | their account with us. |

---

This voucher is then passed in turn to the positions section (which records the transaction and updates the net exposure position of the bank), the foreign exchange correspondence section (which confirms the deal with the counterparty and makes the payment) and then the bank's own accounting department to make the necessary book entry transfers.

The quoting bank is now long $3,192,600 and short £2,000,000 compared with its initial position. This may not be a position it wishes to sustain and in any case the forex desk is in business to make a profit from trading currencies. The chief forex dealer might decide to change the quote to 60–65, thereby raising the price of sterling against the dollar. At these prices, another customer might call and agree to sell £2,000,000 at 1.5960. The quoting bank has therefore sold £2,000,000 at 1.5963 and bought back £2,000,000 at 1.5960 making a profit of:

$$\text{Profit} = £2,000,000(1.5963 - 1.5960) = \$600.$$

Another possible scenario is that market rates change before the quoting bank has time to react. For example, market rates might rise suddenly to 65–70. Bank ABC was smart to have unloaded its dollars. The quoting bank could cover its position at market rates by buying back sterling from yet another bank at 1.5970. In this case it would make a loss:

$$\text{Loss} \;=\; £2,000,000\,(1.5963 - 1.5970) \;=\; -\$1,400.$$

A cheaper alternative would be to change its quote to 66–71 and hope to have its bid hit for £2,000,000 in which case its loss would be reduced:

$$\text{Loss} \;=\; £2,000,000\,(1.5963 - 1.5966) \;=\; -\$600.$$

A quoting bank must also ensure that its bid rate is never higher than another bank's offer. For example if the following were to be observed for \$ per £:

|        | **Buying rate** (bid) | **Selling rate** (offer) |
|--------|-----------------------|--------------------------|
| Bank A | 1.5958                | 1.5963                   |
| Bank B | 1.5964                | 1.5969                   |

then an arbitrageur could buy sterling at 1.5963 from Bank A and immediately resell to Bank B at 1.5964 making a riskless arbitrage profit of one pip per pound or \$100 per £1m traded. In tranquil markets this is not likely to be possible, but in volatile markets it can happen for very short periods until Bank A realizes that it is being constantly lifted and Bank B realizes it is being constantly hit. The arbitrageur does, however, face *execution risk*, the risk that he buys sterling at 1.5963 from Bank A but Bank B changes its quote to, say, 60–65 before the arbitrageur is able to sell off the sterling to it: the arbitrageur would make a loss of three pips per pound in this case.

In recent years there has been an increase in trading in *cross currencies*, i.e., in currencies other than the dollar, e.g., yen against the D-mark. In such cases, *exchange cross rates* have to be determined and this is done using the quotes involving the dollar. For example, suppose we wanted to calculate the ¥/DM cross-rate. We would use the mid rates for the ¥/\$ and DM/\$ as follows:

$$
\left(88.355 \cdot \frac{¥}{\$}\right) \Big/ \left(1.38825 \cdot \frac{DM}{\$}\right) \;=\; \left(88.355 \cdot \frac{¥}{\$}\right)\left(\frac{1}{1.38825} \cdot \frac{\$}{DM}\right)
$$
$$
=\; \frac{88.355}{1.38825}\left(\frac{¥}{\$} \cdot \frac{\$}{DM}\right)
$$
$$
=\; 63.6449 \quad ¥/DM.
$$

If we wanted to calculate the DM/£ cross-rate, we would use the mid rates for DM/\$ and \$/£ as follows:

$$
\left(1.38825 \cdot \frac{DM}{\$}\right)\left(1.59605 \cdot \frac{\$}{£}\right) \;=\; 1.38825 \cdot 1.59605 \left(\frac{DM}{\$} \cdot \frac{\$}{£}\right)
$$
$$
=\; 2.2157 \quad DM/£.
$$

Large banks trading directly in sterling and D-marks might quote a spread around these mid rates of, say, 2.2154–2.2160. But this would be for interbank deals. Bank customers would have to pay a much wider spread, based on the intermediate exchange via the dollar. Suppose that a bank customer wishes to sell sterling and buy D-marks. The bank would buy the sterling from the customer in exchange for dollars at the bid rate for sterling ($1.5958 per £) and then exchange the dollars into D-marks at the bid rate for dollars (DM1.3880 per $). This implies that the bid rate for sterling (offer rate for D-marks) is:

$$
\begin{aligned}
\text{Bid rate (sterling)} &= \left(1.3880 \cdot \frac{\text{DM}}{\$}\right) \left(1.5958 \cdot \frac{\$}{£}\right) \\
&= 1.3880 \cdot 1.5958 \left(\frac{\text{DM}}{\$} \cdot \frac{\$}{£}\right) \\
&= 2.2150 \quad \text{DM}/£.
\end{aligned}
$$

Suppose instead that a bank customer wishes to sell D-marks and buy sterling. The bank would buy the D-marks from the customer in exchange for dollars at the offer rate for dollars (DM1.3885 per $) and then exchange the dollars into sterling at the offer rate for sterling ($1.5963 per £). This implies that the offer rate for sterling (bid rate for D-marks) is:

$$
\begin{aligned}
\text{Offer rate (sterling)} &= \left(1.3885 \cdot \frac{\text{DM}}{\$}\right) \left(1.5963 \cdot \frac{\$}{£}\right) \\
&= 1.3885 \cdot 1.5963 \left(\frac{\text{DM}}{\$} \cdot \frac{\$}{£}\right) \\
&= 2.2165 \quad \text{DM}/£.
\end{aligned}
$$

With bid-offer rates of 2.2150–2.2165, nonbank customers face a spread of 15 pips rather than 6 pips for interbank deals.

## 7.1.2 Forward foreign exchange transactions

Banks not only engage in spot currency transactions, they also engage in *forward foreign exchange transactions*, that is, for delivery on a day further ahead than two business days which is the settlement or value date for spot transactions. We can distinguish between an *outright transaction*, which is a single forward transaction, either purchase or sale, and a *swap transaction*, which is the combination of a spot transaction (either purchase or sale) and the opposite forward transaction (either sale or purchase).

Forward foreign exchange rates are usually quoted not in levels, but as differences between spot and forward rates, i.e. as *premiums* or *discounts* with respect to spot rates; these differentials are called *forward points* or sometimes *swap points*, even if there is no underlying swap transaction involved. When the forward rate is expressed in levels, it is known as a *forward outright rate*. One of the reasons why forward rates are generally expressed as premiums or discounts is that even when spot rates change there is frequently no change in the premium or discount so that fewer overall changes are needed using this method.

We might observe the following spot and forward rates:

| | DM/$ | | ¥/$ | | $/£ | |
|---|---|---|---|---|---|---|
| | **Bid** | **Offer** | **Bid** | **Offer** | **Bid** | **Offer** |
| Spot | 1.3880 | 1.3885 | 88.3300 | 88.3800 | 1.5958 | 1.5963 |
| 1 month | 4 | 6 | 3500 | 2800 | 101 | 98 |
| 2 month | 16 | 18 | 6850 | 6100 | 188 | 184 |
| 3 month | 26 | 29 | 1.0950 | 1.0150 | 269 | 265 |
| 6 month | 64 | 69 | 2.7000 | 2.4150 | 471 | 464 |
| 12 month | 143 | 153 | 4.0550 | 3.9550 | 806 | 786 |

The first task is to identify which currencies are trading at a forward premium and which at a forward discount. To help us do this we should remember two things: first, the forward bid price must always be lower than the forward offer price, and second, the forward bid-offer spread must always increase with term to delivery. So if the number on the bid side is lower than the number on the offer side, we know that the currency is trading at a forward premium and the premium is *added to* the spot rate. On the other hand, if the number on the bid side is larger than the number on the offer side, we know that the currency is trading at a forward discount and the discount is *subtracted from* the spot rate.

To illustrate, we can take the three-month rates. In the case of DM/$, the dollar is trading at a premium against the D-mark:

$$
\begin{array}{lll}
& \text{DM/\$ spot rate} & 1.3880 \; - \; 1.3885 \\
+ & \text{3-month premium} & \underline{\quad 26 \; - \quad\quad 29} \\
= & \text{forward rate} & 1.3906 \; - \; 1.3914
\end{array}
$$

and the spread is 5 pips on the spot rate and 8 pips on the forward rate. In the case of ¥/$, the dollar is trading at a discount against the yen:

$$
\begin{array}{lll}
& \text{¥/\$ spot rate} & 88.3300 \; - \; 88.3800 \\
- & \text{3-month discount} & \underline{1.0950 \; - \quad 1.0150} \\
= & \text{forward rate} & 87.2350 \; - \; 87.3650
\end{array}
$$

and the spread is 500 pips on the spot rate and 1300 pips on the forward rate. In the case of $/£, sterling is trading at a discount against the dollar:

$$
\begin{array}{lll}
& \text{\$/£ spot rate} & 1.5958 \; - \; 1.5963 \\
- & \text{3-month discount} & \underline{\quad 269 \; - \quad\quad 265} \\
= & \text{forward rate} & 1.5689 \; - \; 1.5698
\end{array}
$$

and the spread is 5 pips on the spot rate and 9 pips on the forward rate.

Sometimes the premium or discount is expressed not in absolute terms but as a percentage per annum of the spot rate. So, for example, the 3-month forward bid rate on DM/$ is standing at a percentage premium of:

$$
\begin{aligned}
\text{Percentage premium} \; &= \; \frac{0.0026}{1.3880} \cdot \frac{12}{3} \cdot 100 \\
&= \; 0.75\% \quad \text{p.a.}
\end{aligned}
$$

on the spot bid rate, while the 3-month forward offer rate on $/£ is standing at a percentage discount of:

$$\text{Percentage discount} = \frac{0.0265}{1.5963} \cdot \frac{12}{3} \cdot 100$$
$$= 6.64\% \quad \text{p.a.}$$

on the spot offer rate.

The same procedure used to calculate spot cross rates can also be used to calculate *forward cross rates*. For example, suppose a customer wants to sell six-month forward sterling against six-month forward D-marks. What is the forex dealer's bid rate for sterling? The dealer sells six-month forward sterling (to be received from the customer) against dollars (i.e. buys dollars) at the six-month forward bid rate for sterling of $1.5487 per £, i.e. the spot rate of 1.5958 *less* the 6-month forward discount of 0.0471. At the same time, the dealer buys six-month forward D-marks (to be delivered to the customer) against dollars (i.e. sells dollars) at the six-month forward bid rate for dollars of DM1.3944 per $, i.e. the spot rate of 1.3880 *plus* the six-month forward premium of 0.0064. This implies that the bid rate for six-month forward sterling (offer rate for D-marks) is:

$$\text{Bid rate (sterling)} = \left(1.3944 \cdot \frac{DM}{\$}\right)\left(1.5487 \cdot \frac{\$}{£}\right)$$
$$= 1.3944 \cdot 1.5487 \left(\frac{DM}{\$} \cdot \frac{\$}{£}\right)$$
$$= 2.1595 \quad DM/£.$$

Suppose that another customer wants to buy three-month forward D-marks against three-month forward yen. What is the forex dealer's rate for D-marks? The dealer buys three-month forward D-marks (to be delivered to the customer) against dollars (i.e. sells dollars) at the three-month forward bid rate for dollars of DM1.3906 per $, i.e. the spot rate of 1.3880 *plus* the three-month forward premium of 0.0026. At the same time, the dealer sells three-month forward yen (to be received from the customer) against dollars (i.e. buys dollars) at the three-month forward offer rate for dollars of ¥87.3650 per $, i.e. spot rate of 88.3800 *less* the three-month forward discount of 1.0150. Thus the offer rate for three-month forward D-marks (bid rate for yen) is:

$$\text{Offer rate (D-marks)} = \left(1.3906 \cdot \frac{DM}{\$}\right) \Big/ \left(87.3650 \cdot \frac{¥}{\$}\right)$$
$$= \left(1.3906 \cdot \frac{DM}{\$}\right)\left(\frac{1}{87.3650} \cdot \frac{\$}{¥}\right)$$
$$= \frac{1.3906}{87.3650}\left(\frac{DM}{\$} \cdot \frac{\$}{¥}\right)$$
$$= 0.0159 \quad DM/¥.$$

In practice, this would be quoted as DM1.59 per ¥100.

Sometimes banks will offer forward rates for *broken dates*, i.e. for dates lying between the standard contract dates (of 1, 2, 3, 6 and 12 months ahead). The rates will be based on linear interpolation between the rates available on the nearest standard contracts on either side of the required date. Suppose a customer wanted to buy dollars against D-marks for delivery in two months and 10 days. The spread between the three-month offer premium and two-month offer premium is 11 pips (29 pips – 18 pips) or 0.367 pips per day for a 30-day month (i.e. 11/30). Therefore the bank's offer rate for dollars against D-marks two months and 10 days forward will be 1.3907 DM/$, i.e. the spot rate of 1.3885 *plus* the 2-month forward premium of 0.0018 *plus* (0.0000367 × 10 days).

## 7.2   Exchange rate risk

When investing abroad, an investor has to take into account a number of factors that are not relevant when investing in the domestic economy. Examples of these are *transaction costs*, *taxes* and *political risk*. Transaction costs may be higher than in the domestic economy. For example, the costs involved in trading in futures and options in the USA for a UK (or other overseas) resident are higher than the costs involved for a US resident.  There are also transaction costs involved in acquiring and/or disposing of the required foreign exchange. Similarly, an investor may be liable for both income and capital gains tax in two countries: the country of residence and the country where the investment is held.  Generally, however, double taxation treaties exist between countries.  Under such treaties, UK investors will pay income tax on, say, foreign share dividends at the higher of the investor's marginal income tax rate in the UK and the marginal income tax rate in the country in which the investment is held. This means that, where the investor's marginal tax rate is higher abroad than in the UK, he will not be liable to additional income tax in the UK, but nevertheless will suffer a higher tax burden on an overseas investment than a comparable UK investment. Political risk is the risk that an investment abroad may be expropriated by the overseas government. Less severely, the overseas government might unexpectedly introduce factors that render an overseas investment less attractive, e.g. the imposition of capital controls, additional taxes or transaction costs.

However, the most important factor influencing overseas investments is *exchange rate risk*. This is the risk that adverse movements in the exchange rate (between the country where the investment is held and the country where the investor is domiciled) will reduce the return from an investment, when the return is measured in the domestic currency.

To illustrate, suppose that at the beginning of the year a UK investor exchanges sterling for dollars to invest in US securities. The spot exchange rate is $e_0 = £2$ per £. He requires $50,000 to purchase 2000 shares at $25 per share. The sterling equivalent is £12.50 per share or £25,000 for the investment. The shares are held for a year and then sold for $27 each. In addition, a $2 dividend is paid. The holding period return in US dollars, $r_\$$, is therefore:

$$r_\$ = \frac{27 + 2 - 25}{25}$$
$$= 0.16 \quad (16\%).$$

However, the return when measured in sterling depends on what has happened to the exchange rate during the course of the year. The sterling return, $r_£$, is determined as follows:

$$r_£ = \frac{P_1/e_1}{P_0/e_0} - 1 \tag{7.1}$$
$$= \frac{1 + r_\$}{1 + s} - 1,$$

where:

$$P_0 = \text{beginning-of-year dollar price of security;}$$
$$P_1 = \text{end-of-year dollar price of security (including dividend);}$$
$$e_0 = \text{beginning-of-year exchange rate (\$ per £);}$$
$$e_1 = \text{end-of-year exchange rate (\$ per £);}$$
$$s = (e_1/e_0) - 1 = \text{rate of appreciation of the exchange rate (i.e.}$$
$$\text{appreciation of sterling against the dollar).}$$

The beginning-of-year exchange rate was $e_0 = \$2$ per £. Suppose that the end-of-year exchange rate was $e_1 = \$1.50$ per £. This implies that:

$$s = \frac{1.50}{2.00} - 1 = -0.25;$$

in other words, the exchange rate has depreciated by 25 per cent. In this case:

$$r_£ = \frac{1.16}{0.75} - 1$$
$$= 0.547 \quad (54.7\%).$$

The sterling rate of return is 54.7 per cent, nearly three times the dollar rate of return.

However, suppose instead that the end-of-year exchange rate was $e_1 = \$2.50$ per £. This implies that:

$$s = \frac{2.50}{2.00} - 1 = 0.25,$$

so that the exchange rate has appreciated by 25 per cent. In this case:

$$r_£ = \frac{1.16}{1.25} - 1$$
$$= -0.072 \quad (-7.2\%).$$

The sterling rate of return is negative. Even though the dollar investment was a good one, the adverse movement in the exchange rate (from the view point of a dollar investor) has resulted in the investor making a loss in terms of sterling. This demonstrates precisely the nature of exchange rate risk.

Exchange rate risk affects not only investors but also companies engaged in international trade and/or with operations in foreign countries. For such organisations, exchange rate risk comes in two forms: transaction risk and translation risk.

*Transaction risk* is the risk arising from invoicing in a foreign currency. For example, consider the case of a UK producer exporting goods to the US. Ideally, the UK exporter would like to invoice in sterling. But this passes the exchange rate risk on to the US buyer who may be unwilling to accept this. In addition, there may be other suppliers, such as those based in Germany, Japan and the US. The US supplier will naturally invoice in dollars and so will face no currency risk. The German and Japanese suppliers may choose to invoice in Deutschmarks and yen, respectively, but historically these two currencies have been less volatile than sterling and as a consequence the US buyer may prefer to deal with either of these two suppliers over the UK supplier. In all these cases, the UK exporter faces the *economic risk* of not making the sale to the US buyer. To eliminate this economic risk, the UK exporter has to invoice in dollars and hence take on the transaction risk of receiving lower sterling proceeds than anticipated as a result of a fall in the value of the dollar against sterling.

*Translation risk* is the risk to the balance sheet from having assets and/or liabilities denominated in a foreign currency. For example, consider a company with the following balance sheet when the exchange rate is 1.50 $/£:

|  | *Assets (£)* |  | *Liabilities (£)* |
|---|---|---|---|
| Sterling assets | 10,000 | Sterling loan | 15,000 |
| Dollar assets ($15,000) | 10,000 | Share capital | 5,000 |
|  | 20,000 |  | 20,000 |

Suppose that the exchange rate rises to 2.00 $/£:

|  | *Assets (£)* |  | *Liabilities (£)* |
|---|---|---|---|
| Sterling assets | 10,000 | Sterling loan | 15,000 |
| Dollar assets ($15,000) | 7,500 | Share capital | 2,500 |
|  | 17,500 |  | 17,500 |

*Memorandum item*: translation loss = £2,500.

In this case, the appreciation of sterling results in a translation loss to the company when it compiles its sterling balance sheet. This could lead to a breach of its covenants. For example, when it initially raised the sterling loan, the company might have agreed that its gearing (ratio of debt to total liabilities) should not exceed 80 per cent and that the value of shareholders' capital should not fall below £3,000. With an exchange rate of $2.00 per £, both these covenants are breached: the company's gearing has risen to:

$$\frac{£15,000}{£17,500} = 0.86 \quad (86\%),$$

and shareholders' funds have fallen to £2,500. The company would have to issue shares to the value of at least £1,250 to bring its gearing down to 80 per cent:

$$\frac{£15,000}{£17,500 + £1,250} = 0.8 \quad (80\%).$$

Alternatively, the company could match assets and liabilities in the same currency. Suppose that the original balance sheet when the exchange rate is $1.50 per £ is:

|  | *Assets (£)* |  | *Liabilities (£)* |
|---|---|---|---|
| Sterling assets | 10,000 | Sterling loan | 5,000 |
| Dollar assets ($15,000) | 10,000 | Dollar loan ($15,000) | 10,000 |
|  |  | Share capital | 5,000 |
|  | 20,000 |  | 20,000 |

When the exchange rate rises to $2.00 per £ the balance sheet becomes:

|  | *Assets (£)* |  | *Liabilities (£)* |
|---|---|---|---|
| Sterling assets | 10,000 | Sterling loan | 5,000 |
| Dollar assets ($15,000) | 7,500 | Dollar loan ($15,000) | 7,500 |
|  |  | Share capital | 5,000 |
|  | 17,500 |  | 17,500 |

There is now no translation loss, and gearing at 71 per cent (i.e. £12,500/£17,500) and shareholders' capital at £5,000 are well within covenant limits.

The accounting conventions with translation exposures are as follows. Gains and losses on foreign currency assets and liabilities usually go to or come from reserves as the case may be. The exception is when foreign currency borrowings exceed the level of assets being matched. In this case, any gain or loss on the excess borrowings go into the profit and loss account. To illustrate, suppose that the above company makes profits on its UK activities of £1,000 and a profit on its US activities of $1,500. The profit and loss account is as follows:

| | *$1.50/£* | *$2.00/£* |
|---|---|---|
| UK profits (£) | 1,000 | 1,000 |
| US profits (£) | 1,000 | 750 |
| | 2,000 | 1,750 |

An appreciation of sterling reduces the value of US profits.

Exchange rate risk can be hedged using forward currency transactions. Many companies engaged in international trade use forward contracts to avoid speculating on the exchange rate; these are known as *commercial forward operations*. Suppose a UK importer purchases goods from the US, invoiced in dollars and payable in three months. To remove the risk of an increase in the value of the dollar (fall in the value of sterling), the importer buys three-month forward dollars, thereby locking in the dollar price of the imports and fixing the equivalent sterling cost of the imports with certainty. Alternatively, suppose a UK exporter knows he will have Deutschmark receipts in one month's time. To remove the risk of a fall in the value of the D-mark (rise in the value of sterling), he could sell the D-marks forward at the one-month forward rate. Not to undertake these forward operations is tantamount to speculating on a fall in the value of the dollar in the first example and a rise in the value of the D-mark in the second.

Companies and institutions also engage in *financial forward operations* to hedge the exchange rate risk from capital transactions. As we have seen above, foreign currency assets (e.g. deposits, shares, bonds, property, loans to subsidiaries) lose value if the foreign currency falls in value relative to the domestic currency. This risk can be hedged by selling the foreign currency forward. Conversely, foreign currency liabilities (e.g. borrowing in overseas capital markets) increase in value if the foreign currency rises relative to the domestic currency. This risk can be hedged by buying the foreign currency forward.

To illustrate this, we can consider the following example. A UK-based investor has the choice of investing in a three-month sterling deposit at 11 per cent per annum or a three-month dollar deposit at 5 per cent per annum. The bid rate for spot sterling (offer rate for spot dollars) is $1.5958 per £, the offer rate for spot sterling (bid rate for spot dollars) is $1.5963 per £ and the discount on the three-month forward rate is 269–265 pips. For every pound invested in the UK, the investor will receive £1.0275 back in three months' time, i.e. £1[1 + (0.11/4)]. Alternatively, the investor could exchange the pound into dollars at the spot bid rate (for sterling) of $1.5958 per £, invest this sum for three months at 5 per cent, generating $1.6157 in three months' time, i.e. $1.5958[1 + (0.05/4)], while contracting with the bank to sell these dollar proceeds forward at the three month forward offer rate (for sterling) of $1.5698 per £, i.e. the spot offer rate of 1.5963 *less* the discount of 0.0265. This gives a certain sterling value (i.e. one that is completely hedged for exchange rate risk) of:

$$\frac{1.5958\,[1 + (0.05/4)]}{1.5698} = £1.0293,$$

which implies an equivalent sterling interest rate of 11.71 per cent, i.e. $2.93 \times 4$. So even though the dollar interest rate is less than the sterling interest rate, it is possible to end up with a higher return by investing in the US and fully hedging the exchange rate risk. In this case, the rate is also higher than the rate of 11 per cent that is available on the three-month sterling deposit.

It is also possible to use forward currency transactions to take on exchange rate risk, i.e. for speculation. This involves an outright forward purchase of currency A against currency B if it is believed that currency A will appreciate relative to B in the near future. The speculator does not intend to take delivery of A in exchange for B at maturity; rather he intends to offset the forward transaction by means of an opposite spot transaction at maturity. The advantage of this arrangement is that no funds are needed up front to support this type of speculative activity. To illustrate, suppose that a speculator believes that the dollar will appreciate against sterling over the next three months, so he buys three-month dollars forward at $1.5689 per £, i.e. the spot bid rate for sterling (offer rate for dollars) of 1.5958 *less* the 3-month forward discount of 0.0269. Suppose after three months, the spot rate is 1.5325–1.5335. The speculator buys dollars at $1.5689 per £ but immediately resells them at the spot offer rate for sterling (bid rate for dollars) of $1.5335 per £. This gives a profit per dollar of £0.0147. This is because the dollars were purchased for £0.6374 (i.e. 1/1.5689) and sold for £0.6521 (i.e. 1/1.5335). This profit was generated without the speculator putting up any of his own capital, but it certainly was not riskless. This is because the dollar could have fallen in value and the speculator would then have made a loss. Suppose that after three months the spot exchange rate was 1.6535–1.6545 rather than 1.5325–1.5335. In this case, the dollars that were purchased for £0.6374 were sold for £0.6044 (i.e. 1/1.6545), giving a loss per dollar of £0.0330.

## 7.3   Covering foreign exchange transactions

This section illustrates two ways of covering the risk associated with foreign exchange transactions. The first makes use of the money markets and the second uses swaps.

### 7.3.1   Covering forward transactions

When a bank engages in a forward foreign exchange transaction with a customer, it is agreeing to buy one currency (from the customer) and sell another (to the customer) at some future date (greater than two business days' ahead). If it does not already own the currency it is selling, it must arrange to acquire that currency on or before the forward delivery date. It is unlikely that the bank will wait until the actual delivery date before buying the currency in the spot market (actually two business days prior to the forward delivery date). Instead it is likely to cover its position by using one of two methods: the money market method or the swap method.

With the *money market method*, the bank borrows the currency it is agreeing to buy from the customer, exchanges it at the spot rate into the currency it is agreeing to sell to the customer and then puts this on deposit until the forward transaction takes place, thereby enabling the currency borrowed to be repaid using the currency supplied by the customer on the forward transaction date. For example, suppose that a customer wishes to buy D-marks against dollars in three months' time. The bank observes the following spot exchange rates for DM/$:

Spot      1.3880–1.3885

and the following eurocurrency interest rates:

|                        |             |
|------------------------|-------------|
| Three month (dollar)   | 5.75–5.875  |
| Three month (D-mark)   | 6.5–6.625.  |

Suppose that the bank quotes the customer a forward bid rate for dollars of DM1.3895 per \$ (i.e. the bank will buy dollars from the customer in exchange for D-marks at this rate). The bank then borrows dollars at the three-month offer rate of 5.875 per cent. It exchanges the dollars into D-marks at the interbank spot bid rate for dollars (offer rate for D-marks) of DM1.3880 per \$ (i.e. another possibly larger quoting bank buys the dollars off this bank in exchange for D-marks). It then deposits the D-marks at the three-month bid rate of 6.5 per cent. For each D-mark required in three months' time, the bank would need to have:

$$\frac{1}{1 + (0.065/4)} = DM\,0.9840098$$

at the beginning, so that with the interest earned, there would be exactly enough to supply the D-mark required. To get DM 0.9840098 at the beginning of the period, the bank would need to borrow \$0.7089407 (i.e. 0.9840098/1.3880) and the repayment on this after three months would be:

$$0.7089407[1 + (0.05875/4)] = \$0.7193533.$$

The bank would need a three-month forward bid exchange rate for dollars of at most DM1.3901 per \$ (i.e. 1/0.7193533) to cover its borrowing costs. Since the bank quoted the customer a three-month forward bid exchange rate for dollars (offer rate for D-marks) of DM1.3895 per \$, the bank would make a profit. Suppose that the customer wanted to buy DM10m. At the quoted rate of DM1.3895 per \$, the bank would receive from the customer \$7,196,833 (i.e. 10,000,000/1.3895) in three months' time. The bank only needs \$7,193,727 (i.e. 10,000,000/1.3901) to meet the customer's requirements using the money market method. Hence it makes a profit of \$3,106 (i.e. \$7,196,833 - \$7,193,727) on the deal.

With the *swap method*, the bank buys the currency required by the customer in the interbank market at the current spot offer rate for that currency. It will subsequently deliver this currency to the customer in exchange for the currency received from the customer at the quoted forward bid rate agreed with the customer. In the meantime, it has no use for this currency, so it swaps out of it by selling it at the current spot bid rate and simultaneously agreeing to a forward purchase at the forward offer rate. So the swap method involves two swaps: a spot purchase and a forward sale at one set of exchange rates, with a simultaneous spot sale and forward purchase at another set of exchange rates. Because the swaps are exactly offsetting and have identical durations, the bank uses negligible amounts of its own capital with this method. Also the absolute level of exchange rates is not important. The bank's net profit depends on the difference between the two sets of forward premiums or discounts implied by the two swaps. Suppose that the three-month interbank forward exchange rates for DM/\$ are:

|                      |               |
|----------------------|---------------|
| Three-month forward  | 1.3906–1.3914. |

The bank buys D-marks at the current spot offer rate for D-marks (spot bid rate for dollars) of 1.3880. In three months' time these D-marks will be delivered to the customer at the forward bid rate for dollars (forward offer rate for D-marks) of 1.3895 quoted by the bank to its customer (notice that this is lower than the interbank forward bid rate for dollars of 1.3906). But since the D-marks are not needed for three-months and would otherwise have to be paid for using dollars, they are sold in the interbank market at the current spot bid rate for D-marks (spot offer rate for dollars) of 1.3885. At the same time, the bank takes out a forward contract to buy D-marks in three months' time at the interbank forward offer rate for D-marks (forward bid rate for dollars) of 1.3914. In the first swap, the bank buys D-marks at $0.7204611 per DM (i.e. 1/1.3880) and sells them at $0.7196833 per DM (i.e. 1/1.3895) and so makes a loss of $0.0007778 per DM. In the second swap, the bank sells D-marks at $0.7202016 per DM (i.e. 1/1.3885) and buys them back at $0.7187005 per DM (i.e. 1/1.3914) and so makes a profit of $0.0015011 per DM. Taking the two swaps together the bank makes a profit of $0.0007233 per DM. Again if the customer wishes to buy DM10m, the bank would make a profit of $7,233 (i.e. 0.0007233 × 10m). In this particular example, the bank makes a larger profit using the swap method compared with the money market method.

## 7.3.2   Covering spot transactions

When a bank engages in a spot foreign exchange transaction, it is agreeing to buy one currency and sell another in two working days' time. When it does not already own the currency it is selling, it is effectively creating a short position in that currency. In this case, the bank is said to be running an open foreign exchange position on a spot basis. The resulting short position must be financed. There are a number of ways of doing this.

The first is by borrowing in the money market. The bank must arrange to borrow the currency sold so that it can deliver against the short position. At the same time, the currency purchased must be placed on deposit. Suppose that dollars are purchased and sterling is sold short. The difference between the interest paid on the sterling borrowed and the interest earned on the dollars deposited represents the cost of running a short sterling position on a spot basis. For example, suppose that three month sterling interest rates are 12.625–12.75 and three month eurodollar interest rates are 5.75–5.875. In this case, sterling can be borrowed at 12.75 per cent and dollars can be deposited at 5.75 per cent, so the funding cost of the three-month short position is 7 per cent per annum. The main disadvantage of this method is that the bank is committing itself to running its short position for the fixed term of the loan and deposit, e.g. three months. The bank might find that it wants to unwind its position sooner than this.

A second and more convenient method of running a short position is through a series of day-to-day swap transactions which gives the bank the choice of continuing or unwinding its position on a daily basis. Suppose it is Monday and sterling is sold spot against dollars at 1.5958, value Wednesday (i.e. settlement must take place on Wednesday). On Tuesday, the bank executes a one-day swap transaction, value Wednesday: this is known as a *tomorrow/next* or *tom/next* operation. Sterling is purchased against dollars, value Wednesday, and simultaneously sold against dollars, value Thursday. By doing this, the bank maintains its desired short sterling/long dollars position, but settlement (which would require borrowing sterling and depositing dollars) is delayed for one day. This operation can be carried out again on Wednesday and on subsequent days for as long as the bank wishes to preserve its short position.

These one-day swap operations are effectively a series of one-day forward purchases of sterling, and so the one-day swap exchange rate will depend on the one-day forward premium or discount on the spot rate. Suppose for example that the one-day forward discount is 0.0004–0.00035, implying that the bid rate for one-day forward sterling is at a discount of 4 pips with respect to the spot rate. So the cost of a one-day swap is 4 pips on a spot rate of 1.5958, implying an annual cost of:

$$\frac{(0.0004)(365)}{1.5958} \cdot 100 \;=\; 9.15\%.$$

This annual cost is only constant if the one-day forward discount (i.e. the daily swap rate) also remains constant over time. Since this is unlikely, the actual cost of the swap can only be ascertained after the full set of swap transactions is completed.

As another example, we can consider a bank which receives a three-month deposit in a currency, e.g. Italian lire (ITL), which its other customers do not immediately wish to borrow. The bank accepts the lire but swaps them into dollars, invests in dollars for three months in the money market before swapping back into lire on the maturity date of the deposit. This swap enables the bank to service its customer as well as determine the interest rate on the deposit. Suppose that the bank observes the following spot and forward exchange rates for ITL/$:

|                     |                     |
|---------------------|---------------------|
| Spot                | 1612.250–1612.300   |
| Three month forward | 1633.500–1633.650   |

and the following eurodollar interest rates:

|              |             |
|--------------|-------------|
| Three months | 5.75–5.875. |

The lire are exchanged into dollars at the spot offer rate for dollars (ITL1612.300 per $). The dollars are placed on deposit for three months at the eurodollar bid rate of 5.75 per cent. At the same time, a three-month forward contract is taken out to sell the dollars forward back into lire at the three-month forward bid rate for dollars (1633.500). So every lira is converted into 1/1612.300 dollars which are invested for three months at 5.75 per cent to give $[1 + (0.0575/4)]/1612.300$ dollars which, in turn, are sold forward back into lire to give:

$$\frac{1633.500}{1612.300}\left(1 + \frac{0.0575}{4}\right) \;=\; \text{ITL}1.0277129.$$

This implies that the bank could make an annual equivalent return from this swap transaction of 11.085 per cent (i.e. $0.0277129 \times 4 \times 100$). The bank could accept the lira deposit at 10.75 per cent, say, and make a profit of 0.335 per cent. So the bank can pay a rate of interest on the lira deposit which is higher than the rate that the bank gets on the dollar deposit because of the depreciation of the lira against the dollar implied by the difference between the spot and forward exchange rates.

As yet another example we can consider the case of a bank which receives a request for a six-month loan in a currency, e.g. Belgian francs, in which it does not regularly deal. The bank again executes a swap transaction by borrowing dollars for six months, swapping them into Belgian francs, lending these to the customer for six months, while simultaneously executing a six-month forward repurchase of the dollars in order to repay the dollar loan. Suppose that the following spot and forward rates for BFr/$ are available:

|                   |                   |
|-------------------|-------------------|
| Spot              | 28.5420–28.5570   |
| Six month forward | 28.2150–28.2400   |

and that the following eurodollar interest rates are available:

Six months        5.875–6.0.

The bank borrows six-month dollars at the eurodollar offer rate of 6 per cent, implying that, for every dollar borrowed, \$1.03 must be repaid in six months' time. These dollars are exchanged into Belgian francs at the spot dollar bid rate of BFr28.5420 per \$. The Belgian francs are lent to the customer at a rate $r$ (to be determined) which must be high enough to cover the cost of the dollars borrowed. At the same time the dollars are repurchased at the six-month forward offer rate for dollars BFr28.2400 per \$. The minimum lending rate in Belgian francs to the bank's customer ($r_{min}$) solves the following equation:

$$\frac{28.5420}{28.2400} \left(1 + \frac{r_{min}}{2}\right) = 1.03,$$

or:

$$r_{min} = \left(1.03 \cdot \frac{28.2400}{28.5420} - 1\right) \cdot 2$$

$$= 0.0382 \quad (3.82\%).$$

To make a profit on the deal, the bank would charge a higher rate of interest than this, e.g. 4 per cent. But even this rate of interest is lower than the interest cost of borrowing dollar funds, because of the appreciation of the Belgian franc against the dollar implied by the difference between the spot and forward exchange rates.

## 7.4   The fair pricing of foreign currency

There are a number of ways in which to consider whether or not foreign currency or the exchange rate is fairly valued. We will consider five of them.

### 7.4.1   Consistent cross exchange rates

In equilibrium, there should be a consistent relationship between exchange rates. This means that, if $e_0^{ij}$ is the exchange rate between currency $i$ and currency $j$ (units of $j$ per unit of $i$), the following relationship should hold between any three currencies:

$$e_0^{12} e_0^{23} e_0^{31} = 1. \tag{7.2}$$

For example, suppose that currency 1 is sterling, currency 2 is dollars and currency 3 is Deutschmarks. If $e_0^{23} = 1.50$ (i.e. DM 1.50 per \$) and $e_0^{31} = 0.33$ (i.e. £0.33 per DM), then in equilibrium, we must have:

$$e_0^{12} = \frac{1}{e_0^{23} e_0^{31}}, \tag{7.3}$$

that is:

$$e_0^{12} = \frac{1}{(1.50)(0.33)}$$

$$= 2.00 \quad (\text{i.e. \$2 per £}).$$

Equation (7.2) therefore provides one method of determining the fair exchange rate between sterling and dollars, on the assumption that an equilibrium relationship already exists between, say, sterling and Deutschmarks and between dollars and Deutschmarks.

If the actual sterling-dollar exchange rate differs from 2.00, then an arbitrage opportunity exists. Suppose, for example that the actual sterling-dollar exchange rate was 1.90 instead of 2.00. This means that £1 would buy \$1.90 by directly exchanging sterling for dollars. But by exchanging sterling for Deutschmarks and then Deutschmarks for dollars, £1 would buy \$2.00. Therefore an arbitrageur could make virtually riskless profits by exchanging sterling for Deutschmarks, Deutschmarks for dollars, and dollars for sterling:

£1 buys DM3      (i.e. £1/£0.33 per DM)

DM3 buys \$2      (i.e. DM3/DM1.50 per \$)

\$2 buys £1.05      (i.e. \$2/\$1.90 per £).

This arbitrage opportunity raises the attractiveness of sterling and reduces the attractiveness of dollars. Hence the sterling-dollar exchange rate will appreciate until equilibrium is restored at $e_0 = \$2$ per £.

## 7.4.2  Purchasing power parity

The relationship given in (7.2) is a valid way of determining the fair sterling-dollar exchange rate only if the sterling-Deutschmark and Deutschmark-dollar relationships are already fair. It would be useful to have a way of determining the fair sterling-dollar exchange rate independently of knowing whether these other relationships were equilibrium ones.

One way of doing this is to use the *purchasing power parity* (PPP) theory, also known as the *law of one price*. This states that individuals will value currencies for the bundle of goods that can be purchased with them. With this theory, exchange rates will adjust so that the same bundle of goods costs the same in all countries. This implies that the exchange rate between two countries (e.g. the UK and USA) will equal the ratio of price levels between the two countries:

$$e_0 = \frac{P_{\$0}}{P_{£0}}, \tag{7.4}$$

where:

$$P_{£0} = \text{beginning-of-year price level in the UK;}$$
$$P_{\$0} = \text{beginning-of-year price level in the USA.}$$

So, for example, if the price level were twice as high in the USA as in the UK, we would need £1 in order to buy \$2 worth of US goods:

$$e_0 = \frac{P_{\$0}}{P_{£0}} = \frac{2P_{£0}}{P_{£0}} = 2.0 \quad \text{(i.e. \$2 per £).}$$

In practice, the PPP theory is not usually expressed as in (7.4) in terms of price levels, mainly because of the difficulties involved in determining an appropriate base year for computing the price-level indices. Instead, the theory is usually expressed in terms of changes in price levels in different countries, that is, in terms of differential inflation rates.

With this version of the theory, the change in the exchange rate over a period will equal the differential inflation rates between the two countries. Taking (7.4) for the end of the year and dividing by (7.4) for the beginning of the year gives:

$$\frac{e_1}{e_0} = \frac{P_{\$1}/P_{\$0}}{P_{\pounds1}/P_{\pounds0}}$$

$$= \frac{1+\pi_\$}{1+\pi_\pounds}, \tag{7.5}$$

or:

$$1+s = \frac{1+\pi_\$}{1+\pi_\pounds},$$

or:

$$s = \frac{e_1-e_0}{e_0} = \frac{e_1}{e_0} - 1$$

$$= \frac{\pi_\$ - \pi_\pounds}{1+\pi_\pounds}, \tag{7.6}$$

where:

$$\pi_\pounds = \text{inflation rate in the UK};$$
$$\pi_\$ = \text{inflation rate in the US}.$$

In other words, the rate of appreciation of the exchange rate, $s$ (expressed in $ per £), increases with the US inflation rate and decreases with the UK inflation rate.

Equation (7.6) assumes that we know what the UK and US inflation rates will be over the course of the year. However, at the beginning of the year we cannot know for certain what the inflation rates will be; we can only have expectations about what they will be. The version of (7.6) using expectations is (where $E(s)$ is the expected value of $s$ and so on):

$$E(s) = \frac{E(e_1)-e_0}{e_0}$$

$$= \frac{E(\pi_\$)-E(\pi_\pounds)}{1+E(\pi_\pounds)}. \tag{7.7}$$

This says that the expected rate of appreciation of the exchange rate increases with the expected US inflation rate and decreases with the expected UK inflation rate.

Equation (7.7) is a theory explaining the expected rate of appreciation of the exchange rate. Alternatively, for a given expected future spot exchange rate it is a theory explaining the current spot rate; or for a given current spot rate it is a theory explaining the expected future spot rate.

Under the *expectations hypothesis*, the forward exchange rate is equal to the expected future spot rate; i.e.:

$$f_1 = E(e_1), \tag{7.8}$$

where $f_1$ is the current forward exchange rate for one year ahead.

Substituting (7.8) in (7.7) provides us with another version of the PPP theory:

$$\frac{f_1 - e_0}{e_0} = \frac{E(\pi_\$) - E(\pi_£)}{1 + E(\pi_£)}. \tag{7.9}$$

Equation (7.9) says that the *percentage forward premium*, $(f_1 - e_0)/e_0$ increases with the expected US inflation rate and decreases with the expected UK inflation rate.

To illustrate, suppose that $E(\pi_\$) = 0.05$ (5%), $E(\pi_£) = 0.10$ (10%) and $e_0 = 2.0$. In this case, rearranging (7.9), the implied forward rate is:

$$f_1 = \left(\frac{0.05 - 0.10}{1 + 0.10} + 1\right) \cdot 2.0 = 1.91,$$

and the implied forward premium is:

$$\frac{f_1 - e_0}{e_0} = \frac{1.91 - 2.0}{2.0} = -0.045 \quad (-4.5\%),$$

i.e., sterling is expected to depreciate against the dollar by 4.5 per cent to reflect the differential inflation rates between the UK and the USA.

There are a number of problems with the PPP theory. For instance, most price-level indices include goods and services that are not traded internationally. Also, transport costs, tariffs, sluggish price adjustments, and so on, reduce the degree to which exchange rates reflect relative price levels in the short run. We can think of PPP as being a theory of the long-run determination of exchange rates. In the short run, however, other factors are likely to have a more important influence on the course of exchange rates.

The exchange rate in (7.4) is called the *nominal exchange rate*: it measures the relative prices between two countries. A related measure is the *real exchange rate* which measures relative prices *in a common currency:*

$$e_0^r = e_0 \cdot \frac{P_{£0}}{P_{\$0}}. \tag{7.10}$$

From (7.4), it is clear that if PPP holds then the real exchange rate will equal unity.

The real exchange rate can be used to convert real values into a common currency. Suppose that the nominal value of a firm in sterling is $V_{£0}$. The real value in sterling is found by dividing the nominal value in sterling by the UK price level $(V_{£0}/P_{£0})$. The real value of the firm in dollars is found by multiplying the real value in sterling by the real exchange rate:

$$\begin{aligned}
\text{Real value of the firm in dollars} &= e_0^r \cdot \frac{V_{£0}}{P_{£0}} \\
&= e_0 \cdot \frac{P_{£0}}{P_{\$0}} \cdot \frac{V_{£0}}{P_{£0}} \\
&= e_0 \cdot \frac{V_{£0}}{P_{\$0}}. \tag{7.11}
\end{aligned}$$

This is equivalent to taking the nominal value of the firm in sterling, converting it into nominal dollars and dividing by the US price level. A common mistake is to take the real value of the firm in sterling $(V_{£0}/P_{£0})$, multiply by the nominal exchange rate $(e_0)$ and call this value the real value in dollars.

### 7.4.3   International Fisher effect

The most important factor that is likely to affect the exchange rate in the short term is interest rates. This is because capital flows tend to respond more rapidly to changes in relative interest rates than trade flows tend to respond to changes in relative prices.

One method of demonstrating this is known as the *international Fisher effect*. This states that, in the absence of transaction costs and restrictions on capital movements, real rates of interest will be equal in all countries; arbitrage will ensure that this is the case.

The Fisher equations for the UK and the USA are as follows (see also Chapter 2):

$$(1+r_£) \quad = \quad (1+\rho_£)[1+E(\pi_£)], \tag{7.12}$$

and:

$$(1+r_\$) \quad = \quad (1+\rho_\$)[1+E(\pi_\$)], \tag{7.13}$$

where:

$$\rho_£ \quad = \quad \text{real interest rate in the UK;}$$
$$\rho_\$ \quad = \quad \text{real interest rate in the USA.}$$

The international Fisher effect says that:

$$\rho_£ \quad = \quad \rho_\$. \tag{7.14}$$

Substituting (7.14) into (7.12) and equating to (7.13) yields:

$$\frac{1+r_£}{1+E(\pi_£)} \quad = \quad \frac{1+r_\$}{1+E(\pi_\$)}, \tag{7.15}$$

which on rearranging yields:

$$\frac{r_\$-r_£}{1+r_£} \quad = \quad \frac{E(\pi_\$)-E(\pounds)}{1+E(\pi_£)}. \tag{7.16}$$

Substituting (7.16) into (7.9) gives:

$$\frac{f_1-e_0}{e_0} \quad = \quad \frac{r_\$-r_£}{1+r_£}. \tag{7.17}$$

Equation (7.17) says that the percentage forward premium increases with the US nominal interest rate and decreases with the UK nominal interest rate. Alternatively, for a given forward exchange rate, it is a theory explaining the current spot rate; or for a given current spot rate, it is a theory explaining the forward rate.

To illustrate, suppose that $r_£ = 0.1330$ (13.30%), $r_\$ = 0.0815$ (8.15%) and $e_0 = 2.0$. In this case, rearranging (7.15), the implied forward rate is:

$$f_1 \quad = \quad \left(\frac{0.0815-0.1330}{1+0.1330}\right) \cdot 2.0 \quad = \quad 1.91,$$

and the implied forward premium is:

$$\frac{f_1 - e_0}{e_0} \quad = \quad \frac{1.91 - 2.0}{2.0} \quad = \quad -0.045 \quad (-4.5\%),$$

i.e., sterling is expected to depreciate against the dollar by 4.5 per cent to compensate for the lower US interest rate.

In this example, the implied forward rate and implied forward premium are the same as in the last example. This followed because the expected inflation rates in the two examples were identical, namely $E(\pi_£) = 0.10$ and $E(\pi_\$) = 0.05$. Using the nominal interest rates and the expected inflation rates given, the two Fisher equations (7.12) and (7.13) imply that:

$$\rho_£ \quad = \quad \frac{1 + r_£}{1 + E(\pi_£)} - 1 \quad = \quad \frac{1 + 0.1330}{1 + 0.10} - 1 \quad = \quad 0.03 \quad (3\%),$$

and:

$$\rho_\$ \quad = \quad \frac{1 + r_\$}{1 + E(\pi_\$)} - 1 \quad = \quad \frac{1 + 0.0815}{1 + 0.05} - 1 \quad = \quad 0.03 \quad (3\%).$$

The real rates of interest are the same in both countries at 3 per cent. The nominal interest rate in the UK is higher than in the USA because the expected inflation rate is higher. But the nominal rate is just sufficiently higher than in the USA to equate the real rates, via the two Fisher equations (7.12) and (7.13). Thus the international Fisher effect holds in this example.

## 7.4.4 Covered interest rate parity

If the international Fisher effect holds, then so does *covered interest rate parity*. This states that nominal interest rates from investments that are *hedged* (or *covered*) for exchange rate risk will be equal in all countries. Again, arbitrage will ensure that this is the case.

Consider, for example, the following two investments. The first is an investment of £1 in the UK at $r_£$. At the end of the year:

$$\text{Return on investment 1} \quad = \quad (1 + r_£). \tag{7.18}$$

The second is an investment of £1 in the USA. The £1 is exchanged at the spot exchange rate, $e_0$, into $\$e_0$ and invested at $r_\$$. At the same time, the dollar proceeds from the investment are sold forward at $f_1$, the forward exchange rate, thereby protecting the US investment from adverse movements in the exchange rate. At the end of the year:

$$\text{Return on investment 2} \quad = \quad \frac{e_0}{f_1}(1 + r_\$). \tag{7.19}$$

Equating the two returns and rearranging gives:

$$\frac{f_1}{e_0} \quad = \quad \frac{1 + r_\$}{1 + r_£}. \tag{7.20}$$

Equation (7.20) says that, when covered interest parity holds, the ratio of the forward to the spot rate equals the ratio of (one *plus*) relative interest rates. In (7.20), $r_£$ is sometimes known as the *base interest rate* and $r_\$$ as the *terms interest rate*.

That covered interest rate parity is a variant of the international Fisher effect is very easily demonstrated as follows. If we subtract unity from each side of (7.20) and rearrange, we arrive at (7.17), the relevant exchange rate equation if the international Fisher effect holds.

### 7.4.5   Uncovered interest rate parity

If both PPP and the international Fisher effect hold simultaneously, then so does *uncovered interest rate parity*. This states that nominal interest rates from investments that are unhedged (or uncovered) for exchange rate risk will be equal in all countries. In other words, if uncovered interest rate parity holds, then there is no exchange rate risk to be concerned about: international investment does not provide an additional source of risk compared with domestic investment.

We can illustrate uncovered rate parity as follows. Suppose that the spot exchange rate is $e_0 = 2.0$, the real interest rate in all countries is $\rho = 0.03$, $E(\pi_£) = 0.10$ and $E(\pi_\$) = 0.05$. If PPP holds then, from (7.5):

$$\frac{e_1}{e_0} = \frac{1 + E(\pi_\$)}{1 + E(\pi_£)}, \tag{7.21}$$

where $e_1$ is the end of year exchange rate; that is:

$$e_1 = \left(\frac{1 + 0.05}{1 + 0.10}\right) \cdot 2.0 = 1.91,$$

i.e., the actual end-of-year exchange rate (not just the forward rate) will equal 1.91. If the international Fisher effect holds, then we can derive the nominal interest rates using:

$$\begin{aligned}
(1 + r_£) &= (1 + \rho)[1 + E(\pi_£)] \\
&= (1 + 0.03)(1 + 0.10) \\
&= 1.1330,
\end{aligned}$$

that is:

$$r_£ = 0.1330 \quad (13.3\%),$$

and:

$$\begin{aligned}
(1 + r_\$) &= (1 + \rho)[1 + E(\pi_\$)] \\
&= (1 + 0.03)(1 + 0.05) \\
&= 1.0815;
\end{aligned}$$

that is:

$$r_\$ = 0.0815 \quad (8.15\%).$$

An investment of £1 in the UK will return £1.133 after one year. If, instead, the investment of £1 is converted into dollars at the spot exchange rate, we will get \$2. If this is invested, we get a return of \$2.1630 (i.e. \$2(1 + 0.0815)) after one year. If this is then converted back to sterling at the end of the year at the spot rate $e_1 = 1.91$, we get £1.133.

So the two investments generate the same return if both PPP and the international Fisher effect hold, in which case exchange rate risk is unimportant. But in practice, these two effects do not hold exactly. This leaves exchange rate risk as a feature that remains to be hedged. Hedging exchange rate risks is considered in Chapter 16.

## Selected references

Buckley, A. (1996), *Multinational Finance*, Philip Allan, Oxford.

Copeland, T.E. and Weston, J.F. (1988), *Financial Theory and Corporate Policy*, Addison Wesley, Reading, Mass. (Chapter 21.)

Grabbe, J. (1996), *International Financial Markets*, Prentice Hall, Englewood Cliffs, N.J.

Rutterford, J. (1993), *Introduction to Stock Exchange Investment*, Macmillan, London. (Chapter 11.)

Solnik, B. (1996), *International Investments*, Addison Wesley, Reading, Mass.

## Exercises

1  What are the main risks involved with investing outside your country of residence?

2  What is exchange rate risk?

3  Compare and contrast purchasing power parity and covered interest rate parity as theories determining the exchange rate.

4  You observe the following currency quotes:

|       | *Bid*   | *Offer* |
|-------|---------|---------|
| DM/$  | 1.5000  | 1.5005  |
| ¥/$   | 100.500 | 100.600 |
| $/£   | 1.4815  | 1.4825  |

At what rate:

  a)  will the forex dealer buy D-marks against dollars?

  b)  will the forex dealer buy dollars against yen?

  c)  can a customer sell yen against dollars?

  d)  can a customer sell sterling against dollars?

  e)  will the forex dealer sell yen against dollars?

  f)  will the forex dealer sell dollars against D-marks?

  g)  can a customer buy sterling against dollars?

  h)  will the forex dealer buy dollars against sterling?

  i)  can a customer buy dollars against yen?

  j)  can a customer sell D-marks against dollars?

  k)  will the forex dealer buy yen against dollars?

  l)  will the forex dealer buy sterling against dollars?

5 Suppose that we observe the following bid and offer exchange rates and interest rates in Swiss francs and US dollars:

|                                      | *Bid*   | *Offer* |
| ------------------------------------ | ------- | ------- |
| Spot exchange rate (SFr/$)           | 1.1592  | 1.1602  |
| 3 month Swiss interest rate (%)      | 2.625   | 2.75    |
| 3 month US interest rate (%)         | 5.75    | 5.875   |

Calculate the three-month forward bid and offer exchange rates for dollars against Swiss francs if covered interest parity holds.

6 A customer wants to buy £10m against dollars three-month forward from a bank. The following interbank interest rates and exchange rates are available:

| 3-month sterling (%)       | 6.71875–6.75    |
| -------------------------- | --------------- |
| 3-month dollars (%)        | 5.65625–5.8125  |
| Spot exchange rate ($/£)   | 1.5448–1.5458   |

The bank quotes the customer a three-month forward exchange rate of 1.5440 $/£.

   a) Calculate the three-month forward exchange rate on the assumption that covered interest parity holds.

   b) Demonstrate how the bank would cover its position using both the money market and a swap.

   c) What is the bank's profit using each of these methods?

7 A German company issues a sterling bond to finance an investment in the UK. If the sterling-Deutschmark interest rate is expected to be fairly volatile over the life of the bond, what type of currency risk does the German company face?

# Chapter 8

# Forwards and futures

In this chapter, we consider forward contracts and futures contracts, the differences between them and how they are priced.

## 8.1 Forward and futures contracts

### 8.1.1 Forward contracts

A *forward contract* is an agreement between two counterparties that fixes the terms of an exchange that will take place between them at some future date. The contract specifies: what is being exchanged (e.g. cash for a good, cash for a service, a good for a good, a good for a service, cash for cash, etc.), the price at which the exchange takes place, and the date (or range of dates) in the future at which the exchange takes place. In other words, a forward contract locks in the price today of an exchange that will take place at some future date. A forward contract is therefore a contract for *forward delivery* rather than a contract for immediate or *spot* or *cash delivery*, and generally no money is exchanged between the counterparties until delivery.

Forward contracts have the advantage of being tailor-made to meet the requirements of the two counterparties, in terms of both the size of the transaction and the date of forward delivery. However, one disadvantage of a forward contract is that it cannot be cancelled without the agreement of both counterparties. Similarly, the obligations of one counterparty under the contract cannot generally be transferred to a third party. In short, the forward contract is neither very liquid nor very marketable. Another disadvantage is that there is no guarantee that one counterparty will not default and fail to deliver his obligations under the contract. This is more likely to occur the further away the spot price is at the time of delivery from the price that was agreed at the time the contract was negotiated (i.e. the forward price). It will always be the case that it would have been better for one of the counterparties not to have taken out the forward contract but to have waited and transacted in the spot or cash market at the time called for delivery. If the spot price is higher than the forward price, the counterparty taking delivery (the buyer) gains and the counterparty making delivery (the seller) loses, and vice versa when the spot price is below the forward price. The greater the difference between the spot and forward prices, the greater the incentive for the losing counterparty to renege (i.e. the greater the *credit risk*).

### 8.1.2   Futures contracts

A *futures contract* is also an agreement between two counterparties that fixes the terms of an exchange that will take place between them at some future date. But it is very different from a forward contract and has been designed to remove many of the disadvantages of forward contracts. However, the cost of achieving this has been to remove some of the advantages of forward contracts as well.

Futures contracts are standardized agreements to exchange specific types of good, in specific amounts and at specific future delivery or maturity dates. For example, there might be only four contracts traded per year, with the following delivery months: March, June, September and December. This means that the details of the contracts are not negotiable as with forward contracts. The big advantage of having a standardized contract is that it can be exchanged between counterparties very easily. Traditionally, futures contracts were traded on a central regulated exchange by *open outcry*, whereby traders congregated periodically in a *pit* on the floor of the exchange to buy and sell contracts, with every negotiated price being heard by other traders. When an order was executed, the two traders filled out clearing slips, which were then matched by the exchange. The order was confirmed with customers, and a futures contract came into existence. Increasingly, pit trading is being replaced, both in the UK and elsewhere by electronic trading.

The number of contracts outstanding at any time is known as the *open interest* at that time. Futures contracts eliminate the problems of illiquidity and credit risk associated with forward contracts by introducing a clearing house, a system of marking to market and margin payments, and a system of price limits.

The *clearing house* guarantees fulfilment of all contracts by intervening in all transactions and becoming the formal counterparty to every transaction. The only credit risk is therefore with the clearing house. It is also possible to unwind a futures contract at any time by performing a *reversing trade*, so futures contracts are generally extremely liquid (at least for the near maturing contracts).

The clearing house withstands all the credit risk involved in being the counterparty to every transaction, by using the system of daily *marking to market*. At the end of every day's trading, the profits or losses accruing to the counterparties as a result of that day's change in the futures price have to be received or paid. Failure to pay the daily loss results in default and the closure of the contract against the defaulting counterparty. The credit risk to the clearing house has now disappeared because accumulated losses are not allowed to build up. Even a single day's loss is covered by a deposit that each counterparty must make when the contract is first taken out. This deposit is known as *initial margin* and is set equal to the maximum daily loss that is likely to arise on the contract. As the price of the contract goes against one of the counterparties, the resulting loss is met from that counterparty's initial margin and is paid over to the other counterparty as profit. As the margin account falls below a particular threshold (the *maintenance margin level*), it has to be topped up with additional payments known as *variation margin*. (Such payments have to be made immediately in response to a *margin call* from the clearing house.)

The buyer of a futures contract is said to be *long the contract* and will make profits if the futures price rises. The seller of a futures contract is said to be *short the contract* and will make profits if the futures price falls.

**Example 8.1 (Daily marking to market)** *This example illustrates the transactions involved in the system of daily marking to market. As the following table shows, both counterparties put up initial margin on day 1 of £200, which is 20 per cent of the value of the contract (i.e., 20 per* *cent of the* futures price, *or the* daily closing *or* settlement price*) at the beginning of day 1.*

| | Opening position | Day 1 | 2 | 3 | 4 | 5 |
|---|---|---|---|---|---|---|
| Futures price | 1000 | 1100 | 1200 | 1050 | 950 | 900 |
| **Buyer (long)** | | | | | | |
| Initial margin | 200 | – | – | – | – | – |
| Variation margin | – | – | – | – | – | 50 |
| Margin account | 200 | 300 | 400 | 250 | 150 | 150 |
| Accumulated net gains | – | 100 | 200 | 50 | −50 | −100 |
| **Seller (short)** | | | | | | |
| Initial margin | 200 | – | – | – | – | – |
| Variation margin | – | 50 | 100 | – | – | – |
| Margin account | 200 | 150 | 150 | 300 | 400 | 450 |
| Accumulated net gains | – | −100 | −200 | −50 | 50 | 100 |
| Maintenance margin level | £150 | | | | | |

*At the close of business on day 1, the futures price has risen to £1100. The buyer of the contract has made £100 profit which he receives from the seller of the contract. The seller can take only £50 from the margin account, which cannot fall below £150, the maintenance margin level; the other £50 comes in the form of a variation margin payment. At the end of day 2, the futures price has risen to £1200. The buyer receives a further £100 from the seller who has to pay an equivalent amount as variation margin. However, by the end of day 3, the futures price has fallen to £1050 and the buyer has to pay £150 over to the seller. By the end of day 5, when the buyer closes the contract, the buyer's accumulated net loss is £100 while the seller's accumulated net gain is also £100. This means that the seller has made a return of 50 per cent on his initial investment of £200 in just five days while the buyer has lost 50 per cent of his initial investment. But during the same period the futures price has fallen by just 10 per cent.*

This demonstrates the effect of leverage in futures contracts. Because the initial margin payments are a small fraction of the value of the contract, the percentage gains or losses to the counterparties are magnified in comparison with the changes in the futures price. Futures trading is exactly like betting with a bookmaker (in this case the clearing house) on the price of the underlying good, with daily clearing of bets.

The clearing house is also protected from excessive credit risk through the operation of a system of daily *price limits*. During any trading day, the futures price can lie within a band centred on the *settlement price* at the close of business on the previous trading day. If the futures price rises above the upper limit of the band, the market will close *limit-up*. If the futures price falls below the lower limit of the band, the market will close *limit-down*. The market can close for the remainder of the trading day or for a much shorter period such as half an hour, depending on the exchange. The idea is to ensure an orderly market by giving market participants a cooling-off period with a chance to reassess their positions.

The problem with price limits, of course, is that futures contracts are rendered completely illiquid: a position cannot be closed out at any price when trading is suspended. The use of limit pricing can lead to considerable differences between the settlement price of a futures contract and the underlying equilibrium price. If the equilibrium price has moved substantially and suddenly, the limit pricing system could mean that the market is effectively closed for several days at a time. The market will open each day but will close immediately limit-up or limit-down, and this pattern will repeat itself daily until the settlement price has reached the equilibrium price. It is because of these distortions that many exchanges will not operate limits during the delivery month of the contract.

The explanation for the futures price jumping suddenly lies in what is happening in the market for the underlying good, i.e. in the spot or cash market. There is a close relationship between futures prices and spot prices, especially as the delivery date approaches. On the delivery date itself, the settlement price of the futures contract is determined by the spot price. This is why futures contracts are known as *derivative securities*, because they are derivative of the underlying cash market goods.

Before the delivery date, the futures price could be above or below the spot price. The difference between the two prices is known as the *basis*:

$$\text{Basis} \quad = \quad \text{Futures price} - \text{Spot price}. \qquad (8.1)$$

If the futures price exceeds the spot price, the basis is positive (a situation known as *contango*). The futures price tends to fall over time towards the spot price, equalling the spot price on the delivery day, at which time the basis is zero.[1] If the futures price is less than the spot price, the basis is negative (a situation known as *backwardation*). The futures price tends to rise over time towards the spot price, equalling the spot price on the delivery date, so again the basis is zero at delivery. These relationships are shown in Figure 8.1.

Similar relationships hold for cycles of futures contracts with different delivery dates, as shown in Figure 8.2. If the spot price is not expected to change over time, then in contracts with a positive basis the futures price in the contracts with nearby delivery dates will be lower than the futures price in the contracts with distant delivery dates (a situation known as *normal contango*). On the other hand, when the basis is negative, near maturing contracts will have higher futures prices than distant maturing contracts (a situation known as *normal backwardation*).

A final feature of futures contracts to be considered is the *delivery* (or *settlement*) *process*. Most open futures positions are closed out before delivery by taking out an offsetting position (e.g. the seller of a contract buys an equivalent contract), but the delivery process is important in ensuring that the futures price converges on the spot price on the delivery date. If it were not for the possibility of physical delivery of the underlying cash market good by the seller of the futures contract to the buyer, there would be no mechanism to guarantee convergence of futures and spot prices. If the basis were significantly positive just prior to the delivery day, it would be possible to make substantial arbitrage profits by selling futures contracts and at the same time buying the underlying cash market goods in order to deliver them to the buyers of the contracts. On the other hand, if the basis were significantly negative just prior to the delivery day, it would be possible to make arbitrage profits by

---

[1]The definition of the basis given here (i.e. as futures price *minus* spot price) is, as Hull (1993, p.34) points out, frequently used when the futures contract is on a financial security. However, there is an alternative definition of the basis (i.e. spot price *minus* futures price) which is in common usage with commodity futures contracts and also on many financial futures exchanges. The reason that this alternative definition is common with commodity futures is that the futures price is typically below the spot price so that the basis is a positive number and it is easier to work with positive rather than negative numbers. However with financial futures, it is usually the case that the futures price is higher than the spot price, so that the basis is negative under this alternative definition. If the basis *falls* (gets more negative), this is because the futures price has *risen* relative to the spot price. The author finds this definition of the basis confusing to work with. It is also not consistent with other standard usage in finance. For example, a change in price over time is usually defined as the later price *minus* the earlier price (rather than the earlier price *minus* the later price). To illustrate, if the price today is 100 and the price in one year's time is 110, then the price has *increased* by +10 per cent. Users of the alternative definition of the basis, if they are being consistent, would have to say that the price has *fallen* by -10 per cent! Practitioners in the futures markets who read this book should beware the definition of the basis that is used throughout this text.

**Figure 8.1** Contango and backwardation in futures contracts

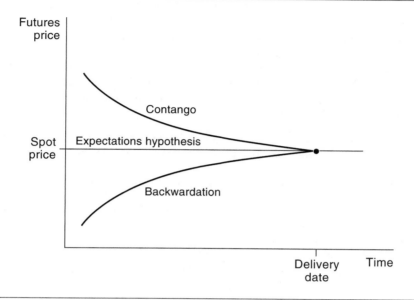

**Figure 8.2** Normal contango and normal backwardation in a cycle of futures contracts

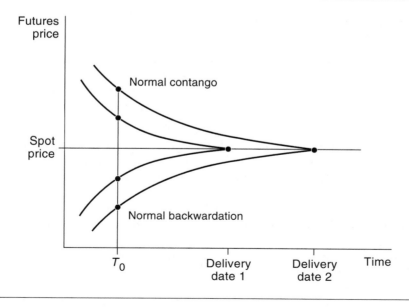

buying futures contracts, taking delivery and then selling the goods in the cash market. So to avoid significant arbitrage profits, the futures and spot prices must converge.

The delivery process itself is determined by the futures exchange and involves a sequence of steps that must be completed in a specific order and at specific times. Because the clearing house is the counterparty to every transaction, it is also involved in the delivery process. The delivery process is initiated by either the buyer (the long) or the seller (the short) (depending on the contract) notifying the clearing house that he intends to take or make delivery. The clearing house then matches long and short positions and *assigns* a short to make delivery to a long. The delivery process is completed or settled by the short delivering an eligible cash market good to the long and the long making payment to the short at the *invoice price* or *amount*.

If there is more than one type of eligible cash market good that can be delivered against the contract, then the short will choose the one that is *cheapest to deliver*. This means that the futures contract will always be priced off the cheapest-to-deliver eligible cash market good. However, not all futures contracts are settled by the delivery of a cash market good; some are settled for cash.

So far, we have discussed futures contracts in general terms and have referred to contracts being defined in terms of 'goods'. It is certainly true that most futures contracts deal with commodities (e.g. aluminium, barley, cattle, citrus, cocoa, coffee, copper, corn, cotton, crude oil, gasoline, gold, heating oil, hogs, lead, lumber, nickel, oats, palladium, palm oil, plywood, pork bellies, potatoes, propane, rapeseed, rice, rubber, rye, silver, soybeans, sugar, tin, wheat, wool and zinc). But we are mostly interested in futures contracts related to financial instruments, i.e. in *financial futures contracts*. These were first traded in the Chicago Mercantile Exchange in 1972. In contrast with commodity futures where most contracts lead to the *physical delivery* of the underlying commodity, most financial futures are *cash-settled* which means that cash rather than a financial instrument is exchanged against the *settlement price* of the contract.

## 8.2   Financial futures contracts

In the UK, all financial futures contracts are traded on the London International Financial Futures and Options Exchange (LIFFE) which opened in 1982. Members of LIFFE include banks, member-firms of the LSE, money and commodity brokers, discount houses and individual traders (known as *locals*) who trade on their own account. More than half the membership of LIFFE is based outside the UK. All members will have met stringent capital adequacy requirements before being accepted.

Originally, trading on LIFFE took place as follows. On receiving a customer order in a member's office, the order was phoned to the member's booth on the LIFFE trading floor, specifying sale or purchase, contract type, delivery month and quantity. The order slip was carried by a *runner* to a *trader* in the pit. Runners were identified by the gold jackets that they wear, while traders were identified by their scarlet jackets or house jackets together with badges carrying the trading initials of their firm. The trader indicated his orders by open outcry and officially sanctioned hand signals. A LIFFE official was responsible for ensuring an orderly pit and for arbitrating in the case of disputed trades. To enhance efficient trading, the *LIFFE Order Transit System* (LOTS) was developed. This enabled members to enter orders and trade execution details and to review the current status of orders on a real-time basis via the LIFFE systems network, EASy. Once executed, the details of the order (including the trading counterparty) were confirmed with the client and recorded on a clearing slip. Clearing slips are collected by LIFFE officials and the details entered on LIFFE's *Trade Registration System* (TRS) and

*Clearing Processing System* (CPS). These systems provided real-time trade matching, allocation and position keeping, and also allowed any reporting errors to be corrected immediately. Matched deals were registered with LIFFE's clearing house, the London Clearing House (LCH). Once a trade was registered, each party had a contractual obligation with LCH and not with the original counterparty. Simultaneously, LIFFE officials, called *price reporters*, relayed information on the trades together with current bids and offers to quote vendors for them to disseminate to the general public via LIFFE's *Price Distribution System* (PDS). The LCH clears and settles trades on a 'principal-to-principal' basis which means that the client's broker acts as a principal in the trade (this contrasts with the 'agency' system where the broker acts as an agent for the end-user who remains a principal in the transaction).

In 1989, LIFFE introduced an *Automated Pit Trading* (APT) system. APT imitated open outcry trading on a computer screen: trading was conducted via a workstation in members' offices linked to a central network. APT allowed after-hours trading in most contracts, as well as exclusive trading in certain contracts: for example, the Japanese Government Bond future was traded exclusively via APT. Another enhancement to open outcry was *Automated Trade Order Matching* (ATOM) which provided users with a central limit order book where orders were stored and then executed on APT as trading conditions were satisfied.

However, increasing competition from other exchanges has forced LIFFE to make increasing use of electronic trading systems, for which trading costs are between three and ten times lower than for open outcry. For example, the Deutscheterminbörse (DTB), the Swiss Options and Financial Futures Exchange (SOFFEX) and the French MATIF have developed *Eurex*, a single electronic trading platform covering all German, Swiss and French derivatives. The Chicago Board of Trade (CBOT) has linked up with Eurex and there are plans for a further link with the Tokyo Futures Exchange (TFE) and the Singapore International Monetary Exchange (SIMEX). This would permit global trading in derivatives using a single trading platform.

In November 1998, LIFFE introduced an *electronic trading platform* called *LIFFE Connect*. LIFFE Connect is an anonymous quote-driven trading system that operates on a strict *price-time priority basis*, with automatic matching of buy and sell orders on the central order book, so that the first end-user who accepts a quoted bid or offer price gets the deal. There are still registered market-makers, but trades are no longer allocated between market-makers on a *pro-rata* basis as under the open outcry system. Instead, a point and click technology ensures immediate order execution. Firm bid and offer prices, together with the total size of buy and sell orders will be visible on the screen and will be updated in real time. LIFFE Connect provides the trading platform, but LIFFE members have to provide the 'front-end'. These front-ends can be purchased off-the-shelf from *independent software vendors* (ISVs) or can be customized to meet the specific requirements of LIFFE members, such as real-time risk management or straight-through processing of customer orders. The front-ends are linked to LIFFE Connect via an *application programming interface* (API) which enables the front-ends to integrate with existing LIFFE systems such as TRS and CPS. The first contracts to be traded via LIFFE Connect were individual equity options; at the same time the use of APT in this class of contracts ceased. Futures trading via LIFFE Connect was introduced in 1999. LIFFE Connect was designed to run alongside the open outcry system, but its immediate success in reducing spreads has led to a decline in the use of open outcry.

We can see, therefore, that LIFFE is a *hybrid* exchange with its contracts being traded by open outcry and on electronic trading platforms. Some contracts are currently traded only in the pit, others during the pit for most of their trading hours but with additional hours available for APT trading, whilst some are traded only on LIFFE Connect. The variety of trading platforms available for each contract will, of course, continue to change in response to demand from LIFFE members and their clients, and to competition from other financial centres.

LIFFE uses a portfolio-based margining system called *London SPAN* (Standard Portfolio Analysis of Risk). In the case of LIFFE futures contracts, initial margins depend on what is called a *futures scanning range*. The futures scanning range is set equal to the largest daily loss that can reasonably be expected to occur in the relevant futures contract, based on recent historical price movements. Futures contracts (both long and short) in the same underlying security are pooled together into *portfolios* and the initial margin for the net futures position is based on the formula:

$$\text{Scanning risk}\quad=\quad\text{Net futures position}\times\text{Futures scanning range}. \tag{8.2}$$

For a long futures position, the *worst case scenario* indicating the maximum likely loss on the futures position is 'futures down 3/3 (i.e. 100%) of scanning range', while for a short futures position, the worst case scenario is 'futures up 3/3 (i.e. 100%) of scanning range'. In addition to the scanning risk, there are other factors that LIFFE periodically takes into account when determining initial margin:

$$
\begin{aligned}
\text{Initial margin}\quad=\quad & \text{Scanning risk}\\
& +\ \text{Spot month charge}\\
& +\ \text{Inter-month spread charge}\\
& -\ \text{Inter-commodity spread credit.}
\end{aligned}
\tag{8.3}
$$

The *spot month charge* allows for the fact that futures prices become more volatile as the expiry date approaches. The *inter-month spread charge* allows for the fact that futures contracts with different delivery months do not have perfectly correlated price movements and this leads to a spread risk. The *inter-commodity spread credit* allows for the fact that different underlying securities may have correlated price movements and this may help to reduce risk across different portfolios of futures contracts. LIFFE can take any or all these three factors into account, but does not necessarily do so at every point in time. Initial margin liabilities can be covered directly in cash (in sterling, dollars, Deutschmarks, French francs, Swiss francs, pesetas, lire, euro or yen) or in collateral including UK Treasury bills and gilts, sterling CDs, US Treasury bills and bonds, German, Spanish or Italian bills or bonds, bank guarantees or UK equities. The collateral is valued at market prices and then subject to a discount or *haircut* determined by the exchange. When the portfolio involves options as well as futures on the same underlying security, other factors have to be taken into account as we show in Chapter 9.

A further development has been the introduction, in April 1999, of a *block trading facility* which is intended to facilitate large orders but without diminishing the role of existing trading mechanisms. This facility enables LIFFE members and those who qualify as *wholesale clients* to transact business of significant size on-exchange without the price uncertainties or execution delays that might otherwise occur in the execution of orders of this size. Block trades are available for the majority of LIFFE's financial and equity contracts, may take place at prices different from the price prevailing on the appropriate trading platform, and are subject to minimum contract size thresholds.

There are three classes of financial futures contracts traded on LIFFE: short-term interest rate contracts, long-term interest rate contracts, and stock index contracts. However, note that LIFFE is constantly introducing new contracts, deleting contracts, and changing the specifications of existing contracts. For example, LIFFE used to trade currency futures contracts, but these are no longer traded.

## 8.2.1 Short-term interest rate futures

There are currently six short-term interest rate contracts traded on LIFFE: a three-month EURIBOR contract, a three-month euro LIBOR contract, a three-month sterling (short sterling) contract, a three-month euroswiss contract, a three-month euroyen (TIBOR) contract and a three-month euroyen (LIBOR) contract. The specifications of two of these contracts are shown in Tables 8.1 and 8.2. The specification of the Chicago Mercantile Exchange (CME) three-month eurodollar interest rate contract is shown in Table 8.3. As we shall see in later chapters, this contract is useful in certain applications. It is, however, no longer offered by LIFFE. We shall concentrate attention on the short sterling contract.

**Table 8.1** LIFFE three-month sterling (short sterling) interest rate futures contract

| | |
|---|---|
| **Unit of trading** | £500,000 |
| **Delivery months** | March, June, September, December, and two serial months, such that 22 delivery months are available for trading, with the nearest three delivery months being consecutive calendar months |
| **Delivery day** | First business day after the last trading day |
| **Last trading day** | 11:00, third Wednesday of the delivery month |
| **Quotation** | 100.00 *minus* rate of interest (%) |
| **Minimum price movement** | |
|     **Tick size** | 0.01 (%) |
|     **Value** | £12.50 |
| **Initial margin** | £500 |
| **Spread margin** | £225 |
| **Trading hours** | 08:05–16:10 |
| **APT trading hours** | 16:15–18:00 |

*Contract standard:* cash settlement based on the Exchange Delivery Settlement Price.

*Exchange Delivery Settlement Price (EDSP):* based on the British Bankers' Association London interbank offered rate (BBA LIBOR) for three-month sterling deposits at 11:00 on the last trading day. For the June 1998 delivery month onwards, the settlement price will be 100.00 *minus* the BBA LIBOR rounded to three decimal places. Where the EDSP rate is not an exact multiple of 0.005, it will be rounded to the nearest 0.005 or, where the EDSP rate is an exact uneven multiple of 0.0025, to the nearest lower 0.005 (e.g. a BBA LIBOR of 6.43750 becomes 6.435).

The three-month short sterling contract (often referred to as 'ST3') has a face value of £500,000. When this contract first began to trade in 1982, the buyer of a contract (the long) expected to be allocated a £500,000 three-month sterling time deposit at an eligible bank on the delivery date; the time deposit facilities were arranged by the contract seller (the short). Because of the inconvenience of one party having to arrange time deposit facilities on behalf of another counterparty, the contract terms were later changed to *cash settlement*. The delivery day is the first business day after the last trading day which is the third Wednesday of the delivery month. There are four delivery months per year: March, June, September and December, plus *serial months*. These are additional months, added to permit trading in months other than the four principal quarterly delivery months. As can be seen

**Table 8.2** LIFFE three-month euro LIBOR interest rate futures contract

| | |
|---|---|
| **Unit of trading** | €1,000,000 |
| **Delivery months** | March, June, September, December, and two serial months such that 18 delivery months are available for trading, with the nearest three delivery months being consecutive calendar months |
| **Delivery day** | First business day after the last trading day |
| **Last trading day** | 11:00, two business days prior to the third Wednesday of the delivery month |
| **Quotation** | 100.00 *minus* rate of interest (%) |
| **Minimum price movement** | |
|     **Tick size** | 0.005 (%) |
|     **Value** | €12.50 |
| **Initial margin** | €450 |
| **Spread margin** | €300 |
| **Trading hours** | 07:30–16:10 |
| **APT trading hours** | 16:15–18:00 |

*Contract standard:* cash settlement based on the Exchange Delivery Settlement Price.

*Exchange Delivery Settlement Price (EDSP):* based on the British Bankers' Association London interbank offered rate (BBA LIBOR) for three-month euro deposits at 11:00 on the last trading day. The settlement price will be 100.00 *minus* the BBA LIBOR rounded to three decimal places. Where the EDSP rate is not an exact multiple of 0.005, it will be rounded to the nearest 0.005 or, where the EDSP rate is an exact uneven multiple of 0.0025, to the nearest lower 0.005 (e.g. a BBA LIBOR of 6.43750 becomes 6.435).

**Table 8.3** CME three-month eurodollar interest rate futures contract

| | |
|---|---|
| **Unit of trading** | US$1,000,000 |
| **Delivery months** | March, June, September, December, four serial months and spot month |
| **Delivery day** | First business day after the last trading day |
| **Last trading day** | 11:00 London time on the second London bank business day immediately preceding the third Wednesday of the contract month |
| **Quotation** | 100.00 *minus* rate of interest (%) |
| **Minimum price movement** | |
|     **Tick size** | 0.01 (%) |
|     **Value** | $25.00 |
| **Initial margin** | $500 |
| **Spread margin** | $250 |

from Table 8.1, serial months are added such that 22 delivery months are available for trading, with the nearest three delivery months being consecutive calendar months. Details of available contracts are published periodically by LIFFE in a *trading calendar*.

As with all short-term interest rate contracts, the ST3 contract is quoted on an index or *price equivalent* basis; i.e. the futures price is given as: 100.00 *minus* interest rate (%). This preserves the standard inverse relationship between prices and interest rates: the lower the interest rate, the higher the futures price. For example, if the price of a June ST3 contract is 90.50, this means that an interest rate of 9.5 per cent (100.00 − 90.50) can be locked in for three months on a June sterling time deposit.

The minimum price movement (or *tick size*) on a ST3 contract is one basis point (i.e. $1/100^{\text{th}}$ of 1 per cent or 0.01 per cent):

$$\text{Tick size} \quad = \quad 0.01\% \text{ of interest for 3 months}. \tag{8.4}$$

This implies a *tick value* of:

$$\begin{aligned} \text{Tick value} \quad &= \quad 0.0001 \cdot \frac{3}{12} \cdot £500{,}000 \\ &= \quad £12.50. \end{aligned} \tag{8.5}$$

This means that, because the smallest permissible amount by which interest rates can move is 0.01 per cent (i.e. 0.0001), the smallest change in the price of the ST3 contract is £12.50. To illustrate, if an individual buys 10 ST3 contracts at 90.50 and closes the position 20 days later with a reversing sale of 10 contracts at 90.55, the profit is:

$$\begin{aligned} \text{Profit} \quad &= \quad \text{Number of contracts} \times \text{Number of ticks gain} \times \text{Value per tick} \\ &= \quad 10 \times 5 \times £12.50 \quad = \quad £625.00, \end{aligned}$$

since the number of ticks gain is 5, i.e. $(90.55 - 90.50)/0.01$, where 0.01 is the tick size.

The initial margin on the ST3 contract is £500. With all LIFFE contracts, the maintenance margin level is set at the initial margin level. This means that, if the margin account on the ST3 contract falls below £500, variation margin payments have to be made. In the last example, at the time of the sale of the 10 contracts on day 20, the individual will have £5000 (10 contracts × £500) in his margin account as initial margin and £625 as variation margin. The profit of £625 has therefore been made with capital of £5000, a return over 20 days of 12.5 per cent, and an effective return (*re*) of:

$$\begin{aligned} re \quad &= \quad [(1.125)^{365/20} - 1] \cdot 100 \\ &= \quad 758.1\% \quad \text{p.a.} \end{aligned}$$

There is a lower level of initial margin on *spread* positions. A spread position is a simultaneous long and short position in different months of the same futures contract, e.g. long one June ST3 contract and short one September ST3 contract. Because the daily price movements in a spread are likely to be lower than in the individual contracts, the initial margin is lower.

If the ST3 contract goes to delivery, it will be cash settled, as the following example involving a June ST3 contract purchased at 90.50 shows. The clearing house announces the *exchange delivery settlement price* (EDSP) which equals 100.00 *minus* the settlement interest rate. The *settlement interest rate* is the British Bankers' Association London interbank offered rate (BBA LIBOR) for three-month sterling deposits at 11:00 on the last trading day. Suppose that the settlement interest rate is 8.75 per cent. In this case the EDSP is 91.25. Since the contract was initially purchased at 90.50, this implies that the long's margin account for this contract contains £500 initial margin *plus* £937.50 in variation margin (i.e. $[(91.25 - 90.50)/0.01]$ ticks $\times$ £12.50 per tick), totalling £1437.50. This sum is returned to the long as final settlement.

When the long originally bought the June futures contract at 90.50, he was expecting to lock in a three-month sterling interest rate of 9.50 per cent. We can demonstrate that this is indeed the case. The spot interest rate in June is only 8.75 per cent but the long's variation margin equals £937.50, so his net worth has increased by £937.50. Thus the implied futures rate ($rf$) is:

$$rf = \left( \frac{\text{Variation margin}}{F} \cdot \frac{365}{91} \right) + rs. \tag{8.6}$$

In this case we get:

$$rf = \left( \frac{937.50}{500,000} \cdot \frac{365}{91} \right) + 0.0875 = 0.095 \quad (9.50\%),$$

as required.

## 8.2.2 Long-term interest rate futures

There are five government bond contracts (or long-term interest rate contracts) traded on LIFFE: a long-gilt contract, a five-year gilt contract, a German government bond (Bund) contract, an Italian government bond (BTP) contract, and a Japanese bond (JGB) contract. The specifications of three of the contracts are shown in Tables 8.4 to 8.6. In 1999, LIFFE introduced the *EURIBOR Financed Bond* (or LIFFE*EFB*) contract; this is a cash-settled bond futures contract that is priced off the swap yield curve (see section 10.3.1) rather than the yield curve for government bonds, thereby making it a suitable instrument for hedging positions in corporate bonds.[2] We shall concentrate our attention on the long-gilt contract.

The long gilt contract trades an imaginary or notional gilt with a yield to maturity (YTM) of 7 per cent. The face value of the contract is £100,000 nominal and the value of a tick (minimum price movement of £0.01 per £100 nominal) is £10.00 (i.e. £0.01 $\times$ £100,000/£100). If an individual buys a long gilt futures contract at a price of 91.38 and later sells a contract at 91.23 he will have made a loss of £150.00 (i.e. 15 ticks $\times$ £10.00 per tick).

The contract requires physical delivery of a real gilt, and any eligible gilt with a maturity of between 8.75 and 13 years can be delivered. (Table 8.7 shows a list of deliverable gilts for a typical LIFFE June long gilt contract.) However, only the bond that is *cheapest to deliver* (CTD) from the point of view of the short will be delivered. The CTD bond can be delivered on any business day of the delivery month, but in practice only two days are ever used. If the current yield on the CTD bond exceeds the money market interest rate, the bond will be delivered on the last business day of the month, because the short earns more by holding on to the bond than by delivering it and investing the proceeds in the money market; otherwise the bond will be delivered on the first business day of the month. Some bonds are not eligible for delivery, such as index-linked, partly paid, convertible or variable-rate bonds.

---

[2]The contract can also be interpreted as a forward-starting, cash-settled swap contract. The name *EURIBOR Financed Bond* is used since it defines the components of an interest rate swap (section 10.3.1), whereby the floating-rate leg (based on EURIBOR) is used to finance the fixed-rate leg. The result is a series of fixed (notional) cash flows, identical to those of a bond, which are discounted using EURIBOR money market rates, thus giving the contract the sensitivity of a swap.

**Table 8.4** LIFFE long gilt futures contract

| | |
|---|---|
| **Unit of trading** | £100,000 nominal value notional gilt with 7% coupon |
| **Delivery months** | March, June, September, December, such that the nearest three delivery months are available for trading |
| **First notice day** | Two business days prior to the first day of the delivery month |
| **Last notice day** | First business day after the last trading day |
| **Delivery day** | Any business day in delivery month (at seller's choice) |
| **Last trading day** | 11:00, two business days prior to the last business day in the delivery month |
| **Quotation** | Per £100 nominal |
| **Minimum price movement** | |
|     **Tick size** | £0.01 |
|     **Value** | £10 |
| **Initial margin** | £2000 |
| **Spread margin** | £250 |
| **Connect trading hours** | 08:00–18:00 |

*Contract standard:* delivery may be made of any gilts on the List of Deliverable Gilts in respect of a delivery month, as published by the Exchange on or before the tenth business day prior to the first notice day of such delivery month. Holders of long positions on any day within the notice period may be delivered against during the delivery month. All gilt issues included in the list will have the following characteristics:

1. having terms as to redemption such as provide for redemption of the entire gilt issue in a single instalment on the maturity date falling not earlier than 8.75 years from, and not later than 13 years from, the first day of the relevant delivery month;

2. having no terms permitting or requiring early redemption;

3. bearing interest at a single rate throughout the term of the issue payable in arrears semi-annually (except in the case of the first interest payment period which may be more or less than six months);

4. being denominated and payable as to the principal and interest only in pounds and pence;

5. being fully paid or, in the event that the gilt issue is in its first period and is partly paid, being anticipated by the Board to be fully paid on or before the last notice day of the relevant delivery month;

6. not being convertible;

7. not being in bearer form;

8. having been admitted to the Official List of the London Stock Exchange;

9. being anticipated by the board to have on one or more days in the delivery month an aggregate principal amount outstanding of not less than £1.5 billion which, by its terms and conditions, if issued in more than one tranche or tap or issue, is fungible.

*Exchange Delivery Settlement Price (EDSP):* the LIFFE market price at 11:00 on the second business day prior to settlement day. The invoicing amount in respect of each deliverable gilt is to be calculated by the price factor system. Adjustment will be made for full coupon interest accruing as at settlement day.

**Table 8.5** LIFFE German Government bond (Bund) futures contract

| | |
|---|---|
| **Unit of trading** | €100,000 nominal value notional German government bond with 6% coupon |
| **Delivery months** | March, June, September, December, such that the nearest three delivery months are available for trading |
| **Delivery day** | Tenth calendar day of delivery month. If such a day is not a business day in Frankfurt then the delivery day will be the next following Frankfurt business day |
| **Last trading day** | 11:00 Frankfurt time, two Frankfurt business days prior to the delivery day |
| **Quotation** | Per €100 nominal value |
| **Minimum price movement** | |
|     **Tick size** | €0.01 |
|     **Value** | €10 |
| **Initial margin** | €1,200 |
| **Spread margin** | €120 |
| **APT Trading hours**[a] | 07:00–17:55 |

*Contract standard:* delivery may be made of any Bundesanleihen with 8.5–10.5 years remaining maturity as at the tenth calendar day of the delivery month, providing that any such Bund has a minumum amount in issue of €2 billion as listed by LIFFE. Delivery may be made via accounts at (i) Deutscher Börse Clearing AG, (ii) Euroclear, or (iii) Cedel S.A.

*Exchange Delivery Settlement Price (EDSP):* the LIFFE market price at 11:00 Frankfurt time on the last trading day. The invoicing amount in respect of each deliverable Bund[b] to be calculated by the price factor system. A final list of deliverable Bunds and their price factors will be announced by the Exchange ten market days prior to the last trading day of the delivery month. Adjustments will be made for full coupon interest accruing as at the delivery day.

[a]Unless otherwise indicated all times are London times.
[b]For the purpose of the contract, Bund means 'Anleihe der Bundesrepublik Deutschland'.

**Table 8.6** LIFFE Japanese Government bond (JGB) futures contract

| | |
|---|---|
| **Unit of trading** | ¥100,000,000 face value notional long-term Japanese government bond with 6% coupon |
| **Delivery months** | March, June, September, December, such that two delivery months are available for trading |
| **Delivery day** | Next business day |
| **Last trading day** | 16:00, one business day prior to Tokyo Stock Exchange last trading day |
| **Quotation** | Per ¥100 face value |
| **Minimum price movement** | |
| Tick size | ¥0.01 |
| Value | ¥10,000 |
| **Initial margin** | ¥1,600,000 |
| **Spread margin** | ¥800,000 |
| **APT Trading hours** | 07:00–16:00 |

*Contract standard:* all open positions on LIFFE at the close of a business day will be closed out automatically at the first subsequent opening price on the Tokyo Stock Exchange for the same delivery month, and cash settlement made accordingly through variation margin. Unless deferred as a result of there being no TSE opening price (e.g. in the event of a TSE holiday), settlement will be on the next business day.

*Price limit:* (1) ¥1.00 from Tokyo Stock Exchange closing price. If limit is hit, price limits are removed one hour later for the remainder of the day. (2) No limit during the last trading hour on each day.

When the bond is delivered, the long pays the short an invoice amount:

$$\text{Invoice amount} = \left( \frac{\text{Settlement price}}{100} \times \text{Price factor} \times \text{Nominal value of gilt} \right) + \text{Accrued interest}. \tag{8.7}$$

The settlement price (or the *exchange delivery settlement price*, EDSP) is the trading price (per £100 nominal) for the futures contract on the last day of trading.

The *price factor* (or *conversion factor*) determines the appropriate price of the bond that is delivered. It is calculated as being the price per £1 nominal at which the bond delivered has a yield to maturity of 7 per cent. The price factors are calculated for the first day of the delivery month, and adjustments have to be made for accrued interest where the first day of the delivery month does not coincide with a coupon payment date. Ignoring accrued interest, the price that a bond has to have to give a yield to maturity of 7 per cent is given by:

$$P = \sum_{t=1}^{2T} \frac{d/2}{\left(1 + \frac{0.07}{2}\right)^t} + \frac{100}{\left(1 + \frac{0.07}{2}\right)^{2T}}$$

$$= \frac{d}{0.07} \cdot \left[ 1 - \frac{1}{(1.035)^{2T}} \right] + \frac{100}{(1.035)^{2T}}. \tag{8.8}$$

This is the price that a bond with a 7 per cent YTM will have on the next coupon payment date. The following adjustments to (8.8) have to be made for accrued interest:

$$P = \frac{1}{(1.035)^{N_1/182.5}} \cdot \left\{ \frac{d}{2} + \frac{d}{0.07} \left[ 1 - \frac{1}{(1.035)^{2T}} \right] + \frac{100}{(1.035)^{2T}} \right\}$$
$$- \frac{d}{2} \cdot \frac{N_2 - N_1}{182.5} \tag{8.9}$$

where:

$N_1$ = Number of days between first day of delivery month and next coupon payment date;

$N_2$ = Number of days between last coupon payment date and next coupon payment date.

First the next coupon payment ($d/2$) is added to (8.8) and then the whole sum is discounted back to the first day of the delivery month. This gives the dirty price on that day. To get the clean price we subtract the interest that has been accruing at the rate of $d$ per cent up to that day. The price factor ($PF$) is then given by:

$$PF = P/100. \tag{8.10}$$

There is a different price factor for each eligible bond and for each delivery month. The price factors are published by LIFFE (see Table 8.7).

The invoice amount also includes interest accrued from the previous coupon payment. This arises because the futures contract is traded at a *clean price* and does not include accrued interest payments. However, gilts also trade at a clean price but have accrued interest added on.

We will calculate the CTD for the June long gilt contract. We will assume that the date is 1 April. We will also assume that on 1 April the money market rate of interest is 8 per cent and the long gilt future is trading at 88.19 (per £100 nominal). Table 8.7 also gives the dirty prices of the eligible bonds on 1 April. From these we can determine current yields. All bonds with current yields exceeding the money market rate of 8 per cent would be delivered at the end of June (i.e. in 90 days from 1 April), otherwise they would be delivered at the beginning of June (i.e. in 61 days from 1 April).

The cheapest to deliver of these bonds is the bond that gives the greatest *implied repo rate* to the short from a *cash-and-carry* (or *cost-of-carry*) transaction, i.e. a strategy of buying the bond (with borrowed funds) in the cash market and selling it into the futures market. Consider the Treasury 8 per cent 2014. The cash outflow (per £100 nominal) from this strategy is as follows:

|   | | | |
|---|---|---|---|
|   | Price of bond, 1 April | | £99.13 |
| + | Interest cost, 1 April–30 June | £99.13 [0.08(90/365)] | 1.96 |
|   | | | £101.09 |

The bond (whose price includes 134 days' accrued interest on 1 April from the previous coupon payment date of 18 November) has to be financed at the money market rate of 8 per cent for the 90 days between 1 April and 30 June, when the bond (if it happens to be the CTD) is delivered into the futures market.

The cash inflow (per £100 nominal) as a result of the strategy is:

**TABLE 8.7** Long gilt contract — deliverable gilts, price factors and accrued interest

(Contract Month: June)

| Stock | Coupon (%) | Redemption date | Price (£) (1 April) | Current yield (% p.a.) | Price factor[a] | Daily accrued[b] (£) | Initial accrued[c] (£) | Delivery days[d,e] | Implied repo rate (% p.a.) (1 April) |
|---|---|---|---|---|---|---|---|---|---|
| 1 Treasury | 8 | 08 Sep 2013 | 99.00 | 8.08 | 1.0845542 | 27.3972 | 2301.36 | 123**67890**34567**01234**7890 | −11.25 |
| 2 Treasury | 8 | 18 May 2014 | 99.13 | 8.07 | 1.0821387 | 27.3972 | 356.14 | 123**67890**34567**01234**7890 | −3.01 |
| 3 Conversion | 7.5 | 25 Oct 2014 | 95.25 | 7.87 | 1.0359796 | 26.0274 | 936.98 | 123**67890**34567**01234**7890 | −4.07 |
| 4 Conversion | 7.5 | 18 Apr 2015 | 95.50 | 7.85 | 1.0338262 | 26.0274 | 1119.18 | 123**67890**34567**01234**7890 | −5.95 |
| 5 Exchequer | 8.5 | 20 Sep 2015 | 103.63 | 8.20 | 1.1225681 | 28.7672 | 2071.24 | 123**67890**34567**01234**7890 | −16.57 |
| 6 Treasury | 10.5 | 21 Nov 2013–15 | 118.00 | 9.00 | 1.3032131 | 34.2466 | 342.46 | 123**67890**34567**01234**7890 | 3.24 (CTD)[f] |
| 7 Treasury | 6.5 | 16 Jul 2017 | 84.38 | 7.70 | 0.9326328 | 23.2876 | −1071.24 | 123**67890**34567**01234**7890 | −5.87 |

[a] Price factor expressed as a fraction of par.
[b] Accrued interest per day on £100,000 face value.
[c] Accrued interest on £100,000 face value as of the last day of the month prior to the delivery month.
[d] * = non-business day.
[e] Invoicing amount = [(settlement price) × (price factor) × 1000] + (initial accrued) + [(daily accrued) × (delivery day in month)] .
[f] Cheapest to deliver.

|  | Implied clean price of bond, 30 June |  |  |
|---|---|---|---|
|  | (futures price, 1 April × price factor) | £88.19 (1.0821387) | £95.43 |
| + | Accrued interest, 18 November–30 June | £8 [(134 + 90)/365] | 4.91 |
|  |  |  | £100.34 |

The implied price of the bond on 30 June equals the futures price on 1 April multiplied by the price factor for the bond. Because the futures price is quoted clean, accrued interest has to be added to get the implied dirty price on 30 June. Note that the accrued interest is calculated from the same date as was used to calculate the accrued interest when the bond was purchased, namely the previous 18 November. The bond was purchased on 1 April with 134 days' accrued interest and is sold on 30 June with 224 (i.e. 134 + 90) days' accrued interest. However, if there is a coupon payment between 18 November and 30 June, as there is in the case of this bond, the last sentence is not strictly correct. On 18 May, the bond will have paid out a coupon of £4, so the bond when it is sold will actually only have 43 days' accrued interest (i.e. the interest accruing between 18 May and 30 June). In addition, the £4 coupon could be placed on deposit until 30 June and earn an addition 43 days' interest. Nevertheless, for the purpose of calculating the implied repo rate, we can treat the bond as though it has accrued interest continually for 227 days; the error involved in disregarding 43 days' interest on £4 will be negligible.

This cash-and-carry transaction which operates for 90 days from 1 April to 30 June generates a rate of return or *implied repo rate* of:

$$\text{Implied repo rate} = \frac{100.34 - 101.09}{101.09} \cdot \frac{365}{90} = -3.01\% \quad \text{p.a.}$$

It is known as a repo rate because it is equivalent to a *repurchase agreement* with the futures market. A repurchase agreement provides a means for the short to lend money to the futures market: the short agrees to buy a bond with a provision to sell it back to the market at a predetermined price and to receive a rate of interest, the repo rate.

The implied repo rates for all the remaining eligible bonds can be calculated in the same way. The only slight modification to the above formulation is that, if a bond is declared ex dividend between 1 April and 30 June, the interest accrued is negative during the ex dividend period. The repo rates are shown in the final column of Table 8.7. The CTD bond is the Treasury 10.5 per cent 2013–15, which has the largest implied repo rate of 3.24 per cent. When £100,000 nominal of this bond is delivered on 30 June, the invoice amount, assuming a futures settlement price of 91.25, will be:

$$
\begin{aligned}
\text{Invoice amount} &= \left( \frac{\text{Settlement price}}{100} \times \text{Price factor} \times \text{Nominal value of gilt} \right) \\
&\quad + \text{Initial accrued interest} \\
&\quad + (30 \times \text{Daily accrued interest}) \\
&= (0.9125)(1.3032131)(£100,000) + £342.46 + (30)(£34.2466) \\
&= £120,288.05.
\end{aligned}
$$

By paying this amount to the short, the long gets a yield to maturity of 7 per cent on his holding of Treasury 10.5 per cent 2013–15 as required by the futures contract.

Prior to the delivery date, we can calculate the *implied forward yield* on a futures contract as the yield to maturity of the CTD bond calculated as of the delivery date of the futures contract assuming that the price of the CTD bond on that date equals the current futures price multiplied by the price factor of the CTD.

## 8.2.3 Currency futures

LIFFE used to trade currency or exchange rate futures contracts, but they were not a success. This was principally because of the liquidity and flexibility of the forward currency market in London. LIFFE no longer trades currency futures. However currency futures are traded in other centres, most notably on the Chicago Mercantile Exchange (CME). The specifications of four contracts traded on the CME are shown in Table 8.8: sterling, euro, Swiss franc and Japanese yen, all traded against the US dollar. We shall concentrate our attention on the sterling contract.

**Table 8.8** CME currency futures contracts

| *Contract:* | *Sterling* | *Euro* | *Swiss franc* | *Japanese yen* |
|---|---|---|---|---|
| **Unit of trading** | £62,500 | €125,000 | SFr125,000 | ¥12,500,000 |
| **Delivery months** | January, March, April, June, July, September, October, December, and spot months | | | |
| **Quotation** | US$ per £ | US$ per € | US$ per SFr | US$ per ¥100 |
| **Minimum price movement** | | | | |
|     **Tick size** | 0.02¢ per £ | 0.01¢ per € | 0.01¢ per SFr | 0.01¢ per ¥100 |
|     **Value** | $12.50 | $12.50 | $12.50 | $12.50 |

*Contract standard:* currencies will be deliverable in the principal financial centres in the country of issue.

*Exchange Delivery Settlement Price (EDSP):* the CME official closing price on the last trading day.

The sterling contract has a face value of £62,500 and is traded against the US dollar. This means that the buyer of one contract (the long) is expecting to receive £62,500 and to make payment for this in dollars. The seller (the short), on the other hand, is expecting to receive a sum of US dollars (which depends on the price of the contract) and to pay £62,500 for this. The price of the contract is quoted in exactly the same way as foreign exchange is quoted. For example, if the EDSP is 1.62 (i.e. £1 = $1.62), then the invoice amount for the contract is:

$$\text{Invoice amount} = £62,500 \times \$1.62 = \$101,250.$$

The long pays $101,250 to the short and in return receives £62,500. Delivery takes place two business days after the last trading day, the standard settlement period in the foreign exchange market.

The tick size on the sterling contract is 0.02 cents per £, i.e. $0.0002 per £. This implies a tick value for the contract of $12.50 (i.e. $0.0002 × £62,500). To illustrate, suppose an individual buys one sterling contract at a price of 1.62 and later closes his position at 1.6276. The exchange rate change is $0.0076 (i.e. $1.6276 − $1.62). The number of ticks gain is 38 (i.e. $0.0076/$0.0002, where $0.0002 is the tick size). The profit on the deal is therefore $475 (i.e. 38 ticks × $12.50 per tick).

## 8.2.4 Stock index futures

There are eight stock index contracts traded on LIFFE, namely those on the FTSE 100, FTSE 250, FTSE Eurotop 100, FTSE Eurotop 300, FTSE Eurotop 300 excluding UK, FTSE Eurobloc 100, MSCI

(Morgan Stanley Capital International) Euro and MSCI Pan Euro indices. The specifications of the first and third contract are shown in Tables 8.9 and 8.10.

**Table 8.9** LIFFE FTSE 100 index futures contract

| | |
|---|---|
| **Unit of trading** | Valued at £10 per index point (e.g. value £50,000 at 5000.0) |
| **Delivery months** | March, June, September, December (nearest three available for trading) |
| **Delivery day** | First business day after the last trading day |
| **Last trading day** | 10:30, third Friday in delivery month[a] |
| **Quotation** | Index points |
| **Minimum price movement** | |
|     **Tick size** | 0.5 |
|     **Value** | £5 |
| **Initial margin** | £1,000 |
| **Spread margin** | £100 |
| **Trading hours** | 08:35–16:30 |
| **APT trading hours** | 16:46–18:00 |

*Contract standard:* cash settlement based on the Exchange Delivery Settlement Price.

*Exchange Delivery Settlement Price (EDSP):* the EDSP is based on the average of the FTSE 100 index every 15 seconds inclusively between 10:10 and 10:30 (London time) on the last trading day. Of the 81 measured values, the highest 12 and lowest 12 will be discarded and the remaining 57 will be used to calculate the EDSP. Where necessary, the calculation will be rounded to the nearest half index point.

[a]In the event of the third Friday not being a business day, the last trading day shall normally be the last business day preceding the third Friday.

---

The face value of the FTSE 100 contract is £10 per full index point and the futures price is quoted in index points. So a futures price of 1825.0 implies that the value of the contract is £18,250 (i.e. 1825.0 × £10 per index point). The tick size on the contract is 0.5 and the value of a tick is £5.00. (Hence two ticks are equivalent to one full index point, and this is valued at £10.) There are no price limits on the contract throughout its entire duration.

To illustrate, consider an individual buying 20 contracts at 5825.0 who closes his position five days later by selling 20 contracts at 5812.5. The futures price has fallen by 12.5 (i.e. 5825.0 − 5812.5) which is equivalent to 25 ticks (i.e. 12.5/0.5, where 0.5 is the tick size). The individual's loss is:

$$
\begin{aligned}
\text{Loss} &= \text{Number of contracts} \times \text{Number of ticks loss} \times \text{Value per tick} \\
&= 20 \times 25 \times £5.00 \;=\; £2500.
\end{aligned}
$$

If the contract goes to delivery, it clearly has to be settled for cash since it is not possible to deliver a physical index. The invoice amount is determined by the difference between the EDSP and the settlement price on the day before the last trading day. This is because all the variation margin payments due will have been up to the penultimate trading day. All that remains to be settled is the consequence of the movement in the cash index between 8:35 am and 10:30 am on the last trading day. To illustrate, we will reconsider the last example and assume that the individual did not close his position after five

**Table 8.10** LIFFE Eurotop 100 futures contract

| | |
|---|---|
| **Unit of trading** | Valued at €20 per index point (e.g. value €56,000 at 2800.0) |
| **Delivery months** | March, June, September, December (nearest three available for trading) |
| **Delivery day** | First business day after the last trading day |
| **Last trading day** | 13:00 CET (12:00 London time) third Friday in delivery month |
| **Quotation** | Index points (e.g. 2807.0) |
| **Minimum price movement** | |
|     **Tick size** | 0.5 |
|     **Value** | €10 |
| **Initial margin** | €1600 |
| **Spread margin** | €300 |
| **Trading hours** | 10:00–17:00 CET (09:00–16:00 London time) |

*Contract standard:* cash settlement based on the Exchange Delivery Settlement Price.

*Exchange Delivery Settlement Price (EDSP):* the EDSP is based on the average values of the FTSE Euro-top 100 index every fifteen seconds between (and including) 12:40 and 13:00 CET (11:40 and 12:00 London time) on the last trading day. Of the 81 measured values, the highest 12 and lowest 12 will be discarded and the remaining 57 will be used to calculate the EDSP. Where necessary, the calculation will be rounded to the nearest half index point.

days but instead waited for the last trading day which was the following day. His variation margin payments of £2500 have been paid and the average FTSE 100 index during the last 20 minutes of trading is 5810.5, implying an EDSP of 5810.5. The futures price has fallen between the previous close and last trade by 2.0 (i.e. $5812.5 - 5810.5$) or by 4 ticks (i.e. $2.0/0.5$). The invoice amount is therefore:

$$
\begin{aligned}
\text{Invoice amount} &= \text{Number of contracts} \times \text{Number of ticks loss} \times \text{Value per tick} \\
&= 20 \times 4 \times £5.00 = £400.
\end{aligned}
$$

This sum is handed over by the long to the short in final settlement.

Trading in stock index futures is much cheaper than trading in the underlying shares of the index as the following example involving a *round trip* (i.e. purchase and immediate resale) shows:

| | *FTSE 100 index* | |
|---|---|---|
| | *Shares* | *Futures* |
| Average bid-offer spread | 1.00% | 0.10% |
| Stamp duty | 0.50% | 0.00% |
| Commission (×2) | 0.40% | 0.04% |
| | 1.90% | 0.14% |

The cost of a round trip with futures is nearly 14 times lower than the cost involving the underlying shares.

## 8.3   The fair pricing of forward and financial futures contracts

Forward contracts and financial futures contracts perform exactly the same function. Therefore we would expect a forward contract and a financial futures contract with the same specifications to have the same price. We shall therefore concentrate on the pricing of financial futures contracts.

### 8.3.1   Fair pricing with no uncertainty

If there is no uncertainty, the fair price of a financial futures contract can be determined very simply using the *cost-of-carry* (or the *cash-and-carry*) model (the same model that was used to find the CTD bond).

Suppose that an individual can undertake one of the following two investments, one in the cash market and one in the futures market. He could borrow enough to buy an asset in the cash market, hold on to it for $T$ years (earning any income, but bearing any carrying costs, including interest on borrowed funds involved), and then sell it in the cash market and also repay the loan with interest. Alternatively, he could sell a futures contract at the current futures price and, at the end of $T$ years, buy the asset in the cash market to deliver it into the futures market to fulfil the terms of the contract.

The profit under the second strategy is:

$$\text{Profit from strategy 2} \quad = \quad P^f - P_T^s, \tag{8.11}$$

where:

$$
\begin{aligned}
P^f &= \text{current futures price;} \\
P_T^s &= \text{spot price in year } T.
\end{aligned}
$$

Clearly, in a world with complete certainty $P^f = P_T^s$; the futures price must equal the actual future spot price. So the profit from this strategy will be zero. Note that because of complete certainty, there will be no need for either initial margin or variation margin, so strategy 2 involves neither cash inflows nor cash outflows during the life of the contract. Note also, that there are no carrying costs with a futures contract; all the carrying costs are associated with the cash market transactions, but they are not incurred until the end of the period.

The profit under the first strategy is:

$$\text{Profit from strategy 1} \quad = \quad P_T^s - P^s(1 + rT) + dP^s T \tag{8.12}$$

where:

$$
\begin{aligned}
P^s &= \text{current spot price;} \\
P_T^s &= \text{spot price in year } T; \\
r &= \text{annual carry costs, including interest on loan (as a proportion);} \\
d &= \text{gross annual return from holding cash asset (as a proportion).}
\end{aligned}
$$

In (8.12) we assume that simple interest and not compound interest is used (otherwise we would need to use $(1+r)^T$) and that carry costs in the cash market are proportional to price. Carry costs can include such items as insurance, storage and deterioration as well as borrowing costs. The cost of carry is $(r-d)$ and this can be positive or negative.

Both strategies achieve the same outcome, namely the sale of an asset in $T$ years' time; both strategies use none of the individual's own wealth; and both strategies are riskless. Two identical strategies using no wealth and involving no risk (such strategies are known as *arbitrage strategies*) should, in equilibrium, generate the same profit, and that profit should be zero. We know that strategy 2 generates zero profit, and strategy 1 should also generate the same zero profit.

By equating (8.11) and (8.12), we can derive the fair futures price $P_0^f$:

$$
\begin{aligned}
P_0^f &= [1 + (r-d)T)]P^s \\
&= P^s + (r-d)P^s T.
\end{aligned}
\tag{8.13}
$$

The fair futures prices is equal to the current spot price *plus* the cost of carry. It is clear from (8.1) and (8.13) that the basis is equal to the cost of carry:

$$
\begin{aligned}
\text{Basis} &= P_0^f - P^s \\
&= (r-d)P^s T = \text{Cost of carry}.
\end{aligned}
\tag{8.14}
$$

The basis will be positive (contango) if the cost of carry is positive and negative (backwardation) otherwise. Actually, (8.14) is known as the *theoretical* or *carry basis*. The actual basis (sometimes called the *gross basis*) is the sum of the theoretical basis and the *value basis*, where the value basis is the difference between the actual futures prices and the fair futures price (i.e. $P^f - P_0^f$). The value basis measures the degree of under- or over-valuation of the actual futures price.

A similar relationship holds between the prices of futures contracts with different delivery months:

$$
P_2^f = P_1^f + (r-d)P_1^f(T_2 - T_1),
\tag{8.15}
$$

where:

$$
\begin{aligned}
P_1^f &= \text{current price of futures contract with delivery in year } T_1; \\
P_2^f &= \text{current price of futures contract with delivery in year } T_2 \ (T_1 < T_2).
\end{aligned}
$$

The difference between the two futures prices is known as the *spread*, and it is clear from (8.15) that the spread is equal to cost of carry:

$$
\begin{aligned}
\text{Spread} &= P_2^f - P_1^f \\
&= (r-d)P_1^f(T_2 - T_1) = \text{Cost of carry}.
\end{aligned}
\tag{8.16}
$$

If the cost-of-carry (or the spread) is positive, then $P_2^f > P_1^f$ (normal contango), while if the cost-of-carry is negative, then $P_2^f < P_1^f$ (normal backwardation).

If $P_2^f$ exceeded the right-hand side of (8.15), a riskless arbitrage would exist. By holding a long contract for delivery at $T_1$ and a short contract for delivery at $T_2$, it would be possible to take delivery at $T_1$ for $P_1^f$, keep the asset for making delivery at $T_2$ for $P_2^f$, and to make a sure profit. If futures contracts were fairly priced, however, this could not happen.

## 8.3.2 Futures prices and expected spot prices

In a world with uncertainty, the future spot price will not be known with certainty. This means that the futures price is likely to differ from the realized spot price. But the question is: how will it differ?

According to the *expectations hypothesis* (see Chapters 2 and 5), which assumes rational behaviour by risk-neutral investors, the futures price will not differ systematically from the realized spot price. In other words, the current futures price will equal the market average expectation of the future spot price; i.e.:

$$P^f \;=\; E(P^s_T), \tag{8.17}$$

where:

$$
\begin{array}{lcl}
P^f & = & \text{current price of futures contract with delivery in year } T\,;\\
P^s_T & = & \text{spot price in year } T\,;\\
E(\ ) & = & \text{market average expectations operator based on all current information.}
\end{array}
$$

The actual rate of return on a futures position depends both on whether the position is long or short, and on the amount of margin that has to be paid. Suppose that an individual has to put up 100 per cent margin (i.e. has to pay the full amount of the investment $P^f$ from the start) but that this can be invested at the riskless rate $r$. If the individual has a long position, his actual rate of return over the one-year holding period $rh$, assuming $T = 1$ is:

$$
\begin{aligned}
rh & = \frac{(1+r)P^f + (P^s_1 - P^f)}{P^f} - 1 \\[2mm]
   & = r + \frac{P^s_1 - P^f}{P^f}. \tag{8.18}
\end{aligned}
$$

The first term on the right-hand side of (8.18) is the return on the margin payments. The second term is the return on the futures position. If $P^s_1 > P^f$, the long makes a profit on his futures position.

If the individual has a short position, his holding period return is:

$$
rh \;=\; r + \frac{P^f - P^s_1}{P^f}. \tag{8.19}
$$

If $P^s_1 > P^f$, the short makes a loss on his futures position.

If the expectations hypothesis is valid then, from (8.17), expected return from the futures position is zero for both the long and the short. Therefore the overall rate of return is simply the risk-free rate of interest.

The expectations hypothesis may be a good starting point, but it assumes that individuals who take unhedged positions in futures markets (i.e. speculators) expect on average to earn only the risk-free rate. This is rational behaviour only if speculators are *risk-neutral* and are willing to accommodate the demands of hedgers without additional compensation in the form of a risk premium in excess of the risk-free rate. Diagrammatically, the expectations hypothesis is given by the horizontal line in Figure 8.1 (assuming that the expected spot price does not change over time).

There are two other explanations of the relationship between futures prices and expected future spot prices, one consistent with the backwardation relationship and the other consistent with the contango relationship. Both allow for the possibility that speculators might be *risk-averse*.

The backwardation pattern is consistent with the following relationship between speculators and hedgers. Suppose that, on average, hedgers hold long cash market positions and short futures positions. If risk-averse hedgers are going to transfer risks effectively to risk-averse speculators, speculators will on average have to hold long futures positions. To induce speculators to take on net long positions, they have to be compensated with an *expected* return from the long position that exceeds the risk-free rate; i.e., their return must include a risk premium. From (8.18) above, this requires the futures price to be less than the *expected* spot price; and because the basis tends to zero as the delivery date of the futures contract approaches, it also requires the futures price to increase over time. This backwardation relationship is shown in Figure 8.1 (assuming that the expected spot price does not change over time).

The contango pattern is consistent with the following relationship between speculators and hedgers. If hedgers on average hold short cash market positions and long futures positions, risk-averse speculators will have to be induced to take short futures positions on average. This requires that the *expected* return from the short position exceeds the riskless rate. From (8.19) above, this means that the futures price has to be greater than the *expected* spot price and to decline over time. The contango relationship is shown in Figure 8.1 (again assuming that the expected spot price does not change over time).

### 8.3.3 Fair pricing of the short-term interest rate contract

We are now in a position to find the fair price of the futures contracts trading on LIFFE or the CME. We will assume for simplicity that the expectations hypothesis holds, so that there is no risk premium in the futures price. Therefore the formula given by (8.13) is appropriate, although the derivations below involve slight variations on the procedure used to derive (8.13).

We begin with the short-term sterling deposit contract. The current spot price (or present value) of each £100 worth of deposit at maturity is given by:

$$P^s = \frac{100}{1 + rs_2(N_1 + N_2)/365}$$
$$= \frac{100}{[1 + rs_1(N_1/365)][1 + {}_1rf_2(N_2/365)]}, \qquad (8.20)$$

where:

$N_1$ = number of days between current date and delivery date of futures contract (period 1);
$N_2$ = number of days to maturity of time deposit, e.g. 91 days (period 2);
$rs_1$ = spot interest rate for period 1;
$rs_2$ = spot interest rate for periods 1 and 2;
${}_1rf_2$ = forward/futures rate for period 2.

In (8.20) the spot interest rate for both periods (the period over which the futures contract operates *plus* the period over which the deposit operates) is $rs_2$. This spot rate can be decomposed into the interest rates relevant for each period: $rs_1$, the spot rate over the period of the operation of the futures contract, and ${}_1rf_2$, the forward or futures interest rate over the period for which the deposit exists. What the futures market is trying to do is to get an unbiased estimate of ${}_1rs_2$, the spot interest rate over period 2. In other words:

$${}_1rf_2 = E({}_1rs_2). \qquad (8.21)$$

In addition, the carrying or financing costs in the cash market for period 1 are $rs_1$. From (8.13), assuming $d = 0$, since interest is not paid until maturity on this deposit, this implies that the fair futures price is:

$$
\begin{aligned}
P_0^f &= [1 + rs_1(N_1/365)]P^s \\
&= \frac{100}{1 + {_1}rf_2(N_2/365)} .
\end{aligned}
\tag{8.22}
$$

Now, the futures price of the three-month deposit contract on LIFFE is not quoted as in (8.22). In practice, two adjustments are made. First, the futures price is quoted on the basis of an annual interest rate $({_1}rf_2)$, not the quarterly interest rate given in (8.22). Second, the following approximation to the discount factor is used:

$$
\frac{1}{1 + {_1}rf_2} \approx 1 - {_1}rf_2 .
\tag{8.23}
$$

Thus, we get the LIFFE quote for the futures price:

$$
P_0^f = 100 - {_1}rf_2 \, (\%) .
\tag{8.24}
$$

This quotation method is known as the *price equivalent* of the interest rate. For example, if the futures rate is 9.25 per cent, then the fair futures price is 90.75.

### 8.3.4   Fair pricing of the long-term interest rate contract

The cash-and-carry transactions used to determine the CTD bond for a given futures price can also be used to determine the fair price of the futures contract, once the price of the CTD bond is known. The fair futures price is that which gives a zero arbitrage profit relative to the CTD bond from a cash-and-carry transaction involving the purchase of the CTD bond in the cash market (with borrowed funds) and selling it into the futures market on the delivery day.

The cash outflow (per £100 nominal) from the transactions is:

$$
\text{Cash outflow} = \left( P_{CTD} + d_{CTD} \cdot \frac{N_1}{365} \right) \left( 1 + r \cdot \frac{N_2}{365} \right) ,
\tag{8.25}
$$

and the cash inflow (per £100 nominal) is:

$$
\text{Cash inflow} = P^f \cdot PF_{CTD} + d_{CTD} \cdot \frac{N_1 + N_2}{365} ,
\tag{8.26}
$$

where:

$$
\begin{aligned}
P^f &= \text{current futures price;} \\
P_{CTD} &= \text{current clean price of CTD bond (excluding accrued interest);} \\
d_{CTD} &= \text{annual coupon on CTD bond;} \\
PF_{CTD} &= \text{price factor for the CTD bond;} \\
r &= \text{annual money market rate of interest (as a proportion);} \\
N_1 &= \text{number of days between last coupon payment date and current date;} \\
N_2 &= \text{number of days between current date and delivery date of futures} \\
&\quad\;\; \text{contract.}
\end{aligned}
$$

The cash outflow covers the cost of borrowed funds at the money market interest rate. The cash inflow covers the implied clean price of the bond on the delivery day (futures price × price factor), plus the amount of accrued interest on the CTD bond up to the delivery date.

The fair futures price (per £100 nominal) is found by equating cash inflow and cash outflow and solving:

$$
\begin{aligned}
P_0^f &= \frac{1}{PF_{CTD}} \left[ P_{CTD} + d_{CTD} \cdot \frac{N_1}{365} + \left( P_{CTD} + d_{CTD} \cdot \frac{N_1}{365} \right) r \cdot \frac{N_2}{365} \right. \\
&\quad \left. - d_{CTD} \cdot \frac{N_1}{365} - d_{CTD} \cdot \frac{N_2}{365} \right] \\
&= \frac{P_{CTD}}{PF_{CTD}} + \left( r \cdot \frac{N_2}{365} - rc \cdot \frac{N_2}{365} \right) \frac{P_{CTD} + AI}{PF_{CTD}},
\end{aligned}
\tag{8.27}
$$

where:

$$
\begin{aligned}
AI &= d_{CTD}(N_1/365) = \text{accrued interest on CTD bond on the date the} \\
&\quad \text{futures transaction arises;} \\
P_{CTD} + AI &= \text{current dirty price of CTD bond;} \\
rc &= d_{CTD}/(P_{CTD} + AI) = \text{dirty current yield on CTD bond.}
\end{aligned}
$$

Comparing with (8.13), we again see that the fair futures prices equals the current clean price of the CTD bond (divided by the price factor) *plus* the cost of carry. The cost of carry equals the interest cost of holding the cash bond (valued at the bond's dirty price) *less* the accrued interest earned on the cash bond before it is delivered into the futures market on the delivery day (i.e., $d = rc$ in (8.13)).

To illustrate, we will estimate the fair price of the long gilt future on 1 April. The CTD bond is the Treasury 10.5% 2013–15. Its dirty price on 1 April is £118.00 (per £100 nominal), its clean price is £114.15 (i.e. the dirty price *less* 134 days' of accrued interest), and its price factor is 1.3032131. The delivery date for the futures contract is 30 June. This means that there are 90 days of accrued interest between 1 April and 30 June. The money market interest rate is 8 per cent. Therefore from (8.27):

$$
P_0^f = \frac{114.15}{1.3032131} + \left( 0.08 \cdot \frac{90}{365} - \frac{10.5}{118.00} \cdot \frac{90}{365} \right) \frac{118.00}{1.3032131} = 87.39.
$$

The fair futures price is 87.39. When we calculated the CTD gilt, the long gilt futures price was 88.19, which is slightly overpriced compared with the fair price.

We can also use the relationship in (8.27) to derive measures of the responsiveness of futures prices to changes in yields. If we ignore the cost-of-carry term, we have (as an approximation):

$$
\frac{\Delta P_0^f}{\Delta(1+rm)} = \frac{1}{PF_{CTD}} \cdot \frac{\Delta P_{CTD}}{\Delta(1+rm)},
\tag{8.28}
$$

or:

$$
BPV_0^f = \frac{BPV_{CTD}}{PF_{CTD}},
\tag{8.29}
$$

where:

$$BPV_0^f \quad = \quad \text{\textit{basis point value}} \text{ of fair futures price (i.e. change in price of futures}$$
in response to a one basis point change in the interest rate);

$$BPV_{CTD} \quad = \quad \text{basis point value of CTD bond.}$$

Again as an approximation (8.28) can be rewritten:

$$\frac{\Delta P_0^f}{\Delta(1+rm)} \cdot \frac{1+rm}{P_0^f} \quad = \quad \frac{1}{PF_{CTD}} \cdot \frac{\Delta P_{CTD}}{\Delta(1+rm)} \cdot \frac{1+rm}{P_{CTD}/PF_{CTD}} \tag{8.30}$$

$$= \quad \frac{\Delta P_{CTD}}{\Delta(1+rm)} \cdot \frac{1+rm}{P_{CTD}}. \tag{8.31}$$

So, referring to equation (5.52), we can see that the duration of a futures contract equals the duration of the CTD bond.

### 8.3.5   Fair pricing of the currency contract

The fair price of an exchange rate or currency contract can also be determined using arbitrage strategies.

Suppose the objective is to receive sterling in one year's time. Strategy 1 involves the purchase of a futures contract. If the futures price ($per £1) is $P^f$, this means that the individual will exchange $P^f$ dollars for £1 at the end of the year. Strategy 2 involves borrowing dollars at the beginning of the year (at US interest rates, $r_\$$), exchanging them into sterling at the spot exchange rate ($\$P^s$ per £), investing the proceeds at UK interest rates ($r_£$), and at the end of the year using the sterling amount to repay the borrowed dollars with interest. In other words, at the beginning of the year an investor would:

1  borrow $\$P^s/(1+r_£)$,

2  exchange the dollars in the spot market for $£1/(1+r_£)$,

3  lend this sum at UK interest rates for one year.

Then at the end of the year, he would:

1  receive the proceeds of the UK loan:

$$(1+r_£)\left(\frac{£1}{1+r_£}\right) \quad = \quad £1,$$

2  pay off the US loan:

$$(1+r_\$)\left(\frac{\$P^s}{1+r_£}\right) \quad = \quad \$P^s\left(\frac{1+r_\$}{1+r_£}\right).$$

The net effect of strategy 2 is to exchange $P^s(1+r_\$)/(1+r_£)$ dollars for £1 at the end of the year.

The two strategies involve identical outcomes, namely the exchange of dollars for sterling at the end of the year. In both cases, the individual's own money is not involved until the end of the year. The two strategies are therefore identical and in equilibrium will have the same value. In other words, the number of dollars exchanged for £1 at the end of the year will be the same:

$$\left(\frac{1+r_\$}{1+r_£}\right)P^s = P^f, \tag{8.32}$$

or, rearranging and ignoring small-order terms:

$$P_0^f = P^s + (r_\$ - r_£)P^s. \tag{8.33}$$

Once again, the futures price equals the spot price *plus* the net cost-of-carry, the difference between US and UK interest rates (i.e. $r = r_\$, d = r_£$).

Equation (8.33) can be written in the more familiar form:

$$\frac{P_0^f - P^s}{P^s} = r_\$ - r_£. \tag{8.34}$$

This is the *covered interest rate parity* equation. It says that the rate of exchange rate appreciation implied by the futures market will equal the difference between US and UK interest rates.

If $r_£ = 10\%$, $r_\$ = 6\%$ and $P^s = \$1.75$ per £, then from (8.33) we estimate the fair futures price to be:

$$P_0^f = 1.75 + (0.06 - 0.10)1.75 = \$1.68 \text{ per } £.$$

From (8.34), this implies that:

$$\frac{P_0^f - P^s}{P^s} = r_\$ - r_£$$
$$= 0.06 - 0.10 = -0.04 \quad (-4\%).$$

The futures market is expecting sterling to depreciate by 4 per cent against the dollar over the year.

In this example, the futures contract matures in one year's time. If the duration of the contract is less than a year, we would have to take into account the fact that the UK money market assumes a 365-day year, while the US money market assumes a 360-day year. For example, if the futures contract matures in 80 days' time, then:

$$P_0^f = 1.75 + \left(0.06 \cdot \frac{80}{360} - 0.10 \cdot \frac{80}{365}\right) \cdot 1.75$$
$$= \$1.73 \text{ per } £.$$

### 8.3.6 Fair pricing of the stock index contract

The fair price of the stock index futures contract can be calculated in precisely the same way as with the other contracts.

Consider the following two investment strategies. Strategy 1 involves the purchase at the beginning of the year of all the shares in the stock index (i.e. all the shares in the FTSE 100 index with the appropriate weights). At the end of the year, all the shares are sold. The return on this strategy is the change in the value of the cash index over the year *plus* the dividend yield on the shares:

$$\text{Return on strategy 1} \quad = \quad (P_1^s - P^s) + d \cdot P^s, \tag{8.35}$$

where:

$$
\begin{aligned}
P^s &= \text{value of cash index at beginning of the year;} \\
P_1^s &= \text{value of cash index at end of the year;} \\
d &= \text{annual dividend yield on shares.}
\end{aligned}
$$

Strategy 2 involves the purchase of a futures contract and the investment of a sum of money equal to the value of the cash index purchased under strategy 1 (i.e. $P^s$) at the money market rate of interest. The return on this strategy is the difference between the value of the cash index at the end of the year and the futures price *plus* the interest earned on the money market investment:

$$\text{Return on strategy 2} \quad = \quad (P_1^s - P^f) + (1 + r)P^s - P^s. \tag{8.36}$$

Both strategies involve the same cost and have the same risk (resulting from the unknown value of the cash index at the end of the year.) They should therefore have the same return. Equating (8.35) and (8.36) yields the fair futures price:

$$P_0^f \quad = \quad P^s + (r - d)P^s. \tag{8.37}$$

Yet again, the futures price equals the spot price *plus* the cost-of-carry, the difference between money market rates and the dividend yield on the stock index.

To illustrate, consider the case where the spot FTSE 100 index is standing at 5820.0, the money market interest rate is 10 per cent and the dividend yield is 4 per cent. This means that the fair futures price is expected to be:

$$P_0^f \quad = \quad 5820.0 + (0.1 - 0.04)5820.0 \quad = \quad 6169.2.$$

In reality, the calculation is not as simple as it appears in (8.37). Firstly, there are transaction costs involved in setting up the cash index required for strategy 1. These may be sufficiently high to make strategy 1 an infeasible way of replicating the return under strategy 2. Second, the payment of dividends under strategy 1 is neither regular nor certain, unlike the payment of interest under strategy 2. This is because the timing of dividend payments on the 100 shares in the FTSE 100 index is not spread evenly throughout the year, and also, the amount of the dividend payments is not known at the beginning of the year. This leads to the futures price being more volatile than the cash index. To illustrate, suppose that all dividend payments are concentrated on a single day in each quarter. If the dividend yield is 4 per cent per annum, then the quarterly dividend payment is 1 per cent. It is clear from (8.37) that the futures index will rise by 1 per cent on the day the shares go ex dividend, whereas the cash index (which makes no allowances for dividends) will be unchanged.

## Selected references

*British Derivatives Markets Handbook*, Financial Services Authority and Joint Exchanges Committee, London.

Briys, E., Bellalah, M., Mai, H.M., and de Varenne, F. (1998), *Options, Futures and Exotic Derivatives*, Wiley, Chichester.

Dubofsky, D. (1992), *Options and Financial Futures*, McGraw Hill, New York.

Duffie, D. (1989), *Futures Markets*, Prentice-Hall, Englewood Cliffs, NJ.

Edwards, F. and Ma, C. (1992), *Futures and Options*, McGraw-Hill, New York.

Elton, E.J. and Gruber, M.J. (1995), *Modern Portfolio Theory and Investment Analysis*, John Wiley, New York. (Chapter 23.)

Fitzgerald, M.D. (1983), *Financial Futures*, Euromoney Publications, London. (Chapters 1–3.)

Francis, J.C. (1991), *Investments*, McGraw-Hill, Singapore. (Chapter 24.)

Hull, J.C. (1993), *Options, Futures and Other Derivative Securities*, Prentice-Hall, Englewood Cliffs, NJ.

Johnson, R.S. and Giaccotto, C. (1995), *Options and Futures*, West, St. Paul, MN.

Kolb, R. (1997), *Futures, Options and Swaps*, Blackwell, Oxford.

Rutterford, J. (1993), *Introduction to Stock Exchange Investment*, Macmillan, London. (Chapter 6.)

Schwarz, E.W., Hill, J.M., and Schneeweis, T. (1986), *Financial Futures*, Irwin, Homewood, Ill. (Chapter 6.)

Sharpe, W.F., Alexander, G., and Bailey, J. (1995), *Investments*, Prentice-Hall, Englewood Cliffs, NJ. (Chapter 21.)

**Exercises**

1  Explain the terms 'contango' and 'backwardation' in respect of futures markets. What type of behaviour by speculators and hedgers is consistent with these two relationships?

2  You are given the following information for 31 March:

> Spot sterling interest rate (3-month) = 9.25%;
> Forward sterling interest rate (30 June, 3-month) = 9.35%;
> Spot dollar interest rate (3-month) = 6.75%;
> Spot price of cheapest-to-deliver long gilt (Treasury 9%, with coupon payment date of 31 March) = £104.13;
> Price factor of cheapest to deliver long-gilt = 1.1785441;
> Spot sterling-dollar exchange rate = $1.82 per £;
> Spot FTSE 100 index = 5875.6;
> Dividend yield on the FTSE 100 index = 4%.

Assuming that the expectations hypothesis is true, calculate the fair futures prices for the following June contracts:

a)  the short sterling interest rate contract

b)  the long gilt contract

c)  the sterling currency contract

d)  the FTSE 100 stock index contract.

(You may assume that the delivery date for all the contracts is 30 June.)

3  What are the main differences between forward contracts and futures contracts?

4  Discuss the significance of 'marking to market' and 'margin payments' in futures markets.

5  a)   If more than one eligible cash market security can be delivered against a futures contract, which is the only one that will be delivered?

   b)   If more than one day is available for delivering against a futures contract, which is the only day on which delivery will take place?

6  a)   Define the terms 'tick size' and 'tick value'.

   b)   Derive the tick values for the following futures contracts:

| | |
|---|---|
| *Contract* | 3-month eurodollar interest rate contract |
| *Contract size* | $1,000,000 |
| *Tick size* | 0.01 (%) |
| *Contract* | German government bond contract |
| *Contract size* | €100,000 |
| *Tick size* | €0.01 |
| *Contract* | Euro currency contract |
| *Contract size* | €125,000 |
| *Tick size* | 0.01¢ per € |
| *Contract* | FTSE 100 stock index contract |
| *Contract size* | £10 per full index point |
| *Tick size* | 0.5 |

7  Examine the role of carry costs in determining futures prices.

8  What are price factors? What role do they play in futures contracts?

9  You can buy a 14-year 10 per cent Treasury gilt for 99.25 (clean price) on 30 March. The gilt pays coupons on 10 March and 10 September. The three-month interest rate is 8.75 per cent. If the current price of the June long gilt future is 85.88, what is the implied return on a cash-and-carry transaction? The price factor for the gilt is 1.1821387.

10  Calculate the profit or loss from the following transactions in futures contracts:

| Contract | Contract size | Price at purchase | Price at sale | Tick size | Tick value |
|---|---|---|---|---|---|
| Short sterling interest rate contract | £500,000 | 90.25 | 90.75 | 0.01 (%) | £12.50 |
| German government bond contract | €100,000 | 89.16 | 87.28 | €0.01 | €10 |
| Japanese yen currency contract | ¥12,500,000 | 0.7905 | 0.7678 | 0.01¢ per ¥100 | $12.50 |
| FTSE 100 stock index contract | £10 per index point | 6228.0 | 5906.0 | 0.5 | £5.00 |

(Assume one contract is purchased and subsequently sold.)

11  You are given the following information on 10 August:

September long gilt futures price = 96.56

Money market rates:   to 1 September       8.25%
                      to 30 September      8.50%

| Stock | Clean price | Price factor | Last coupon |
|---|---|---|---|
| Treasury 10.5% | 115.34 | 1.2169712 | 19 July |
| Treasury 5.5% | 85.13 | 0.8507193 | 15 June |

Which gilt is the cheapest to deliver, and on what date would you expect delivery on the September contract to be made?

12  You are given the following information for 30 June:

Closing price of short sterling future (29 June) = 90.10;
Settlement interest rate for short sterling contract = 9.88%;
Cheapest to deliver long gilt = Treasury 10.5%;
Last coupon payment for CTD long gilt = 15 March;
Price factor for CTD long gilt = 1.2135991;
Settlement price for long gilt contract = 97.50;
Settlement price for sterling currency contract = 1.8179;
Closing price for FTSE 100 contract (29 June) = 5892.0;
Settlement price for FTSE 100 contract = 5904.0.

Calculate the invoice amounts for the following June contracts, assuming that the delivery date for all contracts is 30 June:

a)  the short sterling interest rate contract (£500,000)

b)  the long-gilt contract (£100,000)

c)  the sterling currency contract (£62,500)

d)  the FTSE 100 stock index contract (£10 per full index point).

# Chapter 9

# Options, warrants and convertibles

In this chapter, we discuss options and the different types of financial option contracts that are traded. We examine the different ways in which options can be combined together, and we consider two different methods for pricing options: the binomial method and the Black-Scholes method. We then analyze some of the most important exotic options that are traded. Finally, we examine two types of securities that have option features attached to them: warrants and convertibles.

## 9.1   Option contracts

The effect of a futures contract is to fix today the future price of some security. This means that with a futures contract, the entire future distribution of the security price is concentrated at a single point, namely the current futures price. For many purposes this may be exactly what is required, but for others it is overly restrictive. An investor may be more certain of price rises than price falls but may nevertheless wish to protect against price falls. The solution in this case is to buy an option contract, in this case a put option contract. The initial purchase of an option is known as an *opening purchase*.

An *option* gives to its holder the right but not the obligation to buy or sell an underlying security at a fixed price (the *exercise price* or *strike price*) at or before a specific date (the *maturity date* or *expiry date*). This right is given by the issuer or *writer* of the option. A *call* option gives the right to buy the security, while a *put* option gives the right to sell the security. In order to give effect to the right to buy or sell, the option has to be *exercised*. A *European* option can be exercised only on the expiry date, whereas an *American* option can be exercised at any time before the expiry date. In return for the insurance offered by the option, a price (i.e. *option premium*) has to be paid.

Table 9.1 shows the premia payable on both call and put options on ABC shares. There are three expiry months and three exercise prices. In London, option contracts trade in units of 1000 shares; the premia in Table 9.1 are in pence per share.

On 1 April, ABC was trading at 115p per share. At the same time, the call option with an exercise price of 115p and an expiry month of June is trading at 9p. Clearly, no one will purchase this option and exercise it immediately because the exercise price is equal to the current share price and so the option has no *intrinsic value*, yet the buyer would still have to pay 9p for such an option. This is

**Table 9.1** Premia on ABC options (1 April)

| Exercise price | Calls | | | Puts | | |
|---|---|---|---|---|---|---|
| | *Jun* | *Sep* | *Dec* | *Jun* | *Sep* | *Dec* |
| 105p | 12 | 22 | 31 | 4 | 11 | 15 |
| 115p | 9 | 17 | 22 | 8 | 16 | 20 |
| 125p | 3 | 4 | 5 | 21 | 26 | 30 |

because there is some chance that the share price will rise above the exercise price before the expiry date and the option will acquire intrinsic value; indeed, if the share price rises above 124p, the buyer can exercise the option and make a profit. The option buyer is prepared to pay something for this possibility, and this component of the option premium is called the *time value* of the option.

The option premium therefore has two components:

$$\text{Option premium} \quad = \quad \text{Intrinsic value} + \text{Time value}. \tag{9.1}$$

For a call option where the share price is trading either at or below the exercise price (i.e. an *at-the-money* or an *out-of-the-money* option), the intrinsic value is zero and the option has only time value. For a call option where the share price is trading above the exercise price (i.e. an *in-the-money* option), the intrinsic value equals:

$$\text{Intrinsic value} \quad = \quad \text{Share price} - \text{Exercise price}. \tag{9.2}$$

**Figure 9.1** Profit and loss profile of the buyer of a call option

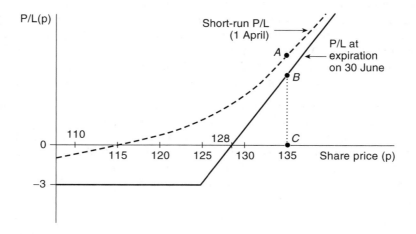

Figure 9.1 shows the profit and loss (P/L) profile for the buyer of a June call option (i.e. a *long* call option) on ABC with an exercise price of 125p when ABC is currently trading at 115p and the premium on the option is 3p. The short-run P/L profile (the broken line) passes through the current share price of 115p. If the share price rose to 135p, the short-run profit on the option would be *AC*, of which *AB* constitutes time value and *BC* constitutes (net) intrinsic value. Over time, the time value of

the option declines and eventually, at expiration, vanishes. If the share price stood at 135p when the option expired in June, the time value component of the profit on the option would be zero ($AB = 0$), but the option could be exercised to give a net intrinsic value profit of $BC$. The premium on the option just prior to expiration would therefore be $BC + 3p$. If, at expiry, the share price was at or below 125p, the option would expire worthless (i.e. without either time value or intrinsic value) and would be *abandoned* by the holder. In this case, the loss would be 3p. The share price has to be above 128p before any profits are made at expiry.

When a call option is sold or *written*, the seller (or *writer*) of the option gives to the buyer the right to purchase shares in return for receiving the premium. This is known as an *opening sale*. Figure 9.2 illustrates the profit and loss profile to the seller of the June call option on ABC (i.e. a *short* call option)

**Figure 9.2** Profit and loss profile of the seller of a call option

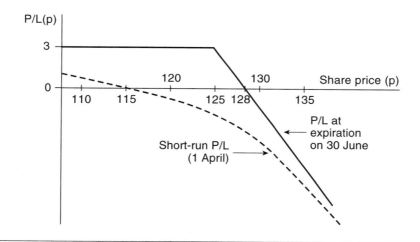

shown in Figure 9.1. It is a mirror image of the call P/L profile about the horizontal zero-profit axis. The maximum profit that the seller can make is the premium. He will make some profit if the price of the share at expiration is less than 128p; but he will make losses, possibly without limit, if the share price moves above 128p. When the option seller owns the underlying shares and writes call options against his holding, the seller is said to be writing *covered calls*. When the seller does not own the underlying shares, then the seller is said to be writing *naked calls*.

Figure 9.3 illustrates the profit and loss profile to the buyer of an in-the-money June put option (i.e. a *long* put option) with an exercise price of 125p when the share price is trading at 115p. The premium on the put option is 21p, which comprises 10p in intrinsic value (the difference between the exercise price and the lower share price: it is worth at least 10p to have the right to sell for 125p an ABC share that can be purchased in the market place for 115p) and 11p in time value. The buyer will make a profit at expiration if the share price falls below 104p.

The profit and loss profile for the seller of the put option (i.e. a *short* put option) considered in Figure 9.3 is given in Figure 9.4. The maximum gain is the 21p premium, while the maximum potential loss is 104p, equal to the exercise price *minus* the premium.

**Figure 9.3** Profit and loss profile of the buyer of a put option

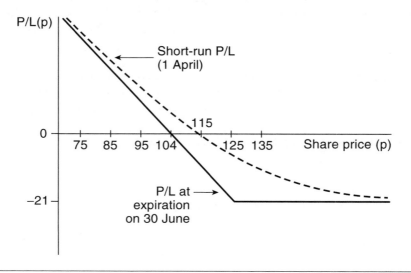

**Figure 9.4** Profit and loss profile of the seller of a put option

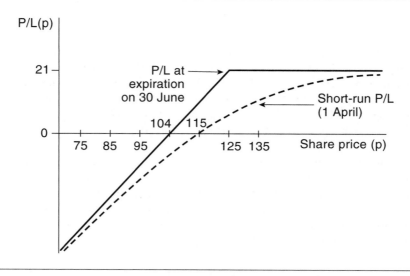

## 9.2 Option combinations

We have just examined the four basic option types: long call, short call, long put and short put. We have seen how their long-run (or expiration) profit and loss profiles consist of combinations of horizontal and diagonal (upward-sloping or downward-sloping at 45°) segments. It is possible to combine these basic option types to create a variety of long-run profit and loss profiles. Such option combinations can involve both put and call options and options with different expiration dates and exercise prices. We will consider some of the most important combinations.

A *straddle* is the combination of a call option and a put option on the same security, with the same exercise price and the same expiry date. The long-run profit and loss profiles of a long straddle and a short straddle are shown in Figure 9.5, where the exercise price is $X$. An individual would buy a

**Figure 9.5** Profit and loss profile: (a) Long straddle, (b) Short straddle

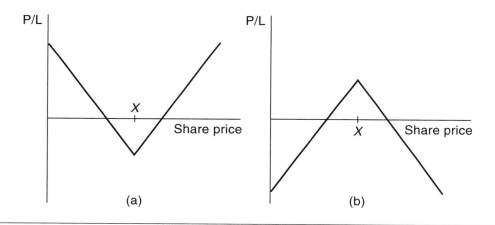

straddle if he expected a big jump in share prices but was not sure of the direction; he would then make a profit if there were either a big rise or a big fall. The seller of a straddle is expecting little or no change in share prices. If he were correct in his beliefs, he would make a profit. If he were to get it wrong and there was either a big rise or a big fall, he would make a loss.

A *strangle* is the combination of a call option and a put option on the same security, with the same expiry dates but different exercise prices. Figure 9.6 shows the long-run profit and loss profiles for a long strangle and a short strangle, where the exercise price on the put is $X_1$ and the exercise price on the call is higher at $X_2$. The strangle is similar to the straddle but extends the range of share price movements over which the seller of the strangle will continue to make profits.

A *strap* is a combination of two calls and one put (all long or all short). A *strip* is a combination of one call and two puts (all long or all short). In either case, the expiry dates are the same but the exercise prices can be the same or different. Figure 9.7 shows the long-run profit and loss profiles for a long strap (with the same exercise prices) and a short strip (with different exercise prices). The long strap is similar to a long straddle but with a steeper right arm as a result of using two call options rather than one. The short strip is similar to a short strangle but with a steeper left arm as a result of using two put options rather than one.

**Figure 9.6** Profit and loss profile: (a) Long strangle, (b) Short strangle

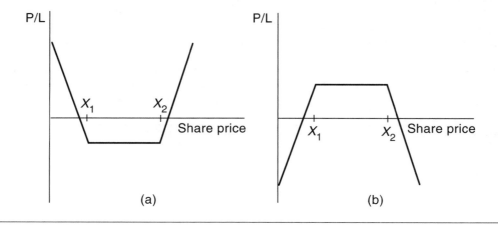

**Figure 9.7** Profit and loss profile: (a) Long strap, (b) Short strip

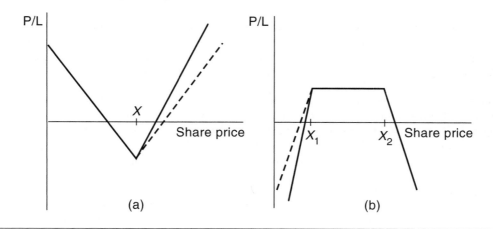

So far we have considered combinations involving either all long options or all short options. Combinations involving mixtures of long and short options are known as *spreads*. *Vertical* (or *cylinder*) *spreads* refer to option combinations with the same expiry date but different exercise prices. *Horizontal* (or *calendar*) *spreads* refer to option combinations with the same exercise prices but different expiry dates. *Diagonal spreads* refer to option combinations with different exercise prices and expiry dates. A spread is said to be *rotated* when the reverse option combination to the standard combination is involved. We will examine some special cases.

A long *butterfly spread* is the combination of a long call with a low exercise price ($X_1$), two short calls with a middle exercise price ($X_2$) and a long call with a high exercise price ($X_3$), all options having the same expiry date. This is shown in Figure 9.8, together with a short butterfly spread. A long

**Figure 9.8** Profit and loss profile: (a) Long butterfly spread, (b) Short butterfly spread

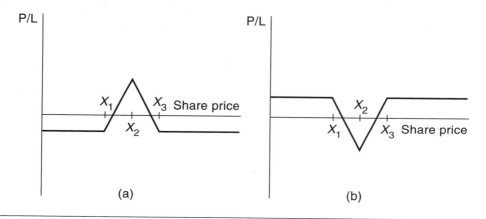

(a)                                     (b)

butterfly spread is very similar to a short straddle (see Figure 9.5(b)) but has the additional advantage of limited downside risk. In fact, a long butterfly spread is the combination of a long strangle and a short straddle. (Note that some authors define Figure 9.8(a) as a short butterfly spread and Figure 9.8(b) as a long butterfly spread.)

A long *condor* is the combination of a long call with a low exercise price ($X_1$), two short calls with different middle exercise prices ($X_2$ and $X_3$) and a long call with a high exercise price ($X_4$), all options having the same expiry date. This is shown in Figure 9.9, together with a short condor. A long condor is very similar to a short strangle (see Figure 9.6(b)), but has the additional advantage of limited downside risk.

A *vertical bull call spread* is a combination of a long call with a low exercise price ($X_1$) and a short call with a high exercise price ($X_2$). A *vertical bull put spread* is a combination of a long put with a low exercise price ($X_1$) and a short put with a high exercise price ($X_2$). Both types of spread give rise to similar long-run profit and loss profiles, as shown in Figure 9.10(a). A vertical bull spread has a bullish middle segment and has limited losses if the share price falls but also limited gains if the share price rises.

A *vertical bear spread* is a combination of a short call (or a short put) with a low exercise price ($X_1$) and a long call (or a long put) with a high exercise price ($X_2$). The long-run profit and loss profile is shown in Figure 9.10(b). It has a bearish middle segment and has limited losses if the share price rises, but also limited gains if the share price falls.

**Figure 9.9** Profit and loss profile: (a) Long condor, (b) Short condor

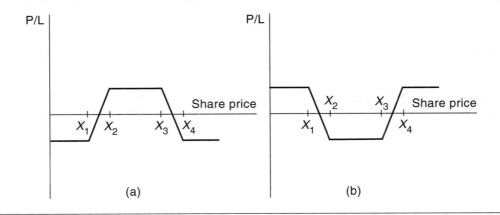

**Figure 9.10** Profit and loss profile: (a) Vertical bull spread, (b) Vertical bear spread

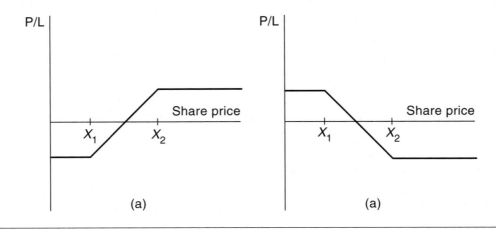

A *rotated vertical bull spread* is a combination of a short put with a low exercise price ($X_1$) and a long call with a higher exercise price ($X_2$). The profit and loss profile is given in Figure 9.11(a). It is designed to profit from a zone of ignorance in an otherwise bullish market, with premium income

**Figure 9.11** Profit and loss profile: (a) Rotated vertical bull spread (b) Rotated vertical bear spread

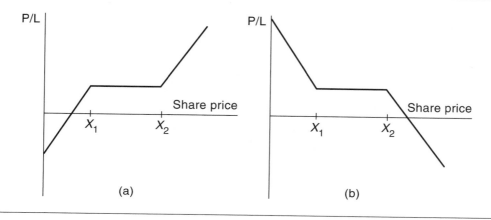

accruing from the sale of the put.

A *rotated vertical bear spread* is a combination of a long put with a low exercise price ($X_1$) and a short call with a high exercise price ($X_2$), as shown in Figure 9.11(b). It is designed to profit from a zone of ignorance in an otherwise bearish market.

Horizontal and diagonal spreads are designed to benefit from the differential effects of the decline in time value on options with different expiry dates. Figure 9.12 (as described by Fitzgerald (1987) Exhibit 4.10) depicts a horizontal spread and a diagonal spread in contrast with a vertical bull spread. The horizontal spread gives the best downside protection, and the vertical bull spread gives the best upside profit and dominates the diagonal spread throughout virtually the entire range of the share price.

The reason why the horizontal and diagonal spreads work in this way is because the time value in the earlier maturing (i.e. June) options declines more rapidly than in the later maturing (i.e. September) options. By June, the June options have only intrinsic value left, while the September $X_1$ and $X_2$ options both have time value. In addition, the September $X_1$ call option will have greater intrinsic value than the September $X_2$ call option. Hence the P/L on the diagonal spread will be lower than that on the horizontal spread if the share price in June is less than $X_2$ and higher if the share price in June is greater than $X_2$. If the short June option expires out-of-money, it will not be exercised against the investor. If, however, the June option has intrinsic value at expiry it will be exercised, but the September option either has the same intrinsic value (in the case of the horizontal spread) or greater intrinsic value (in the case of the diagonal spread), so the investor can always finance the delivery of shares from the sale of the September option. In addition, on the expiry of the June option, the investor could write a September $X_2$ call. This would have the effect of converting the diagonal spread into a vertical bull spread. In the case of the horizontal spread, it would lock in a fixed profit or loss in September, depending on whether or not the premium received from the sale of the September $X_2$ call in June exceeded the premium paid for the earlier purchase of the September $X_2$ call.

**Figure 9.12** Spread profits and losses in June

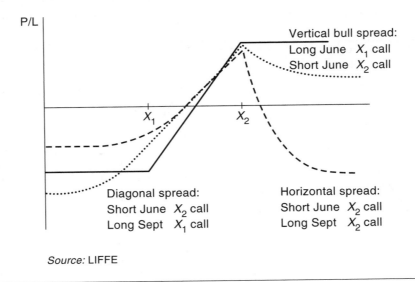

Source: LIFFE

So far, we have considered spreads where an equal number of options have been bought and sold. *Ratio spreads* are spreads involving a larger number of short positions than long positions. *Ratio backspreads* involve a larger number of long positions than short positions.

Looking again at Table 9.1, consider a ratio spread consisting of one long June 105 call on ABC shares at 12p and four short June 125 calls at 3p each. This is an example of a *zero-cost option strategy* (the premium received on the written calls exactly offsets the premium paid on the purchased call) and its profit and loss is shown in Figure 9.13(a). There is zero profit on the ratio spread if at expiry the

**Figure 9.13** Profit and loss profile: (a) Ratio spread, (b) Ratio backspread

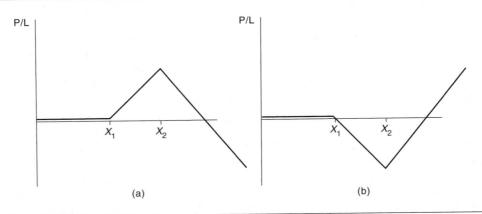

share price is below 105p ($X_1$ in Figure 9.13(a)), since all options expire worthless in this case. The profit on the spread is equal to the intrinsic value of the 105 call if the share price lies between 105p and 125p at expiry, with the profit reaching a maximum of 20p (i.e. the difference between the exercise prices, 125p – 105p) when the share price is 125p ($X_2$ in Figure 9.13(a)). Above 125p, the profit falls away rapidly, and the ratio spread breaks even at 131.67p (i.e. the exercise price of 125p plus one third of maximum profit of 20p, since the position is net short three calls above 125p and so loses 3p for every 1p rise in the share price above 125p). The ratio spread makes losses without limit as the share price rises above 131.67p. Ratio spreads have great upside risk.

In contrast ratio backspreads (using calls) benefit from upward movements in share prices. Consider the ratio backspread consisting of one short June 105 call on ABC shares at 12p and four long June 125 calls at 3p each. This is again a zero-cost strategy and its profit and loss profile is shown in Figure 9.13(b). There is zero profit on the ratio backspread if at expiry the share price is below 105p ($X_1$ in Figure 9.13(b)), since all options expire worthless in this case. The spread makes a loss equal to the intrinsic value of the short 105 call if the share prices lies between 105p and 125p at expiry; the maximum loss is 20p (i.e. the difference between the exercise prices, 125p – 105p) when the share price is 125p ($X_2$ in Figure 9.13(b)). Above 125p, the loss is rapidly reduced as the four long calls get deeper into the money. The ratio spread breaks even at 131.67p and has unlimited potential above this share price.

We have looked at different combinations of options. But it is also possible to form combinations of options and the underlying security. A classic example of this is the *buy-write* which involves the purchase of shares and the simultaneous sale of an out-of-the-money call option on the shares. This strategy can help to reduce the cost of buying the shares as the following example shows. Suppose that it is April 1 and ABC shares are trading at 115p. An investor believes that the shares have long term potential but he does not believe that the shares will rise above 125p before the end of June. He therefore buys 1000 ABC shares at 115p and sells one ABC June 125 call at 3p (see Table 9.1). The cost of the shares is £1150 (i.e. 115p × 1000 shares) and the income from the written call is £30 (i.e. 3p × 1000 shares). The call therefore reduces the effective cost of buying the shares to 112p. So long as the share price remains below 125p before the June option expires, the option will not be exercised and the investor will retain both the shares and the option premium, thereby keeping the effective cost of buying the shares to 112p. On the other hand, if the share price rises above 125p, the option will be exercised and the shares will have to be sold at 125p. This produces an effective sale price for the shares of 128p (i.e. 125p exercise price *plus* 3p premium). Compared with the original purchase price of 115p, this implies a rate of return of 11.3% in only 3 months.

A variant of the buy-write is the *write-buy* which involves the sale of an in-the-money put option which is likely to be exercised against the writer. The writer will be obliged to buy shares at the exercise price but the premium on the put reduces the cost of shares so purchased. Suppose an investor writes a June 125 put on ABC for 21p when ABC is trading at 115p (see Table 9.1). Suppose when the option expires ABC is trading at 110p. The option is exercised and the writer is obliged to buy 1000 ABC shares for 125p. But the effective cost of the shares is only 104p (i.e. 125p exercise price *minus* 21p premium) which is 6p below their market value at the time the option expires.

## 9.3 Financial options contracts

As with futures contracts, there are options on a whole range of commodities. But we are interested in those related to financial securities, i.e. *financial options contracts*.

In London, financial options have been traded on the London International Financial Futures and Options Exchange (LIFFE) since 1992. Prior to this, financial options were traded on two exchanges, the London Traded Options Market (LTOM), part of the London Stock Exchange, where trading in options on cash securities began in 1978, and the London International Financial Futures Exchange (the original LIFFE) where trading in options on both cash securities and futures contracts began in 1986. In 1992, the two exchanges merged to form LIFFE-LTOM, although it is more commonly known just as LIFFE.

Traditionally, the system of trading options on LIFFE has been by *open outcry* in a *pit* on the floor of the exchange. Under this system, the market in each class of option comprises a *crowd* consisting of a *pitch official*, a *board official*, registered *market makers*, and other traders or *broker-dealers*. The pitch official is a LIFFE employee and is there to ensure an orderly market and to intervene as principal between two brokers who have matched orders. The board official is also a LIFFE employee and is there to ensure the execution of public limit orders that have been placed on the *public limit order board* (PLOB). Market makers are able to quote two-way prices and to deal as principal but not to conduct agency business. There are two types of option market maker on LIFFE. An *assigned* market maker is required to make continuous two-way prices in a particular contract; a *nominated* market maker is required to make prices on request. The market makers on LIFFE have the same privileges as other market makers in London, namely stock lending relief and exemptions from stamp duty and stamp duty reserve tax. Broker-dealers can deal as principals, but may not quote two-way prices.

To execute an order, a broker-dealer must approach a board official and ask the price in a manner that is audible to the whole crowd. A market maker will quote bid and offer prices also in an audible manner. The broker-dealer then has the right to deal with any market maker at the quoted prices. There is an *exchange minimum quote size* (EMQS) of 10 contracts, although *market-maker quote sizes* (MMQS) of up to three times the EMQS are permitted. If the broker-dealer challenges the crowd at another price, all market makers are released from their obligation to trade at the quoted prices and may alter their quotations. Once a deal is made, it is recorded on official dealing slips by both the market maker and broker-dealer and these are subsequently matched by the exchange. The number of options contracts outstanding at any time in a particular class of contracts is known as the *open interest* in that class.

*Exchange-traded options* (like exchange-traded futures contracts) have advantages over tailor-made or *over-the-counter options*. They are traded on regulated exchanges. They have highly standardized contract specifications, with trading in specific quantities of securities for delivery in specific months. There are four main expiry months per year: March, June, September and December. However in 1994, LIFFE introduced *serial options*. These have expiry months other than these traditional end-of-quarter months. Their introduction ensures that options expiring in the two nearest serial months and the two nearest quarterly months are always being traded. Since these are options on futures contracts, the serial expiry month options relate to the futures contract at the end of the relevant quarter. For example a January, February or March option will relate to the March future. Most traded options are American, so can be exercised by the option buyer before expiry. Traded options are generally very liquid so can easily be resold. A long options position is cancelled by writing an identical option (known as a *closing sale*), while a short options position is cancelled by buying an identical option (known as a *closing purchase*).

At the end of 1995, LIFFE introduced SOEF (the *Small Order Execution Facility*) to enable brokers to execute automatically client orders of up to 10 lots on LIFFE's equity options at the Autoquote price (which is displayed on screens on the trading floor) if there is no better quote available from the pit. *Autoquote* is LIFFE's own option pricing model. Trades are allocated to market makers on a rota system. Both SOEF and Autoquote have been developed to improve LIFFE's retail market in equity options. SOEF operates between 8.35 and 16.10 in equity options, where the underlying security has at least two market makers. However SOEF does not operate in the following circumstances: on the Monday, Tuesday or Wednesday of the expiry week; when the underlying security price is in backwardation (i.e. the SEAQ best offer is below the SEAQ best bid); when the market in the underlying security has been declared either indicative or fast by the LSE; when the equity options market has been declared fast by LIFFE; when trading in the underlying security has been suspended; or when a series has a contract size of 2,000 or more shares.

In November 1998, LIFFE introduced a screen-based, order-driven trading market for equity options called *LIFFE Connect*. The market is anonymous and orders are matched according to price and time priority. Benefits in comparison with the quote-driven system include: firm prices and reduced execution risk, lower bid-offer spreads, and greater flexibility and market access, especially for private investors.

Options exchanges also operate a clearing house which registers and clears trades, and guarantees the physical delivery of the underlying securities, through a system of margining and marking to market by the seller of a contract. The clearing house at LIFFE is the LCH (London Clearing House). Most option buyers have to pay the full premium at purchase (these are known as *premium paid options*), but for options on futures contracts both buyers and writers are margined and marked to market (these are known as *premium margined options*).

LIFFE uses a portfolio-based margining system called *London SPAN* (Standard Portfolio Analysis of Risk). In the case of LIFFE options contracts, the initial margin depends on two main factors. The first factor is a *scanning range* which is set equal to the largest daily loss that can reasonably be expected to occur in the underlying security, based on recent historical price movements. The second factor is an *implied volatility shift* which equals the largest expected daily change in the volatility of the underlying security, again based on recent historical experience. Options contracts and also any futures contracts (both long and short) in the same underlying security are pooled together into *portfolios*. The initial margin required depends on the components of the overall portfolio, and will be reduced if the portfolio contains offsetting risk components.

The scanning range and implied volatility shift factors are used to calculate a *risk array* under 16 different scenarios concerning changes in the price and volatility of the underlying security. The risk array shows the *value loss* under each of the 16 scenarios and is recalculated daily by the exchange based on the closing prices of options and futures contracts.

An example of a risk array is illustrated in Table 9.2 for a short position in one April call option on ICI shares with an exercise price of 1250p. Each equity option on LIFFE is normally for 1000 shares. On 16 October, the closing premium on this option was 113p per share, ICI itself closed at £12.82 and the scanning range was 120p; short positions are shown as negative. The initial margin for this contract is based on the *spanning risk* for the contract which equals the maximum value loss, i.e. the largest positive number in the value loss column (gains are shown as negative value losses). The spanning risk in this example is £107 which arises under the scenario 'stock price up 3/3 (i.e. 100%) of a scanning range; volatility up'. This means that the exchange estimates that the largest daily movement in the underlying share price is ±£1.20 from the current price of £12.82 and the exchange also estimates that this corresponds to a maximum value loss for each options contract of £107. The worst case scenario for a short option position is a combination of a large rise in the price of the underlying security and an increase in volatility. An *extreme move* is twice the scanning range. The last two scenarios in the table are intended for deep out-of-the-money options whose premiums do not change much even when there is a large change in the price of the underlying; the value losses in these cases are designed to cover 35% of the loss on the position.

**Table 9.2** Margining equity options on LIFFE

| Line | Value Loss | Scenario | |
|------|------------|----------|---|
| 1 | $-1 \times \quad -6$ | Stock price unchanged; | Volatility up |
| 2 | $-1 \times \quad 7$ | Stock price unchanged; | Volatility down |
| 3 | $-1 \times \quad -37$ | Stock price up 1/3; | Volatility up |
| 4 | $-1 \times \quad -28$ | Stock price up 1/3; | Volatility down |
| 5 | $-1 \times \quad 23$ | Stock price down 1/3; | Volatility up |
| 6 | $-1 \times \quad 37$ | Stock price down 1/3; | Volatility down |
| 7 | $-1 \times \quad -71$ | Stock price up 2/3; | Volatility up |
| 8 | $-1 \times \quad -64$ | Stock price up 2/3; | Volatility down |
| 9 | $-1 \times \quad 47$ | Stock price down 2/3; | Volatility up |
| 10 | $-1 \times \quad 62$ | Stock price down 2/3; | Volatility down |
| **11** | $\mathbf{-1 \times -107}$ | **Stock price up 3/3;** | **Volatility up** |
| 12 | $-1 \times -102$ | Stock price up 3/3; | Volatility down |
| 13 | $-1 \times \quad 67$ | Stock price down 3/3; | Volatility up |
| 14 | $-1 \times \quad 82$ | Stock price down 3/3; | Volatility down |
| 15 | $-1 \times \quad -77$ | Stock price up extreme move (cover 35% of loss) | |
| 16 | $-1 \times \quad 37$ | Stock price down extreme move (cover 35% of loss) | |

On top of the scanning risk, there are other factors that LIFFE periodically takes into account when determining initial margin:

$$\text{Initial margin} \quad = \quad \text{Scanning risk}$$
$$+ \quad \text{Spot month charge}$$
$$+ \quad \text{Inter-month spread charge}$$
$$- \quad \text{Inter-commodity spread credit}. \qquad (9.3)$$

The *spot month charge* allows for the fact that options prices become more volatile as the expiry date approaches. The *inter-month spread charge* allows for the fact that options contracts with different delivery months do not have perfectly correlated price movements and this leads to a spread risk. The *inter-commodity spread credit* allows for the fact that different underlying securities may have correlated price movements and this may help to reduce the risk across different portfolios of options contracts. LIFFE can take any or all these three factors into account but does not necessarily do so at every point in time. Initial margin liabilities can be covered directly in cash (in sterling, dollars, Deutschmarks, lire, Swiss francs, pesetas, euros or yen) or in collateral including UK Treasury bonds or bills, sterling CDs, US Treasury bonds, German, Spanish or Italian government bonds or bills, bank guarantees or UK equities.

Under normal conditions, the initial margin depends only on the scanning risk and so in the above example the initial margin is £107. The *total margin* is determined as follows:

$$\text{Total margin} \quad = \quad \text{Initial margin} + \text{Net liquidation value}. \qquad (9.4)$$

The *net liquidation value* (NLV) is the value of the option position at the closing premium. For short option positions, the NLV is a debit, while for long option positions, the NLV is a credit. In the above example when the closing premium is 113p, the NLV is £1130 debit (113p × 1000 shares). Therefore:

$$\text{Total margin} \quad = \quad £107 + £1130 \quad = \quad £1237 \text{ debit}.$$

The total margin payable covers the current value of the position plus any change in the value of the position under the worst case scenario of the share price and volatility both rising.

Long option positions are either premium paid or premium margined. Premium margined positions involve lower margin payments as the following example, again using Table 9.2, shows. Because we are discussing a long position we ignore the '$-1\times$' part of the value loss column. The maximum value loss or initial margin is £82 which arises under the scenario 'stock price down 3/3 (i.e. 100%) of scanning range; volatility down'. The NLV is £1130 which is a credit for a long position. Therefore:

$$\text{Total margin} \quad = \quad £1130 - £82 \quad = \quad £1048 \text{ credit}.$$

This is a credit in the margin account and can be used against debit margins for other portfolios.

During the period between the exercise of an option and the delivery of the underlying security, the position continues to be margined to protect the exchange against adverse security price movements. The initial margin for an exercised option is equal to the scanning range. Using the above example of ICI shares, the initial margin is 120p per share or £1200 per contract. In addition, *contingent margin* is taken into account. This equals the intrinsic value of an option, that is, the difference between the security's closing price and the option's exercise price. In the case of an ICI 1250 call when ICI is trading at £12.82, then:

$$\text{Contingent margin} \quad = \quad (12.82 - 12.50) \cdot 1000 \quad = \quad £320 \text{ credit}.$$

For an in-the-money option, the contingent margin is a credit. Therefore:

$$\begin{aligned} \text{Total margin} \quad &= \quad \text{Initial margin} - \text{Contingent margin} \\ &= \quad £1200 - £320 \quad = \quad £880 \text{ debit}. \end{aligned}$$

For a writer who was assigned, the contingent margin would be a debit so the total margin would be £1520 debit (i.e. £1200 + £320).

Table 9.3 shows how to determine the margin for a portfolio of options, in this case equity options. The portfolio consists of:

$1 \times$ Short assigned ICI call with an exercise price of 1200 (closing price = £12.82);

$1 \times$ Short April ICI put with an exercise price of 1300 (closing premium = 74p);

$5 \times$ Long April ICI calls with an exercise price of 1250 (closing premium = 113p).

The table shows that each risk array is multiplied by position size. We then sum across each row to derive the total loss under each scenario. The largest total loss is £642 given in line 12. This equals the initial margin for the overall portfolio. In this case, the total initial margin would have been £1681 (i.e. £1200 for the assigned call (line 11) + £71 for the put (line 13) + £410 for the calls (line 14)). This demonstrates how London SPAN exploits offsetting risks on positions to reduce the overall initial margin.

The total margin is again the sum of initial margin, NLV for the options and the contingent margin for the delivery position:

$$\begin{aligned} \text{Total} \quad = \quad &-£642 & &(\text{initial margin}) \\ &-£749 & &(\text{NLV for put} = 74\text{p} \times 1000) \\ &+£5650 & &(\text{NLV for calls} = 5 \times 113\text{p} \times 1000) \\ &-£820 & &(\text{CM for delivery} = [£12.82 - £12.00] \times 1000) \\ = \quad &£3448 \text{ credit}. \end{aligned}$$

**Table 9.3** Margining a portfolio of equity options on LIFFE

| Line | Assigned call | Short put 1300 strike | Long call 1250 strike | Total loss (£) |
|------|------|------|------|------|
| 1 | $-1 \times$ 0 | $-1 \times -14$ | $5 \times -6$ | $-16$ |
| 2 | $-1 \times$ 0 | $-1 \times$ 14 | $5 \times$ 7 | 21 |
| 3 | $-1 \times -400$ | $-1 \times$ 1 | $5 \times -37$ | 214 |
| 4 | $-1 \times -400$ | $-1 \times$ 28 | $5 \times -28$ | 232 |
| 5 | $-1 \times$ 400 | $-1 \times -31$ | $5 \times$ 23 | $-254$ |
| 6 | $-1 \times$ 400 | $-1 \times -3$ | $5 \times$ 37 | $-212$ |
| 7 | $-1 \times -800$ | $-1 \times$ 13 | $5 \times -71$ | 432 |
| 8 | $-1 \times -800$ | $-1 \times$ 39 | $5 \times -64$ | 441 |
| 9 | $-1 \times$ 800 | $-1 \times -50$ | $5 \times$ 47 | $-515$ |
| 10 | $-1 \times$ 800 | $-1 \times -24$ | $5 \times$ 62 | $-466$ |
| 11 | $-1 \times -1200$ | $-1 \times$ 24 | $5 \times -107$ | 641 |
| **12** | **$-1 \times -1200$** | **$-1 \times$ 48** | **$5 \times -102$** | **642** |
| 13 | $-1 \times$ 1200 | $-1 \times -71$ | $5 \times$ 67 | $-794$ |
| 14 | $-1 \times$ 1200 | $-1 \times -64$ | $5 \times$ 82 | $-726$ |
| 15 | $-1 \times -840$ | $-1 \times$ 20 | $5 \times -77$ | 435 |
| 16 | $-1 \times$ 840 | $-1 \times -64$ | $5 \times$ 37 | $-591$ |

When an option buyer exercises the option (by completing an *exercise notice*), he will be *assigned* an option writer by the clearing house. The option writer is chosen randomly and has no choice over the matter. Once he is exercised against (and notified of this through an *assignment notice*), he will have to deliver a cash security or a futures contract if he has written a call option, or will have to receive a cash security or a futures contract if he has written a put option. The day following the issue of an exercise notice is known as the *bargain date*. (This is the date on which the option writer receives the assignment notice.) The *value date* is the last day on which it is possible to deliver the underlying security. This will depend on the usual settlement period in the relevant cash market security. For example, FTSE 100 index options and gilt options are settled the day following the bargain date, currency options are settled two days following the bargain date, and individual stock options are settled five days following the bargain date.

A specific price (the exercise price) has to be paid in exchange for the cash security or the futures contract. In the case of a cash security full payment is required at delivery, but in the case of a futures contract full payment is not required; instead, the margining and marking to market of the futures position begins to operate. This can have dramatic savings on both costs and credit lines. Some examples of this are discussed below. (Note: LIFFE constantly changes contracts and contract specifications.)

## 9.3.1 Equity options

On LIFFE, there are *equity options*, sometimes also called *individual stock options*, on more than 70 shares (see Tables 9.4 and 9.5). The contract size is normally for 1000 shares. There are three different expiry cycles: January, April, July, October; February, May, August, November; and March, June, September, December. The option premium is quoted in pence per share, so that a single options contract for 1000 shares would cost £100 if the premium was 10p. The options are premium paid.

**Table 9.4** LIFFE equity options contracts

| | |
|---|---|
| **Unit of trading** | One option normally equals rights over 1000 shares |
| **Expiry months** | January Cycle (J): means the three nearest expiry months from Jan, Apr, Jul, Oct cycle |
| | February Cycle (F): means the three nearest expiry months from Feb, May, Aug, Nov cycle |
| | March Cycle (M): means the three nearest expiry months from Mar, Jun, Sep, Dec cycle |
| **Exercise day** | Exercise by 17:20 on any business day, extended to 18:00 for all series on a last trading day |
| **Settlement day** | Settlement day is six business days after the day of exercise/last trading day |
| **Last trading day** | 16:20, third Wednesday of the expiry month |
| **Quotation** | Pence per share |
| **Minimum price movement** | |
|     **Tick size** | 0.5 pence per share |
|     **Value** | £5.00 |
| **Trading hours** | 09:05–16:20 |

*Contract standard:* delivery will be 1000 shares (or other such number of shares as determined by the terms of the contract).

*Option premium:* premium is payable in full by the buyer on the business day following a transaction.

*Exercise price and exercise price intervals:* pence, e.g. 240, 260, 280. The interval between exercise prices is set according to a fixed scale determined by the Exchange.

*Introduction of new exercise prices:* additional exercise prices will be introduced on the business day after the underlying share price has exceeded the second highest, or fallen below the second lowest, available exercise price.

---

The exercise price interval (see Table 9.1) differs for different shares, ranging from 5p for share prices up to 50p, to 200p for share prices in excess of 4000p. There are also *position limits* on the number of contracts that an investor can hold, ranging from 5000 contracts on the shares of companies with issued share capital of £500 million or less, up to 20,000 contracts on the shares of companies with issued share capital in excess of £1000 million.

To illustrate, we will consider ICI options with an exercise price of 1000p. The July call is trading at 43p and the July put is trading at 2p. ICI shares are trading at 1038p. The buyer of a July 1000 call has the right to buy 1000 ICI shares at 1000p between now and July. The cost of the contract is:

$$\text{Cost of call} \;=\; 1000 \times 43\text{p} \;=\; £430.$$

If the buyer exercises the call, he receives 1000 ICI shares from the option writer and pays him £10,000 (i.e. $1000 \times 1000\text{p}$). The total cost of the shares is therefore £10,430. If at the time of exercise the share price was 1075p, he would have made a profit on the transaction of £320 (i.e. $£10,750 - £10,430$), ignoring transaction costs.

**Table 9.5** Companies with LIFFE equity options, as at 24th May 1999

| Company | Expiry Cycle | Company | Expiry Cycle |
|---|---|---|---|
| Abbey National | J | Imperial Tobacco Group | F |
| Alliance & Leicester | F | Invensys | F |
| Allied Domecq | J | Kingfisher | F |
| Allied Zurich | J | Ladbroke Group | F |
| Anglo American | F | Land Securities | J |
| ASDA Group | J | LASMO | F |
| AstraZeneca | J | Lloyds TSB Group | M |
| BAA | J | Lonmin | M |
| Bass | J | LucasVarity | F |
| BG | M | Marks & Spencer | J |
| Blue Circle Industries | F | National Power | J |
| Boots Co | J | National Westminster Bank | J |
| BP Amoco | J | Norwich Union | M |
| British Aerospace | F | Orange | M |
| British Airways | J | P & O Steam Navigation Co | F |
| British American Tobacco | J | Prudential Corporation | F |
| British Biotech | M | Railtrack Group | M |
| British Sky Broadcasting Group | M | Reed International | J |
| British Steel | J | Reuters Group | J |
| British Telecommunications | F | Rio Tinto | F |
| Cable & Wireless | J | Rolls-Royce | F |
| Cadbury Schweppes | F | Royal & Sun Alliance Insurance Group | J |
| Carlton Communications | F | Safeway | J |
| Centrica | M | Sainsbury, J. | J |
| CGU | J | Scottish Power | M |
| Diageo | F | Shell Transport & Trading Co | J |
| Dixons Group | M | SmithKline Beecham | J |
| EMI Group | M | Standard Chartered | J |
| Gallaher Group | F | Tarmac | M |
| General Electric Co | F | Tesco | F |
| Glaxo Wellcome | J | Thames Water | J |
| Granada Group | M | Tomkins | M |
| Great Universal Stores | M | Unilever | M |
| Halifax | J | United Biscuits (Holdings) | F |
| Hanson | F | Vodafone Group | J |
| HSBC Holdings | J | Woolwich | J |
| Imperial Chemical Industries | J | | |

The buyer of a July 1000 put has the right to sell 1000 ICI shares at 1000p between now and July. The cost of the contract is:

$$\text{Cost of put} = 1000 \times 2p = £20.$$

If the buyer exercises the put, he delivers 1000 ICI shares to the option writer and receives from him £10,000. If at the time of exercise the share price was 950p, he would have made a profit of £480 (i.e. £10,000 − £9500 − £20), ignoring transaction costs.

The holder of a traded option (unlike the giver of a traditional option - see section 9.3.6) does not have the right to receive any dividends paid on the share during its life, unless the option is exercised and the shares acquired before they are marked ex dividend. However, in the case of a rights or scrip issue on the underlying share, LIFFE adjusts the exercise price and the number of shares in the contract.

The settlement cycle for *result of option* (RO) equity bargains is as follows. The last trading day for equity options is the third Wednesday of the month. The transfer of shares under an RO bargain depends on the London Stock Exchange's CREST rolling settlement system. The transfer takes place five business days ($T + 5$) after the booking details have been sent to CREST. The transfer will therefore be six business days after an exercise notice has been submitted to the LCH ($E + 6$). This means that when a writer has been assigned, the shares purchased by the writer for delivery to the long will be settled on the same day as the shares underlying the RO bargain. If an equity option is exercised when a share is cum dividend or cum rights, the RO bargain must reflect this. For example, if an option holder exercises on a Friday, the writer will not receive notification of assignment until Monday by which time the shares might have been marked ex-dividend. If the writer is naked (in other words does not own the underlying shares) he will have to buy the shares on the Monday, negotiating a special cum dividend bargain to satisfy the RO bargain. Shares can be marked ex-dividend on any Monday, but the LSE has published guidelines for setting ex-dividend dates. For shares to go ex-dividend on a particular Monday, the company must have made an announcement to this effect by the Tuesday of the previous week at the latest, otherwise the ex-dividend date must be deferred until the following Monday. This is to give equity option traders sufficient time to respond to the announcement.

Since January 1988, it has been possible to trade options on foreign shares on LIFFE. Such options are known as *international traded options*. The first international traded options were on French shares: Peugeot SA, STE Nationale Elf-Aquitaine (SNEA) and Saint Gobain. The contract size in these options is for 100 shares; the expiry cycle is March, June, September, December; the premium is quoted in French francs.

## 9.3.2 Interest-rate options

Exchange-traded options on cash gilts used to be traded on the London Stock Exchange, an example being £50,000 nominal of Conversion 9.5 per cent 2005. Such contracts were not a success, largely because option holders did not especially want to end up with the particular bonds deliverable under the contract.

However, a particular type of option on specific gilts is still trading. First introduced in 1987, such options are called *negotiated options* and they use the same trading framework as gilt warrants (see section 9.5.1). They are known as negotiated options because their terms and conditions are negotiated between two parties. Because they are bespoke products, they will not be transferable to third parties. The buyer of a negotiated option will be able to exercise it, abandon it or sell it back to the original writer (if the writer so agrees), but will not be able to sell it to a third party. Negotiated options are therefore similar to over-the-counter options although they are arranged through LIFFE rather than off-the-exchange as with most OTC products. They are also similar to traditional options in the sense that they are non-transferable. However, they differ from traditional options since they are designed to be used by institutional investors rather than private clients. The minimum size of the contract at £100,000 nominal value reflects their intended use by professional investors. Everything else about the option is fully negotiable: the exercise price is negotiable, the life of the option is negotiable (up to a maximum of twelve months), the provision for exercise is negotiable (e.g. the option can be European or American), the premium is negotiable, and the payment (if any) of margin is negotiable. But once the terms of the contract have been established, they cannot be changed.

On LIFFE, there are options on a number of interest rate futures contracts: e.g., the three-month short sterling interest rate, the three-month euro LIBOR interest rate, the long gilt and the German government bond futures contracts. The contract specifications are very similar in each case (see Tables 9.6 to 9.9). On exercise, one futures contract is delivered. The delivery months are March, June, September and December, with serial months added in some cases. These options can be exercised on any business day and delivery takes place on the following business day. In-the-money options are automatically exercised on the last trading day. The tick sizes and tick values per contract are as follows: short sterling (0.01 per cent, £12.50 or 0.005 per cent, £6.25), euro LIBOR (0.005 per cent, €12.50), long gilt (£0.01, £10), and the German government bond futures contract (€0.01, €10).

To illustrate the short-term interest rate futures option contract, we will examine a call option on the December short sterling futures contract with an exercise price of 90.00 (implying a three-month interest rate of 10 per cent). The premium is 0.70 (i.e. 70 ticks). The buyer of the call is buying the right between now and December to buy a December short sterling futures contract at a price of 90.00:

$$\text{Cost of call} \quad = \quad 70 \text{ ticks} \times £12.50 \quad = \quad £875.$$

Suppose that the price of the December contract rises to 91.50. The buyer decides to exercise the call. He buys a December short sterling futures contract at 90.00 which is marked to market at 91.50. The margin account is credited with £1875 (i.e. [(91.50 − 90.00)/0.01] ticks × £12.50 per tick), giving a net profit on the transaction of £1000 (i.e. £1875 − £875).

As another example, we can consider the case of a corporate treasurer who wishes to ensure a maximum borrowing rate in the future if interest rates rise but who also wishes to benefit if interest rates fall. In other words, the corporate treasurer wants to create an *interest rate cap*. He can do this by buying a short sterling put option. For example, suppose that the March short sterling 90.00 put option has a premium of 0.30 (i.e. 30 ticks), giving a total cost of:

$$\text{Cost of put} \quad = \quad 30 \text{ ticks} \times £12.50 \quad = \quad £375.$$

The put locks in a maximum future borrowing rate of:

$$\text{Maximum future borrowing rate} \quad = \quad (100.00 - 90.00) + 0.30 \quad = \quad 10.30\%.$$

We can consider two possible outcomes. First, interest rates rise to 11 per cent at expiry. The put expires making a profit of 0.70 (i.e. the intrinsic value of the put, 1.00 *minus* the cost of put, 0.30). Therefore the effective borrowing rate is:

$$\text{Effective borrowing rate} \quad = \quad 11.00 - 0.70 \quad = \quad 10.30\%.$$

**Table 9.6** LIFFE option on three-month sterling (short sterling) interest rate futures contract

| | | |
|---|---|---|
| **Unit of trading** | One three-month sterling futures contract | |
| **Expiry months** | March, June, September, December, such that six expiry months are available for trading | |
| **Delivery day** | Delivery on the first business day after the exercise day | |
| **Exercise/expiry day** | Exercise by 17:00 on any business day prior to the last expiry day/trading day and until 11:45 on the last trading day | |
| **Last trading day** | 11:00, last trading day of the three-month sterling futures contract | |
| **Price unit** | 0.01 (i.e. 0.01%) | |
| **Minimum price movement** | When the price unit value is: | |
| | $\geq 3$ price units | $< 3$ price units |
| **Tick size** | 0.01 | 0.005 |
| **Value** | £12.50 | £6.25 |
| **Trading hours** | 08:07–16:05 | |

*Contract standard:* assignment of one three-month sterling futures contract for the delivery month at the exercise price.

*Exercise price intervals:* 0.25, (i.e. 0.25%), e.g. 92.50, 92.75, 93.00, 93.25, etc; and 0.125, (i.e. 0.125%) e.g. 94.00, 94.125, 94.50, etc for contracts where the underlying futures contract is the front month quarterly delivery month.

*Introduction of new exercise prices:* thirteen exercise prices will be listed for each new series. Additional exercise prices will be listed when the three-month sterling futures contract settlement price is within 0.12 of the sixth highest or lowest existing exercise price, or as deemed necessary by the Exchange.

*Option price:* the contract price is not paid at the time of purchase. Option positions, as with futures positions, are marked to market daily giving rise to positive or negative variation margin flows. If an option is exercised by the buyer, the buyer is required to pay the original contract price to the Clearing House and the Clearing House will pay the original option price to the seller on the following business day. Such payments will be netted against the variation margin balances of buyer and seller by the Clearing House.

---

Second, interest rates fall to 9 per cent at expiry. The put expires worthless but still cost 0.30. Therefore in this case the effective borrowing rate is:

$$\text{Effective borrowing rate} \;=\; 9.00 + 0.30 \;=\; 9.30\%.$$

To illustrate the long-term interest rate futures option contracts, we will examine a put option on the March long gilt futures contract with an exercise price of 96 (i.e. £96 per £100 nominal). The tick size is £0.01 per £100 nominal for the £100,000 contract, giving a tick value for the contract of £10 (i.e. £100,000 × £0.01/£100). The premium is 2.11 (i.e. 211 ticks). The buyer of the put is buying the right to deliver between now and March one long gilt futures contract at a price of 96:

$$\text{Cost of put} \;=\; 211 \text{ ticks} \times £10.00 \;=\; £2110.00.$$

Suppose that the price of the March contract falls to 93.00 and the buyer exercises. He sells a March long gilt futures contract for 96.00 which is marked to market at 93.00. The margin account is credited

**Table 9.7** LIFFE option on three-month euro LIBOR interest rate futures contract

| | |
|---|---|
| **Unit of trading** | One three-month euro LIBOR futures contract |
| **Expiry months** | March, June, September and December, and two serial months such that eight expiry months are available for trading, with the nearest three expiry months being consecutive calendar months |
| **Delivery day** | Delivery on the first business day after the exercise day |
| **Exercise/expiry day** | Exercise by 17:00 on any business day prior to the expiry day and until 11:45 on the last trading day |
| **Last trading day** | Two business days prior to the third Wednesday of the expiry month at 11:00 for both serial expiry months and for quarterly expiry months |
| **Price unit** | 0.01 (i.e. 0.01%) |
| **Minimum price movement** | |
|     Tick size | 0.005 |
|     Value | €12.50 |
| **Trading hours** | 07:32–16:10 |

*Contract standard:* assignment of one three-month euro LIBOR futures contract for the delivery month at the exercise price. The futures delivery month associated with each option expiry month shall be:

    March in respect of January, February and March expiry months;

    June in respect of April, May and June expiry months;

    September in respect of July, August and September expiry months; and

    December in respect of October, November and December expiry months.

*Exercise price intervals:* 0.25, (i.e. 0.25%) e.g. 94.00, 94.25, 94.50 etc; and 0.125, (i.e. 0.125%) e.g. 94.00, 94.125, 94.25 etc for contracts where the underlying futures contract is the front month quarterly delivery month.

*Introduction of new exercise prices:* nine exercise prices will be listed for each new series. Additional exercise prices will be listed when the three-month euro LIBOR futures contract settlement price is within 0.12 of the fourth highest or lowest existing exercise price, or as deemed necessary by the Exchange.

*Option price:* the contract price is not paid at the time of purchase. Option positions, as with futures positions, are marked to market daily giving rise to positive or negative variation margin flows. If an option is exercised by the buyer, the buyer is required to pay the original contract price to the Clearing House and the Clearing House will pay the original option price to the seller on the following business day. Such payments will be netted against the variation margin balances of buyer and seller by the Clearing House.

**Table 9.8** LIFFE option on long gilt futures contract

| | |
|---|---|
| **Unit of trading** | One long gilt futures contract |
| **Expiry months** | March, June, September and December (nearest two available for trading) plus two additional serial months, such that four expiry months are available for trading, which include the nearest three consecutive calendar months |
| **Delivery day** | Delivery on the first business day after the exercise day |
| **Exercise day** | Exercise by 17:00 on any business day, brought forward to 10:45 on the last trading day |
| **Expiry day** | Expiry at 10:45 on the last trading day |
| **Last trading day** | 10:00, six business days prior to the first day of the expiry month |
| **Quotation** | Multiples of £0.01 |
| **Minimum price movement** | |
|     **Tick size** | £0.01 |
|     **Value** | £10 |
| **Trading hours** | 08:02–16:15 |

*Contract standard:* assignment of one long gilt futures contract for the delivery month at the exercise price. The futures delivery month associated with each option expiry month shall be:

    March in respect of January, February and March expiry months;
    June in respect of April, May and June expiry months;
    September in respect of July, August and September expiry months; and
    December in respect of October, November and December expiry months.

*Exercise price intervals:* £0.50, e.g. £102.00, £102.50 etc.

*Introduction of new exercise prices:* thirteen exercise prices will be listed for each new series. Additional exercise prices will be listed when the long gilt futures contract settlement price is within £0.50 of the sixth highest or lowest existing exercise price, or as deemed necessary by the Exchange.

*Option price:* the contract price is not paid at the time of purchase. Option positions, as with futures positions, are marked to market daily giving rise to positive and negative variation margin flows. If an option is exercised by the buyer, the buyer is required to pay the original contract price to the Clearing House and the Clearing House will pay the original option price to the seller on the following business day. Such payments will be netted against the variation margin balances of buyer and seller by the Clearing House.

**Table 9.9** LIFFE option on German government bond (Bund) futures contract

| | |
|---|---|
| **Unit of trading** | One Bund futures contract |
| **Expiry months** | March, June, September and December (nearest two available for trading) plus two additional serial months, such that four expiry months are available for trading, which include the nearest three consecutive calendar months |
| **Delivery day** | Delivery on the first business day after the exercise day |
| **Exercise day** | Exercise by 17:00 on any business day, brought forward to 10:45 on the last trading day |
| **Expiry day** | Expiry at 10:45 on the last trading day |
| **Last trading day** | 10:00, six business days prior to the first day of the expiry month |
| **Quotation** | Multiples of €0.01 |
| **Minimum price movement** | |
|     Tick size | €0.01 |
|     Value | €10 |
| **Trading hours** | 07:02–16:15 |

*Contract standard:* assignment of one Bund futures contract for the delivery month at the exercise price. The futures delivery month associated with each option expiry month shall be:

    March in respect of January, February and March expiry months;
    June in respect of April, May and June expiry months;
    September in respect of July, August and September expiry months; and
    December in respect of October, November and December expiry months.

*Exercise price intervals:* €0.50, e.g. €90.00, €90.50 etc.

*Introduction of new exercise prices:* nine exercise prices will be listed for each new series. Additional exercise prices will be listed when the Bund futures contract settlement price is within €0.25 of the fourth highest or lowest existing exercise price, or as deemed necessary by the Exchange.

*Option price:* the contract price is not paid at the time of purchase. Option positions, as with futures positions, are marked to market daily giving rise to positive and negative variation margin flows. If an option is exercised by the buyer, the buyer is required to pay the original contract price to the Clearing House and the Clearing House will pay the original option price to the seller on the following business day. Such payments will be netted against the variation margin balances of buyer and seller by the Clearing House.

with £3000 (i.e. [96 − 93] × 100 ticks × £10 per tick), giving a net profit on the transaction of £890 (i.e. £3000 − £2110).

In 1998, LIFFE introduced one-year *mid-curve options*, allowing investors to take a view on interest rates between the short and long ends of the yield curve. The option is on a three-month interest rate futures contract with a delivery month twelve months ahead. For example, the underlying for a December 1998 mid-curve option is a December 1999 future, rather than a December 1998 future as with a conventional option.

### 9.3.3   Currency options

Currency options are no longer traded on LIFFE. They were withdrawn due to insufficient demand. However, a number of currency options are traded on, for instance, the Philadelphia Stock Exchange (PSE) against the US dollar: sterling, Canadian dollar, Japanese yen, Swiss franc, Deutschmark, French franc, euro and Australian dollar. These options are traded on a March, June, September and December cycle plus the nearest two months, giving a total of six options. The expiry date is the Saturday preceding the third Wednesday of the expiry month.

The sterling contract, for example, has a contract size of £31,250, the premium is quoted in US cents per £1 and the exercise price interval is 0.5 cents. The minimum tick size is 0.01 cents per £ or $3.125 per contract. The buyer of a sterling call option will receive sterling and deliver dollars if he exercises the option. So a long sterling call option is equivalent to a long dollar put option. To illustrate, we will consider a September sterling call option with an exercise price of 1.575 (i.e. $1.575 per £1) and a premium of 2.98 cents. The buyer has the right to purchase between now and September £31,250 for $49,218.75 (i.e., £31,250 × $1.575):

$$\text{Cost of call} \quad = \quad £31,250 \times \$0.0298 \quad = \quad \$931.25 \,.$$

PSE options are cleared and settled by the Options Clearing Corporation. The OCC handles the payment of premiums and manages the transfer of currencies when an option is exercised; the settlement date of the option is four business days after the option is exercised.

### 9.3.4   Stock index options

The range of stock index options offered by LIFFE was considerably broadened in May 1999 and now includes options on the FTSE 100, FTSE Eurotop 100, FTSE Eurobloc 100, FTSE Eurotop 300, FTSE Eurotop 300 (ex. UK), MSCI Euro and MSCI Pan Euro cash indices. We shall concentrate our attention on the FTSE 100 index option.

There are three versions of the LIFFE FTSE 100 index option traded: American, European and FLEX (see Tables 9.10 to 9.12). The value of the contract is  £10 × FTSE 100 cash index level (or 1000 units at 1p per unit). Settlement is for cash on the next business day following exercise or expiry. The premium is quoted in pence per unit of the contract (equivalent to the same number of index points). The tick size is 0.5p per unit or £5 per contract. The American option has expiry months of June and December plus the nearest four months. The European option has expiry months of March, June, September and December plus the nearest four months. The FLEX option (which stands for *flexible exchange*) has European-style exercise but the expiry date can be any business day within two years from the date that the contract is made. In addition any exercise price can be chosen, not simply

**Table 9.10** LIFFE FTSE 100 index option (American style exercise) (SEI)

| | |
|---|---|
| **Unit of trading** | Valued at £10 per index point (e.g. value £50,000 at 5000.0) |
| **Expiry months** | June and December plus such additional months so that the four nearest calendar months are always available for trading |
| **Exercise day** | Exercise by 16:45 on any business day, extended to 18:00 for expiring series on the last trading day |
| **Last trading day** | 10:30, third Friday of the expiry month[a] |
| **Settlement day** | Settlement day is the first business day after the day of exercise/last trading day |
| **Quotation** | Index points |
| **Minimum price movement** | |
|     **Tick size** | 0.5 |
|     **Value** | £5.00 |
| **Trading hours** | 08:35–16:30 |

*Contract standard:* cash settlement based on a daily settlement price for non-expiring series or the exchange delivery settlement price for expiring series.

*Daily Settlement Price:* the daily settlement price is the FTSE 100 index value published at 16:30 (London time), rounded to the nearest half index point.

*Exchange Delivery Settlement Price (EDSP):* the EDSP is based on the average values of the FTSE 100 index every 15 seconds inclusively between 10:10 and 10:30 (London time) on the last trading day. Of the 81 measured values, the highest 12 and lowest 12 will be discarded and the remaining 57 will be used to calculate the EDSP. Where necessary, the calculation will be rounded to the nearest half index point.

*Option premium:* is payable in full by the buyer on the business day following a transaction.

*Exercise price and exercise price intervals:* the interval between exercise prices is determined by the time to maturity of a particular expiry month and is either 50 or 100 index points.

*Introduction of new exercise prices:* additional exercise prices will be introduced on the business day after the underlying index level has exceeded the second highest, or fallen below the second lowest, available exercise price.

[a]In the event of the third Friday not being a business day, the last trading day shall normally be the last business day preceding the third Friday.

**Table 9.11** LIFFE FTSE 100 index option (European style exercise) (ESX)

| | |
|---|---|
| **Unit of trading** | Valued at £10 per index point (e.g. value £50,000 at 5000.0) |
| **Expiry months** | March, June, September and December plus such additional months so that the three nearest calendar months are always available for trading |
| **Exercise** | Exercise by 18:00 for expiring series on the last trading day (an option can only be exercised on the last trading day) |
| **Last trading day** | 10:30, third Friday of the expiry month[a] |
| **Settlement day** | Settlement day is the first business day after the last trading day |
| **Quotation** | Index points |
| **Minimum price movement** | |
|     **Tick size** | 0.5 |
|     **Value** | £5.00 |
| **Trading hours** | 08:35–16:30 |

*Contract standard:* cash settlement based on the exchange delivery settlement price.

*Exchange Delivery Settlement Price (EDSP):* the EDSP is based on the average values of the FTSE 100 index every 15 seconds inclusively between 10:10 and 10:30 (London time) on the last trading day. Of the 81 measured values, the highest 12 and lowest 12 will be discarded and the remaining 57 will be used to calculate the EDSP. Where necessary, the calculation will be rounded to the nearest half index point.

*Option premium:* is payable in full by the buyer on the business day following a transaction.

*Exercise price and exercise price intervals:* the interval between exercise prices is determined by the time to maturity of a particular expiry month and is either 50 or 100 index points.

*Introduction of new exercise prices:* additional exercise prices will be introduced on the business day after the underlying index level has exceeded the second highest, or fallen below the second lowest, available exercise price.

---

[a]In the event of the third Friday not being a business day, the last trading day shall normally be the last business day preceding the third Friday.

**Table 9.12** LIFFE FTSE 100 index FLEX option (European style exercise)

| | |
|---|---|
| **Unit of trading** | Valued at £10 per index point (e.g. value £50,000 at 5000.0) |
| **Expiry date** | Any business day within two years from the date the contract is made |
| **Exercise** | Exercise by 18:00 on the expiry date <br> (an option can only be exercised on the last trading day) |
| **Last trading day** | 10:30 on the expiry date |
| **Settlement day** | Settlement day is the first business day after the expiry date |
| **Quotation** | Index points or percentage of an index figure |
| **Minimum price movement** | |
|     **Tick size** | 0.5 index points |
|     **Value** | £5.00 |
| **Trading hours** | 09:15–16:15 |

*Contract standard:* cash settlement based on the exchange delivery settlement price.

*Exchange Delivery Settlement Price (EDSP):* the EDSP is based on the average values of the FTSE 100 index every 15 seconds inclusively between 10:10 and 10:30 (London time) on the last trading day. Of the 81 measured values, the highest 12 and lowest 12 will be discarded and the remaining 57 will be used to calculate the EDSP. Where necessary, the calculation will be rounded to the nearest half index point.

*Option premium:* is payable in full by the buyer on the business day following a transaction.

*Exercise price:* is agreed by the parties to the contract. A FTSE 100 index FLEX option contract may not be made with an exercise price and expiry date which are the same as the exercise price *and* last trading day of an existing series of the standard FTSE 100 index option (European style exercise) contract.

*Novation:* if a standard FTSE 100 index option (European style exercise) is made available for trading with an exercise price and last trading day which are the same as the exercise price and expiry date of an existing FTSE 100 index FLEX option contract, then such contract shall be replaced by novation by a standard FTSE 100 index option (European style exercise) contract.

those established by the exchange. However a FLEX option will not be introduced if a European option with the same terms already exists. Also if the exchange introduces a European option with the same terms as the FLEX option, the FLEX option will be converted into the European option, a process called *novation*.

While FLEX options can only be traded on LIFFE's trading floor, they are not traded by the normal open outcry method. Instead trading involves the following seven steps:

1 Member makes a *request for quotes* (RFQ) to the exchange official responsible for administering FLEX business, specifying the flexible features that are required.

2 Exchange official enters details of RFQ into a PC sited at the FTSE 100 FLEX post (which is located on LIFFE's trading floor) and validates that the terms of the RFQ fall within the FLEX contract specification.

3 Exchange official summons FLEX registered market makers to the FLEX post and informs them of the RFQ.

4 At the end of the *request response time* period (RRT), which is normally set to 10 minutes, the originating member asks 'what's there?'.

5 Market makers (and other brokers, if they wish) respond with bid/offer quotes.

6 If best bid or offer is acceptable, the originating member accepts it. If the best bid or offer is not acceptable the originating member may seek a better price by requesting a *quote extension time* (QET). This enables market makers to reassess their price quotes and gives the broker a chance to refer back to his client.

7 At the end of the QET the originating member re-establishes the best bid/offer and either executes his order or concludes that the price is still unacceptable.

The exchange calculates a daily settlement price for every existing FLEX option series using Autoquote.

We can illustrate the use of a stock index option as follows. If an individual buys one FTSE 100 June 5800 call option at a premium of 30 (i.e. 30p per unit or 30 index points or 60 ticks), he has the right between now and June to buy the index at a level of 5800:

$$\text{Cost of call} \quad = \quad £10 \times 30 \quad (\text{or } 60 \text{ ticks} \times £5) \quad = \quad £300.$$

If the option is exercised, the buyer receives from the writer the difference between the spot price and the exercise price of the index multiplied by £10. So if the index is standing at 5870 when the option is exercised, the buyer receives from the writer £700 (i.e. [5870 − 5800] × £10), a profit of £400.

## 9.3.5 Restricted-life traded options

Restricted-life traded options were introduced in 1988 so that institutional investors could use options during takeover bids (instead of taking a position in the cash market). This class of option will only be introduced, at the discretion of the exchange, once a takeover bid has been announced. The class has a two-four-six-month expiry cycle. At the end of the last expiry month, the exchange will decide whether to renew the restricted life option, to convert it to a standard option (with a three-six-nine-month expiry cycle), or to withdraw the option.

The first example of restricted-life options was on the shares of Rank Hovis McDougall. They were introduced in July 1988 with a September-November-January expiry cycle. Each investor was subject to a position limit of 5000 contracts.

### 9.3.6   Traditional options

The London Stock Exchange also offers what are called *traditional* (or *conventional*) *options*. These differ from the options just discussed because they are not negotiable and they also have their own terminology. For example, the buyer of a traditional option is known as the *giver* (of the premium), while the writer is known as the *taker* (of the premium). The premium is known as the *option money*. The arranger of the deal between giver and taker is called the *option dealer*.

A traditional option has the following characteristics. It can be offered on any traded share or gilt. It has a maximum life of three months. It can be exercised (or *declared*) on any day up to 1pm. It can be either a call option, a put option or a double option (that is, a call and a put combined, although if the call is exercised then the put is automatically cancelled and vice versa). It can be purchased or written only through member-firms of the LSE and cannot be sold to a third party; i.e., it is not tradable. Unlike traded options, the holder of a traditional option is entitled to all dividends, rights and powers in the underlying security, provided that the option is exercised, even if exercise takes place after the security has gone ex dividend or ex rights, etc. For example, the dividend is paid as 'cash in lieu of dividend' since clearly no dividend voucher can be raised against the option.

### 9.3.7   Over-the-counter options

In recent years, there has been a growth in *over-the-counter* (OTC) *options*. These have the same relationship to traded options as forward contracts have with futures. In other words, OTC options are tailor-made contracts in terms of size and expiry dates, and are not traded on regulated exchanges. In addition, there are no troublesome margining requirements to take into account.

But this additional flexibility is bought at the cost of reduced liquidity and increased risk of default. The buyers and sellers of OTC options deal directly with each other and not through a centralized exchange. This means that prospective buyers and sellers have to telephone around in order to discover the best prices. And since there are likely to be fewer counterparties willing to undertake the opposite transaction in tailor-made as opposed to standardized products, this is likely to diminish liquidity and raise spreads. Similarly, the risk of default is increased since there is no clearing house acting as guarantor and no margining or marking to market, as with exchange-traded options. Users of forward contracts face the same problems of diminished liquidity and increased risk of default.

Nevertheless, there have been very few defaults in the OTC options market, which is now larger than the market for exchange-traded options. The most important OTC options contracts are the OTC currency and interest rate options contracts, with contracts having maturities in excess of those available on exchange-traded contracts being the most popular. Banks and other financial institutions (such as pension funds) have found that writing options has proved to provide a useful additional source of income.

In 1984, a group of banks formed LICOM, the *London Interbank Currency Options Market* as a means of standardizing trading practice with OTC currency options. Many banks in other parts of the world such as New York now use LICOM terms for price quotation and settlement. Two types of bank participate in LICOM. First, intermediary banks which deal directly with clients and then wish to lay off this risk using LICOM. Second, there are market-making banks which quote two-way prices that are transmitted on interdealer brokers' screens. While LICOM has established standard operating procedures, it does not operate a clearing house, so that the credit risk with LICOM options still remains with the counterparties to the transaction. Also it is only possible to close an options position using the same bank.

## 9.4 The fair pricing of options contracts

### 9.4.1 Factors influencing the premium

There are five factors that influence the price or premium at which an option contract is traded. We will consider these factors for a European call option, which was the first type of option to be priced theoretically. The premium for a European call option depends on:

$$P^C = F(P^S, X, T, r, \sigma^2),$$
$$\;\;\;\;\;\;\;\;\; (+) \;\; (-) \;\; (+) \;\; (+) \;\; (+)$$

(9.5)

where:

$$
\begin{array}{rcl}
P^C & = & \text{premium on a European call option;} \\
P^S & = & \text{spot price of the underlying security;} \\
X & = & \text{exercise price;} \\
T & = & \text{time to expiry;} \\
r & = & \text{riskless rate of interest;} \\
\sigma^2 & = & \text{variance (or volatility) of the return on the underlying security.}
\end{array}
$$

It is clear that the higher the share price, the more valuable the option, so that $P^C$ in (9.5) will be positively related to $P^S$. Similarly, the lower the exercise price, the more valuable the option, so that $P^C$ will be negatively related to $X$. The greater the time to maturity, the greater the time value of the option, so that $P^C$ will be positively related to $T$.

An increase in the riskless rate of interest increases the value of the option because the money saved by purchasing the option rather than the underlying security can be invested at the riskless rate of interest until the option expires. An increase in $r$ increases the attractiveness of holding the option relative to the underlying security and hence raises the option premium.

An increase in the variance of the share price increases the value of the option. This is because an increase in variance increases the chance that the share price will lie in the tails of the distribution of the share price when the option expires. However, only the distribution of the share price above the exercise price is relevant for option pricing. This is because the maximum loss on the option is the premium paid, whereas the potential gains on the option are unlimited. Therefore an increase in the chance of the share price lying in the tail of the distribution above the exercise price increases the value of the option, while the same increase in the chance of the share price lying in the tail of the distribution below the exercise price does not decrease the value of the option symmetrically. This is because the option is worthless at expiry when the share price is below the exercise price, whether it is just below or far below. Consequently $P^C$ in (9.5) is positively related to $\sigma^2$. This is demonstrated in Figure 9.14, which shows that the proportion of the distribution with the high variance lying below

**Figure 9.14** The effect of increasing variance on the option premium

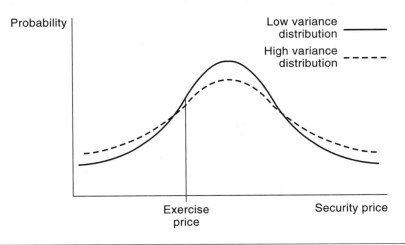

the exercise price is greater than with the distribution with the low variance. Since the option buyer is paying a premium to lose the distribution below the exercise price, the greater the proportion of the distribution lost, the greater the premium. The proposition can also be demonstrated using a simple arithmetic example. Consider Table 9.13, which shows the payoffs to call options on a low-variance share and a high-variance share in three states of the world. The option payoff from the high-variance share is at least as great in all states of the world as, and greater in at least one state of the world than, the option payoff from the low-variance share. This is a definition of *stochastic dominance*, and, if one option payoff pattern stochastically dominates that of another, the option will have a higher value.

If a share pays dividends during the period, this will also affect the price of an option on the share, even though the holder of an option is not entitled to receive any dividends unless they also own the underlying share. When shares are declared ex-dividend, this will have the effect of lowering the share price. This, in turn, will have the effect of reducing the price of a call option on the share and increasing the price of a put option. Changes to a company's capital structure can also affect the share price. Examples are: capitalization issues, rights issues, sub-divisions, consolidations, demergers, takeovers, privatization instalments and warrant issues. In cases such as these, the exchange will alter the exercise price or the number of shares underlying an option, so as to leave both option holders and writers unaffected by the changes made.

## 9.4.2   Boundary conditions for options

Before deriving the exact formula for pricing options, it will be useful to derive some boundary conditions for the option premium. This time we will consider the boundary conditions for an American call option.

**Table 9.13** Payoffs on low and high variance shares

| State of the world | Probability | Low variance share | | High variance share | |
|---|---|---|---|---|---|
| | | Share price at expiry | Option payoff if $X=45p$ | Share price at expiry | Option payoff if $X=45p$ |
| Slump | 0.2 | 40p | 0p | 20p | 0p |
| Normal | 0.6 | 50p | 5p | 50p | 5p |
| Boom | 0.2 | 60p | 15p | 80p | 35p |

The option must have a positive value throughout its life because there is always some chance, however small, that it will expire in the money. Therefore it must be the case that:

$$P^C \geq 0. \tag{9.6}$$

An American call option must have a value at least as high as its intrinsic value. If this were not the case, then someone could buy the option, exercise it immediately and earn a riskless arbitrage profit. Therefore it must be the case that:

$$P^C \geq P^S - X. \tag{9.7}$$

A call option cannot be worth more than the underlying security; i.e., no one is going to pay more for the option on a security than the security itself. Therefore:

$$P^C \leq P^S. \tag{9.8}$$

A call option with a low exercise price will be worth more than a call option with a high exercise price:

$$P^C(X_1) > P^C(X_2) \quad \text{if } X_2 > X_1. \tag{9.9}$$

This follows from (9.7).

A call option with a greater time to expiry will be worth more than a call option with a shorter time to expiry:

$$P^C(T_1) > P^C(T_2) \quad \text{if } T_1 > T_2. \tag{9.10}$$

This again follows from (9.7), where the right-hand side of (9.7) is the (intrinsic) value of the shorter ($T_2$) option at expiry and the left-hand side is the value of the longer ($T_1$) option.

The value of a call option will always be greater than the value of the security price *minus* the discounted value of the exercise price:

$$P^C \geq P^S - Xe^{-rT}. \tag{9.11}$$

This is a stronger condition than (9.7) and is proved by stochastic dominance. Consider two portfolios A and B. Portfolio A consists of a share with current price $P^S$. Portfolio B consists of a European call option on the share with current premium $P^C$ and exercise price $X$ *plus* a riskless pure discount

**Table 9.14** The current and terminal values of two portfolios

| Portfolio | Current value | Value at expiry | |
| :---: | :---: | :---: | :---: |
| | | $P_T^S < X$ | $P_T^S \geq X$ |
| A | $V^A = P^S$ | $V_T^A = P_T^S$ | $V_T^A = P_T^S$ |
| B | $V^B = P^C + X e^{-rT}$ | $V_T^B = 0 + X$ | $V_T^B = (P_T^S - X) + X$ |
| | | $V_T^B > V_T^A$ | $V_T^B = V_T^A$ |

bond paying $X$ on the expiry date $(T)$ of the option. The current price of the bond is $X e^{-rT}$. The payoffs to the two portfolios at the expiry date of the option depend on whether the share price at expiry $(P_T^S)$ is less than the exercise price $(X)$, in which case the option expires worthless, or exceeds the exercise price, in which case the option is worth the intrinsic value $P_T^S - X$. The current value of the two portfolios are $V^A$ and $V^B$ and the terminal values are $V_T^A$ and $V_T^B$, as shown in Table 9.14. Because portfolio B stochastically dominates portfolio A at expiry, its current value must exceed that of A. Hence:

$$P^C + X e^{-rT} \geq P^S,$$

or:

$$P^C \geq P^S - X e^{-rT}. \tag{9.12}$$

Combining (9.6) and (9.12) implies that:

$$P^C \geq \max(0, P^S - X e^{-rT}), \tag{9.13}$$

i.e. that the value of a European call option cannot be less than the current security price *minus* the discounted value of the exercise price. In addition, an American call option must be worth more than a European call option because it can be exercised at any time and not just at maturity. Therefore:

$$P^{CA} \geq P^{CE} \geq \max(0, P^S - X e^{-rT}), \tag{9.14}$$

where $P^{CA}$ is the price of an American call and $P^{CE}$ is the price of a European call.

There are two implications of (9.14). One is that an American call option (on a non-dividend-paying share) will never be exercised before maturity. This is because, for $r, T > 0$:

$$P^C \geq P^S - X e^{-rT} > P^S - X. \tag{9.15}$$

Since $P^S - X$ is all that would be received if the option were exercised, (9.15) suggests that it would be better to sell the option than to exercise it.

The second implication of (9.14) concerns the risk-free rate. If the risk-free rate increases, the discounted value of the exercise price falls and this increases the value of the option.

Figure 9.15 shows the boundary conditions for a European call option premium. The option premium will lie in the area $OABC$.

While it is never optimal to exercise early an American call option on an non-dividend paying share, this is not necessarily the case with an American put option on a non-dividend paying share.

**Figure 9.15** Boundary conditions for a call option

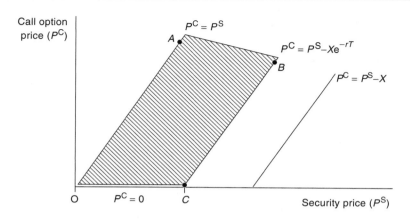

Indeed, if the put is sufficiently in-the-money, it actually becomes optimal to exercise early. It is easy to demonstrate this. Suppose that an American put has an exercise price of £2.00 and the underlying share price is very close to zero. The option holder could wait for the share price to get even lower, so that the option is even deeper in-the-money. But the share price can never become negative, and so the intrinsic value of the option can never exceed £2.00. In addition, if the option is exercised, the proceeds of (nearly) £2.00 can be invested and thereby earn additional interest. Also the share price could recover and this would lower the value of the option. Under these circumstances, it becomes optimal to exercise the option immediately.

We can demonstrate this formally as follows. Consider two portfolios A and B. Portfolio A consists of a riskless pure discount bond paying X on the expiry date ($T$) of the option. Portfolio B consists of a share with current price $P^S$ and an American put option on the share with current premium $P^{PA}$ and exercise price X. The current price of the bond is $Xe^{-rT}$. If the option is exercised at time $\tau < T$, portfolio A is worth $Xe^{-r\tau}$, while portfolio B is worth X. Hence portfolio B is worth more than portfolio A at any time before expiry. On the expiry date, portfolio A is worth X, while portfolio B is worth $\max(X, P^S_T)$. Hence portfolio B is worth at least as much as portfolio A at expiry if not more. Portfolio B therefore stochastically dominates portfolio A. This implies the following boundary condition for the price of an American put:

$$P^{PA} \geq X - P^S, \tag{9.16}$$

since it is always possible to exercise the option immediately. However for sufficiently low $P^S$, it actually becomes optimal to exercise the option, at which point:

$$P^{PA} = X - P^S. \tag{9.17}$$

This implies that at this low price (shown as A in Figure 9.16), the value of the option is equal to its intrinsic value. Its time value falls to zero: no one will be prepared to pay for the chance that the option moves even deeper into the money, since if interest rates are positive, investors are foregoing interest earned by not exercising early. It becomes optimal to exercise if point A is reached in Figure 9.16.

Another implication of this analysis is that if an American put is sometimes worth its intrinsic value, and an American put is always worth more than a European put, it must follow that a European

**Figure 9.16** The American put option

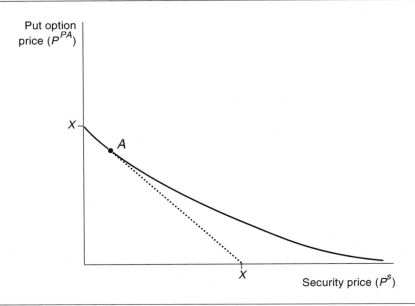

**Figure 9.17** The European put option

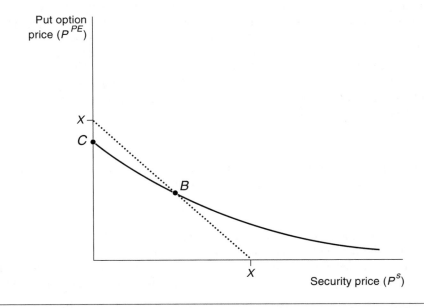

put can sometimes be worth *less* than its intrinsic value. This is demonstrated in Figure 9.17. The point at which the price of the European put equals its intrinsic value is denoted B in Figure 9.17. This point must occur at a higher security price than point A in Figure 9.17. This is because at point B in Figure 9.17 the following holds:

$$P^{PA} \geq X - P^S = P^{PE} > Xe^{-rT} - P^S.$$

The first inequality shows that an American put is worth at least its intrinsic value. The last inequality shows that a European put is worth more than the discounted value of the exercise price *minus* the security price. This follows because the European put cannot be exercised before maturity and is proved using an argument that is exactly analogous to the one used to derive the inequality in (9.12) above in the case of European calls. Given the first inequality and the assumed equality $P^{PE} = X - P^S$, it follows that the American put price is higher than $P^{PE}$ at point B and so must touch the 45° intrinsic value line to the left of B (i.e. A in Figure 9.16 is to the left of B in Figure 9.17). It also follows that the European put price must be everywhere below the 45° line in the case where the share price is below the point corresponding to B in Figure 9.17. In particular at point C where $P^S = 0$, then the European put price is $P^{PE} = Xe^{-rT} < X$.

### 9.4.3   The binomial model of the fair European call option price

The simplest model for determining the price of an option is the *binomial model* (see Cox, Ross and Rubinstein (1979)), and the simplest type of option to price is the European call option on a security that makes no cash payments (e.g. a non-dividend-paying share).

The binomial model assumes a discrete-time one-period world in which the security price follows a stationary binomial stochastic process so that at the end of the period it can be higher or lower than at the start of the period, as shown in Figure 9.18. We assume the following notation:

$$
\begin{array}{rcl}
P^S & = & \text{current security price (e.g. 50p);} \\
q & = & \text{probability that security price will rise (e.g. 0.5);} \\
1 - q & = & \text{probability that security price will fall (e.g. 0.5);} \\
r & = & \text{risk-free rate of interest (e.g. } r = 0.1\text{);} \\
u & = & \text{multiplicative upward movement in security price, } u > 1 + r \text{ (e.g. 1.32);} \\
d & = & \text{multiplicative downward movement in security price, } d < 1 \text{ (e.g. 0.68).}
\end{array}
$$

With these assumptions, the security price will increase to $uP^S$ (i.e. 66p) with probability $q = 0.5$, or decrease to $dP^S$ (i.e. 34p) with probability $1 - q = 0.5$. It is necessary that $u > (1 + r) > d$, otherwise there would be opportunities for riskless arbitrage.

Now we consider a call option on the security with an exercise price of 45p. It is clear from Figure 9.19 that the expiry value of the option has to be either $P_u^C = \max(0, uP^S - X) = 21p$ or $P_d^C = \max(0, dP^S - X) = 0$ and there is a 50 per cent probability that it could be either. What is the value of the call at the beginning of the period?

To answer this question, we need to examine the return on a *riskless hedge portfolio* constructed from a long position in the underlying security and a short position in $h$ units of the call option (where $h$ is the *hedge ratio*). The value of the riskless hedge is given by:

$$V^H = P^S - hP^C. \tag{9.18}$$

**Figure 9.18** A one-period binomial stochastic process for a security price

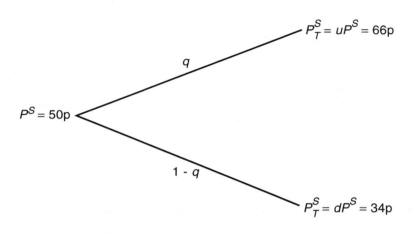

**Figure 9.19** Expiry value of a one-period call option

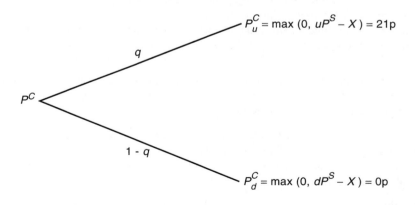

**Figure 9.20** Expiry value of riskless hedge portfolio

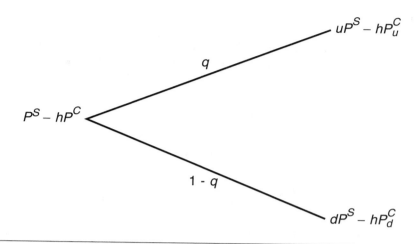

Figure 9.20 shows the expiry value of the riskless hedge portfolio. We can use the fact that a riskless hedge portfolio must have the same terminal value in all states:

$$uP^S - hP_u^C = dP^S - hP_d^C, \tag{9.19}$$

in order to determine the appropriate hedge ratio, $h$, i.e., the number of call options to be written against the underlying security:

$$
\begin{aligned}
h &= \frac{P^S(u-d)}{P_u^C - P_d^C} \\
&= \frac{50(1.32 - 0.68)}{21 - 0} \\
&= 1.52.
\end{aligned}
\tag{9.20}
$$

A riskless hedge portfolio is constructed from one security and 1.52 short call options. Substituting $h = 1.52$ into (9.19), implies that the riskless hedge portfolio has a terminal value of 34p in all states of the world, so that any increase in the value of the share component is always exactly offset by the fall in the value of the option component.

Because the hedge portfolio is riskless, it must be the case that the current value of the portfolio can be found by discounting the known terminal value by the riskless rate of interest:

$$P^S - hP^C = \frac{uP^S - hP_u^C}{1+r}. \tag{9.21}$$

Substituting (9.20) into (9.21) and solving for $P^C$, we get the fair price of the call option ($P_0^C$):

$$P_0^C = \frac{fP_u^C + (1-f)P_d^C}{1+r}, \tag{9.22}$$

where:

$$f = \frac{1 + r - d}{u - d}$$

and is the conditional probability that the option will expire worth $P_u^C$ (it is sometimes also called the *hedging probability*). Note that $f$ does not depend on $q$, the probability that the security price will rise during the period. From (9.22), it is clear that the fair option premium is simply the discounted value of the expected expiry value of the option.

Using the numerical values above, we get:

$$
\begin{aligned}
P_0^C &= \frac{\left(\dfrac{1.1 - 0.68}{1.32 - 0.68}\right) 21 + \left[1 - \left(\dfrac{1.1 - 0.68}{1.32 - 0.68}\right)\right] 0}{1.1} \\
&= \frac{(0.65625)21 + (0.34375)0}{1.1} = 12.53\text{p}.
\end{aligned}
$$

From (9.21) and (9.22), it is clear that the fair option premium depends on all the factors given in (9.5): the current security price ($P^S$), the exercise price ($X$), the time to expiry ($T = 1$ in the one-period model since the period is one year), and the variance of the security price is determined by $u$, $d$ and $q$. The variance of the security price implied by $u$, $d$ and $q$ can be found as follows. The expected terminal value of the security price is:

$$
\begin{aligned}
E(P_T^S) &= quP^S + (1 - q)dP^S \\
&= 0.5(1.32)(50) + 0.5(0.68)(50) = 50\text{p},
\end{aligned}
$$

and the variance is (assuming zero covariance since $u$ and $d$ are independent of each other):

$$
\begin{aligned}
\text{Var}(P_T^S) &= q[uP^S - E(P_T^S)]^2 + (1 - q)[dP^S - E(P_T^S)]^2 \\
&= 0.5(66 - 50)^2 + 0.5(34 - 50)^2 = 256.
\end{aligned}
$$

If the annual standard deviation of the return on a security is given by $\sigma$, then the values of $u$ and $d$ consistent with this are given respectively by:

$$u = e^\sigma \quad \text{and} \quad d = \frac{1}{u} = e^{-\sigma}.$$

If the time horizon differs from one year and extends to, say, $T$ years, then we have:

$$u = e^{\sigma\sqrt{T}} \quad \text{and} \quad d = e^{-\sigma\sqrt{T}}.$$

### 9.4.4   The Black-Scholes model of the fair European call option price

The binomial model assumes a discrete-time stationary binomial stochastic process for security price movements. In the limit, as the discrete-time period becomes infinitely small, this stochastic process becomes a *diffusion process* (also called a *continuous-time random walk*, an *Ito process*, or *geometric Brownian motion*). This was the process assumed by Black and Scholes (1973) in their derivation of the option pricing formula. As with the binomial model, Black and Scholes begin by constructing a riskless hedge portfolio, long in the underlying security and short in call options. This portfolio generates the riskless rate of return, but the internal dynamics of the portfolio are driven by the diffusion process for the security price. The structure of the hedge portfolio can be put into a form that is identical to the heat equation in physics. Once this was recognized, the solution to the equation was easily derived.

The Black-Scholes formula for the fair price of the call option is:

$$P_0^C = P^S N(d_1) - X e^{-rT} N(d_2), \qquad (9.23)$$

where:

$P_0^C$ = fair price of call option;
$P^S$ = current price of security;
$X$ = exercise price;
$r$ = riskless rate of interest;
$T$ = time to expiry in fractions of a year (e.g. one quarter, $T = 0.25$; one year, $T = 1.00$);
$\sigma$ = instantaneous standard deviation (or volatility);
$d_1$ = $\frac{\ln(P^S/X) + rT}{\sigma\sqrt{T}} + \frac{1}{2}\sigma\sqrt{T} = \frac{\ln(P^S/Xe^{-rT})}{\sigma\sqrt{T}} + \frac{1}{2}\sigma\sqrt{T}$;
$d_2$ = $d_1 - \sigma\sqrt{T}$;
$N(d_i)$ = cumulative probability distribution for standard normal variate from $-\infty$ to $d_i$.

Again, the formula in (9.23) depends on all the factors given in (9.5): $P^S$, $X$, $T$, $r$ and $\sigma^2$, the instantaneous variance of the security price. All these factors are readily observable (i.e. $P^S$, $X$, $T$ and $r$) except for the variance, which has to be estimated. There are two main ways of estimating $\sigma^2$.

The first method uses historical data on the security's price movements and calculates the variance based on log price relatives. We will illustrate this using Table 9.15 which lists the average weekly price for a share for the previous eleven weeks, together with the corresponding price relatives and log price relatives.

**Table 9.15** Weekly share prices

| Week | Share price $P_t^S$ (pence) | Price relative $P_t^S/P_{t-1}^S$ | Log price relative $\ln(P_t^S/P_{t-1}^S)$ |
|------|------|------|------|
| 1 | 48.39 | — | — |
| 2 | 50.78 | 1.0494 | 0.048209 |
| 3 | 53.09 | 1.0455 | 0.044486 |
| 4 | 47.48 | 0.8943 | −0.111680 |
| 5 | 50.00 | 1.0531 | 0.051714 |
| 6 | 52.60 | 1.0520 | 0.050693 |
| 7 | 48.62 | 0.9243 | −0.078682 |
| 8 | 46.57 | 0.9578 | −0.043079 |
| 9 | 49.21 | 1.0567 | 0.055140 |
| 10 | 50.54 | 1.0270 | 0.026668 |
| 11 | 52.61 | 1.0410 | 0.040129 |
| Arithmetic mean | 50.00 | | 0.008360 |
| Variance | 4.923 | | 0.003858 |
| Standard deviation | 2.219 | | 0.062119 |

The arithmetic mean is calculated as:

$$\text{Arithmetic mean} \;=\; \bar{X} \;=\; \frac{\sum\limits_{t=1}^{N} X_t}{N}, \tag{9.24}$$

where:

$$
\begin{aligned}
X_t &= P_t^S \text{ or } \ln(P_t^S/P_{t-1}^S); \\
N &= \text{number of observations}; N = 11 \text{ for } P_t^S; N = 10 \text{ for } \ln(P_t^S/P_{t-1}^S).
\end{aligned}
$$

The variance is calculated as:

$$\text{Variance} \;=\; \sigma^2 \;=\; \frac{\sum\limits_{t=1}^{N} (X_t - \bar{X})^2}{N-1}, \tag{9.25}$$

and the standard deviation is the square root of the variance.

The variances and standard deviations given in the table are weekly variances and standard deviations. But we need annual variances and standard deviations for the Black-Scholes formula. The annual variance is given by:

$$\text{Annual variance} \;=\; \text{Weekly variance} \times 52, \tag{9.26}$$

implying, for the share price:

$$\text{Annual variance} \;=\; 4.923 \times 52 \;=\; 256,$$

and, for the log price relative:

$$\text{Annual variance} \;=\; 0.003858 \times 52 \;=\; 0.200658.$$

The annual standard deviation is given by:

$$\text{Annual standard deviation} \;=\; \text{Weekly standard deviation} \times \sqrt{52}, \tag{9.27}$$

implying, for the share price:

$$\text{Annual standard deviation} \;=\; 2.219 \times \sqrt{52} \;=\; 16,$$

and, for the log price relative:

$$\text{Annual standard deviation} \;=\; 0.062119 \times \sqrt{52} \;=\; 0.447948.$$

The appropriate variance estimator for the Black-Scholes model is the annual variance of the log price relatives. However, what is usually quoted in the options pricing literature is *volatility*, which is the annual standard deviation of the log price relatives expressed as a percentage. For the case in point:

$$\text{Volatility} \;=\; 44.79\%,$$

meaning that $\sigma = 0.4479$. As we have seen, this is equivalent to an annual standard deviation for the share price of 16.

The second method of estimating $\sigma^2$ uses (9.23) in reverse. It takes the current market option premium for call options with a particular exercise price and term to expiry, together with the current price of the security and riskless rate of interest, and solves for the standard deviation. In other words, this method calculates the volatility implied by the market option premium itself. The problem is that there can be different *implied volatilities* even for the same expiry date, so that the different volatility estimates have to be combined into a single composite volatility estimate. Nevertheless, this method provides a theoretically superior estimate of volatility because it is essentially forward-looking. In other words, it provides an estimate of the volatility around the forward price of the underlying security for the expiry date of the option. The first method uses backward-looking historical data.

To illustrate, the Black-Scholes model, we will use the same data as for the binomial model, i.e. $P^S = 50$p, $X = 45$p, $r = 0.1$, $T = 1$, $\sigma = 0.4479$ (implying an annual variance for the share price of 256, the same as for the binomial model). From (9.23), we have:

$$d_1 = \frac{\ln(50/45) + 0.1(1)}{0.4479 \cdot \sqrt{1}} + \frac{1}{2} \cdot 0.4479 \cdot \sqrt{1} = 0.68245,$$

and:

$$d_2 = 0.68245 - 0.4479 \cdot \sqrt{1} = 0.23455.$$

Using cumulative normal distribution tables (see Appendix C), we get:

$$N(d_1) = N(0.68245) = 0.7525,$$

and:

$$N(d_2) = N(0.23455) = 0.5927.$$

(Note that: (a) linear interpolation is used if $d_1$ or $d_2$ lies between the relevant numbers in the table, e.g. $d_1$ lies about a quarter of the way between 0.68 and 0.69 in the tables; (b) if normal distribution tables which present only the upper half of the standard normal distribution are used, then 0.5 has to be added to the result; e.g., with $d_1$, the normal distribution table gives a value of 0.2525 and 0.5 has to be added to this to give $d_1 = 0.7525$.)

Substituting these values into (9.23) gives:

$$P_0^C = 50(0.7525) - 45e^{-0.1}(0.5927) = 13.49\text{p},$$

of which 5p is intrinsic value and 8.49p is time value. Comparing with the binomial model, we see that the Black-Scholes model predicts a slightly higher price for the option. There could be a number of reasons for the discrepancy. First, the variance estimate is approximate and it may not be the case that the true annual variance is 52 times the weekly average variance. Second, the Black-Scholes model is a continuous-time model requiring an estimate of the instantaneous variance; however, what we have estimated is an annual variance.

There is a well-known polynomial approximation to the cumulative normal distribution function $N(x)$. This is given as follows:

$$N(x) = 1 - H(x) \qquad \text{for } x \geq 0,$$
$$N(x) = H(x) \qquad \text{for } x < 0,$$

where:

$$
\begin{aligned}
H(x) &= N'(x)(0.436184k - 0.120168k^2 + 0.937298k^3); \\
N'(x) &= \frac{1}{\sqrt{2\pi}} \cdot e^{-x^2/2}; \\
k &= \frac{1}{1 + 0.33267\,|x|}; \\
\pi &= 3.1415927.
\end{aligned}
$$

For example, if $x = 0.68245$, then:

$$
\begin{aligned}
k &= 0.8149755, \\
N'(x) &= 0.3160649, \\
H(x) &= 0.2474851,
\end{aligned}
$$

and:

$$
N(x) = 1 - 0.2474851 = 0.7525148.
$$

## 9.4.5  Properties of the Black-Scholes model: the Greeks

We can now examine some of the properties of the Black-Scholes model. We are particularly interested in the sensitivity of the option premium to changes in the determining factors: $P^S$, $T$, $\sigma^2$ and $r$.

**Option delta.**   The first sensitivity factor is called *delta* ($\delta$). It measures the change in the option premium as the security price moves one point. From the Black-Scholes formula, the option delta is given by:

$$
\text{Delta} = \frac{\partial P^C}{\partial P^S} = N(d_1). \tag{9.28}
$$

From (9.28), it is clear that delta always lies between zero and unity. In the above example, delta = 0.7525.

From (9.28), delta measures the slope of the option price profile with respect to the security price (at the current value of the security price). This is shown in Figure 9.21(a). As the share price rises, delta approaches unity, while as the share price falls delta approaches zero. Delta is also equal to the slope of the short-run profit and loss profile as shown in Figure 9.1.

Delta is also related to the riskless hedge ratio. The value of the hedge portfolio is given by (9.18) and its rate of change over time is given by:

$$
\frac{dV^H}{dt} = \frac{dP^S}{dt} - h \cdot \frac{dP^C}{dt}. \tag{9.29}
$$

If the hedge portfolio is riskless, the value of (9.29) will be (approximately) zero, implying that (using (9.28)):

$$
h = \frac{dP^S}{dP^C} = \frac{1}{N(d_1)} = \frac{1}{\text{delta}}. \tag{9.30}
$$

**Figure 9.21** Sensitivity factors for a call option: (a) Delta $= \partial P^C / \partial P^S$, (b) Gamma $= \partial^2 P^C / \left( \partial P^S \right)^2$, (c) Theta $= \partial P^C / \partial T$, (d) Kappa $= \partial P^C / \partial \sigma^2$

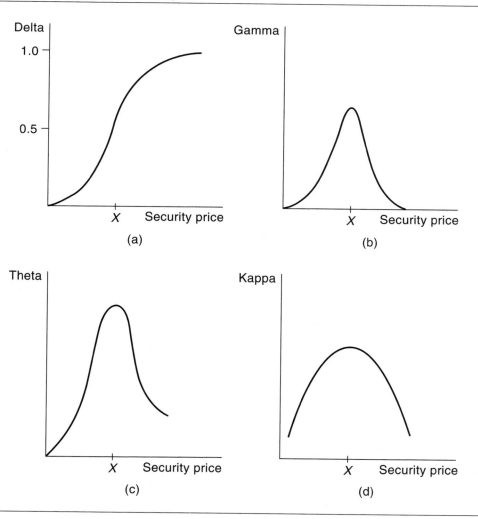

So delta is the inverse of the hedge ratio. To illustrate, if delta = 0.7525, then $h = 1.33$. Given that a standard options contract in the UK is for 1000 shares, this implies that to hedge 1000 shares it is necessary to write 1.33 call options (or, to hedge 3000 shares 4 calls have to be written). Again note the discrepancy with the binomial model where, using the same data, the hedge ratio was estimated to be 1.52.

For long calls and short puts, the delta is positive, while for short calls and long puts, the delta is negative. One of the key characteristics of deltas is that they are linearly additive. This means the delta for a portfolio of options is easy to calculate. A portfolio consisting of ten long 125p calls with delta of 0.8, five short 135p calls with delta of –0.55, fifteen short 125p puts with delta of 0.15 and ten long 145p puts with delta of –0.75 will have a portfolio delta of:

$$\text{Portfolio delta} \quad = \quad 10(0.8) + 5(-0.55) + 15(0.15) + 10(-0.75) \quad = \quad 0.$$

Therefore the portfolio is totally riskless for small changes in the underlying security price. Delta can therefore be used as a measure of both option risk and option portfolio risk.

Having interpreted $N(d_1)$, it is interesting to give an interpretation to $N(d_2)$. While not immediately obvious, $N(d_2)$ can be interpreted as the probability that the option will finish in the money. This can be demonstrated as follows. The terminal value of a call option is equal to the expected value of the payoff at expiry:

$$
\begin{aligned}
P_T^C &= E\{\max[(P_T^S - X), 0]\} \\
&= \Phi E\left[(P_T^S - X) \mid P_T^S > X\right] + (1 - \Phi)0 \\
&= \Phi E\left[(P_T^S - X) \mid P_T^S > X\right],
\end{aligned}
\tag{9.31}
$$

where $\Phi$ is the conditional probability that the option expires in the money, $E\left[(P_T^S - X) \mid P_T^S > X\right]$ is the expected payoff conditional on the option expiring in the money, and $(1 - \Phi)$ is the conditional probability that the option expires worthless. The Black-Scholes formula (9.23) evaluated at the expiry date can be rearranged in a way that is consistent with (9.31):

$$
P_T^C = N(d_2)\left[P^S e^{rT}\frac{N(d_1)}{N(d_2)} - X\right].
\tag{9.32}
$$

Comparing (9.31) and (9.32), we see that:

$$
\Phi = N(d_2)
\tag{9.33}
$$

is the probability that the call ends up in the money, and that:

$$
E\left[(P_T^S - X) \mid P_T^S > X\right] = P^S e^{rT}\frac{N(d_1)}{N(d_2)} - X
\tag{9.34}
$$

is the expected in-the-money payout. In the above example, $N(d_2) = 0.59$, implying that there is a 59 per cent probability that the option will expire in the money.

**Option gamma.**   From Figure 9.21(a), it is clear that, as the security price changes, so does the option delta. This is because the short-run price profile for the option is not linear. *Gamma* ($\gamma$), the second sensitivity factor, measures the change in delta as the share price moves one point. In other words, it is the second derivative of the option premium with respect to the share price:

$$\text{Gamma} = \frac{\partial \text{delta}}{\partial P^S} = \frac{\partial^2 P^C}{(\partial P^S)^2}. \tag{9.35}$$

So, for example, if the share price moves from 50p to 51p and this leads the delta on the 45p call option to move from 0.75 to 0.77, this means that the gamma of the 45p call option is 0.02. The average delta over the range of a price change is delta $\pm \frac{1}{2}$ gamma, depending on whether the security price rose or fell. The gamma function is symmetric about the current share price: see Figure 9.21(b). For a European call or put on a non-dividend paying share:

$$\text{Gamma} = \frac{N'(d_1)}{P^S \sigma \sqrt{T}}, \tag{9.36}$$

where:

$$N'(d_1) = \frac{1}{\sqrt{2\pi}} \cdot e^{-(d_1)^2/2}. \tag{9.37}$$

So the gamma of a call is equal to the gamma of a put.

A long options position has positive gamma, while a short options position has negative gamma. Options with high gamma require more frequent hedge adjustments than options with low gamma in order to maintain an overall delta-neutral (i.e. delta equal to zero) position for a combination of an option and the underlying security. Gamma is high if the option is close to expiry, close to the exercise price or has low volatility.

**Option theta.** The third sensitivity factor is *theta* ($\theta$), which measures the change in the option premium as the time to expiry increases:

$$\text{Theta} = \frac{\partial P^C}{\partial T}. \tag{9.38}$$

For a European call option on a non-dividend paying share:

$$\text{Theta} = -\frac{P^S}{2} \cdot \frac{N'(d_1)\sigma}{\sqrt{T}} - rXe^{-rT}N(d_2). \tag{9.39}$$

For a European put option on a non-dividend paying share:

$$\text{Theta} = -\frac{P^S}{2} \cdot \frac{N'(d_1)\sigma}{\sqrt{T}} + rXe^{-rT}N(-d_2). \tag{9.40}$$

Theta is an increasing function of the security price (see Figure 9.21(c)). Time is always against the holder of an option, so theta is always negative for a long position in an option. An option is an asset whose time-value decays over time according to the square root of time (see Figure 9.22). For example: suppose that an option priced at 5p with 10 days to expiry has a theta of 0.5. This means that, *ceteris paribus*, the following day the option price will fall to 4.5p. Similarly if an option with 4 months to expiry costs 80p, the same option with 2 months to expiry would cost 20p and, with 1 month to expiry, it would cost 5p.

**Figure 9.22** The decay of time value

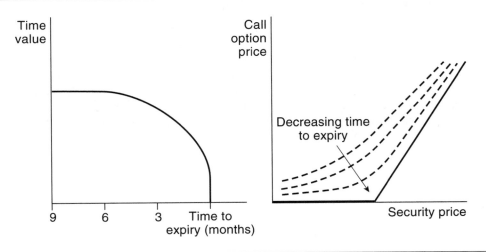

**Option kappa.** The fourth sensitivity factor is *kappa* ($\kappa$) (also known as lambda, sigma, epsilon, eta or vega), which measures the change in the option premium following a 1 per cent change in security price volatility or variance:

$$\text{Kappa} = \frac{\partial P^C}{\partial \sigma^2}. \tag{9.41}$$

For a European call or put option on a non-dividend paying share:

$$\text{Kappa} = P^S N'(d_1)\sqrt{T}. \tag{9.42}$$

Kappa decreases with the square root of time. It is high if the option has a long time to expiry or is close to the money or has a high absolute implied volatility. The kappa function is symmetric about the current security price, as illustrated in Figure 9.21(d).

**Option rho.** The fifth sensitivity factor is *rho* ($\rho$), which measures the change in the option premium following a change in the interest rate:

$$\text{Rho} = \frac{\partial P^C}{\partial r}. \tag{9.43}$$

For a European call option on a non-dividend paying share:

$$\text{Rho} = XTe^{-rT}N(d_2). \tag{9.44}$$

For a European put option on the share:

$$\text{Rho} = -XTe^{-rT}N(-d_2). \tag{9.45}$$

## 9.4.6   Pricing a European put option

Once we know the value of a European call option, we can use it to calculate the value of a European put option written on the same underlying security with the same exercise price and expiration date. We can do this using the *put-call parity* theorem of Stoll (1969).

Stoll shows that it is possible to create a riskless hedge portfolio by combining long positions in the security and the put option with a short position in the call option (with the same exercise price $X$ and expiry period $T$). At expiration, if the price of the security equals or exceeds the exercise price $(P_T^S \geq X)$, then the value of the portfolio is:

|   | Value of security | $P_T^S$ |
|---|---|---|
| + | Value of put option | 0 |
| − | Value of call option | $-(P_T^S - X)$ |
| = | | $X$, |

while if the price of the share is less than the exercise price $(P_T^S < X)$, then the value of the portfolio is:

|   | Value of security | $P_T^S$ |
|---|---|---|
| + | Value of put option | $X - P_T^S$ |
| − | Value of call option | 0 |
| = | | $X$. |

So in either case, the value of the portfolio at expiration is $X$. Such a portfolio is completely riskless and will therefore earn a riskless return $r$. Hence the value of the portfolio at the beginning of the period if it earns a riskless return of $r$ is $Xe^{-rT}$.

Therefore the following relationship (known as the put-call parity relationship) must hold for European options at the beginning of the period:

$$P^S + P^P - P^C = Xe^{-rT},$$

or, rearranging:

$$P^P = P^C - P^S + Xe^{-rT}, \qquad (9.46)$$

where $P^P$ is the premium on the put option. Therefore, once we know $P^C$ (using the Black-Scholes model) we can easily determine $P^P$. It is also easy to see that the delta of a put option (i.e. $\partial P^P / \partial P^S$) is equal to $N(d_1) - 1$.

**Example 9.1 (European put option pricing)** *Using the same data as for the call option, namely:*

$$P^S = 50p, \ X = 45p, \ T = 1, \ r = 0.1, \ P^C = 13.5p,$$

*we have, using (9.46):*

$$P^P = 13.5 - 50 + 45e^{-(0.1)(1)} = 4.22p.$$

Put-call parity is only valid for European options on non-dividend paying shares. However it is possible to derive some boundary conditions on the relationship between American put and call option prices on non-dividend paying shares. Since $P^{PA} > P^{PE}$ (because early exercise is a valuable right) and $P^{CA} = P^{CE}$ (because the American option will not be exercised early if the share does not pay dividends, the right of early exercise has no value in the case of American calls), it follows from (9.46) that:

$$P^{PA} > P^{CA} - P^S + Xe^{-rT}, \tag{9.47}$$

or:

$$P^{PA} - P^{CA} > Xe^{-rT} - P^S. \tag{9.48}$$

Further, a portfolio consisting of a European call option *plus* a sum of cash equal to $X$ (and earning $r$) must be worth more than a portfolio consisting of an American put option *plus* a share, i.e.:

$$P^{CE} + X > P^{PA} + P^S. \tag{9.49}$$

This follows because if the put is exercised early (at $\tau$, say) the portfolio containing the put is worth $X$ (since the share is sold for $X$) whereas the portfolio containing the call option is worth at least $Xe^{r\tau}$. But if the put is not exercised, the portfolio containing the put is worth $\max(P_T^S, X)$ at expiry whereas the portfolio containing the call is worth $\max(P_T^S, X) + X(e^{r\tau} - 1)$. The portfolio with the call stochastically dominates the portfolio with the put, thereby confirming the result in (9.49). Also since $P^{CE} = P^{CA}$, it follows that:

$$P^{CA} + X > P^{PA} + P^S, \tag{9.50}$$

or:

$$X - P^S > P^{PA} - P^{CA}. \tag{9.51}$$

Combining (9.48) and (9.51) yields the boundary condition:

$$X - P^S > P^{PA} - P^{CA} > Xe^{-rT} - P^S. \tag{9.52}$$

### 9.4.7   Modifications to the Black-Scholes model

Finally, we will briefly consider a number of modifications to the Black-Scholes model examined above.

**The payment of dividends.**   The basic Black-Scholes formula (9.23) is valid for a European call option on a share that does not pay dividends. It is also valid for an American call option on a non-dividend-paying share since such an option will not be exercised early; it is more profitable to sell rather than to exercise. However, the payment of dividends requires the Black-Scholes model to be modified slightly.

When dividends are paid, there is the possibility of early exercise in order to receive the dividend payment on the delivered share. Nevertheless, it can be shown that the only time that it becomes profitable to exercise an American call option (apart from on the expiry date) is just prior to the ex dividend date. Suppose that the share price falls by exactly the amount of the dividend, $d$, when a dividend is paid; i.e., it falls to $P^S - d$. If the call option is exercised just prior to the ex dividend date, the option holder receives $P^S - X$ (i.e. $d + (P^S - d) - X$). If the option is not exercised, the option holder's position is worth $P^{CA}(P^S - d, X, T)$. It becomes profitable to exercise early whenever:

$$P^S - X > P^{CA}(P^S - d, X, T). \tag{9.53}$$

However, if the present value of the dividends is less than the present value of the interest earned on an investment equal to the exercise price, then the American call option will not be exercised before expiry.

The opposite result holds for an American put option. If the present value of the dividends is greater than the present value of the interest earned on an investment equal to the exercise price, then the American put will not be exercised before expiry.

To illustrate the effect of dividend payments, we will consider a European call option on a share paying dividends continuously with a constant dividend yield, $d$. The Black-Scholes model in this case becomes (Merton (1973)):

$$P^C = P^S e^{-dT} N(d_1) - X e^{-rT} N(d_2), \tag{9.54}$$

where:

$$d_1 = \frac{\ln(P^S e^{-dT}/X) + rT}{\sigma\sqrt{T}} + \frac{1}{2}\sigma\sqrt{T} = \frac{\ln(P^S/X) + (r-d)T}{\sigma\sqrt{T}} + \frac{1}{2}\sigma\sqrt{T};$$

$$d_2 = d_1 - \sigma\sqrt{T}.$$

The basic Black-Scholes formula (9.23) is also valid for a European call option on a cash stock index with no dividend payments, while (9.54) is also valid for a European call option on a cash stock index with a constant dividend yield, $d$.

In the case where dividend payments occur at discrete intervals during the remaining life of the option, the correct procedure is to subtract the present value of these future dividends from the current share price and then to apply the original Black-Scholes model using this discounted share price.

The only general procedure for valuing an American call option on a dividend-paying share is to use the binomial model (see Black (1975)). At each step, it is necessary to check whether it is optimal to exercise the option just prior to an ex dividend date or to hold on to the option for one more period.

We can illustrate the use of the binomial model using the following example. Suppose that a share is currently valued at £2.00, but over the course of the year, it could either fall by 20 per cent to £1.60 or rise by 25 per cent to £2.50. The share will pay a dividend of 40p at the end of the year. Once the dividend has been paid the share price will fall either to £1.20 (i.e. £1.60 – £0.40) or to £2.10 (i.e. £2.50 – £0.40). During the second year, the share price will again fall from the ex dividend price by 20 per cent or rise by 25 per cent. The possible share prices at the end of years 1 and 2 are shown in Figure 9.23. Figure 9.24 shows the possible values of a two-year American call option on this share. The option has an exercise price of £1.50 and we assume that the interest rate is 10 per cent. The options can be valued using equation (9.22) above with $r = 0.1$, $u = 1.25$, $d = 0.8$ and $f = 0.667$. The options are valued using the cum dividend prices of the underlying share, since as we argued above, it is only ever optimal to exercise just prior to a dividend distribution.

The procedure for determining the initial value of the option involves starting at the end of the period and working backwards, and at each stage deciding whether it would be optimal to continue

**Figure 9.23** Possible share prices at the end of one and two years

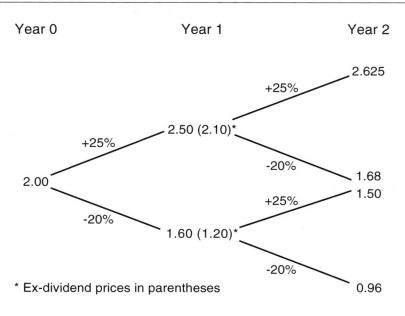

**Figure 9.24** Possible option values at the end of one and two years

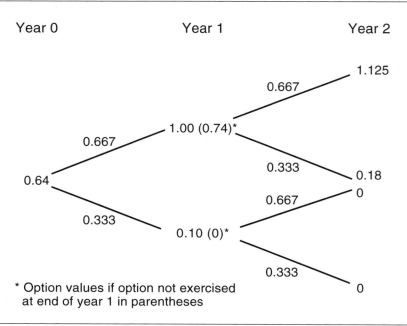

holding the option or to exercise it (this procedure is an application of *dynamic programming*). So starting at the end of year 2, Figure 9.24 shows the intrinsic values of the option on its maturity date on the basis of the four possible outcomes for the share price over two years: *uu*, *ud*, *du* and *dd*. The value of the option at the end of year 1, in the case where the option is not exercised, is found by using equation (9.22). In the case where the share price rose during year 1, we have:

$$P_1^C = \frac{0.667(1.125) + 0.333(0.18)}{1.1} = £0.74.$$

In the case where the share price fell during year 1, the option will expire worthless at the end of year 2, whether the share price subsequently rose during year 2 or fell. Therefore the option will also be worthless at the end of year 1, if it is not exercised at the end of year 1.

We must check whether the option would be more valuable if it was exercised at the end of year 1. This involves calculating the intrinsic value of the option at the end of year 1. In the case where the share price rose during year 1, the intrinsic value of the option at the end of year 1 is £1.00, i.e. share price (£2.50) minus exercise price (£1.50). In the case where the share price fell during year 1, the intrinsic value of the option at the end of year 1 is £0.10, i.e. share price (£1.60) minus exercise price (£1.50). It is clear that in each case, the option is worth more if it is exercised at the end of year 1 than if it is held until expiry. Therefore we can predict that it will be exercised early at the end of year 1. The intrinsic values on exercise are used to find the initial value of the option. Again using (9.22) we have:

$$P_0^C = \frac{0.667(1.00) - 0.333(0.10)}{1.1} = £0.64.$$

**Options on futures contracts.** The modification to the Black-Scholes formula when the call option is on a futures contract is straightforward (see Black (1976)):

$$P^C = e^{-rT}[FN(d_1) - XN(d_2)], \tag{9.55}$$

where:

$$F = \text{current futures price};$$

$$d_1 = \frac{\ln(F/X)}{\sigma\sqrt{T}} + \frac{1}{2}\sigma\sqrt{T};$$

$$d_2 = d_1 - \sigma\sqrt{T}.$$

Similarly, the modification to the put-call parity formula when the put option is on a futures contract is:

$$
\begin{aligned}
P^P &= P^C - e^{-rT}[F - X] \\
&= e^{-rT}[FN(d_1) - XN(d_2)] - e^{-rT}[F - X] \\
&= e^{-rT}[F(N(d_1) - 1) - X(N(d_2) - 1)] \\
&= e^{-rT}[XN(-d_2) - FN(-d_1)].
\end{aligned}
\tag{9.56}
$$

A variation on (9.55) is an *at-the-money forward* (ATMF) option where the exercise price, $X$, is set equal to the forward price, $F$. Puts and calls trade at the same premium which can be shown to be approximately equal to (in percentage terms):

$$P^C \;=\; P^P \;\approx\; \frac{1}{2.5} \cdot e^{-rT} \sigma \sqrt{T}.$$

For example, a three-month ATMF call option with 15 per cent volatility and an interest rate of 10 per cent has a premium of:

$$P^C \;\approx\; \frac{1}{2.5} \cdot e^{-0.1(0.25)} 15\sqrt{0.25} \;=\; 2.93\%$$

of the forward price.

In the case where the option is on an interest-rate future, we have to take into account the inverse relationship between interest rates and prices. For example, a put option on a futures price with an exercise price of 90 (i.e. 100 − 10) is equivalent to a call option on interest rates with an exercise price of 10%. A corporate treasurer with a loan might buy a call option on an interest-rate futures contract from a bank if he thought interest rates might rise in the future. If the bank is also providing the loan, it is conventional for the premium to be charged when the option expires rather than when it starts, so the premium must be compounded to the expiry date. In this case the call option is priced as follows:

$$P^C \;=\; r_x N(-d_2) - r_f N(-d_1), \tag{9.57}$$

where:

$$
\begin{aligned}
r_f &= \text{interest rate implied by futures price (i.e. 100 − futures price);} \\
r_x &= \text{interest rate implied by exercise price (i.e. 100 − exercise price);} \\
d_1 &= \ln\!\left(\frac{r_f}{r_x}\right) \Big/ \sigma\sqrt{T} + \tfrac{1}{2}\sigma\sqrt{T}; \\
d_2 &= d_1 - \sigma\sqrt{T}; \\
\sigma &= \text{annual standard deviation of 3-month interest rates;} \\
T &= \text{time to expiry of option in years.}
\end{aligned}
$$

**Options on currency contracts.**    The modification to the Black-Scholes formula when the call option is on a currency option is:

$$P^C \;=\; e^{-r_\$ T} P^S N(d_1) - e^{-r_\pounds T} X N(d_2), \tag{9.58}$$

where:

$$
\begin{aligned}
P^S &= \text{spot rate of currency to be delivered in foreign units of domestic currency (e.g. \$ per £);} \\
r_\pounds &= \text{domestic riskless rate of interest;} \\
r_\$ &= \text{foreign riskless rate of interest;} \\
d_1 &= \left[\ln(P^S/X) + (r_\pounds - r_\$)T\right] \big/ \sigma\sqrt{T} + \tfrac{1}{2}\sigma\sqrt{T}; \\
d_2 &= d_1 - \sigma\sqrt{T}.
\end{aligned}
$$

The put option premium is determined by:

$$P^P \;=\; P^C - P^S + e^{-r_\pounds T} X. \tag{9.59}$$

## 9.5 Exotic options

Any option that is not a straightforward conventional option is known as an *exotic option*. We can classify exotic options in the following ways.

The first type of exotic option is *nonstandard* options, options with features that differ from standard options. One example is the *Boston option* where the premium is paid when the option is exercised, rather than at the beginning of the contract. If the exercise price is set equal to the forward price at the start of the option, Boston options are called *break forwards, forwards with optional exit* and *cancellable forwards*. With a *money-back option*, the premium is repaid on the option expiry date. With an *instalment option*, the premium increases if the price of the underlying security passes certain prespecified threshold levels. With a *ratchet option*, the exercise price improves (from the holder's viewpoint) if the price of the underlying security passes certain threshold levels. Another example of a nonstandard option is the *Bermudan* (or *modified American*) *option*. This is an American option, but early exercise is restricted to certain dates during the life of the option. With a *forward start option* the premium is paid at the beginning of the contract, but the option does not come into effect until some time in the future. Finally, a *binary* (or *digital* or *cash-or-nothing*) *option* pays out a fixed predetermined sum if the price of the underlying security reaches the exercise price, regardless of how much the option is in-the-money; otherwise it pays nothing. A variation on this is the *range digital* (or *double-no-touch*) *option* which pays out a fixed sum if the price of the underlying security lies within a specified range (or *corridor*), and nothing if it moves outside this range.

The second type of exotic option involves *option combinations*. These are options which can be interpreted as combinations of other options and possibly a forward contract as well. They are often designed to have zero cost. An example is a *range forward contract* (also known as a *zero-cost collar*, *flexible forward, cylinder option, option fence, min-max* and *forward bond*). This consists of a long forward contract combined with a long put with a low exercise price ($X_1$) and a short call with a high exercise price ($X_2$), as shown in Figure 9.25. The exercise prices are chosen so that the price of the call equals the price of the put and since the value of the forward is zero, the range forward contract can be

**Figure 9.25** Range forward contract

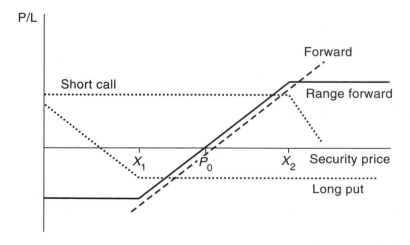

sold at zero cost. The buyer of the contract will make profits if the price of the underlying is above $P_0$ on the expiry date.

The third type of exotic option is *barrier options* (or *limited dependent options*). Here the payout depends on whether the price of the underlying security hits a certain level or barrier during a certain period of time. One example is the *knock-out* or *vanishing* option which is automatically cancelled when the price of the underlying hits a certain barrier. In the case of a knock-out call option, the barrier, $B$, is generally below the exercise price (i.e. $B < X$ or $B$ is out-of-the-money relative to $X$) and such options are also known as *down-and-out* options. They involve an automatic stop-loss component if the security price falls below $B$. An equivalent put option is known as an *up-and-out* option and in this case $B > X$ (i.e. $B$ is out-of-the-money relative to $X$). An example of an up-and-out option is a put on the FTSE 100 index that is automatically cancelled if the index rises by 1 per cent. These options are also known as *out-of-the-money knock-out* options. However, it is also possible for the barrier ($B$) to be in-the-money relative to the exercise price ($X$). Such options are known as *in-the-money* (or *reverse*) *knock-out* options. The premium on out-of-the-money knock-outs increases with both time to expiry and volatility. However, the premium on in-the-money knock outs decreases with time to expiry and with volatility, because there is a greater chance that the barrier will be hit and that the option will be cancelled. Because of this risk, the premium on in-the-money knock outs is much lower than that on standard options.

In contrast, a *down-and-in* option is a call option that starts only if a barrier, $B$ ($< X$), is hit, while an *up-and-in* option is a put that starts only if a barrier, $B$ ($> X$), is hit. These are examples of *knock-in* options. The price of a European down-and-in call option is given by (see Rubinstein (1991)):

$$P^C = P^S \left(\frac{B}{P^S}\right)^\lambda N(d_1) - Xe^{-rT} \left(\frac{B}{P^S}\right)^{\lambda-2} N(d_2), \tag{9.60}$$

where:

$$\lambda = (2r + \sigma^2)/\sigma^2;$$
$$d_1 = \ln(B^2/P^S X)/\sigma\sqrt{T} + \lambda\sigma\sqrt{T};$$
$$d_2 = d_1 - \sigma\sqrt{T}.$$

The price of a European up-and-in put option is:

$$P^P = Xe^{-rT} \left(\frac{B}{P^S}\right)^{\lambda-2} N(-d_2) - P^S \left(\frac{B}{P^S}\right)^\lambda N(-d_1). \tag{9.61}$$

A standard call is the sum of knock-out and knock-in calls (this is demonstrated in Figure 9.26 in the case of in-the-money options). Therefore the price of a European down-and-out call is equal to the price of a standard European call *minus* the price of a related down-and-in call. In the same way, the price of a European up-and-out put is equal to the price of a standard European put *minus* the price of corresponding up-and-in put.

Variations on these barrier options include: *rebate* (the option pays out a predetermined sum, typically the initial premium, at the knock-out barrier); *double barriers* (two barrier levels); *partial window* (the option can knock out for only a part of the option's life); *capped call* (the option pays out a predetermined sum at maturity if the barrier is hit at any time during life of the option); *second chance*

**Figure 9.26** The relationship between standard options and barrier options

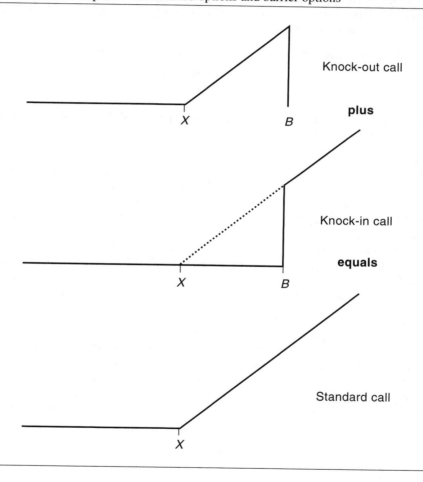

(the option knocks out only if the barrier is breached for two consecutive days); *two factor* (the option knocks out on a second security); and *sloping knock outs* (the barrier level changes during life of option).

The fourth type of exotic option is *time-dependent options*. These are options whereby the holder has the right to determine the nature of the option after a specified period of time. The most common example of such options are *chooser* (or *preference* or *as-you-like-it*) *options* which give the holder the right to choose whether the option is a call or a put. Suppose that the holder can make this choice $\tau$ periods to expiry when the underlying security price is $P_\tau^S$. We suppose that the option originally has $T(>\tau)$ periods to expiry. Suppose also that both of the options underlying the chooser option are European with the same exercise price. In this case, put-call parity can be used to price the chooser option and this will equal the larger of the values of the two options:

$$
\begin{aligned}
\max(P^C, P^P) &= \max(P^C, P^C + Xe^{-r\tau} - P_\tau^S) \\
&= P^C + \max(0, Xe^{-r\tau} - P_\tau^S) \\
&= P^C + P_\tau^P .
\end{aligned}
\tag{9.62}
$$

Hence a chooser option is the sum of a call option with a maturity of $T$ and exercise price $X$, and a put option with a maturity of $(T - \tau)$ and an exercise price of $Xe^{-r\tau}$.

The fifth type of exotic option is *multiple asset* (or *multiple factor*) *options*. The value of such options depends on the relationship between the prices of two or more assets rather than on the price of a single asset. We can consider some examples. With a *basket option* the payout depends on the cumulative performance of a basket of securities. A *difference* (or *spread*) *option* has an exercise price equal to the difference between the prices of two different securities, e.g. a call option to buy the spread between 3 month sterling LIBOR and 3 month dollar LIBOR at 250 basis points. A *rainbow* (or *out-performance*) *option* pays out the greatest appreciation from two or more specified markets, e.g. a call option that pays the greater of the gains on the FTSE 100 or S&P 500 indices. A *quanto* (or *second currency*) *option* pays in one currency on the basis of the movement in the price of a security in another currency, e.g. the percentage gain in the Nikkei 225 index but payable in US dollars based on a notional sum.

Another example of a multiple asset option is the *exchange option*, an option to exchange one asset for another. For example a stock tender offer is an option to exchange the shares of one company for those of another. In this case the exercise price is not fixed, but is equal to the price of the shares being exchanged. The value of such an option was first determined by Margrave (1978). Suppose that the shares being given up are priced at $P_1^S$ and yield $r_1$ and the shares being received in exchange are priced at $P_2^S$ and yield $r_2$. Suppose further that the volatilities of the shares and the correlation between them are given respectively by $\sigma_1$, $\sigma_2$ and $\rho$. The price of a European call option on this exchange is:

$$
P^C = P_2^S e^{-r_2 T} N(d_1) - P_1^S e^{-r_1 T} N(d_2),
\tag{9.63}
$$

where:

$$
\begin{aligned}
d_1 &= \frac{\ln(P_2^S/P_1^S) + (r_1 - r_2)T}{\sigma\sqrt{T}} + \tfrac{1}{2}\sigma\sqrt{T}; \\
d_2 &= d_1 - \sigma\sqrt{T};
\end{aligned}
$$

and:

$$
\sigma^2 = \sigma_1^2 + \sigma_2^2 - 2\rho\sigma_1\sigma_2
$$

is the volatility of $P_2^S/P_1^S$. Comparison with the Black-Scholes model indicates that an exchange option is equivalent to $P_1^S$ standard European call options on a share priced at $P_2^S/P_1^S$ with a strike price of 1, a risk free interest rate of $r_1$ and a dividend yield on the asset of $r_2$. It immediately follows from this that a rainbow option giving the greatest appreciation on two securities is equivalent to a portfolio comprising one of the securities *plus* an exchange option for the other security:

$$\max(P_1^S, P_2^S) = P_1^S + \max(P_2^S - P_1^S, 0). \tag{9.64}$$

A final example of a multiple asset option is a *compound option* which is an option on an option. There are four types of compound option: a call on a call, a put on a call, a call on a put, and a put on a put. Such options have two exercise prices and two expiry dates. For example, in the case of a call on a call, the holder has the right on the first expiry date $T_1$ to pay the first exercise price $X_1$ and receive a call option. The second call option gives the holder the right to purchase the underlying security at the second exercise price $X_2$ on the second expiry date $T_2$. The first option will only be exercised at $T_1$ if the second option is in the money at that time. The value of a compound option was first determined by Geske (1979).

The price of a European call on a call is:

$$P^{CC} = P^S M(a_1, b_1; \rho) - X_2 e^{-rT_2} M(a_2, b_2; \rho) - e^{-rT_1} X_1 N(a_2), \tag{9.65}$$

where:

$$a_1 = \frac{\ln(P^S/P_1^S) + rT_1}{\sigma\sqrt{T}} + \tfrac{1}{2}\sigma\sqrt{T}$$

$$a_2 = a_1 - \sigma\sqrt{T}$$

$$b_1 = \frac{\ln(P^S/X_1) + rT_2}{\sigma\sqrt{T_2}} + \tfrac{1}{2}\sigma\sqrt{T_2}$$

$$b_2 = b_1 - \sigma\sqrt{T_2}$$

$$\rho = \sqrt{\frac{T_1}{T_2}},$$

and $P_1^S$ is the share price at time $T_1$ that makes the option premium at time $T_1$ equal to $X_1$. If the actual share price is above $P_1^S$ at $T_1$, the first option will be exercised, otherwise it will expire valueless. $M(a, b; \rho)$ is the cumulative bivariate normal distribution function evaluated at $a$ for the first variable and at $b$ for the second variable, and $\rho$ is the correlation between the two variables.

The price of a European put on a call is:

$$P^{PC} = X_2 e^{-rT_2} M(-a_2, b_2; -\rho) - P^S M(-a_1, b_1; -\rho) + e^{-rT_1} X_1 N(-a_2). \tag{9.66}$$

The value of a European call on a put is:

$$P^{CP} = X_2 e^{-rT_2} M(-a_2, -b_2; -\rho) - P^S M(-a_1, -b_1; -\rho) + e^{-rT_1} X_1 N(-a_2). \tag{9.67}$$

The value of a European put on a put is:

$$P^{PP} = P^S M(a_1, -b_1; -\rho) - X_2 e^{-rT_2} M(a_2, -b_2; -\rho) + e^{-rT_1} X_1 N(a_2). \tag{9.68}$$

$M(a,b;\rho)$ can be calculated as follows (see Hull (1993), App. 10B). If $a \leq 0$, $b \leq 0$, and $\rho \leq 0$:

$$M(a,b;\rho) = \frac{\sqrt{1-\rho^2}}{\pi} \sum_{i,j=1}^{4} A_i A_j f(B_i, B_j),$$

where:

$$f(x,y) = \exp[a'(2x - a') + b'(2y - b') + 2\rho(x - a')(y - b')];$$

$$a' = \frac{a}{\sqrt{2(1-\rho^2)}}; \quad b' = \frac{b}{\sqrt{2(1-\rho^2)}};$$

$$A_1 = 0.3253030; \quad A_2 = 0.4211071; \quad A_3 = 0.1334425; \quad A_4 = 0.006374323;$$
$$B_1 = 0.1337764; \quad B_2 = 0.6243247; \quad B_3 = 1.3425378; \quad B_4 = 2.2626645.$$

Where the product of $a$, $b$ and $\rho$ is negative or zero, one of the following identities can be used:

$$M(a,b;\rho) \equiv N(a) - M(a,-b;-\rho),$$
$$M(a,b;\rho) \equiv N(b) - M(-a,b;-\rho),$$
$$M(a,b;\rho) \equiv N(a) + N(b) - 1 + M(-a,-b;\rho).$$

Where the product of $a$, $b$ and $\rho$ is positive, the identity:

$$M(a,b;\rho) \equiv M(a,0;\rho_1) + M(b,0;\rho_2) - \delta$$

can be used in conjunction with the previous results, where:

$$\rho_1 = \frac{(\rho a - b)\mathrm{sgn}(a)}{\sqrt{a^2 - 2\rho ab + b^2}}; \quad \rho_2 = \frac{(\rho b - a)\mathrm{sgn}(b)}{\sqrt{a^2 - 2\rho ab + b^2}};$$

$$\delta = \frac{1 - \mathrm{sgn}(a)\mathrm{sgn}(b)}{4}; \quad \mathrm{sgn}(x) = \begin{cases} +1 & \text{when } x \geq 0, \\ -1 & \text{when } x < 0. \end{cases}$$

The last type of exotic option that we will consider are *path-dependent options*. These are options where the payoff and sometimes the actual structure of the option itself depends on the particular path taken by the underlying security price over the life of the option. We can consider some examples.

*Look-back options* give the right to buy (in the case of the call) at the lowest recorded price or to sell (in the case of the put) at the highest recorded price during the life of the option; in other words, the exercise price is not fixed but set equal to the most favourable price (from the holder's viewpoint) that the underlying security achieved prior to the option's expiry. *Look-back strike* (or *ladder*) *options* are look-back options in which the setting of the exercise price occurs over a period of time that is less than the full period to expiry. *Capped look-back options* combine a look-back option with a cap. *Hi-lo options* pay out the difference between the highest and lowest prices recorded on a security during the life of the option; this option is useful if volatility is expected to rise over the life of the option.

Valuation formulae for look-back options have been derived by Goldman et al. (1979). If $P^S_{\min}$ is the minimum recorded price of the security, $P^S_{\max}$ is the maximum recorded price of the security and $P^S_T$ is the final price of the security, then the terminal value of a look-back call is:

$$P^C_T = \max(0, P^S_T - P^S_{\min}), \tag{9.69}$$

and the terminal value of a look-back put is:

$$P_T^P = \max(0, P_{\max}^S - P_T^S).\tag{9.70}$$

The price of a look-back call at the beginning is:

$$P^C = P^S N(a_1) - P^S \frac{\sigma^2}{2r} N(-a_1) - P_{\min}^{S^*} e^{-rT} \left[ N(a_2) - \frac{\sigma^2}{2r} e^{\lambda_1} N(-a_3) \right],\tag{9.71}$$

where $P_{\min}^{S^*}$ is the lowest price achieved by the underlying security to date and:

$$
\begin{aligned}
a_1 &= \frac{\ln(P^S/P_{\min}^{S^*}) + rT}{\sigma\sqrt{T}} + \tfrac{1}{2}\sigma\sqrt{T}; \\[2mm]
a_2 &= a_1 - \sigma\sqrt{T}; \\[2mm]
a_3 &= \frac{\ln(P^S/P_{\min}^{S^*}) - rT}{\sigma\sqrt{T}} + \tfrac{1}{2}\sigma\sqrt{T}; \\[2mm]
\lambda_1 &= \frac{-(2r - \sigma^2)\ln(P^S/P_{\min}^{S^*})}{\sigma^2}.
\end{aligned}
$$

The price of a look-back put at the beginning is:

$$P^P = P_{\max}^{S^*} e^{-rT} \left[ N(b_1) - \frac{\sigma^2}{2r} e^{\lambda_2} N(-b_3) \right] + P^S \frac{\sigma^2}{2r} N(-b_2) - P^S N(b_2),\tag{9.72}$$

where $P_{\max}^{S^*}$ is the highest price achieved by the underlying security to date and:

$$
\begin{aligned}
b_1 &= \frac{\ln(P_{\max}^{S^*}/P^S) - rT}{\sigma\sqrt{T}} + \tfrac{1}{2}\sigma\sqrt{T}; \\[2mm]
b_2 &= b_1 - \sigma\sqrt{T}; \\[2mm]
b_3 &= \frac{\ln(P_{\max}^{S^*}/P^S) + rT}{\sigma\sqrt{T}} - \tfrac{1}{2}\sigma\sqrt{T}; \\[2mm]
\lambda_2 &= \frac{(2r - \sigma^2)\ln(P_{\max}^{S^*}/P^S)}{\sigma^2}.
\end{aligned}
$$

Other examples of path-dependent options are *Asian* (or *average price*) *options* and *average strike price options*. Asian options pay out the difference between the exercise price and the average price of the security recorded during the life of the option; such an option is useful if volatility is expected to fall over the life of the option. The payoff from an Asian call is:

$$P^C = \max(0, P_{av}^S - X),\tag{9.73}$$

where $P_{av}^S$ is the average price of the underlying over the life of the security, while the payoff from an Asian put is:

$$P^P = \max(0, X - P_{av}^S).\tag{9.74}$$

In contrast, the payoff from an average strike price call is:

$$P^C = \max(0, P_{av}^S - P^S),$$ (9.75)

while the payoff from an average strike price put is:

$$P^C = \max(0, P^S - P_{av}^S).$$ (9.76)

The call ensures that if a security is purchased periodically over a given period, the average price paid is above the terminal price. The put ensures that if a security is sold periodically over a given period, the average price received is below the terminal price.

If $P_{av}^S$ is equal to the geometric average price over the period, then Kemna and Vorst (1990) have shown that an Asian option is the same as a standard option with a dividend yield equal to $0.5\,(r + d + \sigma^2/6)$ and a volatility of $\sigma/\sqrt{3}$ where $d$ is the dividend yield on the underlying security. However, for most Asian options, $P_{av}^S$ is equal to the arithmetic average price over the period. In this case, Turnbull and Wakeman (1991) have shown that an Asian option is the same as a standard option with dividend yield equal to:

$$d_A = r - \frac{\ln M_1}{T},$$ (9.77)

and volatility equal to:

$$\sigma_A^2 = \frac{\ln M_2}{T} - 2(r - d_A),$$ (9.78)

where:

$$M_1 = \frac{e^{(r-d)T} - 1}{(r-d)T},$$

and:

$$M_2 = \frac{2e^{(2(r-d)+\sigma^2)T}}{(r-d+\sigma^2)(2r-2d+\sigma^2)T^2} + \frac{2}{(r-d)T^2}\left[\frac{1}{2(r-d)+\sigma^2} - \frac{e^{(r-d)T}}{r-d+\sigma^2}\right].$$

## 9.6   Warrants and convertibles

Warrants and convertibles are instruments that have option features attached to them and they are used by corporations (and sometimes governments) to raise additional finance at some future date following their issue (warrants), or to change the form of that finance at some future date (convertibles). It is these option features that can make them attractive to investors. They are sometimes said to act as 'sweeteners' to make the instruments to which they are attached easier to sell.

### 9.6.1   Warrants

An *equity warrant* is an option issued by a firm to purchase a given number of shares in that firm at a given exercise price at any time before the warrant expires. If the warrant is exercised, the firm issues new shares at the exercise price and so raises additional finance. A *bond warrant* is an option to purchase more of the firm's bonds. A warrant generally has a longer maturity than a conventional option (e.g. five years), and some warrants are perpetual.

Warrants are usually attached to debt instruments such as bonds (known as *host bonds*). Sometimes they are detachable from these instruments and so can be traded separately; sometimes they are non-detachable. Equity warrants do not carry any of the rights of shareholders until they are exercised; for example, they pay no dividends and do not have voting rights. However, warrant holders are protected from changes to the underlying share price, such as those resulting from stock splits or stock dividends, through a corresponding adjustment to the exercise price of the warrant. (The same is true of ordinary options.) Bond warrants can either be exercised into the same class of bonds as the host bond or into a completely different class of bond.

Other types of warrant include *naked warrants* (where no host bond is issued), *interest-bearing warrants*, and *currency warrants* (which enable investors to buy bonds denominated in a different currency from the host bond).

In valuing a warrant, it is important to recognize that the exercise of the warrant (unlike the exercise of an ordinary option) will increase the number of shares outstanding. This will have the effect of diluting earnings per share and hence reducing the share price. It follows from this that a warrant can be valued in exactly the same way as an American call option, but with account taken of this dilution effect.

As with ordinary options, the value of a warrant has two components, an intrinsic value (which in warrant terminology is called the *formula value*) and a time value (which in warrant terminology is known as the *premium* over the formula value):

$$\text{Warrant value} \ = \ \text{Formula value} + \text{Premium}. \tag{9.79}$$

The formula value is determined by the following equation:

$$\begin{aligned} \text{Formula value} \ = \ &(\text{Share price} - \text{Exercise price}) \\ &\times \text{Number of new shares issued if warrant is exercised}. \end{aligned} \tag{9.80}$$

If the exercise price exceeds the share price, the formula value is zero and the warrant is said to be out-of-the-money. If the share price exceeds the exercise price, the warrant is in-the-money and the formula value is positive. The time value is always positive if there is still some time left to expiry. However, as with ordinary options, the time value declines as the expiry date approaches and on the expiry date itself, the time value is zero.

**Example 9.2 (Formula value)** *We have the following data:*

$$\begin{aligned} \textit{Share price} \ &= \ \textit{£2.75} \\ \textit{Exercise price} \ &= \ \textit{£2.50} \end{aligned}$$

*If two new shares will be issued if the warrant is exercised then, from (9.80):*

$$\text{Formula value} \ = \ £(2.75 - 2.50) \times 2 \ = \ £0.50.$$

The *percent premium* of the warrant is given by:

$$\text{Percent premium} \;=\; \frac{\text{Warrant value} - \text{Formula value}}{\text{Share price} \times \text{Number of new shares issued if warrant is exercised}}. \qquad (9.81)$$

If the warrant is trading in the market place at £1.00, then, using the data in the above example:

$$\text{Percent premium} \;=\; \frac{£1.00 - £0.50}{£2.75 \times 2} \;=\; 9.09\%.$$

The fair price of a warrant is determined by the following formula:

$$\text{Warrant value} \;=\; \frac{P^{CA}}{1+q} \times \text{Number of new shares issued if warrant is exercised}, \qquad (9.82)$$

where $q$ is the proportionate increase in the number of shares outstanding if all the warrants are exercised, and $P^{CA}$ is the value of an American call option with the same exercise price and expiry date as the warrant. For example, if the exercise of the warrants implies a 25 per cent increase in the number of shares outstanding (i.e. if $q = 0.25$), if two shares are issued if the warrant is exercised, and if the price of the American call option is £1.25, then the fair warrant value would be given by:

$$\text{Warrant value} \;=\; \frac{£1.25}{1.25} \times 2 \;=\; £2.00.$$

A warrant is attractive to investors because, if the firm is successful, the warrant can be exercised and the holder can receive high-value shares at the much lower exercise price.

Most warrants traded are issued by corporations and exercise into shares. However, the LSE and Bank of England operate a market in *gilt warrants* which can be exercised into UK government bonds.

## 9.6.2   Convertibles

A *convertible* is a bond (or sometimes a preference share) that is convertible at some future date into common stock (in the case where the convertible is issued by a corporation) or into another bond, known as a *conversion bond* (in the case where the issuer is a government). The conversion is at the option of the holder of the convertible, although it can be forced if the convertible is callable by the firm. A convertible is therefore a means of transforming debt into equity at some future date. This contrasts with a warrant, where the warrant holder retains ownership of the host bond when the warrant is exercised.

The *conversion ratio* defines the number of shares of common stock received in return for the bond. The *conversion price* is the price paid for the shares when conversion takes place:

$$\text{Conversion price} \;=\; \frac{\text{Par value of bond}}{\text{Conversion ratio}}. \qquad (9.83)$$

If the conversion ratio is 20 (i.e. if 20 shares are received in return for the bond with a par value of £100), then the conversion price is:

$$\text{Conversion price} \;=\; \frac{£100}{20} \;=\; £5.00.$$

The *percentage conversion premium* is the percentage by which the conversion price exceeds the current share price. It shows the percentage by which the share price must rise before the bond is likely to be called. If the current price of the share is £3.70, then:

$$\text{Percentage conversion premium} \;=\; \frac{\text{Conversion price} - \text{Share price}}{\text{Share price}} \tag{9.84}$$

$$=\; \frac{£5.00 - £3.70}{£3.70} \;=\; 35.14\%.$$

The *conversion value* of the bond is given by:

$$\text{Conversion value} \;=\; \text{Share price} \times \text{Conversion ratio}, \tag{9.85}$$

and shows the current value of the shares received in exchange for the bond. If the current share price is £3.70, then the current conversion value is given by:

$$\text{Conversion value} \;=\; £3.70 \times 20 \;=\; £74.00.$$

If the bond is trading at £82.50, then the *percentage conversion price premium*, or the percentage by which the current bond price exceeds the current conversion value, is given by:

$$\text{Percentage conversion price premium} \;=\; \frac{\text{Price of bond} - \text{Conversion value}}{\text{Conversion value}} \tag{9.86}$$

$$=\; \frac{£82.50 - £74.00}{£74.00} \;=\; 11.49\%.$$

This shows the percentage by which the share price must rise before the bond is converted. As with warrants, convertibles are protected from dilution of the share price resulting from stock dividends or stock splits: the conversion ratio is raised (and the conversion price lowered) by the percentage amount of any stock dividend or split.

A convertible is similar to a straight bond with a warrant attached to it. Its fair price will therefore be related to the price of a straight bond and the price of a call option, taking into account both the dilution effect of the new shares issued on and the interest payments saved by conversion.

The proportionate increase in the number of shares outstanding if all bonds are converted is:

$$q \;=\; \frac{\text{Number of convertible bonds} \times \text{Conversion ratio}}{\text{Number of shares outstanding before conversion}}. \tag{9.87}$$

The fair price of the convertible is given by:

$$\text{Price of convertible} \;=\; \text{Price of straight bond} + \frac{P^{CA}}{1+q} \times \text{Conversion ratio}, \tag{9.88}$$

where $P^{CA}$ is the value of an American call option with an exercise price equal to the conversion price and an expiration date equal to the maturity date of the bond. The price of the straight bond is calculated in precisely the same way as a standard bond in the same risk class.

Equation (9.88) gives the fair price of a convertible bond if the bond is not callable. However, most convertible bonds are callable at the option of the firm before their maturity dates. The firm can therefore force conversion when the share price has risen to the point where the value of the shares received on conversion equals the call price of the bond. Since the firm has a clear incentive to call the bond when this occurs, the call price puts an effective upper limit on the price of the convertible given in (9.88).

It is possible to calculate the likely call date using the following formula:

$$\text{Call price} \;=\; \text{Current share price} \times (1+g)^t \times \text{Conversion ratio}, \tag{9.89}$$

where $g$ is the expected growth rate in the share price and $t$ is time in years. Suppose that the call price of the bond is £110 (i.e. exceeds the face value by £10), the conversion ratio is 20, and the current share price is £3.70 and is growing at 8.25 per cent per year. Given that the RHS of (9.89) is the conversion value of the convertible in $t$ years' time, it can be determined that the conversion value will equal the call price five years' hence. Therefore the bond is likely to be called in five years time.

Returning to (9.88), we can see that the price of the convertible depends on the price of a straight bond with five years to maturity (and a terminal value of £110) and a call option with five years to expiration. If the straight bond has a fair price of £63.30, the call option has a fair price of £1.20, and the proportionate increase in the number of shares is 25 per cent, then the fair price of the convertible is:

$$\text{Price of convertible} \;=\; £63.30 + \frac{£1.20}{1.25} \times 20 \;=\; £82.59.$$

Now because a convertible is a combination of a straight bond and an option, we can see how it might be attractive to investors. We know from option valuation theory that the value of an option *increases* with the variance of the underlying share. But we also know from bond valuation theory that the value of a bond *decreases* with the variance of the underlying share because the risk of default is increased. Therefore attaching an option to a bond helps to limit the downside risk in high-risk companies while at the same time preserving the upside potential if the firm is successful because of the right to convert into shares. There is a similar effect in terms of the income generated by the convertible. In a new high-risk company, the dividend income from shares is likely to be very low. The interest income on the convertible will be much higher initially. However, if the firm is successful, dividend income will grow over time and eventually will exceed interest income. The optimal conversion date from the viewpoint of the holder of the convertible rather than the issuer is therefore at this cross-over point (see Figure 9.27). Another advantage of investing in convertibles follows from possible legal restrictions. Some pension fund trustees are faced with legal restrictions on the equity content of their portfolio. Convertibles qualify as *narrow-range investments* under the 1961 Trustee Investment Act. They therefore provide an indirect means of circumventing such barriers.

# Appendix A: Accounting issues with options and futures contracts

There are four principal accounting issues in respect of options and futures contracts: the valuation of open positions; the recognition of profit and loss; consideration of any underlying asset or liability; and the treatment of margins. We deal with each of these factors in turn.

The valuation of exchange-traded options and futures positions is relatively straightforward because such positions are marked to market on a daily basis. This means that net open positions in options and futures can be readily valued at closing settlement prices. Accounting conventions now

**Figure 9.27** Optimal conversion date for a convertible

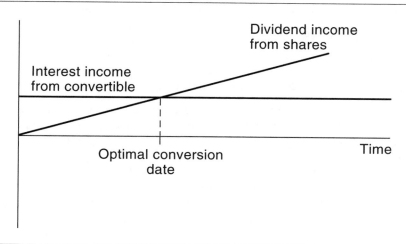

adopt the marked-to-market evaluation approach. In the past, an accruals approach was used. This meant that a profit or a loss was recognised only when a position was closed out. But this approach leaves open the possibility of manipulation, i.e., selectively closing a position to take either a profit or a loss, depending on what was required by the user. The marked-to-market approach removes this possibility.

Once a profit or loss has been determined, the second issue concerns the accounting period in which it should be recognized. The answer depends on the purpose underlying the open position in options or futures, in particular on whether the purpose is for trading or for hedging.

With open trading positions, the situation is again straightforward. With the profit or loss on trading transactions determined on a marked-to-market basis, the whole of the profit or loss should be recognized immediately. Since options and futures traders decide on a daily basis whether to maintain an open position or to close it out, the taking of profits or losses on a daily basis simply acknowledges the impact of the trader's decision in the period in which the decision is made. Recognizing profits or losses only when positions are closed out again leads to the possibility of manipulation discussed above.

The accounting treatment of hedging transactions is somewhat different. The profit or loss on options or futures hedging strategies should be recognised over the same period of time as the loss or profit on the asset or liability being hedged. This may mean that profits or losses on options or futures hedges should be brought forward in the balance sheet for recognition at a later date. For example, suppose that an investor has a three month sterling deposit and is concerned that interest rates will fall and so hedges his position by buying a call option on the sterling short term interest rate futures contract. Suppose further that on the rollover date for the deposit, interest rates are lower and the option is showing a profit. It is appropriate to recognize the profit on the option transaction over the same period as the lower interest income on the sterling deposit.

However, in order to avoid profit manipulation (e.g. carrying losses forward), it is essential to differentiate trading transactions from hedging transactions. A hedging transaction must satisfy three criteria. The first is *intent*. If an option or futures transaction is intended to be a hedging transaction, it should be identified and documented as such and both the asset or liability being hedged and the planned period of exposure should be specified. The second is *correlation*. There should be a high degree of correlation between the value of the asset or liability being hedged and the price of the hedging instrument. The third is *certainty of execution*. When a hedge is anticipatory (i.e. is related to a transaction that is likely to occur in the future), there should be a high degree of certainty that the transaction will actually be executed. If these criteria are not satisfied, then it is very difficult to distinguish a hedging transaction from a trading transaction.

The third accounting issue is the balance sheet treatment of the securities underlying the options and futures contracts. Again this depends on whether or not the options and futures transactions are trading transactions or hedging transactions. In the case of trading transactions, the underlying securities should not be included in the balance sheet, either as assets or liabilities, since legal title to the securities does not pass until exercise and delivery is effected. In the case of hedging transactions, the balance sheet position depends on how the assets and liabilities being hedged are valued in the balance sheet. If they are valued at market prices, then the profit and losses on hedging transactions should be recognized immediately. If they are valued at cost, then the profit and losses on hedging transactions should be deferred and only recognized on the sale of the asset or extinction of liability. The book value of a hedged asset or liability should not be compared with its market value in isolation, since this might suggest an apparent write-off to the profit and loss account even though a hedging profit that offsets the write-off might have been made.

The final accounting issue is the treatment of margin payments in the margin account held with the broker executing options and futures transactions. Initial margin should be treated as an amount due from the broker when an option or futures position is closed. Free cash in the margin account should be treated as repayable on demand. Variation margin payments represent daily profits and losses on open positions. In the case of trading transactions, these profits and losses should be recognized immediately. In the case of hedging transactions, the profits and losses should be carried in the balance sheet until the hedging exposure is removed.

This appendix was based on: *Futures and Options: Accounting and administration*, LIFFE Administration and Management.

## Appendix B: Taxation issues with options and futures contracts

The tax treatment of options and futures contracts revolves around whether a particular transaction is considered to be a trading transaction or a capital transaction and whether a trading or capital transaction gives rise to a tax liability or to an exemption. The treatment also depends on whether the option user is an institution or an individual. We take each type of user in turn.

The main Acts of Parliament dealing with the institutional taxation of options and futures are the Income and Corporation Taxes Act 1988 and the Taxation of Chargeable Gains Act 1992. In the case of pension funds and authorized unit trusts, all profits from dealings in options and futures are exempt from tax whether they arise from capital or trading transactions. The exemption applies irrespective of the frequency of transactions in options or futures. In the case of authorized unit trusts and approved investment trusts, profits from capital transactions are exempt from tax, but profits from trading transactions will be subject to income tax. A transaction will be regarded as a capital transaction if its intention is to: 1) reduce economic risk in a portfolio, either by hedging or through the use of options and futures as a preliminary step in implementing an investment strategy (e.g. pre-positioning or asset switching), or 2) reduce the cost of an underlying transaction which has either taken place or is intended to take place. The Inland Revenue requires documentation evidencing the intention of the fund manager in order to determine whether a transaction qualifies for capital treatment. In the case of banks, building societies and insurance companies, their profits from transactions in options and futures are treated as trading income which is subject to schedule D income tax.

The main acts of parliament dealing with the individual taxation of options and futures are the Income and Corporate Taxes Act 1988 and the Finance Act 1994. These acts stipulate that an individual's profits from options and futures are subject to capital gains tax, unless they can be shown to arise from a trading activity in which case they are subject to schedule D income tax against which legitimate expenses can be offset. In reality, the Inland Revenue will not accept an individual's use of options and futures as trading transactions unless the individual already has an established track record of trading in securities.

The general rules governing capital gains tax (CGT) are as follows. It is charged on net capital gains arising during a fiscal year (which ends on 5 April) and is payable on the following 1 December. Losses can be used to offset gains and unused losses can be carried forward indefinitely.

The specific rules governing CGT in respect of options and futures are as follows:

- Bought option, expires unexercised — premium loss arises when option expires: however, for out-of-the-money options that would otherwise be valueless, LIFFE operates a 'cabinet bid' facility which allows holders to sell their options for £1 per contract thereby establishing a loss before expiry;

- Written option, expires unallocated — premium gain arises when option was written;

- Bought option, subsequently sold — gain or loss arises on date of sale;

- Written option, subsequently bought to close — gain or loss arises on day of writing: cost of closing purchase is treated as incidental expense of opening sale;

- Bought call option, subsequently exercised — exerciser effectively acquires shares at the option exercise price *plus* the option premium on the day on which the exercise notice is delivered;

- Bought put option, subsequently exercised — exerciser effectively disposes of shares at the option exercise price on the day on which the exercise notice is delivered: option premium is an allowable expense of sale;

- Written call option, subsequently exercised — writer effectively sells shares on the day of notification of exercise, for exercise price *plus* premium received;

- Written put option, subsequently exercised — writer effectively acquires shares on the day of notification of exercise, for exercise price *minus* premium received;

- Long or short futures position, subsequently closed out or expires — accumulated variation margin generates a gain or loss on date of closure or expiry.

Capital gains generate a CGT charge. Premium gains are also taxable under CGT. Capital and premium losses can be used to offset current or future gains.

This appendix was based on: *Taxation of LIFFE Futures and Options for UK Institutional Investors*, LIFFE Administration and Management, and *Tax Guide for Private Clients*, LIFFE Administration and Management.

# Appendix C: Standard normal distribution table

|  | 0.00 | 0.01 | 0.02 | 0.03 | 0.04 | 0.05 | 0.06 | 0.07 | 0.08 | 0.09 |
|---|---|---|---|---|---|---|---|---|---|---|
| 0.0 | 0.0000 | 0.0040 | 0.0080 | 0.0120 | 0.0160 | 0.0199 | 0.0239 | 0.0279 | 0.0319 | 0.0359 |
| 0.1 | 0.0398 | 0.0438 | 0.0478 | 0.0517 | 0.0557 | 0.0596 | 0.0636 | 0.0675 | 0.0714 | 0.0753 |
| 0.2 | 0.0793 | 0.0832 | 0.0871 | 0.0910 | 0.0948 | 0.0987 | 0.1026 | 0.1064 | 0.1103 | 0.1141 |
| 0.3 | 0.1179 | 0.1217 | 0.1255 | 0.1293 | 0.1331 | 0.1368 | 0.1406 | 0.1443 | 0.1480 | 0.1517 |
| 0.4 | 0.1554 | 0.1591 | 0.1628 | 0.1664 | 0.1700 | 0.1736 | 0.1772 | 0.1808 | 0.1844 | 0.1879 |
| 0.5 | 0.1915 | 0.1950 | 0.1985 | 0.2019 | 0.2054 | 0.2088 | 0.2123 | 0.2157 | 0.2190 | 0.2224 |
| 0.6 | 0.2257 | 0.2291 | 0.2324 | 0.2357 | 0.2389 | 0.2422 | 0.2454 | 0.2486 | 0.2517 | 0.2549 |
| 0.7 | 0.2580 | 0.2611 | 0.2642 | 0.2673 | 0.2703 | 0.2734 | 0.2764 | 0.2794 | 0.2823 | 0.2852 |
| 0.8 | 0.2881 | 0.2910 | 0.2939 | 0.2967 | 0.2995 | 0.3023 | 0.3051 | 0.3078 | 0.3106 | 0.3133 |
| 0.9 | 0.3159 | 0.3186 | 0.3212 | 0.3238 | 0.3264 | 0.3289 | 0.3315 | 0.3340 | 0.3365 | 0.3389 |
| 1.0 | 0.3413 | 0.3438 | 0.3461 | 0.3485 | 0.3508 | 0.3531 | 0.3554 | 0.3577 | 0.3599 | 0.3621 |
| 1.1 | 0.3643 | 0.3665 | 0.3686 | 0.3708 | 0.3729 | 0.3749 | 0.3770 | 0.3790 | 0.3810 | 0.3830 |
| 1.2 | 0.3849 | 0.3869 | 0.3888 | 0.3907 | 0.3925 | 0.3944 | 0.3962 | 0.3980 | 0.3997 | 0.4015 |
| 1.3 | 0.4032 | 0.4049 | 0.4066 | 0.4082 | 0.4099 | 0.4115 | 0.4131 | 0.4147 | 0.4162 | 0.4177 |
| 1.4 | 0.4192 | 0.4207 | 0.4222 | 0.4236 | 0.4251 | 0.4265 | 0.4279 | 0.4292 | 0.4306 | 0.4319 |
| 1.5 | 0.4332 | 0.4345 | 0.4357 | 0.4370 | 0.4382 | 0.4394 | 0.4406 | 0.4418 | 0.4429 | 0.4441 |
| 1.6 | 0.4452 | 0.4463 | 0.4474 | 0.4484 | 0.4495 | 0.4505 | 0.4515 | 0.4525 | 0.4535 | 0.4545 |
| 1.7 | 0.4554 | 0.4564 | 0.4573 | 0.4582 | 0.4591 | 0.4599 | 0.4608 | 0.4616 | 0.4625 | 0.4633 |
| 1.8 | 0.4641 | 0.4649 | 0.4656 | 0.4664 | 0.4671 | 0.4678 | 0.4686 | 0.4693 | 0.4699 | 0.4706 |
| 1.9 | 0.4713 | 0.4719 | 0.4726 | 0.4732 | 0.4738 | 0.4744 | 0.4750 | 0.4756 | 0.4761 | 0.4767 |
| 2.0 | 0.4772 | 0.4778 | 0.4783 | 0.4788 | 0.4793 | 0.4798 | 0.4803 | 0.4808 | 0.4812 | 0.4817 |
| 2.1 | 0.4821 | 0.4826 | 0.4830 | 0.4834 | 0.4838 | 0.4842 | 0.4846 | 0.4850 | 0.4854 | 0.4857 |
| 2.2 | 0.4861 | 0.4864 | 0.4868 | 0.4871 | 0.4875 | 0.4878 | 0.4881 | 0.4884 | 0.4887 | 0.4890 |
| 2.3 | 0.4893 | 0.4896 | 0.4898 | 0.4901 | 0.4904 | 0.4906 | 0.4909 | 0.4911 | 0.4913 | 0.4916 |
| 2.4 | 0.4918 | 0.4920 | 0.4922 | 0.4925 | 0.4927 | 0.4929 | 0.4931 | 0.4932 | 0.4934 | 0.4936 |
| 2.5 | 0.4938 | 0.4940 | 0.4941 | 0.4943 | 0.4945 | 0.4946 | 0.4948 | 0.4949 | 0.4951 | 0.4952 |
| 2.6 | 0.4953 | 0.4955 | 0.4956 | 0.4957 | 0.4959 | 0.4960 | 0.4961 | 0.4962 | 0.4963 | 0.4964 |
| 2.7 | 0.4965 | 0.4966 | 0.4967 | 0.4968 | 0.4969 | 0.4970 | 0.4971 | 0.4972 | 0.4973 | 0.4974 |
| 2.8 | 0.4974 | 0.4975 | 0.4976 | 0.4977 | 0.4977 | 0.4978 | 0.4979 | 0.4979 | 0.4980 | 0.4981 |
| 2.9 | 0.4981 | 0.4982 | 0.4982 | 0.4983 | 0.4984 | 0.4984 | 0.4985 | 0.4985 | 0.4986 | 0.4986 |
| 3.0 | 0.4987 | 0.4987 | 0.4987 | 0.4988 | 0.4988 | 0.4989 | 0.4989 | 0.4989 | 0.4990 | 0.4990 |

This table can be used to calculate $N(d_i)$, the cumulative normal distribution functions needed for the Black-Scholes model of option pricing. If $d_i > 0$, add 0.5 to the relevant number above. If $d_i < 0$, subtract the relevant number above from 0.5.

**Selected references**

Black, F. (1976), 'The Pricing of Commodity Contracts', *Journal of Financial Economics*, 3, 167–79.

Black, F. (1975), 'Fact and Fantasy in the Use of Options', *Financial Analysts Journal,* July/August, 36–72.

Black, F. and Scholes, M. (1973), 'The Pricing of Options and Corporate Liabilities', *Journal of Political Economy*, 81, 637–54.

Bookstaber, R. (1991), *Option Pricing and Investment Strategies*, McGraw-Hill, London.

Briys, E., Bellalah, M., Mai, H.M., and de Varenne, F. (1998), *Options, Futures and Exotic Derivatives*, Wiley, Chichester.

Connolly, K.B. (1997), *Buying and Selling Volatility*, Wiley, Chichester.

Cox, J.C., Ross, S.A. and Rubinstein, M. (1979), 'Option Pricing: A Simplified Approach', *Journal of Financial Economics*, 7, 229–63.

Cox, J.C. and Rubinstein, M. (1985), *Options Markets*, Prentice-Hall, Englewood Cliffs, NJ.

Das, S. (1995), 'From Genesis to Revelation: An Overview of Exotic Options', *IFR Financial Products*, No.10, January 25.

Dubofsky, D. (1992), *Options and Financial Futures*, McGraw-Hill, New York.

Edwards, E. and Ma, C. (1992), *Futures and Options*, McGraw-Hill, New York.

Elton, E.J. and Gruber, M.J. (1995), *Modern Portfolio Theory and Investment Analysis*, John Wiley, New York. (Chapter 22.)

*Financial Derivatives and Risk Management*, IFR Publishing, London.

Financial Times Survey (1989), 'Financial Futures and Options', *Financial Times* (London), 8 March.

Fitzgerald, M.D. (1987), *Financial Options*, Euromoney Publications, London. (Chapters 1–4, 6–8.)

Francis, J.C. (1991), *Investments*, McGraw-Hill, Singapore. (Chapters 22 and 23.)

Gemmill, G. (1993), *Options Pricing*, McGraw Hill, London.

Geske, R. (1979), 'The Valuation of Compound Options', *Journal of Financial Economics*, 7, 63–81.

Gibson, R. (1991), *Option Valuation*, McGraw-Hill, New York.

Goldman, B., Sosin, H. and Gatto, M.A. (1979), 'Path-Dependent Options: Buy at the Low, Sell at the High', *Journal of Finance*, 34, 1111–27.

Hull, J.C. (1993), *Options, Futures and Other Derivative Securities*, Prentice-Hall, Englewood Cliff, NJ.

*IFR Financial Products*, IFR Publishing, London.

Johnson, R.S. and Giaccotto, C. (1995), *Options and Futures*, West Publishing Co., St. Paul, MN.

Kemna, A. and Vorst, A. (1990), 'A Pricing Method for Options Based on Average Asset Values', *Journal of Banking and Finance*, 14, 113–29.

Kolb, R. (1994), *Options*, Kolb Publishing Company, Miami, FL.

Kolb, R. (1997), *Futures, Options and Swaps*, Blackwell, Oxford.

*Margining for Equity and Index Options*, London Clearing House.

Magrabe, W. (1978), 'The Value of an Option to Exchange One Asset for Another', *Journal of Finance*, 33, 177–86.

Merton, R. (1973), 'The Theory of Rational Option Pricing', *Bell Journal of Economics and Management Science*, 4, 141–83.

Natenberg, S. (1994), *Option Volatility and Pricing*, Irwin Professional, Chicago.

Nelken, U. (ed.)(1996), *The Handbook of Exotic Options*, Irwin, Chicago.

Ritchken, P. (1987), *Options*, HarperCollins, Cleveland, Ohio.

Rubinstein, M. (1991), 'Breaking down the Barriers', *Risk*, September.

Rutterford, J. (1991), *Introduction to Stock Exchange Investments*, Macmillan, London. (Chapter 7.)

Sharpe, W.F., Alexander, G. and Bailey, J. (1995), *Investments*, Prentice-Hall, Englewood Cliffs, NJ. (Chapter 20.)

Stoll, H.R. (1969), 'The Relationship Between Put and Call Option Prices', *Journal of Finance,* 24, 802–24.

Turnbull, S.M. and Wakeman, L.M. (1991), 'A Quick Algorithm for Pricing European Average Options', *Journal of Financial and Quantitative Analysis*, 26, 377–89.

*Understanding London SPAN*, London Clearing House.

Weston, J.F. and Copeland, T.E. (1992), *Managerial Finance*, Dryden Press, Chicago. (Chapter 12.)

Wilmott, P., Howison, S. and Dewynne, J. (1995), *The Mathematics of Financial Derivatives*, Cambridge University Press, Cambridge.

**Exercises**

1  In what direction do the following variables influence the price of a call option on an individual security?

a) the current price of a security

b) the expected future price of a security

c) the exercise price

d) the riskless rate of interest

e) the maturity date of the option

f) the variance of the price of the underlying security.

2 a) What is the difference between an American option and a European option?

   b) What is the difference between an in-the-money option and an out-of-the-money option?

3 You buy a December call option on ABC shares with an exercise price of 120p for 8p and sell a December call option with an exercise price of 130p for 3p. What is the maximum profit at expiry that you can achieve on your spread position, and under what conditions will it arise?

4 a) Use an option diagram to show the profit and loss profile of a call option: (i) before expiry and (ii) at expiry.

   b) Indicate the effects on the position of the profit and loss profile of (i) an increase in the volatility of the price of the underlying security and (ii) the passage of time.

5 What are the differences between:

   a) an options straddle and an option spread?

   b) a strangle, a strap and a strip?

6 What are the differences between vertical, horizontal and diagonal options spreads?

7 What advantages do exchange-traded options have over-the-counter options? What disadvantages do they have?

8 What are the differences between premium-paid and premium-margined options? Give an example of each type of option.

9 a) Ignoring transaction costs, what is the value of one contract on the following options on ABC shares trading in the UK (ABC shares are currently trading at 100p)?

   (i)  April 80p calls with a premium of 25p

   (ii) April 90p puts with a premium of 6p

   b) If ABC shares are trading at 85p on the expiry date of the April options, calculate the net profit from

   (i)  a long position in the April calls and

   (ii) a short position in the April puts,

   both established at the premiums given in a).

10 You buy one short sterling 90.00 put option at 0.25.

   a) Calculate the total premium paid.

   b) What is the maximum future borrowing rate that you lock in?

   c) Calculate the effective borrowing rate if on the expiry date of the option:

   (i)  the three-month interest rate is 9 per cent

   (ii) the three-month interest rate is 11 per cent.

11 An investor believes that there are likely to be major moves in the German bond market in the near future and so decides to sell 100 strangles using the following June options on German government bond futures when the June future is trading at 93.49–93.50:

> June 93.00 put, trading at 0.47–0.51, implied volatility 7.8%;
> June 94.00 call, trading at 0.42–0.46, implied volatility 7.3%.

Two weeks later the investor closes his position by buying 100 strangles when the June future is trading at 93.29–93.30:

> June 93.00 put, trading at 0.26–0.30, implied volatility 7.5%;
> June 94.00 call, trading at 0.11–0.15, implied volatility 7.1%.

a) Calculate the profit or loss on the strangle.

b) Provide an explanation for why this profit or loss occurred.

12 Why will an American call option on a non-dividend-paying share never be exercised before maturity?

13 Ignoring transaction costs, the creation of an option contract involves a zero-sum game being played between the buyer and the writer. The buyer gains or loses exactly the opposite of what the writer gains or loses. How therefore can both enter into the contract expecting a positive return?

14 What is a riskless hedge portfolio? How would you construct such a portfolio using call options?

15 Using the simple one-period binomial option pricing model, find the value of a call option with an exercise price of 90p when the underlying security price is currently trading at 97p and has the same chance to rise to 115p or fall to 85p. The riskless interest rate is 10 per cent.

16 a) Given that the price of a non-dividend-paying share is 25p and has a volatility of 35 per cent, use the Black-Scholes model to determine the value of a call option that has an exercise price of 23p and 91 days to expiry. The riskless interest rate is 10 per cent.

b) How many call options must you write in order to create a riskless hedge, given that you own 132,000 shares?

17 Calculate the implied volatility on a security given the following information: a call option on the security has a premium of 3.5p, the security itself is trading at 50p, the call has an exercise price of 51p and has 120 days to maturity, and the riskless interest rate is 12 per cent.

18 What is the delta of an option? Why is it a useful concept?

19 What is put-call parity? Why is it important?

20 How is the Black-Scholes formula for a call option modified if:

a) the underlying security pays dividends?

b) the underlying security is a futures contract?

21 What are the main similarities and differences between options and warrants?

22 Why are convertible bonds attractive to investors? When is it optimal to convert a convertible bond?

23 Why are convertible bonds attractive to issuers? When is it optimal to call a convertible bond?

24 What are the main differences between traded and traditional options?

25 What are the main similarities and differences between exchange-traded options and OTC options?

26 Explain how writing covered calls can enhance portfolio return at little risk.

27 Show how writing put options gives a similar outcome to underwriting.

28 What are the main types of exotic option now available?

29 Consider the following index portfolio of FTSE 100 futures, American FTSE 100 options (SEI) and European FTSE 100 options (ESX):

> 2 × Short SEI December calls with an exercise price of 2500;
> 1 × Long ESX March put with an exercise price of 2625;
> 4 × Long December FTSE futures.

Suppose that the index closed at 2574, and the SEI and ESX options closed at 144 and 99 respectively. Suppose also that the following risk arrays have been calculated by LIFFE:

| Line | SEI call 2500 | ESX put 2625 | FTSE future | Total loss (£) |
|------|---------------|--------------|-------------|----------------|
| 1  | −2 × −100 | 1 × −175 | 4 ×      0 | 25    |
| 2  | −2 ×  145 | 1 ×  175 | 4 ×      0 | −115  |
| 3  | −2 × −230 | 1 ×  −95 | 4 ×  −500 | −1635 |
| 4  | −2 ×    0 | 1 ×  255 | 4 ×  −500 | −1745 |
| 5  | −2 ×   30 | 1 × −260 | 4 ×   500 | 1680  |
| 6  | −2 ×  280 | 1 ×   90 | 4 ×   500 | 1530  |
| 7  | −2 × −370 | 1 ×  −15 | 4 × −1000 | −3275 |
| 8  | −2 × −150 | 1 ×  325 | 4 × −1000 | −3375 |
| 9  | −2 ×  155 | 1 × −350 | 4 ×  1000 | 3340  |
| 10 | −2 ×  140 | 1 ×    0 | 4 ×  1000 | 3720  |
| 11 | −2 × −515 | 1 ×   55 | 4 × −1500 | −4915 |
| 12 | −2 × −305 | 1 ×  395 | 4 × −1500 | −4995 |
| 13 | −2 ×  270 | 1 × −445 | 4 ×  1500 | 5015  |
| 14 | −2 ×  530 | 1 × −100 | 4 ×  1500 | 4840  |
| 15 | −2 × −310 | 1 ×  144 | 4 × −1050 | −3436 |
| 16 | −2 ×  249 | 1 × −208 | 4 ×  1050 | 3494  |

a) Calculate the initial margin for the calls, put and futures separately.

b) Calculate the initial margin for the portfolio comprising the calls, put and futures combined. How much initial margin is saved by using the portfolio approach to margining?

c) Calculate the net liquidation value for the options.

d) Calculate the total margin for the portfolio of options and futures.

# Chapter 10

# Synthetic securities

In this the final chapter on security valuation, we examine synthetic securities, that is, securities that are either constructed from basic securities or deconstructed from basic securities. We begin by analyzing the four basic building blocks of synthetic securities, and then examine some important examples of synthetic securities: synthetic options, synthetic futures, swaps, forward rate agreements, caps, floors and collars, bundled and unbundled securities.

## 10.1   The basic building blocks of synthetic securities

A *synthetic security* (or *proxy*) is simply a 'security' that is 'constructed' from combinations of two or more basic securities. This construction process is known as *financial engineering*.

There are just four basic securities that are needed to construct any form of synthetic security: shares (in the case of equity-based synthetics), riskless bonds, call options and put options. Figure 10.1 shows the (long-run) profit and loss profiles of the four basic securities as a function of the underlying share price.

Panel (a) depicts the profit and loss profile for a share. The origin represents the initial purchase or sale price of the share. If the share was purchased, then the upward-sloping line represents the profit and loss profile as the share price changes with respect to the original purchase price. If the share was sold short, then the downward-sloping line shows the profit and loss profile as the share price changes with respect to the original sale price. Panel (b) shows the profit and loss profile for long and short positions in a pure discount (zero-coupon) riskless bond. A long bond is equivalent to lending and a short bond is equivalent to borrowing. Given that the bond is riskless, the profit and loss will be independent of the share price. Panel (c) shows the profit and loss for long and short positions in a call option on the share, with the exercise price equal to the initial share price (i.e. for an option that is at-the-money). Panel (d) shows the profit and loss profile for a put option.

The following relationship holds between the four building blocks:

$$S + P = B + C, \tag{10.1}$$

where:

**Figure 10.1** The four basic building blocks of synthetic securities:  (a) Shares, (b) Riskless bonds, (c) Call options, (d) Put options

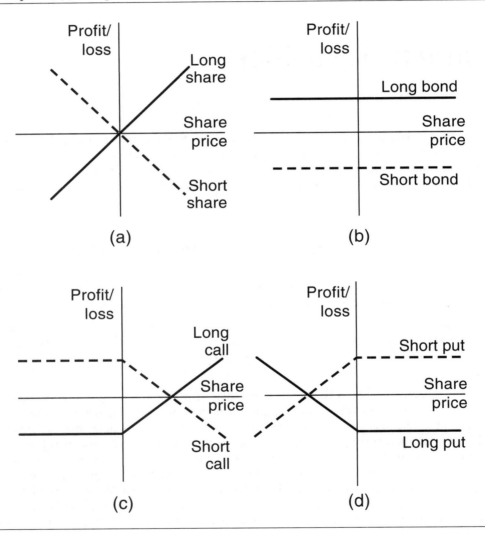

| | | |
|---|---|---|
| $S$ | = | one share; |
| $B$ | = | one riskless pure discount bond with maturity value $X$; |
| $C$ | = | one call option (with exercise price $X$ and time to maturity $T$) written on the share; |
| $P$ | = | one put option (with exercise price $X$ and the same expiry date as the call) written on the share. |

**Figure 10.2** Combining a share and a long put option

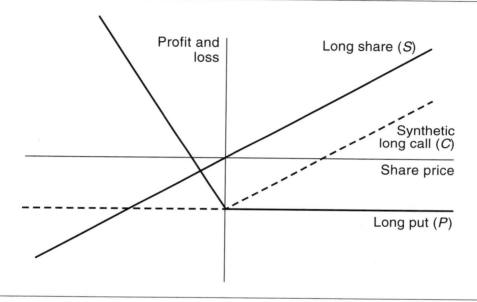

This can be demonstrated graphically. Figure 10.2 shows the effect of combining the share and the long put option. The result, which is achieved by vertically summing the two profit and loss profiles, is a synthetic long call (the dotted line in Figure 10.2). Figure 10.3 shows the effect of combining a long call option and a riskless bond. The result is another synthetic long call. The investment in the riskless bond can be altered to ensure that the profit and loss profiles of the two synthetic calls in Figures 10.2 and 10.3 are identical, in which case (10.1) is proved.

Equation (10.1) is a relationship between the quantities of the basic building blocks. A similar relationship holds between the prices of the securities. On the expiry date, the following relationship holds:

$$P_T^S + P_T^P = P_T^B + P_T^C, \tag{10.2}$$

where:

| | | | |
|---|---|---|---|
| $P_T^S$ | = | | price of share on expiry date of the options; |
| $P_T^B$ | = | $X$ = | price of riskless bond on expiry date of the options; |
| $P_T^C$ | = | | price of call option at expiry; |
| $P_T^P$ | = | | price of put option at expiry. |

**Figure 10.3** Combining a long call option and a riskless bond

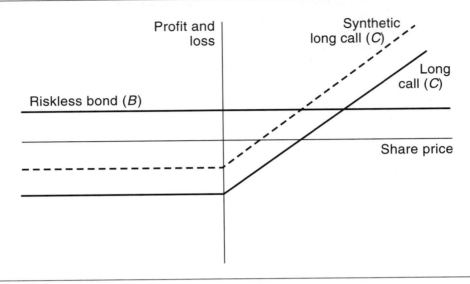

In order to find the four current prices, we recognize that the relationship in (10.1) is riskless (i.e. that $S + P - C$ is equivalent to a riskless bond and so must be riskless). Therefore we can discount the terminal prices in (10.2) back to current prices at the risk-free rate, $r$:

$$P^S + P^P = e^{-rT}X + P^C. \tag{10.3}$$

Equation (10.3) can also be used to determine the fair price of any one building block, once we know the fair prices of the remaining three building blocks. For example, the fair price of a put is given by:

$$P_0^P = P_0^C - P_0^S + e^{-rT}X, \tag{10.4}$$

where the subscript 0 indicates the fair price. We have seen this relationship before, because it is nothing more than the put-call parity relationship for determining the fair price of a European put (see section 9.4.6).

It can be shown that any share-based synthetic security is a function of two or more of these building blocks. Other types of synthetic securities, such as currency-based or bond-based synthetic securities, can be constructed if the underlying security in (10.1) is a currency or a risky bond rather than a share.

## 10.2   Synthetic options and futures

It is easy to see how *synthetic options* and *futures* can be constructed using the four building blocks.

We have already seen (Figure 10.2) that a synthetic long call can be constructed from a combination of a long share and a long put. A synthetic short call can be constructed by combining a short share and a short put (Figure 10.4).

**Figure 10.4** Synthetic short call

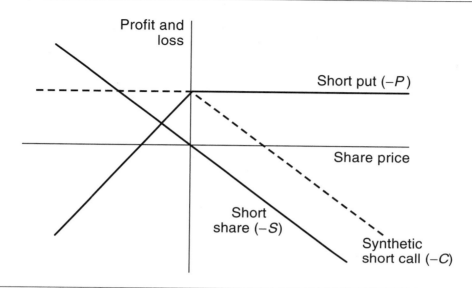

A synthetic long put can be constructed from a long call and a short share (Figure 10.5). A synthetic short put can be constructed from a short call and a long share (Figure 10.6).

A synthetic long future can be constructed from a long call and a short put (Figure 10.7), whereas a synthetic short future can be constructed from a short call and a long put (Figure 10.8). The exercise price of all these options must equal the current forward price of the underlying security.

Synthetic futures (with a particular set of characteristics) can also be constructed from combinations of real futures (with a different set of characteristics), as the following examples illustrate.

The sale of June–September long gilt straddle is equivalent to a synthetic short September Treasury bill future, since both involve three-month rates over the same period on government instruments. This can be seen from an examination of Figure 10.9. On 1 April, a fund manager buys a June long gilt future trading at 100.50 and sells a September long gilt future trading at 100.75. Suppose that he holds both contracts until maturity. This means that on 30 June he will take delivery of £100 nominal of the CTD gilt at a purchase price of £100.50 (transaction AB in Figure 10.9). We assume for simplicity that the CTD is a 7 per cent coupon gilt and so has a price factor of 1.0. Its purchase will be financed from the proceeds of the sale of the September gilt. The implied borrowing cost will be calculated shortly. The fund manager holds onto the gilt and receives accrued interest on the bond of £1.75 per £100 nominal at C (transaction BC). On 30 September the fund manager delivers the £100 nominal of the 7 per cent CTD gilt and receives £100.75 (transaction CD). Finally, the proceeds from the sale are used to repay the loan taken out to finance the gilt purchase on 30 June. The implied borrowing cost, $r$, is found from the following calculation:

$$100.50[1+r(92/365)] = 100.75+1.75,$$

implying a borrowing cost of 7.90 per cent. The right-hand side of the equation measures the income received from the straddle as of 30 September, while the left-hand side measures the expenditure

**Figure 10.5** Synthetic long put

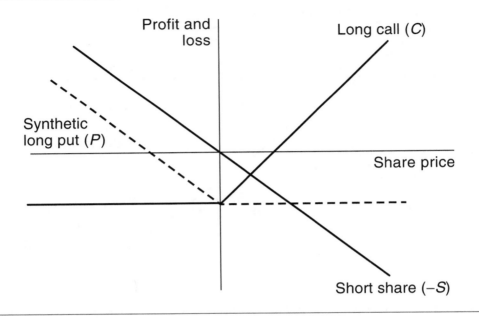

**Figure 10.6** Synthetic short put

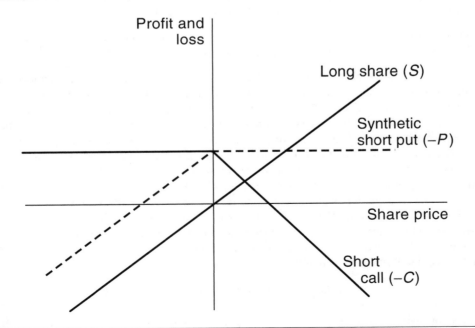

**Figure 10.7** Synthetic long future

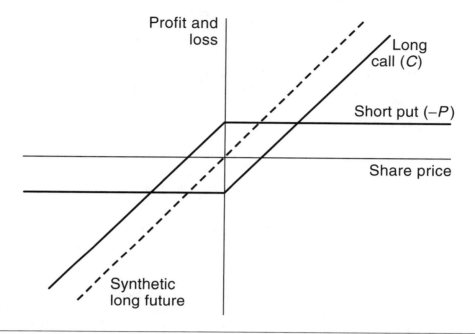

**Figure 10.8** Synthetic short future

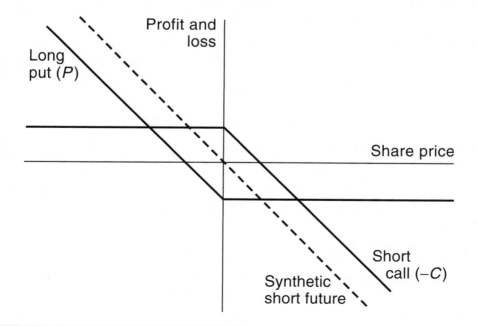

**Figure 10.9** Synthetic Treasury bill future

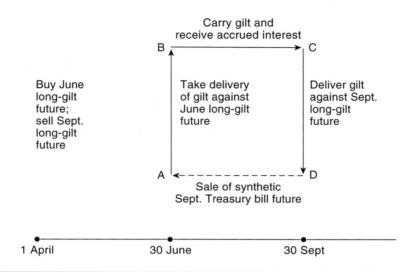

incurred in maintaining the straddle as of the same date. But the three-month borrowing cost of 7.90 per cent p.a. is identical to the sale of a September Treasury bill for 98.05 (i.e., $100/[1 + 0.079(92/365)]$). So a long June–September long gilt straddle is equivalent to the sale of a synthetic September Treasury bill future which is a three-month loan at the Treasury bill rate (transaction DA).

Synthetic US interest rate futures can be constructed by combining UK interest rate futures and currency futures. This can be seen from an examination of Figure 10.10. On 1 April, the fund manager buys a June sterling exchange rate futures contract trading at \$1.6027 per £ and sells a September exchange rate futures contract trading at \$1.6135 per £. He also buys a June three-month sterling time deposit futures contract trading at 89.05, implying a UK rate of interest between June and September of 10.95 per cent (100 − 89.05). Suppose again that he holds all contracts to maturity. This means that on 30 June he converts \$1 into £0.6239 (i.e. 1/1.6027) (transaction AB in Figure 10.10). The £0.6239 is then invested at 10.95 per cent for 92 days, at the end of which it is worth

$$£0.6239[1 + 0.1095(92/365)] \; = \; £0.6411$$

(transaction BC). On 30 September, the £0.6411 is converted back into \$1.0344 (i.e. 0.6411 × 1.6135) (transaction CD). If the original \$1 had been borrowed, this sum could have been used to repay that loan with interest. The implied interest rate on the loan over 92 days is 13.65 per cent p.a. (transaction DA in Figure 10.10). So the three futures contracts purchased on 1 April are equivalent to the sale of a synthetic June US interest rate future which is equivalent to a three-month dollar loan at 13.65 per cent per annum.

It should be obvious from these examples that the main assumption underlying synthetic securities is the absence of riskless arbitrage. The second example works on the basis of the forward interest rate parity assumption holding, so that riskless arbitrage profits from setting up the synthetic are not possible. This is the principal condition for pricing new synthetic securities.

Synthetic futures are useful where the real future is not traded. For example, there are many currencies in which a short-term interest rate future is not traded, e.g. the Swiss franc. A synthetic

**Figure 10.10** Synthetic US interest rate future

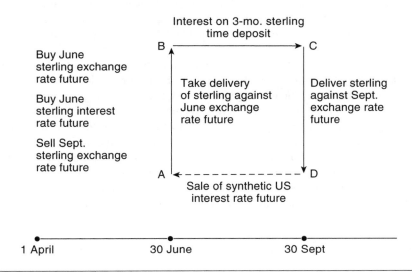

three-month Swiss franc interest rate future could be constructed from US dollar-Swiss franc exchange rate contracts and the three-month eurodollar deposit contract.

Similarly, synthetic options are useful when the corresponding real option is not traded. An important example is *cross-rate options*, that is, currency options that do not involve the US dollar on one side of the transaction. Most traded currency options involve the US dollar, e.g. the sterling contract and the Deutschmark contract both involve exchanging the contract currency into US dollars. However, suppose that someone wanted to buy sterling directly with Deutschmarks. In the absence of a direct sterling-Deutschmark call option, a synthetic (cross-rate) sterling-Deutschmark call option could be constructed through the simultaneous purchase of a sterling call option and a Deutschmark put option. Suppose that the sterling call option has an exercise price of $1.50 per £1 and that the Deutschmark put option has an exercise price of DM1.50 per $1. If the put option is exercised DM2.25 could be exchanged for $1.50 (i.e. 1.5 × DM1.50 per $1 = DM2.25 per $1.50). If the call option is then immediately exercised, the $1.50 can be exchanged for £1. This implies that the two options can be exercised to give an exchange of Deutschmarks for sterling at an effective exchange rate of DM2.25 per £1. In contrast, if an individual wanted the option to exchange sterling for Deutschmarks, this could be effected by buying both a sterling put option and a Deutschmark call option to create a synthetic (cross-rate) sterling-Deutschmark put option.

## 10.3 Swaps

*Swaps* (or *contracts for differences*) are synthetic securities involving combinations of two or more basic building blocks. Most swaps currently operating involve combinations of two or more cash market securities (e.g. a fixed interest rate security combined with a floating interest rate security, possibly also combined with a currency transaction). Standard swaps are known as *plain vanilla swaps*. However, there are also swaps that involve a futures or forward component, as well as swaps that involve an option component. The market for swaps is organized by members of the International Swaps and Derivatives Association (ISDA). There are three relevant dates with any swap: the *trade date* (on which the terms of the swap are agreed), the *effective date* (on which the interest rates begin to accrue) and the *termination* (or *maturity*) *date* (on which the swap payments end).

Institutional investors in the UK (such as pension funds) have been involved in swap agreements since the late 1960s when they took out parallel or back-to-back currency loans to finance their overseas investments in a way that was compatible with UK exchange control regulations then in force. The loan operated as follows. There was a matching agreement between a UK investor and an overseas counterparty, whereby the counterparty purchased overseas assets for the UK investor, who in turn purchased an equivalent amount of sterling assets for the foreign institution. While it involved no direct exchange of principal, this method of overseas investment was clearly very cumbersome and was made even more complicated in the period before June 1979 by additional Bank of England regulations which required every $100 of currency loan to be covered by $115 of dollar assets, with the additional dollar assets being purchased with investment currency at a premium above the official rate.

The back-to-back currency loan was the precursor to the currency swap, the first example of this being between IBM and the World Bank in 1981. The swap market can be said to date from this time. The main types of swap are interest rate swaps, basis swaps, fixed-rate currency swaps, currency coupon swaps, and asset swaps. All these swaps work on the principle that different institutions have different comparative advantages, and that, as a result, there can be gains from any two institutions trading with each other. We will examine each of them in turn.

### 10.3.1   Interest rate swaps

Interest rate swaps are the most important type of swap in terms of volume of transactions. An *interest rate swap* (or *coupon swap*) is an agreement between two counterparties to exchange fixed interest rate payments for floating interest rate payments in the same currency calculated with reference to an agreed notional amount of principal (hence the alternative name, *contract for differences*). The principal amount, which is equivalent to the value of the underlying assets or liabilities that are 'swapped', is never physically exchanged but is used merely to calculate interest payments. The purpose of the swap is to transform a fixed-rate liability into a floating-rate liability and vice versa. The liability so transformed is therefore a synthetic security comprising the difference between two cash market liabilities. The floating rate that is used in most interest rate swaps is calculated with reference to LIBOR; if the floating rate is LIBOR itself with no margin above or below, then the swap is known as a *LIBOR flat swap*. Most interest rate swaps are in US dollars, but those in yen, sterling, Swiss francs and Deutschmarks are also important. Interest rate swaps have a similar structure to interest rate futures contracts in the sense that the terms of the future obligations under the swap are determined today.

The motive underlying an interest rate swap is to exploit a comparative advantage and to make a gain from trade. To illustrate this, we will consider Figure 10.11, which shows the interest rate swap established between Bank A and Bank B with funds provided by two companies, Company I and Company II. Bank A has a credit rating of AAA while B has one of BBB. The cost of borrowing directly from the companies is as follows:

**Figure 10.11** Interest rate swap

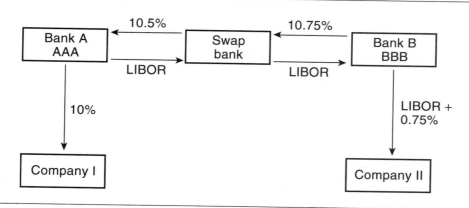

|  | **Bank A (AAA)** | **Bank B (BBB)** | **Comparative advantage of A over B** |
|---|---|---|---|
| Fixed-rate loans | 10% | 12% | 2% |
| Floating-rate loans | LIBOR + 0.25% | LIBOR + 0.75% | 0.5% |

While A has an absolute advantage in borrowing both fixed-rate and floating-rate funds, it has a *comparative advantage* in fixed-rate loans, giving B a comparative advantage in floating-rate loans. A swap is therefore feasible if A would prefer to have a floating-rate loan and B would prefer to have a fixed-rate loan. Company I is willing to make fixed-rate loans to (or purchase the bonds of) AAA banks at a fixed rate of 10 per cent. Company II is willing to make variable rate loans to BBB companies at LIBOR + 0.75 per cent.

If the swap is executed using the services of a swap bank intermediary, Bank A will make floating-rate payments to Bank B and, in return, B will make fixed-rate payments to A as indicated in Figure 10.11. The effect of the swap on each counterparty involved might be as follows:

| Bank A: | Borrows fixed at | 10% |
|---|---|---|
|  | Receives from swap bank | (10.5%) |
|  | Pays to swap bank | LIBOR |
|  |  | LIBOR − 0.5% |

and so effectively borrows floating-rate funds (i.e. has created a synthetic floating-rate loan) at LIBOR − 0.5 per cent, which is less than the rate at which it can borrow these funds directly from the market (i.e. LIBOR + 0.25 per cent, a saving of 0.75 per cent).

| Bank B: | Borrows floating at | LIBOR + 0.75% |
|---|---|---|
|  | Receives from swap bank | (LIBOR) |
|  | Pays to swap bank | 10.75% |
|  |  | 11.5% |

and so effectively borrows fixed-rate funds (i.e. has created a synthetic fixed-rate loan) at 11.5 per cent, which is less than the rate at which it could borrow such funds directly from the market (i.e. 12 per cent, a gain from trade of 0.5 per cent).

|                | The swap bank: | Pays A          | (10.5%)  |
|                |                | Receives from A | LIBOR    |
|                |                | Pays B          | (LIBOR)  |
|                |                | Receives from B | 10.75%   |
|                |                |                 | 0.25%    |

and so makes 0.25 per cent out of the deal.

The companies involved do not gain directly from the swap itself; they just receive the market return on their loans. However, it is conceivable that, if the bargaining position of the two companies is sufficiently strong, some of the gains made by the two counterparties could be shared with them. Company I might be able to negotiate a return of 10.25 per cent rather than 10 per cent, and company II might be able to negotiate a return of LIBOR + 1 per cent rather than LIBOR + 0.75 per cent.

When a swap bank makes a quote on an interest rate swap, it does so on the following terms: it may, for example, quote 45–55 (or $T + 45$–55) for a 3-year swap. This means that the swap bank is willing either to pay a fixed rate of 45 basis points over the yield on three-year government (Treasury) bonds and receive LIBOR, or to receive a fixed rate of 55 basis points over the yield on three-year government bonds and pay LIBOR.

The floating rate payments on a swap (with the exception of the first payment) are, of course, not known when the swap is taken out, but we can calculate the break-even payments, as the following example illustrates. Consider a one-year interest rate swap against 6 month LIBOR on a notional sum of £10m. Suppose that the annual fixed rate is 9.5 per cent p.a. (annual bond basis), while the first LIBOR payment is 8.75 per cent (semi-annual money market basis). The second LIBOR payment in six months' time is unknown at the beginning of the year. The payment on the fixed leg is:

$$£10,000,000 \times 0.095 = £950,000.00.$$

The first floating payment is:

$$£10,000,000 \times 0.075 \times \frac{182}{365} = £373,972.60.$$

The difference of £576,027.40 is available for paying the second floating payment on £10m and also for paying the interest on the funds needed to borrow the first floating payment of £373,972.60 over the second six month period until the fixed payment of £950,000.00 is made. The break-even floating interest rate is determined by solving:

$$576,027.40 = 10,373,972.60 \times r \times \frac{183}{365}$$

that is,

$$r = 0.1107,$$

or 11.07 per cent (semi-annual money market basis). This is the same as the forward interest rate for the second six month period.

Interest rate swaps help to generate another type of yield curve called the *swap yield curve*. A *swap yield* is the fixed rate payment (as a proportion of the notional principal) that equates the present value of the fixed rate leg of the swap to the expected present value of the floating rate leg where the floating rate leg is valued using a combination of spot and forward yields. The swap yield so determined is therefore the fair rate for the swap and the present value so determined is therefore the fair price for (both legs of) the swap. Dealing at the swap yield therefore implies that an expected zero-sum game is being played between the two counterparties to the swap: if realized floating rates over the life of the swap differ from the forward rates, then one counterparty will gain at the expense of the other.

Suppose that we have the following spot and forward yields:

| Year | Spot yield (%) | Forward yield (%) |
|------|----------------|-------------------|
| 1 | 10.00 | 10.00 |
| 2 | 10.26 | 10.53 |
| 3 | 10.81 | 11.92 |

Suppose also that we have a LIBOR flat swap on a notional principal of £100. The expected floating rate cash flows on the swap are found by multiplying the notional principal by the forward rates, on the grounds that the forward rates represent the market's best expectation about what the spot floating rates will be in the future. The present values of these expected floating rate cash flows is found by discounting them using the spot yields. Hence for a one-year swap, the present value of the floating rate cash flows is:

$$\frac{£10}{1.10} = £9.09.$$

For a two-year swap, the present value of the floating rate cash flows is:

$$\frac{£10}{1.10} + \frac{£10.53}{(1.1026)^2} = £17.75,$$

while for a three-year swap, the present value of the floating rate cash flows is:

$$\frac{£10}{1.10} + \frac{£10.53}{(1.1026)^2} + \frac{£11.92}{(1.1081)^3} = £26.51.$$

These are also the present values of the fixed rate cash flows:

$$\frac{£X}{1.10} = £9.09,$$

implying that the one-year fixed rate cash flow is £10:

$$\frac{£X}{1.10} + \frac{£X}{(1.1026)^2} = £17.75,$$

implying that the two-year fixed rate cash flows are £10.25 per year, and:

$$\frac{£X}{1.10} + \frac{£X}{(1.1026)^2} + \frac{£X}{(1.1081)^3} = £26.51,$$

implying that the three-year fixed rate cash flows are £10.75. Given that the notional principal of the swap is £100, the one-, two- and three-year swap yields are, respectively, 10.00 per cent, 10.25 per cent and 10.75 per cent.

Notice that in the case of a LIBOR flat swap, the swap yields are identical to the par yields (see section 5.5.5). This is why an interest rate swap that is priced using par yields is sometimes known as a *par swap*. Take, for example, a three-year par swap on a notional principal of £100. The three-year par yield (swap yield) is 10.75 per cent. The fixed rate leg of the swap involves making a series of payments of £10.75 at the end of each of the next three years together with a notional return of principal of £100. These cash flows have a present value, when discounted at the three-year par yield (swap yield), equal to par (£100):

$$100 = \frac{10.75}{(1.1075)} + \frac{10.75}{(1.1075)^2} + \frac{110.75}{(1.1075)^3}.$$

The analysis also shows that an interest rate swap is in reality a series of forward interest rate contracts, with the payments being valued at the corresponding spot rates. However an interest rate swap differs slightly from a forward rate agreement (see section 10.4 below): in the former case undiscounted interest payments are exchanged between two counterparties at the end of each floating rate period, whereas in the latter case, a single discounted interest rate payment is made by one counterparty to the other, at the beginning of each floating rate period. Also it should be noted that this method of valuing swaps is not completely correct since it ignores default risk. If one counterparty defaults, the complete sequence of forward contracts will be voided. Therefore the credit risk of the counterparty should be taken into account when valuing swaps.

As an alternative to viewing interest rate swaps as a series of forward interest rate contracts, it is possible to view them as the difference between a long position in one bond and a short position in another bond. One of the bonds is a fixed-coupon bond, while the other is a floating rate note. In each case, the par value of the bond will equal the notional principal of the swap. In the case of the fixed-coupon bond, the coupon will equal the par yield of the same term; in the case of the FRN, the coupon will equal LIBOR. The coupons will be discounted at the appropriate spot yield.

We can illustrate this using the above example of a three-year par swap on a notional principal of £100. The three-year par yield is 10.75 per cent, so the fixed coupon bond pays £10.75 annually for three years. At the beginning of the swap, its price will be:

$$P_{FC} = \frac{£10.75}{1.10} + \frac{£10.75}{(1.1026)^2} + \frac{£110.75}{(1.1081)^3} = £100.$$

The first coupon on the FRN will be paid at the end of the first year, and will equal the current one-year spot rate (£10). At the time a coupon is paid the FRN always equals its par value, so at the beginning of the swap, its price will be:

$$P_{FRN} = \frac{£110}{(1.10)} = £100.$$

This implies that at the beginning of a swap, its value is always zero:

$$P_{Swap} = P_{FC} - P_{FRN} = 0. \tag{10.5}$$

Note that this is the value of the swap to the counterparty receiving fixed and paying floating. The value of the swap to the other counterparty is:

$$P_{Swap} = P_{FRN} - P_{FC}, \tag{10.6}$$

which is also zero at the beginning. The value is also zero for both counterparties at the end of the swap.

However, during its life, a swap's value can be positive or negative. Suppose that six months into the life of the swap, the following spot yields are observed:

| Year | Spot yield (%) |
|------|----------------|
| 0.5  | 10.50          |
| 1.5  | 10.75          |
| 2.5  | 11.00          |

The value of the two bonds will now be:

$$P_{FC} = \frac{£10.75}{(1.1050)^{0.5}} + \frac{£10.75}{(1.1075)^{1.5}} + \frac{£110.75}{(1.11)^{2.5}} = £104.77,$$

and:

$$P_{FRN} = \frac{£110}{(1.1050)^{0.5}} = £104.64.$$

The value of the swap to the floating rate payer is:

$$P_{Swap} = £104.77 - £104.64 = £0.13,$$

while its value to the fixed rate payer is $-£0.13$. As with the treatment of swaps as a series of forward interest rate contracts, this way of valuing swaps should ideally take into account counterparty credit risk.

### 10.3.2  Basis swaps

*Basis swaps* are the same as floating/floating interest rate swaps. This means that floating-rate payments calculated on one basis are swapped for floating-rate payments on another basis. The main examples are the US dollar prime rate – US dollar LIBOR swap, US dollar commercial paper – US dollar LIBOR swap, and the 1 month US dollar LIBOR – 6 month US dollar LIBOR swap. A variation is a *quanto swap* where LIBOR is set in one currency and paid in another.

### 10.3.3  Currency swaps

*Currency swaps* are agreements to exchange payments in one currency for those in another. Sometimes the principal is exchanged as well as the interest payments. The structure of a currency swap is similar to a forward or futures contract in foreign exchange. There are two types of currency swap: fixed-rate currency swaps and currency coupon swaps.

Most currency swaps involve the US dollar on one side of the transaction, but cross-rate currency combinations such as the Deutschmark-yen are also important. Many eurobonds are now issued in unusual currencies such as the Danish krone, the Australian dollar or the New Zealand dollar solely for the purpose of being swapped into a major currency.

**Fixed-rate currency swaps.**  *Fixed-rate currency swaps* have three main components: the principal amounts, the exchange rate, and two fixed interest rates. At the beginning of the swap, two principal amounts are 'exchanged' between the two counterparties at an agreed exchange rate. The exchange rate is usually the spot rate (the average of the bid and offer rates) and, in this case, the currency swap is known as a *par swap*. This exchange of principal can be either 'notional' (no physical exchange takes place) or 'real' (a physical exchange is made). In either case, the significance of the principal is that it is used to determine both the interest payments under the swap and the re-exchange of principal when the swap matures. The interest payments that are made depend on both the principal amounts and the interest rates that are fixed at the beginning of the swap. On maturity, the principal amounts are re-exchanged between the two counterparties at the initial exchange rate. Notice that with currency swaps, unlike with interest rate swaps, there is generally an exchange of principal. This is because each counterparty raises funds in one currency but wants the use of funds in the currency raised by the other counterparty. Hence there is a need to exchange principal. An alternative to the par swap is the *outright swap*. With this type of swap, the re-exchange of principal amounts between the two counterparties does not occur at the original spot exchange rate, but at the implied forward exchange rate, taking into account both interest rate differentials between the two currencies and the term of the swap (see equation (7.20)).

Fixed-rate currency swaps therefore allow fixed-rate liabilities in one currency to be transformed into fully hedged fixed-rate synthetic liabilities in another currency. Again, the motivation behind the swap is to exploit comparative advantage. To illustrate this we will consider Figure 10.12, which shows the fixed-rate currency swap agreed between UK Company A and US Company B for principal

---

**Figure 10.12** Fixed-rate currency swap

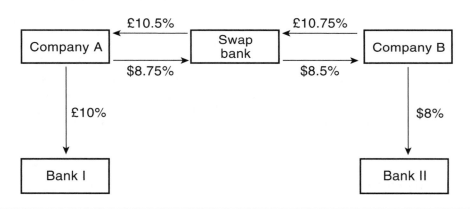

---

amounts of £100 million and $150 million and a spot exchange rate of £1 = $1.50. The cost of borrowing directly from banks is as follows:

|  | Company A (UK) | Company B (US) | Comparative advantage of A over B |
|---|---|---|---|
| Fixed-rate sterling loans | 10% | 11% | 1% |
| Fixed-rate dollar loans | 9% | 8% | (1%) |

Company A has a comparative advantage in raising fixed-rate sterling finance and B has one in raising fixed-rate dollar funds. A swap is therefore possible if A prefers to have a dollar loan (e.g. in order to finance a US subsidiary) and B prefers to have a sterling loan (e.g. in order to invest in the UK). Bank I is willing to lend fixed-rate sterling to A for 10 per cent, while Bank II is willing to lend fixed-rate dollars to B for 8 per cent.

If the swap is transacted through a swap bank, Company A will give Company B £100 million and in return receive $150 million from B. During the term of the swap, interest payments might be exchanged between the counterparties as indicated in Figure 10.12.

| | | |
|---|---|---|
| Company A: | Borrows fixed-rate sterling at | 10% |
| | Receives from the swap bank for its sterling asset | (10.5%) |
| | Pays to the swap bank for its dollar debt | 8.75% |
| | | 8.25% |

and so effectively borrows fixed-rate dollars (i.e. has created synthetic fixed-rate dollars) at 8.25 per cent, which is less than the rate at which it can borrow these funds directly from the market (9 per cent, a saving of 0.75 per cent).

| | | |
|---|---|---|
| Company B: | Borrows fixed-rate dollars at | 8% |
| | Receives from the swap bank for its dollar asset | (8.5%) |
| | Pays to the swap bank for its sterling debt | 10.75% |
| | | 10.25% |

and so effectively borrows fixed-rate sterling (i.e. has created synthetic fixed-rate sterling) at 10.25 per cent, which is less than the rate at which it could borrow these funds directly from the market (11 per cent, a saving of 0.75 per cent).

The swap bank makes 0.5 per cent out of the deal. Given the size of the swap, this means that both companies save £750,000 ($1,125,000) for each year that the swap is in place and that the swap bank makes £500,000 ($750,000) annually. When the swap matures, the principal amounts are re-exchanged at the original exchange rate by A returning B's $150 million and B returning A's £100 million.

Strictly speaking, the above calculations of the effective interest rates paid by the two companies on synthetic dollars and synthetic sterling are not completely correct. This is because one percentage point of interest on a dollar basis does not equal one percentage point of interest on a sterling basis when the interest rates on dollars and sterling differ. To correct for this, the interest rate has to be rescaled by a *basis conversion factor*. This is found as follows. Suppose that the swap depicted in Figure 10.12 lasts for three years and that annual payments of interest are made at the end of each of the three years. One percentage point of interest in sterling over three years has a present value at the sterling interest rate of 10 per cent of

$$P_£ = 1 \times \left[ \frac{1 - (1.1)^{-3}}{0.1} \right] = 2.486852\%.$$

In contrast, one percentage point of interest in dollars over three years has a present value at the dollar interest rate of 8 per cent of:

$$P_\$ = 1 \times \left[ \frac{1 - (1.08)^{-3}}{0.08} \right] = 2.577097\%.$$

Hence, over the life of the swap one percentage point of interest in sterling is worth 0.9649819 (i.e. 2.486852/2.577097) percentage points of interest on a dollar basis; equivalently, one percentage point of interest in dollars is worth 1.0362889 (i.e. 1/0.9649819) percentage points of interest on a sterling basis. These are the basis conversion factors. Therefore, the effective rate on the synthetic dollars borrowed by Company A is 8.27 (i.e. $[10.0 - 10.5] \times 0.9649819 + 8.75$) which is 2 basis points higher than the rate quoted above. Similarly, the effective rate on the synthetic sterling borrowed by Company B is 10.23 per cent (i.e. [8.0 − 8.5] × 1.0362889 + 10.75) which is 2 basis points less than the rate quoted above.

When a swap bank makes a quote on a fixed-rate currency swap, it does so on the following terms. The bank might quote 5.60–5.70 per cent in dollars and 7.25–7.35 per cent in Deutschmarks. This means that the swap bank expects either:

- to pay 5.60 per cent in dollars and receive 7.35 per cent in Deutschmarks; or

- to receive 5.70 per cent in dollars and pay 7.25 per cent in Deutschmarks.

As another example, we can consider a bank engaging in a *forward-against-forward* transaction. This is effectively a forward fixed-rate currency swap which is hedged for overall changes in the level of exchange rates, but leaves the bank exposed to changes in exchange rate differentials. Suppose the bank observes the following spot and forward exchange rates for $/£:

|          | *Bid*  | *Offer* |
|----------|--------|---------|
| Spot     | 1.5958 | 1.5963  |
| 3 months | 269    | 265     |
| 6 months | 471    | 464     |

Suppose further that the bank believes that UK interest rates will have to rise in four or five months' time if inflationary expectations are going to be contained, while US interest rates are not expected to change. This view implies that (due to covered interest parity) sterling should depreciate against the dollar in four or five months' time. To back this view, the bank could sell six-month forward sterling against dollars, buy three-month forward sterling against dollars (both on a swap basis, see section 7.3) and hope that three-month forward sterling in three months' time can be repurchased on more favourable terms than currently available. Because forward sterling is trading at a discount to spot, what the bank is hoping is that this discount will widen over the next three months, so that the forward sterling that will be repurchased in three months' time can be repurchased at a wider discount.

On the basis of the above spot and forward rates, the bank sells six-month forward sterling against dollars on a swap basis. This means that the bank buys sterling at the spot offer rate of $1.5963 per £ and sells it six-month forward at the six-month forward bid rate of $1.5487 per £ (i.e. 1.5958–0.0471), i.e. at a discount of 476 pips (i.e. 1.5487–1.5963). At the same time, the bank buys three-month forward sterling against dollars on a swap basis. In other words, the bank sells sterling at the spot bid rate of $1.5958 per £ and buys it three-month forward at the three-month forward offer rate of $1.5698 per £ (i.e. 1.5963–0.0265), i.e. at a discount of 260 pips (i.e. 1.5498–1.5958). This implies that the bank is short three months forward sterling in three months' time at a net discount of 216 pips (i.e. 476–260). It will gain from this position if the discount widens.

Suppose in three months' time the bank observes the following spot and forward exchange rates for $/£:

|          | *Bid*  | *Offer* |
|----------|--------|---------|
| Spot     | 1.4725 | 1.4730  |
| 3 months | 392    | 388     |

As the bank had anticipated, sterling has fallen against the dollar, but this is not important for the transaction. What is important is that the three-month forward discount has widened. The bank can therefore close out the second three months of the initial six-month transaction by buying three-month forward sterling against dollars on a swap basis. This means that the bank sells sterling at the spot bid rate of $1.4725 per £ and buys it three-month forward at the three-month forward offer rate of $1.4342 per £ (i.e. 1.4730–0.0388), i.e. at a discount of 383 pips (i.e. 1.4725–1.4342). The bank has therefore sold forward sterling against the dollar at a discount of 476 pips and bought forward sterling against the dollar at discounts of 260 pips and 383 pips, giving a profit of 167 pips (i.e. 383 + 260 – 476). Equivalently, the bank has sold three-month forward sterling in three months' time at a discount of 216 pips and repurchased it at a discount of 383 pips, again giving a profit of 167 pips (i.e. 383 – 216). This implies that for every £1m exchanged in this forward-against-forward transaction, the bank makes a profit of $16,700. However, this profit is not risk free since it depends on the bank's expectations of future movements in interest rates and exchange rates being fulfilled.

**Currency coupon swaps.** The other type of currency swap is the *currency coupon swap* or cross-currency interest rate swap. This is a combination of an interest rate swap and a currency swap. The format of the swap is identical to that of a fixed-rate currency swap with both initial and final exchange of principal (at the initially agreed exchange rate), but one or both of the interest payments involved are on a floating-rate basis. So, for example, fixed-rate dollars could be swapped for floating-rate sterling.

Currency swaps can be priced in the same way as interest rate swaps, namely as the difference between two bonds or as a series of forward contracts.

Consider a fixed-rate currency swap involving US dollars and sterling. The value of the swap (in sterling) to the counterparty paying sterling interest rates is:

$$P_{Swap} = (P_\$/e_0) - P_£, \tag{10.7}$$

where:

$$
\begin{aligned}
P_£ &= \text{price of the sterling bond underlying the swap;} \\
P_\$ &= \text{price of the dollar bond underlying the swap;} \\
e_0 &= \text{spot exchange rate (\$ per £).}
\end{aligned}
$$

Suppose that the spot exchange rate is $2 per £, that the principal amounts of the swap in the two currencies are £100 and $200, that the swap lasts two years, with interest payments of 8% p.a. in sterling and 5% p.a. in dollars at the end of each year and that the following spot yields are observed in the two currencies:

| Year | Spot yield | |
|:---:|:---:|:---:|
| | Sterling (%) | Dollars (%) |
| 1 | 7 | 3 |
| 2 | 9 | 5 |

This implies that:

$$P_£ = \frac{8}{1.07} + \frac{108}{(1.09)^2} = £98.38,$$

and:

$$P_\$ = \frac{10}{1.03} + \frac{210}{(1.05)^2} = \$200.18.$$

The value of the swap is:

$$P_{Swap} = \frac{200.18}{2} - 98.38 = £1.71.$$

If we wish to view a currency swap as a series of forward foreign exchange contracts, we need to calculate the forward exchange rates implied by the relationship between current spot interest rates and exchange rates. We do this using the equation for covered interest parity (cf. equation (7.20)):

$$f_i = \left(\frac{1+r_{\$i}}{1+r_{£i}}\right)^i \cdot e_0, \tag{10.8}$$

where:

$$
\begin{array}{rcl}
f_i & = & i^{th} \text{ year forward exchange rate;} \\
r_{£i} & = & i^{th} \text{ year sterling spot yield;} \\
r_{\$i} & = & i^{th} \text{ year dollar spot yield.}
\end{array}
$$

Using (10.8) we get:

$$f_1 = \left(\frac{1.03}{1.07}\right) \cdot 2 = \$1.92523 \text{ per } £,$$

$$f_2 = \left(\frac{1.05}{1.09}\right)^2 \cdot 2 = \$1.85590 \text{ per } £.$$

The swapping of interest payments involves the receipt of £8 per year and the payment of $10 per year. The risk-free interest rate in sterling is 7 per cent for the year 1 swap and 9 per cent for the year 2 swap. The present value of the two forward contracts corresponding to these swap payments is therefore (in sterling):

$$\frac{(10/1.92523) - 8}{1.07} = -£2.62,$$

and:

$$\frac{(10/1.85590) - 8}{(1.09)^2} = -£2.20.$$

The final exchange of principal involves paying £100 and receiving $200. The value of the forward contract corresponding to this swap is:

$$\frac{(200/1.85590) - 100}{(1.09)^2} = £6.53.$$

The total value of the swap is:

$$P_{Swap} = 6.53 - 2.62 - 2.20 = £1.71,$$

which is the same value as in the case as treating a swap as the difference between two bonds.

### 10.3.4 Asset swaps

*Asset swaps* combine an asset and a swap to create a synthetic asset. So, for example, a fixed-rate asset can be converted into a floating-rate asset in the same currency or in a different currency. To illustrate, we will consider a pension fund, which can purchase in the market-place fixed-rate bonds yielding 10 per cent p.a. or floating-rate notes (FRNs) yielding LIBOR, and a bank, which can also buy bonds yielding 10 per cent or can lend to house-buyers at LIBOR + 0.5 per cent. The pension fund decides to purchase the bond and swap it directly with the bank without using the services of a swap bank. The mechanics of the swap are indicated in Figure 10.13.

**Figure 10.13** Asset swap

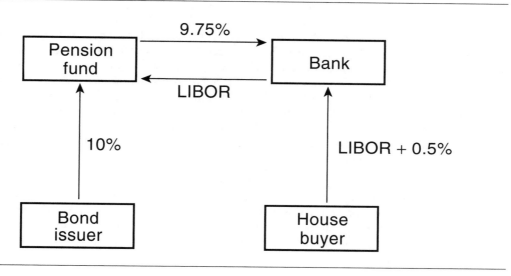

| The pension fund: | Purchases the bond yielding | 10% |
| | Pays to the bank | (9.75%) |
| | Receives from the bank | LIBOR |
| | | LIBOR + 0.25% |

and so has created a synthetic FRN yielding LIBOR + 0.25 per cent, which is higher than the yield on an FRN in the market (LIBOR).

| The bank: | Lends to house-buyers at | LIBOR + 0.5% |
| | Receives from the pension fund | 9.75% |
| | Pays to the pension fund | (LIBOR) |
| | | 10.25% |

and so has created a synthetic bond yielding 10.25 per cent, which is greater than the yield on the bond in the market (10 per cent).

Another example is the *equity swap* where the return on an equity portfolio is swapped for a floating-rate return linked to LIBOR, e.g. LIBOR + 1.5 per cent. If the return on the equity portfolio is negative, then the bank will pay the equity fund manager both the floating-rate amount as well as the loss on equity. The fund manager would execute this swap if he believed that share prices were going to fall and/or short-term interest rates were going to rise.

### 10.3.5  More esoteric swaps

These are the main type of swap. But other more complicated swaps have been executed. *Circus swaps* combine interest rate and currency swaps. *Forward swaps* are swaps that are executed on a future date but on which the terms are agreed today. A *swaption* is an option on a swap giving the holder the right but not the obligation to execute the swap on a future date with the terms agreed today. A *callable swap* gives the fixed-rate payer the right to terminate the swap before the maturity date. An *index swap* is one in which the payments depend on an index, such as the retail price index, a stock index or an index of bond prices. A *zero-coupon swap* is one in which the fixed-rate payments are compounded over the life of the agreement at some agreed rate of interest and are paid on the maturity date. *Amortizing swaps* (or *step-down* or *decreasing swaps*) involve the principal declining according to a fixed schedule, whereas *drawdown swaps* (or *accreting* or *step-up* or *increasing swaps*) involve the principal increasing over time, as in the case of the financing of a large construction project. A *rollercoaster swap* is designed to match the principal to that of the underlying financing requirement which may vary up or down over the life of the swap. *Seasonal swaps* have alternating periods of positive and zero principal amounts. The last five swaps are all classed as *tailored swaps* since the principal amount of the swap at any time is tailored to suit the requirements of the counterparties.

Let us consider an example of a swaption. Suppose that a construction company is bidding for a major building contract and wants to lock in the cost of borrowed funds, but is not sure that it will get the contract. The company might buy a swaption for a premium of 1.5 per cent of the principal amount for the right but not the obligation to swap three-year money fixed at 10 per cent in 6 months' time. The premium of 1.5 per cent amortized in arrears over three years at 10 per cent is 0.60 per cent per annum, found by solving $X$ in:

$$1.5 \;=\; \frac{X}{1.1} + \frac{X}{(1.1)^2} + \frac{X}{(1.1)^3}\,.$$

This raises the cost of borrowed funds to 10.60 per cent if the swaption is exercised. The company is therefore in-the-money if interest rates rise above 10.60 per cent. The swaption will not be exercised if interest rates are below 10 per cent and the company will lose the premium of 1.5 per cent of the principal amount, but at least it will have contained its borrowing costs if it does win the contract. European swaptions can only be exercised on the maturity date of the swaption, whereas American options can be exercised on any day up to expiry. *Extendable swaptions* give the holder the right, but not the obligation, to extend the life of the swaption at a predetermined rate.

In contrast, a spot interest rate swap locks in a current fixed-interest rate, while a forward interest rate swap locks in a fixed interest rate at some date in the future. The three types of swap are illustrated in Figure 10.14. The current rate might be 9 per cent, so a current swap pays fixed-for-floating at 9 per cent fixed. If the yield curve is upward sloping, the one-year forward rate will be above the spot rate at, say, 10 per cent. So a one-year forward swap will pay fixed-for-floating at 10 per cent in one year's time. A one-year swaption might also pay a fixed rate of 10 per cent if exercised, but involves a premium of 0.5 per cent. The swaption will be exercised in a year's time if the market interest rate then is above 10.5 per cent (i.e. the exercise price (10 per cent) *plus* the premium of 0.5 per cent). But the swaption will not be exercised if the market interest rate is below 10.5 per cent in a year's time,

**Figure 10.14** Interest rate swaps: spot swaps, forward swaps and swaptions

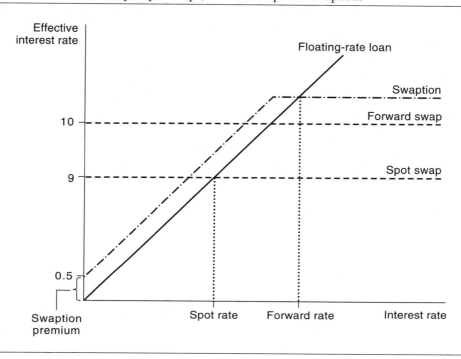

since any floating rate borrower who had bought the swaption would wish to benefit from being able to borrow at rates below 10.5 per cent.

There are also swaps that are not linked to any financial product, but are instead linked to the value of an underlying physical commodity. These are called *commodity swaps*. The main examples are energy products (e.g. West Texas Intermediate, Brent Crude, jet fuel, kerosene, gasoline, natural gas) and metals (e.g. gold, copper, aluminium, zinc, nickel). An example might be a swap between an airline and an oil company in which the airline pays a fixed oil price to an oil company and receives the spot oil price over the life of the swap (typically up to five years). The airline buys jet oil in the spot market paying for it with the spot oil price receipts from the swap; it benefits by being able to plan its activities over the next five years on the basis of stable oil price payments to the oil company. The oil company benefits from receiving a fixed price on its future oil sales.

### 10.3.6 The risks involved in swaps

It is important to examine the risks involved in executing swaps. There are two main types of risk facing the counterparties, *credit risk* and *position* or *market risk*. Credit risk is the risk that the other counterparty will default on his obligation. Position or market risk is the risk that market interest rates or exchange rates will diverge from the rates agreed in the swap, leading to a position loss for one counterparty.

While credit as such is not extended when a swap is executed, there is a risk that the promised payments and receipts under the swap are not, in fact, made. The present value of these future payments and receipts (discounted at the swap rates or the opportunity borrowing and lending rates) represents the extent of exposure. Credit risk declines as the swap approaches maturity. Position or market risk, however, varies over the life of the swap according to the extent of movements in interest rates. The two types of risk are not unrelated. For example, a swap might be showing a position gain but the other party might then default. There is also *gap risk*, the risk that the counterparties to a swap may have differing maturity dates for the debt that they wish to swap, thereby creating what is called a *gap*.

The swap bank that *warehouses* a swap by taking out a futures hedge until the other leg of the swap is executed faces a *spread risk*. This is the risk that the difference between the swap price and the futures price moves in an adverse direction.

Until 1987 swaps were treated, in terms of accounting convention, as off-balance-sheet items. This meant that banks and companies devoted very little capital to support their swap market activities, which resulted in such activities generating high rates of return in terms of capital employed. But in 1987 the Bank of England and the US Federal Banking Supervisory Authorities agreed on a common risk ratio framework for treating swaps and other off-balance-sheet items. This resulted in more capital being employed to support swap positions.

### 10.3.7   The uses of swaps

In discussing swaps, it has been argued that they worked if different counterparties had different comparative advantages. In a sense, therefore, swaps are the outcome of market imperfections (either temporary or permanent) of one kind or another. Market imperfections can be interpreted in the broadest sense to include differences in the regulatory regimes covering the counterparties as well as imperfections in the internal structure of the market.

These market imperfections give rise to arbitrage possibilities, and swaps are one example of the exploitation of such possibilities. For example, swaps can result from two counterparties arbitraging between different exchange control regimes, different supervisory authorities, different tax authorities or even different accounting conventions.

Similarly, swaps can result from arbitraging between segmented markets that arise from different perceptions of credit risk, interest rate risk or exchange rate risk by investors, or from differential access to information, market liquidity, transactions costs, etc. Counterparties are willing to arbitrage these differentials in a way that the market apparently is not. As an example, banks can raise fixed-rate funds more cheaply than companies, while companies can raise floating-rate funds relatively cheaply but would prefer to have fixed-rate debt; hence an interest rate swap is executed which benefits both counterparties. Another example occurs when a currency swap can be executed more cheaply than a forward foreign exchange contract which has an almost identical structure.

Another type of market imperfection is incompleteness, and swaps can be used to extend existing markets. Swaps can be executed in sizes and maturities that are not available by direct funding and hence are more flexible than the underlying instruments. For example, interest rate swaps can be interpreted as an extension of the interest rate futures market, which is liquid only out to maturities of around 18 months. Similarly, currency swaps are seen as extensions to the forward currency market.

So the first use of swaps is as an arbitrage instrument. The second use is as a hedging instrument. A company with floating-rate debt that expected interest rates to rise could execute an interest rate swap and hence secure a low fixed rate for its debt funding. Similarly, a pension fund holding fixed-coupon bonds that expected interest rates to rise could execute an asset swap and earn a return related to LIBOR. Of course, given the capital loss that would be expected on the bonds, it might still be better for the pension fund to sell the bonds rather than undertake the swap. The hedging possibilities of swaps depend, as with all hedging instruments, on both price volatility and differential expectations concerning directions of movements in prices. Third, swaps can be used for speculation, that is, for taking a view on the direction of future movements in interest rates or exchange rates. The final use of swaps is as an instrument for asset and liability management. On the liability side swaps can be used to reduce funding costs, while on the asset side they can be used to increase returns. This last factor is of particular value to net investors such as pension funds.

Finally, we can examine the future of the swap market. Two countervailing trends appear to be discernible. First, swaps are designed to overcome market imperfections. The very success of swaps in doing this is likely to reduce or even eliminate those imperfections and hence to lead to a declining use of swaps.

However, in the opposite direction, the swap market itself is becoming more efficient. Initially, swaps were matched deals between two counterparties using the services of an intermediary swap bank. The swap bank acted as principal by making separate agreements with each counterparty. Early swaps were therefore illiquid instruments. Later, the swap banks began market-making in swaps through the establishment of swap warehouses. They would undertake one leg of the swap with one counterparty while hedging their position in the futures market until the other leg of the swap could be executed. The liquidity in swap markets has been further enhanced by standardizing both the dealing terms and the documentation involved in swaps. For example, since 1985, as a result of moves by ISDA, the interest rate swap has traded as a standardized instrument. Nevertheless, for most swaps, secondary-market activity remains very low. For example, only about 5 per cent of asset swaps are traded in secondary markets. Therefore in order to unwind a swap, a counterparty is forced to take one of the following measures: he can try to assign the rights and obligations under the swap to the swap bank or a third party in return for a payment equal to the present value of the future income streams arising from the swap; alternatively, he can take out a reverse swap with another counterparty.

## 10.4  Forward rate agreements

The market in *forward rate agreements* (FRAs) began in the early 1980s as an offshoot of the inter-bank market in forward/forward interest rate agreements. Within five years, the FRA market had an annual turnover of around $500 million. London is the centre of the FRA market because of its connections with the eurodollar market. Most FRAs (about 90 per cent) are in sterling or dollars, although there is a growing market in Deutschmark and yen FRAs. The average size of an FRA is £5 million for sterling FRAs and $10 million for dollar FRAs. However, some agreements can be for as much as £100 million. Virtually all FRAs are quoted in LIBOR. Most are for 3-6s (i.e. three-month LIBOR in three months' time), but there are other combinations available, e.g. 9-15s (six-month LIBOR in nine months' time). FRAs are implemented using standard British Bankers Association documentation.

FRAs are equivalent to forward contracts in short-term interest rate swaps and so combine many of the features of forward or futures contracts and of swaps. In other words, FRAs are equivalent to synthetic forward swap contracts. An FRA is a contract between two counterparties to swap short-term interest rate payments over an agreed period at some date in the future. The buyer of an FRA locks in a fixed rate of interest, while the seller locks in a floating rate. As with a standard swap, no exchange of principal is involved. Instead, on the settlement date of the FRA, one counterparty makes a single cash payment to compensate the other counterparty for any difference between the agreed interest rate and the spot interest rate at the time the FRA is taken out.

The payment made is determined by the following formula:

$$\text{Payment made} = \frac{(rs - rf) \times (N/365) \times B}{1 + rs(N/365)}, \tag{10.9}$$

where:

$$
\begin{aligned}
rs &= \text{spot or settlement interest rate;} \\
rf &= \text{interest rate agreed at the time FRA is taken out;} \\
B &= \text{notional principal involved;} \\
N &= \text{term to maturity of the FRA in days.}
\end{aligned}
$$

The amount paid is discounted to the settlement date at the spot rate of interest. This is because the full payment of the obligations under the FRA is made on the settlement date, even though the interest rate differences apply to the full term of the FRA.

If the spot rate ($rs$) exceeds the agreed rate ($rf$), then the payment is made by the seller of the FRA to the buyer; otherwise the payment is made by the buyer to the seller.

**Example 10.1 (FRA)** *On 1 April LIBOR was 8.28 per cent and a corporate treasurer decided to buy an FRA from a bank with the following specification. The FRA fixed a three-month rate of 8.5 per cent in three months' time on a notional sum of £10 million. The settlement date of the agreement is therefore 1 July and the term to maturity of the FRA is 92 days (from July 1 to September 30).*

*On 1 July the spot rate was 9.5 per cent, so the bank had to make the following payment to the corporate treasurer:*

$$\text{Payment made} = \frac{(0.095 - 0.085) \times (92/365) \times £10,000,000}{1 + 0.095(92/365)} = £24,616.04.$$

*Had the spot rate been only 8.0 per cent of 1 July, the corporate treasurer would have had to make the following payment to the bank:*

$$\text{Payment made} = \frac{(0.085 - 0.080) \times (92/365) \times £10,000,000}{1 + 0.080(92/365)} = £12,353.64.$$

It is clear from the example that the buyer of the FRA is locking in a fixed interest rate. Suppose the corporate treasurer had intended to borrow £10 million for three months at the spot market rate (plus 1 per cent) on 1 July. The payments made to the corporate treasurer by the bank on 1 July allow the treasurer to lock in an effective fixed three-month borrowing rate of 9.5 per cent (i.e. 8.5 + 1 per cent). The bank as seller of the contract is committed to making floating-rate payments related to the spot rate on the settlement date.

The bank's commission for undertaking the FRA might be 5 basis points or £5000 (i.e. £10,000,000 × 0.0005). There are no other front-end fees to pay; e.g., there are no broker's commissions to pay, since the FRA is established directly with the bank, rather than through a broker.

FRAs are tailor-made agreements so they can be flexible in terms of size, duration and term to maturity. Short-term interest rate futures contracts, in contrast, have specified contract sizes and delivery dates and a single term to maturity of three months. Also, futures contracts involve margin payments and marking to market; with FRAs, on the other hand, the size of the contract is negotiable (although there is generally a minimum contract size of 250,000), as are the delivery dates (although few agreements are for periods of more than two years ahead). Also, FRAs can be drawn up for terms to maturity of other than three months. In addition, there is no system of margining and marking to market with FRAs. However, FRAs are more difficult to liquidate than futures contracts. So FRAs are more flexible than futures contracts, but they are also less liquid and involve more credit risk.

FRAs tend to be priced off the nearest short-term interest rate futures contract. So the FRA in the above example would be priced off the June sterling deposit contract. If this was priced at 91.50, then the agreed rate on the FRA would be exactly in line with the implied interest rate on the June future.

Most FRAs, as the above example illustrates, are used for hedging purposes and provide an alternative to the futures market. However, they can also be used for speculation (i.e. for taking a view on future interest rate movements) and for arbitrage.

Recent developments in the FRA market include: *interest rate guarantees* (or IRGs), which are equivalent to options on FRAs; long-dated FRAs (or LDFRAs), e.g. two-year LIBOR in five years; and *synthetic agreements for forward exchange* (or SAFEs), which are identical to FRAs but for which settlement is made against forward/forward exchange rates rather than interest rates.

## 10.5 Caps, floors and collars

Caps, floors and collars are examples of *synthetic interest rate options* that are provided over-the-counter mainly by banks, making them flexible, individually-customized products. They are linked to changes in the following interest rates: LIBOR, the Treasury bill rate, commercial paper rate and prime rate.

An interest rate *cap* is an agreement between two counterparties to place an upper limit (called the *cap level*) on the interest rate paid by one counterparty on a notional amount of floating rate loan over a specified time period. The cap buyer (typically a company) benefits from having this upper limit and this benefit is provided by the cap seller (typically a bank) in return for an upfront premium paid by the buyer. The term of the agreement can be up to ten years. In effect the cap seller is selling a synthetic interest rate call option to the buyer. The cap buyer limits the losses incurred on a floating rate loan if interest rates rise (see Figure 10.15): the combined effect of a floating-rate loan and a short call option is a synthetic short put option (cf. Figure 10.6). (If the cap is expressed in terms of price equivalents (i.e. 100 – interest rate (%)), the bank is selling a synthetic interest rate put option to the company.)

The cap works as follows. The counterparties agree that on specific rate-setting days during the term of the cap, the cap level is compared with the spot value of a specified benchmark interest rate. For example, the benchmark might be three-month LIBOR and there might be four rate-setting days per year. If, on a particular rate-setting day, the spot rate exceeds the cap level, the seller compensates the buyer for the difference in these two interest rates until the next rate-setting day. If the spot rate equals or is below the cap level, the seller makes no payment and the buyer pays the market rate on funds borrowed. The amount paid (if any) depends only on the spot interest rate on the rate-setting days and not on what happens to interest rates between these rate-setting days.

The payment is determined by the following formula:

$$\text{Payment made} = \frac{\max[(rs-rx),0] \times (N/365) \times B}{1+rs(N/365)}, \tag{10.10}$$

**Figure 10.15** Interest rate cap

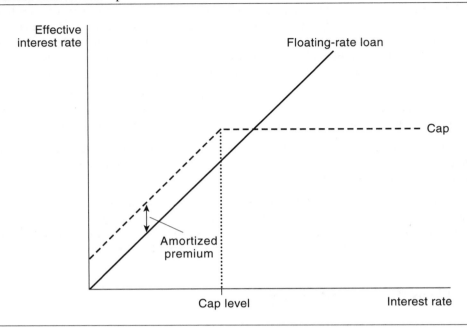

where:

$$
\begin{aligned}
rs &= \text{spot interest rate on rate-setting day;} \\
rx &= \text{cap rate;} \\
B &= \text{notional principal involved;} \\
N &= \text{number of days until next rate-setting day.}
\end{aligned}
$$

The amount paid (if any) is discounted to the beginning of the period using the spot interest rate.

**Example 10.2 (Cap)** *Suppose a bank quotes the following terms for a cap on 3-month LIBOR:*

| | |
|---|---|
| *Cap level:* | *9%* |
| *Term:* | *2 years* |
| *Rate setting frequency:* | *Quarterly* |
| *Payment:* | *Quarterly in advance* |
| *Notional principal:* | *£10m* |
| *Cap premium:* | *0.6% or £60,000* |

*Suppose a buyer takes out this cap and, on the first rate-setting date, three-month LIBOR is 8 per cent, then no payment is made. However, suppose that on the second rate-setting date, three-month LIBOR is 9.5 per cent, and that there are 91 days until the third rate-setting date, then the following amount is paid to the buyer by the seller on the second rate-setting date:*

$$
Payment\ made \quad = \quad \frac{(0.095 - 0.090) \times (91/365) \times £10,000,000}{1 + 0.095(91/365)} \quad = \quad £12,177.33 .
$$

In this example, the cap premium charged by the bank is an upfront fee of 0.6 per cent of the principal or £60,000. Alternatively, the premium might be amortized over the life of the cap to give an annual fee. For example, the premium might be amortized at 8 per cent to give a fee of 0.336 per cent (or £33,600) payable annually in arrears, found by solving for $X$ in:

$$0.6 = \frac{X}{1.08} + \frac{X}{(1.08)^2}.$$

This raises the effective cap level to 9.336 per cent.

It is clear that a cap is a type of interest rate option: the holder has an option which will be exercised if the spot rate on the rate setting date exceeds the cap rate. The premium on this option therefore reflects the cost to the bank of providing this option to its customer. The customer pays the bank the premium in exchange for the option. Alternatively, if the bank also provides the loan, the premium would be rolled up into the interest charge. In either case, the option can be valued using Black's (1976) model. Since $rs$ in (10.10) is not known until the rate-setting day, it can be replaced by the relevant forward rate, $rf$. If we also assume that the forward rate has constant volatility, $\sigma_f$, Black's model for valuing each component of a cap (known as a *caplet*) is:

$$P^c = \frac{\tau B}{1 + \tau \cdot rf} \cdot e^{-rT} \cdot [rf \cdot N(d_1) - rx \cdot N(d_2)], \tag{10.11}$$

where:

$$d_1 = \frac{\ln(rf/rx)}{\sigma_f \sqrt{T}} + \tfrac{1}{2} \sigma_f \sqrt{T};$$

$$d_2 = d_1 - \sigma_f \sqrt{T};$$

and:

$\tau$ = rate-setting frequency (e.g. quarterly);
$T$ = length of time from beginning of cap to payment date of caplet.

The option premium on the cap is the sum of the option premiums on the individual caplets.

An interest rate *floor* is an agreement between two counterparties to place a lower limit (called the *floor level*) on the interest rate earned by one counterparty on a notional amount of floating-rate deposit over a specified time period. The floor buyer (typically a company with surplus funds on deposit) benefits from having this lower limit and this benefit is provided by the floor seller (typically a bank) in return for an upfront premium paid by the buyer. In effect, the floor seller is selling a synthetic interest rate put option to the buyer. The floor buyer limits the losses incurred on a floating rate deposit if interest rates fall (see Figure 10.16): the combined effect of a floating rate deposit and a synthetic long put is a synthetic long call option. (If the floor is expressed in terms of price equivalents, the bank is selling a synthetic interest rate call option to the depositor.)

An interest rate *collar* is a combination of a cap and a floor. The buyer of a collar purchases a cap and sells a floor: the proceeds from selling the floor reduce the cost of the cap. The seller of a collar does the opposite, i.e. sells a cap and buys a floor. For example, a company paying three-month LIBOR on its £10m loan from a bank, could reduce the 0.6 per cent cost of its two-year, 9 per cent cap in the above example, by selling a two-year 7 per cent floor at, say, 0.4 per cent. For a net of 0.2 per

---

**Figure 10.16** Interest rate floor

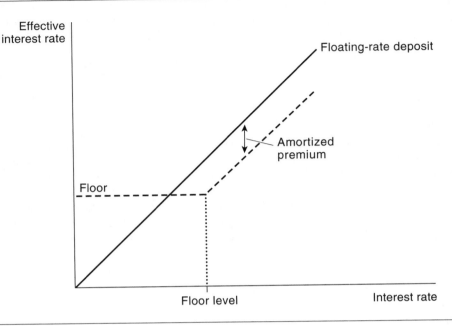

cent or £20,000, the company could ensure that its funding costs always lay between 7 and 9 per cent over the next two years.

There are also *forward caps, forward floors* and *forward collars* as well as options on the above products with the names of *captions, floortions* and *collartions*.

## 10.6  Bundled and unbundled securities

Finally in this chapter, we can consider the case of synthetic securities that result from the processes of *bundling* and *unbundling*.

### 10.6.1  Bundled securities

*Bundled securities* are marketable securities that result from the bundling or packaging together of a set of non-marketable assets, a process that is also known as *securitization*. Securitization has been defined as the case where 'a lending institution's assets are removed in one way or another from the balance sheet ... and are funded instead by investors who purchase a negotiable financial instrument evidencing the indebtedness, without recourse (or, in some cases, with limited recourse) to the original lender' (Henderson and Scott (1988), p.2). In the case where there remains some limited recourse, an estimate of the liability for the recourse remains on the balance sheet.

One of the earliest examples of securitization comes from the US mortgage market where residential mortgage loans made by an original lender (known as the *originator*) are packaged up and sold on to investors who receive the interest and principal payments made by the borrowers of the initial loans.

The original lender benefits in a number of ways. First, removing assets from the original lending institution's balance sheet removes its risk exposure and enhances its liquidity position. These benefits increase with the maturity of the loans. In the case of mortgage loans, for example, the commitment can be for 25 years or more. The maturity mismatching is obvious when it is recognized that the bulk of these loans are financed from deposits that are withdrawable on demand. Second, it is possible that, as a result of securitization, the packaged loans are funded at a lower rate than that charged by the original lending institution. This implies that the package of loans can be sold off at a higher value than the lending institution implicitly values them. In other words, securitization must add value and this additional value must accrue to the original lender. Third, as a result of securitization, the total funding available to the lending institution may well increase as a result of its access to capital markets; in other words, it may become less dependent on its traditional deposit base. Fourth, by reducing the amount of debt on the original lending institution's balance sheet, it can dramatically improve the institution's leverage ratio.

The main advantage of securitization to the investor is that it offers a marketable asset-backed instrument to invest in. Often the instrument offers two layers of security: the original assets and credit enhancement. The original assets will provide good security if they are well-diversified and homogeneous in respect of quality, terms and conditions (e.g. repayment structure and maturity of assets). Diversified assets reduce the risk of a single drastic failure, while homogeneous assets reduce the problems of evaluation. If there is no liquidity in the original loans (i.e. no secondary market), then investors will often require *credit enhancement* in the form of an insurance contract, letters of credit, recourse to the issuer, subordination of a second tranche which absorbs losses first, over-collateralization or a reserve fund, for the instrument to be sold at a price that is acceptable to the original lender. In this way, securitization can provide a better credit risk for the investor than for the original lender.

The main costs of securitization are the transaction costs involved in packaging the original assets, mainly fees to investment banks and lawyers, etc.

Securitization began in the US housing market in 1970 when the Government National Mortgage Association (GNMA or 'Ginnie Mae'), which was authorized to guarantee the principal and interest on securities issued by other lenders and backed by the Federal Housing Administration, began issuing *mortgage pass-through certificates*. A pass-through is a security representing ownership in a pool of mortgages. The mortgages themselves are sold through a grantor trust and the certificates are sold in the capital markets. As with standard mortgages, the interest and amortized principal are paid monthly. Later *mortgage-backed bonds* (or MBBs) were issued with semi-annual payments and maturities of between 5 and 12 years; that is, on terms that are familiar to traditional bondholders. In 1983, *collateralized mortgage obligations* (or CMOs) were first traded with collateral provided by mortgages issued by the Federal Home Loans Mortgage Corporation. These are multi-tranche pay-through bonds in which the interest payments, amortization payments and principal repayments are made in separate tranches.

Because all these securities are asset-backed and guaranteed by the government, they carry little additional risk compared with US Treasury securities with the same terms. They can therefore be priced on the basis of the prices of the corresponding US Treasury securities. However, they do face one type of risk that is not present with Treasury securities and this is *prepayment risk*. This is the risk that mortgages will be paid off early, a risk that increases when mortgages have been taken out at high fixed interest rates and interest rates have subsequently fallen. This risk increases the required return on such investments compared with corresponding US Treasury securities, and is determined by comparing different prepayment scenarios. However, the structure of CMOs is designed to reduce prepayment risk to a minimum.

Securitization in the UK mortgage market began in 1985 when the Mortgage Intermediary Note Issuer (No.1) Amsterdam BV was established solely for the purpose of securitizing 1200 mortgages of BankAmerica Finance Ltd. Shortly afterwards a number of other institutions were established with similar objectives: the National Home Loans Corporation, the Household Mortgage Corporation, the Mortgage Corporation, the Mortgage Funding Corporation and First Mortgage Securities. Barclays Bank securitized £175m worth of home loans in 1989.

A second major example of securitization was the establishment of the eurocommercial paper (ECP) market, beginning in 1970. This market enabled borrowers to raise short-term finance from investors at lower cost than equivalent-maturity bank loans. In other words, the ECP market has led to the international securitization of commercial bank loans, with the commercial banks replacing loan income with fee income from arranging ECP issues rather than providing loans.

A third example is provided by the securitization of commercial property. In the UK, this has been achieved through vehicles such as the Single Asset Property Company (or SAPCO) and the Single Property Ownership Trust (or SPOT), otherwise known as the Single Property Unit Trust (or SPUT). In 1986, *property income certificates* (or PINCs) were first listed on the LSE. PINCs comprise an income certificate and an equity share. The income certificate provides a contractual right to receive a share of the property's income flow, while the equity share is an ordinary share in a specially created management company for the particular property.

As a fourth example, we have the securitization of export credits. In the UK, this has been achieved through Credit For Export PLC (or CFX) which was established in 1984.

As a final example, we have the repackaging of UK FRNs into fixed-rate bonds. The repackaged securities have been marketed as BECS (*bearer eurodollar collateralized securities*) by Barclays and as MECS (*marketable eurodollar collateralized securities*) by Merrill Lynch.

We can conclude by saying that securitization is a process that involves the replacement of credit markets with capital markets.

## 10.6.2   Unbundled securities

*Unbundled* (or *stripped*) *securities* result from the process of unbundling, that is, breaking down a particular security into various components and selling off each component separately. The classic example of a security that has been stripped in this way is a fixed-coupon, fixed-maturity bond in which the coupon component is traded separately from the principal component. The coupons provide an annuity and can be priced using the annuity yield curve (see section 5.5.6). The principal is equivalent to a zero-coupon bond which can be priced using the spot yield curve (see section 5.5.4); each individual coupon can also be treated as a zero-coupon bond. The value of the annuity component is given by (assuming annual coupon payments):

$$P_a = \sum_{t=1}^{T} \frac{d}{(1+ra_T)^t}, \tag{10.12}$$

where:

$$P_a \quad = \quad \text{price of a } T\text{-year annuity;}$$
$$d \quad = \quad \text{annual fixed coupon payment;}$$
$$T \quad = \quad \text{number of years to maturity;}$$
$$ra_T \quad = \quad \text{annuity yield for a } T\text{-year annuity.}$$

The value of the zero-coupon bond component is given by:

$$P_z \; = \; \frac{B}{(1+rs_T)^T} \, , \tag{10.13}$$

where:

$$P_z \quad = \quad \text{price of a } T\text{-year zero-coupon bond;}$$
$$B \quad = \quad \text{par value of the bond;}$$
$$rs_T \quad = \quad \text{spot yield for year } T.$$

It will be attractive for an institution to purchase and then strip a security in this way whenever:

$$P_a + P_z \; > \; P_d \, , \tag{10.14}$$

where $P_d$ is the dirty price of the bond.

Examples of stripped bonds are *STAGS* (sterling transferable accruing government securities) and *ZEBRAS* (zero-coupon eurosterling bearer or registered accruing securities). These are coupon-stripped gilts which have been issued respectively by Quadrex Securities and S.G. Warburg.

An official *gilt stripping* facility was introduced by the Bank of England in 1997, via the Gilts Settlements Office. The GSO will both strip gilts into their component parts and reconstitute gilts from their constituent components. One example of a strippable gilt is Treasury 8% 2020. The minimum strippable amount is £10,000 nominal and the amount increases in units of £10,000 nominal. Stripped coupons from different strippable gilts (with the same coupon payment dates) are fully fungible. Strippable gilts pay interest gross (whether or not in stripped form), with tax accounted for on an annual basis for those liable for UK tax. Strips offer the following advantages over coupon-paying bonds: more accurate management of cash flows, more precise matching of liabilities, elimination of reinvestment risk, and higher duration and convexity than the underlying coupon-paying gilt.

## Selected references

Beaumont, P. (1992), *Fixed-Income Synthetic Assets*, Wiley, New York.

Beidleman, C. (ed.)(1991), *Interest Rate Swaps*, Business One Irwin, Homewood Ill.

Black, F. (1976), 'The Pricing of Commodity Contracts', *Journal of Financial Economics*, 3, 167–79.

Bonsall, D. (ed.)(1990), *Securitisation*, Butterworths, London.

Briys, E., Bellalah, M., Mai, H.M., and de Varenne, F. (1998), *Options, Futures and Exotic Derivatives*, Wiley, Chichester.

Dattatreya, R. and Hotta, K. (1994), *Advanced Interest Rate and Currency Swaps*, Probus, Chicago, Ill.

Decovny, S. (1998), *Swaps*, Prentice Hall, Hemel Hempstead.

Dickens, P. (1988), 'Fast Forward with FRAs', *Corporate Finance*, April, Euromoney Publications, London.

Euromoney (1987), 'Swaps: New Moves', *Euromoney Supplement*, July, Euromoney Publications, London.

Euromoney (1987), 'The International Swap Market', *Euromoney Supplement*, September, Euromoney Publications, London.

Galitz, L. (1994), *Financial Engineering*, FT Pitman Publishing, London.

Hammond, G. (1987), 'Recent Developments in the Swap Market', *Bank of England Quarterly Bulletin*, February, 66–79.

Henderson, J. and Scott, J. (1988), *Securitisation*, Woodhead-Faulkner, Cambridge.

Kolb, R. (1997), *Futures, Options and Swaps*, Blackwell, Oxford.

Marshall, J. and Kapner, K. (1993a), *Understanding Swaps*, Wiley, New York.

Marshall, J. and Kapner, K. (1993b), *The Swaps Market*, Kolb Publishing, Miami, Fl.

Smith, C. and Smithson, C. (1990), *Handbook of Financial Engineering*, Harper Business Books, New York.

Sundaresan, S. (1997), *Fixed Income Markets and Their Derivatives*, South-Western College Publishing, Cincinnati.

*Swaps and Financial Derivatives*, IFR Publishing, London.

Taylor, F. (1996), *Mastering Derivatives Markets*, FT Pitman Publishing, London.

Tucker, A. (1991), *Financial Futures, Options and Swaps*, West, St. Paul, MN.

Vittas, D. (1986), 'The New Market Menagerie', *The Banker*, June, 16–27.

**Exercises**

1  Examine the principles and objectives of 'financial engineering'.

2  Explain how you would use a call option, a put option and a riskless zero-coupon bond to create a synthetic short security.

3  Explain how to construct a synthetic call option. How will its price compare with a real traded call option?

4  Since synthetic securities are constructed as linear combinations of basic building blocks, the pricing of synthetic securities is straightforward. Discuss.

5 Interest rate swaps are incompatible with an efficient market. Discuss.

6 Two banks can borrow from the corporate sector on the following terms:

|  | Bank A | Bank B |
|---|---|---|
| Fixed-rate loans | 11.5% | 11% |
| Floating-rate loans | LIBOR + 0.75% | LIBOR + 0.5% |

Design a suitable interest rate swap between the two banks. What is the maximum size of the swap (as a rate of interest) that can be made between the two banks?

7 Using an example, show carefully how a swap works. Why does it work?

8 What is an asset swap? Illustrate using an example.

9 Examine the risks involved in swap transactions.

10 Do you think the swap market will survive into the next century?

11 What are: FRAs, ERAs, caps, collars and floors?

12 What is 'securitization'? Illustrate with three examples.

13 What is coupon-stripping? Illustrate with an example.

14 A corporate treasurer is offered the following interest rate swap rates by a bank:

| Term (years) | Gilt yield (semi-annual) | Swap rates |
|---|---|---|
| 3 | 7.50 | 50–55 |
| 5 | 7.70 | 60–65 |
| 7 | 8.00 | 70–75 |
| 10 | 8.60 | 80–85 |

Calculate the full quotes if the treasurer wishes to:

a) Pay 3 year fixed on a semi-annual basis

b) Pay 10 year fixed on an annual basis

c) Receive 5 year fixed on a semi-annual basis

d) Receive 7 year fixed on an annual basis.

15 Two companies can borrow in the currency markets on the following terms:

|  | Company A | Company B |
|---|---|---|
| Fixed-rate dollars | Treasuries + 60 | Treasuries + 180 |
| Floating-rate sterling | LIBOR + 15 | LIBOR + 160 |

The spot exchange rate is $1.50 per £. The two companies engage in a two-year swap transaction on a notional principal of £100m using the services of a swap bank. Company A takes 60 per cent of the arbitrage gain, Company B takes 24 per cent and the swap bank takes 16 per cent. Show how the swap works and calculate the payments made by the two companies if the yield on Treasuries is 7 per cent and LIBOR is 5 per cent in year 1 and 5.5 per cent in year 2.

16 A German company wishes to borrow five-year, fixed-interest US dollars to finance a US investment programme. But the company has never accessed the US dollar bond market before. However, it could borrow five-year, fixed-interest euros at 9 per cent p.a. Five-year dollar-euro currency swaps are quoted at 6.50–6.63 per cent for fixed-interest dollars and 9.15–9.25 per cent for fixed-interest DMs.

    a) Design a swap transaction that provides fixed-interest dollars for the company.

    b) Calculate the company's net cost of borrowing dollars through the swap.

17 Seven-year sterling bonds are yielding 9 per cent per annum and seven-year sterling-dollar cross-currency coupon swaps are quoted at 8.50–8.65 per cent per annum for fixed-rate sterling against dollar LIBOR. Calculate the net return on synthetic dollar floating-rate notes.

18 Consider the following (fixed-to-fixed) zero-coupon currency swap. £10% p.a. is payable against the receipt of $6% p.a. on a principal amount of £100m when the spot exchange rate is $1.50 per £ and the term of the swap is three years.

    a) Determine the cash flows under the swap.

    b) Show how a zero-coupon currency swap can be used to determine the forward exchange rate. What is the three-year forward exchange rate in this case?

# Part III

# PORTFOLIO ANALYSIS, MANAGEMENT AND PERFORMANCE MEASUREMENT

In the third part of the book, we examine the use of securities in constructing portfolios, in managing portfolios and in contributing to portfolio performance.

Drawing on the ideas developed in Part II, we begin with a discussion of an efficient market. If the financial markets are efficient, then we would expect securities to be fairly priced most, if not all, the time. Whenever market inefficiencies occur, the securities will be mispriced, and this gives rise, even if only for very short periods of time, to speculation and arbitrage opportunities. We examine how these opportunities can be exploited. But the bulk of this part of the book is concerned with portfolios of securities. We examine the reasons for investors holding portfolios, concentrating, in particular, on the aversion to risk held by most investors. Given this risk aversion, we examine how useful portfolios are in diversifying certain types of risk. Having demonstrated that most risk can be diversified, we show how the pricing of assets depends on that risk which cannot be diversified, however well a portfolio is diversified. Having done this, we are in a position to analyse the structuring and management of portfolios of securities. We examine the efficacy of both passive and active portfolio management strategies. Then we examine how to measure the performance of a portfolio of securities. Finally we examine how portfolio values can be protected using hedging or risk management strategies.

# Chapter 11

# Market efficiency: theory and evidence

In this chapter, we discuss a number of different concepts of *market efficiency* and also the empirical evidence that has been collected in support of them.

## 11.1 Allocative, operational and informational efficiency

The role of markets in a competitive economy is to allocate scarce resources between competing ends in a way that leads to these scarce resources being used most productively. This means that the highest bidder for the resources gets to use them. When this occurs markets are said to be *allocatively efficient*. The role of financial markets is to allocate investable resources in a way that is allocatively efficient.

A market is said to be *operationally efficient* when the transaction costs of operating in the market (namely, the market-maker's spread and the broker's commission) are determined competitively. In other words, the market operates in a competitive environment with market-makers and brokers earning normal profits (and not monopoly profits) on their activities. A strict definition of operational efficiency implies that the transaction costs of making a market are zero. However, in the real world, markets would not exist if the people who operated them were not compensated for doing so.

A market is said to be *informationally efficient* if the current market price 'instantaneously and fully reflects all relevant available information'. We will analyze this statement in some detail below, but will assume for the moment that it is valid.

A market is said to be *perfectly efficient* if it is simultaneously allocatively efficient, operationally efficient and informationally efficient.

While the three components of perfect market efficiency are interrelated, we will assume that securities markets are allocatively and operationally efficient; our main interest in this chapter concerns whether they are informationally efficient. And although informational efficiency is only one component of market efficiency, we will adopt the convention of treating the terms 'informational efficiency' and 'market efficiency' interchangeably; i.e., when the finance literature speaks of market efficiency it is generally speaking exclusively about informational efficiency.

## 11.2    The EMH, the fair game model and random walk

The statement that market prices 'instantaneously and fully reflect all relevant available information' is known as the *efficient market hypothesis* (EMH). If the statement is true, it means that the market prices of securities will always equal the fair or fundamental values of those securities, or that, if market and fundamental prices are not equal, then the difference between them is sufficiently small that, given transaction costs, this difference cannot be exploited profitably. In short, if the EMH is true, securities markets will be in *continuous stochastic equilibrium.* (This concept is discussed in greater detail below.)

The best way of explaining the EMH is by using the *fair game model.* A fair game is one in which there is no systematic difference between the *actual* return on the game and the *expected* return before the game is played. In terms of securities, the securities market is a fair game if there is no systematic difference between the actual and expected returns on securities. Mathematically, this can be written:

$$r_{i,t+1} = E(r_{i,t+1} \mid \Omega_t) + \varepsilon_{i,t+1}, \tag{11.1}$$

where:

$$r_{i,t+1} \quad = \quad \text{actual return on security } i \text{ in period } t+1;$$
$$E(r_{i,t+1} \mid \Omega_t) \quad = \quad \text{expected return on security } i \text{ in period } t+1, \text{ conditional on } \Omega_t, \text{ the set of information available in period } t;$$
$$\varepsilon_{i,t+1} \quad = \quad \text{expectation or prediction error on security } i \text{ in period } t+1.$$

The error in predicting the actual outcome, $\varepsilon_{i,t+1}$, has to be, in statistical terms, a *non-systematic* (or *white noise) error*, if the securities market is a fair game. A non-systematic error has three statistical properties: *consistency* (or *unbiasedness*), *independence*, and *efficiency*.

The prediction error will be *consistent* (or *unbiased*) if its expected return, conditional on $\Omega_t$, is zero:

$$\begin{aligned} E(\varepsilon_{i,t+1} \mid \Omega_t) &= E[r_{i,t+1} - E(r_{i,t+1} \mid \Omega_t) \mid \Omega_t] \\ &= E(r_{i,t+1} \mid \Omega_t) - E(r_{i,t+1} \mid \Omega_t) \\ &= 0. \end{aligned} \tag{11.2}$$

This simply means that on average, over a large sample of observations, the prediction error will be zero.

The prediction error will be *independent* if it is uncorrelated with the expected return:

$$\begin{aligned} E[\varepsilon_{i,t+1} E(r_{i,t+1} \mid \Omega_t) \mid \Omega_t] &= E(r_{i,t+1} \mid \Omega_t) E(\varepsilon_{i,t+1} \mid \Omega_t) \\ &= 0, \end{aligned} \tag{11.3}$$

which follows from (11.2).

The prediction error will be *efficient* if it is both contemporaneously and serially uncorrelated. Mathematically, this requires the following three equalities to hold:

$$E(\varepsilon_{i,t+1} \varepsilon_{j,t+1} \mid \Omega_t) = 0; \tag{11.4}$$
$$E(\varepsilon_{i,t+1} \varepsilon_{i,t} \mid \Omega_t) = 0; \tag{11.5}$$
$$E(\varepsilon_{i,t+1} \varepsilon_{j,t} \mid \Omega_t) = 0. \tag{11.6}$$

Equality (11.4) says that the prediction error for the $i^{th}$ security is contemporaneously uncorrelated with the prediction error on the $j^{th}$ security (where $j$ is any other security). Equalities (11.5) and (11.6) say that the prediction error on the $i^{th}$ security is uncorrelated with the previous period's prediction error on either the $i^{th}$ or the $j^{th}$ security.

If any of the equalities (11.2) to (11.6) did not hold, then it would be possible to improve the prediction of $r_{i,t+1}$ in (11.1) by using a very simple mechanical rule. For example, suppose that $\varepsilon_{i,t+1}$ is *serially correlated* as follows:

$$\varepsilon_{i,t+1} = \rho_i \varepsilon_{i,t} + e_{i,t+1}, \tag{11.7}$$

where $e_{i,t}$ is white noise. This means that (11.5) is violated, since:

$$
\begin{aligned}
E(\varepsilon_{i,t+1}\varepsilon_{i,t} \mid \Omega_t) &= \rho_i E(\varepsilon_{i,t}^2 \mid \Omega_t) + E(\varepsilon_{i,t} e_{i,t+1} \mid \Omega_t) \\
&= \rho_i \sigma_i^2 + 0 = \rho_i \sigma_i^2 \neq 0,
\end{aligned} \tag{11.8}
$$

where $\sigma_i^2$ is the conditional variance of $\varepsilon_{i,t}$. The best prediction of $r_{i,t+1}$ is now (cf. (11.1)):

$$E(r_{i,t+1} \mid \Omega_t) + E(\varepsilon_{i,t+1} \mid \Omega_t) = E(r_{i,t+1} \mid \Omega_t) + \rho_i \varepsilon_{i,t} \neq E(r_{i,t+1} \mid \Omega_t); \tag{11.9}$$

i.e., by adding an amount which is proportional to the previous period's prediction error, the prediction can be improved. We want to rule out possibilities such as (11.9) and so will assume that equalities (11.2) to (11.6) hold.

So a fair game is defined by equations (11.1) to (11.6). As a simple example of a fair game, consider tossing a coin that has a 55 per cent chance of heads and a 45 per cent chance of tails. If your information set is such that you know that the expectation of heads is 55 per cent, then the game of tossing this particular coin is fair. If, on the other hand, you are told that the coin is a fair one, then the game would be unfair. Similarly, if your information set is such that the return on securities is expected to be 15 per cent and the actual return on securities averages out at 15 per cent, then the securities market is a fair game and the efficient markets hypothesis is valid.

We have spent some time examining the prediction error in (11.1). We now want to spend time examining the formation of expectations $E(r_{i,t+1} \mid \Omega_t)$. Again, the EMH provides some guidance. If the EMH is valid, then securities markets will be in *continuous stochastic equilibrium*. This, as we have already seen, means that security prices always equal their fair or fundamental values. Any change in fundamental values will be reflected immediately in market prices. But the only factor that would cause fundamental values to change would be new information: if there is no new information about a particular security, we will not expect its fundamental value to change at all. However, new information or 'news' is, by definition, unpredictable: otherwise it is not 'news'. Therefore we would expect the return on securities to change in response to new information in a direction and by an amount that is also unpredictable. This, in turn, implies that the best estimate of the return on a security tomorrow is the return on the security today. This is because, even though tomorrow's return will almost certainly differ from today's return, it differs in a way that is completely unpredictable, and hence the best estimate is still today's return. So if the EMH is true, we would expect to have:

$$E(r_{i,t+1} \mid \Omega_t) = r_{i,t}. \tag{11.10}$$

Substituting this into (11.1) gives:

$$r_{i,t+1} = r_{i,t} + \varepsilon_{i,t+1}. \tag{11.11}$$

Equation (11.11) is known as a *random walk* (or a *martingale* or *Brownian motion*). It says simply that the return on a security tomorrow is equal to the return on a security today *plus* an amount that depends on the new information generated between today and tomorrow, which is unpredictable, given today's information set, $\Omega_t$.

Equation (11.11) defines a random walk for the returns on securities where the return includes capital gains as well as income payments. There is a similar equation for the prices of securities:

$$P_{i,t+1} = g_{i,t+1} + P_{it} + \varepsilon'_{i,t+1}, \tag{11.12}$$

where $g_{i,t+1} = r_{i,t+1} \times P_{it}$. Because the expected return on securities is positive, $g_{i,t+1}$ will have a positive expectation. Over time, security prices can be expected to drift upwards. Equation (11.12) therefore defines a *random walk with positive drift* (or a *submartingale*). Had $g_{i,t+1}$ had a negative expectation, then (11.12) would have defined a *random walk with negative drift* (or a *supermartingale*).

## 11.3    The EMH and information

We have considered the EMH in terms of the fair game model and have also considered the implication of the EMH for the evolution of security returns and prices over time. But we have said very little about the information set, $\Omega_t$, that conditions expectations.

Fama (1965, 1970) argued that expectations can be conditioned on three sets of information:

1  the *weak-form* information set, which contains only data on the previous history of the prices of the security under consideration;

2  the *semi-strong-form* information set which contains all publicly available information;

3  the *strong-form* information set, which contains all known information, whether or not it is publicly available (i.e., it contains private *inside information* as well as public information).

More recently, the definition of efficient markets has been altered to state that prices reflect available information only to the extent that the marginal benefits of exploiting the information exceed the transaction costs incurred in doing so (Jensen (1978)).

There are three main versions of the EMH corresponding to the three different information sets.

1.  The *weak-form EMH* says that current security prices instantaneously and fully reflect all information contained in the past history of security prices. In other words, past prices provide no information about future prices that would allow an investor to earn excess returns (over a passive buy-and-hold strategy) from using active trading rules based on historical prices.

2.  The *semi-strong-form EMH* says that current security prices instantaneously and fully reflect all publicly available information about securities markets. If the hypothesis is true, then when any new information (i.e. news) becomes public, it is very rapidly incorporated into security prices. Good news will lead to a rise in prices and bad news will lead to a fall in prices, but once this has happened no further predictable price changes can be expected to occur. In short, this version of the EMH implies that there are no learning lags in the dissemination of publicly available information that can give rise to profitable trading rules. Similarly, if news does not lead to any change in security prices, then if the semi-strong-form EMH is true, we can infer that the news contained no relevant information.

3. The *strong-form EMH* says that current security prices instantaneously and fully reflect all known information about securities markets including privately available inside information. This implies that the markets respond so quickly that not even someone with the most valuable piece of inside information can trade profitably on the basis of it.

## 11.4    The EMH and an information-efficient equilibrium

According to the EMH, security prices fully reflect all available information. But how does this process occur? The answer depends on whether the markets are fully aggregating information or only averaging information. In a market that is *fully aggregating information*, even if a piece of information is held only by a single individual, it will be fully reflected in security prices as though every participant in the market is fully aware of that piece of information. In a market that is *averaging information*, security prices will only reflect the average impact of different pieces of information. This is because not every individual is equally well-informed and the response of security prices to new information depends on the balance between 'informed' and 'uninformed' investors.

A strong-form efficient market requires information to be fully aggregating: if this is the case, then not even insiders can exploit their informational advantage. A semi-strong-form efficient market requires only that the market is averaging information. Since the latter case is the most likely in practice, we shall concentrate attention on a market that is averaging information and examine the kind of equilibrium that may result in such a market.

In an information-averaging market there is an important distinction between 'informed' and 'uninformed' investors. Informed (or smart) investors (e.g. institutional investors or rich private clients) invest in costly research and aim to use their superior information to take trading positions and hence to make excess returns. Current security prices respond to the activities of the informed investors. Uninformed investors (sometimes called *noise traders*), on the other hand, do not invest in collecting information, but, by seeing what is happening to security prices, they can infer the information acquired by the informed traders. In this way, all investors become informed.

Is it better to be an informed investor, or an uninformed investor? The choice is between paying for costly information and using it to generate excess returns, or saving on information costs and allowing others to ensure that prices reflect available information. The answer depends on which strategy leads to the greatest return after costs.

Suppose that every investor decides it is better to be informed. Suppose also that information costs are 4 per cent of a security's price and that transaction costs add another 4 per cent. In return, investors can use the information acquired to generate a gross return of 6 per cent. Hence their net return is −2 per cent. Since everyone is paying for information, no one has a competitive advantage over any other investor. Suppose now that someone decides not to bother to pay for information. His gross return falls from 6 per cent to, say, 5 per cent, but his information costs fall from 4 per cent to zero. He still has to pay transaction costs, but his net return is 1 per cent, 3 per cent more than if he paid for information. Because of the higher return, other investors decide not to buy information either, so the number of uninformed investors begins to grow. As it does so, however, the market becomes more and more inefficient and the return to all investors begins to fall. In the limit, everyone becomes an uninformed investor and the gross return falls to, say, 3 per cent. After transaction costs this means that the net return is −1 per cent. Now suppose that one investor decides to pay for information. Suppose that his gross return from doing this is 10 per cent. After transaction and information costs, his net return is

2 per cent. Because of the higher return, other investors decide to buy information, so the number of informed investors begins to increase. As it does so, the market becomes more and more efficient and the return to informed investors begins to fall.

Clearly, an equilibrium with either all investors being informed or all investors being uninformed is unstable. For a stable equilibrium to exist, it must be the case that there is a balance between informed and uninformed investors. And that balance will occur when the net return to both investment strategies is zero (the standard result for a competitive equilibrium). Such an equilibrium is known as a Grossman-Stiglitz (1980) *information-efficient equilibrium*. In the example above, the gross return to uninformed investors has to be 4 per cent in equilibrium, and the gross return to informed investors has to be 8 per cent. The equilibrium percentage of informed investors ($\theta_I$) is found by solving:

$$-2(\theta_I) + (1 - \theta_I) \;=\; 0,$$

giving $\theta_I = 33$ per cent.

The information-efficient equilibrium requires both informed and uninformed investors to exist, but after costs both sets of investors will earn the same competitive return. Another implication of the theory is that market prices will reflect the information held by informed investors. A further implication is that security or investment analysts, speculators and arbitrageurs all have an essential role to play in ensuring that security markets are efficient. We examined the role of investment analysis in Chapter 6. In the next chapter, we turn to speculation and arbitrage.

## 11.5   Tests of the efficient markets hypothesis

### 11.5.1   Evidence favouring the efficient markets hypothesis

The early evidence seemed remarkably consistent with the hypothesis that financial markets were indeed efficient.

The most important early test of the weak-form EMH was the test of a particular technical trading rule called the *k% filter rule* (Alexander (1961) and Fama and Blume (1966)). A *k%* filter rule operates as follows: buy a security if its price has risen *k%* above a previous low, hold until the price falls *k%* from the next high, then sell and go short, hold the short position until the price rises *k%* from the next low, then cover the short position and go long. If there are systematic patterns over time in security prices, then a filter rule should earn excess returns over a buy-and-hold strategy. The key question is: what is the optimal size of *k*? If *k* is too small (e.g. if $k = 0.5$ per cent) then trading in a security will be excessive and high transactions costs will be incurred. If *k* is too large (e.g. $k = 20$ per cent), then, even though transaction costs are not high, many turning points will be missed. The early evidence showed that the size of the filter is irrelevant, because, whatever its size, no filter rule can systematically generate excess returns (after transaction costs) over a buy-and-hold strategy. This test provided strong evidence that securities markets are weak-form-efficient: security prices incorporate any information embodied in past prices far too rapidly for there to be a profitable trading rule based on the movement of past prices.

One of the most important early tests of the semi-strong-form EMH was to see whether the information contained in company reports (particularly earnings announcements contained in company reports) leads to significant changes in security prices following the public release of the reports (Ball and Brown (1968)). If the semi-strong-form EMH is true, then no trading rule based on the announcements can lead to positive excess returns (after adjusting for risk and transaction costs) because security prices will either have responded too quickly to the information contained in the announcements, leaving no further predictable price changes to be exploited, or will not have responded at all, because the announcement contained no relevant information. Certainly, if the EMH is true, it would be too late for an investor to wait until the announcement is reported in the financial press the following day.

The evidence indicated that, once an adjustment has been made for risk and transaction costs, most (i.e. about 90 per cent) of the adjustment to earnings occur *before* the announcement is made. In other words, the market is correctly anticipating earnings changes before they are announced to the public. This is because investors are utilizing more immediate sources of information (such as stockbrokers' reports) to make decisions about whether to buy or sell a particular share. If the information being acquired about the company is good, the share price will be increasing and most of the increase will have occurred before the favourable earnings announcement is made by the company itself. The opposite outcome will occur if the news about the company is unfavourable. These results are shown in a stylized way in Figure 11.1. With 'good news' companies, about 90 per cent (on average) of the increase in

---

**Figure 11.1** Price changes preceding and succeeding earnings announcements

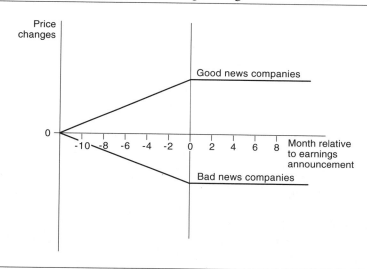

---

the share price takes place in the twelve months prior to the announcement and only 10 per cent of the increase takes place in the subsequent six months. A similar result occurs with 'bad news' companies. The evidence therefore indicates that securities markets are semi-strong-form-efficient in the sense that no trading rule based on exploiting the information embodied in public earnings announcements will generate excess returns compared with a buy-and-hold strategy.

Another important early test was based on price changes around a large block trade (Kraus and Stoll (1972), Dann, Mayers and Raab (1977)). A large block of, say, 10,000 shares sold by a large investor might be sold because the investor has discovered some bad news about a company. The news would initially be the private information of the investor, but the information content of the news could be inferred once the block trade had taken place. If the news is bad, this should permanently lower the share price. But it is possible that the markets initially overreact to the announcement of the block trade and the share price falls by more than the difference between the old and the new (lower) equilibrium price before rising to this new price level. In other words, there might be price pressures at the time of a block trade that enable investors to make positive excess returns (after adjusting for risk and transactions costs) from buying shares in a company just after a block trade has been announced and selling later. The evidence for this is presented in a stylized way in Figure 11.2. The evidence presented in the above studies indicates that the price pressures at the time of a block sale were such

**Figure 11.2** Price changes preceding and succeeding announcements of block trades

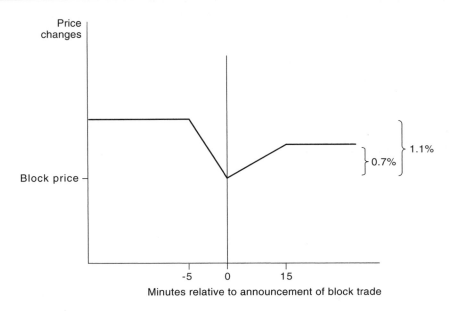

that prices did fall (by an average of 1.1 per cent) as a result of the sale and then rose (by an average of 0.7 per cent afterwards). But the important point is that the recovery in price took only 15 minutes on average to occur, thereby indicating how fast financial markets adjust to new, unexpected information, such as a block trade. The conclusion from these studies is that while block sales do contain important information in the sense that the post-block price is permanently lower, financial markets appears to be semi-strong-form efficient, because no excess profits are available more than a few minutes after news of the block sale becomes publicly available.

There have been other tests of the semi-strong-form EMH. For example, tests have been made of whether publicly announced changes in the discount rate by the Bank of England affect present values and hence security prices. The evidence indicates that the market correctly predicts a change in the discount rate and that most of the adjustment to security prices takes place before the announcement is made. Hence after the announcements made, there is no trading rule based on exploiting the information about discount rate adjustments that will generate excess returns compared with a buy-and-hold strategy.

As another example, there were tests based on leading and lagging securities. If particular securities consistently lead the business cycle and others consistently lag, then it would be possible to design a rule for trading in the lagging securities once the change in the prices of the leading securities had been observed. However, there was no evidence that particular securities consistently lead while others consistently lag the business cycle.

All this early evidence suggested that securities markets are not only weak-form-efficient, they are also semi-strong-form-efficient. It appeared from the early evidence that no trading rule based on exploiting publicly available information can be used consistently to generate excess returns over a buy-and-hold strategy once adjustments for risk and transaction costs are taken into account.

The evidence for the strong-form EMH is conflicting. Despite the fact that insider trading is illegal in a number of countries (it has been illegal in the UK since 1980), there is evidence that it can lead to excess returns after adjusting for risk and transaction costs. One has only to think of the cases of Ivan Boesky in the USA and Geoffrey Collier in the UK. These two cases illustrate that insiders can make large profits, but not without some risk, especially the risk of getting caught!

This is evidence against the strong-form version of the EMH. But it is evidence based on illegal behaviour. There is different evidence, which is based not on the illegal use of information but rather on the legal acquisition and use of information, which suggests that even the strong form of the EMH may hold. The alternative evidence comes from the performance of unit trusts (or mutual funds, as they are known in the USA). Unit trusts spend a great deal of time, effort and money on research into companies. In other words, they generate information about company performance. This information is not public information; it is private information, although it is not illegal inside information. The question is: do unit trusts earn sufficient excess returns on a risk-adjusted basis from using this information to cover their research costs? The evidence shows that, on average, unit trusts do make just enough risk-adjusted excess returns to cover their research costs. In other words, unit trusts, on average, make the same return adjusted for risk and costs as a buy-and-hold strategy (Jensen (1968), Ippolito (1989)).

Most of the early tests of efficient markets were performed on the equity market, but similar results were obtained in the bond market. In the case of bonds, testing centred on whether the expectations hypothesis was supported by the data. Modigliani and Sutch (1966) and Modigliani and Shiller (1973), for example, used averages of ex post realised short-term interest rates as proxies for ex ante forecasts of short-term interest rates to test whether these forecasts explained the term structure; the tests confirmed the expectations hypothesis. Meiselman (1962) calculated one-year forward rates implied by the yield curve such as:

$$_1rf_2 = \left[(1+rs_2)^2/(1+rs_1)\right] - 1,$$

where $rs_1$ and $rs_2$ are one- and two-year spot rates. He found that revisions to these implied forward rates over time were highly correlated with forecasting errors in the models that he used to predict future interest rates and concluded that this was further evidence in support of the expectations hypothesis. Even more evidence came in the form of a study by Malkiel (1966) who found that changes in the relative supplies of bonds at different maturities had no effect on interest rate differentials at these maturities. This indicated that bonds at different maturities were perfect substitutes for each other, so that the supply of a bond of a particular maturity could be increased without changing its relative price *vis-à-vis* other bonds. This is exactly what is implied by the expectations hypothesis which says that interest rates for bonds of one particular maturity are related only to interest rates on bonds of adjacent maturities not on their relative supplies.

Testing for efficient markets began in the early 1960s and for a 20-year period during the 60s and 70s, the evidence indicated that securities markets were both weak-form and semi-strong-form-efficient. Using either information on lagged security prices or any currently available public information, it appeared that it was not possible to generate excess returns for risks and transactions costs. Securities markets also appeared to be strong-form-efficient on the basis of using privately-generated information.  However, they appeared to be strong-form-inefficient on the basis of using private (but illegal) inside information.  With this exception, the early evidence on the EMH was overwhelming. Smart, rational investors in pursuit of profit opportunities collectively acted in a way that made financial markets efficient in the sense that security prices instantaneously and fully reflected all relevant information, so that the vast majority of investors could be confident of trading at fair prices.  During this period, the efficient markets hypothesis became almost an act of faith.  The period coincided with the rational expectations revolution that was taking place in other parts of economics, especially macroeconomics (Muth (1961) and Begg (1982) for a survey).  Any evidence that was found to be inconsistent with the EMH was sacrilegious, inconsistent with rational behaviour by individuals and clearly wrong; and any heretic coming forward with such evidence found it very difficult to get his results published.

But the evidence would not go away and could not indefinitely be swept under the carpet.  From the beginning of the 1980s that evidence did start to appear in the academic literature.  It was the start of the so-called *anomalies* literature, that is, the publication of research papers presenting evidence of *empirical regularities* that appear to be inconsistent with the EMH and which defy rational economic explanations.

## 11.5.2   Evidence against the efficient markets hypothesis

In terms of the weak-form EMH, some professional traders have long believed, despite the early evidence on filter rules, that profitable technical trading rules based only on the past history of security prices do in fact exist.  One example is the *double moving average rule*.  The trader uses a short (e.g. 10 day) and a long (e.g. 60 day) moving average of security prices.  When the short moving average rises above the long moving average, this is a signal to purchase the security and when the short moving average falls below the long moving average, this is a signal to sell the security.  Brock, Lakonishok and LeBaron (1992) showed that this rule, when applied to US equity prices between 1897 and 1986, generated above average returns of about 17 per cent per annum.  Another example is the *trading range breakout rule* (or *channel rule*) which signals a buy instruction when a day's closing price is above the highest price recorded over the last 100 (say) trading days as long as the previous day's closing price was below the highest price; similarly a sell instruction is signalled when the closing price on two consecutive days moves from being above to being below the lowest price recorded over the previous 100 trading days.  Brock et al. showed that this trading rule when also applied to US equity prices generated returns of nearly 18 per cent per year.  This builds on earlier evidence by Logue and Sweeney (1977) and Sweeney (1986) which also found that a range of filter rules applied to foreign exchange movements generated excess returns compared with a buy-and-hold strategy.  Similar results have been obtained in the derivatives markets.  For example, Taylor (1992) has examined double moving average, trading range break out and filter rules on a number of currency futures contracts (sterling, Deutschmark, Swiss franc and yen) traded on the Chicago Mercantile Exchange between 1981 and 1987.  He found that over the period, an investment strategy based on a combination of these rules could have generated average excess returns above the risk free rate of more than 7 per cent per annum.

In terms of the semi-strong-form EMH a whole range of negative results has emerged since the early 1980s for each class of security: shares, bonds, foreign exchange, futures and options.

In terms of shares, one of the earliest class of anomalies to be identified is the *calendar effects*, significant excess returns associated with specific times of the day, days of the week, or months of the year. The five most persistent of these calendar effects are: the *January effect*, the *turn-of-the-month effect*, the *Monday* (or *weekend*) *effect*, the *day-end effect* and the *holiday effect*. Rozeff and Kinney (1976), using data on equities listed on the New York Stock Exchange, found that, between 1904 and 1974, the average return on shares in January exceeded the average return on shares for the other eleven months by 3.06 per cent. Ariel (1987) found that returns during the first half of any month (defined to include the last business day of the previous month) were much higher than the returns during the second half of the month. Lakonishok and Smidt (1988) found that the turn-of-the-month effect was actually concentrated in the first three trading days of the month. French (1980) and Gibbons and Hess (1981) found that the average return on shares was negative on Mondays whereas it was positive for the other days of the week. The French study, for example, found that the average returns on US shares over the period 1953 to 1977 for each day of the week (beginning on Monday) were as follows: –0.17 per cent, 0.02 per cent, 0.10 per cent, 0.04 per cent and 0.09 per cent. Harris (1986, 1989) found that the negative return for Mondays was actually concentrated in the first hour of trading on Monday morning and that thereafter Monday's share price movements behaved in the same way as on other days of the week; in particular Harris found that there was a significant upward movement in prices during the last half hour of trading for every day of the week, including Mondays. Ariel (1990) found that returns on the two trading days prior to national holidays in the US (especially Labor Day, Thanksgiving and Good Friday) were between 9 and 14 times higher than the average daily returns for the rest of the year. All these calendar effects seem to be inconsistent with the semi-strong-form EMH, since they are examples of empirical regularities that could be exploited by a simple trading rule to generate excess returns.

Another set of anomalies that has been found in respect of shares is related to the characteristics of the firms that issue the shares. It has been discovered that it is possible to generate excess returns by trading on the basis of such publicly-available information about a firm as its size, its market-to-book ratio and its earnings yield (earnings-price ratio).

Banz (1981) was the first to identify the *small firm effect*, i.e. the positive excess returns that could be generated by investing in small companies with low stock market capitalizations (sometimes called *small cap stocks*). Banz found that by investing in the smallest 20 per cent of firms quoted on the New York Stock Exchange over the period 1936 to 1988, it was possible to generate differential returns above the largest 20 per cent of firms of 19.8 per cent per year. There also appears to be a connection between the small firm effect and the January effect. Keim (1983) found that, over the period 1963 to 1979, the excess return generated by small cap shares over large cap shares was concentrated in the first five trading days of January: 26.3 per cent of the excess return was generated in those five days, whereas if the small firm effect was spread evenly over the year, only 0.4 per cent of the excess return would accrue over this period.

Fama and French (1992) examined the relationship between the return on securities and market-to-book ratios, earnings-price ratios and firm size. The *market-to-book ratio* is the ratio of the market value of a firm's share to its book value, using the firm's latest balance sheet; it is often used to divide shares into two categories: *growth shares* (which have high market-to-book ratios) and *value shares* (which have low market-to-book ratios). Fama and French found a strong negative relationship between returns and market-to-book ratios. Firms with the lowest 1/12th market-to-book ratios had higher average returns than firms with the highest 1/12th market-to-book ratios (1.83 per cent per month compared with 0.30 per cent per month over the period 1963-1990). This result suggests that value shares tend to outperform growth shares: the great value investor Warren Buffet has known this for years. Fama and French also found a strong positive relationship between returns and earnings-price ratios. Firms with the largest 1/12th earnings-price ratios had higher average returns than firms with the lowest 1/12th earnings-price ratio (1.72 per cent per month compared with 1.04 per cent per month). Since value shares tend to have higher earnings-price ratios than growth shares, this result provides further evidence for the conclusion that value shares outperform growth shares. Finally Fama and French also found a strong negative relationship between returns and firm size: the shares of smaller firms tended to have higher average returns than the shares of larger firms (1.64 per cent per month compared with 0.90 per cent per month on average), again confirming the existence of the small firm effect. All these results are incompatible with semi-strong-form market efficiency since it should not be possible to earn excess returns on the basis of characteristics of firms that are readily observable.

As a final illustration of evidence against the semi-strong-form EMH in respect of equity markets, we can consider the *volatility tests* conducted by Shiller (1981) and LeRoy and Porter (1981). Shiller, for example, began with the concept of the *perfect foresight price* ($P_0^*$) of a share as equalling the discounted value of the future dividends on a share on the assumption that all these future dividends are known with certainty:

$$P_0^* = \sum_{t=1}^{\infty} \frac{d_t}{(1+r)^t}. \tag{11.13}$$

If the financial markets are efficient, then the actual share price will equal the expectation of the perfect foresight price, conditional on all publicly available information at time $t = 0$ (i.e. $\Omega_0$):

$$P_0 = E(P_0^* \mid \Omega_0). \tag{11.14}$$

Now, (11.14) implies that:

$$P_0^* = P_0 + \varepsilon_0, \tag{11.15}$$

where $\varepsilon_0$ is a white noise prediction error at time $t = 0$ that is uncorrelated with $P_0$. This in turn implies that:

$$
\begin{aligned}
\text{Cov}(P_0^*, P_0) &= \text{Cov}(P_0 + \varepsilon_0, P_0) \\
&= \text{Cov}(P_0, P_0) + \text{Cov}(\varepsilon_0, P_0) \\
&= \sigma^2(P_0),
\end{aligned}
\tag{11.16}
$$

where $\text{Cov}(P_0^*, P_0)$ is the covariance between $P_0^*$ and $P_0$, and $\sigma^2(P_0)$ is the variance of $P_0$. From the definition of the correlation coefficient:

$$\rho(P_0^*, P_0) = \frac{\text{Cov}(P_0^*, P_0)}{\sigma(P_0^*)\sigma(P_0)}, \tag{11.17}$$

we substitute from (11.16) to obtain:

$$\sigma(P_0) = \rho(P_0^*, P_0)\sigma(P_0^*). \tag{11.18}$$

Since the maximum value of the correlation coefficient between $P_0^*$ and $P_0$ is unity, Shiller was able to obtain an upper bound to the variability of the actual share price $P_0$, given the variability of the perfect foresight price $P_0^*$:

$$\sigma(P_0) \leq \sigma(P_0^*). \tag{11.19}$$

An alternative form of the *variance bound* can be found by recognizing that the infinite geometric sum (11.13) can be derived from the recursive relationship:

$$P_0^* = \frac{d_1 + P_1^*}{1+r}, \tag{11.20}$$

or:

$$(P_1^* - P_0^*) + d_1 - rP_0^* = 0. \tag{11.21}$$

Taking expectations of (11.21) conditional on $\Omega_0$ and rearranging we get:

$$P_1 - P_0 + d_1 - rP_0 = u_0, \tag{11.22}$$

where $u_0$ is the error in predicting the price (i.e. the *price innovation*) at time $t = 0$ (and depends on $\varepsilon_0$ and the errors in predicting $P_1$ and $d_1$). Now in an efficient market, the price innovation $u_0$ will be uncorrelated with the price $P_0$ (i.e. $\text{Cov}(P_0, u_0) = 0$), which implies:

$$\text{Cov}(P_1, P_0) + \text{Cov}(d_1, P_0) - (1+r)\sigma^2(P_0) = 0. \tag{11.23}$$

We can show that (where $\Delta P = P_1 - P_0$):

$$
\begin{aligned}
\text{Cov}(P_1, P_0) &= \text{Cov}(P_1, P_1 - \Delta P) \\
&= \text{Cov}(P_1, P_1) - \text{Cov}(P_0 + \Delta P, \Delta P) \\
&= \sigma^2(P_1) - \text{Cov}(\Delta P, \Delta P) - \text{Cov}(P_0, P_1 - P_0) \\
&= \sigma^2(P_1) - \sigma^2(\Delta P) - \text{Cov}(P_1, P_0) + \sigma^2(P_0). 
\end{aligned} \tag{11.24}
$$

Shiller assumed that share prices were stationary, i.e. $\sigma^2(P_1) = \sigma^2(P_0)$, so that (11.24) becomes:

$$\text{Cov}(P_1, P_0) = \sigma^2(P_0) - \tfrac{1}{2}\sigma^2(\Delta P). \tag{11.25}$$

He also assumed that the correlation between $d_1$ and $P_0$ was a constant $\rho$ so that (11.23) becomes:

$$r\sigma^2(P_0) - \rho\sigma(d)\sigma(P_0) + \tfrac{1}{2}\sigma^2(\Delta P) = 0. \tag{11.26}$$

This quadratic equation in $\sigma(P_0)$ has the solution:

$$\sigma(P_0) = \left[\rho\sigma(d) \pm \sqrt{\rho^2\sigma(d)^2 - 2r\sigma(\Delta P)^2}\right] \Big/ 2r. \tag{11.27}$$

Since we need to have $\sigma(P_0) \geq 0$ and $\rho^2 \leq 1$, this leads to the restriction:

$$\sigma(\Delta P) \leq \sigma(d) \Big/ \sqrt{2r}. \tag{11.28}$$

The two inequalities (11.19) and (11.28) state respectively that, if the semi-strong EMH holds, then the volatility of the perfect foresight share price should exceed the volatility of the actual share price, and the volatility of dividends (divided by the square root of twice the firm's cost of capital, which Shiller assumes to be a constant) should exceed the volatility of share price changes. Shiller showed using price and aggregate dividend data on the Standard and Poor Index between 1871 and 1979 that both these inequalities were violated. He estimated the following: $\sigma(P^*) = 7.51$, $\sigma(P) = 47.2$, $\sigma(d) = 1.28$, $\sigma(d)/\sqrt{2r} = 4.26$, and $\sigma(\Delta P) = 24.3$. Both variance bounds (11.19) and (11.28) are exceeded by a factor of six. In other words, share prices exhibited *excess volatility*, i.e. they were more volatile than implied by the volatility of the fundamental variables that were supposed to determine share prices. Shiller concluded that this was inconsistent with market efficiency and even suggested that it was inconsistent with rational behaviour by investors. Rather he interpreted this as being consistent with *fashions and fads* in investor behaviour. DeBondt and Thaler (1985) also showed that the share market appears to overreact: they found that shares whose price has fallen dramatically over a three-year period would show excess returns of 6.1 per cent per year over the subsequent three years. Most of the evidence against the semi-strong-form EMH that has been gathered since the early 1980s has dealt with shares. We now consider the evidence in the case of the other main classes of security.

In the case of bonds, Shiller (1979) found that long-term interest rates were excessively volatile compared with the volatility of short term interest rates if the expectations hypothesis is valid. He showed that the variance bound in the case of bonds was:

$$\sigma(rh) \ \leq \ \sigma(r) \Big/ \sqrt{2r} \, , \tag{11.29}$$

where $rh$ is the holding period return $[(P_{B,t+1} - P_{Bt} + d)/P_{Bt}]$, $r$ is the short-term rate, and $\sigma(rh)$ and $\sigma(r)$ are the standard deviations of the holding period return and the short term rate, respectively. Shiller found that for US data between 1857 and 1987 the volatility of holding period returns exceeded the variance bound by 1.14 times. The excess volatility, while present with bonds, is much less than for shares, however.

In contrast, Sargent (1972) generated results that conflicted with those of Shiller (1979), but nevertheless were still inconsistent with the expectations hypothesis. Sargent discovered that short term interest rates followed a random walk and he argued that this feature should be incorporated into expectations of future short-term interest rates. But he found that revisions to expected short-term interest rates over time were less than implied by the random walk result, i.e. they changed by less than the full extent of actual interest rate changes ($\Delta r_t = r_t - r_{t-1}$). This, in turn, implied that long term interest rates were less volatile than suggested by changes in short-term interest rates if the expectations hypothesis is valid. So, for example, with an upward sloping yield curve, an increase in short-term rates generates a smaller increase in long term rates than is consistent with the expectations hypothesis; as a result, the yield curve flattens. There is also a delay in this effect occurring, so that a profitable trading rule emerges: sell long term bonds when short term rates rise, since long term interest rates are likely to rise (bond prices to fall) in the future.

In terms of exchange rates, there is also some evidence of semi-strong form inefficiency. If market participants are risk-neutral, then the forward exchange rate should be an unbiased predictor of the future spot exchange rate. This can be tested through the estimation of the following regression equation:

$$e_t \ = \ a + b f_t, \tag{11.30}$$

where $e_t$ is the spot exchange rate and $f_t$ is the forward exchange rate from the previous period. If $f_t$ is an unbiased predictor of $e_t$, such that $f_t = E(e_t \mid \Omega_{t-1})$, then in (11.30) we would expect to find $a = 0$ and $b = 1$. Bilson (1981), Frenkel (1981) and Baillie, Lippens and McMahon (1983), using data for the 1970s, found that semi-strong form efficiency can be rejected (since they found $a \neq 0$ and $b < 1$) for sterling, the French franc and the Canadian dollar (all against the US dollar) but not for the Deutschmark, the Italian lira or the Swiss franc (also against the US dollar). However there is another possible explanation. Participants in the currency market might be risk-averse rather than risk-neutral and this means that they need to be compensated for the risks that they take. The compensation takes the form of a risk premium embodied in the forward exchange rate; the risk premium could be time-varying and might be expected to decline as the delivery date approaches. So all we can say strictly is that the joint hypotheses of risk-neutrality and semi-strong market efficiency is rejected by the data.

Another set of tests, based on the covered interest parity hypothesis, provides better support for semi-strong-form efficiency. Tests of covered interest parity have been based on the estimation of the following regression equation:

$$\ln\left(f_t/e_{t-1}\right) = a + b \ln\left[\left(1 + r_{\$,t-1}\right)/\left(1 + r_{\pounds,t-1}\right)\right],$$

where $r_\$$ and $r_\pounds$ are respectively the foreign and domestic interest rates. Frenkel and Levich (1975, 1977), using end-of-day data from the eurocurrency markets, found that, in general, covered interest parity held and that any deviation from it could not be profitably exploited because of the size of transaction costs. Taylor (1987) used high frequency data on foreign exchange markets recorded every 10 minutes over a three-day period: he found that covered interest parity held except temporarily during periods of turbulence.

Elton, Gruber and Rentzler (1984) and Cavanaugh (1987) examined the semi-strong-form efficiency of the futures market. Elton et al. examined the efficiency of US Treasury bill futures between 1976 and 1982. They began by recognizing that there were two ways in which investors could purchase an M-day T-bill. The first was by direct purchase of an M-day T-bill in the spot market. The second was by purchasing a (M+91)-day T-bill in the spot market and simultaneously selling a T-bill future for delivery in M days; then, in M days' time, deliver what is now a 91-day T-bill into the futures market to fulfil the short futures contract. In an efficient market, the two portfolios should yield the same return. Elton et al. tested this by examining an arbitrage strategy that involved the purchase of the cheaper portfolio and financing this by shorting the dearer portfolio. They found that excess returns could be made from this strategy, indicating that the US T-bill futures market was not efficient. Cavanaugh examined the efficiency of currency futures contracts. He found evidence of serial correlation in the daily change in the prices of the sterling and Canadian dollar futures contracts. Members of the exchange who pay only market-makers' spreads could make excess returns from trading on the basis of this serial dependence compared with a buy-and-hold strategy. However ordinary investors who have to pay brokers' commissions as well as market-makers' spreads could not make positive excess returns.

Manaster and Rendleman (1982) and Tucker (1987) examined the efficiency of the options market. Manaster and Rendleman used the Black-Scholes model in reverse to derive the option market's implied equilibrium share price, conditional on the actual option premium, the share's volatility, the exercise price, the risk free interest rate and the expiry time. If the difference between the actual and the implied share price is correlated with subsequent movements in the actual share price, then this means that the options market generates information that is not fully taken into account in the cash market for shares. Manaster and Rendleman tested this hypothesis using data on end-of-day equity option premiums on all listed options exchanges for the period April 1973 to June 1976. They found a statistically significant relationship between implied and actual price differences and future share price movements, but this relationship was not sufficiently strong to generate excess profits once transactions costs were taken into account.

Tucker (1987) undertook a similar study using currency options, but instead of comparing the implied equilibrium exchange rate (calculated under the assumption of covered interest parity) with the actual spot exchange rate, he compared it with the forward exchange rate. When the implied spot rate exceeds the actual spot rate, the currency options market is predicting that the forward exchange rate is undervalued so that profits can be made through the forward purchase of currency. Using data on options for sterling, the Deutschmark, Swiss franc and Japanese yen over the period November 1983 to August 1984, Tucker found that differences between the implied and actual exchange rates were significantly related to movements in the forward rate. This result is similar to that found by Manaster and Rendleman, and Tucker's conclusion about the profitability of trading rules based on the evidence is also similar, namely that the relationship was not sufficiently strong to generate positive excess returns once transaction costs were taken into account.

Beckers (1981) looked at options market efficiency in another way by comparing the implied volatility from the Black-Scholes model with the actual volatility observed in security prices. He found that the implied measure of volatility was biased and, in particular, that options that were either deep out-of-the-money or deep in-the-money had much higher implied volatilities than at-the-money options, a phenomenon that has been called *volatility with a smile* (see Figure 11.3 and Gemmill (1993), Chapter 7). This is inconsistent with market efficiency since there should be a single measure of implied volatility consistent with a single options series.

**Figure 11.3** Volatility with a smile

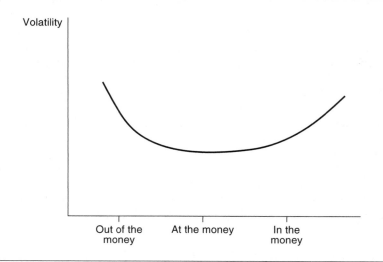

It was possible to publish evidence against the strong-form EMH even during the golden years of the EMH in the 60s and 70s. For example, Lorie and Niederhoffer (1968) and Jaffe (1974) examined the profitability of the trading strategies of insiders, such as company directors and large shareholders. In the US, it is not illegal for designated insiders to trade, but they must register their purchases and sales with the Securities and Exchange Commission. Insiders will have access to privileged information about companies although it is illegal for them to trade on the basis of this information if it is not in the public domain. Nevertheless the studies by Lorie and Niederhoffer and by Jaffe found that insiders purchased shares in their companies prior to rises in share prices and sold shares prior to falls and earned positive excess returns from this strategy. In the UK, a unit trust called the Pointon-BRI Director Dealings Unit Trust and run by BRI Asset Management has been established to exploit this result.

More recently studies by Dimson and Marsh (1984) and Elton, Gruber and Grossman (1986) have shown that positive excess returns could be gained from investing in portfolios of securities formed on the basis of forecasts of security returns provided by a group of investment analysts. These forecasts were based, not on illegal information, but on the costly acquisition of private information. Dimson and Marsh examined 3,364 one-year ahead forecast returns on the top 200 UK shares made by 35 different investment analysts during 1981 and 1982. They found that the average correlation coefficient between actual and forecast returns was 0.08 (8 per cent). Since the squared correlation coefficient is the proportion explained, this implies that 0.64 per cent $\left[(0.08)^2 \times 100\right]$ of the actual return on the UK shares is explained by the investment analysts' forecasts. This appears to be a relatively small percentage explained and there were also wide differences in the forecasting ability of the different analysts: the correlation coefficients for analysts ranged from –0.19 (–19 per cent) to +0.26 (+26 per cent). Further, past forecasting successes were not a good guide to future forecasting successes. However, when the forecasts of the analysts were pooled, the correlation between the actual returns and the average pooled forecast was 0.12 (12 per cent). Although this is 50 per cent higher than the average for the unpooled forecasts, it still indicates that there is only a small amount of information in the combined forecasts of the analysts. Despite this, when a portfolio was constructed on the basis of these forecasts, the performance of the portfolio exceeded that of the market by 2.2 per cent. Furthermore, more than half the information contained in the forecasts was incorporated into share prices within one month of the publication of the forecasts. Similar results were found by Elton, Gruber and Grossman based on forecasts made by 720 US investment analysts. These results indicate that financial markets are not strong-form efficient, since the payment for investment analysis does pay dividends, although only if the analysts' forecasts are pooled. But the results also indicate that the financial markets respond fairly rapidly to the information contained in the forecasts.

Strong-form efficient markets tests have also been conducted in markets other than the equity market, e.g. the foreign exchange market. For example, Bilson (1983) examined the performance of currency forecasting services which generate privately available forecasts for their subscribers. He found that it was possible to generate privately available forecasts for their subscribers. Blake, Beenstock and Brasse (1986) found that exchange rate forecasts had about the same predictive power as the forward rate which, as we have seen, is not, in general, a particularly good predictor of future spot exchange rates. This evidence suggests that the foreign exchange market is inefficient at least when combined with the joint hypothesis of risk-neutrality.

So with the possible exception of the options market, a substantial body of evidence accrued during the 1980s which suggested that the financial markets were not as efficient as the evidence from the 1960s and 1970s once suggested. However, from the second half of the 1980s onwards, there has been a counter-attack from supporters of the efficient markets hypothesis as we shall now see.

## 11.5.3   Are the financial markets efficient?

Supporters of the efficient markets hypothesis have responded to the evidence questioning the existence of financial market efficiency in one of two ways. First, they have attacked the theoretical foundations of the analyses that have concluded that financial markets are inefficient. Second, they have tried to account for anomalies that have been identified, arguing that those researchers who have found them offer no theory to explain them.

The classic theoretical attack has been that on the volatility tests. The excess volatility results of Shiller (1979, 1981) have been criticized by a number of researchers, e.g. Flavin (1983), Kleidon (1986) and Marsh and Merton (1986). The main criticism centres on the assumption used by Shiller to detrend his actual and perfect foresight price series, $P$ and $P^*$. He detrended these variables by multiplying them by the factor $e^{-gt}$ where $g$ is the average growth rate in prices over the entire sample period. Kleidon showed that this was an invalid procedure if dividends followed a random walk rather than the constant deterministic growth trend assumed by Shiller. In particular, Kleidon argued that if the log of dividends followed a random walk with constant positive drift, then it was possible to find apparent excess volatility in share prices even when the efficient markets model (11.13) to (11.15) was valid. In other words, the excess volatility could be a spurious consequence of assuming a deterministic trend in a model where the underlying dividend process was generated by a nonstationary random walk process. This is because it is possible to fit a trend line through a random walk process even if the random walk has no drift component: the estimated trend is entirely spurious and it is invalid to extrapolate it. Flavin used a similar argument to criticize Shiller's variance bounds test in the bond market. Marsh and Merton proved these results analytically. They show that if the dividend process is random walk, then the variance bound specified by Shiller will always be violated in a finite sample, even if the efficient markets model (11.13) to (11.15) is true.

There have been a number of attempts to address the anomalies literature. For example, Sullivan, Timmermann and White (1998) show that the calendar effects can be completely explained by *data snooping*, whereby the same data set that was used originally to identify a calendar effect is also used to test hypotheses about the effect. As they argue: "In the limited sample sizes typically encountered in economic studies, systematic patterns and apparently significant relations are bound to occur if the data are analyzed with sufficient intensity" (p.2). They show that, although the small number of calendar effects that have been publicly reported are statistically significant when examined in isolation, this significance disappears when the full set of 9,500 possible calendar trading rules are examined simultaneously. Similarly, a low market-to-book ratio might indicate that a firm is in financial difficulties, with its future earnings particularly sensitive to market conditions, so that the firm's shares would need to offer a higher return than otherwise to induce investors to hold them. Finally, it has been argued that investors might irrationally prefer large firms and this drives down yields.

In any event, some of the most blatant anomalies have disappeared after researchers had identified them and recognition of this has changed the nature of the debate. It has become now not so much a debate about whether the financial markets are efficient or inefficient, but a debate about 1) the speed with which the financial markets become efficient and 2) whether some market participants are fully rational. Market efficiency is therefore not just about whether prices fully reflect available information, it is also about winners and losers. If financial markets are inefficient, then this means that *smart* (informed) *investors* can use mechanical trading rules to earn excess profits at the expense of so-called *noise* (uninformed) *traders* (Campbell and Kyle (1993)). It is clear why consistent winners stay in the game, but why should consistent losers?

The early versions of the EMH argued that the activities of smart investors would quickly bankrupt noise traders and drive them out of the market and this would make prices efficient (Friedman (1953), for example, argued this). But now it is believed that the complete arbitraging away of all these anomalies is unlikely, largely because smart investors do not have sufficient resources to do so. But without complete arbitrage, it is not necessarily in the interests of smart investors to keep prices efficient. We know that experiments on mass psychology show that noise traders have a tendency to overreact to news (Tversky and Kahneman (1982)), extrapolate trends (De Bondt (1993)) or become overconfident and take on excessive risk (Shleifer and Summers (1990)). Smart investors therefore know that if they see that noise traders have become excessively bullish about a share, it might pay them to run with the herd, rather than try to short what they know to be an overvalued share. Smart investors are still using information efficiently, by taking into account the behaviour of noise traders, but the share prices that emerge might well appear to be inefficient to any independent observer.

Black (1986) argued that noise trading was necessary for a fully functioning financial system. Without noise, there would be no misinterpretation of information, no differences of opinion on price, and hence no trading: in short, no financial system. Shleifer and Summers (1990) go on to explain the presence of noise traders using the concept of *limited arbitrage*. Smart investors and noise traders co-exist in financial markets. The smart investors act on information but have an aversion to risk. While the actions of noise traders cannot affect the fundamental prices of securities, they can increase the risk present in the market. The larger the number of noise traders operating in the market, the greater the noise content of securities prices. This implies larger potential pricing anomalies. Informed traders therefore face greater potential profits but also greater risks. They can therefore never be absolutely sure that their information has not already been incorporated into securities prices and that they are not just trading on the basis of noise themselves. So the existence of potential profit opportunities does not necessarily imply markets are inefficient since these profit opportunities are not riskless.

The presence of noise traders and the consequential limited arbitrage opportunities available to smart investors can lead to excess volatility and mean reversion. Fundamental values respond to information, but securities prices respond to both information and noise. A big increase in noise, say as a result of the fashions and fads favoured by noise traders, can induce *excess volatility* in security prices (Shiller (1989), Chapter 2). It is also possible for the effect of noise to be cumulative, so that prices temporarily overshoot their long-run fundamental values before returning slowly to equilibrium. This is known as *mean reversion* (Shiller (1989), Chapter 1). If smart investors acquire a piece of good information about a firm, they will buy the firm's shares causing a jump in the share price. Noise traders observe the increase in price and increase their demand for the share. This causes the price to rise even more (it is now well above fundamental values) and smart investors begin to unload their shares onto the market. The share price peaks and begins to fall. Noise traders panic and also begin to sell their shares, further depressing the price which may now undershoot the fundamental value. Smart investors begin to buy back the undervalued shares and their actions restore the share price to its fundamental value. Because the noise traders buy shares if they observe share prices rising and sell shares if they observe share prices falling, they are sometimes called *positive feedback traders*; had they adopted the contrarian strategy of selling shares while they are still rising, and buying them while they are still falling, then they would be called *negative feedback traders* (Cutler et al. (1990)).

Mean reversion implies that the returns on securities are *serially correlated* and hence predictable. Consistent with this, Lo and MacKinlay (1988) found that the weekly returns on shares in the US were positively correlated over short periods, while Poterba and Summers (1988) found that returns on US shares were negatively correlated over long periods. All this suggests that share prices do not follow random walks: noise traders could not survive if they did (De Long et al. (1991)). Timmermann (1993, 1995) has shown that in a simple present value model with a constant growth rate in dividends, it is possible for recursive but incomplete learning by rational investors about the process generating 'fundamentals' concerning the firm to induce a transmission mechanism that allows relatively small shocks to fundamentals to have large but transitory effects on stock prices. This, in turn, implies that recursive learning can generate both excess volatility and mean reversion.

But who are the persistent losers? A number of candidates have been suggested. The first is central banks obliged to act under political pressure. Central banks, charged with the task of managing the exchange rate, are believed to be the biggest losers in the foreign currency market, for example; this is well illustrated by the experience of the Bank of England on Black Wednesday, 16 September 1992, when smart investors forced the UK out of the European Exchange Rate Mechanism at the net cost to the Bank of at least £1bn. Another candidate is pension fund managers. While they could not be considered to be naive investors, pension fund managers are under very strong pressures from their sponsoring companies to perform and risk being fired if they cannot justify poor performance. This leads pension fund managers to have an excessive weight in shares that could subsequently be justified to sponsors if need be (after all, as the saying goes, nobody got fired for buying IBM). But all pension managers take the same view and this helps to make such shares overpriced and hence more likely (ironically) to underperform; evidence of underperformance by pension funds can be found in Lakonishok, Shleifer and Vishny (1992) and Blake, Lehmann and Timmermann (1999). Finally, there are individual investors whose investment behaviour might be driven by mood rather than by any rational assessment of particular securities. Evidence for this comes from the performance of investment trusts whose investors are almost entirely individuals rather than institutions. Investment trusts trade at a discount to their net asset value and it has been argued that the size of the discount (itself a sign of a market inefficiency) might be a signal of the degree of collective pessimism or optimism of individual investors.

Can we conclude from all this that financial markets are efficient? Perhaps the last word should go to Ball (1994), p.33, one of the earliest researchers in the field: 'The answer is both yes and no. On the one hand, the research provides insights into stock price behaviour that were previously unimaginable. On the other hand, the theory of efficient markets (like all theories) is an imperfect and limited way of viewing stock markets, as research has come to show. No theory can explain all the data with which it is confronted. Thus, in spite of the rapid early accumulation of much seemingly-supporting evidence, the subsequent accumulation of considerable anomalous evidence, directly or indirectly calling 'efficiency' into question, should be no surprise. The documented anomalous price behaviour includes apparent under-reaction, apparent over-reaction and the variation of expected returns as a function of day-of-the-week, month, size, market-book ratio, dividend yield, earnings yield and other variables that have been difficult to rationalize. It is the variety and volume, not the mere existence, of the accumulated evidence that has been surprising'.

## Selected references

Alexander, S.S. (1961), 'Price Movements in Speculative Markets: Trends or Random Walks', *Industrial Management Review*, May, 7–26.

Ariel, R.A. (1987), 'A Monthly Effect in Stock Returns', *Journal of Financial Economics*, 18, 161–74.

Ariel, R.A. (1990), 'High Stock Returns Before Holidays: Existence and Evidence on Possible Causes', *Journal of Finance*, 45, 1611–26.

Baillie, R., Lippens, R. and McMahon, P. (1983), 'Testing Rational Expectations and Efficiency in the Foreign Exchange Market', *Econometrica*, 51, 553–64.

Ball, R. (1994), 'The Development, Accomplishment and Limitations of the Theory of Stock Market Efficiency', *Management Finance*, 20, 3–47.

Ball, R., and Brown, P. (1968), 'An Empirical Evaluation of Accounting Income Numbers', *Journal of Accounting Research*, Autumn, 159–78.

Banz, R. (1981), 'The Relationship Between Return and Market Value of Common Stock', *Journal of Financial Economics*, 9, 3–18.

Beckers, S. (1981), 'Standard Deviations Implied in Options Prices as Predictors of Future Stock Price Variability', *Journal of Banking and Finance*, 5, 363–81.

Begg, D. (1982), *The Rational Expectations Revolution in Macroeconomics*, Philip Allan, Oxford.

Bilson, J. (1981), 'The Speculative Efficiency Hypothesis', *Journal of Business*, 54, 435–51.

Bilson, J. (1983), 'The Evaluation and Use of Foreign Exchange Rate Forecasting Services', in R.J. Herring (ed.), *Managing Foreign Exchange Risk*, Cambridge University Press, Cambridge.

Black, F. (1986), 'Noise', *Journal of Finance*, 41, 529–43.

Black, F., Jensen, M., and Scholes, M. (1972), 'The Capital Asset Pricing Model: Some Empirical Tests', in M. Jensen (ed.) *Studies in the Theory of Capital Markets*, Praeger, New York.

Blake, D., Beenstock, M. and Brasse, V. (1986), 'The Performance of UK Exchange Rate Forecasters', *Economic Journal*, 96, 986–99.

Blake, D., Lehmann, B.N., and Timmermann, A. (1999), 'Asset Allocation Dynamics and Pension Fund Performance', *Journal of Business*, forthcoming.

Brock, W., Lakonishok, J., and LeBaron, B. (1992), 'Simple Technical Trading Rules and the Stochastic Properties of Stock Returns', *Journal of Finance*, 47, 1731–64.

Campbell, J., and Kyle, A. (1993), 'Smart Money, Noise Trading and Stock Price Behaviour', *Review of Economic Studies*, 60, 1–34.

Cavanaugh, K. (1987), 'Price Dynamics in the Foreign Currency Futures Market', *Journal of International Money and Finance*, 6, 295–314.

Cuthbertson, K. (1996), *Quantitative Financial Economics: Stocks, Bonds and Foreign Exchange*, Wiley, Chichester.

Cutler, D., Poterba, J. and Summers, L. (1990), 'Speculative Dynamics and the Role of Feedback Traders', *American Economic Review*, 80, 63–68.

Dann, L., Mayers, D. and Raab, R. (1977), 'Trading Rules, Large Blocks and the Speed of Adjustment', *Journal of Financial Economics*, 8, 3–22.

De Bondt, W. (1993), 'Betting on Trends: Intuitive Forecasts of Financial Risk and Return', *International Journal of Forecasting*, 9, 355–71.

De Bondt, W., and Thaler, R. (1985), 'Does the Stock Market Overreact', *Journal of Finance*, 40, 793–805.

De Long, J., Shleifer, A., Summers, L., and Waldmann, R. (1991), 'The Survival of Noise Traders in Financial Marets', *Journal of Business*, 64, 1–20.

Dimson, E., and Marsh, P. (1984), 'An Analysis of Broker's and Analysts' Unpublished Forecasts of UK Stock Returns', *Journal of Finance*, 39, 1257–92.

Elton, E., Gruber, M., and Grossman, S. (1986), 'Discrete Expectational Data and Portfolio Performance', *Journal of Finance*, 41, 699–712.

Elton, E., Gruber, M., and Rentzler, J. (1984), 'Intra-Day Tests of the Efficiency of the Treasury Bill Futures Market', *Review of Economics and Statistics*, 66, 129–37.

Fama, E.F. (1965), 'Random Walks in Stock Market Prices', *Financial Analysts Journal*, September-October, 3–7.

Fama, E.F. (1970), 'Efficient Capital Markets: A Review of Theory and Empirical Work', *Journal of Finance*, 25, 383–417.

Fama, E.F., and Blume, M. (1966), 'Filter Rules and Stock Market Trading Profits', *Journal of Business*, 39, 226–41.

Fama, E.F. and French, L.R. (1992), 'The Cross-Section of Expected Stock Returns', *Journal of Finance*, 47, 427–65.

Fama, E., and MacBeth, J. (1973), 'Risk, Return and Equilibrium: Empirical Tests', *Journal of Political Economy*, 71, 607–636.

Flavin, M. (1983), 'Excess Volatility in the Financial Markets: A Reassessment of the Empirical Evidence', *Journal of Political Economy*, 91, 929–56.

Francis, J.C. (1991), *Investments*, McGraw-Hill, Singapore. (Chapter 18.)

French, K. (1980), 'Stock Returns and the Weekend Effect', *Journal of Financial Economics*, 8, 55–69.

Frenkel, J. (1981), 'The Collapse of PPP in the 1970s', *European Economic Review*, 16, 145–65.

Frenkel, J., and Levich, R. (1975), 'Covered Interest Arbitrage: Unexploited Profits', *Journal of Political Economy*, 83, 325–38.

Frenkel, J., and Levich, R. (1977), 'Transaction Costs and Interest Arbitrage: Tranquil Versus Turbulent Periods', *Journal of Political Economy*, 85, 1209–26.

Friedman, M. (1953), 'The Case for Flexible Exchange Rates', in *Essays in Positive Economics*, University of Chicago Press, Chicago.

Gemmill, G. (1993), *Option Pricing*, McGraw-Hill, London.

Gibbons, M. and Hess, P. (1981), 'Day of the Week Effects and Asset Returns', *Journal of Business*, 54, 579–96.

Grossman, S.J., and Stiglitz, J. (1980), 'On the Impossibility of Informationally Efficient Markets', *American Economic Review*, 70, 393–408.

Harris, L. (1986), 'How to Profit from Intradaily Stock Returns', *Journal of Portfolio Management*, 12, 61–64.

Harris, L. (1989), 'A Day-End Transaction Price Anomaly', *Journal of Financial and Quantitative Analysis*, 24, 29–45.

Ippolito, R. (1989), 'Efficiency with Costly Information: A Study of Mutual Fund Performance, 1965-84', *Quarterly Journal of Economics*, 104, 1–23.

Jaffe, J. (1974), 'Special Information and Insider Trading', *Journal of Business*, 47, 410–428.

Jensen, M. (1968), 'The Performance of Mutual Funds in the Period 1945-64', *Journal of Finance*, 23, 389–416.

Jensen, M. (1978), 'Some Anomalous Evidence Regarding Market Efficiency', *Journal of Financial Economics*, 6, 95–101.

Keim, D. (1983), 'Size-Related Anomalies and Stock Return Seasonality: Further Empirical Evidence', *Journal of Financial Economics*, 12, 13–32.

Kleidon, A. (1986), 'Variance Bounds Tests and Stock Valuation Models', *Journal of Political Economy*, 94, 953–1001.

Kraus, A., and Stoll, H.R. (1972), 'Price Impacts of Block Trading on the New York Stock Exchange', *Journal of Finance*, 27, 569–88.

Lakonishok, J., Shleifer, A., and Vishny, R.W. (1992), 'The Structure and Performance of the Money Management Industry', *Brookings Papers: Microeconomics*, 339–91.

Lakonishok, J. and Smidt, S. (1988), 'Are Seasonal Anomalies Real? A Ninety-Year Perspective', *Review of Financial Studies*, 1, 403–25.

LeRoy, S., and Porter, R. (1981), 'The Present-Value Relation: Tests Based on Implied Variance Bounds', *Econometrica*, 48, 555–574.

Lo, A., and MacKinlay, A. (1988), 'Stock Market Prices do not follow Random Walks', *Review of Financial Studies*, 1, 41–66.

Logue, D., and Sweeney, R. (1977), 'White Noise in Imperfect Markets: The Case of the Franc/Dollar Exchange Rate', *Journal of Finance*, 32, 761–8.

Lorie, J., and Niederhoffer, V. (1968), 'Predictive and Statistical Properties of Insider Trading', *Journal of Law and Economics*, 11, 35–53.

Malkiel, B. (1966), *The Term Structure of Interest Rates*, Princeton University Press, Princeton.

Malkiel, B. (1996), *A Random Walk Down Wall Street*, W.W. Norton, New York.

Manaster, S., and Rendleman, R. (1982), 'Options Prices as Predictors of Equilibrium Stock Prices', *Journal of Finance*, 37, 1043–57.

Marsh, T., and Merton, R. (1986), 'Dividend Variability and Variance Bounds Tests for the Rationality of Stock Market Prices', *American Economic Review*, 76, 483–98.

Meiselman, D. (1962), *The Term Structure of Interest Rates*, Prentice-Hall, Englewood Cliffs, NJ.

Modigliani, F., and Shiller, R. (1973), 'Inflation, Rational Expectations and the Term Structure of Interest Rates', *Economica*, 40, 12–43.

Modigliani, F., and Sutch, R. (1966), 'Innovations in Interest Rate Policy', *American Economic Review*, 56, 178–97.

Muth, J.F. (1961), 'Rational Expectations and the Theory of Price Movements', *Econometrica*, 28, 315–35.

Poterba, J., and Summers, L. (1988), 'Mean Reversion in Stock Prices: Evidence and Implications', *Journal of Financial Economics*, 22, 27–59.

Rozeff, M., and Kinney, W. (1976), 'Capital Market Seasonality: The Case of Stock Returns', *Journal of Financial Economics*, 3, 379–402.

Rutterford, J. (1993), *Introduction to Stock Exchange Investment*, Macmillan, London. (Chapter 10.)

Sargent, T. (1972), 'Rational Expectations and the Term Structure of Interest Rates', *Journal of Money, Credit and Banking*, 4, 74–97.

Shiller, R. (1979), 'The Volatility of Long-Term Interest Rates and Expectations Models of the Term Structure', *Journal of Political Economy*, 87, 1190–2119.

Shiller, R. (1981), 'Do Stock Prices Move Too Much to be Justified by Subsequent Changes in Dividends', *American Economic Review*, 71, 421–36.

Shiller, R. (1989), *Market Volatility*, MIT Press, Cambridge, Mass.

Shleifer, A., and Summers, L. (1990), 'The Noise Trader Approach to Finance', *Journal of Economic Perspectives*, 4, 19–33.

Sullivan, R., Timmermann, A., and White, H. (1998), 'The Dangers of Data-driven Inference: The Case of Calendar Effects in Stock Returns', Discussion Paper 304, Financial Markets Group, London School of Economics.

Sweeney, R. (1986), 'Beating the Foreign Exchange Market', *Journal of Finance*, 41, 163–82.

Taylor, M. (1987), 'Covered Interest-Rate Parity: A High Frequency, High Quality Data Study', *Economica*, 54, 429–38.

Taylor, S. (1992), 'Rewards Available to Currency Futures Speculators: Compensation for Risk or Evidence of Inefficient Pricing?', *Economic Record*, 68 (Special Issue on Futures Markets), 105–16.

Timmermann, A. (1993), 'How Learning in Financial Markets Generates Excess Volatility and Predictability in Stock Prices', *Quarterly Journal of Economics*, 108, 1135–45.

Timmermann, A. (1995), 'Volatility Clustering and Mean Reversion of Stock Returns in an Asset Pricing Model with Incomplete Learning', Discussion Paper, University of California, San Diego.

Tucker, A. (1987), 'Foreign Exchange Option Prices as Predictors of Equilibrium Forward Exchange Rates', *Journal of International Money and Finance*, 6, 283–94.

Tversky, A., and Kahneman, D. (1982), 'Evidential Impact of Base Rates', in D. Kahneman, P. Slovic and A. Tversky (eds.), *Judgement under Uncertainty: Heuristics and Biases*, Cambridge University Press, Cambridge.

Weston, J.F. and Copeland, T.E. (1992), *Managerial Finance*, Dryden Press, Chicago. (Chapter 4.)

## Exercises

1 Define the terms 'allocative efficiency', 'operational efficiency' and 'informational efficiency' in respect of financial markets.

2 Distinguish between 'weak-form', 'semi-strong-form' and 'strong-form' versions of market efficiency.

3 If securities markets are fully efficient, then investment analysis is a waste of time and money. Discuss.

4 If securities markets are fully efficient, then the errors in predicting the returns on securities will satisfy the properties of 'consistency', 'independence' and 'efficiency'. Explain these terms.

5 Explain the random walk model of security returns. On what grounds is the model justified?

6 How would you go about testing the different versions of market efficiency?

7 Explain Grossman and Stiglitz's notion of an 'information-efficient equilibrium' in financial markets.

8 What is the evidence for the efficient markets hypothesis?

# Chapter 12

# Speculation and arbitrage

In the last chapter, we discussed a number of different concepts of market efficiency. In this chapter we examine the consequences of different forms of market efficiency for speculating and arbitraging in different types of securities.

The aim of a speculator is to make money by willingly taking on risk. In contrast, the aim of an arbitrageur is to make money without taking on any risk at all. In Appendix A of this chapter, we examine the case of the collapse of Barings Bank which involved an apparent arbitrage operation that went badly wrong: what the management of the bank believed to be purely an arbitrage operation turned out to be pure speculation, with disastrous consequences.

## 12.1  Speculation

### 12.1.1  The process of speculation

*Speculators* (or *traders*) are not especially interested in the role that they have to play in making security markets efficient. They are simply interested in taking either a short or a long position in a particular security in the hope of making a quick short-term profit. They believe that they have better information than other market participants about whether a security is overpriced or underpriced compared with its fair or fundamental value. Fundamental analysis plays an important role in influencing their position-taking strategies. If they think that a security is overpriced they take short positions, while if they believe that it is underpriced they take long positions. Similarly, they could accept that a security is fairly priced currently, but believe that they have superior information indicating that the fair price and hence the market price is about to rise or fall. Again, they could take long or short positions to back their views. This type of trading is known as *open position* (or *directional*) *trading*. If, on the other hand, speculators believe that the prices of two securities are out of line with each other, they will buy the relatively underpriced security and short the relatively overpriced security. This is known as *spread trading*.

In a sense, though, speculators are keen supporters of the efficient markets hypothesis (in its semi-strong form), because they believe that their information is superior to other market participants (such as *noise traders*, see Chapter 11), which allows them to take their positions earlier than the other participants. They can then sit back and wait for the slower investors to recognize the mispricing and to move *en masse* in or out of the security and so act to correct the mispricing. The speculators can then take their profits and run.

It is important for speculators that any mispricing is rapidly corrected because they do not like to hold extended positions. Most speculators do not like to hold positions lasting several days. Indeed, many do not like to hold positions overnight. They prefer any mispricing to be corrected in a matter of hours or even minutes. Speculators who hold positions lasting more than one day are known as *long-duration traders*; those who will not hold overnight positions are known as *day traders*; those who take positions for only a few minutes are known as *scalpers*.

There are two main reasons for not holding extended positions. First, extended position-taking has to be financed and this can be expensive. Speculators prefer not to use any capital at all to fund their position-taking, instead relying on delays arising from the settlement process for securities to provide a 'free' source of finance. This will work, however, only if the mispricing is corrected before the position has to be settled, and, depending on the security, settlement periods last from one day to two weeks. Second, and more importantly, speculators are taking *uncovered* (i.e. *unhedged*) positions. This is extremely risky. It leaves them open to sudden adverse price movements that have nothing to do with the relative mispricing of the underlying security. Consider for example a speculator taking a long position in a share on Friday 16 October 1987, believing it to be relatively underpriced. Suppose that by Monday the relative mispricing had been more than corrected and was showing a 5 per cent relative overpricing. This is splendid — apart from the fact that the absolute value of every share on the planet (including this one) had fallen by about 30 per cent in the meantime. Speculators must know when to run their profits and cut their losses, otherwise their financing costs and their risks become excessive.

While fundamental analysis is important to speculators, this does not necessarily mean that all speculators will take the same view of a particular security. This is because fundamental analysis does not and cannot provide absolute answers about the fair value of a security. The analysis performed by some speculators can lead them to believe that the security is overvalued, while the analysis performed by others leads them to believe that the same security is undervalued. There can be a wide diversity of view about the security. And this is essential for the liquidity of the market. If everyone believed that a security was overvalued, for example, then everyone would be trying to sell and no one would be willing to buy. The market in the security would become highly illiquid, and there would be a sharp mark-down in the security price by market-makers but with little or no actual trading in the security itself. A diversity of views, on the other hand, will give rise to a good flow of both buy and sell orders and the market will exhibit good liquidity.

Nor is fundamental analysis the only method of analysis used by speculators. There are certain groups of speculators called *technical analysts* or *chartists* who use bar charts and point-and-figure charts to detect patterns in the time series of security prices. Different patterns are given different names, such as 'head and shoulders', 'triangles', 'rectangles' and 'double tops'. Technical analysts argue that these patterns repeat themselves over time, and so once a particular pattern starts to form, this aids them in predicting and hence speculating on the future course of prices (see Appendix B).

So speculation involves the exploitation of any mispricing of securities. But the question is: should the exploitation of securities mispricing take place in the cash market or in the market for derivatives, i.e. the futures and options markets? There are problems with operating in the cash market. For one thing, it is often difficult to short cash market securities in sufficient volume to make the speculation worthwhile. For another, cash markets may actually be less liquid than the corresponding derivatives market; this is important for opening and closing positions quickly. The big advantage of speculating using futures and options is that they are highly leveraged bets; only a small amount of capital has to be put upfront to take on large long or short positions. Also transactions costs may be higher in the cash market (e.g., stamp duty is payable in the cash market, but not in the derivatives market). We shall therefore concentrate attention on analyzing trading strategies in futures and options markets.

## 12.1.2 Trading strategies with futures

Three key features about trading with futures are volatility, leverage and marking to market. Trading in financial futures began in the 1970s because of extreme interest rate and exchange rate volatility resulting from the introduction of floating exchange rates and the increase in world interest rates arising from the inflationary pressures caused by the two oil price shocks. If money, capital and foreign exchange markets were ever to stabilize, it is very likely that futures (and options) markets would disappear. High volatility implies that there can be large price changes over very short time periods. High leverage and marking to market, on the other hand, imply that those price changes can lead to magnified profits and losses.

For example, it takes an initial margin payment of only £500 to establish a long position of £500,000 in short-term sterling interest rates by purchasing one LIFFE short sterling futures contract. For every basis point (0.01 per cent) change in interest rates, the value of the contract will change by £12.50. If interest rates fall by 1 per cent (100 basis points), the value of the contract will rise by 100 basis points and the trader will make a profit of £1250, giving a rate of return of 250 per cent on capital employed. Of course, if interest rates rise by 1 per cent, the trader will make a 250 per cent loss.

**Open position trading.** Open position trading with financial futures involves backing a view on the future direction of interest rate, exchange rate or share price movements. It is sometimes also known as *directional trading*. For example, if a speculator believes that interest rates are going to fall (e.g. because he believes that favourable money supply figures are about to be announced) and hence that futures prices are going to rise, he will want to buy futures contracts. Similarly, if he believes that share prices are going to fall (e.g. because he believes that the stock market has become overheated and is due for a correction), he will want to sell futures contracts.

**Example 12.1 (Open position trading: buying futures contracts)** *A speculator believes that interest rates are going to fall (futures prices are going to rise) and buys one December short sterling futures contract on LIFFE at 90.50 (i.e. 100 − 9.50):*

| Day | Action | Futures price | Initial margin (£) | Variation margin (£) | Net profit (£) |
|-----|--------|---------------|--------------------|----------------------|----------------|
| 1 | Buy 1 contract | 90.50 | −500.00 | 0 | −500.00 |
| 2 | Hold | 90.00 | − | −625.00 | −1125.00 |
| 3 | Hold | 90.25 | − | +312.50 | −812.50 |
| 4 | Hold | 90.75 | − | +625.00 | −187.50 |
| 5 | Sell 1 contract | 91.25 | +500.00 | +625.00 | 937.50 |

*On day 1, the speculator buys one contract and puts up initial margin of £500. On day 2, interest rates have risen 50 basis points. The markets have initially responded to the lower-than-expected money supply figures by increasing interest rates on fears of credit tightening. The futures price has fallen by*

*50 ticks (i.e. 0.5%/0.01) and the position is showing a loss of £625 (i.e. 50 ticks × £12.50 per tick). However on day 2, the markets reassess their view, fears of credit rationing subside, and interest rates begin to ease. The futures price begins to rise. By day 5, the position is showing a net profit and the speculator decides to close his position by selling one contract, making an overall profit of £937.50 or 188 per cent on capital employed of £500.*

**Example 12.2 (Open position trading: selling futures contracts)** *A speculator believes that share prices are going to fall and sells one December FTSE 100 futures contract on LIFFE at 2400.0 (the date is Friday 16 October 1987):*

| Day | Action | Futures price | Initial margin (£) | Variation margin (£) | Net profit (£) |
|-----|--------|---------------|--------------------|----------------------|----------------|
| 1 | Sell 1 contract | 2400.0 | −1,000.00 | 0 | −1,000.00 |
| 2 | Hold | 2000.0 | − | +4,000.00 | +3,000.00 |
| 3 | Buy 1 contract | 1600.0 | +1,000.00 | +4,000.00 | +8,000.00 |

*On day 1, the speculator sells one contract and puts up £1000 as initial margin. On (business) days 2 and 3, the price of the contract drops like a stone, by 400 points or 800 ticks (i.e. 400/0.5) on each day. Therefore the daily profit is £4,000 (i.e. 800 ticks × £5 per tick). On day 3, the speculator closes his position by buying one contract and walks away with a profit of £8,000, or 800 per cent on an investment of £1000. This again demonstrates the leverage effect of futures contracts: the market has fallen by 33 per cent, but the value of the futures contract has changed by 800 per cent.*

**Spread trading.** Spread trading involves the simultaneous purchase and sale of related financial futures contracts. The speculator is taking a view on what is going to happen to the *difference* between two futures prices. Spread trading has two advantages over open position trading. First, because it is a trade based on differences, it is likely to be less risky than a trade based on levels. Second, as a result of lower risk, the initial margin requirements are lower on a spread trade in the same contract. Spread trading is an example of non-directional trading.

There are two main types of spread trade. The first is an *intra-contract spread trade* (or *straddle trade*). This involves buying and selling different maturities of the same futures contract on the same exchange, e.g. the purchase of a September three-month sterling deposit future and the sale of a December future. The second is an *inter-contract spread trade*, which involves buying and selling different types of futures contracts on the same or different exchanges, e.g. the purchase of a June sterling deposit future and the sale of a June eurodollar deposit future.

In the case of intra-contract spreads, *buying the spread* (or *putting on a bull spread*) involves the purchase of the distant (e.g. December) contract and the sale of the nearby (e.g. June) contract. A speculator will buy the spread if he thinks that the spread will widen (i.e. become more positive, or become less negative). *Selling the spread* (or *putting on a bear spread*) involves the sale of the distant contract and the purchase of the nearby contract. A speculator will sell the spread if he thinks that the spread will narrow (i.e. become less positive, or become more negative).

LIFFE has introduced (in 1997) a *Spread Trading Facility* (STF) for inter-contract spreads. Prior to the STF, spread traders had to execute one leg of the spread in one trading pit and then move to another trading pit to execute the other leg. Prices might have changed adversely during this process, creating a particular type of *execution risk* known as *leg risk*. The STF allows the spread trade to be implemented in a single trading pit. For example, in the short sterling pit, buying the short sterling-eurodollar spread involves the purchase of the short sterling contract and the simultaneous sale of the eurodollar contract.

A special case of spread trading is known as *basis trading*. This involves buying or selling a futures contract and simultaneously executing the opposite transaction in the underlying cash security. For example, buying the basis involves the purchase of the future and the sale of the cash security. In this case the speculator is expecting the basis to widen. The popularity of basis trading is such that LIFFE has introduced (in 1995) a *Basis Trade Facility* (BTF) for bonds whereby the futures leg of a basis trade is executed at a single price thereby avoiding another type of execution risk known as *delay risk*. This is the risk that the required number of futures contracts cannot be acquired in one transaction at the same price, with the possibility that the profit opportunity is lost by the time the required contracts are in place.

Whether trading the spread or trading the basis, the speculator is not concerned with what is happening to the absolute level of prices; he is concerned only with what is happening to the differences between prices. But the difference between prices cannot be unbounded, since the theory of futures prices provides a theoretical upper limit to the size of the spread (distant futures price *minus* nearby futures price) or the basis (futures price *minus* cash price). From Chapter 8, we know that the spread and the basis cannot exceed the cost-of-carry, i.e. the net cost of buying the security on one date and delivering it into the futures market at a later date. The net cost is the difference between the interest cost of borrowing the funds to buy the security and the income accruing on the security while it is held for delivery. If the cost-of-carry is expected to increase (say, because short-term interest rates are expected to increase), then a speculator might decide to buy the basis or the spread.

**Example 12.3 (Buying the basis)** *Suppose that it is 1 April and the June long gilt future is trading at 92.38, while the cheapest-to-deliver long gilt is the Treasury 10.5 per cent 2013–15 with a price factor of 1.3032131. The CTD bond is trading at a dirty price of £118 per £100 nominal and money market interest rates are 8 per cent. A basis trader believes that short term interest rates are going to rise and so decides to buy the basis:*

$$\text{Basis} = P^f - \frac{P_{CTD}}{PF_{CTD}}, \tag{12.1}$$

*where:*

$$
\begin{aligned}
P^f &= \text{price of the long gilt future;} \\
P_{CTD} &= \text{price of the CTD bond;} \\
PF_{CTD} &= \text{price factor for the CTD bond.}
\end{aligned}
$$

*On 1 April, the basis is:*

$$\text{Basis} = 92.38 - \frac{118.00}{1.3032131} = 1.83.$$

*However, the trader wants to hedge against absolute changes in prices. Ignoring cost-of-carry terms, the relationship between changes in the futures price and the price of the CTD bond is given by:*

$$\Delta P^f = \frac{1}{PF_{CTD}} \cdot \Delta P_{CTD}, \tag{12.2}$$

*where:*

$$\Delta P^f \quad = \quad \text{change in the price of the long gilt future;}$$
$$\Delta P_{CTD} \quad = \quad \text{change in the price of the CTD bond.}$$

*It follows from (12.2) that the futures price moves by less than the cash bond if the price factor ($PF_{CTD}$) exceeds unity and by more otherwise. This relationship can be used to hedge the CTD bond:*

$$\text{Number of contracts} \quad = \quad \frac{\text{Face value of cash bond}}{\text{Face value of futures contract}} \times PF_{CTD}. \qquad (12.3)$$

   *Suppose the trader wants to implement the basis trade on £1,000,000 nominal of the CTD bond. This implies that the number of futures contracts that need to be purchased against the sale of £1,000,000 nominal of the CTD bond is:*

$$\text{Number of contracts} \quad = \quad \frac{£1,000,000}{£100,000} \times 1.3032131 \quad \approx \quad 13,$$

*where the contract size for the long gilt future is £100,000. Any proceeds from the sale of the bond will be placed in the money market. The trader implements the basis trade and 20 days later observes that the future is trading at 92.88 and the CTD bond is trading at £118.25. The basis has now widened:*

$$\text{Basis} \quad = \quad 92.88 - \frac{118.25}{1.3032131} \quad = \quad 2.14,$$

*and the trader closes his position by selling the basis.*

   *The overall profit is calculated as follows. The futures contracts were bought at 92.38 and sold at 92.88, giving a profit of 50 ticks per contract. Therefore:*

$$\text{Profit on futures} \quad = \quad \text{Number of contracts} \times \text{Number of ticks gained} \times \text{Tick value}$$
$$= \quad 13 \times 50 \times £10 \quad = \quad £6,500.$$

*The 10,000 CTD bonds were sold at £118 and repurchased at £118.25, giving a loss of £0.25 per bond. So:*

$$\text{Loss on bonds} \quad = \quad \text{Number of bonds} \times \text{Loss per bond}$$
$$= \quad 10,000 \times £0.25 \quad = \quad £2,500.$$

*Also the proceeds from the sale of the bonds could be placed on deposit for 20 days earning interest at 8 per cent:*

$$\text{Interest earned on proceeds from sale of bonds} \quad = \quad £1,180,000 \times 0.08 \times \frac{20}{365}$$
$$= \quad £5,172.60.$$

*So the total profit from the basis trade was £9,172.60 (i.e. £6,500 – £2,500 + £5,172.60).*

**Example 12.4 (Buying an intra-contract spread)** *A speculator believes that the cost-of-carry is going to rise and so decides to buy a short-term interest rate spread on the three-month short sterling future on LIFFE. On day 1, he buys one September future at 90.00 and sells one June future at 89.50:*

$$\text{Spread} \quad = \quad 90.00 - 89.50$$
$$= \quad 0.50 \quad (\text{or 50 basis points or ticks}).$$

*On day 5, he sells a spread, by selling one September future at 89.00 and buying one June future at 88.25:*

$$\text{Spread} = 89.00 - 88.25$$
$$= 0.75 \quad (\text{or 75 basis points or ticks}).$$

*The profit on the spread trade is:*

$$\text{Profit} = (75 - 50) \text{ ticks} \times £12.50 \text{ per tick}$$
$$= 25 \text{ ticks} \times £12.50 \text{ per tick} = £312.50.$$

*Since his initial (spread) margin was only £225, the speculator has made 139 per cent profit on capital employed.*

The same cost-of-carry analysis carries over to longer-term securities such as the LIFFE long gilt contract. This is because the spread between, say, the June and September long gilt futures prices contains an implicit three-month interest rate for the June-September period. (See Chapter 10 for more details.) Suppose a speculator buys the June contract and sells the September contract. If he took delivery of a gilt under the June contract and held it for redelivery under the September contract, he would accrue interest on the gilt at the current yield and gain the spread between the two contracts.

To illustrate, we will calculate the implicit interest rate between June and September when the June long gilt is trading at 91.28 and the September long gilt is trading at 91.50. The current yield on the June gilt future (which has a 7 per cent coupon) is:

$$\text{Current yield} = \frac{7}{91.28} = 0.0767 \quad (7.67\%).$$

The yield equivalent of the spread 0.22 (i.e., $91.50 - 91.28$) on an annual basis is:

$$\text{Spread yield} = \frac{0.22}{91.28} \times \frac{365}{91} = 0.0097 \quad (0.97\%).$$

Adding the spread yield to the current yield gives the implicit three-month interest rate:

$$\text{Implicit interest rate} = 7.67 + 0.97 = 8.64\%.$$

If a speculator expects the actual three-month rate to be lower than the implicit interest rate, then he is expecting the spread to narrow. He therefore sells the spread.

**Example 12.5 (Selling an intra-contract spread)** *On day 1, a speculator sells one September long gilt future on LIFFE at 91.50 and simultaneously purchases one June future at 91.28:*

$$\text{Spread} = 91.50 - 91.28 = 0.22 \quad (\text{or 22 ticks}).$$

*On day 5, he buys the spread by buying the September future at 91.38 and selling the June future at 91.22:*

$$\text{Spread} = 91.38 - 91.22 = 0.16 \quad (\text{or 16 ticks}).$$

*The profit on the spread trade is 6 ticks:*

$$\text{Profit} = (22 - 16) \times £10$$
$$= 6 \text{ ticks} \times £10 = £60,$$

*or 24 per cent on capital employed, since the initial (spread) margin is £250.*

*The implicit three-month interest rate with the new prices is:*

$$\text{Implicit interest rate} \quad = \quad \frac{7}{91.22} + \frac{0.16}{91.22} \times \frac{365}{91} \quad = \quad 8.38\%,$$

*so the speculator was correct in his belief both about the fall in interest rates and about the narrowing of the spread.*

Another complicated spread trade is the *butterfly spread trade*. This is an example of an intra-contract trade involving three maturities of futures contracts which together form two spreads. A butterfly spread is composed of two spreads, a bull and a bear spread, but with a common middle contract. The speculator is taking a view on the relationship between the two spreads. A butterfly spread trade is used when the middle contract looks out of line with the contracts for the delivery months on either side, but it is not clear which contract(s) will adjust in order to correct the anomaly.

To illustrate, we will consider the sterling currency future for June, September and December:

| *June* | *September* | *December* |
|--------|-------------|------------|
| 1.7010 | 1.7020      | 1.7100     |

The September contract looks relatively undervalued. The June-September spread is 5 ticks (i.e. $(1.7020 - 1.7010)/0.0002$ where 0.0002 is the tick size in \$ per £); the September-December spread is 40 ticks (i.e. $(1.7100 - 1.7020)/0.0002$). The question is: will the June and December prices fall, or will the September price rise? It is impossible to say, but what we can say is that the June-September spread is likely to widen and the September-December spread is likely to narrow, so that the *butterfly spread* (which equals the September-December spread *minus* the June-September spread) is expected to narrow. The speculator therefore buys the June-September spread and sells the September-December spread; i.e., he sells the butterfly spread. As Example 12.6 shows, the profit from this strategy is \$500.

**Example 12.6 (Butterfly spread)** *On day 1, the following prices for the sterling currency future are observed:*

| *Contract:* | *June* | *September* | *December* |
|-------------|--------|-------------|------------|
| *Futures price:* | *1.7010* | *1.7020* | *1.7100* |

*The speculator sells the butterfly spread:*

| | |
|---|---|
| Buy 1 × September contract    1.7020 ⎫ | June–September spread = 5 ticks |
| Sell 1 × June contract    1.7010 ⎭ | |
| Sell 1 × December contract    1.7100 ⎫ | September–December spread = 40 ticks |
| Buy 1 × September contract    1.7020 ⎭ | |

$$\text{Butterfly spread} \quad = \quad 40 - 5 \quad = \quad 35 \text{ ticks}$$

*On day 3, the prices are as follows:*

| *Contract:* | *June* | *September* | *December* |
|-------------|--------|-------------|------------|
| *Futures price:* | *1.7050* | *1.7100* | *1.7140* |

*The speculator reverses his trades:*

$$
\left.\begin{array}{ll}
\text{Sell } 1 \times \text{September contract} & 1.7100 \\
\text{Buy } 1 \times \text{June contract} & 1.7050
\end{array}\right\} \quad \text{June–September spread } = 25 \text{ ticks}
$$

$$
\left.\begin{array}{ll}
\text{Buy } 1 \times \text{December contract} & 1.7140 \\
\text{Sell } 1 \times \text{September contract} & 1.7100
\end{array}\right\} \quad \text{September–December spread } = 20 \text{ ticks}
$$

$$
\text{Butterfly spread} \;=\; 20 - 25 \;=\; -5 \text{ ticks}
$$

*The profit from selling the butterfly spread, which has narrowed is:*

$$
\begin{aligned}
\text{Profit} \;&=\; -(-5 - 35) \text{ ticks} \times \$12.50 \text{ per tick} \\
&=\; 40 \text{ ticks} \times \$12.50 \text{ per tick} \;=\; \$500.
\end{aligned}
$$

Inter-contract spreads are more risky than intra-contract spreads, and this is reflected in the initial margin requirements. The spread trader would have to pay the full amount of initial margin on both legs of the trade.

A classic example of an inter-contract spread trade is known as *trading the yield curve*. The yield on the sterling short sterling futures contract is a short-term (three-month) interest rate. The implied yield on the gilt futures contract is a long-term (10 to 15-year) interest rate. Together, they define the yield curve that the market is expecting on the delivery dates of the contracts. If a speculator believed that the yield curve was going to tilt upwards or downwards, he could back his view with an inter-contract spread.

Suppose, for example, that the speculator believed that the yield curve was going to steepen, so that long-term rates were expected to rise relative to short-term rates. He could back his view by selling the spread, by selling the gilt future and buying the short sterling future; i.e., he would be expecting the spread between futures prices to narrow. (Interest rates are expected to widen, so prices are expected to narrow.)

However, there are a number of complications that have to be taken into account. The speculator is taking a view on changes in relative interest rates, i.e. on relative shifts in the yield curve. But he wants to protect himself from changes in absolute interest rates, i.e. from parallel shifts in the yield curve. Also, the sizes of the two contracts differ: the gilt contract has a nominal value of £100,000 whereas the short sterling contract has a nominal value of £500,000.

The problem of parallel shifts in the yield curve arises because of the nonlinear response of gilt prices, and hence gilt futures prices, to interest rate changes (see e.g. Chapter 5). One measure of interest rate sensitivity that is used in bond pricing is duration:

$$
\Delta P \;=\; -D \times P \times [\Delta rm/(1 + rm)], \tag{12.4}
$$

where:

$$
\begin{aligned}
D \;&=\; \text{duration of the bond;} \\
P \;&=\; \text{price of the bond;} \\
rm \;&=\; \text{yield to maturity on the bond.}
\end{aligned}
$$

This measure can be used to determine the number of long gilt futures contracts compared with the number of deposit contracts required to hedge against a parallel shift in the yield curve. The problem does not arise with the short sterling contract because the price change and the interest rate change are linearly related.

The problem of the different contract sizes is handled as follows. A one percentage point change in price is equivalent to 100 ticks for both the gilt and short sterling contracts. However, the value of a gilt tick is £10 and the value of a short sterling tick is £12.50. Therefore a one percentage point change in the value of the gilt contract is equal to £1000, whereas a one percentage point change in the value of the short sterling contract is equal to £1250.

We can determine the number of short sterling contracts necessary to hedge one long gilt contract using:

$$h = \frac{D \times P_g^f \times 1000}{P_d^f \times 1250}, \tag{12.5}$$

where:

$$h = \frac{\text{Number of short sterling contracts}}{\text{Number of gilt contracts}},$$

and where:

$$
\begin{aligned}
P_g^f &= \text{gilt future price;} \\
P_d^f &= \text{short sterling futures price.}
\end{aligned}
$$

If $P_g^f = 91.50$, $P_d^f = 87.25$ and $D = 11.92$ years, then we need ten short sterling contracts for each long gilt contract to hedge against parallel shifts in the yield curve. In other words, the inter-contract spread would be established by selling one long gilt future and buying ten short sterling futures contracts.

Another example of an inter-contract spread trade is a *cross-currency yield spread* using bond futures contracts. Again the aim is to benefit from movements in relative yields rather from movements in absolute yields. This means that the spread should be set up in such a way that it is hedged against general parallel movements in international yield curves and merely exposed to a widening or narrowing of the yield spread. If a speculator believes that the yield spread between two bond futures contracts is going to *widen*, he should *buy* the contract with the *lower* yield and *sell* the contract with the *higher* yield. This is because the speculator believes that the contract with the lower yield is going to rise in price, while the contract with the higher yield is going to fall in price. If the speculator believes that the yield spread between two bond futures contracts is going to *narrow*, he should *buy* the contract with the *higher* yield and *sell* the contract with the *lower* yield.

We can illustrate a cross-currency yield spread using the long gilt and Bund futures contracts. Each contract will be priced off the cheapest-to-deliver bond that is eligible for delivery under the terms of each contract. Suppose that the CTD under the long gilt contract is the Treasury 10.5 per cent 2013–15, while the CTD under the Bund contract is the Bund 8 per cent 2012:

|  | *Treasury 10.5%* | *Bund 8%* |
|---|---|---|
| Dirty price ($P_d$) | £118.00 | €101.66 |
| Price factor ($PF$) | 1.3032131 | 1.145064 |
| Modified duration ($MD$) | 9.723 | 6.549 |
| Yield to maturity | 9.33% | 7.82% |

Suppose also that the long gilt future is priced at 91.66 while the Bund future is priced at 87.87. The responsiveness of a bond's price (in money terms) to a basis point change in yield is called the *basis point value* (*BPV*) or *risk* of a bond:

$$BPV = \Delta P = \frac{MD \cdot Pd}{10,000}. \tag{12.6}$$

For the gilt we have $BPV_g = 0.11473$, while for the Bund we have $BPV_b = 0.06658$. This shows that the price of the gilt is 72 per cent more responsive to a parallel yield curve shift than the price of the Bund.

The futures price responds to changes in the CTD bond as follows:

$$
\begin{aligned}
\Delta P^f &= \frac{1}{PF_{CTD}} \cdot \Delta P_{CTD} \\
&= \frac{BPV_{CTD}}{PF_{CTD}} \\
&= \frac{MD_{CTD} \cdot P_{CTD}}{PF_{CTD} \cdot 10,000}.
\end{aligned} \tag{12.7}
$$

For the gilt contract, we have $\Delta P_g^f = 0.088036$ (i.e. 0.11473/1.3032131), while for the Bund contract, we have $\Delta P_b^f = 0.058145$ (i.e. 0.06658/1.145064). This shows that the price of the gilt future is 51 per cent more responsive to a parallel yield curve shift than the price of the Bund future.

In order to hedge a cross-currency yield spread against changes in the level of international interest rates, the trader has to take into account the relative responsiveness of the two futures prices to changes in yields. He also has to take into account both the different sizes of the futures contracts and the exchange rate between the currencies of the two contracts. The long gilt contract is for £100,000 nominal and the Bund contract is for €100,000 and let us also suppose that the spot exchange rate ($e_0$) €1.56 per £.

We can determine the number of Bund contracts necessary to hedge one gilt contract using:

$$
\begin{aligned}
h &= \frac{BPV_g}{BPV_b} \cdot \frac{\text{Face value of long gilt futures contract}}{\text{Face value of bund futures contract}} \cdot e_0 \tag{12.8} \\
&= \frac{0.11473}{0.06658} \cdot \frac{£100,000}{€100,000} \cdot €1.56 \text{ per } £ = 2.69,
\end{aligned}
$$

where:

$$h = \text{hedge ratio} = \frac{\text{Number of Bund contracts}}{\text{Number of gilt contracts}}.$$

This means that to hedge against parallel yield curve shifts, the speculator would have to trade Bund and gilt contracts in the ratio of 2.69 Bund contracts for every gilt contract, i.e. 269 Bund contracts per 100 gilt contracts.

The current yield spread between the two bonds is 1.51 per cent (i.e. 9.33 − 7.82). Suppose that the speculator believes that the yield spread will widen. He decides to buy 269 Bund contracts and sell 100 gilt contracts. Suppose that 5 days later, the speculator observes that the long gilt future is priced at 92.25, the Bund future is priced at 88.28, the CTD gilt has a yield to maturity of 9.11%, the CTD Bund has a yield to maturity of 7.12%, and the exchange rate is €1.62 per £. The yield spread has widened to 1.99 per cent (i.e. 9.11 − 7.12) as anticipated by the speculator. There was also a downward shift in both the UK and German yield curves, but the speculator was hedged against this shift. The speculator decides to unwind his position at this point. The gilt future increased in price by 59 ticks (i.e. 92.25 − 91.66) and the Bund future increased in price by 41 ticks (i.e. 88.28 − 87.87). The speculator makes a profit on the spread as follows:

$$
\begin{aligned}
\text{Profit on Bund futures} \;=\;& 269 \text{ contracts} \times 41 \text{ ticks profit} \times \text{\euro}10 \text{ per tick} \\
=\;& \text{\euro}110,290 \;=\; \pounds68,080.25 \quad (\text{at } \text{\euro}1.62 \text{ per } \pounds),
\end{aligned}
$$

and:

$$
\begin{aligned}
\text{Loss on gilt futures} \;=\;& 100 \text{ contracts} \times 59 \text{ ticks loss} \times \pounds10 \text{ per tick} \\
=\;& \pounds59,000.
\end{aligned}
$$

So the overall profit is £9,080.25 (i.e. £68,080.25 − £59,000).

### 12.1.3   Trading strategies with options

One of the most important features of an option as a trading instrument is the nonlinear response of the option premium to changes in the price of the underlying security. From Figure 12.1, it can be seen that a deep in-the-money call option has the same profit and loss profile as the underlying security, in the

**Figure 12.1** The relationship between the call option premium and the security

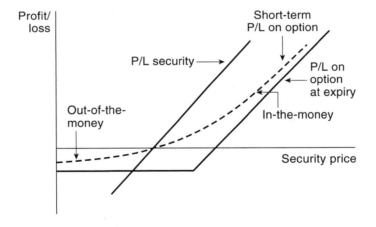

sense that the option premium increases one-for-one with the security price. This implies that a deep in-the-money call option has a delta of unity. A deep out-of-the-money call option, on the other hand, is very insensitive to security price movements and has a delta of almost zero. As a trading instrument, therefore, a call option is extremely desirable, because it behaves like the underlying security in a bull market but has strictly limited risk in a bear market. In other words, it has unlimited upside potential, but great downside protection.

Another important feature is the degree of leverage afforded by options. The delta of a call option is always less than or equal to unity. As long as the option premium is less than the security price *times* the option delta, the elasticity of the option premium with respect to the share price will exceed unity. In this case, the option is a highly geared trading instrument, since there will be more than a one per cent change in the option price for a one per cent change in the security price.

A further feature of options is their response to increases in volatility. Most securities will fall in value if there is an increase in volatility, since this implies an increase in risk. However, with options, an increase in volatility increases the price of the option, as we saw from the Black-Scholes formula (see Chapter 9). This feature can be used for trading purposes.

**Open position trading.** Open position trading with financial options involves backing a view on the future direction of interest rate, exchange rate or share price movements. The same strategies used with futures can be used with options, but options have the advantage of limited risk. For example, a call option can be purchased if the speculator believes that a security price is going to increase, but the call has limited downside risk if the security price falls. Similarly, a put option can be purchased if the speculator believes that a security price is going to fall, but the put has limited upside risk if the security price rises. It is often more profitable to trade using out-of-the-money options, since they are cheaper to buy and hence offer greater leverage.

**Example 12.7 (Open position trading)** *A speculator believes that the price of ABC shares is going to increase and so decides to buy an out-of-the-money call option on ABC:*

*Day 1*    Price of ABC = 115p

| Exercise price | Calls | | |
|---|---|---|---|
| | June | September | December |
| 105p | 12 | 22 | 31 |
| 115p | 9 | 17 | 22 |
| 125p | 3 | 4 | 5 |
| 135p | 1 | 2 | 3 |

On day 1, the speculator buys 10 June 135 call options at 1p (each contract is for 1000 shares):

$$\text{Cost} \; = \; 10 \text{ contracts} \times 1000 \text{ shares} \times £0.01 \; = \; £100.00 \,.$$

*Day 8*    Price of ABC = 125p

| Exercise price | Calls | | |
|---|---|---|---|
| | June | September | December |
| 105p | 25 | 36 | 48 |
| 115p | 19 | 28 | 35 |
| 125p | 10 | 12 | 14 |
| 135p | 5 | 7 | 9 |

On day 8, the speculator sells 10 June 135 call options at 5p:

$$\text{Revenue} \; = \; 10 \text{ contracts} \times 1000 \text{ shares} \times £0.05 \; = \; £500 \,.$$

*So even though the share price itself has risen by less than 9 per cent, the out-of-the-money call has risen by 500 per cent; and the speculator has made money even though the option is still out-of-the-money. If the share price had fallen rather than risen, the maximum loss that the speculator would have borne would be £100.*

We have seen that delta is a measure of option price risk. It can also be used to control risks when trading a combination (or portfolio) of options. Consider the following example. Suppose that, on the basis of the Black-Scholes fair price model, a speculator believes that the 125p call options are underpriced in the market and that the 135p calls are overpriced. Clearly, he should sell the overvalued options and buy the undervalued options; i.e., he should undertake a *relative valuation trade* based on price. But he should put these transactions together in such a way that the position has no overall price risk; i.e., he should trade on the basis of relative mispricing, but should protect himself against an overall jump in option price levels. This means he should undertake a *delta-neutral* (or a *delta-ratio*) trade. Suppose that the 125p calls have a delta of 0.8 and the 135p calls have a delta of 0.55. The appropriate hedge ratio is therefore 0.8/0.55 = 1.45. If the speculator buys 100 of the 125p calls and sells 145 of the 135p calls, this trade will be delta-neutral and so will have no additional price risk. If the speculator is correct in his assessment about relative misvaluation, the 125p calls premium will increase and the 135p calls premium will fall, and he will make a profit.

If delta measures the slope of the profit and loss profile with respect to the share price, then gamma measures the curvature. A speculator should look for options or option combinations with high positive gammas since the deltas for such options move more rapidly in the holder's favour whether the underlying share price rises or falls. Consider, for example, a *straddle* consisting of a long 115p call option and a long 115p put option with the same expiration date. Suppose that the straddle is delta-neutral with the delta of the call equal to 0.5 and the delta of the put equal to –0.5. If the straddle is gamma-positive (e.g. if gamma = 0.02), then whatever the subsequent movement in the share price, the straddle will make a profit. This can be seen from Figure 12.2. At *A*, where the straddle is ini-

---

**Figure 12.2** Profit and loss profile for a delta-neutral, gamma-positive straddle

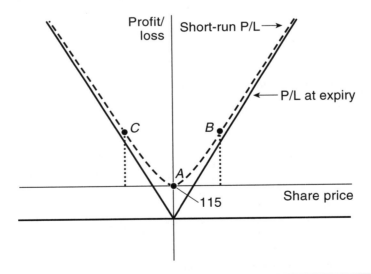

---

tially established at the current share price of 115p, the straddle delta is zero. Because the straddle is gamma-positive, the straddle delta will become positive if the share price rises and negative if the share price falls. This is precisely what is required if the straddle is to show a profit whatever happens to the underlying share price. At *B*, for example, following a rise in the share price, the delta of the call will have risen to, say, 0.6 and the delta of the put will have increased by less to, say, –0.4, giving a positive overall straddle delta of 0.2. On the other hand at $C$, following a fall in the share price, the delta of the call will have fallen to, say, 0.4 and the delta of the put will have fallen by less to, say, $-0.6$, giving a negative overall straddle delta of $-0.2$.

So far we have considered trading on the basis of prices. An alternative to this is to trade on the basis of volatility (i.e. *trading volatility*). As the Black-Scholes formula indicates, the price of a call option increases if the security price increases or if security price volatility increases. However, it is possible for the price of a call option to fall because the security price has fallen, even if there is a large increase in volatility. So a volatility trader has to protect against adverse price movements. This is achieved by using a *delta-neutral strangle* (a long strangle composed of a long call with a high exercise price and a long put with a low exercise price and combined in such a way that the delta is zero).

**Example 12.8 (Volatility trading: buying a delta-neutral strangle to buy volatility)** *A speculator believes that the volatility of ABC shares is going to increase and so decides to buy a delta-neutral strangle to protect against adverse price movements in the underlying security:*

> **Day 1** Price of ABC $= 115p$
> Price of June 125 call $= 3p$     Delta $= 0.50$
> Price of June 105 put $= 6p$     Delta $= -0.25$
> Ratio of 105 puts to 125 calls $= 0.50/0.25 = 2$.

*The speculator buys one June 125 call for 3p and two June 105 puts for 6p each:*

$$\text{Cost} \;=\; (1 \text{ call} \times 1000 \text{ shares} \times £0.03) + (2 \text{ puts} \times 1000 \text{ shares} \times £0.06) \;=\; £150.00\,.$$

> **Day 15** Price of ABC $= 105p$
> Price of June 125 call $= 2p$
> Price of June 105 put $= 9p$

*The speculator sells one June 125 call for 2p and two June 105 puts for 9p each:*

$$\text{Revenue} \;=\; (1 \text{ call} \times 1000 \text{ shares} \times £0.02) + (2 \text{ puts} \times 1000 \text{ shares} \times £0.09) \;=\; £200.00\,.$$

*So even though the share price has fallen, the puts have gained more than the call has lost and the speculator makes a profit of £50. Similarly, volatility can be sold by selling a strangle.*

The Black-Scholes model assumes that the underlying security price is normally distributed. In practice, this assumption can be violated in one of two ways. First, the true underlying distribution can have fatter tails than implied by the normal distribution (this property is known as leptokurtosis); second, the true underlying distribution can be skewed rather than be symmetric like the normal distribution. It is possible to trade both these features using options and option combinations such as straddles and strangles.

It is possible to estimate the leptokurtosis effect by comparing the premium on an out-of-the-money option with that on an at-the-money option. A common procedure for doing this is to compare the premium on a long delta-neutral straddle (which is sometimes also known as a 50 per cent delta straddle since it is composed of two 50 per cent (i.e. 0.5) delta at-the-money options) with the premium on a long 25 per cent delta strangle (i.e. a strangle composed of an out-of-the-money call and an out-of-the-money put with exercise prices set at the point where the deltas are ±25 per cent (i.e. ±0.25)). The excess premium on the strangle compared with that of the straddle is a direct measure of the excess volatility in the tails of the distribution of the security price. For example, if the at-the-money volatility is 10 per cent and the (percentage) premium on the strangle is 0.30 per cent, then the volatility in the tails is 10.30 per cent. This follows because the volatility of a strangle equals the average volatility of the 25 per cent delta call and put in excess of the average volatility of the at-the-money options; the premium difference between the strangle and the straddle will be directly proportional to the difference in average volatilities. An increase in leptokurtosis implies an increase in the tails of the distribution compared with the centre. This view could be traded by buying a strangle and selling a straddle; this is equivalent to buying a butterfly spread, which is long volatility in the wings and short volatility in the centre (see Figure 9.8(a)).

It is possible to estimate the skew effect using a 25 per cent delta *risk reversal* (R/R). This shows the volatility difference between a 25 per cent delta call and a 25 per cent delta put. For example, a 0.40 per cent R/R of calls over puts implies that if the 25 per cent delta put is valued (in percentage terms) at 10 per cent, then the 25 per cent delta call is valued at 10.40 per cent. An anticipated increase in right-side skewness, for example, could be traded by buying the 25 per cent delta call and selling the 25 per cent delta put; this is equivalent to buying a rotated vertical bull spread (see Figure 9.11(a)).

By altering the delta of the strangle and risk reversal, it is possible to build up the *smile curve*, that is, the graph of the implied volatility of an option as a function of the option delta (see Figure 12.3).

**Figure 12.3** Smile curve

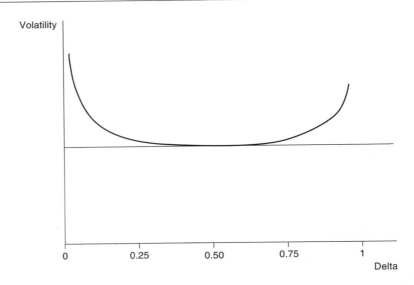

The smile curve in Figure 12.3 is relevant for a particular maturity of option. It is also possible to vary the maturity of the option and build up a *volatility term structure* (see Figure 12.4). Under normal conditions, volatility will be constant over time, but if there is expected to be some short-term turbulence in the markets before normal conditions returns (say, because an election is approaching), then the volatility term structure will be inverted. This view could be traded by buying near-maturity

**Figure 12.4** Volatility term structure

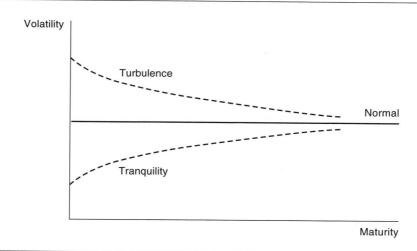

options and selling distant maturing options; in other words by selling a calendar spread. Just as it is possible to calculate forward yields from the term structure of interest rates, so is it possible to estimate forward volatility from the volatility term structure (cf. (5.36)):

$$_s\sigma_\ell = \sqrt{\frac{\sigma_\ell^2 N_\ell - \sigma_s^2 N_s}{N_\ell - N_s}}, \tag{12.9}$$

where:

$\sigma_s^2$ = volatility over the short period;
$\sigma_\ell^2$ = volatility over the long period;
$N_s$ = number of days in short period;
$N_\ell$ = number of days in long period;
$_s\sigma_\ell$ = forward volatility over the period beginning after $N_s$ days and ending after $N_\ell$ days.

**Spread trading.**   As with futures, spread trading involves the simultaneous purchase and sale of related financial options contracts. We have seen examples of options spread trades before. For instance, the delta-neutral relative valuation trade considered in the last section was really a spread trade because it involved the purchase and sale of options. Similarly, many of the option combinations considered in Chapter 9 are spread trades. *Vertical* (or *cylinder*) spreads are option combinations with the same expiry date but different exercise prices. *Horizontal* (or *calendar*) spreads are option combinations with the same exercise prices but different expiry dates. *Diagonal* spreads are option combinations with different exercise prices and expiry dates. We can consider a couple of examples of spread trades.

One example is a *calendar put spread*. Suppose that on May 25, a speculator believes that, although there is unlikely to be a major change in share prices immediately, share prices will tend to drift down in the near future. The speculator therefore decides to buy the following calendar put spread on the FTSE 100 index when the FTSE 100 index is 3780:

$$\begin{array}{ll} \text{Buy September 3700 put at} & 60 \\ \text{Sell June 3700 put at} & 25 \end{array}$$

$$\text{Cost} \;=\; (60-25)\cdot\pounds10 \;=\; \pounds350.$$

Ten days later (June 4), the speculator sells the calendar put spread when the FTSE 100 index is 3720:

$$\begin{array}{ll} \text{Sell September 3700 put at} & 90 \\ \text{Buy June 3700 put at} & 15 \end{array}$$

$$\text{Revenue} \;=\; (90-15)\cdot\pounds10 \;=\; \pounds750.$$

The profit is therefore £400. The speculator has benefited both from the anticipated directional move in the index and also from the faster time decay of the nearby June option compared with the more distant September option.

Another example of a spread trade is a *relative valuation trade* based on volatility (i.e. another type of volatility trade). A speculator seeks to sell high-volatility (i.e. high-price) options and buy low-volatility (i.e. low-price) options. Just as there can only ever be a single share price consistent with any options series on the same security with the same expiration date, so there can only ever be a single measure of share price volatility consistent with that options series. If two different options with the same expiration date give rise to different implied volatilities, then one is mispriced and the speculator can execute a relative valuation trade in expectation of the relative misvaluation being corrected. Again, the trade should be delta-neutral to protect against price risk.

Another example is a *butterfly spread trade*, which, as with futures contracts, can be used if the price of a contract looks out of line with the prices of contracts with exercise prices on either side, but it is not clear which contract(s) will adjust to correct the anomaly. To illustrate, we will consider the Philadelphia Stock Exchange sterling exchange rate call option for September with exercise prices 165 ($1.65), 170 ($1.70) and 175 ($1.75). The spot exchange rate is $1.70 and the option premiums are:

| **Exercise price:** | 165 | 170 | 175 |
|---|---|---|---|
| **Option premium:** | 6.30 cents | 5.25 cents | 1.70 cents |

The 170 contract looks relatively overpriced; i.e., the 165–170 spread of –1.05 cents or –105 ticks (i.e. –1.05/0.01 where 0.01 cents per £ is the tick size) is too high (i.e., less negative) compared with the 170–175 spread of –3.55 cents or –355 ticks (i.e. –3.55/0.01). A speculator would expect the 165–170 spread to narrow (i.e., become more negative) and the 170–175 spread to widen (i.e., become less negative). He therefore sells the 165–170 spread and buys the 170–175 spread, i.e., he buys the butterfly spread.

**Example 12.9 (Butterfly spread)** *On the morning of day 1, the spot exchange rate is $1.70 per £ and the following prices for the Philadelphia Stock Exchange sterling exchange rate call option contract for September are observed:*

| *Exercise price:* | *165* | *170* | *175* |
|---|---|---|---|
| *Option premium:* | *6.30 cents* | *5.25 cents* | *1.70 cents* |

*The speculator buys the butterfly spread:*

| | | |
|---|---|---|
| Sell 1 × 170 contract | 5.25 cents | } 165–170 spread = −105 ticks |
| Buy 1 × 165 contract | 6.30 cents | |
| Buy 1 × 175 contract | 1.70 cents | } 170–175 spread = −355 ticks |
| Sell 1 × 170 contract | 5.25 cents | |

$$\text{Butterfly spread} = -355 - (-105) = -250 \text{ ticks}$$

*By the afternoon of day 1, sterling has weakened against the dollar, the spot exchange rate is now $1.67 per £ and the option prices are now as follows:*

| **Exercise price:** | *165* | *170* | *175* |
|---|---|---|---|
| **Option premium:** | *4.10 cents* | *2.40 cents* | *0.90 cents* |

*The speculator reverses his trades:*

| | | |
|---|---|---|
| Buy 1 × 170 contract | 2.40 cents | } 165–170 spread = −170 ticks |
| Sell 1 × 165 contract | 4.10 cents | |
| Sell 1 × 175 contract | 0.90 cents | } 170–175 spread = −150 ticks |
| Buy 1 × 170 contract | 2.40 cents | |

$$\text{Butterfly spread} = -150 - (-170) = 20 \text{ ticks}$$

*The profit from buying the butterfly spread, which has widened is:*

$$\begin{aligned} \text{Profit} &= [20 - (-250)] \text{ ticks} \times \$3.125 \text{ per tick} \\ &= 270 \text{ ticks} \times \$3.125 \text{ per tick} = \$843.75. \end{aligned}$$

*The initial investment is calculated as follows (each contract has a nominal value of £31,250):*

- *purchase of 1 × 165 contract at 6.30 cents per £,*

$$\$0.0630 \times £31,250 = \$1,968.75;$$

- *purchase of 1 × 175 contract at 1.70 cents per £,*

$$\$0.0170 \times £31,250 = \$531.25;$$

- *sale of 2 × 170 contracts at 5.25 cents per £,*

$$2 \times \$0.0525 \times £31,250 = \$3,281.25;$$

- *net initial investment,*

$$\$1,968.75 + \$531.25 - \$3,281.25 = -\$781.25.$$

*So, from a negative investment, a positive profit accrues. The speculator has found a* money machine. *It is not likely that such an opportunity will be available for very long, and indeed the anomaly is corrected the same day in this example.*

## 12.2   Arbitrage

### 12.2.1   The process of arbitrage

Arbitrageurs, unlike speculators, are very interested in the role that they have to play in making securities markets efficient. The role of arbitrageurs is to correct pricing anomalies. In an efficient market, it should not be possible to buy a security on one market and immediately resell it on another market at a higher price. For example, US dollars traded in New York should not trade at a higher price than US dollars traded in London (at least, not when both markets are open simultaneously). If they were selling at a higher price in New York, it would be possible to sell sterling in London and buy dollars and simultaneously resell the dollars for sterling in New York and collect an arbitrage profit.

The point about arbitrage is that the profits accruing to an arbitrage trade should be riskless, or as near to riskless as is practicably possible. It is not physically possible to buy dollars in London and resell them in New York exactly simultaneously. There is bound to be a delay between the two transactions, even if it is only a matter of seconds. And during that delay it is possible for the pricing anomaly to be corrected and hence for the arbitrage profit to disappear. Nevertheless, we will assume that arbitrage is a procedure for generating (nearly) riskless profits.

The reason for stressing the (nearly) riskless nature of arbitrage profits is to make a distinction between arbitrage and speculation. Many speculative trades appear to have the characteristics of an arbitrage trade. For example, some of the valuation trades with futures and options discussed above are designed to profit from some perceived under- or over-valuation of the market price of the future or option compared with its fundamental value. Similarly, some of the spread trades with futures and options are designed to correct pricing anomalies between related contracts (e.g. the butterfly spread). But the point is that such trades are not riskless. The pricing anomaly may persist for some time during which the speculator (willingly) bears risk. So we wish to distinguish between speculation, in which a speculator hopes to make profits by taking on risk, and arbitrage, in which an arbitrageur hopes to make profits at minimal risk.

As well as being important for ensuring that security markets are efficient, arbitrage also has an important role in determining the fair value of securities in the first place. The principle of fair valuation is based on the absence of riskless arbitrage profits. This is especially clear from the Black-Scholes formula for determining the fair price of a call option. In Chapter 9, we derived the Black-Scholes formula by constructing a *riskless hedge portfolio*. This consisted of a long position in the underlying security and *h* short positions in the call option (where *h* is the hedge ratio).

The riskless hedge portfolio is also an *arbitrage portfolio* if:

1  it uses no net wealth;

2  it is riskless;

3  it generates a rate of return in excess of the riskless rate of interest.

We know that the riskless hedge portfolio is riskless. (This is true by construction.) It also uses no net wealth, because it is self-financing (i.e., the proceeds from the sale of the call options *plus* borrowing at the riskless rate finance the purchase of the underlying security). The real question therefore is: does the riskless hedge portfolio generate a return in excess of the riskless rate and so leave a risk-free arbitrage profit after paying back the borrowed funds at the riskless rate? If the answer is yes, then the riskless hedge is an arbitrage portfolio (or a *money machine*). But an arbitrage portfolio cannot exist in equilibrium, and neither can a riskless hedge portfolio that generates an excess return. It is the condition that a risk-free arbitrage profit cannot exist in equilibrium that allows us to determine the fair price of the call option.

While explicit in the determination of the fair price of options, the absence of a risk-free arbitrage profit is also implicit in the determination of the fair prices of the other securities discussed in Part II above: money market instruments, bonds, shares, futures and swaps. It should not be possible to generate risk-free arbitrage profits on any of these securities in equilibrium.

One factor that is common to both speculative trades and arbitrage trades is transaction costs. In calculating the profits on the speculative trading examples in the last section, we ignored transaction costs. But they can substantially reduce and even eliminate trading profits. For example, the bid-offer spread on options can be as high as 30 per cent of the option premium for the private investor, so there would have to be significant pricing anomalies for an investor to make net profits after paying this size of spread. The same applies to arbitrage profits. Arbitrageurs therefore have to construct *arbitrage bands* within which a potential arbitrage trade is not profitable after transaction costs are taken into account. Only if a pricing anomaly is large enough to lie outside the band will it be profitable to undertake an arbitrage trade.

As with speculative trading, it is often more effective to undertake an arbitrage trade using futures and options rather than using the underlying cash market security. We shall therefore concentrate attention on arbitrage strategies using futures and options.

There are two main types of arbitrage trade: *box arbitrages* and *conversion arbitrages*. The former use only combinations of derivative instruments (i.e. futures and options), the latter use combinations of cash market securities and derivative instruments.

## 12.2.2 Arbitrage strategies with futures

Arbitrage strategies with futures can never be entirely riskless. This is because of marking to market. Even if there is a guaranteed profit at delivery, variation margin calls can arise at any time before delivery and the financing costs of these calls can eliminate any arbitrage profits. Similarly, as noted before, transaction costs can also eliminate arbitrage profits.

**Box arbitrages.** The main principles of arbitrage can be demonstrated using the time-security grid. Figure 12.5 demonstrates a potential *box arbitrage* using four futures contracts: the June and September sterling-dollar currency futures contracts (denoted STG), the June three-month eurodollar interest rate futures contract (denoted ED3), and the June three-month short sterling futures contract (denoted ST3). The direction of the arrows follows the convention:

| | |
|---|---|
| Horizontal right-pointing arrow: | Investment or going long |
| Horizontal left-pointing arrow: | Borrowing or going short |
| Vertical arrows: | Exchange of one security (or derivative security) for another. |

An arbitrageur is going to investigate the possibility of whether a box arbitrage exists for the June-September period. The current date is 15 April. On this date, the following futures prices are available:

**Figure 12.5** Futures box arbitrage

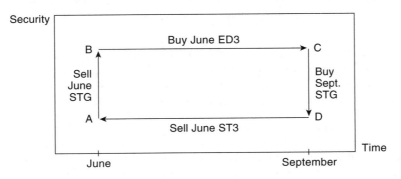

STG — sterling-dollar foreign exchange futures contract
ED3 — 3-month eurodollar deposit futures contract
ST3 — 3-month short sterling futures contract

|           | *STG*  | *ED3* | *ST3* |
|-----------|--------|-------|-------|
| June      | 1.7265 | 89.50 | 88.25 |
| September | 1.7121 | 89.50 | 88.50 |

The arbitrageur begins at A in Figure 12.5 by borrowing £1 at 11.75 per cent, the rate of interest implied by the June ST3 contract (i.e. 100 − 88.25). He then follows the time-security grid around in a clockwise direction, undertaking the following transactions (note that the eurodollar money market assumes a 360-day year, whereas the sterling money market assumes a 365-day year):

Transaction AB:   £1 exchanged into $1.7265

Transaction BC:   $1.7265 invested at 10.50% (i.e. 100 − 89.50)
for 91 days = $1.7265 × [1 + (0.1050 × (91/360))] = $1.7723

Transaction CD:   $1.7723 exchanged into £ at $1.7121 = £1.0352

Transaction DA:   Repay £1 loan plus interest at 11.75% (i.e. 100 − 88.25)
for 91 days = £1 × [1 + (0.1175 × (91/365))] = £1.0293

$$\text{Box arbitrage profit} \ = \ £1.0352 - £1.0293 \ = \ £0.0059.$$

So a riskless box arbitrage profit of £0.0059 for each £1 invested is possible as long as the futures contracts are held until delivery. If we made the trade with one ST3 contract of £500,000, then the arbitrage profit would be £2950 (i.e. £500,000 × £0.0059).

**Conversion arbitrages.**   The most important type of *conversion arbitrage* using a combination of futures and cash market securities is the *cash-and-carry arbitrage*. This has an important role to play in the determination of fair futures prices (see Chapter 8). We know that the basis (the difference between the futures price and the cash market price) cannot exceed the cost-of-carry in equilibrium, otherwise an arbitrage profit exists.

**Figure 12.6** Futures conversion arbitrage

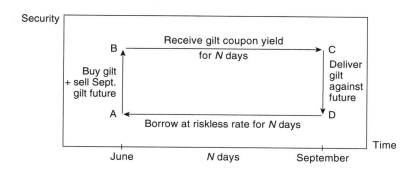

A long cash-and-carry (see Figure 12.6) involves borrowing funds at money market rates in June and using the proceeds to purchase a gilt, while simultaneously selling a gilt futures contract to lock in the price at which the gilt can be sold (transaction AB); receiving the coupon yield on the gilt for $N$ days between June and September (transaction BC); delivering the gilt against the future in September (transaction CD); and repaying the loan with interest using the proceeds from the sale of the gilt (transaction DA). This strategy will give rise to an *implied repo rate*. If this rate exceeds the cost of borrowed funds or, equivalently, if the basis exceeds the cost-of-carry (i.e. market interest rate *less* coupon yield on the gilt), then a riskless long cash-and-carry arbitrage exists.

A short cash-and-carry involves shorting a gilt (and paying the coupon yield) and using the proceeds to invest in the money market, at the same time buying a future to lock in the repurchase price of the gilt. Again, a repo rate is implied by this strategy. If that rate is less than that earned in the money market, a short cash-and-carry arbitrage profit exists. However the profit, if it exists, is not riskless; this is because, on the delivery of the futures contract, the arbitrageur will receive the cheapest-to-deliver (CTD) gilt, which may not be the same as the gilt that he has sold short. He therefore has to switch out of the CTD gilt into the gilt that he has sold short, which he then delivers to his long. He therefore incurs a *switch ratio risk*, which implies that the short cash-and-carry arbitrage can never be entirely riskless.

As another example of a conversion arbitrage, we can consider *program trading arbitrages*. It is argued that program traders have been responsible for some of the wild fluctuations in stock indices in recent years, especially in the USA. They use computer software which triggers instructions to buy or sell stock index futures contracts. *Buy programs* trigger instructions to buy shares (i.e. to buy the cash stock index) and sell stock index futures whenever the data that is fed into the computer indicates that a long cash-and-carry arbitrage exists. Similarly, *sell programs* trigger instructions to sell shares (i.e. to sell the cash stock index) and buy stock index futures whenever the data indicates that a short cash-and-carry arbitrage exits.

We will illustrate program trading arbitrages as follows. As we know from Chapter 8, the fair futures price, $P_0^f$, is given by:

$$P_0^f = P^s + [(r-d) \cdot (N/365)]P^s, \qquad (12.10)$$

where:

$$
\begin{aligned}
P^s &= \text{current level of the cash index;} \\
P_0^f &= \text{fair price of the futures contract;} \\
r &= \text{money market interest rate (annual);} \\
d &= \text{dividend yield on the cash index (annual);} \\
N &= \text{number of days between settlement and delivery;} \\
P^f &= \text{current price of the futures contract.}
\end{aligned}
$$

If $P^f > P_0^f$, so that the basis (i.e. $P^f - P^s$) exceeds the cost-of-carry (i.e. $P_0^f - P^s$), a buy program arbitrage exists. If $P^f < P_0^f$, so that the basis is less than the cost-of-carry, a sell program arbitrage exists.

The excess return from the buy program is given by:

$$
\text{Excess return from buy program} \;=\; \frac{P^f - P^s}{P^s} \cdot \frac{365}{N} + (d - r). \tag{12.11}
$$

The excess return from the sell program is given by:

$$
\text{Excess return from sell program} \;=\; (r - d) - \frac{P^f - P^s}{P^s} \cdot \frac{365}{N}. \tag{12.12}
$$

**Example 12.10 (Buy program opportunity)** *We have the following data:*

$$
\begin{aligned}
P^s &= 1800 \\
P^f &= 1890 \\
r &= 0.10\,(10\%) \\
d &= 0.04\,(4\%) \\
N &= 91 \; days
\end{aligned}
$$

*From (12.11), the excess return is:*

$$
\begin{aligned}
\text{Excess return} &= \frac{1890 - 1800}{1800} \cdot \frac{365}{91} + (0.04 - 0.10) \\
&= 0.1405 \quad (14.05\%).
\end{aligned}
$$

**Example 12.11 (Sell program opportunity)** *We have the following data:*

$$
\begin{aligned}
P^s &= 1800 \\
P^f &= 1810 \\
r &= 0.10\,(10\%) \\
d &= 0.04\,(4\%) \\
N &= 91 \; days
\end{aligned}
$$

*From (12.12), the excess return is:*

$$
\begin{aligned}
\text{Excess return} &= (0.10 - 0.04) - \frac{1810 - 1800}{1800} \cdot \frac{365}{91} \\
&= 0.0377 \quad (3.77\%).
\end{aligned}
$$

### 12.2.3 Arbitrage strategies with options

As with futures, transaction costs can more than offset any arbitrage profits. Again, both box and conversion arbitrages can be used.

**Box arbitrages.** With options, a *box arbitrage* uses four options to create two synthetic securities, one long and one short, at different effective prices.

**Figure 12.7** Options credit box arbitrage

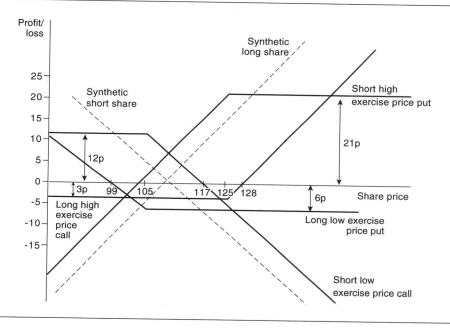

Suppose that on 1 April, the following June option prices are observed on ABC shares when the current share price is 115p:

| Exercise price | June calls | June puts |
|---|---|---|
| 105p | 12 | 6 |
| 115p | 9 | 12 |
| 125p | 3 | 21 |

A *credit box arbitrage* trade consists of the following transactions on 1 April (see Figure 12.7):

|   |   | **Revenue** |
|---|---|---|
| A: | Sale of low exercise price (e.g. 105p) call | +12p |
| B: | Purchase of low exercise price (e.g. 105p) put | −6p |
| C: | Purchase of high exercise price (e.g. 125p) call | −3p |
| D: | Sale of high exercise price (e.g. 125p) put | +21p |
|   | Net credit | 24p |

Transactions A and B create a synthetic short ABC share with an effective price of 105p on the expiry date (i.e., the arbitrageur has the right to sell one ABC share for 105p on the expiry date). Transactions C and D create a synthetic long ABC share with an effective price of 125p on the expiry date (i.e., the arbitrageur has the right to buy one ABC share for 125p on the expiry date). On the expiry date of the options, there will be a loss on these sets of transactions equal to the difference in exercise prices (i.e., 20p), since one synthetic share is being sold at expiry (for 105p) for less than another synthetic share is being bought at expiry (for 125p). However, since this is more than offset by the net credit that is collected at the beginning of the transaction (which will also earn interest), a credit box arbitrage exists. In other words, the arbitrageur has discovered that the net cash inflow will exceed the difference between the exercise prices:

$$\text{Profit at expiry} \quad = \quad (\text{Net credit} \times \text{Interest factor}) - (\text{Difference in exercise prices}). \quad (12.13)$$

Suppose that the interest rate is 12 per cent per annum and the position is held for 60 days, then:

$$\text{Profit} \quad = \quad \left[ 24\text{p} \cdot \left( 1 + 0.12 \cdot \frac{60}{365} \right) \right] - (125\text{p} - 105\text{p}) \quad = \quad 4.47\text{p}.$$

This profit is guaranteed on 1 April as long as the position is held to the expiry date of the options and none of the options is exercised before expiry.

A *debit box arbitrage* trade consists of the opposite set of trades:

|   |                                                  | *Revenue* |
|---|--------------------------------------------------|-----------|
| A: | Purchase of low exercise price (e.g. 105p) call  | −12p      |
| B: | Sale of low exercise price (e.g. 105p) put        | +6p       |
| C: | Sale of high exercise price (e.g. 125p) call      | +3p       |
| D: | Purchase of high exercise price (e.g. 125p) put   | −21p      |
|   | Net debit                                         | 24p       |

Transactions A and B now create a synthetic long ABC share with an effective price of 105p at expiry, while transactions C and D now create a synthetic short ABC share with an effective price of 125p at expiry. On the expiry date of the options, there will be a gain on the transactions equal to the difference in exercise prices, since one synthetic share is being sold for more than another one is being purchased. If this gain more than offsets the net debit (*plus* financing costs), then a debit box arbitrage occurs. In other words, the arbitrageur hopes that the net cash outflow will be less than the difference in exercise prices:

$$\text{Profit at expiry} \quad = \quad (\text{Difference in exercise prices}) - (\text{Net debit} \times \text{Interest factor}). \quad (12.14)$$

It is obvious that in this case the debit box arbitrage will show a net loss:

$$\text{Profit} \quad = \quad (125\text{p} - 105\text{p}) - \left[ 24\text{p} \cdot \left( 1 + 0.12 \cdot \frac{60}{365} \right) \right] \quad = \quad -4.47\text{p}.$$

**Conversion arbitrages.** A *conversion arbitrage* is similar to a box arbitrage but, instead of using two synthetic securities constructed from four options, it uses one synthetic security constructed from two options and the underlying cash market security itself. Using the same information as before, a conversion arbitrage trade involves the following set of transactions on 1 April:

|   |   |   | *Revenue* |
|---|---|---|---|
| A: | Purchase of ABC × Interest factor | −115p × [1+0.12 × (60/365)] | −117.27p |
| B: | Sale of low exercise price (e.g. 105p) call × Interest factor | +12p × [1+0.12 × (60/365)] | +12.24p |
| C: | Purchase of low exercise price (e.g. 105p) put × Interest factor | −6p × [1+0.12 × (60/365)] | −6.12p |
| D: | Sale of synthetic ABC at expiry | | +105p |
| | | Net profit | −6.15p |

At the beginning of the transaction, one ABC share is purchased for 115p with borrowed funds (interest at 12 per cent per annum). Simultaneously, a 105p call is sold and a 105p put is purchased, creating the sale of an ABC share on the expiry date (60 days later) for 105p. In other words, the ABC share bought on 1 April for 115p will be sold for 105p on the expiry date. Taking account of interest payments, the position shows an overall net loss of 6.15p. This loss is guaranteed on 1 April, as long as the position is held to the expiry date of the options and the options are not exercised before expiry. The opposite of a conversion arbitrage trade is a *reversal arbitrage trade*. This involves a short position in the underlying security together with a synthetic long position created from a long call and a short put with a lower exercise price than the current share price (in this case 105p). When the synthetic security is purchased on the expiry date for 105p, the position makes a guaranteed profit of 6.15p.

Of course, both conversion and reversal arbitrage trades could have been carried out with options having a higher exercise price than the current share price. In the case of 125p options, the conversion arbitrage would have shown a loss of 10.62p, while the reversal arbitrage would have shown a profit of 10.62p. So it would have been more profitable to have undertaken the reversal using the higher exercise price options.

Even if an arbitrage profit net of transactions and interest rate costs does exist, another factor must be addressed. All the options used as arbitrage instruments are American options. This means that any of the options can be exercised before the expiration date. The arbitrage profit exists only on the expiration date, and the arbitrage profit can be destroyed by early exercise. Exercise is likely to take place when it is least advantageous to the arbitrageur. In addition, puts are more likely to be exercised than calls, and in-the-money calls are most likely to be exercised just prior to a dividend payment. So the arbitrageur has to trade off the arbitrage profit against the risk of early exercise. He can do something to mitigate this danger: by selling out-of-the-money puts, for example.

# Appendix A: When turbo-arbitrage turns into speculation — the collapse of Barings Bank

Barings was Britain's oldest merchant bank: it was founded in 1762 by Sir Francis Baring. In 1803, it helped to finance the Louisiana Purchase. In 1818, the Duc de Richelieu stated: 'There are six great powers in Europe: England, France, Prussia, Austria, Russia and Baring Brothers'. In 1886, Barings floated Guinness on the London Stock Exchange. In 1890, its Argentine loans soured and it was rescued by the Bank of England. In February 1995, Barings Bank collapsed with debts of £827m as a consequence of speculative losses on futures trading made by a single 'rogue trader', Mr Nick Leeson, based in the Singapore office of a subsidiary company, Barings Securities. This time the Bank of England did not succeed in rescuing the bank. Instead it had to be rescued by the Dutch bank ING (International Netherlands Group) which bought the bank for the nominal sum of £1. This appendix examines the causes and consequences of this collapse.

Leeson went to work in Singapore in March 1992 as a settlements clerk in the back office of Barings Securities, with the job of clearing and settling the deals executed by Barings traders on the floor of the Singapore International Monetary Exchange (SIMEX). Very soon he was put in charge of the back office. Shortly after this, he was allowed to trade on behalf of Barings himself, while remaining in charge of the back office. It is very unusual for someone to have both back office and front office responsibilities; it is even more unusual for a trader to be allowed to clear and settle his own deals. In any event, Leeson's trading activities were supposed to be confined to stock index futures arbitrage between SIMEX and the Osaka Securities Exchange in Japan. Both SIMEX and Osaka traded identical futures contracts on the Nikkei 225 index, the main price index for Japanese shares. Leeson's job was to arbitrage any price differences that emerged between SIMEX and Osaka. This involved buying Nikkei 225 futures on the cheaper exchange and simultaneously selling the same number of contracts on the dearer exchange, leaving a risk-free arbitrage profit. However, what Leeson began to do was to write option straddles on the Nikkei 225 index. This is not an arbitrage strategy, but a speculative one which will make profits if the index does not move much before the options expire, but which will lose money if there is either a large rise or a large fall in the index.

In July 1992, Leeson opened account number 88888 in the Barings internal accounting system. Initially details of the account were included in reports back to London, but soon Leeson arranged for the computer system to be altered so that account 88888 was excluded from all these reports except one. Leeson then started to use this account to hide any trading losses he made: the losses were made to appear as though they were made by a client rather than by Barings. He was therefore able to report higher profits. By the end of 1992, account 88888 had a cumulative loss of £2m. By the end of 1993, the cumulative loss was £23m, while the reported profits before tax for the Barings Group as a whole were £100m. Leeson's bonus for 1993 was £130,000. By the end of 1994, the total losses had risen to £208m. Barings Group reported profits for that year were £205m, with Leeson's apparent contribution to those profits amounting to £28.5m. Leeson was due to pick up a bonus of £450,000. Within Barings he was regarded as 'almost a miracle worker' and as a 'turbo-arbitrageur'.

At the beginning of 1995, things started to go really wrong for Leeson. He took the view that the Japanese stock market, which had been falling steadily for some time, was about to stabilize. In other words, he expected the trading range of the Nikkei 225 index to narrow. To back this view, Leeson wrote 40,000 option straddles on the Nikkei 225 index which would make profits if the index stayed in the range 18,500 - 19,500. Unfortunately for Leeson, there was a massive earthquake in Kobe on the night of 17 January 1995. This had the effect of driving down the Nikkei: on 23 January the index fell 1000 points to below 17,800. His straddles were showing a massive loss rather than the profit he expected. In an effort to reverse these losses, Leeson attempted singlehandedly to drive up the Japanese market through massive purchases of Nikkei 225 futures contracts. But the market kept falling, and Leeson had to make massive margin payments to SIMEX on both his short straddles and long futures positions. By 26 February when the bank collapsed, account 88888 was showing cumulative losses of £827m.

In July 1995, the Bank of England issued a report on the Barings collapse (*Board of Banking Supervision Report on Barings*, HMSO). The report argued that the collapse was caused by 'a failure of controls of management and other internal controls of the most basic kind'. The bank's executives were unsure of their specific responsibilities and did not even understand the nature of the derivatives arbitrage business carried out in Singapore. The executives, including Mr Peter Baring, chairman, and Mr Andrew Tuckey, deputy chairman, were criticized for not understanding that Leeson could not possibly have made the profits from derivatives arbitrage that he was reporting, but there was 'no informal analysis or appraisal of the issue'. The report listed nine warning signs that the executives ignored, such as: Leeson's responsibilities were not segregated between the front and back offices, he was not adequately supervised (e.g., the regional operations manager for south-east Asia, Leeson's immediate boss, did not deal adequately with warnings from SIMEX identifying irregularities in account 88888), and Leeson kept asking London for further 'top-up payments' to cover his margin payments to SIMEX, but Barings treasury department failed to clarify whether these payments were for client trading or for Barings' own trading account. The bank's executives were also criticized for not responding to market rumours about Leeson's trading that were reaching London by late January. Finally, the executives were criticized for failures in reporting to the bank's regulators, in particular, for submitting inaccurate returns to the Bank of England and the Securities and Futures Authority. During January and February 1995, the parent bank advanced £760m to the Singapore subsidiary. These were reported as 'trade credits' in the returns (i.e., sums passing through the bank to fund clients' trading), rather than their true purpose as 'lending to affiliates'.

The report also criticized the Bank of England's monitoring of Barings' capital adequacy and risk exposure position during the period in question. The Barings Group was the first banking group to be monitored on a *solo consolidated* basis, whereby one set of capital and exposure standards was applied to both the parent bank (Baring Brothers and Co) and its securities house subsidiary (Baring Securities Ltd). The more usual monitoring procedure is *solo plus*, whereby the bank and securities arm are treated separately for regulatory purposes, with their own individual capital and exposure requirements. The Bank of England was criticized for failing to consider all the consequences of solo consolidation for dealing with systemic risk within an integrated banking firm. The Bank was also criticised for offering Barings an informal concession that permitted it to exceed limits on its exposure to the Osaka Securities Exchange. The concession was granted in 1993 by a junior officer of the Bank, apparently without reference to more senior management at the Bank. The report proposed that the Bank should apply more stringent criteria before granting solo consolidation in the future. It also called for greater collaboration between regulators both domestically and internationally to help bridge the gap in securities regulation, whereby the SFA was responsible for regulating the domestic business of UK-based securities houses, while the regulation of overseas subsidiaries was the responsibility of overseas regulators.

Finally, the report offered some lessons for the future: it argued that 'rapid product innovation and sophisticated technology, alongside vastly improved communications systems, have to be understood and managed actively'. It went on to state that 'Barings' experience shows it to be absolutely essential that top management understand the broad nature of all the material activities of the institution for which they are responsible'. Managers should make regular visits to overseas offices where trading is being conducted and talk to traders, risk managers and office managers about their activities. There should be 'clearly defined lines of responsibility and accountability covering all activities' and 'there must be no gaps and no room for any confusion' over each manager's responsibilities. But the clearest lessons from the Barings collapse relate to the risk from not separating front and back office functions and the woeful lack of understanding of derivatives by senior management at Barings: in October 1993, Barings chairman, Peter Baring had stated: 'Derivatives need to be well controlled and understood, but we believe we do that here'.

Mr Leeson was sentenced to a six and half year prison sentence for fraud. He wrote about his experiences in *Rogue Trader* (published by Little, Brown). The incident led directly to the ending of the City of London as a British-run gentleman's club: during the remainder of 1995, a number of small, undercapitalized British merchant banks sold out to larger, better capitalized European investment banks (e.g. Warburgs went to Swiss Bank Corporation, Morgan Grenfell went to Deutsche Bank, and Kleinworts went to Dresdner Bank). Finally the Bank of England's role as a regulatory authority was seriously undermined. In 1997, this function was transferred to the Financial Services Authority.

# Appendix B: Technical analysis

*Technical analysis* (or *chartism*) is based on the assumption that the stock market follows *trends* that depend on the attitudes of investors towards a range of economic, political and psychological factors. The skill of the technical analyst is to identify changes in these trends at an early stage and to establish and maintain an investment position until a *reversal* of a trend is signalled. The simplest tool used to implement this strategy is the *point and figure chart*:

```
                                                        X
                                                        X
        X               X                              X_B
        X      O        X      O      X_b               X
        X      O        X      O      X       O         X
        X      O_s              O      X       O         X
        X                       O_S    X       O         X
                                 O     X
                                 O
```

where:

| | | |
|---|---|---|
| $X$ | = | price rises during a given time interval (e.g. hour or day); |
| $O$ | = | price falls during a given time interval; |
| $S$ | = | sell signal, since previous lowest price ($s$) has been exceeded; |
| $B$ | = | buy signal, since previous highest price ($b$) has been exceeded. |

The main techniques used to identify trends and reversals are: price patterns, trend lines, moving averages, Dow theory and Elliot wave theory.

**B.1 Price patterns.**   The nature of price patterns is illustrated in Figures 12.8 and 12.9. Figure 12.8 shows a typical stock market cycle in which there are three trends: two *primary* and one *secondary*. The two primary trends are the *bull market* or *rising trend* (A to B) and the *bear market* or *declining trend* (C to D). The secondary trend is a transitional phase that separates the two major market movements. Sometimes a strong bullish market can suddenly go into reverse as in Figure 12.9, but this is not common.

The transitional phase provides an important indicator to the technical analyst, since it signals the turning point between rising and falling markets. During the transitional phase, the balance of sentiment changes in favour of the bears and the increasing weight of sellers pushes the trend of price movements downwards. The reverse process occurs at the end of the bear market.

The transitional phase is characterized by clearly identifiable price patterns and formations. A typical example is the *rectangle*. The rectangle in Figure 12.10 marks the turning point between bull and bear markets and this is known as a *reversal* pattern. The reversal patterns at market peaks are called *distribution* patterns, while those at market troughs are known as *accumulation* patterns. The area around the AA line is known as a *resistance level*, since the market shows a resistance to a further price rise. The BB line is called the *support level*, since buyer support keeps prices above BB.

In contrast, the rectangle in Figure 12.11 interrupts temporarily the progress of a bull market and this is known as a *continuation* or *consolidation* pattern. During the formation period of a rectangle,

**Figure 12.8** Typical stock market cycle

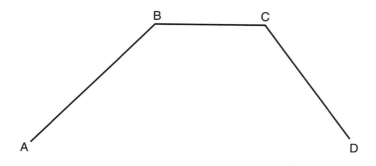

**Figure 12.9** Untypical reverse

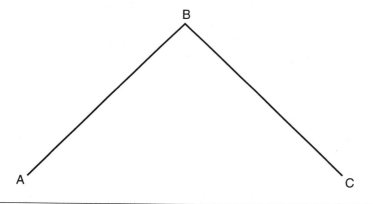

**Figure 12.10** Rectangle with reversal

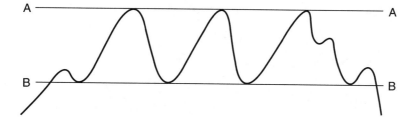

**Figure 12.11** Rectangle with continuation

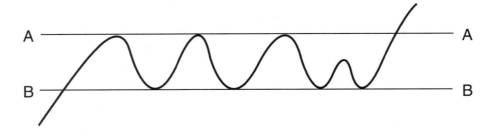

**Figure 12.12** Rectangle with completed top

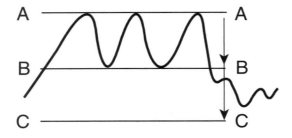

**Figure 12.13** Turnover-price chart

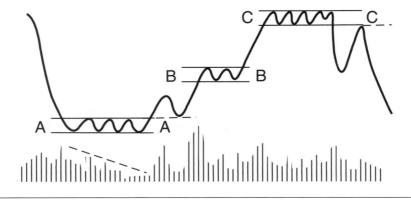

it is impossible to know beforehand which way the price will eventually break, but technical analysts usually assume that the prevailing trend will continue, until there is hard evidence to the contrary. The significance given to a price pattern depends on its *size* and *depth*. The greater the time a pattern takes to complete and the larger the price fluctuation contained within the formation, the more substantial the ensuing breakout is likely to be. This is because of the greater build-up of stock by like-minded investors.

Figure 12.12 shows a rectangle which has formed and completed a top. The *measuring implication* or *objective level* of the formulation is the vertical distance between lines AA and BB projected downward from line BB by the same distance, i.e. the line CC. The measuring implication tends to become a support level where the price trend is temporarily halted.

A valid *breakout* can be confirmed by either a change in price or a change in turnover. A 3 per cent *price penetration* of the boundaries of a formation is generally taken as evidence that a breakout is valid. *Turnover* or *volume* (the number of shares changing hands) is generally correlated with the trend. Turnover grows with a rising price trend and declines with a falling price trend. Figure 12.13 depicts a turnover-price chart. The turnover is indicated by the vertical lines at the bottom of the chart. Turnover increases marginally as the price reaches a low, but as the accumulation pattern forms, activity falls. The downward trend line of the trading activity supports the validity of the breakout.

The principal price patterns are listed below:

1. A *head and shoulders* (H and S) formation comprises a substantial rally (the head) surrounded by two small rallies (the shoulders), see Figure 12.14. The first shoulder is the penultimate thrust of a bull market and the second is the first rally of an onsetting bear market. Turnover is normally highest during the formation of the left shoulder and also on the build up to the head. However, the formation of the right shoulder is always associated with lower turnover. The baseline of the two shoulders is called the *neckline*. The measuring implication for this price formation is the vertical distance between the head and the neckline projected downward the same distance from the neckline.

   Figure 12.15 illustrates an *inverted head and shoulders* pattern at a market trough. Turnover is generally highest at the bottom of the left shoulder and during the formation of the head. It declines on the right shoulder but then expands substantially on the breakout.

2. A *double top* comprises two peaks separated by a trough. The main characteristic of a double top is that the second top is formed with less volume than the first and signals the end of a bull market. Figure 12.16 illustrates a double top and Figure 12.17 depicts *double bottom*.

3. *Broadening formations* result when a series of two or more rallies widen out in size so that peaks and troughs follow two divergent trendlines. Figure 12.18 depicts a *flattened bottom*, while Figure 12.19 depicts a *flattened top*. Activity is generally high during the rally phases.

4. *Triangles* are frequently occurring but unreliable price patterns. They may show either consolidation or reversal formations. Figure 12.20 shows the typical pattern of a triangle: a series of two or more rallies narrow in size so that peaks and troughs follow two convergent trendlines. Triangles are the opposite of broadening formations.

**Figure 12.14** Head and shoulders

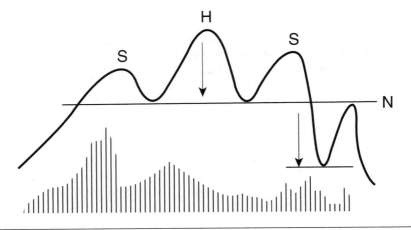

**Figure 12.15** Inverted head and shoulders

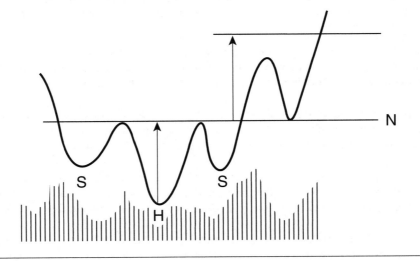

**Figure 12.16** Double top

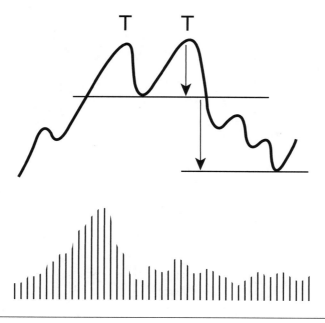

**Figure 12.17** Double bottom

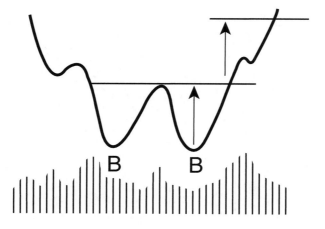

**Figure 12.18** Flattened bottom

**Figure 12.19** Flattened top

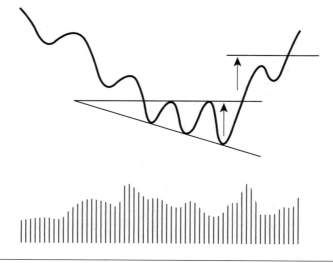

**Figure 12.20** Triangles

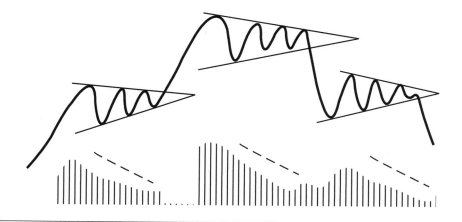

**B.2 Trendlines.**   A trendline is a straight line which touches either a series of ascending bottoms in a bull market (Figure 12.21) or the tops of a series of descending valley peaks in a bear market (Figure 12.22).

A *break* in trend arising from the *penetration* of a trendline results in either an actual trend reversal or a deceleration in the pace of an existing trend.  The significance of a trendline depends on the frequency with which it has been touched, its length and its slope.  A trendline constitutes a support or a resistance level and each successful test of the line's strength (i.e. without breach) adds to the authority of the trend line.  The greater the length of the line, the greater is its *strength*.  Shallow trends are more likely to be sustainable than steeper trends, so a break in a shallow trend is more significant than a break in a steep trend.

Trendlines have measuring implication when they are broken.  With a rising trendline, the vertical distance between the peak and the trendline is measured ($A_1$ in Figure 12.23).  This distance is then projected down from the point at which the violation occurs ($A_2$).  This projection is known as a *price objective*.  When prices fall below the objective, as in Figure 12.24, this line can become one of resistance to the next major rally or support for a subsequent *reaction*.

At the beginning of a new primary bull market, the first intermediate rally is likely to be relatively steep and the advance unsustainable.  The first trendline (AA in Figure 12.25) derived from the first rally is likely to be violated quickly.  A new trendline is then constructed using the bottom of the first intermediate decline (AB).  This new line is less steep.  When this trendline is violated, a third trendline is constructed (AC).  These lines are known as *fan lines*.  The *corrective fan principle* states that once the third trendline has been violated, the end of the bull market is confirmed.

**B.3 Moving averages**   Moving averages are used to smooth out the fluctuations in security prices, so that the underlying trend is more clearly discernible.  Three types of moving average are used in technical analysis: simple, weighted and exponential.

**Figure 12.21** Upward trendline

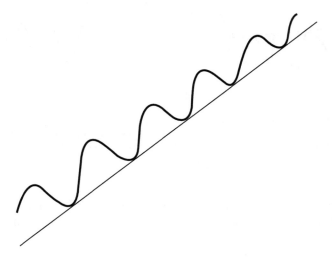

**Figure 12.22** Downward trendline

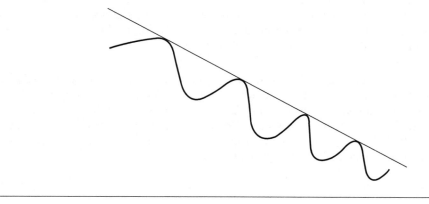

**Figure 12.23** Broken trendline and price objective

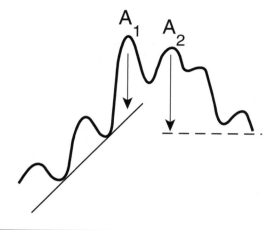

**Figure 12.24** Price objective becoming resistance level

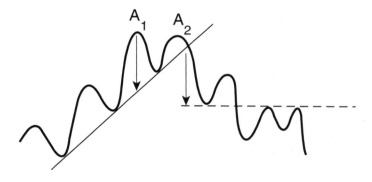

**Figure 12.25** Fan lines

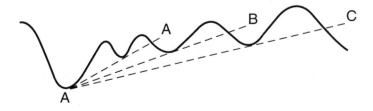

An *N*-period *simple moving average* is given by:

$$\bar{X}_t \;=\; \frac{1}{N} \sum_{i=0}^{N-1} X_{t-i},$$

that is, the last $N$ observations in a sequence are summed and the result divided by $N$. In the next period, a new observation ($X_{t+1}$) is added to the sum and the oldest observation ($X_{t-N-1}$) is dropped, and so on.

Changes in the trend of the security price being measured are indicated by a crossover between the moving average and the price itself. A change from a rising to a declining market occurs when the price moves below its moving average, and vice versa for a change from a declining to a rising market. Similarly, there can be shorter moving averages (e.g. 10-week) and longer moving averages (e.g. 30-week), and the beginning of a falling market is indicated when the shorter moving average moves below the longer moving average. When the shorter moving average crosses the longer moving average from below when both are rising, this is a buy signal and is known as a *golden cross*.

In interpreting moving averages, the following factors should be taken into account:

1 Since a moving average is just a smoothed version of a trend, the average itself involves regions of both support and resistance. For example, in a bull market, falls in security prices are frequently reversed because of support at the moving-average level. Similarly, a rally in a bear market sometimes meets resistance at the moving average level and turns down.

2 If the moving average is flat or has changed direction, a price crossover is generally taken as confirmation that the previous trend has been reversed.

3 If the crossover of a moving average occurs while the moving average is still following the prevailing trend, this constitutes an initial warning that a trend reversal has taken place. Confirmation is signalled by a flattening of or switch in direction of the moving average itself.

4 The greater the length of a moving average, the greater is the significance of a crossover. A crossover of a 24-month moving average, which is smoothing out a very long-term trend, is much more important than a crossover of a 10-day moving average.

5 The significance of the *trend channel* implied by the moving average depends on the width of the *Bollinger band* surrounding the moving average: these are flexible lines above and below a moving average which expand when prices become more volatile and contract when prices become more tranquil. A narrow Bollinger band is indicative of a strong trend channel.

A *weighted moving average* gives greater weight to more recent observations:

$$\bar{X}_t^W \;=\; \frac{1}{N} \sum_{i=0}^{N-1} \lambda_i X_{t-i}.$$

The only real restriction on the $\lambda_i$ is that $\lambda_0 > \lambda_1 > \lambda_2 > \dots > \lambda_{N-1} > 0$, although in most cases the weights are chosen in such a way that they sum to unity:

$$\lambda_i \;=\; \frac{\lambda_i^*}{\sum \lambda_i^*}.$$

One example of a weighted moving average is known as a *Coppock index*.

Another special case is the *exponential moving average*:

$$\bar{X}_t^E \;=\; \frac{1}{N}\sum_{i=0}^{N-1}\frac{1-\lambda}{1-\lambda^{N-1}}\lambda^i X_{t-i},$$

where $0 < \lambda < 1$.

The purpose of using weighted moving averages is to capture trend reversals more quickly, but with weighted moving averages, trend reversals are signalled by a change in direction rather than a crossover.

**B.4 Dow theory and Elliot wave theory**   *Dow theory* argues that markets move in definite waves that are predictable. A refinement of this approach is *Elliot wave theory* which predicts that a bull market consists of a series of bull cycles, with each bull cycle having five positive waves followed by three negative waves (Figure 12.26(a)). In contrast, a bear market consists of a series of bear cycles, with each bear cycle having five negative waves followed by three positive waves (Figure 12.26(b)).

**Figure 12.26** Elliot waves: (a) in a bull market; (b) in a bear market

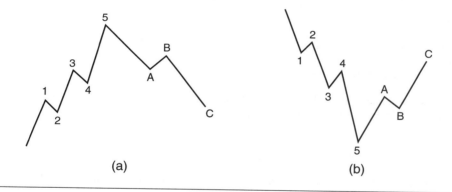

**Selected references**

Achelis, S. (1995), *Technical Analysis from A to Z*, McGraw Hill, New York.

Fitzgerald, M.D. (1983), *Financial Futures*, Euromoney Publications, London. (Chapters 6 and 7.)

Fitzgerald, M.D. (1987), *Financial Options*, Euromoney Publications, London. (Chapters 4, 6, 7 and 8.)

Lefèvre, E. (1994), *Reminiscences of a Stock Operator*, John Wiley, New York.

Malkiel, B. (1996), *A Random Walk Down Wall Street*, W.W. Norton, New York.

**Exercises**

1  What role does arbitrage have to play in financial markets? Provide *two* examples of potential arbitrages.

2  What is the difference between 'valuation trading' and 'volatility trading' using options?

3  You are given the following set of call option premiums on ABC shares when ABC is trading at 100p:

| Exercise price | 75p | 85p | 95p |
|---|---|---|---|
| September | 26 | 19 | 10 |
| December | 27 | 19 | 15 |

  a)  Which is the most attractive buy if:

      i)  a stagnant market is expected?

      ii)  a take-over bid is expected?

  b)  Might writing options be a better bet under these circumstances?

4  What are the differences between speculation and arbitrage?

5  What is the difference between 'open position trading' and 'spread trading'? Use examples to illustrate your answer.

6  Both speculators and arbitrageurs believe in semi-strong-form market efficiency and believe that pricing anomalies will soon be corrected. There is therefore no essential difference between speculation and arbitrage. Discuss.

7  What are the advantages and disadvantages of trading strategies using futures and options compared with trading strategies using cash market securities?

8  What is the difference between an 'intra-contract spread trade' and an 'inter-contract spread trade'? Illustrate your answer with an example.

9  What is the difference between 'spread trading' and 'basis trading'? Illustrate your answer with an example.

10  You expect short-term interest rates to rise relative to long-term interest rates. How would you trade this view?

11  Design a strategy that a trader might follow if the following set of eurodollar futures prices are observed:

| September | 93.10 |
|---|---|
| December | 93.00 |
| March | 93.80 |

12  A trader observes the following set of FTSE 100 futures prices:

| June | 1925.0 |
|---|---|
| September | 1952.0 |
| December | 1959.0 |

and buys 10 butterfly spreads. Two days later he observes the following set of prices:

| | |
|---|---|
| June | 1894.0 |
| September | 1900.0 |
| December | 1906.0 |

and he unwinds his futures position. Calculate his butterfly spread profit or loss. What was the rate of return on capital employed on an annualized basis?

13 Why are options such useful trading instruments?

14 The availability of individual stock options and stock index options makes it possible to make positive returns in a bear market. Discuss.

15 How can stock index futures contracts be used to increase the rate of return on money market investments?

16 A trader believes that a convertible gilt is undervalued. Design a trade that will profit from a return of the gilt to correct pricing.

17 A speculator believes that the 105p calls on ABC shares are overvalued, while the 115p calls are undervalued. How can he trade this relative mispricing, while protecting himself from overall price risk?

18 Design a strategy that a trader might follow if he observed the following set of June sterling currency call option premiums:

| | |
|---|---|
| 170 | 7.50 |
| 175 | 3.40 |
| 180 | 2.65 |

19 A trader observes the following set of June sterling currency call option premiums:

| | |
|---|---|
| 170 | 7.50 |
| 175 | 3.40 |
| 180 | 2.65 |

and sells 10 butterfly spreads. Later that day he observes the following set of premiums:

| | |
|---|---|
| 170 | 8.45 |
| 175 | 5.65 |
| 180 | 3.85 |

and unwinds his options position. Calculate his butterfly spread profit or loss. What was the rate of return on capital employed on an annualized basis?

20 Can an arbitrage ever be entirely riskless?

21 What is the difference between a 'box arbitrage' and a 'conversion arbitrage'?

22 What are the risks involved with arbitrage strategies involving futures and options?

23 On 15 May, you observe the following set of sterling interest rates and three-month sterling interest rate futures contracts:

| Interest rates | Futures prices | |
|---|---|---|
| 1-mo. 10.875–11 | June | 88.89 |
| 2-mo. 10.9375–11.0625 | September | 87.26 |
| 3-mo. 11–11.0625 | December | 87.03 |
| 4-mo. 11–11.125 | | |
| 5-mo. 11–11.125 | | |
| 6-mo. 11.0625–11.1875 | | |
| 7-mo. 11.125–11.25 | | |

a) Can you identify any arbitrage possibilities? If so, how would you implement them?

b) Would your answer be different if the September futures price were 88.83?

c) Would your answer be different if the September futures price were 89.00?

24 You observe the following set of options prices on ABC shares on 20 March, when ABC is trading at 100p:

| Exercise price (p) | June calls | June puts |
|---|---|---|
| 95 | 10 | 5 |
| 100 | 7 | 9 |
| 105 | 3 | 15 |

Money market interest rates on 20 March are as follows:

| 1-mo. | 10–10.125 |
|---|---|
| 2-mo. | 10–10.125 |
| 3-mo. | 10.0625–10.1875 |

If the expiry date for the options is on 20 June, design:

a) two box arbitrages,

b) two conversion arbitrages.

25 It is 1 April and a trader expects a movement in short-term UK interest rates but is not sure of the direction. He believes the current level of volatility implied by the prices of options on short sterling futures does not reflect the expected higher volatility. He observes the following:

| | |
|---|---|
| June short sterling future | 91.30 |
| June 91.25 call option | 0.23 |
| June 91.25 put option | 0.19 |
| Implied volatility | 14% |

and backs his view by buying 50 of the June 91.25 straddles. Calculate the trader's overall profit or loss if he sells the straddles on 16 April on the following terms:

| | |
|---|---|
| June short sterling future | 91.72 |
| June 91.25 call option | 0.48 |
| June 91.25 put option | 0.05 |
| Implied volatility | 17% |

26    a) What is the main trading rationale for calendar spreads?

b)   A trader observes the following prices on 15 February:

| | |
|---|---|
| March short sterling future | 91.57 |
| June short sterling future | 91.69 |
| March 91.50 call option (expires 15 March) | 0.18 |
| June 91.50 call option (expires 14 June) | 0.40 |

He buys 100 of the March-June 91.50 call calendar spreads. Calculate his profit or loss if the spreads are sold on 15 March when the following prices are observed:

| | |
|---|---|
| March short sterling future EDSP | 91.53 |
| June short sterling future | 91.67 |
| March 91.50 call option | 0.00 |
| June 91.50 call option | 0.37 |

# Chapter 13

# Portfolio analysis and asset pricing

So far, we have discussed the characteristics of different securities taken individually. In this chapter, we examine the reasons for putting securities together in a portfolio. We begin by examining the trade-off that investors wish to make between risk and return. We go on to examine the way in which portfolios generate risk and return and the way in which diversification can help reduce risk without sacrificing return. We then integrate the consumption and production of risk and return across all investors to determine the market equilibrium price of risk, the market portfolio and the optimal structure of individual portfolios. Once we have determined market equilibrium conditions, we can decompose total risk into undiversifiable market risk and diversifiable specific risk. This decomposition allows us to price inefficient portfolios and individual securities, since only the undiversifiable component of risk is priced in equilibrium. The capital asset pricing model is the equilibrium pricing model that arises from this analysis. An alternative asset pricing model based on the absence of arbitrage possibilities is also discussed.

## 13.1  Portfolio analysis

### 13.1.1  Choice under uncertainty: the consumption of risk and return

It is rare to find investors concentrating their entire wealth in a single security. Instead, they tend to invest in a diversified portfolio of securities. The reason for this is that, while all investors like the idea of achieving high returns on their investments, most tend to dislike the high risks that are often associated with anticipated high returns. In other words, most investors have an aversion to risk.

A *risk-averse* investor is someone who, given the choice between two investments with the same expected return, will always choose the less risky investment. A *risk-neutral* investor is someone who is indifferent to risk; i.e., he does not take risk into account when he is making his investment decisions; given the choice between two investments with the same expected return but different risks, he is indifferent to which one he selects. A *risk-loving* investor is someone who enjoys taking on risks and, given the choice between two investments offering the same expected return but different risks, will always select the investment offering greater risk. This is because there is some chance of achieving a very high realized return, even though there is also a chance of receiving a disastrous return.

The reason that most investors are risk-averse is that they have *diminishing marginal utility of wealth*. This follows because their *utility functions* are *concave* functions of wealth. Figure 13.1 depicts a concave utility function defined on an individual's wealth. As the level of the individual's

---

**Figure 13.1** A concave utility function exhibiting diminishing marginal utility of wealth

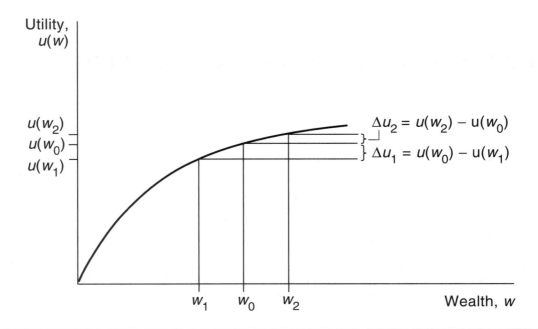

---

wealth increases, so does the level of utility or satisfaction that he derives from owning wealth. However, the level of utility or satisfaction increases at a diminishing rate as wealth increases. In other words, additional or marginal increments to wealth increase utility by successively smaller amounts, so that investors with concave utility functions possess diminishing marginal utility of wealth.

One important implication of this is that, for any level of wealth, a given fall in wealth leads to a bigger fall in utility than the same increase in wealth leads to a rise in utility. This can be seen by examining Figure 13.1 again. Suppose the initial level of wealth is $w_0$, implying a utility level of $u(w_0)$. If wealth falls by the amount $\Delta w_1 = w_0 - w_1$, utility falls by the amount $\Delta u_1 = u(w_0) - u(w_1)$. If, on the other hand, wealth increases by the same amount $\Delta w_2 = w_2 - w_0$, utility increases by the amount $\Delta u_2 = u(w_2) - u(w_0)$. When there is diminishing marginal utility, $\Delta u_1$ is always greater than $\Delta u_2$.

We can use this property of a concave utility function to demonstrate why a risk-averse investor will always choose the less risky investment when two investments offer the same expected return. Suppose that a risk-averse investor has two choices of where to invest his entire wealth, $w_0/(1 + r_f)$. He could put all of it into a riskless security earning $r_f$ per cent per year; at the end of the year, his wealth will be $w_0$ with certainty and his certain level of utility will be $u(w_0)$. Alternatively, he could put it into a portfolio of risky securities which also generates expected wealth of $w_0$ at the end of the year. Suppose, however, that the actual wealth at the end of the year will be $w_1$ or $w_2$. If the distribution of wealth in the risky portfolio is symmetric (equivalently, if risk is symmetric), so that there is an equal probability of 50 per cent of end-of-year wealth being $w_1$ or $w_2$, expected wealth will be $w_0$, but the expected utility of wealth will be less than $u(w_0)$ since:

$$
\begin{aligned}
\text{Expected utility from risky investment} \quad &= \quad \tfrac{1}{2}u(w_1) + \tfrac{1}{2}u(w_2) \\
&= \quad \tfrac{1}{2}\left[u(w_0) - \Delta u_1\right] + \tfrac{1}{2}\left[u(w_0) + \Delta u_2\right] \\
&= \quad u(w_0) + \tfrac{1}{2}\left(\Delta u_2 - \Delta u_1\right) \quad < \quad u(w_0) \\
&= \quad \text{Expected utility from riskless investment}, \quad (13.1)
\end{aligned}
$$

because $\Delta u_1 > \Delta u_2$.

The investor's expected utility from a risky investment will always be less than his utility from a certain investment with the same expected return, as long as the investor is risk-averse and has a concave utility function. It therefore follows that a risk-averse investor will never select a risky investment offering the same expected return as a risk-free investment.

Risk-neutral investors have linear (straight-line) utility functions exhibiting constant marginal utility of wealth and will therefore be indifferent between the choice of a riskless investment and a risky investment offering the same expected return. This is because for such investors $\Delta u_1 = \Delta u_2$. Risk-loving investors have convex utility functions exhibiting increasing marginal utility of wealth and will therefore prefer the risky investment because in this case $\Delta u_2 > \Delta u_1$.

We have discussed risk aversion in terms of the utility of wealth and the expected utility of wealth. But neither utility nor expected utility are objectively measurable concepts. It is impossible to compare directly the utility of one investor against that of another. We need to find a different way of measuring the choice or the trade-off between risk and return.

We can do this by taking a Taylor's expansion of the expected utility function. But we make one slight modification. Rather than deal with a utility function defined on the level of wealth invested in a risky portfolio, we intend to deal with a utility function defined on the return on the risky portfolio, i.e. on the difference between the value of wealth in the portfolio at the end of the period and the value at the beginning. We therefore take a second-order Taylor's expansion of the expected utility of the return on the portfolio (about the expected return on the portfolio):

$$
\begin{aligned}
E[u(r_p)] \quad &\equiv \quad \bar{u} \\
&= \quad E\left[u(\bar{r}_p) + u'(\bar{r}_p)(r_p - \bar{r}_p) + \tfrac{1}{2}u''(\bar{r}_p)(r_p - \bar{r}_p)^2\right] \\
&= \quad u(\bar{r}_p) + u'(\bar{r}_p)E(r_p - \bar{r}_p) + \tfrac{1}{2}u''(\bar{r}_p)E(r_p - \bar{r}_p)^2 \\
&= \quad u(\bar{r}_p) + \tfrac{1}{2}u''(\bar{r}_p)\sigma_p^2, \quad (13.2)
\end{aligned}
$$

where:

$$E \quad = \quad \text{expectations operator;}$$

$\bar{u} \equiv E[u(r_p)] \quad = \quad$ expected utility where the utility function is concave and is defined on the return on the risky portfolio;

$r_p \quad = \quad$ realized return on the risky portfolio;

$\bar{r}_p = E(r_p) \quad = \quad$ expected return on the portfolio;

$\sigma_p^2 = E(r_p - \bar{r}_p)^2 \quad = \quad$ variance of the return on the portfolio;

$u(\bar{r}_p) \quad = \quad$ utility function evaluated at $r_p = \bar{r}_p$, the expected return on the portfolio;

$u'(\bar{r}_p) = du/d\bar{r}_p \quad = \quad$ first derivative of $u$ with respect to $\bar{r}_p$ (or the *change* in $u$ in response to a small change in $\bar{r}_p$);

$u''(\bar{r}_p) = d^2u/d\bar{r}_p^2 \quad = \quad$ second derivative of $u$ with respect to $\bar{r}_p$;

$\quad = \quad$ rate of change of marginal utility (negative since marginal utility is diminishing when the utility function is concave and there is risk aversion).

Equation (13.2) says that, if we take a second-order Taylor's expansion of the utility function and then take expectations, we can derive an approximation to expected utility which depends on the expected return on the portfolio and the variance of the return on the portfolio. Put another way:

$$\bar{u} \quad = \quad \bar{u}(\bar{r}_p, \sigma_p^2). \tag{13.3}$$

This is useful, because expected return and variance are much more easy to measure than expected utility. Also, variance corresponds to the risk of the portfolio: the higher the variance, the greater the risk. This means that (13.2) is very useful indeed for discussing the choice between risk and return.

We can demonstrate the usefulness of (13.2) by finding the set of *indifference curves* associated with it. Indifference curves satisfy the property that expected utility is constant along them. We can impose this property by totally differentiating (13.2) and setting the result to zero:

$$d\bar{u} \quad = \quad u'(\bar{r}_p)d\bar{r}_p + \tfrac{1}{2}u'''(\bar{r}_p)\sigma_p^2 d\bar{r}_p + \tfrac{1}{2}u''(\bar{r}_p)d\sigma_p^2 \quad = \quad 0. \tag{13.4}$$

We will assume that $u'''(\bar{r}_p)$, the third derivative of $u(\bar{r}_p)$ with respect to $\bar{r}_p$, is zero. Imposing this assumption on (13.4) and rearranging, we get:

$$d\bar{u} \quad = \quad d\bar{r}_p + \tfrac{1}{2} \cdot \frac{u''(\bar{r}_p)}{u'(\bar{r}_p)} \cdot d\sigma_p^2$$

$$= \quad d\bar{r}_p - R_A d\sigma_p^2 \quad = \quad 0, \tag{13.5}$$

where:

$$R_A \quad \equiv \quad -\tfrac{1}{2} \cdot \frac{u''(\bar{r}_p)}{u'(\bar{r}_p)} \quad = \quad \text{Coefficient of absolute risk aversion;} \tag{13.6}$$

$$R_T \quad \equiv \quad \frac{1}{R_A} \quad = \quad \text{Coefficient of risk tolerance.}$$

If we now reintegrate (13.5), we derive the following linearized set of indifference curves:

$$\bar{r}_p \quad = \quad \bar{u} + R_A \sigma_p^2, \tag{13.7}$$

or:

$$\bar{r}_p = \bar{u} + \frac{1}{R_T}\sigma_p^2. \tag{13.8}$$

There is a different indifference curve for every utility level, $\bar{u}$. Figure 13.2 shows the set of indifference curves in mean-variance space, while Figure 13.3 shows the same set of indifference curves in mean-standard deviation space, for expected utility levels $\bar{u}_0$, $\bar{u}_1$ and $\bar{u}_2$.

There are several important points to note about these indifference curves. First, they are convex; concave utility functions give rise to convex indifference curves. Second, expected utility is measured by the intercept term; i.e., it is equal to the level of expected return when the variance of the portfolio is zero.

Third, the slope of the indifference curve depends on the size of $R_A$, the *coefficient of absolute risk aversion*, or its reciprocal, $R_T$, the *coefficient of risk tolerance*. $R_A$ measures the degree of risk aversion. Because marginal utility is positive ($u' > 0$) and diminishing ($u'' < 0$), $R_A$ is positive. Its size is dominated by the size of $u''$. If $u''$ is large (in absolute terms) so that the utility function in (13.1) is highly concave (implying extreme risk aversion), then $R_A$ will be large. If there is little risk aversion so that $u''$ is small (in absolute terms), then $R_A$ will also be small. If $R_A$ is large, then the indifference curves in Figures 13.2 and 13.3 will be steep. This makes sense, because indifference curves measure the trade-off between expected return and risk necessary to keep the investor's expected utility level constant. If $R_A$ is large then the individual will have to have a big increase in expected return to compensate him for taking on an additional unit of variance (or risk).

So we have looked at choice under uncertainty. We have shown that a risk-averse investor who makes investment choices based on the expected utility of the return on his investment portfolio is equivalently making investment choices based on the expected return and variance of the portfolio. There is a trade-off between return and variance (or risk). The greater the degree of risk aversion, the greater the trade-off. In short, we can think of investors as 'consuming' risk and return. We can also think of their portfolios as 'producing' risk and return.

## 13.1.2   Portfolios under uncertainty: the production of risk and return

The return on a portfolio is the weighted average of the returns on the individual securities held in the portfolio, where the weights are the value-weighted proportions of each security in the total portfolio:

$$r_p = \sum_{i=1}^{N} \theta_i r_i, \tag{13.9}$$

where:

$r_p$ = return on the risky portfolio;
$N$ = number of securities in the portfolio;
$r_i$ = return on the $i$th security in the portfolio;
$\theta_i$ = value-weighted proportion of the portfolio held in the $i$th security with $\sum_{i=1}^{N} \theta_i = 1$.

The expected return on the portfolio is given by the weighted average of the expected returns on the individual securities:

$$\bar{r}_p = \sum_{i=1}^{N} \theta_i \bar{r}_i, \tag{13.10}$$

**Figure 13.2** Indifference curves in mean–variance space

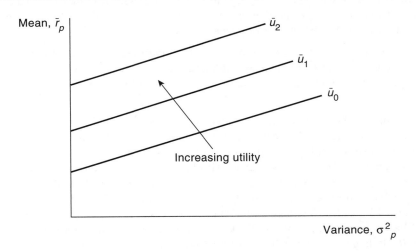

**Figure 13.3** Indifference curves in mean–standard deviation space

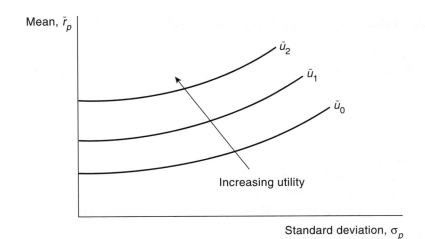

where:

$$
\begin{aligned}
\bar{r}_p &= E(r_p) &= \text{expected return on the portfolio;} \\
\bar{r}_i &= E(r_i) &= \text{expected return on the } i\text{th security.}
\end{aligned}
$$

Using (13.9) and (13.10), the variance of the return on the portfolio (or the portfolio risk) is given by:

$$
\begin{aligned}
\sigma_p^2 &= E(r_p - \bar{r}_p)^2 \\
&= E\left[\sum_{i=1}^N \theta_i(r_i - \bar{r}_i)\right]^2 \\
&= \sum_{i=1}^N \sum_{j=1}^N \theta_i \theta_j \sigma_{ij} \\
&= \sum_{i=1}^N \sum_{j=1}^N \theta_i \theta_j \sigma_i \sigma_j \rho_{ij},
\end{aligned}
\tag{13.11}
$$

where:

$$
\begin{aligned}
\sigma_p^2 &= \text{variance of the return on the risky portfolio;} \\
\sigma_{ii} &= \sigma_i^2 = E(r_i - \bar{r}_i)^2 = \text{variance of the return on the } i\text{th security;} \\
\sigma_i &= \sqrt{E(r_i - \bar{r}_i)^2} = \text{standard deviation of the return on the } i\text{th security;} \\
\sigma_{ij} &= E(r_i - \bar{r}_i)(r_j - \bar{r}_j) = \text{covariance between the returns on the } i\text{th and } j\text{th securities;} \\
\rho_{ij} &\equiv \sigma_{ij}/\sigma_i \sigma_j = \text{correlation between the returns on the } i\text{th and } j\text{th securities.}
\end{aligned}
$$

The standard deviation of the portfolio ($\sigma_p$), which is an alternative measure of portfolio risk, is simply the square root of portfolio variance. It has the advantage over portfolio variance of being measured in the same units as expected return.

**Example 13.1 (Portfolio expected return, variance and standard deviation)** *A portfolio contains two risky assets denoted $x_1$ and $x_2$. The total wealth in the portfolio is therefore $w = x_1 + x_2$. The proportion of the total portfolio held in $x_1$ is $\theta_1 = 0.4$ and the proportion of the total portfolio held in $x_2$ is $\theta_2 = (1 - \theta_1) = 0.6$. The two assets generate the following sets of expected returns, standard deviations and correlation:*

$$
\begin{aligned}
\bar{r}_1 &= 0.20 \quad (20\%) & \sigma_1 &= 0.75 \quad (75\%) \\
\bar{r}_2 &= 0.16 \quad (16\%) & \sigma_2 &= 0.50 \quad (50\%) \\
& & \rho_{12} &= -0.60 \quad (-60\%)
\end{aligned}
$$

*Given this information, we can derive:*

$$
\begin{aligned}
\bar{r}_p &= \theta_1 \bar{r}_1 + \theta_2 \bar{r}_2 \\
&= 0.4(0.20) + 0.6(0.16) \\
&= 0.176 \quad (17.6\%),
\end{aligned}
$$

*and:*

$$
\begin{aligned}
\sigma_p^2 &= \theta_1^2\sigma_1^2 + \theta_2^2\sigma_2^2 + 2\theta_1\theta_2\sigma_1\sigma_2\rho_{12} \\
&= (0.4)^2(0.75)^2 + (0.6)^2(0.50)^2 + 2(0.4)(0.6)(0.75)(0.50)(-0.60) \\
&= 0.072,
\end{aligned}
$$

*and:*

$$
\sigma_p = 0.2683 \quad (26.83\%).
$$

As the above example illustrates, the return and risk produced by the portfolio depends on two sets of factors: the returns and risks of the individual securities in the portfolio, and the proportions of each security held in the portfolio. The first set of factors is parametric to the portfolio investor, in the sense that he has no control over the returns and risks of the individual securities. The second set of factors are choice variables, in the sense that the investor can choose the proportions of each security in the portfolio. The first set of factors influences the degree of diversification available from combining assets together in a portfolio. The second set of factors will depend on the degree of risk aversion by the portfolio investor.

### 13.1.3   Diversification

Diversification is the process of combining securities in a portfolio with the aim of reducing total risk, but without sacrificing portfolio return.

Our preferred measure of portfolio risk is the standard deviation of the portfolio return, since it is measured in the same units as return. In the above example, the expected return on the portfolio was 17.6 per cent and the standard deviation of the portfolio was 26.83 per cent. If the actual returns on the portfolio are *normally distributed*, then there is a 95 per cent probability that the actual return on the portfolio will lie within two standard deviations of the expected return. In the case in point, two standard deviations is 53.66 per cent (i.e. $2 \times 26.83$ per cent), implying that the actual return will lie between −36.06 and 71.26 per cent with 95 per cent probability (see Figure 13.4).

It is clear from the last example that diversification does help to reduce risk. The portfolio standard deviation at 26.83 per cent is lower than the standard deviation on either of the two securities taken separately (75 or 50 per cent). Yet the expected return on the portfolio (17.6 per cent), while not as high as the expected return on $x_1$ (20 per cent), is higher than the expected return on $x_2$ (16 per cent).

The explanation for this lies in the degree of correlation between the returns on the two securities. We will examine three cases: (a) when security returns are perfectly positively correlated, (b) when security returns are perfectly negatively corrected, and (c) when security returns are uncorrelated.

**Diversification when security returns are perfectly positively correlated.**   We will consider again the two-asset portfolio in the above example, but will assume that $\rho_{12} = 1.0$ rather than $\rho_{12} = -0.6$. When $\rho_{12} = 1.0$ (i.e. 100 per cent), the two assets' returns are perfectly positively correlated, as shown in Figure 13.5(a). The two returns always move up and down together.

**Figure 13.4** The normal distribution

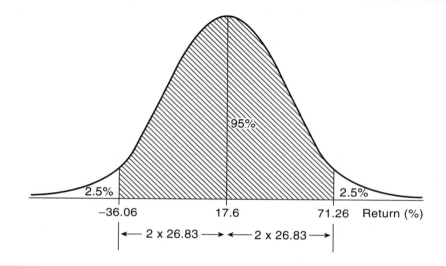

**Figure 13.5** Returns on two securities: (a) Perfectly positively correlated returns; (b) Perfectly negatively correlated returns; (c) Uncorrelated returns

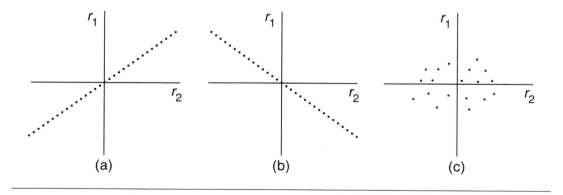

The expected return on the illustrative portfolio is unchanged as a result of changing the correlation between the two assets:

$$\bar{r}_p = \theta_1 \bar{r}_1 + \theta_2 \bar{r}_2, \tag{13.12}$$

giving $\bar{r}_p = 17.6$ per cent, but the variance of the returns on the portfolio is now:

$$\begin{aligned} \sigma_p^2 &= \theta_1^2 \sigma_1^2 + \theta_2^2 \sigma_2^2 + 2\theta_1 \theta_2 \sigma_1 \sigma_2 \\ &= (\theta_1 \sigma_1 + \theta_2 \sigma_2)^2, \end{aligned} \tag{13.13}$$

while the standard deviation is:

$$\sigma_p = \theta_1 \sigma_1 + \theta_2 \sigma_2, \tag{13.14}$$

which is simply a weighted average of the standard deviations of the returns on the individual securities; for the illustrative portfolio $\sigma_p = 60$ per cent.

From (13.12) and (13.14), it is clear that, when $\rho_{12} = 1$, $\bar{r}_p$ and $\sigma_p$ are linearly related to each other as $\theta_1$ and hence $\theta_2$ (which equals $(1 - \theta_1)$) change. This is shown in Figure 13.6, which depicts the *portfolio opportunity set* for this two-asset portfolio. The portfolio opportunity set is the set of all possible feasible portfolios with different combinations of $x_1$ and $x_2$. At $A$ all the portfolio is held in $x_1$ (i.e. $\theta_1 = 1$) and at $B$ all the portfolio is held in $x_2$ (i.e. $\theta_1 = 0$). At $P$ we have the portfolio in the example above with $\theta_1 = 0.4$.

**Figure 13.6** Portfolio opportunity set when security returns are perfectly positively correlated

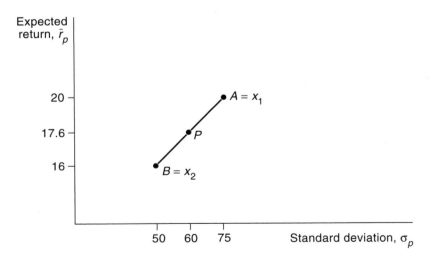

The portfolio opportunity set when $\rho_{12} = 1$ is linear, and it follows from this that there are no benefits from diversification. This is because every portfolio gives a risk-return configuration that is simply a linear combination of the risk-return configurations of $x_1$ and $x_2$. It is not possible to sacrifice risk without sacrificing some return.

**Diversification when security returns are perfectly negatively correlated.** When $\rho_{12} = -1$ (i.e. $-100$ per cent), the two assets' returns are perfectly negatively correlated, as shown in Figure 13.5(b). The two returns always move in exactly opposite directions.

The expected return on the illustrative portfolio is the same as before at 17.6 per cent (calculated using (13.12)), but the variance of the returns on the portfolio is now:

$$\sigma_p^2 = \theta_1^2\sigma_1^2 + \theta_2^2\sigma_2^2 - 2\theta_1\theta_2\sigma_1\sigma_2$$
$$= (\theta_1\sigma_1 - \theta_2\sigma_2)^2, \tag{13.15}$$

while the standard deviation is:

$$\sigma_p = \theta_1\sigma_1 - \theta_2\sigma_2. \tag{13.16}$$

For the illustrative portfolio, we get:

$$\sigma_p = (0.4)(0.75) - (0.6)(0.5) = 0.$$

In other words, the portfolio, although it contains two risky assets, has no risk at all. This result follows for two reasons. The result requires that the two assets be perfectly negatively correlated. It also requires that the relative portfolio proportions have the following relationship to the relative standard errors (derived by setting $\sigma_p$ in (13.16) to zero):

$$\frac{\theta_1}{\theta_2} = \frac{\sigma_2}{\sigma_1}. \tag{13.17}$$

This means that, if we set $\theta_1$ and $\theta_2$ ($= 1 - \theta_1$) as follows:

$$\theta_1 = \frac{\sigma_2}{\sigma_1 + \sigma_2}, \qquad \theta_2 = \frac{\sigma_1}{\sigma_1 + \sigma_2}, \tag{13.18}$$

and $\rho_{12} = -1$, then the portfolio is entirely riskless. The illustrative portfolio happened to have $\theta_1$ and $\theta_2$ determined in this way and so has no risk, as shown by point $P$ in Figure 13.7, which lies on the portfolio opportunity set.

Other points on the portfolio opportunity set are shown by the linear segments $PA$ and $PB$ in Figure 13.7. Portfolios with proportions in $x_1$ between $\theta_1 = 1$ and $\theta_1 = 0.4$ lie on $PA$, while portfolios with proportions in $x_1$ less than 0.4 lie on $PB$. Movements from $B$ to $P$ both reduce risk and increase expected return. Portfolio $P$ therefore dominates all portfolios between $P$ and $B$ because it has both higher expected return and lower risk. No rational investor (whether risk-averse or not) should select a portfolio lying on $PB$ when portfolio $P$ is available. Movements from $A$ to $P$ reduce both expected return and risk. But the reduction in risk takes place at a relatively greater rate when $\rho_{12} = -1$ than when $\rho_{12} = 1$; in other words, the line segment $AP$ is much flatter than the line segment $AB$. The effect of this can be seen by comparing portfolios $P$ and $P'$ in Figure 13.7. $P$ is the illustrative portfolio when $\rho_{12} = -1$, and $P'$ is the illustrative portfolio when $\rho_{12} = 1$. The benefits from diversification when securities are negatively correlated are clear.

**Diversification when security returns are uncorrelated.** The last case was an extreme example of the benefits of diversification. But it is unlikely in reality that many securities are perfectly negatively correlated, although the principle of hedging using futures and options is based on exploiting perfectly negative correlations, as we shall see in Chapter 16.

**Figure 13.7** Portfolio opportunity set when security returns are perfectly negatively correlated

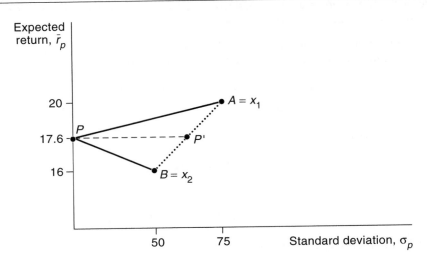

Nevertheless, there are benefits from diversification whenever asset returns are less than perfectly positively correlated. There are even benefits when security returns are entirely uncorrelated, as will now be demonstrated. When $\rho_{12} = 0$ (i.e. 0 per cent), the two securities' returns are uncorrelated, as shown in Figure 13.5(c).

The expected return on the illustrative portfolio is again the same as before at 17.6 per cent (calculated using (13.12)), but the variance of the returns on the portfolio is:

$$\sigma_p^2 \; = \; \theta_1^2 \sigma_1^2 + \theta_2^2 \sigma_2^2, \tag{13.19}$$

while the standard deviation is:

$$\sigma_p \; = \; (\theta_1^2 \sigma_1^2 + \theta_2^2 \sigma_2^2)^{\frac{1}{2}}. \tag{13.20}$$

For the illustrative portfolio, we have $\sigma_p = 0.424$ (i.e. 42.4 per cent). The illustrative portfolio is shown as point $P$ in Figure 13.8. Again, the benefits of diversification when assets are less than perfectly correlated are clear, as can be seen by comparing portfolios $P$ and $P'$ (the illustrative portfolio when $\rho_{12} = 1$).

While $P$ is the portfolio when $\theta_1 = 0.4$ and $\theta_2 = 0.6$, it is not the *minimum standard deviation portfolio* (unless $\rho_{12} = -1$). The minimum standard deviation portfolio when $\rho_{12} = 0$ is represented by $H$ in Figure 13.8. It is found by differentiating $\sigma_p$ in (13.20) with respect to $\theta_1$, setting the result to zero and solving for $\theta_1$. This gives:

$$\theta_1 \; = \; \frac{\sigma_2^2}{\sigma_1^2 + \sigma_2^2}, \qquad \theta_2 \; = \; \frac{\sigma_1^2}{\sigma_1^2 + \sigma_2^2}, \tag{13.21}$$

as the portfolio proportions required to generate $H$. In our case $\sigma_1^2 = (0.75)^2 = 0.5625$ and $\sigma_2^2 = (0.50)^2 = 0.25$, indicating that $\theta_1 = 0.31$ and $\theta_2 = 0.69$. With these portfolio proportions, we get

**Figure 13.8** Portfolio opportunity set when security returns are uncorrelated

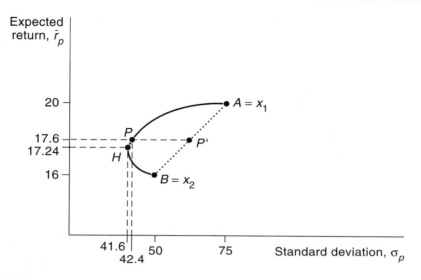

$\bar{r}_p = 17.24$ per cent and $\sigma_p = 41.6$ per cent as the expected return and standard deviation of the minimum standard deviation portfolio, $H$.

The rest of the portfolio opportunity set is given by *APHB* in Figure 13.8. Again, $H$ dominates all points along *HB*, so that a rational investor will not hold portfolios along *HB* when $H$ is available.

**Increasing the benefits from diversification.**   So far, we have considered a portfolio with two assets with uncorrelated returns. The benefits from diversification increase as more and more assets with uncorrelated returns are included in the portfolio. Suppose that $N$ securities are included in the portfolio. In this case, the standard deviation of the portfolio is:

$$\sigma_p = \left(\theta_1^2\sigma_1^2 + \theta_2^2\sigma_2^2 + \cdots + \theta_N^2\sigma_N^2\right)^{\frac{1}{2}}. \tag{13.22}$$

If each security has an equal weight in the portfolio (i.e. if $\theta_i = 1/N$) and, for simplicity, the same variance (i.e. $\sigma_i^2 = \sigma^2$), then (13.22) becomes:

$$\sigma_p = \left[\left(\frac{1}{N}\right)^2\sigma^2 + \left(\frac{1}{N}\right)^2\sigma^2 + \cdots + \left(\frac{1}{N}\right)^2\sigma^2\right]^{\frac{1}{2}}$$

$$= \left[N\left(\frac{1}{N}\right)^2\sigma^2\right]^{\frac{1}{2}}$$

$$= \left(\frac{1}{N}\right)^{\frac{1}{2}}\sigma. \tag{13.23}$$

As $N$ increases, the portfolio standard deviation is reduced towards zero, as shown in Figure 13.9.

---

**Figure 13.9** Risk and the number of securities in the portfolio

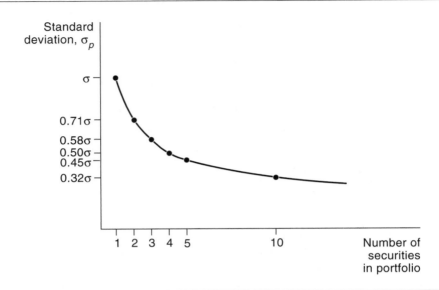

This result follows because of *risk-pooling*: as more and more uncorrelated risks are pooled together, total risk is reduced. It is also known as the *insurance principle*: insurance companies like to take on more and more uncorrelated risks.

### 13.1.4  The minimum standard deviation portfolio opportunity set and the efficient set

Instead of dealing with just two assets, we will continue the analysis using all the assets in the economy. Suppose that there are $N$ assets in the economy. We are interested in constructing portfolios using some or all of these assets. A portfolio can consist of one asset, two assets, all the way up to $N$ assets. It can also contain the same assets as another portfolio but with different weights. The set of every possible portfolio so constructed is shown in Figure 13.10 as the shaded set $AHBQ$. This is the economy's *portfolio opportunity set* as long as everyone has the same expectations concerning risks and returns (i.e. as long as expectations are *homogeneous*). It takes this convex shape because it consists of portfolios containing assets that are less than perfectly correlated, as shown in Figure 13.8.

Not every portfolio in the portfolio opportunity set is an interesting one to investigate. For example, we should not be particularly interested in portfolios that were clearly dominated by other portfolios. One portfolio will *dominate* another if it has either a lower standard deviation and the same expected return, or a higher expected return and the same standard deviation. Portfolios that are dominated by other portfolios are known as *inefficient* portfolios. Clearly, all portfolios in the interior of the portfolio opportunity set (such as $P_1$, $P_2$ and $P_3$) are dominated by portfolios on the left-hand boundary of the portfolio opportunity set, $AHB$ in Figure 13.10. This left-hand boundary is known as the *minimum standard deviation portfolio opportunity set*. It is convex for reasons already discussed.

**Figure 13.10** The minimum standard deviation portfolio opportunity set and the efficient set

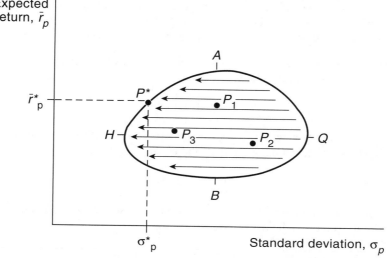

The *efficient set* is that part of the minimum standard deviation portfolio opportunity set that does not contain inefficient portfolios. All portfolios lying between $H$ and $B$ in Figure 13.10 are inefficient because they are dominated by portfolios lying along $AH$. $AH$ contains the set of all efficient portfolios and is known as the efficient set.

One method of calculating the efficient set uses the *quadratic programming* technique and is known as the *Markowitz method* (after Markowitz, 1959). Suppose, for example, that we wanted to find the portfolio $P^*$ that is on the efficient set, $AH$, in Figure 13.10. This portfolio has an expected return of $\bar{r}_p^*$ and is therefore the portfolio with the smallest standard deviation having this expected return. The objective is to find the portfolio proportions $\theta_i$ that minimize the portfolio standard deviation subject to $\bar{r}_p^*$ being obtained and to the portfolio proportions summing to unity. Formally, we wish to:

$$\left. \begin{aligned} \text{Minimize with respect to } \theta_i : \qquad \sigma_p &= \left( \sum_{i=1}^{N} \sum_{j=1}^{N} \theta_i \theta_j \sigma_{ij} \right)^{\frac{1}{2}} \\[2mm] \text{subject to:} \qquad \sum_{i=1}^{N} \theta_i \bar{r}_i &= \bar{r}_p^* \quad \text{and} \quad \sum_{i=1}^{N} \theta_i = 1. \end{aligned} \right\} \qquad (13.24)$$

The solution to this problem gives the portfolio proportions $\theta_i$ of the portfolio $P^*$. By changing the expected level of return $\bar{r}_p^*$, we can find all the different portfolios that lie on the efficient set. One of the main problems with the Markowitz method, however, is the huge number of covariance coefficients required to calculate $\sigma_p$. For example, if there are 500 securities in the economy, we need 125,000 independent covariance coefficients to calculate $\sigma_p$ in (13.24). A simpler model, due to Sharpe (1963), will be discussed later.

### 13.1.5    The efficient set when there is a riskless security

So far, we have calculated the efficient set when there are only risky securities in the portfolio. What happens to the efficient set if, in addition to the risky securities, there is a riskless security and that riskless security can be both lent (i.e. invested in) and borrowed at a single riskless interest rate?

Initially, we will consider a portfolio consisting of a single risky security, $x_1$, and a riskless security, $x_f$. The expected return on the portfolio is:

$$\bar{r}_p = \theta_1 \bar{r}_1 + \theta_2 r_f, \qquad (13.25)$$

where $r_f$ is the riskless rate of return, $\theta_1$ is the proportion of wealth held in the risky security, and $\theta_2 = 1 - \theta_1$. The standard deviation of the portfolio is simply:

$$\sigma_p = \theta_1 \sigma_1, \qquad (13.26)$$

which follows because, by definition, the risk-free interest rate has zero variance ($\sigma_f^2 = 0$) and is uncorrelated with the return on the risky asset ($\sigma_{1f} = 0$).

---

**Figure 13.11** Portfolio opportunity set with a risky and a riskless asset

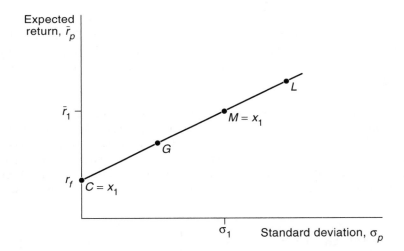

---

Equations (13.25) and (13.26) imply a linear portfolio opportunity set as shown in Figure 13.11. At $C$, the investor invests the entire portfolio in the riskless asset; the portfolio return is $r_f$ and the portfolio risk is zero. At $M$, the investor invests the entire portfolio in the risky asset, with expected return $\bar{r}_1$ and expected risk $\sigma_1$. At $G$, which lies between $C$ and $M$, part of the portfolio is invested in the risky asset (i.e. $0 < \theta_1 < 1$) and the rest is invested in the riskless asset (i.e. is lent out at the riskless rate). At $L$, which lies to the right of $M$, the investor invests more than 100 per cent of the portfolio in the risky asset. This is achieved by borrowing at the riskless rate and investing the proceeds together with the original portfolio in the risky asset. In other words, the riskless asset has been sold short in order to invest in the risky asset: the investor has employed leverage to enhance both expected return and risk.

Having found the portfolio opportunity set for the riskless asset and a single risky asset, we can find the portfolio opportunity set and the efficient set when the riskless asset is combined with all the risky assets in the economy. This is shown in Figure 13.12. For example, when the riskless asset is combined with the risky portfolio $K$, this generates the portfolio opportunity set $CKP$. Similarly, when the

**Figure 13.12** Capital market line

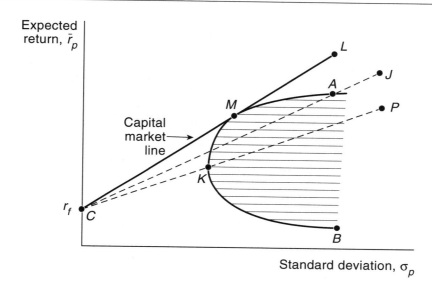

riskless asset is combined with the risky portfolio $A$, this generates the portfolio opportunity set $CAJ$. This portfolio opportunity set dominates $CKP$ because every portfolio on $CAJ$ has a higher expected return than every portfolio on $CKP$ with the same standard deviation. The portfolio opportunity set that is not dominated by any other is that which results from combining the riskless asset with the risky portfolio $M$ in Figure 13.12. Portfolio $M$ is the portfolio that lies at the point of tangency between the line segment $CML$ and the convex set of risky portfolios $AMKB$. When there is a riskless asset that can be borrowed and lent at the same riskless rate of interest, the efficient set comprises all portfolios that are combinations of the riskless asset and the risky portfolio $M$. In Figure 13.12 this implies that the efficient set is the line segment $CML$.

The striking feature about the efficient set when there is a riskless asset is that it is linear. The efficient set is also known as the *capital market line*, because portfolios along it are derived from borrowing and lending at the riskless rate of interest in the capital market. The slope of the capital market line shows the rate at which risk and return can be traded off against each other from the production side. This is discussed in greater detail in the next section.

## 13.1.6 Market equilibrium, portfolio optimality and the pricing of efficient portfolios

We have discussed risk and return from the consumption side: the slope of the indifference curve in expected return–standard deviation space shows the rate at which the investor is *willing* to trade off risk and return. We have also discussed risk and return from the production side: the slope of the efficient set or capital market line shows the rate at which the investor is *able* to trade off risk and return. We can now bring the consumption and production sides together and examine market equilibrium and portfolio optimality.

---

**Figure 13.13** Market equilibrium and the market portfolio

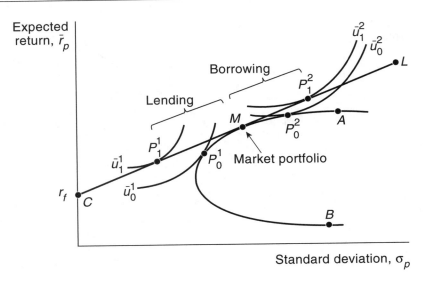

Figure 13.13 brings together the consumption and production sides of the risk-return relationships. It shows the efficient set of risky portfolios, *AMB*, and the capital market line, *CML*. It also shows the indifference curves of two risk-averse investors. Investor 1 has indifference curves labelled $\bar{u}_0^1$ and $\bar{u}_1^1$, whereas investor 2 has indifference curves labelled $\bar{u}_0^2$ and $\bar{u}_1^2$. Investor 1 is more risk-averse than investor 2, so has steeper indifference curves, implying that he requires a larger increase in expected return to compensate him for a given increase in risk.

Without the possibility of riskless borrowing and lending, investor 1 would maximize his utility by selecting portfolio $P_0^1$, determined by the point of tangency between investor 1's indifference curve $\bar{u}_0^1$ and the efficient set of risky portfolios. Similarly, investor 2 would optimize by selecting portfolio $P_0^2$. Without riskless borrowing and lending, therefore, different investors would hold different risky portfolios depending on their degree of risk aversion.

When riskless borrowing and lending is introduced, however, all investors can improve their utility. The efficient set now becomes the capital market line, *CML* in Figure 13.13, which dominates all portfolios in the set of risky portfolios apart from portfolio *M*. Investor 1 can increase his utility level from $\bar{u}_0^1$ to $\bar{u}_1^1$ by holding portfolio $P_1^1$ instead of $P_0^1$, and investor 2 can increase his utility level from $\bar{u}_0^2$ to $\bar{u}_1^2$ by holding portfolio $P_1^2$ instead of $P_0^2$. But how are the equilibrium portfolios $P_1^1$ and $P_1^2$ constructed? They are constructed exclusively from linear combinations of portfolio *M* and the riskless asset. Investor 1 will exchange portfolio $P_0^1$ for portfolio *M* and then trade-in part of *M* in order to invest in (i.e. lend out) the riskless asset, ending up with portfolio $P_1^1$. Investor 2 will exchange portfolio $P_0^2$ for *M* and then borrow at the riskless rate to invest in even more of *M*, thereby ending up with portfolio $P_1^2$.

So whatever the risk preferences of investors, all investors will, in equilibrium and assuming that there are homogeneous expectations concerning risks and return, hold portfolio $M$ together with either borrowing or lending at the riskless rate. Portfolio $M$ therefore assumes a very special significance in portfolio analysis. It is known as the *market portfolio* of risky assets. The market portfolio is defined as the portfolio of all the assets in the economy with weights equal to their relative market values. This means that the $i$th asset in the market portfolio has the following weight:

$$\theta_i = \frac{\text{Market value of } i\text{th asset}}{\text{Market value of all assets in the economy}}. \tag{13.27}$$

In *market equilibrium*, all assets must be held voluntarily. Equilibrium is achieved when the market value of each asset is such that there is a balance between the supply of the asset and the demand for the asset. This is true for both the risky assets and the riskless asset; in the latter case this is equivalent to a balance between borrowing and lending at the riskless rate of interest. Market equilibrium therefore requires two things. First, it requires that the riskless interest rate is such that the amount of funds borrowed matches the amount of funds lent. In terms of Figure 13.13 (and assuming that all investors are either like investor 1 or like investor 2), this means that the distance $MP_1^1$ (the total amount of lending) equals the distance $MP_1^2$ (the total amount of borrowing). Second, it requires that all investors hold the market portfolio as part of their own portfolios, since the market portfolio is the only portfolio for which all the risky assets are in equilibrium simultaneously. But from Figure 13.13, the only portfolio of risky assets that *all* investors will *want* to hold as part of their own portfolios is portfolio $M$, the tangency portfolio between the capital market line and the convex opportunity set of risky portfolios. Portfolio $M$ is also the only portfolio that *all* investors will be *able* to hold, since the assets in the portfolio are valued at market equilibrium prices; if the portfolio is valued at *any other* set of prices, there will be an excess demand or excess supply for the underlying securities in the portfolio which will lead to price movements that restore market equilibrium. Therefore it must be the case that portfolio $M$ is the market equilibrium portfolio.

Once we have the market portfolio and the riskless interest rate, we can calculate the *market* or *equilibrium price of risk*. The market price of risk is simply equal to the slope of the capital market line (see Figure 13.14):

$$\text{Market price of risk} = \frac{\bar{r}_m - r_f}{\sigma_m}, \tag{13.28}$$

where:

$$
\begin{aligned}
r_f &= \text{riskless rate of interest;} \\
\bar{r}_m &= \text{expected return on the market portfolio;} \\
\sigma_m &= \text{standard deviation of the market portfolio.}
\end{aligned}
$$

Equation (13.28) shows that the market price of risk is equal to the *excess return* or *risk premium* on the market (over the riskless rate) per unit of risk. It measures the increase in expected return required to compensate an investor for bearing an additional unit of risk. This can be seen more clearly when we examine the equation for the capital market line (CML):

$$\bar{r}_p = r_f + \left( \frac{\bar{r}_m - r_f}{\sigma_m} \right) \sigma_p, \tag{13.29}$$

where:

**Figure 13.14** Portfolio optimality and the market price of risk

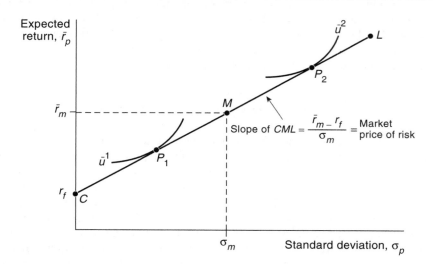

$$\bar{r}_p \; = \; \text{expected return on a portfolio along the CML;}$$
$$\sigma_p \; = \; \text{standard deviation of a portfolio along the CML.}$$

From (13.29), $\partial \bar{r}_p / \partial \sigma_p$ measures the *marginal rate of transformation* (MRT) between risk and return, and this equals the market price of risk (13.28).

For example if $r_f = 0.09$ (9 per cent), $\bar{r}_m = 0.18$ (18 per cent) and $\sigma_m = 0.30$ (30 per cent), then the market price of risk is 0.3 (i.e. $(0.18 - 0.09)/0.30$) and the equation for the CML is:

$$\bar{r}_p \; = \; 0.09 + 0.3\sigma_p,$$

implying that the marginal rate of transformation between risk and return is 0.3.

As long as there are homogeneous expectations concerning risk and return, every investor will agree that (13.28) is the market price of risk and also equals the marginal rate of transformation between risk and return. Every investor will also agree that all efficient portfolios will be priced in equilibrium according to (13.29). In other words, the rate of return required on an efficient portfolio to be held in equilibrium will be given by $\bar{r}_p$ in (13.29) if its level of risk is given by $\sigma_p$. Alternatively, in terms of prices rather than returns, the equilibrium price of an efficient portfolio will be $£1/(1 + \bar{r}_p)$ for every £1 expected from the portfolio at the end of the year.

Every investor's *optimal portfolio* will be formed from a combination of the market portfolio and the riskless asset. The precise combination of the market portfolio and the riskless asset depends on the degree of risk aversion. An investor with a high degree of risk aversion, such as investor 1 in Figure 13.14 with indifference curve $\bar{u}^1$, will hold positive quantities of the riskless asset in his optimal portfolio, $P_1$. An investor with a low degree of risk aversion, such as investor 2 with indifference curve $\bar{u}^2$, will hold negative quantities of the riskless asset in his optimal portfolio, $P_2$. But the conditions for portfolio optimality will be the same for both investors, namely that the optimal portfolio is determined at the point where the indifference curve is tangential to the CML. At this point the slope of the indifference curve (which measures the *marginal rate of substitution* (MRS) between risk and return) equals the slope of the CML (which measures the marginal rate of transformation (MRT) between risk and return):

$$MRS_1 \; = \; MRS_2 \; = \; MRT \; = \; \frac{\bar{r}_m - r_f}{\sigma_m}, \tag{13.30}$$

where:

$MRS_i$ = marginal rate of substitution between risk and return for investor $i$, $i = 1, 2$;
$MRT$ = marginal rate of transformation between risk and return (= market price of risk).

Equation (13.30) is a standard optimality condition in economics which can be used to calculate the proportions of the market portfolio and the riskless asset in the optimal portfolio. It can be shown (using (13.7) and (13.26), assuming that the market portfolio replaces the single risky security, $x_1$) that the marginal rate of substitution between risk and return is given by:

$$MRS \; = \; 2\theta_m R_A \sigma_m, \tag{13.31}$$

which is increasing in the individual investor's degree of risk aversion (i.e. if the investor has steeper indifference curves), in the proportion of his portfolio in the market, and in market risk. Substituting (13.31) into (13.30) and rearranging gives:

$$\begin{aligned}
\theta_m \; &= \; \frac{1}{2} \cdot \left[ \frac{\bar{r}_m - r_f}{\sigma_m^2} \right] \cdot \frac{1}{R_A} \\
&= \; \frac{1}{2} \cdot \left[ \frac{\bar{r}_m - r_f}{\sigma_m^2} \right] \cdot R_T
\end{aligned} \tag{13.32}$$

as the optimal proportion of the investor's portfolio invested in the market portfolio. The optimal proportion increases if the excess return on the market increases, or if the investor's degree of risk tolerance increases, and decreases if the variance of the market portfolio increases.

To illustrate, suppose that $r_f = 0.09$, $\bar{r}_m = 0.18$ and $\sigma_m = 0.30$. If investor 1 has $R_T = 1$, then, using (13.32):

$$\theta_m \; = \; \frac{1}{2} \cdot \left[ \frac{0.18 - 0.09}{(0.30)^2} \right] \cdot 1 \; = \; 0.50 \quad (50\%).$$

So investor 1's optimal portfolio is invested 50 per cent in the market portfolio and 50 per cent in the riskless asset. Similarly, if investor 2's degree of risk tolerance is 3, then his optimal portfolio will have 150 per cent of his wealth invested in the market portfolio and have borrowings equal to 50 per cent of his wealth.

Therefore $\theta_m$, the proportion of an individual investor's optimal portfolio in the market portfolio, is the only choice variable that needs to be determined by the investor himself. Everything else is determined by the market. The proportions of each security in the market portfolio are determined by market equilibrium conditions. The riskless interest rate is set to balance the supply and demand for loans. The only variable that the investor has to choose is $\theta_m$, and this depends on his degree of risk aversion.

Equation (13.26) can be used to calculate portfolio risks:

$$\sigma_p \; = \; \theta_m \sigma_m. \tag{13.33}$$

If $\sigma_m = 0.30$, then the risk in investor 1's portfolio is 15 per cent, whereas the risk in investor 2's portfolio is 45 per cent.

### 13.1.7   Pricing inefficient portfolios and the decomposition of total risk

In equilibrium, efficient portfolios along the CML (i.e. combinations of the market portfolio and the riskless asset) are priced according to (13.29) and their risk is determined by (13.33). But how are inefficient portfolios (i.e. those in the interior of the portfolio opportunity set, such as $P_1$, $P_2$ and $P_3$ in Figure 13.10) priced in equilibrium? Even if no rational risk-averse investor would hold such portfolios in equilibrium, they must still have a price. And how will the price of an inefficient portfolio depend on the standard deviation of the portfolio return? To answer these questions, we must analyze total portfolio risk in greater detail and decompose it into its constituent components.

We have associated the riskiness of the portfolio with the standard deviation of the portfolio. And we have seen how diversification can reduce the standard deviation of a portfolio of assets compared with assets held individually if the returns on those assets are less than perfectly correlated. We have also seen that, even where a portfolio does contain a diversified collection of assets, it is still possible for an even more diversified portfolio to dominate it in the sense of having a lower standard deviation but the same expected return. The most diversified portfolio of all is the market portfolio, and this dominates all other risky portfolios. So we will begin the analysis by decomposing *total risk* into two main components: *diversifiable risk* and *undiversifiable risk*.

**Table 13.1** Diversifiable and undiversifiable risk

| Number of securities in portfolio | Standard deviation of portfolio returns, $\sigma_p$ (% per month) | Correlation with return on the market portfolio |
|:---:|:---:|:---:|
| 1 | 7.0 | 0.54 |
| 2 | 5.0 | 0.63 |
| 3 | 4.8 | 0.75 |
| 4 | 4.6 | 0.77 |
| 5 | 4.6 | 0.79 |
| 10 | 4.2 | 0.85 |
| 15 | 4.0 | 0.88 |
| 20 | 3.9 | 0.89 |

*Source:* Wagner and Lau (1971)

Table 13.1 and Figure 13.15 show the effect of diversification on total risk using portfolios constructed from equally weighted and randomly selected securities on the New York Stock Exchange. As the number of securities in the portfolio is increased, the total portfolio risk, as measured by the portfolio standard deviation, falls, but at a diminishing rate. After about ten securities are included in the portfolio, there is little additional reduction in risk. This demonstrates that, however, diversified a portfolio, there is some level of risk that cannot be diversified away. So some risk is diversifiable, while some risk is not. (Comparing Figures 13.9 and 13.15, we observe that in Figure 13.9 only uncorrelated securities are included, whereas in Figure 13.15 all types of randomly selected securities are included.) The benefits of diversification are even more apparent when the portfolio is diversified internationally, as can be seen from Figure 13.16 which compares a portfolio constructed only from US securities with a portfolio constructed from international securities. But Figure 13.16 also makes clear that, even with international diversification, some risk remains undiversifiable.

But what is the undiversifiable risk related to? A clue is provided by the third column of Table 13.1. As the standard deviation of the portfolio return falls, the correlation between the portfolio return

**Figure 13.15** Diversifiable and undiversifiable risk

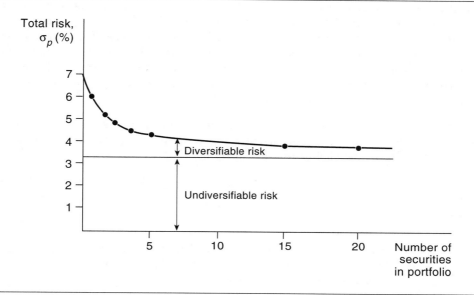

**Figure 13.16** The benefits of international diversification

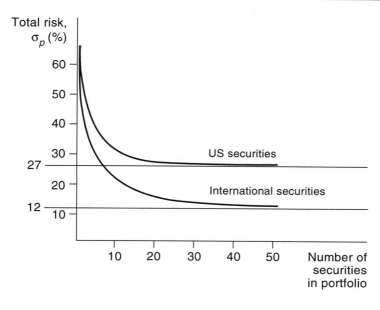

*Source:* Solnik (1974)

and the return on the market portfolio increases. In other words, the evidence indicates that highly diversified portfolios have returns that are highly correlated with the market. This makes sense. We would expect the level of undiversifiable risk to be related to the state of the economy in the form of, say, the business cycle. A good proxy for the business cycle is the return on the market portfolio or market index. In other words, undiversifiable risk can be associated with the *systematic risk* in the economy. The world is an inherently risky place and that risk has to be borne by someone, namely the holders of risky securities; not all of it can be diversified away. Because the state of the stock market is a good proxy for the business cycle (in fact, the stock market is a *leading indicator* of the business cycle), undiversifiable risk is also known as *market risk*.

The *market index model* (or simply the *market model*) (due to Sharpe (1963)) postulates a linear relationship between the return on a security and the return on the market, and can be used to decompose total risk into diversifiable and undiversifiable components:

$$r_{i,t} = \gamma_i + \beta_i r_{m,t} + \varepsilon_{i,t}, \tag{13.34}$$

where:

$$
\begin{aligned}
r_{i,t} &= \text{total return (capital gain plus income) on the } i\text{th security in year } t; \\
r_{m,t} &= \text{total return (capital gain plus income) on the market in year } t; \\
\varepsilon_{i,t} &= \text{an independent random error term;} \\
\gamma_i, \beta_i &= \text{intercept and slope coefficients.}
\end{aligned}
$$

Equation (13.34) is sometimes called the *characteristics line* of the $i$th security, and it has all the characteristics of a regression equation. It has a *systematic* component $(\gamma_i + \beta_i r_{m,t})$, in which the return on the $i$th security is systematically explained by the return on the market. The component of the return on the $i$th security not explained by the market is $\varepsilon_{i,t}$. This is sometimes known as the *unsystematic* or *specific* or *idiosyncratic* component of the security's return, because it is not systematically related to the market return or indeed to the return on any other security. This component has the following properties:

$$
\begin{aligned}
E(\varepsilon_{i,t}) &= 0, \\
E(\varepsilon_{i,t}^2) &= \text{Var}(\varepsilon_{i,t}) = \eta_i^2, \\
E(\varepsilon_{i,t} r_{m,t}) &= \text{Cov}(\varepsilon_{i,t}, r_{m,t}) = 0, \\
E(\varepsilon_{i,t} \varepsilon_{j,t}) &= \text{Cov}(\varepsilon_{it}, \varepsilon_{j,t}) = 0.
\end{aligned}
\tag{13.35}
$$

These properties state that $\varepsilon_{i,t}$ has a zero mean and a constant variance $(\eta_i^2)$, and is uncorrelated with (i.e. has a zero covariance with) both the return on the market and the unsystematic component of the return on any other security. These are exactly the same properties as the independent random error term in a standard regression model.

Since (13.34) is a regression equation, we know how to calculate the intercept and slope coefficients, $\gamma_i$ and $\beta_i$. The slope coefficient is calculated as follows:

$$
\begin{aligned}
\beta_i &= \frac{\text{Cov}(r_{i,t}, r_{m,t})}{\text{Var}(r_{m,t})} \\
&= \frac{\sigma_{im}}{\sigma_m^2}, \tag{13.36}
\end{aligned}
$$

where:

$$\begin{aligned} \text{Cov}(r_{i,t}, r_{m,t}) &= \sigma_{im} = \text{covariance between } r_{i,t} \text{ and } r_{m,t}; \\ \text{Var}(r_{m,t}) &= \sigma_m^2 = \text{variance of } r_{m,t}. \end{aligned}$$

Thus $\beta_i$ is proportional to the covariance between the $i$th security and the market. The intercept coefficient is calculated as follows:

$$\gamma_i = \bar{r}_i - \beta_i \bar{r}_m, \tag{13.37}$$

where:

$$\begin{aligned} \bar{r}_i &= \text{mean of } r_{i,t}; \\ \bar{r}_m &= \text{mean of } r_{m,t}. \end{aligned}$$

**Example 13.2 (The market model)** *We are given the following information concerning the ith security and the market:*

$$\begin{aligned} \bar{r}_i &= 0.18 \quad (18\%) & \sigma_i &= 0.35 \quad (35\%) \\ \bar{r}_m &= 0.15 \quad (15\%) & \sigma_m &= 0.25 \quad (25\%) \\ & & \sigma_{i,m} &= 0.053 \end{aligned}$$

*Using these data we calculate:*

$$\beta_i = \frac{0.053}{(0.25)^2} = 0.85,$$

*and:*

$$\gamma_i = 0.18 - 0.85(0.15) = 0.0525.$$

*The market model or characteristics line is therefore:*

$$r_{i,t} = 0.0525 + 0.85 r_{m,t} + \varepsilon_{i,t}.$$

Figure 13.17 shows a graph of the characteristics line, illustrating the systematic component of the return on the $i$th security and the unsystematic component. Also, the slope coefficient $\beta_i$ is positive, so that there is a positive relationship between the $i$th security and the market: a 1 percentage point increase in the expected return on the market leads to a 0.85 percentage point increase in the expected return on the security.

The market model can also be used to decompose total risk into diversifiable and undiversifiable risk. Using (13.34), we have:

$$\begin{aligned} \text{Var}(r_{i,t}) &= \text{Var}(\gamma_i + \beta_i r_{m,t} + \varepsilon_{i,t}) \\ &= \beta_i^2 \text{Var}(r_{m,t}) + 2\beta_i \text{Cov}(r_{m,t}, \varepsilon_{i,t}) + \text{Var}(\varepsilon_{i,t}) \\ &= \beta_i^2 \text{Var}(r_{m,t}) + \text{Var}(\varepsilon_{i,t}), \tag{13.38} \end{aligned}$$

**Figure 13.17** The characteristics line

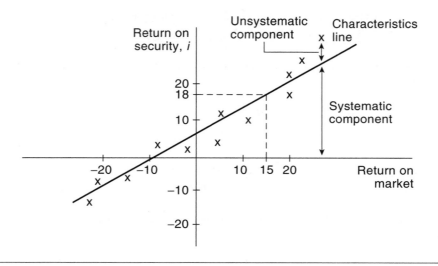

or:

$$\sigma_i^2 \; = \; \beta_i^2 \sigma_m^2 + \eta_i^2, \tag{13.39}$$

since $\text{Cov}(r_{mt}, \varepsilon_{it}) = 0$. The first component on the right-hand side of (13.38) or (13.39) is *undiversifiable risk* (also called *systematic* or *market risk*). The second component is *diversifiable risk* (also called *specific* or *unsystematic* or *idiosyncratic* or *residual risk*). Therefore we have the following decomposition:

$$
\begin{aligned}
\text{Total risk} \;\; &= \;\; \text{Undiversifiable risk} + \text{Diversifiable risk} \\
&= \;\; \text{Market risk} + \text{Specific risk}. \tag{13.40}
\end{aligned}
$$

Using the data from the last example, we can decompose the total risk on the security into its diversifiable and undiversifiable components. Total risk is:

$$\text{Var}(r_{i,t}) \;\; = \;\; \sigma_i^2 \;\; = \;\; (0.35)^2 \;\; = \;\; 0.1225,$$

and systematic risk is:

$$\beta_i^2 \text{Var}(r_{m,t}) \;\; = \;\; \beta_i^2 \sigma_m^2 \;\; = \;\; (0.85)^2 (0.25)^2 \;\; = \;\; 0.0452.$$

Therefore:

$$\text{Total risk} \;\; = \;\; \text{Undiversifiable risk} + \text{Diversifiable risk},$$

or:

$$0.1225 \;\; = \;\; 0.0452 + 0.0773.$$

Of the total risk, 37 per cent is undiversifiable, while 63 per cent is diversifiable.

It is good to have a high proportion of the total risk of a security constituting diversifiable risk. This is because diversifiable risk can be almost entirely eliminated by relatively low-cost diversification. The effect of combining a large number of securities in a diversified portfolio is that the independent random error components of their returns cancel each other out. This leaves only the undiversifiable risk of the security as the important measure of risk that an investor is going to be concerned about.

We can demonstrate the assertion that only undiversifiable risk is important as follows. The relevant measure of risk for any security in equilibrium is that security's contribution to the total risk of the portfolio. This is calculated by finding the change to the portfolio standard deviation as the share of a particular security in the portfolio is increased. Since $\sigma_p$ is the square root of (13.11), we have for the $i$th security:

$$
\begin{aligned}
\frac{\partial \sigma_p}{\partial \theta_i} &= \frac{1}{2\sigma_p}\left(2\theta_i\sigma_i^2 + 2\sum_{j\neq i}^{N}\theta_j\sigma_{ij}\right) \\
&= \theta_i\frac{\sigma_i^2}{\sigma_p} + \sum_{j\neq i}^{N}\theta_j\frac{\sigma_{ij}}{\sigma_p} \\
&= \theta_i\frac{\sigma_i^2}{\sigma_p} + \frac{\sigma_{ip}}{\sigma_p} \\
&= \text{Variant risk} + \text{Covariant risk}.
\end{aligned}
\tag{13.41}
$$

So the contribution of the $i$th security to total portfolio risk has two components: one that depends on the variance of the $i$th security (and is therefore known as *variant risk*), and one that depends on the covariance between the $i$th security and the rest of the portfolio (and is therefore known as *covariant risk*).

But the variant risk can be completely diversified away. This can be seen most clearly in an equally-weighted portfolio with $\theta_i = 1/N$. As $N \to \infty$, the variant risk vanishes, leaving only the covariant risk. If the portfolio in question is the market portfolio, so that $\theta_i$ is the value-weighted proportion of the $i$th security, then (13.41) becomes:

$$
\begin{aligned}
\frac{\partial \sigma_m}{\partial \theta_i} &= \theta_i\frac{\sigma_i^2}{\sigma_m} + \frac{\sigma_{im}}{\sigma_m} \\
&\approx \frac{\sigma_{im}}{\sigma_m} \\
&= \beta_i\sigma_m,
\end{aligned}
\tag{13.42}
$$

(cf. (13.36)). The share of the $i$th security in the market portfolio is so small that again variant risk is negligible. This leaves only covariant risk as the relevant measure of risk - in this case, the covariance of the $i$th security with the market relative to the standard deviation of the market (or, equivalently, the coefficient $\beta_i$ times the standard deviation of the market). Thus we have two more names to add to our list of alternative names for undiversifiable and diversifiable risk: covariant risk and variant risk.

So we are now in a position to answer the questions raised at the beginning of this section. The appropriate measure of risk for an efficient portfolio is the standard deviation or variance of the return; i.e., the appropriate measure is total risk. This is because, for an efficient portfolio, total risk equals undiversifiable risk, since by construction an efficient portfolio has no specific risk. However, total risk is not the appropriate measure of risk for inefficient portfolios or individual securities (which are examples of inefficient portfolios). This is because inefficient portfolios are not well diversified. Because diversification is a low-cost means of reducing total risk, only the component of total risk that cannot be diversified is the appropriate measure for pricing inefficient portfolios and individual securities. And we found that the reason that some risk is undiversifiable is because it is correlated with the market, which in turn is correlated with the business cycle, which, in turn, reflects the underlying riskiness of the economy; and this latter risk has to be borne by someone. Therefore the pricing of inefficient portfolios and individual securities should depend only on the undiversifiable risk embodied in them.

So far, we have looked at portfolios of securities, both efficient and inefficient. All efficient portfolios lie along the CML and as such are all perfectly correlated with the market portfolio, which is the most diversified portfolio of all. Thus all efficient portfolios contain no diversifiable risks, so along the CML total risk equals undiversifiable risk. All inefficient portfolios contain, by definition, some diversifiable risks. The diversifiable component of the risk of inefficient portfolios will not be priced in equilibrium because that risk could be eliminated at low cost. No one is going to be willing to pay for a risk that can be eliminated at very low cost. Only undiversifiable risk will be priced in equilibrium.

The analysis of this section, which was applied to portfolios, can also be used to determine the equilibrium price or return on an individual security. This is done in the next section.

But before then, it can be demonstrated how the *Sharpe method*, which uses the market model, simplifies the procedure for calculating the efficient portfolio opportunity set compared with the Markowitz method (see (13.24)). Using (13.34) and (13.35), the covariance between the $i$th and $j$th securities' returns is given by:

$$\sigma_{ij} = \beta_i \beta_j \sigma_m^2 + \eta_{ij}, \tag{13.43}$$

where:

$$\eta_{ij} = \begin{cases} \eta_i^2 & \text{if } i = j, \\ 0 & \text{if } i \neq j. \end{cases}$$

So all the covariances can be calculated once we know the market model for each security. If there are 500 securities, we only need 500 market models to calculate 125,000 independent covariance coefficients, a dramatic simplification on the Markowitz method. We can substitute (13.43) into (13.24) and calculate the efficient set using quadratic programming.

We can also use (13.43) to calculate the variance of the portfolio by substituting it into (13.11):

$$\sigma_p^2 = \sum_{i=1}^{N} \sum_{j=1}^{N} \theta_i \theta_j \sigma_{ij}$$

$$= \sum_{i=1}^{N} \sum_{j=1}^{N} \theta_i \theta_j (\beta_i \beta_j \sigma_m^2 + \eta_{ij})$$

$$= \sum_{i=1}^{N} \sum_{j=1}^{N} \theta_i \theta_j \beta_i \beta_j \sigma_m^2 + \sum_{i=1}^{N} \theta_i^2 \eta_i^2$$

$$= \text{Market risk of portfolio} + \text{Specific risk of portfolio}. \tag{13.44}$$

## 13.2   Asset pricing

In this section, we examine the equilibrium pricing of individual securities. Two models of asset prices are considered: the capital asset pricing model and the arbitrage pricing model.

### 13.2.1   The capital asset pricing model

The *capital asset pricing model* (CAPM) was developed by Sharpe (1963) and Lintner (1965). It is valid for all types of securities, including shares and bonds. However, there is a version of the CAPM that is especially suitable for bonds. We will consider both versions.

**The general version of the CAPM**

**Derivation.**   The CAPM is an equilibrium model of asset pricing, based explicitly on utility maximization and a given portfolio opportunity set. In other words, equilibrium asset prices are determined in a way that balances the supply of assets with the demand for assets.

Suppose that there are $h = 1, \dots, H$ investors and $i = 1, \dots, N$ risky securities and riskless debt which is denoted $N+1$ in the following matrix:

$$\textit{Investors}$$

| $\textit{Securities}$ | $1$ | $\cdots$ | $h$ | $\cdots$ | $H$ | $\sum_{h=1}^{H} \omega_{ih}$ |
|---|---|---|---|---|---|---|
| $1$ | $\omega_{11}$ | $\cdots$ | $\omega_{1h}$ | $\cdots$ | $\omega_{1H}$ | $\theta_1$ |
| $2$ | $\omega_{21}$ | $\cdots$ | $\omega_{2h}$ | $\cdots$ | $\omega_{2H}$ | $\theta_2$ |
| $\vdots$ | $\vdots$ | $\ddots$ | $\vdots$ | $\ddots$ | $\vdots$ | $\vdots$ |
| $i$ | $\omega_{i1}$ | $\cdots$ | $\omega_{ih}$ | $\cdots$ | $\omega_{iH}$ | $\theta_i$ |
| $\vdots$ | $\vdots$ | $\ddots$ | $\vdots$ | $\ddots$ | $\vdots$ | $\vdots$ |
| $N$ | $\omega_{N1}$ | $\cdots$ | $\omega_{Nh}$ | $\cdots$ | $\omega_{NH}$ | $\theta_N$ |
| $N+1$ | $-\omega_{N+1,1}$ | $\cdots$ | $-\omega_{N+1,h}$ | $\cdots$ | $-\omega_{N+1,H}$ | $0$ |
| $\sum_{i=1}^{N+1} \omega_{ih}$ | $\varphi_1$ | $\cdots$ | $\varphi_h$ | $\cdots$ | $\varphi_H$ | $\sum_{h=1}^{H} \sum_{i=1}^{N+1} \omega_{ih} = 1$ |

The elements of the matrix are explained as follows. A typical element $\omega_{ih}$ is the proportion of the total market invested by investor $h$ in security $i$. Similarly, $\omega_{N+1,h}$ is the proportion of the total market taken up by investor $h$ in riskless debt. The column sums give the budget constraints for the investors: $\varphi_h$ is the proportion of the investor $h$'s wealth in total wealth. The row sums give the market equilibrium constraints for individual securities: $\theta_i$ is the proportion of security $i$ in the total market. Similarly, the sum of riskless debt across all investors must be zero.

Suppose that each individual investor $h$ has a utility function of the form:

$$\bar{u}_h = \bar{u}_h(\bar{r}_{ph}, \sigma_{ph}^2), \tag{13.45}$$

where:

$$\bar{r}_{ph} = \left(\frac{1}{\varphi_h}\right)\left(\sum_{i=1}^{N} \omega_{ih}\bar{r}_i - \omega_{N+1,h}r_f\right) \tag{13.46}$$

is the expected return on investor $h$'s portfolio, and:

$$\sigma_{ph}^2 = \left(\frac{1}{\varphi_h}\right)^2\left(\sum_{i=1}^{N}\sum_{j=1}^{N}\omega_{ih}\omega_{jh}\sigma_{ij}\right) \tag{13.47}$$

is the variance of the return on investor $h$'s portfolio. Investor $h$'s budget constraint is:

$$\left(\frac{1}{\varphi_h}\right)\left(\sum_{i=1}^{N}\omega_{ih} - \omega_{N+1,h}\right) = 1. \tag{13.48}$$

The objective of investor $h$ is to maximize (13.45) subject to (13.48). The first-order conditions for a maximum are (where $\lambda_h$ is the Lagrange multiplier for investor $h$):

$$\frac{\partial \bar{u}_h}{\partial \bar{r}_{ph}} \cdot \frac{\partial \bar{r}_{ph}}{\partial \omega_{ih}} + \frac{\partial \bar{u}_h}{\partial \sigma_{ph}^2} \cdot \frac{\partial \sigma_{ph}^2}{\partial \omega_{ih}} + \lambda_h\left(\frac{1}{\varphi_h}\right) = \frac{\partial \bar{u}_h}{\partial \bar{r}_{ph}}\left(\frac{1}{\varphi_h}\right)\bar{r}_i$$

$$+ \frac{\partial \bar{u}_h}{\partial \sigma_{ph}^2}\left[2(1/\varphi_h)^2\sum_{j=1}^{N}\omega_{jh}\sigma_{ij}\right] + \lambda_h\left(\frac{1}{\varphi_h}\right)$$

$$= 0, \quad i = 1,\ldots,N, \tag{13.49}$$

and:

$$\frac{\partial \bar{u}_h}{\partial \bar{r}_{ph}} \cdot \frac{\partial \bar{r}_{ph}}{\partial \omega_{N+1,h}} + \frac{\partial \bar{u}_h}{\partial \sigma_{ph}^2} \cdot \frac{\partial \sigma_{ph}^2}{\partial \omega_{N+1,h}} - \lambda_h\left(\frac{1}{\varphi_h}\right) = \frac{\partial \bar{u}_h}{\partial \bar{r}_{ph}}[-(1/\varphi_h)r_f] - \lambda_h\left(\frac{1}{\varphi_h}\right)$$

$$= 0. \tag{13.50}$$

By substituting (13.50) into (13.49) we can eliminate $\lambda_h$:

$$\frac{\partial \bar{u}_h}{\partial \bar{r}_{ph}}(\bar{r}_i - r_f) + \frac{\partial \bar{u}_h}{\partial \sigma_{ph}^2}\left[2\left(\frac{1}{\varphi_h}\right)^2\sum_{j=1}^{N}\omega_{jh}\sigma_{ij}\right] = 0, \quad i = 1,\ldots,N. \tag{13.51}$$

Equation (13.51) is an equilibrium relationship that must hold for all investors, $h = 1,\ldots,H$, and for all securities, $i = 1,\ldots,N$.

Since (13.51) holds for all securities, it also holds for ratios of pairs of securities. Taking securities $i$ and $k$, we have:

$$\frac{\dfrac{\partial \bar{u}_h}{\partial \bar{r}_{ph}}(\bar{r}_i - r_f)}{\dfrac{\partial \bar{u}_h}{\partial \bar{r}_{ph}}(\bar{r}_k - r_f)} = \frac{-\dfrac{\partial \bar{u}_h}{\partial \sigma_{ph}^2}\left[2\left(\dfrac{1}{\varphi_h}\right)^2\sum_{j=1}^{N}\omega_{jh}\sigma_{ij}\right]}{-\dfrac{\partial \bar{u}_h}{\partial \sigma_{ph}^2}\left[2\left(\dfrac{1}{\varphi_h}\right)^2\sum_{j=1}^{N}\omega_{jh}\sigma_{kj}\right]},$$

which simplifies to:

$$\frac{\bar{r}_i - r_f}{\sum\limits_{j=1}^{N} \omega_{jh}\sigma_{ij}} = \frac{\bar{r}_k - r_f}{\sum\limits_{j=1}^{N} \omega_{jh}\sigma_{kj}}.$$

(13.52)

In market equilibrium, the following relationship must hold for all securities:

$$\sum_{h=1}^{H} \omega_{jh} = \theta_j, \quad j = 1, \ldots, N.$$

(13.53)

Summing (13.52) across all investors $h = 1, \ldots, H$ and applying (13.53) gives:

$$\frac{\bar{r}_i - r_f}{\sum\limits_{j=1}^{N} \theta_j\sigma_{ij}} = \frac{\bar{r}_k - r_f}{\sum\limits_{j=1}^{N} \theta_j\sigma_{kj}} = \pi,$$

(13.54)

where $\pi$ is a common ratio for all securities.

Multiplying both the numerator and denominator of (13.54) by $\theta_k$ and summing over all securities $k = 1, \ldots, N$ gives:

$$\frac{\sum\limits_{k=1}^{N} (\bar{r}_k\theta_k - r_f\theta_k)}{\sum\limits_{k=1}^{N} \sum\limits_{j=1}^{N} \theta_k\theta_j\sigma_{kj}} = \frac{\bar{r}_m - r_f}{\sigma_m^2} = \pi,$$

(13.55)

where:

$$\begin{aligned}
\bar{r}_m &= \text{expected return on the market portfolio;} \\
\sigma_m^2 &= \text{variance of the return on the market portfolio.}
\end{aligned}$$

Equation (13.55) indicates that, if we sum over all securities and investors, and impose market equilibrium conditions, we end up, as we would expect, with the market portfolio.

Substituting (13.55) into (13.54) and rearranging gives us the capital asset pricing model:

$$\bar{r}_i = r_f + \frac{\bar{r}_m - r_f}{\sigma_m} \cdot \frac{\sigma_{im}}{\sigma_m},$$

(13.56)

or:

$$\bar{r}_i = r_f + (\bar{r}_m - r_f)\beta_i,$$

(13.57)

where:

$$\begin{aligned}
\sigma_{im} &= \sum_{j=1}^{N} \theta_j\sigma_{ij} = \text{covariance of the return on the $i$th security with the return on} \\
& \qquad\qquad\qquad \text{the market;} \\
\beta_i &= \frac{\sigma_{im}}{\sigma_m^2} = \text{beta of $i$th security.}
\end{aligned}$$

**Risk in the CAPM.** Equations (13.56) and (13.57) can be written in words as follows:

$$\text{Expected return on } i\text{th security} = \left( \begin{array}{c} \text{Price of} \\ \text{time} \end{array} \right) + \left( \begin{array}{c} \text{Price of} \\ \text{risk} \end{array} \times \begin{array}{c} \text{Quantity} \\ \text{of risk} \end{array} \right). \quad (13.58)$$

One difference between the two formulations is that (13.56) expresses the market price of risk in units of total risk (cf. (13.28)), whereas (13.57) employs the absolute price of risk. The other difference is that the measures of the quantity of risk differ slightly. Equation (13.56) uses the covariance of the $i$th security with the market relative to total market risk as measured by the standard deviation of the market. Equation (13.57) uses the covariance of the $i$th security with the market relative to total market risk as measured by the variance of the market. The latter measure is known as the *beta* of the security because it is defined in exactly the same way as the beta coefficients in a regression equation (cf. (13.34) and (13.36)). The beta for the portfolio is simply the value-weighted sum of the betas of the assets in the portfolio:

$$\beta_p = \sum_{i=1}^{N} \theta_i \beta_i. \quad (13.59)$$

But the important point is that both measures define the quantity of risk in precisely the same way, namely as the amount of undiversifiable or systematic or market risk. This is because in an equilibrium model, it is only market risk that is priced: diversifiable risk, because it can be eliminated by low-cost diversification, will not be priced. By this we mean, investors will not in equilibrium be compensated for taking on a risk that could be eliminated by low-cost diversification.

This can be seen more clearly if we compare the capital market line with the security market line. The capital market line is a line plotting expected return against total risk. The *security market line* (SML), on the other hand, is a line plotting expected return against market risk or beta (i.e. it is the graph corresponding to the CAPM (13.57)). The two lines are depicted in Figure 13.18. Point $M$ plots the market portfolio which has total risk of $\sigma_m$ and a beta of unity. (From the definition of beta, the beta of the market portfolio is unity.)

In equilibrium, all securities will be priced so that they lie on the SML. Similarly, in equilibrium all efficient portfolios will be priced so that they lie on the CML. Inefficient portfolios will not lie along the CML but will still be priced in equilibrium to reflect only the undiversifiable risk contained in them. For example, we can consider securities, $A$, $B$ and $C$ in Figure 13.18(a) which have the same expected return but different total risks. But because they have the same expected return, they must, in equilibrium, have the same level of undiversifiable risk, $\beta_A$ in Figure 13.18(b). The fact that the three securities have different total risks is irrelevant for determining their equilibrium prices or returns. This is because the total risk contains a diversifiable component that will not be priced in equilibrium.

The relationship between the CML and the SML can be seen more clearly if we express the SML in a slightly different form. Using (13.56), and recognizing that $\sigma_{im} = \rho_{im}\sigma_i\sigma_m$ where $\rho_{im}$ is the correlation between the return on the $i$th security and the market, we get:

$$\bar{r}_i = r_f + \left( \frac{\bar{r}_m - r_f}{\sigma_m} \right) \sigma_i \rho_{im}. \quad (13.60)$$

The CML is:

$$\bar{r}_p = r_f + \left( \frac{\bar{r}_m - r_f}{\sigma_m} \right) \sigma_p \rho_{pm}. \quad (13.61)$$

**Figure 13.18** The capital market line (a) and the security market line (b)

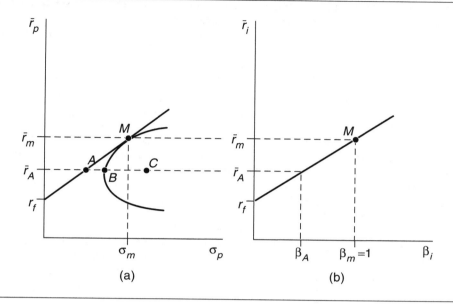

(a)  (b)

Along the CML, all (efficient) portfolios are perfectly correlated with the market, so that $\rho_{pm} = 1$. (This follows because all portfolios along the CML are linear combinations of the market portfolio and the riskless asset, and therefore by construction are perfectly correlated with the market.) Inefficient portfolios and individual securities will not be perfectly correlated with the market, and this is recognized by the SML. The SML shows that undiversifiable risk has two components: the security's total risk $\sigma_i$, and its correlation with the market, $\rho_{im}$. The SML is the correct way of pricing securities whether or not the securities are efficient. It provides a unique relationship between the required return on a security and the amount of undiversifiable risk (measured by $\beta$) contained in it.

We can also compare the CAPM with the market model, given respectively by:

$$\bar{r}_i = r_f + (\bar{r}_m - r_f)\beta_i, \tag{13.62}$$

and:

$$r_{it} = \gamma_i + \beta_i r_{mt} + \varepsilon_{it}, \tag{13.63}$$

or (taking expectations of (13.63)):

$$\bar{r}_i = \gamma_i + \beta_i \bar{r}_m. \tag{13.64}$$

If the CAPM is correct, then this imposes certain restrictions on the regression equation (13.64). Rearranging (13.62), we get:

$$\bar{r}_i = r_f(1 - \beta_i) + \beta_i \bar{r}_m. \tag{13.65}$$

This imposes the restriction that:

$$\gamma_i = r_f(1 - \beta_i). \tag{13.66}$$

The CAPM can be used to determine the *required rate of return* on a security if it is going to be held in equilibrium. Suppose that the riskless rate of interest is 9 per cent and the expected return on the market is 15 per cent. The formula for the CAPM is:

$$\bar{r}_i \;=\; 0.09+(0.15-0.09)\beta_i$$
$$\;=\; 0.09+0.06\beta_i,$$

where the market risk premium is $(\bar{r}_m-r_f)=6$ per cent. If a particular security has the same $\beta$ as the market (i.e. $\beta_i=1$), it will have the same required return, namely $\bar{r}_i=15$ per cent.

If the security has a $\beta$ greater than that of the market (e.g. $\beta_i=1.5$), the security is known as an *aggressive stock*, since its price is more volatile than that of the market: it rises by more than the market in a bull phase and falls by more than the market in a bear phase. Aggressive stocks, because that have more undiversifiable risk in them than the market, have a higher required rate of return than the market: in this case, a required rate of return of 18 per cent.

If the security has a $\beta$ less than that of the market (e.g. $\beta_i=0.5$), the security is known as a *defensive stock*, since its price is less volatile than that of the market: it rises by less than the market in a bull phase and falls by less than the market in a bear phase. Defensive stocks have less undiversifiable risk in them than the market and so require a smaller rate of return: in this case 12 per cent. These securities are shown in Figure 13.19.

**Figure 13.19** The required rate of return on securities

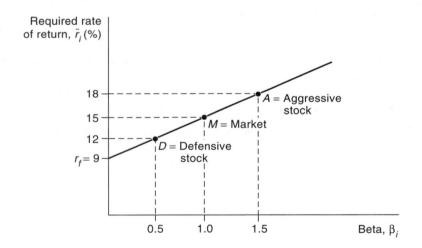

We now have for the first time a measurable concept of risk. This can be immediately related back to the analysis in Chapter 2 which examined the market determination of interest rates. In that chapter, we decomposed the rate of interest into four principal components: a real rate of interest, an inflation premium, a liquidity premium, and a risk premium. The CAPM includes all four components:

$$\bar{r}_i \;=\; r_f+(\bar{r}_m-r_f)\beta_i$$
$$\;=\; f(\text{Real rate, Inflation premium, Liquidity premium})+\text{Risk premium}. \qquad (13.67)$$

The risk-free interest rate $r_f$ accounts for the first three components, while the term $(\bar{r}_m - r_f)\beta_i$ is the risk premium. Again as argued in Chapter 2, it is only the quantity of undiversifiable risk that is included in the risk premium. Comparing (13.58) and (13.67), we see that $r_f$ strictly includes more than the price of time (the real rate of interest); it also includes the inflation and liquidity premiums.

Finally in this section, we will introduce the concept of *alpha*. Alpha measures the *excess return* on a security. It is equal to the difference between the *actual* rate of return on a security and its *required* rate of return using the CAPM (13.57):

$$\begin{aligned} \alpha_i &= r_i - \bar{r}_i \\ &= (r_i - r_f) - (\bar{r}_m - r_f)\beta_i. \end{aligned} \tag{13.68}$$

If a security is *correctly priced*, $\alpha_i = 0$. If a security is *underpriced* (or *oversold*), $\alpha_i > 0$: the security is expected to rise in price and so is worth buying. If a security is *overpriced* (or *overbought*), $\alpha_i < 0$: the security is expected to fall in price and so is worth selling. The alpha for a portfolio of securities is the value-weighted sum of the alphas in the portfolio:

$$\alpha_p = \sum_{i=1}^{N} \theta_i \alpha_i. \tag{13.69}$$

Alpha is used extensively in Chapter 14, dealing with portfolio management.

### Extensions to the CAPM

We can briefly consider two extensions to the CAPM. The first covers the case where the borrowing and lending rates differ. Suppose that the borrowing rate $(r_b)$ exceeds the lending rate $(r_l)$, as is likely to be the case in practice. Figure 13.20 shows the effect of this on the capital market line. The CML is no longer linear and there is no longer a single unique market portfolio. The CML is given by $CM_l M_b L$ in the figure. There is a linear segment $CM_l$ reflecting riskless lending at $r_l$ and there is a linear segment $M_b L$ reflecting riskless borrowing at $r_b$. But any risky portfolio lying between $M_l$ and $M_b$ is consistent with being the market portfolio. There are also two CAPMs and SMLs:

$$\bar{r}_i = r_l + (\bar{r}_{ml} - r_i)\beta_{iml} \quad \text{for } \bar{r}_i < \bar{r}_{ml}, \tag{13.70}$$

and:

$$\bar{r}_i = r_b + (\bar{r}_{mb} - r_b)\beta_{imb} \quad \text{for } \bar{r}_i > \bar{r}_{mb}, \tag{13.71}$$

where $\beta_{iml}$ and $\beta_{imb}$ are the beta coefficients defined with respect to portfolios $M_l$ and $M_b$ respectively.

The second extension covers the case where there is no riskless asset at all. It is still possible for the SML to exist if a *zero-beta security* exists. This is a security which, like the riskless asset itself, has no market risk, although it could still have specific risk, unlike a riskless asset. It therefore has a $\beta$ of zero and an expected return of, say, $\bar{r}_0$. The equation for the CAPM is therefore:

$$\bar{r}_i = \bar{r}_0 + (\bar{r}_m - \bar{r}_0)\beta_i. \tag{13.72}$$

**Figure 13.20** The effect of differential borrowing and lending rates on the capital market line

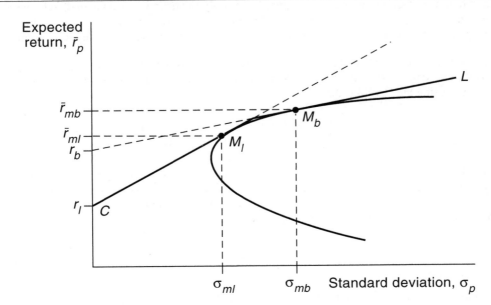

### Tests of the CAPM

Finally, it is interesting to examine the empirical tests of the CAPM. The appropriate test of the CAPM involves running the regression:

$$r_{it} - r_{ft} = a + b\beta_i + \varepsilon_{it}. \tag{13.73}$$

If the CAPM is correct, then we would expect to find that:

1. the intercept $a$ should be zero;

2. the slope coefficient $b$ should equal $(r_{mt} - r_{ft})$;

3. no additional explanatory variable apart from $\beta_i$ should be significant; additional explanatory variables that have been tried include the square of $\beta_i$ ($\beta_i^2$), residual variance (Var($\varepsilon_{it}$)), dividend yield, firm size, price-earnings ratios, market-to-book ratios, and growth rates.

When the model in (13.73) was estimated by Fama and McBeth (1973) and Black, Jensen and Scholes (1972) (see also Elton and Gruber (1995), Chapter 15), the evidence indicated that:

1. the intercept $a$ is estimated to be positive;

2. the slope coefficient $b$ is estimated to be less than $(r_{mt} - r_{ft})$ on average;

3. the coefficient on the square of $\beta_i$ is zero, indicating that there is a linear relationship between excess return and beta, but not a nonlinear (quadratic) relationship;

4 the coefficient on residual variance is zero, indicating that while there is a linear relationship between excess return and systematic risk, there is no relationship between excess return and unsystematic risk;

5 certain additional explanatory variables do have a significant effect: firms with low price-earnings and market-to-book ratios, small firms, and firms with high growth rates and dividend yields all have higher returns than predicted by the CAPM.

One implication of this evidence is that the empirical version of the SML (known as the *empirical market line*) is flatter and has a larger intercept than the theoretical SML; both lines pass through the market portfolio, *M*, and are linear in beta (see Figure 13.21). Another implication is that much of the returns on securities not explained by the market can be explained by certain *anomalies* such as

**Figure 13.21** The security market line and the empirical market line

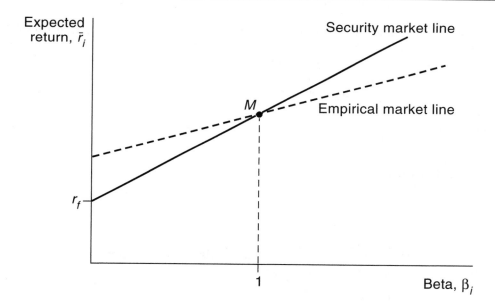

dividend yield, firm size, price-earning ratios, market-to-book ratios and growth rates. Many of these anomalies appeared in the tests of the efficient markets hypothesis discussed in Chapter 11. Indeed, when these efficient markets tests involved calculations of excess returns, the excess returns were calculated from the alpha values using the CAPM (see equation (13.68)).

For example, when a researcher is interested in testing whether firms with low market-to-book ratios outperformed the market, he would form portfolios of assets with low market-to-book values and then compare the actual returns on such portfolios with the returns predicted from the CAPM for portfolios with the same beta. If a positive alpha emerged from this analysis, then this would indicate that there was a market inefficiency, that an anomaly existed and that an additional explanatory variable in the form of a firm's market-to-book ratio could add to the explanatory power of the CAPM equation.

**The bond version of the CAPM**

It is perfectly possible to calculate the beta coefficient for a bond by regressing the rate of return on the bond against the rate of return on the market. The beta coefficient so estimated is a measure of the bond's undiversifiable risk. However, undiversifiable risk is not the only type of risk present in a bond portfolio. Equally important is interest rate risk, and the measure of interest rate risk that we use for bonds in duration (see Chapter 5).

The version of the CAPM that captures the effect of interest rate risk is:

$$\bar{r}_i = r_f + (\bar{r}_m - r_f)\beta_i, \tag{13.74}$$

where:

$$
\begin{aligned}
\bar{r}_i &= \quad \text{expected return on bond } i; \\
\bar{r}_m &= \quad \text{expected return on the market portfolio of bonds;} \\
\beta_i &= \quad D_i/D_m \quad = \quad \text{relative duration, where } D_i \text{ is the duration of the } i\text{th bond} \\
&\qquad \text{and } D_m \text{ is the duration of the market portfolio of bonds.}
\end{aligned}
$$

This formulation (which we can call the *bond market line*) is very similar to that of the general CAPM. It states that, if the interest rate rises by 1 per cent, the return on the $i$th bond will rise by $\beta_i$, i.e. by the relative duration of the bond. Thus duration has precisely the same effect in this model as beta has in the general model: the expected return on a bond is an increasing linear function of its duration, in exactly the same way as the expected return on any security, is an increasing linear function of its beta (see Figure 13.22).

**Figure 13.22** The bond market line

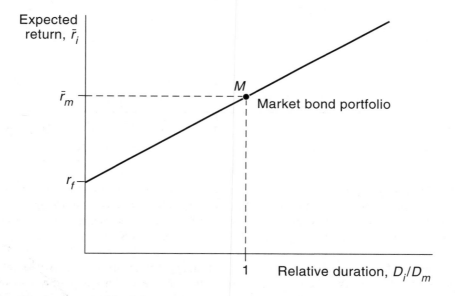

There are two problems with (13.74), however. First, it overstates the effect of changes in short-term interest rates on the returns and prices of long-duration bonds; for example, the effect on a bond with a duration of five years is predicted to be five times that on a bond with a duration of one year, whereas in reality the effect is not that large. Second, by including only a short-term interest rate as an explanatory variable, it is implicitly assumed that, when interest rates do change, there is a parallel shift in the yield curve; in reality, there are rarely parallel yield curve shifts, so to take account of non-parallel yield curve shifts, we use the following model:

$$\bar{r}_i = r_f + (\bar{r}_m - r_f)\beta_i + \kappa_i(\bar{r}_\ell - r_f), \tag{13.75}$$

where $(\bar{r}_\ell - r_f)$, the difference between expected long-term and short-term interest rates, measures the slope of the yield curve.

## The futures and options version of the CAPM

There are also versions of the CAPM relevant for futures and options contracts.

We know that the price of a futures contract on a security equals the current price *plus* the cost of carry (see, for example, equation (8.13) with $T = 1$):

$$P_i^f = [1 + (r_f - d_i)]P_i^s, \tag{13.76}$$

where:

$$
\begin{aligned}
P_i^f &= \quad \text{price of a futures contract on } i\text{th security;} \\
P_i^s &= \quad \text{price of the } i\text{th security;} \\
d_i &= \quad \text{income yield on } i\text{th security;} \\
r_f &= \quad \text{risk free interest rate.}
\end{aligned}
$$

Totally differentiating both sides of (13.76), we get:

$$\frac{dP_i^f}{P_i^f} = \frac{[1 + (r_f - d_i)]P_i^s}{P_i^f} \cdot \frac{dP_i^s}{P_i^s} = \frac{dP_i^s}{P_i^s}, \tag{13.77}$$

using (13.76) again. Taking expectations of (13.77) and substituting from (13.57) we get:

$$
\begin{aligned}
\bar{r}_i^f &= \bar{r}_i^s \\
&= r_f + (\bar{r}_m - r_f)\beta_i^s \\
&= r_f + (\bar{r}_m - r_f)\beta_i^f, \tag{13.78}
\end{aligned}
$$

where:

$$
\begin{aligned}
\bar{r}_i^f &= E(dP_i^f/P_i^f); \\
\bar{r}_i^s &= E(dP_i^s/P_i^s).
\end{aligned}
$$

Equation (13.78) shows that the CAPM for a futures contract is identical to that for the underlying security, and that the beta for a futures contract ($\beta_i^f$) equals that for the underlying security ($\beta_i^s$).

From (9.30), we know that changes in the price of a call option contract are related to changes in the price of the underlying security via the delta of the option:

$$dP_i^c = \delta_i^c dP_i^s,$$

or:

$$\frac{dP_i^c}{P_i^c} = \phi_i^c \cdot \frac{dP_i^s}{P_i^s},$$ (13.79)

where:

$$P_i^c = \text{price of a call option on the } i\text{th security;}$$
$$\delta_i^c = \text{delta of a call option on the } i\text{th security;}$$

and:

$$\phi_i^c = \delta_i^c \cdot \frac{P_i^s}{P_i^c}.$$ (13.80)

Taking expectations of (13.79) and substituting from (13.57) we get:

$$\begin{aligned} \bar{r}_i^c &= \phi_i^c \bar{r}_i^s \\ &= \phi_i^c r_f + (\bar{r}_m - r_f)\phi_i^c \beta_i^s \\ &= r_{fi}^c + (\bar{r}_m - r_f)\beta_i^c, \end{aligned}$$ (13.81)

where:

$$\bar{r}_i^c = E(dP_i^c/P_i^c)$$
$$r_{fi}^c = \phi_i^c r_f.$$

Equation (13.81) is the CAPM for a call option contract and the beta for a call option contract is given by:

$$\beta_i^c = \phi_i^c \beta_i^s.$$ (13.82)

While the option delta is always less than unity, the ratio $P_i^s/P_i^c$ will always be much larger than unity, so $\phi_i^c$ will typically be much greater than unity (the exception is for options that are deep out-of-the-money). This implies that the beta of a call option will generally be much larger than the beta of the underlying security, thereby confirming the much greater responsiveness of option prices to changes in market conditions than the securities underlying these options.

The CAPM for a put option is similar to (13.81) except that $\phi_i^p$ replaces $\phi_i^c$ where:

$$\phi_i^p = \delta_i^p \cdot \frac{P_i^s}{P_i^p} = (\delta_i^c - 1)\frac{P_i^s}{P_i^p},$$ (13.83)

and:

$$P_i^p = \text{price of a put option on the } i\text{th security.}$$

The corresponding beta for a put option is:

$$\beta_i^p = \phi_i^p \beta_i^s.$$ (13.84)

## 13.2.2 The multi-factor model

The CAPM is known as a *single-factor model* since the returns on securities are assumed to be related only to a single factor, namely the embodiment of market risk contained in each security. However, we saw above that, in empirical tests of the CAPM, other factors were found to be important in explaining returns. It was this observation that led to the development of *multi-factor models*. Such models are based on extensions of the market model (13.34) and take the general form:

$$r_{it} \;=\; \gamma_i + \sum_{j=1}^{K} \beta_{ij} F_{jt} + \varepsilon_{it} , \qquad (13.85)$$

where $F_{jt}$ are $K$ factors that have a systematic effect on the returns of each and every security and where $\beta_{ij}$ measures the sensitivity of the return on the $i$th security to the $j$th factor; any specific component of the return on the $i$th asset is contained in $\varepsilon_{it}$ .

One of the earliest users of models such as (13.85) was a US company which began in the early 1970s called Barra which stands for Barr Rosenberg Associates and is named after a former professor of finance at the University of California at Berkeley. Barra identified 70 firm-specific factors that influenced security returns, but pooled these into 13 composite factors: variability in markets, size, growth, earnings-price ratio, market-to-book ratio, earnings variation, financial leverage, trading activity, foreign income, labour intensity, yield, success and low capitalisation. Barra also identified 55 industry-specific factors that could influence returns. In total therefore there were 68 factors (i.e. $K = 68$) that could influence returns in the Barra modelling framework.

More recently, Fama and French (1993) found that most of the variability in monthly share returns could be explained by just three factors: a market factor (i.e. the return on the market index as in the simple market model), a size factor (measured by the difference in returns between a small cap and a large cap index) and a market-to-book factor (measured by the difference in returns between an index of shares with low market-to-book ratios and an index of shares with high market-to-book ratios).

Sharpe (1982) conducted a cross-section multi-factor study and found that factors such as beta (both against an equity index and a bond index), alpha, dividend yield and firm size were statistically significant. For example, he found a dividend yield factor of 0.24, indicating that a share with a dividend yield of 4 per cent would have a return that was 0.24 per cent higher than a share with a dividend yield of 3 per cent, with all other factors being identical.

## 13.2.3 The arbitrage pricing model

The *arbitrage pricing model* (or APT after *arbitrage pricing theory*) was proposed by Ross (1976) as an alternative to the capital asset pricing model (13.57) in which the linear relationship between the expected return ($\bar{r}_i$) and risks ($\beta_i$) depended on the mean–standard-deviation efficiency of the market portfolio. The reason for the proposal lay in the increasing dissatisfaction with the CAPM on both theoretical and empirical grounds. While the CAPM was derived from the first principles of expected utility theory and was consistent with the most widely accepted empirical regularity concerning asset returns, namely their common variability, Ross argued that the assumption underlying expected utility theory made no use of this common variability and that, instead, rationalization of the CAPM was based on the distinction between diversifiable and non-diversifiable risk, a distinction that results from a linear generating process such as the market model (13.34), in which the common variation of returns is due to a single factor and actual returns differ from this common factor by an additive random disturbance, Ross (p.342) argued that the alternative APT 'retains many of the intuitive results' of the CAPM, is based on a linear return generating process as a first principle, and employs no utility assumptions apart from monotonicity and concavity (in other words, greed and risk aversion); the CAPM, in contrast, requires a utility function based on mean and standard deviation. We have seen one version of APT before: that version involved constructing a riskless hedge portfolio and using it to price a European call option (see Chapter 9). A similar procedure is used here to construct an arbitrage portfolio.

Ross began by assuming that individuals believe that security returns are determined by the $K$-factor generating model:

$$r_i = \bar{r}_i + \sum_{j=1}^{K} \delta_j \beta_{ij} + \varepsilon_i, \tag{13.86}$$

where $r_i$ is the actual return on the $i$th security, $\bar{r}_i$ is the expected return on the $i$th security, $\delta_j$ is the zero-mean $j$th factor common to all security returns, and the coefficient $\beta_{ij}$ measures the response (or loading) of the $i$th return to the $j$th common factor. The *common factors* $\delta_j$ are the systematic components of risk, and $\varepsilon_i$ is the unsystematic component of risk peculiar to the $i$th asset alone.

Given the return generating process (13.86), Ross used arbitrage conditions to place restrictions on the individual returns generated by the model. He considered an individual who examines the set of all possible *arbitrage portfolios*, that is, the set of new portfolios of securities, which differ from his existing portfolio but use no additional wealth. This implies that any additional purchases of assets must be financed from the sale of others, so that for all arbitrage portfolios:

$$\sum_{i=1}^{N} \Delta x_i = 0, \tag{13.87}$$

where $\Delta x_i$ is the change in the holding of the $i$th asset (from a portfolio containing $N$ assets). The change in portfolio return from altering the current portfolio is given by:

$$\begin{aligned} \Delta r_p &= \sum_{i=1}^{N} r_i \Delta x_i \\ &= \sum_{i=1}^{N} \bar{r}_i \Delta x_i + \sum_{i=1}^{N} \sum_{j=1}^{K} \delta_j \beta_{ij} \Delta x_i + \sum_{i=1}^{N} \varepsilon_i \Delta x_i. \end{aligned} \tag{13.88}$$

If the arbitrage portfolio is well diversified, then each $\Delta x_i$ will be of order $1/N$ for a portfolio containing $N$ assets, and therefore unsystematic risk can be diversified away and so the last term on the right-hand side of (13.88) will be negligible. In addition, if the individual is able to choose $\Delta x_i$ so that the arbitrage portfolio has no systematic risk either, then:

$$\sum_{i=1}^{N} \beta_{ij} \Delta x_i = 0 \tag{13.89}$$

for all $j$, and the net return from altering the current portfolio is:

$$\Delta r_p = \sum_{i=1}^{N} \bar{r}_i \Delta x_i. \tag{13.90}$$

But in equilibrium, it must be the case that a portfolio that costs nothing (i.e. uses no new resources) and embodies neither systematic nor unsystematic risk (i.e. is riskless to achieve) must generate a certain return of zero, i.e.,

$$\Delta r_p = \sum_{i=1}^{N} \bar{r}_i \Delta x_i = 0, \tag{13.91}$$

otherwise arbitrarily large positive net wealth positions could be achieved without cost or risk. In short, 'no portfolio is an equilibrium ... portfolio if it can be improved upon without incurring additional risk or committing additional resources' (Roll and Ross (1980), p.1078).

Since the restriction in (13.91) must hold for all $\Delta x_i$ satisfying both (13.87) and (13.89), then it must be the case that the $\bar{r}_i$ are spanned by the unit constant and the $\beta_{ij}$ with constant weights $\gamma_0, \gamma_1, \ldots, \gamma_K$, i.e.,

$$\bar{r}_i = \gamma_0 + \sum_{j=1}^{K} \gamma_j \beta_{ij} \tag{13.92}$$

for all $i$, since by multiplying each side of (13.92) by $\Delta x_i$ and summing over $i$ we satisfy (13.87), (13.89) and (13.91) simultaneously. If there is a riskless security, or a zero-beta security if there is no riskless security, then $\beta_{0j} = 0$ and:

$$r_f = \gamma_0. \tag{13.93}$$

Substituting (13.93) into (13.92) gives:

$$\bar{r}_i = r_f + \sum_{j=1}^{K} \gamma_j \beta_{ij}, \tag{13.94}$$

that is, a linear relationship between expected returns and the loadings (or response amplitudes) on the common factors, $\beta_{ij}$. The loadings $\beta_{ij}$ have exactly the same interpretation as the beta coefficient in the CAPM:

$$\beta_{ij} = \frac{\mathrm{Cov}(r_i, \delta_j)}{\mathrm{Var}(\delta_j)}, \tag{13.95}$$

where:

$$\mathrm{Cov}(r_{i,\delta_j}) = \text{covariance between the return on the } i\text{th security and the } j\text{th factor;}$$
$$\mathrm{Var}(\delta_j) = \text{variance of the } j\text{th factor.}$$

Now if there is only a single factor, then (13.94) becomes:

$$\bar{r}_i = r_f + \gamma \beta_i. \tag{13.96}$$

In addition, if we multiply each side of (13.96) by the proportion of the $i$th asset in the market portfolio, and sum over $i$, we get:

$$\gamma = \bar{r}_m - r_f, \tag{13.97}$$

since $\beta_m = 1$ for the market portfolio. If we substitute (13.97) into (13.96), we get (13.57), so that (13.96) and (13.97) are the APT equivalents of the CAPM.

But Ross (1976) argued that the arbitrage pricing approach is 'substantially different from the usual mean-variance analysis and constitutes a related but quite distinct theory' (p.343). He suggested that there are two major differences between APT and the CAPM. The first is that, while the CAPM is a single-factor (i.e. single-beta) generating model, APT is a multiple-factor (i.e. multiple-beta) generating model; i.e., it allows for the possibility of more than one generating factor apart from the market (as with the multi-factor model (13.85) above). The second is that, while it is crucial for the CAPM for the market portfolio to be mean-variance-efficient, APT makes no such requirement and instead relies on the assumption that in market equilibrium there will be no riskless arbitrage profits, and this leads to (13.94), the linear relationship between expected returns and common factors. Indeed, the market portfolio, as such, plays no special role in (13.94), although it is clearly useful in helping to value the risk premia $\gamma_j$. However, any well diversified portfolio (i.e. a portfolio without much systematic risk) could do the same, and Roll and Ross argued that 'in general, $K$ well-diversified portfolios could be found that approximate the $K$ factors *better* than any single market index' (1980, p.1080). So it is clear that APT applies to subsets of the universe of assets, whereas the CAPM applies only to the full universe of assets in the market portfolio.

The APT has been tested by Roll and Ross (1980), Chen, Roll and Ross (1986), Connor and Korajczyk (1986) and Lehmann and Modest (1988). Roll and Ross examined daily data on 42 groups of 30 shares for the period 1962–72. They found, using a statistical technique known as factor analysis, that at least three but no more than six factors were significant in explaining most of the joint variability in the returns on this group of shares. The next task was to identify these factors. Chen et al. argued that the return on a firm's shares was likely to be influenced by any factor that affects either future cash flows from the firm or the rate at which those cash flows are discounted. They therefore concluded that the following four factors would be important: the business cycle as measured by the rate of change of industrial production (since this affects the cash flows of the firm), the rate of inflation (since this affects both cash flows and the discount rate), the term structure of interest rates as measured by the difference in yields between long term and short term bonds (since changes in the term structure affect the discounting of distant cash flows compared with nearby cash flows), and the risk premium as measured by the difference in yields between low-grade (BBB) and high-grade (AAA) bonds (since this affects the market's reaction to risk). Chen et al. found that there was a strong statistical relationship between four of the factors found but not identified by Roll and Ross and these four macroeconomic variables. In other words, Chen et al. were able to identify the four most important common factors explaining security returns. Connor and Korajczyk, and Lehmann and Modest showed that with up to five factors they could explain some of the anomalies associated with the CAPM, e.g. the dividend yield effect, the small firm effect, and the January effect.

### Selected references

Black, F., Jensen, M. and Scholes, M. (1972), 'The Capital Asset Pricing Model: Some Empirical Tests', in Jensen, M. (ed.), *Studies in the Theory of Capital Markets,* Praeger, New York.

Chen, N., Roll, R. and Ross, S. (1986), 'Economic Forces and the Stock Market', *Journal of Business*, 59, 383–403.

Connor, G. and Korajczyk (1986), 'Performance Measurement with the Arbitrage Pricing Theory: A New Framework for Analysis', *Journal of Financial Economics*, 15, 373–94.

Dimson, E. and Marsh, P., *Risk Measurement Service*, London Business School, London, quarterly.

Elton, E.J. and Gruber, M.J. (1995), *Modern Portfolio Theory and Investment Analysis*, John Wiley, New York.

Fama, E. (1976), *Foundations of Finance*, Blackwell, Oxford.

Fama, E. and French, K. (1993), 'Common Risk Factors in the Returns on Stocks and Bonds', *Journal of Financial Economics*, 33, 3–56.

Fama, E. and MacBeth, J. (1973), 'Risk, Return and Equilibrium: Empirical Tests', *Journal of Political Economy*, 71, 607–36.

Francis, J.C. (1991), *Investments*, McGraw-Hill, Singapore. (Chapters 9–11, 19 and 20.)

Lehmann, B. and Modest, D. (1988), 'The Empirical Foundations of the Arbitrage Pricing Theory I: The Empirical Tests', *Journal of Financial Economics*, 21, 213–254.

Lintner, J. (1965), 'The Valuation of Risk Assets and the Selection of Risky Investments in Stock Portfolios and Capital Budgets', *Review of Economics and Statistics*, 47, 13–37.

Markowitz, H. (1959), *Portfolio Selection: Efficient Diversification of Investments*, John Wiley, New York.

Roll, R. and Ross, S.A. (1980), 'An Empirical Investigation of the Arbitrage Pricing Theory', *Journal of Finance*, 35, 1073–1103.

Ross, S.A. (1976), 'The Arbitrage Theory of Capital Asset Pricing', *Journal of Economic Theory*, 13, 341–60.

Rutterford, J. (1993), *Introduction to Stock Exchange Investment*, Macmillan, London. (Chapters 2, 8 and 9.)

Sharpe, W. (1982), 'Factors in New York Stock Exchange Security Returns 1931-79', *Journal of Portfolio Management*, 8, 5–19.

Sharpe, W.F. (1963), 'A Simplified Model for Portfolio Analysis', *Management Science*, 9, 277–93.

Sharpe, W.F. (1964), 'Capital Asset Prices: A Theory of Market Equilibrium under Conditions of Risk', *Journal of Finance,* 19, 425–42.

Sharpe, W.F., Alexander, G., and Bailey, J. (1995), *Investments*, Prentice-Hall, Englewood Cliffs, NJ. (Chapters 6–12.)

Solnik, B.H. (1974), 'Why Not Diversify Internationally rather than Domestically?', *Financial Analysts Journal*, July-August, 48–54.

Wagner, W. and Lau, S. (1971), 'The Effect of Diversification on Risk', *Financial Analysts Journal*, November-December, 48–53.

Weston, J.F. and Copeland, T.E. (1992), *Managerial Finance*, Dryden Press, Chicago. (Chapters 10 and 11.)

**Exercises**

1 Why are most investors risk-averse?

2 Define the coefficient of absolute risk aversion. What does it measure?

3 What is the relationship between the coefficient of absolute risk aversion and the coefficient of risk tolerance?

4 In what sense does a portfolio generate risk and return, and in what sense does an investor consume risk and return?

5 You are told that the expected return on a portfolio is 16 per cent and that the standard deviation of the return is 20 per cent. What does this mean?

6 What is diversification?

7 Encouraging small savers to invest directly in privatization issues is acting against the principles of effective portfolio diversification. Discuss.

8 Compare and contrast:

   a) a security's characteristics line;

   b) the capital market line;

   c) the security market line.

9 You are given the following portfolio:

| Share | Proportion of portfolio | Return | Beta |
|-------|-------------------------|--------|------|
| A | 0.2 | 15.0 | 0.8 |
| B | 0.5 | 16.2 | 1.1 |
| C | 0.3 | 18.9 | 1.3 |

   a) Calculate the return on and beta of the portfolio.

   b) Calculate the alpha values (excess returns) for the individual shares and for the portfolio, assuming that the riskless rate of interest is 9 per cent and the market return is 16 per cent.

   c) Calculate the returns on the individual shares and on the portfolio you would expect next year if the riskless rate of interest were 10 per cent and the market return were expected to be 18 per cent.

   d) How might portfolio performance be improved next year if:

      i) a bull market is expected?

      ii) a bear market is expected?

10 You are given the following information about a portfolio:

| Share | Proportion of portfolio | Beta | Specific risk |
|-------|-------------------------|------|---------------|
| A | 0.4 | 0.92 | 12% |
| B | 0.6 | 1.25 | 10% |

What is the total risk of the portfolio if market risk is 11 per cent?

11  What is the expected return and risk on the following portfolio of securities?

| Share | Proportion of portfolio | Expected return | Standard deviation of returns |
|-------|------------------------|-----------------|-------------------------------|
| A     | 0.7                    | 16%             | 10%                           |
| B     | 0.3                    | 12%             | 8%                            |

The correlation between returns is 60 per cent.

12  The capital asset pricing model and the market model are fully consistent. Assess this statement.

13  How does the capital asset pricing model change if the assumption of being able to borrow and lend at the riskless interest rate is invalid?

14  The market is expected to rise next year by 18 per cent and have a standard deviation of return of 12 per cent. The riskless interest rate is 9 per cent. A share with an expected return of 20 per cent has a standard deviation of return of 25 per cent and a correlation coefficient of return with the market of 0.6. Make a recommendation about whether or not to buy the share.

15  Under what conditions is it possible to construct a portfolio of two risky securities that guarantees a riskless return? Find the proportions of the two securities in the portfolio.

16  The beta of four shares are as follows:

$$\beta_A = 0, \quad \beta_B = 0.5, \quad \beta_C = 1, \quad \beta_D = 1.5.$$

Assuming that the riskless rate of interest is 9 per cent and the expected return on the market is 17 per cent, calculate the expected return on the four shares.

17  Discuss the terms 'systematic risk' and 'non-systematic risk'.

18  Does the arbitrage pricing model have any advantages over the capital asset pricing model?

19  What is the 'efficient frontier'? How would you construct it?

20  Explain one method for identifying mispriced securities.

21  What are the main characteristics of the market portfolio?

22  The following securities are correctly priced according to the security market line:

| Security | Expected return | Beta |
|----------|-----------------|------|
| A        | 10%             | 0.2  |
| B        | 20%             | 1.2  |

a)  Derive the security market line.

b)  What is the expected return on a security with a beta of 1.5%?

c)  What would you do with a security with an expected return of 12 per cent and a beta of 0.5?

23  A risk-free security is a zero-beta security but a zero-beta security is not necessarily risk-free. Do you agree?

24  Diversification pays only when the return on securities are perfectly correlated; when the returns on securities are uncorrelated, there is no benefit from diversification at all. Do you agree?

25  What is the market price of risk?

26  When borrowing and lending rates differ, the concept of the market price of risk is a meaningless one. Discuss.

27  The beta of a security estimated from historical data cannot be a good estimate of the true beta of a security. Discuss.

28  Distinguish between:

   a) the portfolio opportunity set;

   b) the minimum variance portfolio opportunity set;

   c) the efficient set.

29  What is the 'insurance principle'?

30  Distinguish between the Markowitz method and the Sharpe method for constructing the efficient set.

31  Why is the efficient set linear in the presence of a riskless asset?

32  Prove that all portfolios along the capital market line are perfectly correlated with the market portfolio.

33  Why is the market portfolio the tangential portfolio between the capital market line and the efficient set of risky assets?

34  How can the market model be used to decompose total risk into diversifiable and undiversifiable risk?

35  a) What is the appropriate measure of risk for an efficient portfolio?

   b) What is the appropriate measure of risk for an inefficient portfolio?

36  Does beta measure the price of risk or the quantity of risk?

37  Define:

   a) an aggressive security;

   b) a defensive security.

   When would you hold each type of security in your portfolio?

38  Discuss some of the anomalies that have been associated with the capital asset pricing model.

39  Distinguish between:

   a) the security market line;

   b) the empirical market line.

40  You are advised that the shares of small, high-growth companies with low PE ratios and high-dividend yields generate excess returns. How would you test this advice?

41 What is the bond market line? What adjustments have to be made to the bond market line to account for non-parallel shifts in the yield curve?

42 What is an 'arbitrage portfolio'?

43 You are given the following information about a company:

| | |
|---|---|
| Earnings per share forecast, year 1 | 40p |
| Earnings per share forecast, year 2 | 50p |
| Dividend payout rate | 50% |
| Long-run earnings growth rate | 8% |
| Latest dividend | 16p |
| Company alpha | 1.75% |
| Company beta | 1.5 |
| Current share price | 170p |
| Risk-free rate | 10% |
| Expected market return | 16% |

Would you recommend buying or selling the share at its current level?

44 For the market portfolio, how would you measure its

   a) total risk?

   b) market risk?

   c) specific risk?

45 In what way does the market portfolio depend on the riskless rate of interest?

# Chapter 14

# Portfolio management

This chapter considers the functions of portfolio managers and the ways in which they assess their clients' portfolio preferences. It then examines the two main types of portfolio management strategies, passive and active, particularly as they apply to share and bond portfolios.

## 14.1   The functions of portfolio management

A *portfolio manager* (or *fund manager*) is an individual who or company which runs an investment portfolio (or an investment fund) on behalf of a client or the trustees of a client. The portfolio manager can be an employee of the client or an independent organization under contract to the client.

The functions of the portfolio manager are as follows:

1 portfolio structuring and analysis — using the client's utility function to structure an optimal portfolio, and then analyzing the portfolio's expected return and risk;

2 portfolio adjustment — selecting the set of asset purchases and sales as circumstances change;

3 portfolio performance measurement and attribution — measuring the actual performance of the portfolio, identifying the sources of the performance and comparing the performance against that of a predetermined benchmark portfolio.

We examine the first two functions in this chapter. The third, which is sometimes undertaken by an organization independent of the portfolio manager, is examined in the following chapter.

There are two main *types of client* whose portfolios require managing and whose *mandate* the portfolio manager will be seeking. The first is a client with positive net worth (called a *gross investor*) who wishes to have a portfolio of assets that matches his risk-return trade-off; this is the kind of investor that we examined in the last chapter. The second is a client without net worth of his own but who wishes to run a portfolio of assets that matches the contingent liabilities that he faces and is concerned about asset-liability mismatching of one kind or another, especially maturity mismatching; such a client is known as a *net investor*. Examples here are short-term investors such as corporate treasurers or long-term investors such as pension funds.

There are a number of different *management styles* that a fund manager can follow. Which one is appropriate depends on the size and preferences of the client and also on the size and preferences of the fund management group itself.

Clients with small portfolios (e.g. small pension funds) may decide to have their portfolios managed by insurance companies; these are called *insurance-managed portfolios*. Sometimes the funds are *pooled*. This increases the degree of diversification, but no individual attention is given to a specific client's portfolio: every member of the pool has the same set of investments and gets the same return. Alternatively, the funds may be *segregated* and different funds may have different investments.

The most common management style is known as *balanced management*. With this style, the fund manager is responsible for deciding on both the general asset categories that are invested in (such as shares, bonds or money market instruments) and the individual securities within each asset category that are invested in (e.g. ICI shares or medium-term gilts). The first decision is known as the *asset allocation* decision and the second is known as the *security selection* decision. There are two components to the asset allocation decision. The first is *strategic asset allocation* (SAA) which determines the global long-term mix between shares, bonds and cash, based on the fund manager's assessment of long-run expected returns and risks. The second is *tactical asset allocation* (TAA) which involves temporary adjustments to the asset mix away from the SAA based on the fund manager's forecasts of the relative performance of the share, bond or money markets over the short term. TAA is also known as *market timing*. The balanced management approach can apply whether the fund is small and part of an insurance-managed pool or large and employing its own fund management group.

The problem with balanced managers is that they cannot be experts in all markets, especially on a global basis. One solution is to have *specialist managers* in each sector who take the security selection decision. Sitting above the specialists will be an *asset allocation manager*. Another solution is to have *split funding*. This means that a number of balanced managers are appointed. While this does not solve the problem of insufficient expertise in all markets, it forces managers to compete against each other. However, the danger of this is that they may be induced to over-trade the portfolio (this is known as *churning*), so that transaction costs might be excessive. In addition, a *risk manager* has to sit above the individual managers to ensure *overall risk control*.

There are two main types of *portfolio management strategy*: passive and active.

*Passive portfolio management* involves a *buy-and-hold strategy*, that is buying a portfolio of securities and holding them for a long period of time, with only minor and infrequent adjustment to the portfolio over time. Passive portfolio management is consistent with two conditions being satisfied in the securities market: *efficiency* and *homogeneity of expectations*. If securities markets are efficient, then securities will be fairly priced at all times. There will be no misvalued securities and hence no incentive to trade actively in securities. Similarly, if securities markets are characterized by investors who have homogeneous (i.e. identical) expectations of the risks and returns on securities, so that there is a consensus view concerning the market portfolio and the capital market and security market lines, then again, there is no incentive to trade actively in securities. The typical passive investor will be content to hold some linear combination of the riskless asset and the commonly agreed market portfolio, as we saw in the last chapter. Investors with preferences differing from those of the average investor will have portfolios tailored to meet their requirements. But passive portfolio managers do not attempt to beat the market.

*Active portfolio management* involves frequent and sometimes substantial adjustments to the portfolio. Active managers do not believe that securities markets are continuously efficient. Instead, they believe that securities can be misvalued, so that trading in them can lead to excess returns (even after adjusting for risk and transaction costs). Alternatively, active managers believe that there are *heterogeneous* (i.e. divergent) *expectations* of the risks and returns on securities and that they have better estimates than the rest of the market of the true risks and returns on securities. Again, they attempt to use their better estimates to generate excess returns. In short, the objective of active managers is to beat the market.

The market portfolio is a value-weighted average of all the securities in the economy. In the last chapter, we showed that all optimal portfolios could be formed from linear combinations of the market portfolio and the riskless asset. Real-world portfolio structuring is more complicated than this, however. Even with passive portfolios, the portfolio structuring decision is usually broken down into a number of different layers. For example, it is generally decided to break down the overall portfolio into general asset categories, such as shares and bonds. The share portfolio would be managed separately from the bond portfolio, and each portfolio could be either passively or actively managed. Similarly, in the real world there is usually more than a single riskless asset. It is possible to hold portfolios of money market instruments, and the management of such portfolios is known as *treasury portfolio management* (or *money management*).

The marketing of portfolio management services has become extremely important in the 1980s and 90s. Marketing has four main functions: to keep the fund management team aware of new business opportunities resulting from legislative and capital market developments, or the activities of competitors; the origination of new business; the design and implementation of new products and advertizing campaigns; and to ensure that existing clients receive adequate attention.

The origination of new business begins with identifying a potential client, e.g. a company whose pension fund requires managing. The first task is to identify key personnel in the company, using such sources as industry directories or independent consultants. The next step is to obtain a foothold and make contact with the *gatekeeper*, the person in the company whose role is to filter out potential fund managers and to recommend a short list to his superior, usually the finance director. This initial contact can be made by direct communication (*cold calling*), through an established relationship, or again using consultants. The gatekeeper typically reports to a pensions subcommittee which in turn reports successively to the finance committee, the main board and the pension fund trustees. The next step is to exploit the foothold with the aim of taking part in the series of presentations known as the *beauty contest*, which ultimately lead, through preliminary and final heats, to the award of the mandate. As the fund manager crosses each hurdle, the complexity of the presentations increases, since the client's emphasis inevitably switches from the elimination of unsuitable managers to the identification of each competitor's favourable characteristics. The ultimate choice usually depends to some extent on personal prejudice or the 'rapport' generated between the client and the fund management team.

Once the mandate has been won, *client maintenance* becomes another very important task of marketing. This requires constant effort, helped both by efficient administration of the account by a designated *account executive* and, of course, by successful investment performance.

Since the 1980s the most important factor used by trustees for selecting the management group for their pension fund was good investment performance over the preceding two or three years. Without this, it has proved almost impossible for a management group to win a new mandate. Similarly, managers with recent poor investment performance are likely to lose clients. Yet there is much evidence to show that past investment performance has no implication for future investment performance and is therefore unlikely to provide a good guide to selecting a fund manager. A recent piece of evidence for this comes from a report by consultants Mercer Fraser, *Past Performance in Perspective* (1989). The report indicates that most fund managers' investment performance tends to exhibit a cyclical pattern, with a run of good years followed by a run of poor years. No fund management group can expect to deliver systematically good performance over an extended period. The implication is that to replace a manager after a few years of poor performance may turn out to be a short-sighted strategy. However, there is no guarantee that good performance will ultimately be delivered. There does appear to be a definite asymmetry in performance, since a poor management team is capable of delivery systematically poor performance indefinitely. So it is always difficult to distinguish poor cyclical from poor trend performance at least in the short term, say two to three years.

Another feature of the 1980s and 1990s has been the change in the selection process for fund managers. Originally mandates were won through personal contacts between clients and managers. This tended to favour traditional merchant banks. During the 1980s mandates began to be awarded through open competition. As elsewhere in the UK financial services industry during the 1980s, relationship deals have begun to be replaced by transactional deals. This tended to favour newcomers and weaken the position of the traditional fund management groups.

In this chapter, we intend to examine share, bond and treasury portfolio management, both passively and actively; but before we do this, we have to investigate how portfolio managers determine the utility function of their clients.

## 14.2   Assessing the investing client's utility function

It is usually extremely difficult to determine the investing client's utility function with any degree of accuracy. But it is very important for portfolio managers to have a good idea of the utility function, for at least three reasons. First, it is a prerequisite for the initial structuring of a portfolio. Second, it will influence the kinds of portfolio adjustment that can be made. Third, because it affects the initial portfolio structure, it will also influence the portfolio's subsequent performance.

In order to structure a client's portfolio, the portfolio manager must be aware of the most important characteristics of the client, such as tax status, liquidity needs, time horizon (i.e. time period over which investment objectives are to be achieved), risk aversion (or alternatively risk tolerance), other assets and liabilities, preferences (e.g. for high-income bonds or for financial sector securities) and constraints (e.g. restrictions on defence sector or tobacco shares, or prohibitions on holding the securities of companies that compete against the client, or regulatory or legal constraints). All these factors will affect the initial portfolio, adjustments to the portfolio and subsequent performance. It is important for both the client and the portfolio manager to be aware of this from the outset. It is important to isolate the performance of the portfolio manager from, say, the restrictions placed on him by the client. A typical investment-objectives questionnaire is given in the appendix to this chapter.

We can now attempt to infer the utility functions of the two main types of client referred to in the last section: namely, the client interested in maximizing the expected utility of the return on the portfolio (or equivalently, a utility function based on the expected return and variance of the portfolio) and the client interested in minimizing the mismatching between assets and liabilities.

For the investing client interested in maximizing expected utility (the gross investor), the most important characteristic that has to be identified is his degree of risk aversion or risk tolerance. The lower the degree of risk aversion (the higher the degree of risk tolerance), the greater the degree of risk (and expected return) that can be sustained in his portfolio.

A standard procedure for inferring the client's degree of risk tolerance is to ask him to select his preferred combination of general asset categories: say, his preferred mixture of share and bonds.

To help him, the client could be given the portfolio opportunity set derived from holding different combinations of shares and bonds. This is shown in Figure 14.1 as the curved line *BPS*. At *B* the portfolio is invested 100 per cent in bonds, while at *S* the portfolio is invested 100 per cent in shares. Suppose the client picks a particular mix, say 60 per cent shares to 40 per cent bonds. This portfolio is represented by point *P* in the figure. The portfolio manager now has some idea of the *normal* (or *strategic* or *target*) *mix* of shares and bonds. He also has some idea of the client's risk tolerance. This is because *P* must be a tangency point between the portfolio opportunity set and the client's indifference curve.

---

**Figure 14.1** Inferring an investor's risk tolerance

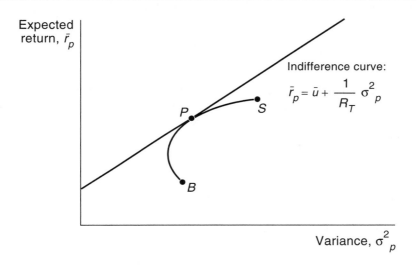

---

In the last chapter, we saw that indifference curves in mean-variance space could be represented by the equation (see, for example, equation (13.8)):

$$\bar{r}_p = \bar{u} + \frac{1}{R_T} \cdot \sigma_p^2,$$ (14.1)

where:

$$\bar{r}_p = \text{expected return on portfolio;}$$
$$\sigma_p^2 = \text{variance of return on portfolio;}$$
$$\bar{u} = \text{constant expected utility level;}$$
$$R_T = \text{degree of risk tolerance.}$$

If the degree of risk tolerance is assumed to be constant, then the indifference curves (one for each level of $\bar{u}$) are linear, as shown in (14.1). If we know *P*, we can calculate the slope of the line tangent at *P* and, given this, derive the degree of risk tolerance:

$$R_T = \frac{1}{\text{Slope of line tangent at } P}.$$ (14.2)

Rewriting (14.1) gives:

$$\bar{u} = \bar{r}_p - \frac{1}{R_T} \cdot \sigma_p^2, \tag{14.3}$$

or:

$$\text{Expected utility} = \text{Expected return} - \text{Risk penalty}. \tag{14.4}$$

This shows that *expected utility* is equivalent to the *risk-adjusted expected return* on the portfolio. It is derived by subtracting a *risk penalty* from the expected return, where the risk penalty depends on the portfolio risk and the client's risk tolerance. For example, if $\bar{r}_p = 0.17$ (17 per cent), $\sigma_p = 0.30$ (30 per cent) and $R_T = 3$, then:

$$\bar{u} = 0.17 - \tfrac{1}{3}(0.30)^2 = 0.14 \quad (14\%).$$

The objective of the portfolio manager is to maximize (14.3), under the assumption that the client's risk tolerance, $R_T$, is known. We can demonstrate this by finding the optimal combination of shares and bonds in the portfolio. (This is the opposite exercise to the one performed above to determine the degree of risk tolerance.)

The objective is to maximize:

$$\bar{u} = \bar{r}_p - \frac{1}{R_T} \cdot \sigma_p^2, \tag{14.5}$$

subject to:

$$\bar{r}_p = \theta_s \bar{r}_s + \theta_b \bar{r}_b, \tag{14.6}$$

$$\sigma_p^2 = \theta_s^2 \sigma_s^2 + 2\theta_s \theta_b \sigma_{sb} + \theta_b^2 \sigma_b^2, \tag{14.7}$$

$$\theta_s + \theta_b = 1, \tag{14.8}$$

where:

$$
\begin{aligned}
\bar{r}_s, \bar{r}_b &= \text{expected returns on shares and bonds;} \\
\sigma_s^2, \sigma_b^2 &= \text{variance of returns on shares and bonds;} \\
\sigma_{sb} &= \text{covariance between returns on shares and bonds;} \\
\theta_s, \theta_b &= \text{proportion of the portfolio in shares and bonds.}
\end{aligned}
$$

If we substitute equations (14.6) to (14.8) into (14.5), we have an unconstrained optimization problem:

$$\max_{\theta_s} \bar{u} = \theta_s \bar{r}_s + (1 - \theta_s)\bar{r}_b - \frac{1}{R_T}\left[\theta_s^2 \sigma_s^2 + 2\theta_s(1 - \theta_s)\sigma_{sb} + (1 - \theta_s)^2 \sigma_b^2\right]. \tag{14.9}$$

Differentiating (14.9) with respect to $\theta_s$, setting the result to zero and solving for $\theta_s$, we get:

$$\theta_s^* = \frac{\sigma_b^2 - \sigma_{sb}}{(\sigma_s^2 - 2\sigma_{sb} + \sigma_b^2)} + \frac{(\bar{r}_s - \bar{r}_b)}{2(\sigma_s^2 - 2\sigma_{sb} + \sigma_b^2)} \cdot R_T \tag{14.10}$$

as the optimal proportion of the portfolio invested in shares. The proportion in shares increases linearly with the degree of risk tolerance, $R_T$, and with the spread between the expected returns on shares and bonds.

The other type of client whose portfolio a fund manager may be managing is one who is concerned about minimizing the mismatching between assets and liabilities (i.e. the net investor). In other words, this type of client is concerned that the value of the assets (or equivalently, the return on the assets) in the portfolio should never be less than the value of the liabilities (or equivalently, the payout on the liabilities). This type of behaviour is known as *safety-first* behaviour.

Of course, in a world of risk it is not possible to guarantee that the return on the assets will never be less than the payout on the liabilities. Instead, the portfolio manager will attempt to minimize the probability that the return on the assets is less than the payout on the liabilities; i.e.:

$$\min \Pr(r_p < r_l), \tag{14.11}$$

where:

$$r_p = \text{rate of return on portfolio of assets;}$$
$$r_l = \text{rate of payout on liabilities.}$$

If the portfolio return is normally distributed, then the optimum portfolio will be the one for which the *expected* return on the portfolio, $\bar{r}_p$, is the maximum number of standard deviations away from $r_l$. This is demonstrated in Figure 14.2. The shaded area is the probability of the return on the portfolio

**Figure 14.2** The safety-first criterion

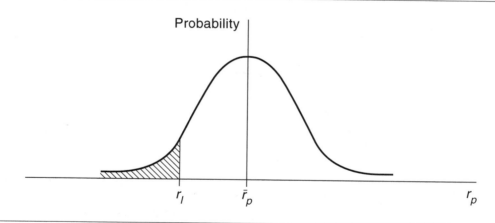

being less than $r_l$. This area is minimized when the number of standard deviations between $\bar{r}_p$ and $r_l$ is maximized. Since the number of standard deviations between $\bar{r}_p$ and $r_l$ is given by $(\bar{r}_p - r_l)/\sigma_p$, then (14.11) is equivalent to:

$$\max k = \frac{\bar{r}_p - r_l}{\sigma_p}. \tag{14.12}$$

To illustrate, suppose that $r_l = 0.1$ (10 per cent) and we have the following two portfolios:

|         | *Portfolio A* | *Portfolio B* |
|---------|:-------------:|:-------------:|
| $\bar{r}_p$ |     0.17      |     0.20      |
| $\sigma_p$  |     0.30      |     0.35      |

For portfolio A, we have:

$$\frac{\bar{r}_p - r_l}{\sigma_p} = 0.23,$$

while for portfolio B, we have:

$$\frac{\bar{r}_p - r_l}{\sigma_p} = 0.29.$$

Therefore portfolio B is preferred.

All portfolios having the same value $k$ in (14.12) will be equally preferred under the safety-first criterion, and this fact allows us to construct indifference curves in mean-standard deviation space, under the safety-first criterion. Rearranging the expression in (14.12), we get:

$$\bar{r}_p = r_l + k\sigma_p \qquad (14.13)$$

as the formula for the indifference curve. As shown in Figure 14.3, all indifference curves pass through (but are clearly not defined at) $r_l$. Also, indifference curves with higher values of $k$ indicate higher utility: the indifference curve $k = k_2$ indicates greater utility than the one with $k = k_1$.

---

**Figure 14.3** The optimal safety-first portfolio

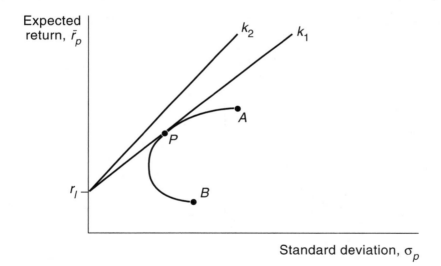

---

Figure 14.3 also shows how the optimal portfolio is selected. The optimal portfolio $P$ is the tangency portfolio between the highest indifference curve and the portfolio opportunity set $APB$.

Having found the client's utility function, the fund manager is now in a position to manage the client's portfolio so as to maximize the utility function. However, it is likely that the share portfolio and bond portfolio will be managed separately. In addition, the fund manager has to decide whether to manage the fund passively or actively. We will consider all these factors in turn.

# 14.3 Passive portfolio management

In this section we will examine the passive management of share and bond portfolios. We will assume initially that the client is interested in maximizing a risk-return utility function, and subsequently that the client is interested in safety first.

## 14.3.1 Passive portfolio management for an expected utility-maximizing client

We will assume that the client is concerned only with risk and return and that his degree of risk tolerance has been assessed; he is not concerned with any other factor. In other words, there are no tax effects, liquidity is not a problem, and the time horizon is effectively infinite. We will also assume that there is a consensus view of the expected returns and risks associated with different securities. Finally, we will assume that it is possible for investors to borrow and lend at the same riskless interest rate. In short, we have the stylized world of the capital asset pricing model and security market efficiency. Such a world justifies passive portfolio management as the appropriate management technique, since investors cannot expect to earn positive (risk-adjusted) excess returns from actively trading portfolios after adjusting for transaction costs.

There are two main types of passive strategy: *buy-and-hold* and *index-matching* (or *indexing*).

Buy-and-hold involves purchasing securities and holding on to them indefinitely or, in the case of fixed-maturity securities (such as money market instruments and bonds), until maturity and then replacing them with similar securities. The return from a buy-and-hold strategy will be dominated by income flows (i.e. dividend and coupon payments) and in the case of shares, by *long-term* capital growth. Expectations of short-term capital gains or losses are ignored; in the case of bonds, capital gains and losses are ignored altogether, because at maturity only the par value of the bond will be received.

Since there is a consensus view that all securities are fairly priced at all times, it does not really matter which securities are bought and held. However, by buying and holding only a few securities, a substantial amount of diversifiable risk might remain in the resulting portfolio.

A version of buy-and-hold that eliminates diversifiable risk is index-matching. Index-matching involves the construction of an *index fund* which is designed to replicate the performance of the market index. This is exactly the kind of portfolio behaviour outlined in the last chapter, in which the optimal portfolio is determined (depending on the degree of risk tolerance) as a combination of the riskless asset and the market portfolio. This is shown in Figure 14.4, where $M$ is the consensus view of the market portfolio and $C$ is the riskless asset. Given the client's indifference curve (and degree of risk tolerance), the optimal portfolio $P$ is invested in the following proportions: $\theta_m$ in the market portfolio, and $(1 - \theta_m)$ in the riskless asset.

Several types of indexing are possible. *Complete indexing* involves the construction of an index fund which exactly matches the underlying market portfolio. In the case of shares, this could be the FTSE-A All Share Index; in the case of bonds, it could be the Salomon Brothers Bond Index; in the case of an international portfolio, it could be the Morgan Stanley Capital International Index. Complete indexing is very expensive. For example, the FTSE-A All Share Index contains more than 800 securities weighted according to their relative market proportions. To construct a portfolio of 800 securities with the same proportions as the index would involve extremely high brokerage commissions (which are ignored by the underlying index). Also, the constituents of the index change quite frequently, and

**Figure 14.4** Passive portfolio management

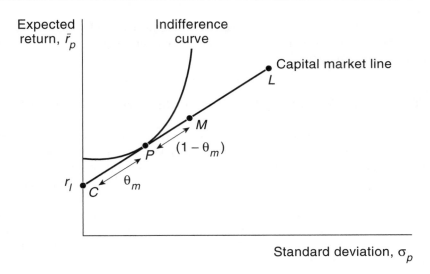

so the rebalancing of the index fund (i.e. selling the deleted securities and purchasing the added securities) involves dealing spreads as well as brokerage commissions (and these are also ignored by the underlying index). A bond index fund is even more expensive to construct. Over time, the average maturity of a bond index will decline unless new long-maturing bonds are added to replace those that mature and automatically drop out of the index. All this shows that exact indexing is not feasible. Three alternatives have been suggested: stratified sampling, factor matching, and comingling.

*Stratified sampling* involves the construction of an index fund based on a sample of securities from the total population (or universe) comprising the index. The idea is to divide the total set of securities into sectors or strata (which are, e.g., industry-based for shares or maturity-based for bonds). An overall sample proportion is selected, say 5 per cent. Then the top 5 per cent of securities that have the highest correlation with the market index are included in the index fund. This procedure limits initial transaction costs and subsequent rebalancing costs but increases the risks of *tracking error*, the error is not exactly replicating the market index.

*Factor matching* (or *risk matching*) is more general than stratified sampling. Stratified sampling involves selecting securities on the basis of a single factor, e.g. industry grouping or maturity range. Factor matching involves the construction of an index fund using securities selected on the basis of a number of factors (or risk indices). The first factor is generally the level of systematic risk, so the selected portfolio must be chosen to have the same level of beta as the market (namely unity). The other factors could be (in the case of shares) sector breakdown, dividend pattern, firm size, financial structure (i.e. debt-equity ratio). The selected index fund would be a portfolio of, say, 50 securities which match the market in terms of the above five factors (or risk indices) and have the highest correlation with the market.

*Comingling* involves the use of *comingled funds* such as *unit trusts* or *investment trusts* (i.e. a company whose assets are the securities of other companies) rather than the explicit formation of an index fund. Comingling may be especially suitable for clients with relatively small portfolios and may provide an acceptable compromise between the transaction costs of complete indexing and the tracking error of stratified sampling.

Apart from the transaction costs involved in setting up and rebalancing, there are other problems with running an index fund. The most important of these concerns income payments on the securities. The total return on an index includes not only capital gains but also income in the form of dividend or coupon payments. In order to match the performance of the index in terms of income, the index fund would have to have the same pattern of income payments as the index. It would also have to make the same reinvestment assumptions. Since the index fund was constructed to replicate the capital structure of the index, it is unlikely to replicate the income pattern (unless exact matching was used). Similarly, the index assumes that gross income payments are reinvested costlessly back into the index on the day that each security becomes ex dividend. In practice, however, these assumptions are violated in four ways. First, the dividend or coupon payment is not made until an average of six weeks after the ex dividend date. Second, the payment is received net of tax. (Non-taxpaying investors such as charities have to wait even longer before receiving a tax rebate.) Third, there are dealing costs of reinvesting income payments. Fourth, the income payments on different securities are going to be trickling in all the time and no fund manager is going to invest small sums of money on the day they are received. Instead, the small sums are going to be accumulated until a suitable large sum is available for reinvestment. The effect of all these factors is that the index fund will begin to drift away from the index and will eventually have to be rebalanced.

Another problem concerns the effect of changing the constituents of the index. When the announcement of the change is made, the price of the security being deleted falls, while the price of the security being added rises. These effects can cause major tracking errors between the index fund and the index.

All these factors lead to the index fund invariably underperforming the index. So it appears that passive fund managers cannot even match the index, let alone beat it. But this appearance is deceptive. The appropriate test is how well an index fund manager performs on a risk-adjusted and transaction-cost-adjusted basis compared with a fund manager pursuing an active strategy.

Despite these problems, passive fund management is increasing in importance as a management strategy. And it is also a sensible strategy, if there is a consensus about the market portfolio's expected return and risk.

The only occasions on which a passive fund manager goes into active mode is either when the client's preferences change, or when the consensus concerning the market portfolio's expected return and risk changes. The first case leads to a new combination of the riskless asset and the market portfolio; the second leads to a rebalancing of the existing index fund.

## 14.3.2 Passive portfolio management for a safety-first client

We will assume that the client has a portfolio of assets and liabilities and has a utility function that satisfies the safety-first criterion. This means that the return on the assets should not be less than the payout on the liabilities. Equivalently, it means that the present value of the portfolio should not be less than the present value of the liabilities. The portfolio management strategies that attempt to deliver these results are known as *asset-liability management* (ALM) strategies.

A pension fund is exactly the kind of client that will have a safety-first utility function. A pension fund has a future stream of pension payments to make and must always generate the right amount of cash at the right time to meet these payments. In addition, a pension fund is not allowed to run a surplus or deficit: it is obliged to ensure that the pension liabilities are neither overfunded nor underfunded. This implies that the pension fund has an obligation to ensure that the present value of the liabilities equals the present value of the assets. Furthermore, the stream of future pension liabilities is reasonably predictable: actuaries are able to make good forecasts of the future number of pensioners, and, since most pensions are only partially indexed against inflation, it is relatively easy to predict the growth in the value of pensions. This suggests that it is desirable to ensure that the future cash flows from assets required to meet the pension payments are also reasonably predictable. This, in turn, suggests that bonds should play a significant role in the portfolios of pension funds. Indeed, in the past, when pensions were not indexed at all, fixed-coupon bonds were the ideal vehicle for meeting pension funds' needs. Today, when there is some indexing of pensions, pension funds will need to have indexed bonds and shares in their portfolios as well.

In this section we will consider some of the passive strategies suitable for the bond portfolios of safety-first clients. The two main types of strategies are *immunization* and *cash flow matching*.

*Classical immunization* was first designed by Redington (1952). It involves the construction of a bond portfolio that has an assured return over a given investment horizon (equal to that of the payout on the client's liabilities), regardless of changes in the level of interest rates. Equivalently, it involves the construction of a bond portfolio with a present value equal to (or, even better, never less than) the present value of the client's liabilities regardless of changes in the level of interest rates. In short, the bond portfolio is *immunized* against interest rate changes.

**Figure 14.5** Classical immunization in terms of present values

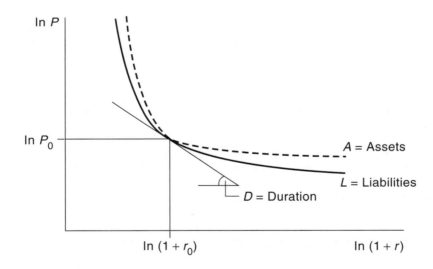

Figure 14.5 shows the effect of immunization in terms of the present values of assets and liabilities (e.g. future pension obligations). $A$ is the present-value profile for the portfolio of bonds and $L$ is the present-value profile for the client's future liabilities. When the current interest rate is $r_0$, the value of both the bonds and the liabilities is $P_0$. When interest rates rise, the present values of both the bonds and the liabilities fall. (The present value of the liabilities falls because lower contributions need to be collected as the interest earned on them increases.) Similarly, when interest rates fall, the present

values of both the bonds and the liabilities rise. But the important point to note is that, whatever happens to interest rates, the present value of the bonds is never less than the present value of the liabilities; indeed, except when the interest rate is $r_0$, the present value of the bonds always exceeds that of the liabilities. This result arises because the bond portfolio is constructed to have the same *duration* and also (at least) the same *convexity* as the liabilities. And this provides the clue as to why immunizing a bond portfolio works.

As we saw in Chapter 5, duration and convexity are first- and second-order measures of interest rate risk. As interest rates rise, the present value of the portfolio falls, but the return from reinvesting the portfolio's cash flows (coupon payments and maturing bonds) increases. A perfectly immunized portfolio exactly balances these offsetting effects, i.e. exactly offsets interest rate risk with reinvestment risk. By constructing the bond portfolio to have a duration equal to the specified investment horizon, both the return on the portfolio and the value of the portfolio will be immunized against interest rate changes. We can demonstrate these results using a portfolio containing a single bond.

**Example 14.1 (Immunizing a bond)** *We will consider a bond with five years to maturity, a current value of £114.28, an annual coupon payment of £13.77 and a yield to maturity of 10 per cent. The duration of the bond is given by:*

$$
\begin{aligned}
\text{Duration} &= \frac{d}{P_d}\left[\frac{(1+r_m)^{T+1}-(1+r_m)-r_m T}{(r_m)^2(1+r_m)^T}\right] + \frac{B}{P}\cdot\frac{T}{(1+r_m)^T} \\
&= \frac{13.77}{114.28}\left[\frac{(1.1)^6-(1.1)-0.1(5)}{(0.1)^2(1.1)^5}\right] + \frac{100}{114.28}\cdot\frac{5}{(1.1)^5} \\
&= 4 \text{ years},
\end{aligned}
$$

*where:*

$$
\begin{aligned}
P_d &= \text{current (dirty) price of the bond;} \\
B &= \text{maturity value of the bond;} \\
T &= \text{years to maturity;} \\
r_m &= \text{yield to maturity.}
\end{aligned}
$$

*If the bond is held for exactly the same time as its duration (i.e. four years) and then sold, its value in four years' time will be the same whatever happens to interest rates (i.e. reinvestment rates). This can be seen from Table 14.1.*

**Table 14.1** The value of the bond in year 4 as reinvestment rates change

| Year | Cash flow | Reinvestment rates | | |
|------|-----------|------|------|------|
| | | 9% | 10% | 11% |
| 1 | 13.77 | $13.77 \times (1.09)^3$ | $13.77 \times (1.1)^3$ | $13.77 \times (1.11)^3$ |
| 2 | 13.77 | $13.77 \times (1.09)^2$ | $13.77 \times (1.1)^2$ | $13.77 \times (1.11)^2$ |
| 3 | 13.77 | $13.77 \times (1.09)$ | $13.77 \times (1.1)$ | $13.77 \times (1.11)$ |
| 4 | 13.77 | 13.77 | 13.77 | 13.77 |
| 5 | 113.77 | $113.77 \times (1.09)^{-1}$ | $113.77 \times (1.1)^{-1}$ | $113.77 \times (1.11)^{-1}$ |
| **Year 4 value** | | 167.30 | 167.30 | 167.30 |

*So whatever happens to reinvestment rates, the value of the investment in the bond by year 4 is always equal to £167.30. This follows because, as interest rates change, the change in the income component of the value of the bond is always exactly offset by the change in the capital component of the bond's value, where the bond is valued at its duration date (i.e. year 4). The income component is given by the sum of the first four elements of the table:*

$$\text{Income component} = £13.77 \left[(1+r)^3 + (1+r)^2 + (1+r) + 1\right].$$

*The capital component is given by the last element of the table:*

$$\text{Capital component} = £113.77(1+r)^{-1}.$$

*If the interest rate falls from 10 to 9 per cent, the income component falls by £0.95 and the capital component rises by £0.95. Similarly, if the interest rate rises from 10 to 11 per cent, the income component increases by £0.93 and the capital component falls by £0.93.*

*If the bond had been held for any other period than its duration, the value of the bond would not be independent of the interest rate. For example, had the bond been held to maturity, its year 5 value would be £182.40 at 9 per cent, £184.10 at 10 per cent and £185.80 at 11 per cent.*

*It follows from the fact that the year 4 value of the bond is constant, regardless of interest rates, that the return from holding the bond must also be constant, regardless of interest rates, if the holding period is equal to the bond's duration. The initial cost of the bond is £114.28 and the duration date value is £167.30; therefore the rate of return over four years is:*

$$\text{Rate of return} = (167.30/114.28)^{1/4} - 1 = 0.10 \quad (10\%),$$

*equal to the original yield to maturity on the bond. By holding a bond for its duration, it is possible to lock in the initial yield to maturity.*

*Now if a fund manager's client has liabilities of £100,000 which arise in four years' time, the fund manager could recommend that the client invest in a portfolio of 598 (i.e. £100,000/£167.30) of the above bonds.*

The same principles apply to portfolios of bonds. The duration of a portfolio of bonds is simply the value-weighted sum of the durations of the individual bonds:

$$D_p = \sum_{i=1}^{N} \theta_i D_i, \tag{14.14}$$

where:

$$
\begin{aligned}
D_p &= \text{duration of the portfolio with } N \text{ bonds;} \\
D_i &= \text{duration of the } i\text{th bond;} \\
\theta_i &= \text{proportion of the } i\text{th bond in portfolio.}
\end{aligned}
$$

It is possible to construct a portfolio with a specified duration from a whole range of bonds with different durations. For example, the portfolio could be constructed from bonds with durations close to that of the liability (a *focused* or *bullet portfolio*), or it could be constructed from bonds with durations distant from that of the liability (a *barbell portfolio*). Consider, for example, a liability with a duration of 10 years and a set of bonds with durations of 4, 9, 11 and 15 years. A focused portfolio would contain the 9- and 11-year duration bonds with weights of 50 per cent each, giving a duration of:

$$0.50\,(9) + 0.50\,(11) \;=\; 10 \text{ years}.$$

A barbell portfolio would consist of the 4- and 15-year duration bonds with weights of 45.5 and 54.5 per cent respectively, giving a duration of:

$$0.455\,(4) + 0.545\,(15) \;=\; 10 \text{ years}.$$

The advantage of a barbell strategy is that a much wider range of portfolios with different durations can be constructed compared with a focused strategy. However, the disadvantage of the barbell strategy is that it has greater *immunization risk* than the focused strategy.

Immunization risk arises whenever there are non-parallel shifts in the yield curve. As the last example showed, the immunization effect works because there were parallel shifts in the yield curve: i.e., the reinvestment rate fell from 10 to 9 per cent at each maturity. If this does not happen, then matching the duration to the investment horizon no longer guarantees immunization. Non-parallel shifts in the yield curve will lead to the income component of the value of the portfolio changing either too much or too little compared with the change in the capital component; i.e., there will be immunization risk. This risk is reduced if the durations of the individual bonds in the immunizing portfolio are close to that of the liabilities (i.e. if a focused portfolio is used). In this case, non-parallel yield curve shifts will affect the individual bonds and the liabilities in a similar way. The effects of non-parallel yield curve shifts are divergent if the durations of the individual bonds in the immunizing portfolio differ much from that of the liabilities (as in a barbell portfolio), even though the duration of the portfolio itself is the same as that of the liabilities.

While immunization is usually regarded as a passive strategy, the portfolio will have to be periodically rebalanced, and therefore an immunization strategy has certain active elements. There are two main reasons for rebalancing: (1) changes in interest rates, and (2) the passage of time. Immunization is effective only for small changes in interest rates; as the change in interest rates increases, its effectiveness decreases. However, the discrepancy always favours the portfolio holder, as shown in Figure 14.6. For example, if the interest rate falls from 10 to 5 per cent, the year 4 value of the portfolio in the last example rises to £167.70, while if the interest rate rises to 20 per cent, the value of the portfolio rises to £168.72. The passage of time will automatically reduce the duration of the portfolio. But the reduction in duration may not occur at the same rate as time decays. For example, after one year the duration of the portfolio might decline by only 0.8 year. So periodically the portfolio has to be rebalanced with respect to both the new reinvestment rate and the remaining investment horizon.

So far, we have considered the construction of an immunized portfolio to meet a single liability at a single future date. More often, however, the portfolio has to meet a schedule of liabilities over time. This involves the construction of a *dedicated portfolio* which is capable of meeting the schedule of liabilities from both the income and the capital components, and which declines to zero on the payment of the last liability. There are two ways of dedicating a portfolio: multi-period immunization, and cash flow matching.

When there are multiple liabilities, it is no longer sufficient simply to match the duration of the portfolio to the average duration of the liabilities as in classical immunization. Instead, it is necessary for each liability payment to be individually immunized (i.e. duration-matched) by a portfolio payment stream. The procedure for doing this is known as *multi-period immunization* and is a straightforward extension of single-period immunization.

**Figure 14.6** Classical immunization in terms of investment horizon values

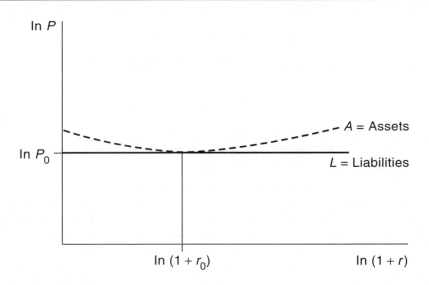

A very simple alternative to multi-period immunization is *cash flow matching*. This involves finding the lowest-cost portfolio that generates a pattern of cash flows that exactly matches the pattern of liability payments. The procedure for doing this is as follows. A bond (the lowest-cost bond, if more than one is available) is purchased with the same maturity and value as the last liability payment. The coupon payments on the bond are held to meet the earlier liabilities. Taking these coupon payments into account, another bond (again the lowest-cost one) is purchased with the same maturity as the penultimate liability payment. Working backwards in this way, all the liabilities can be matched by payments on the bonds in the portfolio. To illustrate, annual liability payments of £1000 for three years could be met by the purchase of nine 11.11 per cent three-year bonds, eight 12.50 per cent two-year bonds and seven 14.29 per cent one-year bonds:

| Number of bonds | Coupon (%) | Maturity (yrs) | Cash flows (£) | | |
|:---:|:---:|:---:|:---:|:---:|:---:|
| | | | *Year 1* | *Year 2* | *Year 3* |
| 9 | 11.11 | 3 | 100 | 100 | 1000 |
| 8 | 12.50 | 2 | 100 | 900 | – |
| 7 | 14.29 | 1 | 800 | – | – |
| | | | 1000 | 1000 | 1000 |

There are two main advantages of cash flow matching over immunization. First, there is no need for duration-matching. Second, there is no need to rebalance the portfolio as interest rates change or with the passage of time. Cash flow matching is therefore a pure passive buy-and-hold strategy. However, in the real world, it is unlikely that bonds exist with the appropriate maturity dates and coupon payments. To guarantee that the liabilities are paid when due in the absence of perfect matching, the cash flow matching strategy would have to be overfunded. In this case, an immunization strategy may well end up meeting the required objectives at lower cost.

*Horizon matching* is a combination of cash flow matching and immunization. For example, we could construct a portfolio which cash-flow-matches the liabilities for the next four quarters, but is immunized for the remaining investment horizon. At the end of the four quarters, the portfolio is rebalanced to cash-flow-match over the subsequent four quarters, and is again immunized for the remaining period.

As a final example of a passive strategy for bonds, we can consider *riding the yield curve*. A yield curve ride is valid in the case where the yield curve is upward-sloping. If this is the case, then a fund manager can buy bonds with maturities in excess of his investment horizon. He proceeds to hold the bonds until the end of his investment period and then sells them. If the yield curve has not shifted during this period, the fund manager will have generated higher returns than if he has bought bonds with the same maturity as his investment horizon. This follows because, as the time to maturity declines, the yield to maturity falls and the price of the bonds rises, thereby generating capital gains (hence the term 'yield curve ride'). These gains will be higher than those available if bonds with the same maturity as the investment horizon are used, because the maturity value of the latter bonds is fixed.

The asset-liability management strategies just discussed rely on a quantitative technique known as *asset-liability modelling*. Pension funds (and other institutional investors, such as insurance companies, which have low net worth (shareholders' funds) in relation to their liabilities) use this technique to help structure their asset portfolios in relation to the maturity structure of their liabilities. Asset-liability modelling begins by making forecasts about how a pension fund's liabilities are going to accrue over a particular time horizon, that might be 5, 10 or 15 years ahead. To do this, assumptions concerning salary growth rates, staff turnover, the age distribution and sex composition of the work-force have to be made. Then forecasts concerning the funding position of the pension scheme have to be made. This involves making projections of future contribution rates and also assessing the value of assets in relation to accrued liabilities. These forecasts and projections are made under different scenarios concerning likely outcomes. Typically three scenarios are adopted: most likely, best-case and worst-case. This provides a realistic range of possible outcomes, and, in the latter case, spells out the extent of the risks that the pension fund trustees face.

There are two main uses of asset-liability modelling. The first is to indicate the consequences of adopting any particular investment strategy. The second is to discover alternative strategies that increase the likelihood of meeting the fund's objectives. Proponents of asset-liability modelling argue that the strategy allows pension funds to generate higher returns without any consequential increase in risk.

The modelling exercise might indicate, for example, that if current investment returns are sustained, there would be no need to change the employer contribution rate into the pension fund over the next 5 years. However, the worst-case scenario might indicate the employer contribution rate might have to rise by 10 per cent over the next 5 years. The exercise therefore allows the employer to plan for this possibility. As another illustration, the modelling exercise might indicate that because a pension fund is maturing, it should switch out of equities into fixed-income bonds, which are more likely to meet pension liabilities with lower risk of employer deficiency payments (this is now a requirement of the 1995 Pensions Act in the UK).

While all this seems eminently sensible, the technique is not without its critics. As with many long-term forecasting exercises, the predictions are only as good as the assumptions used to generate them. Some claim that the assumptions made about future investment returns are likely to be so unreliable that the modelling exercise provides very little of value. Less sceptical proponents of asset-liability modelling argue that the 'models are to be used and not believed', with the usefulness of the technique 'to provide a disciplined quantitative framework for qualitative discussions on investment policies' (Roger Urwin, *Financial Times*, 18 April 1991).

Another problem encountered with the technique comes from fund managers who are concerned that it gives an unwarranted role to outsiders such as actuaries in designing investment strategies, in particular asset allocation strategies. Actuaries have always had a role in determining the value of a pension scheme's liabilities. But with the advent of asset-liability modelling, actuaries have begun to have a role in setting long-term asset allocation over, say, a 10-year horizon. Some fund managers claim they are being reduced to the subsidiary role of determining tactical asset allocation and stock selection relative to this new long-term strategic asset allocation benchmark. However, not all fund managers are critical of the redefinition of their respective roles. Many fund managers have positively welcomed the formal separation of long-term policy decisions from short-term tactical decisions that asset-liability modelling allows.

Another potential problem concerns the interpretation of performance measurement in the light of the technique. Asset-liability modelling justifies different pension funds pursuing very different investment policies. For example, small fast-growing funds might pursue very aggressive investment policies, while large mature funds might adopt passive investment policies. This makes it very difficult to interpret a single performance league table drawn up on the assumption that all funds are pursuing the same objective of maximizing returns. Performance measurement services have begun to take this into account by constructing peer-group performance league tables, drawn up for sub-groups of funds following similar objectives.

## 14.4   Active portfolio management and adjustment

In this section we will examine the active management and adjustment of share, money market and bond portfolios. Active portfolio management is usually not a suitable management strategy for safety-first clients, so we will concentrate our attention on clients who are interested in maximizing expected utility.

### 14.4.1   Active share portfolio management and adjustment

**Portfolio management**

A portfolio will be actively managed whenever it is believed that there are misvalued securities around, or when there are heterogeneous expectations of the risks and returns on securities, so that there is no consensus view of the market portfolio. Expectations of price movements are vitally important with active management. This contrasts with passive management, where expectations are less important but where risk aversion dominates behaviour.

It is still possible to construct the optimal active portfolio (based on the fund manager's own estimation of the risks and returns on different securities), in the same way that the optimal passive portfolio (based on market consensus estimates of the risks and returns on different securities) is constructed. That is, using his estimates of the risks and returns on different securities, the fund manager constructs his efficient set of portfolios. Then, given his assessment of the client's utility function, he constructs the client's optimal portfolio from combinations of the riskless asset and the tangency portfolio with

**Figure 14.7** Structuring the portfolio

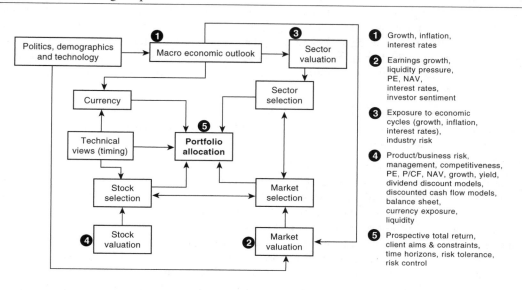

*Source:* Swiss Bank Corporation, Portfolio Management International Division, London

the capital market line (i.e. the fund manager's own version of the 'market' portfolio). However, in practice, an active portfolio is not constructed in this way. Instead, active portfolio management operates around three activities: asset allocation, security selection and market timing.

To simplify the problem of structuring the portfolio, the fund manager breaks it down into two or more stages (see Figure 14.7 for an example of how this is achieved in practice).

**Asset allocation.** At the first stage, the *asset allocation* stage, he decides what proportions of the total portfolio to invest in broad asset categories such as shares, bonds and money market securities. This is sometimes called *strategic asset allocation*. The optimal asset allocation decision has been demonstrated before (see (14.9) and (14.10)). It depends on the client's degree of risk tolerance and on the fund manager's estimates of the risks and returns on shares, bonds and money market securities. The asset allocation decision is extremely important, since it dominates the performance of most portfolios. This is because returns on securities within each asset category are usually highly correlated; i.e., they generally rise together or fall together. This implies that selecting the best-performing asset category is usually more important for performance than selecting the best-performing securities within each asset category. However, restrictions placed on them by trustees or regulators may mean that fund managers do not have a completely free hand in making their asset allocation decisions.

**Security selection.** Having decided on his asset allocation, the fund manager can then proceed to the second stage, called *security selection*. At this stage, the fund manager in charge of a particular asset category selects securities from that category. This is done independently of the securities being selected within another category, so that, for example, any cross-category correlations between bonds and shares are completely ignored when forming the share and bond portfolios. This common feature of hierarchical or stage-by-stage decision-making is known as *separability*: the bond portfolio is separable from the share portfolio. There is sometimes an intermediate stage between asset allocation and security selection, known as *sector selection* (or group selection). At this stage, funds are allocated to different sectors of each category before individual securities are selected from within those sectors. So, for example, with bonds, the sectors could be short-term, medium-term and long-term bonds; with shares, the sectors could be the components of the Standard Industrial Classification (e.g. banks, breweries, electrical, textiles, etc.).

We will assume that the asset allocation decision (and, where appropriate, the sector selection decision) has been made (according to equations such as (14.9) and (14.10) above). We can therefore concentrate our attention on the security selection decision.

Security selection (also called *stock picking*) is important whenever fund managers are prepared to accept the overall consensus for the market as a whole, but believe that certain individual securities are misvalued - in other words, they believe that most shares are fairly priced but a few are either underpriced or overpriced. A good stock picker believes he knows which securities are misvalued. An overpriced security has an expected return that is less than, or a risk estimate that is more than, the market consensus estimate, while an underpriced security has an expected return that is more than, or a risk estimate that is less than, the market consensus estimate. In terms of the capital asset pricing model and the security market line (SML), a security is said to be mispriced when it lies off the SML or has a non-zero *alpha* value. We know from the analysis of the last chapter that a security is fairly priced when its equilibrium expected return ($\bar{r}_i^*$) is given by:

$$\bar{r}_i^* = r_f + (\bar{r}_m - r_f)\beta_i, \qquad (14.15)$$

and so lies on the SML. The difference between the actual expected return ($\bar{r}_i$) and the equilibrium expected return is known as the *alpha* value of the security ($\alpha_i$):

$$\alpha_i = \bar{r}_i - \bar{r}_i^*. \qquad (14.16)$$

For example, suppose that $\bar{r}_m = 0.15$ (15 per cent), $r_f = 0.10$ (10 per cent) and $\beta_1 = 0.75$; then $\bar{r}_1^* = 0.1375$ (13.75 per cent). If $\bar{r}_1 = 0.1475$ (14.75 per cent), then $\alpha_1 = 0.01$ (i.e. 1 per cent). This means that the security offers a 1 per cent higher return than it should be offering, and is therefore underpriced.

When a security's alpha value is positive, the security is underpriced. When a security's alpha value is negative, the security is overpriced. When a security is fairly priced, its alpha value is zero (see Figure 14.8). The alpha for the portfolio ($\alpha_p$) is the value-weighted average of the individual securities in the portfolio:

$$\alpha_p = \sum_{i=1}^{N} \theta_i \alpha_i. \qquad (14.17)$$

The objective of a stock picker is to select portfolios of securities with positive alphas, a procedure that has been called 'the quest for alpha'. In other words, the stock picker will construct portfolios of securities that, in comparison with the market portfolio, have less than proportionate weightings in the overpriced (negative-alpha) securities (since they are expected to fall in price) and more than proportionate weightings in the underpriced (positive-alpha) securities (since they are expected to rise in price). The resulting active portfolio can then be viewed as a combination of the market portfolio and a set of side bets:

**Figure 14.8** Alpha values for shares

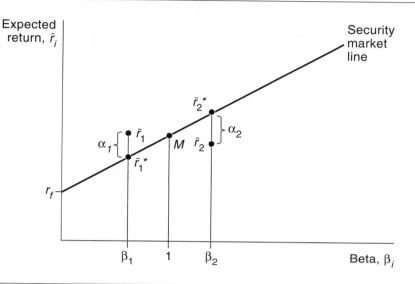

| Shares | Market portfolio weightings (%) | Active portfolio weightings (%) | Side bets |
|---|---|---|---|
| 1 | 1.0 | 0.0 | −1.0 |
| 2 | 2.5 | 3.0 | 0.5 |
| 3 | 0.6 | 0.6 | 0.0 |
| ⋮ | ⋮ | ⋮ | ⋮ |
| N | 0.9 | 0.6 | −0.3 |

In this example, the market portfolio has a 1.0 per cent weighting in share 1, while the fund manager believes the share is heavily overpriced and does not take it into his active portfolio at all. (He would like to sell it short but cannot.) He is therefore taking on a *side bet* against other active managers equal to 1 per cent of his portfolio. This is because the sum of all side bets across each share must be zero. For every fund manager with a lower-than-average weighting in a share, there must be another manager with an above-average weighting; it is a zero-sum game that is being played between managers. The manager takes an opposite view of share 2 and holds a more than average weighting equal to 0.5 per cent of his portfolio. With share 3, he accepts the market consensus and holds the market weighting. And so on.

The active portfolio is therefore equal to the market portfolio plus the set of side bets:

$$A = M + \Delta, \qquad (14.18)$$

where:

$$
\begin{aligned}
A &= \text{active portfolio;} \\
M &= \text{market portfolio;} \\
\Delta &= \text{side bets.}
\end{aligned}
$$

Whether or not the active portfolio is good for the client depends on whether or not the client's utility is increased from using the active portfolio. The client's optimal portfolio is derived (given riskless borrowing and lending opportunities) by combining the active (risky) portfolio and the riskless asset. Therefore the question is whether the active portfolio is on a steeper capital market line than the market portfolio. Figure 14.9 shows two active portfolios in comparison with the market portfolio. One of the

---

**Figure 14.9** Security selection

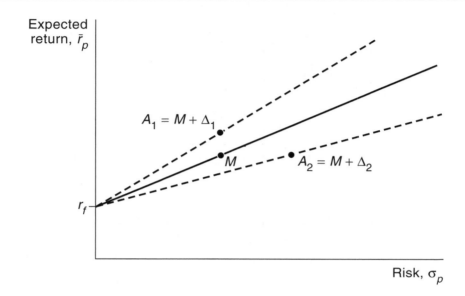

---

active portfolios, $A_1$, with side bets $\Delta_1$, is on a higher CML than the market portfolio, $M$, so that any combination of $A_1$ and the riskless asset will dominate any combination of $M$ and the riskless asset. Portfolio $A_1$ has been put together by a good stock picker and will beat the market. Portfolio $A_2$, on the other hand, combines the market portfolio and a different set of side bets $\Delta_2$. It has been put together by a poor stock picker, and simply results in an increase in risk without a compensating increase in expected return.

How is the optimal active portfolio of risky securities determined? An operational procedure for determining this portfolio has been proposed by Elton and Gruber (1978). Given the fund manager's own estimates of the expected returns and betas on different securities, the fund manager ranks all securities according to their *excess returns to beta* (from the highest to the lowest):

$$\text{Excess return to beta} \;=\; \frac{\bar{r}_i - r_f}{\beta_i}. \tag{14.19}$$

The greater the excess return to beta (ERB), the more desirable the security will be for inclusion in the optimal portfolio. The number of securities in the optimal portfolio depends on a unique cut-off rate $c^*$ for the ERB, such that all securities with ERBs greater than this cut-off rate will be included in the portfolio (and included in the calculation of $c^*$), while all securities with ERBs less than the cut-off rate will be excluded from the portfolio (and excluded from the calculation of $c^*$). The cut-off rate $c_j$

for a portfolio containing the first $j$ securities is given by:

$$c_j = \frac{\sigma_m^2 \sum\limits_{i=1}^{j} \left[(\bar{r}_i - r_f)\beta_i / \eta_i^2\right]}{1 + \sigma_m^2 \sum\limits_{i=1}^{j} (\beta_i^2 / \eta_i^2)}, \qquad (14.20)$$

where:

$$\sigma_m^2 \; = \; \text{variance of the market portfolio;}$$
$$\eta_i^2 \; = \; \text{specific risk of the } i\text{th security.}$$

We can illustrate the cut-off rate using the following data on ten shares together with $r_f = 5$ per cent and $\sigma_m^2 = 10$:

| Share number | Expected return | Beta | Specific risk | Excess return to beta | Cut-off rate |
|---|---|---|---|---|---|
| $i$ | $\bar{r}_i$ | $\beta_i$ | $\eta_i^2$ | $\dfrac{\bar{r}_i - r_f}{\beta_i}$ | $c_j$ |
| 1 | 15.0 | 1.0 | 50 | 10.0 | 1.67 |
| 2 | 17.0 | 1.5 | 40 | 8.0 | 3.69 |
| 3 | 12.0 | 1.0 | 20 | 7.0 | 4.42 |
| 4 | 17.0 | 2.0 | 10 | 6.0 | 5.43 |
| 5 | 11.0 | 1.0 | 40 | 6.0 | 5.45 |
| 6 | 11.0 | 1.5 | 30 | 4.0 | 5.30 |
| 7 | 11.0 | 2.0 | 40 | 3.0 | 5.02 |
| 8 | 7.0 | 0.8 | 16 | 2.5 | 4.91 |
| 9 | 7.0 | 1.0 | 20 | 2.0 | 4.75 |
| 10 | 5.6 | 0.6 | 6 | 1.0 | 4.52 |

The cut-off rates are calculated using (14.20):

$$c_1 = \frac{10[(10)(1.0)/50]}{1 + 10[(1.0)^2/50]} = 1.67,$$

$$c_2 = \frac{10\{[(10)(1.0)/50] + [(12)(1.5)/40]\}}{1 + 10\{[(1.0)^2/50] + [(1.5)^2/40]\}} = 3.69,$$

and so on.

The cut-off rate $c^*$ is determined as follows. We start with the first cut-off rate $c_1 = 1.67$. If $c^* = c_1 = 1.67$, this means that all shares with ERBs greater than 1.67, i.e. shares 1–9, will be included in the optimal portfolio. But only share 1 was used to calculated $c_1$, so $c_1$ is not $c^*$. Similarly, $c_2$ is not $c^*$, because $c_2 = 3.69$ implies that shares 1–6 are included in the optimal portfolio but only shares 1 and 2 were used to compute $c_2$. Proceeding in this way, we find that $c^* = c_5 = 5.45$ and that shares 1–5 are included in the optimal portfolio; shares 6-10 are excluded.

The proportion of the portfolio invested in the $i$th share is given by:

$$\theta_i = \frac{\omega_i}{\sum\limits_{i=1}^{N} \omega_i}, \qquad (14.21)$$

where:

$$\omega_i = \frac{\beta_i}{\eta_i^2}\left(\frac{\bar{r}_i - r_f}{\beta_i} - c^*\right). \tag{14.22}$$

This proportion increases with ERB and decreases with both systematic and specific risk.

The optimal proportions in the active portfolio are shown in the following table together with the market proportions and the side bets:

| Shares | Market portfolio weightings (%) | Active portfolio weightings (%) | Side bets |
|---|---|---|---|
| 1 | 15.0 | 23.5 | 8.5 |
| 2 | 10.0 | 24.6 | 14.6 |
| 3 | 5.0 | 20.0 | 15.0 |
| 4 | 20.0 | 28.4 | 8.4 |
| 5 | 2.5 | 3.5 | 1.0 |
| 6 | 5.0 | 0.0 | −5.0 |
| 7 | 7.5 | 0.0 | −7.5 |
| 8 | 10.0 | 0.0 | −10.0 |
| 9 | 15.0 | 0.0 | −15.0 |
| 10 | 10.0 | 0.0 | −10.0 |
| **Total:** | 100.0 | 100.0 | 0.0 |

As we would expect, shares 1–5 have greater weightings in the active portfolio than the market portfolio. The fund manager is taking out positive side bets against other active managers since he believes these shares are underpriced. Shares 6–10 have zero weightings in the active portfolio. The fund manager believes that these shares are overpriced and he would ideally wish to short-sell them, but is constrained from doing so. He therefore takes out negative side bets against the other active managers. The side bets have to sum to zero, of course.

**Market timing.**  A fund manager engages in security selection when he accepts the overall consensus for the market portfolio but believes that individual securities are misvalued. A fund manager engages in *market timing* when he does not accept the consensus about the market portfolio; in other words, he is more bullish or more bearish than the market. This is shown in Figure 14.10 in the case where the fund manager's estimate of the market portfolio, $A$, is more bullish than the market consensus, $M$. The fund manager's estimation of the capital market line is $CAN$, whereas the market consensus capital market line is $CML$. Had the fund manager accepted the market consensus, then, given his client's indifference curves, the utility-maximizing portfolio would have been $P_2$, a linear combination of $M$ and the riskless asset. However, the fund manager believes that the market portfolio is $A$ and he can increase his client's utility by choosing portfolio $P_3$, a linear combination of $A$ and the riskless asset, with a much higher weighting in $A$. If the fund manager gets it right, the client is better off ($\bar{u}_3$ is a higher indifference curve than $\bar{u}_2$); if the fund manager gets it wrong, the client is worse off. With the same proportions of the market portfolio and the riskless asset as in $P_3$, the equivalent portfolio on $CML$ is $P_1$, which leaves the client with lower utility than at $P_2$ ($\bar{u}_1$ is a lower indifference curve than $\bar{u}_2$).

**Figure 14.10** Market timing

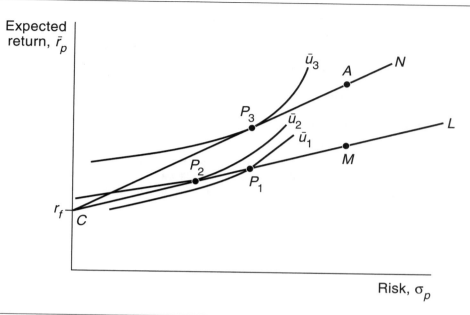

Market timing is equivalent to adjusting the beta of the portfolio over time. If the fund manager is expecting a bull market, he wants to increase the beta of the portfolio (i.e. make it more aggressive). If he is expecting a bear market, he wants to reduce the beta of the portfolio (i.e. make it more defensive). One way of doing this would be to switch into high-beta shares in a bull market and switch out of them in a bear market. However, the transaction costs involved would make this an expensive strategy. An alternative is to keep the portfolio of risky assets (in this case, $A$) constant and raise or lower beta by lowering or raising the proportion of the client's portfolio held in cash. This can be a cheaper alternative, since moving into or out of cash is generally cheaper than moving between different shares. An even cheaper alternative is to use futures or options, and this is examined in Chapter 16.

### Portfolio adjustment

Portfolio adjustment involves the purchase and sale of securities. The objective is to increase the net utility of the client after adjusting for transaction costs. This objective can be expressed in another way: to increase the risk-adjusted return on the portfolio after adjusting for transaction costs.

The net utility function is given by:

$$\bar{u}_n = \bar{r}_p - \frac{\sigma_p^2}{R_T} - c_p,$$

(14.23)

where:

$$\bar{u}_n = \text{net utility;}$$

$$\bar{r}_p = \sum_{i=1}^{N} \theta_i \bar{r}_i = \text{expected return on the portfolio;}$$

$$\sigma_p^2 = \sum_{i}^{N} \sum_{j}^{N} \theta_i \theta_j \sigma_{ij} = \text{variance of the return on the portfolio;}$$

$$R_T = \text{degree of risk tolerance;}$$

$$c_p = \text{costs of adjusting the portfolio.}$$

The costs of adjusting the portfolio will include brokerage commissions, market-makers' spreads and taxes.

The optimal set of adjustments involves *switches* (or *swaps*) between pairs of securities, such that a security with a low marginal net utility is sold and replaced by a security with a higher marginal net utility, where marginal net utility is defined as the change to total utility as an additional unit of a security is bought or sold:

$$\begin{aligned}
\text{Marginal net utility} &= \frac{\partial \bar{u}_n}{\partial \theta_i} \\
&= \frac{\partial \bar{r}_p}{\partial \theta_i} - \frac{1}{R_T} \cdot \frac{\partial \sigma_p^2}{\partial \theta_i} - \frac{\partial c_p}{\partial \theta_i} \\
&= \bar{r}_i - \frac{2}{R_T} \sum_{j=1}^{N} \theta_j \sigma_{ij} - \tau_i,
\end{aligned} \tag{14.24}$$

where $\tau_i$ is the marginal cost associated with trading in the $i$th security. By replacing low marginal net utility securities with high marginal net utility securities, the total net utility of the client increases. When there are no further switches available that lead to low marginal net utility securities being replaced with high marginal net securities, the portfolio has been reoptimized and the switching process stops.

The portfolio adjustment procedure expressed in terms of risk and transaction-cost-adjusted returns is as follows. We can define the net excess return to beta (NERB) as:

$$\text{Net excess return to beta} = \frac{\bar{r}_i - r_f - \tau_i}{\beta_i}. \tag{14.25}$$

The fund manager eliminates from the client's portfolio all securities with NERBs less than $c^*$, the optimal cut-off rate, and replaces them with securities with NERBs greater than $c^*$. Once this has been achieved, the switching process stops and the portfolio has been reoptimized.

One practical method of portfolio adjustment is known as *portfolio trading*. This involves the sale by tender of a large portfolio of shares by an institutional investor. But the potential buyers of the portfolio, generally brokers, do *not* know beforehand the exact composition of the portfolio. They will only be told the current market value of the portfolio and its general characteristics (e.g., the NMS bands of the shares), and they have to make bids on this basis. The composition of the portfolio is kept secret in order to prevent unfavourable share price movements before the portfolio is sold. However, this means that the buyer faces *integrity risk*, the risk that the portfolio contains a number of unmarketable shares. The advantage of portfolio trading to the seller is that the transaction costs involved are quite low, about 0.25 per cent compared with about 1 per cent for more conventional means of unloading shares. In addition, the seller avoids the *execution risks* present when a large portfolio of shares is liquidated over a period of time.

## 14.4.2 Active treasury portfolio management

Portfolios of money market securities are held mainly for liquidity purposes. But there is no reason why they cannot be managed effectively.

Passive management generates very poor returns on capital, as the following example illustrates. Suppose that a bank borrows £1 million for one year at 10.125 per cent and invests it in a one-year certificate of deposit yielding 10.25 per cent. At the end of the year, the bank receives £1,102,500, pays out £1,101,250 and makes a profit of £1250. If the FSA requires that every £40 of loan is supported by £1 of capital, this means that the £1 million loan has to be supported by £25,000 of capital. This gives a rate of return on capital of only 5 per cent (i.e. (£1,250/£25,000) × 100). So the passive strategy of matching assets and liabilities is not very profitable.

Active treasury portfolio management involves a mismatching between assets and liabilities, and also involves a view of the future movement in short-term interest rates. If the treasury manager believes that short-term interest rates are going to rise, he will want the maturity of his liabilities to exceed that of his assets (this is called *positive gapping*), if he believes that interest rates are going to fall, he will want the maturity of his assets to exceed that of his liabilities (this is called *negative gapping*).

To illustrate, we can consider the case where interest rates are expected to rise. The treasury manager borrows £1 million for three months at 10.125 per cent and invests in a one-month CD at 10.25 per cent. At the end of the month, interest rates have risen by 1.5 per cent and he invests in a two-month CD at 11.75 per cent. At the end of three months the loan is repaid. The overall profit is calculated as follows. At the end of three months, the proceeds from the CD are worth:

$$£1,000,000[1+0.1025(30/365)][1+0.1175(61/365)] = £1,028,227.08.$$

The repayment on the loan totals:

$$£1,000,000[1+0.10125(91/365)] = £1,025,243.15.$$

Therefore the profit is £2983.93. On a capital investment of £25,000, this corresponds to a return of 11.94 per cent over three months, or 56.99 per cent over a year. This is a marked improvement on the 5 per cent rate of return from the passive strategy.

Of course, had interest rates fallen rather than risen, the treasury manager could have made a loss. For example, suppose that in the last example interest rates had fallen by 2 per cent. The proceeds from the CD would then be:

$$£1,000,000[1+0.1025(30/365)][1+0.0825(61/365)] = £1,022,328.49,$$

and therefore a loss of £2914.66 would be made. This is equivalent to a loss rate of 11.66 per cent over three months, or 55.44 per cent per year.

We can illustrate the case where interest rates are expected to fall. In this case, the treasury manager wants the maturity of his assets to exceed that of his liabilities. Suppose he buys a three-month CD for £1 million at 10.25 per cent which is financed by a one-month loan at 10.125 per cent. After a month, the loan has to be refinanced, but interest rates have fallen by 1 per cent, so the treasury manager closes the gap by taking out a two-month loan at 9.125 per cent. At the end of three months, the proceeds from the CD are worth:

$$£1,000,000[1+0.1025(91/365)] = £1,025,554.80,$$

and the repayment on the loan totals:

$$£1,000,000\,[1+0.10125(30/365)]\,[1+0.09125(61/365)] \;=\; £1,023,698.83,$$

giving a profit of £1855.97. On the capital investment of £25,000, this corresponds to a return of 7.42 per cent over three months, or 33.17 per cent per year.

An alternative to this would have been to have sold the CD after one month. Suppose that the yield on the CD has fallen to 9.25 per cent at the end of one month. The CD, which has two months to maturity, would be worth its maturity value £1,025,554.80 discounted for two months at 9.25 per cent:

$$£1,025,554.80/\,[1+0.0925(61/365)] \;=\; £1,009,942.20.$$

The repayment of the loan costs:

$$£1,000,000\,[1+0.10125(30/365)] \;=\; £1,008,321.92.$$

The profit is therefore £1620.28, corresponding to a rate of return of 6.48 per cent over one month or 112.46 per cent per year. Clearly, the second alternative is more profitable.

### 14.4.3   Active bond portfolio management and adjustment

**Portfolio management**

As with shares, a bond portfolio will be actively managed whenever there are misvalued bonds around, or when there are heterogeneous expectations about the risks and returns on bonds, so that there is no consensus of the market portfolio for bonds. Similarly, with the asset allocation decision having been made, active bond portfolio management operates around the activities of security selection and market timing. However, there is a difference between share and bond portfolio managers. Most share managers engage in security selection, whereas most bond managers engage in market timing.

A *bond picker* will construct portfolios of bonds that, in comparison with the market portfolio, have less than proportionate weightings in the overpriced bonds (since they are expected to fall in price) and more than proportionate weightings in the underpriced bonds (since they are expected to rise in price). In other words, the portfolio has relatively low weightings in negative-alpha bonds and relatively high weightings in positive-alpha bonds (see (14.16)), where alpha is defined with respect to the bond market line (see Figure 14.11). For example, suppose that $\bar{r}_m = 0.12$ (12 per cent) and $r_f = 0.10$ (10 per cent); then the equation for the bond market line is:

$$\begin{aligned} \bar{r}_i^* &= r_f + (\bar{r}_m - r_f)D_i/D_m \\ &= 0.10 + (0.02)D_i/D_m, \end{aligned}$$

where:

$$\begin{aligned} \bar{r}_i^* &= \text{equilibrium expected return on the } i\text{th bond;} \\ D_i/D_m &= \text{relative duration of the } i\text{th bond.} \end{aligned}$$

**Figure 14.11** Alpha values for bonds

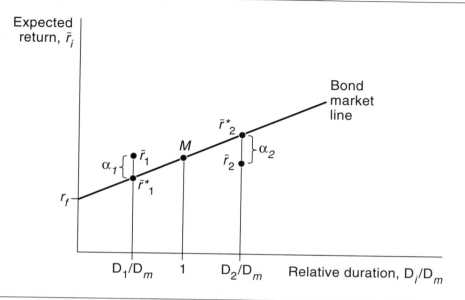

If, for bond 1, $D_1/D_m = 0.5$, then $\bar{r}_1^* = 0.11$ (11 per cent). If $\bar{r}_1 = 0.12$ (12 per cent), then $\alpha_1 = 0.01$ (i.e. 1 per cent). The bond offers a 1 per cent higher return than it should have and is therefore underpriced.

Again, the active bond portfolio can be viewed as a combination of the market portfolio and a set of side bets against other active managers, as in (14.18) above. The determination of the optimal active bond portfolio can be determined using the procedure of Elton and Gruber (1978), with the exception that bonds are ranked according to *excess returns to relative duration*, $(\bar{r}_i - r_f)/(D_i/D_m)$. Similarly, the cut-off point for the optimal portfolio is determined using (14.20) with relative duration replacing beta. The optimal proportions are found using (14.21) and (14.22), again with relative duration replacing beta.

A market timer engages in active management when he does not accept the consensus market portfolio, and is either more bullish or more bearish than the market. Expectations of interest rate changes are therefore a crucial input into successful market timing. A bond market timer is interested in adjusting the relative duration of his portfolio over time. (Market timing with bonds is sometimes called *duration switching* or *rate anticipation switching*.) If the fund manager is expecting a bull market because he is expecting a fall in the general level of interest rates, he wants to increase the duration of his portfolio, by replacing low-duration bonds with high-duration bonds. If the fund manager is expecting a bear market because he is expecting a rise in the general level of interest rates, he wants to reduce the duration of his portfolio, by replacing high-duration bonds with low-duration bonds.

Active bond portfolio management is generally not as profitable as active share portfolio management. There are several reasons for this. First, there are more shares traded than bonds in the UK. The most liquid bonds are UK government bonds, and then only at certain maturities. Because of active trading in these bonds, they are less likely to be mispriced. In addition, the volatility of bond prices is generally much less than that of share prices, so the opportunities for substantial mispricing of bonds are in any case much less than for shares. Further, with only a few bonds suitable for active trading, the portfolio consisting of those bonds will be relatively undiversified and therefore relatively risky, thereby reducing the risk-adjusted excess returns from active trading. The costs of active bond portfolio management can be reduced by using futures and options, and this is examined in Chapter 16.

**Portfolio adjustment**

Bond portfolio adjustment involves the purchase and sale of bonds, i.e. the *switching* or *swapping* of bonds.

There are two main classes of bond switches: anomaly switches and policy switches. An *anomaly switch* is a switch between two bonds with very *similar* characteristics but whose prices (or yields) are out of line with each other. A *policy switch* is a switch between two *dissimilar* bonds because of an anticipated change in the structure of the market (e.g. quality ratings are expected to change), which is expected to lead to a change in the relative prices (or yields) of the two bonds. Policy switches involve greater expected returns, but also greater potential risks than anomaly switches.

The simplest example of an anomaly switch is a *substitution switch*. This involves the exchange of two bonds which are similar in terms of maturity, coupon and quality rating and every other characteristic, but which differ in terms of price (or yield). Since two similar bonds should trade at the same price and yield, then whenever a price (or yield) difference occurs, an arbitrage opportunity emerges. The 'dear' bond is sold and the 'cheap' bond is purchased. Later, if and when the anomaly has been eliminated, the reverse set of transactions is made in order to lock in the profit. The time taken for the elimination of the anomaly is known as the *workout period*. The workout period is important for calculating the rate of return on the switch. The shorter the workout period, the greater the annualized rate of return. If the two bonds have to be held until maturity before the anomaly is corrected, the annualized return from the swap may be negligible.

The following example illustrates a typical substitution switch:

|        | *Date 1* | | | *Date 2* | | | *Profit* | |
|--------|----------|-----------|--------------|----------|-----------|--------------|--------------|--------------|
|        | *Action* | *Price (£)* | *Yield (%)* | *Action* | *Price (£)* | *Yield (%)* | *Price (£)* | *Yield (%)* |
| Bond A | Sell | 100 | 10.00 | Buy  | 100 | 10.00 | 0 | 0.00 |
| Bond B | Buy  | 99  | 10.20 | Sell | 100 | 10.00 | 1 | 0.20 |
|        |      |     |       |      |     |       | 1 | 0.20 |

If, historically, the difference between the clean prices of A and B has never been more than £0.50 and the difference between the yields to maturity has never been more than 0.10 per cent (i.e. 10 basis points), then clearly, at date 1 an anomaly exists and so a substitution switch is made. The cheaper bond B is purchased and the dearer bond A is sold. By date 2 the anomaly has been eliminated. Bond A was correctly priced and its price has not changed between the two dates. Bond B was underpriced and its price rises by £1, while its yield falls by 20 basis points. If dates 1 and 2 are a year apart, the rate of return on capital employed of £100 is only 1 per cent. However, if the two dates are one month apart, the annualized rate of return is 12.68 per cent.

If the coupon and maturity of the two bonds are similar, then a substitution swap involves a one-for-one exchange of bonds. However, if there are substantial differences in coupon or maturity, then the duration of the two bonds will differ. This will lead to different responses if the general level of interest rates changes during the life of the switch. It will therefore be necessary to weight the switch in such a way that it is hedged from changes in the level of interest rates but is still exposed to changes in the anomalous yield differential between the bonds.

To illustrate, suppose that bond A in the last example has a duration of ten years, while bond B has a duration of two years. This means that bond A is five times more responsive to interest rate fluctuations than bond B. To protect against unanticipated shifts in interest rates, the relative investment in the two bonds is determined as follows:

$$\frac{\text{Investment in bond A}}{\text{Investment in bond B}} = \frac{\text{Duration of bond B}}{\text{Duration of bond A}}.$$

Expressing this in terms of nominal amounts:

$$
\begin{aligned}
\text{Nominal of bond B bought} \;=\; & \text{Nominal of bond A sold} \\
& \times \frac{\text{Duration of bond A} \times \text{Dirty price of bond A}}{\text{Duration of bond B} \times \text{Dirty price of bond B}} \\
\approx\; & 5 \times \text{Nominal of bond A sold}.
\end{aligned}
$$

So for every bond A sold, five of bond B have to be bought. Consider what would happen if there was a one-for-one exchange and interest rates fell by 1 per cent. The price of bond A would rise by 10 per cent (i.e. by 1 per cent *times* its duration of 10), from £100 to £110. The price of bond B would rise by 2 per cent (i.e. by 1 per cent *times* its duration of 2), from £100 to £102. Suppose also that the price of B rose by another £1 to £103 to correct the anomaly. So although the relative mispricing has been corrected, the substitution switch has made a loss of £7. Similarly, differences in coupon rates between the two bonds will affect the profitability of the switch, and this has to be taken into account.

Another type of anomaly switch is a *pure yield pickup switch*. This simply involves the sale of a bond with a given yield to maturity and the purchase of a similar bond with a higher yield to maturity. With this switch, there is no expectation of any yield or price correction, so no reverse transactions take place at a later date.

Policy switches are designed to take advantage of an anticipated change. The change could be (1) a shift in interest rates, (2) a change in the structure of the yield curve, (3) a change in a bond's quality rating, or (4) a change in sector relationships.

A shift in interest rates is exactly what a market timer is looking out for. So switching from low-duration to high-duration bonds, if interest rates are expected to fall, is an example of a policy switch. (As we have seen, it is also known as a *duration switch* or *rate anticipation switch*.)

The other changes listed above lead to what are known as *intermarket* (or *intersector*) *spread switches*. Some examples can be given.

Normally the yield curve is a smooth relationship between yield and maturity. But occasionally there may be humps or dips in the curve, as in Figure 14.12. If the humps and dips are expected to disappear, then the prices of bonds (e.g. bond A) on the hump can be expected to rise (their yields will fall) and the prices of bonds (e.g. bond B) in the dip can be expected to fall (their yields will rise). So one example of a switch is the purchase of bond A and the sale of bond B.

A bond whose quality rating is expected to fall will fall in price. To prevent a capital loss, it can be switched for a bond whose quality rating is expected to rise or to remain unchanged. This is the principle underlying *credit spread* (or *relative valuation*) *trading*. The credit spread (above a

**Figure 14.12** Bond switching

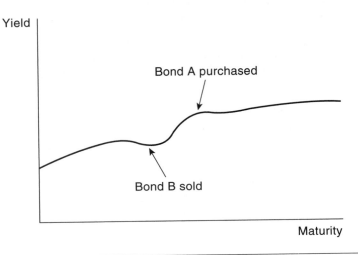

benchmark index based on, say, government bonds or LIBOR) is a measure of the market's assessment of the borrower's ability to repay the interest and principal on the bond. It is possible to hedge the interest rate risk in a corporate bond and leave the bond holder exposed to the credit spread. One way of doing this is via an asset swap in which the trader funds the purchase of the bond at LIBOR, pays over the fixed coupon on the bond to a swap bank and receives from the swap bank LIBOR *plus* the credit spread of, say, 25 basis points: so long as the corporate keeps making the coupon payments on the bond, the trader receives the credit spread for a zero net cost investment. Furthermore, as a result of inefficiencies in the market, similar credits can trade at different spreads: for instance, more liquid issues will trade at finer spreads. As an illustration of how to exploit such inefficiencies, it might be possible for a trader to sell an FRN at LIBOR *minus* 15 basis points and buy a fixed coupon bond which is swapped at LIBOR flat, so that the trader takes out the spread of 15 basis points.

An example of a change in sector relationships is a change in taxes between two sectors. For instance, one sector (e.g. the domestic bond sector) might have withholding taxes on coupon payments, whereas another (e.g. the eurobond sector) might not. If it is anticipated that withholding tax will either be applied to all sectors or will be withdrawn from all sectors, then another switch is possible.

As a final example of a policy switch, we can consider a *bridge swap*. This is demonstrated in Figure 14.13, which shows a one-year horizon rolling yield curve. The eight- and ten-year bonds are selling at lower yields and higher prices than the nine-year bond. A bridge swap involves selling the eight- and ten-year bonds and buying the nine-year bond, thereby selling bonds with an average yield of $r_A$ and buying bonds with an average yield of $r_B$. The bridge swap gain is therefore $(r_B - r_A)$.

## 14.5   Mixed active–passive portfolio management

We have considered pure passive and pure active strategies, but it is possible for fund managers to use mixtures of the two. For example, the asset allocation decision can be passive, with active side bets being placed against other managers. This is known as a *security-selection style* of management.

**Figure 14.13** Bridge swap

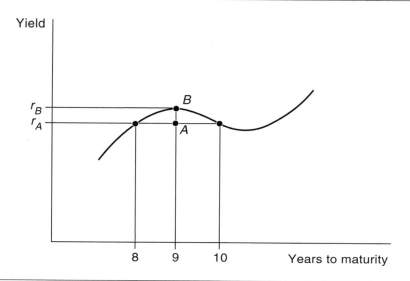

Alternatively, the fund manager might construct passive portfolios of individual securities, but make active asset allocation decisions. This is known as an *asset-allocation style* of management.

Another mixed strategy is *core-satellite* portfolio management. This is a management strategy pursued by very large funds. The fund manager has a large *core portfolio* that is never traded, because doing so would result in adverse market movements. But surrounding the core portfolio is a number of smaller *satellite portfolios*. The satellite portfolios are actively managed and even have the ability to take short positions, because they can borrow securities from the core portfolio; i.e., they can go short against the core (see Figure 14.14).

With bond portfolios, an example of a mixed strategy is *contingent immunization*. The fund manager begins with an active strategy, and continues in this mode until the end of the investment horizon or until the return on the active strategy falls below a threshold level, at which point the bond portfolio is immunized for the remainder of the investment horizon. Another example is when a bond fund manager engages in security selection or market timing within an otherwise immunized portfolio. For instance, the manager might construct an immunized portfolio from underpriced bonds; or he might establish a negative net duration position (i.e., where the duration of the bonds is less than the duration of the liabilities) if he believed interest rates were going to rise.

Another type of mixed active-passive strategy involves options and futures. With one version of this strategy, fund managers have passive portfolios of cash market securities. The portfolio is not traded because of the high transaction costs of trading in the cash market. Instead, the fund managers trade a view on individual securities by buying or selling individual stock options. Similarly, they can engage in market timing and shift the beta of their share portfolio or the duration of their bond portfolio buy buying or selling stock index or gilt options and futures. This is because transaction costs are low (at least for institutional investors) and liquidity is generally high in the markets for derivatives.

With another version of this strategy, what are called *equitized cash portfolios* (or *synthetic equity index funds*) are constructed. The entire value of the portfolio is held passively in money market

**Figure 14.14** Core–satellite portfolios

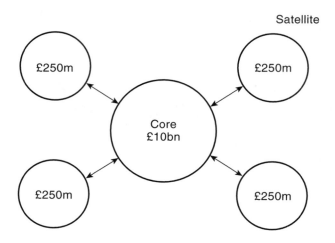

instruments. The active part of the strategy is performed entirely using stock index futures. Yet another version is known as a *90-10 portfolio* (or sometimes a *guaranteed equity bond* or a *capital-protected fund*). In this case, 90 per cent of the portfolio is held in cash and 10 per cent in call options. With money market interest rates at around 10 per cent, the strategy locks in the initial value of the portfolio (since £90(1 + 0.1) ≈ £100), but gains by the intrinsic value of the options if they expire in-the-money.

There are variations on this. For example Kleinwort Benson's *Investor's Deposit Account* keeps the capital sum intact but invests the interest in stock index options on the FTSE 100 index. With deposit rates at 4 per cent, Kleinwort Benson estimate that investors get about half the rise in the FTSE 100 index if they invest for 3 months, 80 per cent of the rise if they invest for 6 months and 120 per cent of the rise if they invest for one year. Another example is Swiss Bank Corporation's *guaranteed return-on-investment* (GROI) units. These involve a money market investment, a purchased call on a stock index (the first GROIs were on the Swiss Market Index) at a low exercise price and a written call on the stock index at a high exercise price. GROIs provide a guaranteed capital return together with the possibility of participating in the performance of the stock market up to a limit implied by the written call. SBC also offer *protected index participation* (PIP) units which are in effect uncapped GROIs, i.e. do not involve the written call.

## 14.6   Investment management styles

The real world of fund management differs somewhat from the stylized analysis outlined above. In this section, we examine the different styles of investment management actually pursued by different fund managers. These styles can be broadly classified into two types: traditional and quantitative. The different styles lead to different *investment strategies*, i.e. systematic trading rules pursued by active managers. We also examine the most important of these.

## 14.6.1 Traditional investment management

*Traditional investment management* relies on the subjective feelings of the fund manager. Traditional active fund managers follow one of two types of investment strategy: continuation strategies and contrarian strategies.

*Continuation* (or *momentum* or *relative strength*) *strategies* are based on the belief that a rise in a particular security price will be followed by another rise (and similarly with price falls) and that this relationship can be exploited by investors. In other words, there is a momentum to security prices over time which leads to a *positive serial correlation* in security price movements. The most important continuation strategy is the pursuit of *winner* or *glamour stocks*, securities which have done well in the recent past and are expected to do well in the future; similarly *loser* or *out-of-favour stocks* with recent poor performance are sold. Another example is based on *earnings underreaction*, a belief that the market initially underreacts to earnings announcements, thereby inducing earnings-based continuations.

*Contrarian* (or *reversal*) *strategies* are based on the belief that the market initially overreacts to news and other information, so that price rises will be followed by subsequent price falls (and vice versa) implying that there is a *negative serial correlation* (also known as *mean reversion*) in share price movements. Contrarian strategies, by definition, run counter to the prevailing mood (or herd instinct) of the market. They involve buying securities when prices are still falling and selling them when prices are still rising, and this can be an uncomfortable experience to have to go through. Contrarian strategies are so-called because they are contrary to the strategies pursued by naive investors simply following the herd. *Naive strategies*, in the view of contrarians, result from extrapolating good past earnings growth too far into the future, or assuming an excessive upward trend in a share price, or merely assuming that a well-run company must be a good investment regardless of the current share price. As a consequence, naive investors invest heavily in glamour stocks which soon become overpriced with respect to fundamental value and disinvest equally heavily in out-of-favour stocks which soon become underpriced with respect to fundamental value. Contrarians believe strongly that this mispricing will be corrected rapidly. The main contrarian strategies are value strategies and tactical asset allocation strategies.

*Value strategies* involve the purchase of securities that have low market prices relative to some measure of fundamental value such as earnings, dividends, historical prices or book values; such securities are called *value stocks*. A typical value strategy might be to buy shares with market-to-book ratios (also called *bargain ratios*) below unity and to sell shares with market-to-book ratios above unity. The positions are unwound when the bargain ratios have returned to unity. One of the simplest value strategies is as follows: buy shares when their dividend yield rises above 6 per cent and sell shares when their dividend yield falls below 4 per cent. This strategy is based on the observation that the average yield on UK shares for most of this century has been about 5 per cent per annum, and that rarely do yields rise above 6 per cent or fall below 4 per cent. Share prices are therefore historically very low when yields are at 6 per cent and historically very high when yields are at 4 per cent. Another simple strategy is: sell shares and buy bonds when the *yield gap* rises above 5 per cent, and sell bonds and buy shares when the yield gap falls below 3 per cent (the yield gap is the difference between the current yield on long-dated bonds and the dividend yield on a share index such as the FTSE-A All Share Index). This strategy is based on the observation that the average yield gap in the UK over the post-war period has been 4 per cent and that rarely does the yield gap rise above 5 per cent or fall below 3 per cent. Share prices are therefore historically very high relative to bond prices when the yield gap is 5 per cent and historically very low when the yield gap is 3 per cent.

*Tactical asset allocation* (TAA), as we have seen, is an investment strategy that makes tactical adjustments to the long-run or strategic asset mix in response to anticipated changes in market conditions. In particular, it exploits the belief that there is positive serial correlation in price movements in the short run but mean reversion in the medium run. This implies that there can be a global *strategic asset allocation*, i.e., an optimal long-run mix of shares and bonds across different countries, based on economic fundamentals, combined with a TAA that embodies short term momentum strategies and medium term contrarian strategies. TAA strategies will involve investment in countries whose recent price performance was negative and disinvest from countries with recent positive price performance; momentum indicators are used to indicate when to invest and disinvest. If TAA strategies are successful, the distribution of returns generated by such strategies will be positively skewed.

**Figure 14.15** Continuation and contrarian signals for US shares

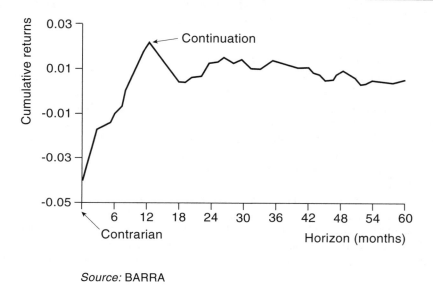

*Source:* BARRA

There are other investment strategies based on picking high growth or high yielding shares. All of the strategies are inconsistent with the efficient markets hypothesis, but they are predicated on the belief that investors can be susceptible to varying degrees of irrational behaviour, such as trying to discern patterns in historical security price movements and using these to predict future price movements. But if sufficient numbers of people are behaving in this way, it becomes sensible to join the herd, so long as you believe you can predict what the herd is going to predict from a given set of share price movements better and faster than they can. In short, it becomes rational to be irrational.

A number of fund management companies have been established to follow continuation and contrarian investment strategies, such as Barra (named after its academic founder Bar Rosenberg) and LSV Asset Management (also named after its academic founders Professors Lakonishok, Shleifer and Vishny). Barra, for example, has identified some very simple continuation and contrarian signals such as those identified in Figure 14.15 (the figure identifies the signals for US shares, but very similar patterns emerge for the UK, Japan and Australia). The figure depicts the relationship between cumulative returns over different horizons varying from one month to 60 months. For the one-month horizon, the figure shows the relationship between the return over the previous month to the return in the subsequent month. The relationship is negative, indicating that, on average, shares that performed well one month will perform badly the next month: this provides a signal for a contrarian investment strategy. For the twelve-month horizon, the figure shows the relationship between the cumulative return over the previous 12 months to the return in the subsequent month. The relationship is positive, indicating that, on average, shares that performed well over the previous 12 months will continue to perform well in the subsequent month: this provides a signal for a continuation investment strategy. Barra does recognize, however, that once news of a successful investment strategy gets out and is adopted by the herd, it soon becomes valueless.

## 14.6.2 Quantitative investment management

*Quantitative* (or *quant*) *investment management* is the term given to a style of portfolio management that is based solely on objective criteria, rather than on the subjective feelings of the fund manager. There are three main types: indexation, rocket science and value-based quant.

*Indexation* (as we saw above in section 14.3.1) is a passive portfolio management strategy in which an index manager builds a portfolio that replicates the performance of a particular market index. This was the first type of quant management, beginning in the US in the early 1980s, and it was the first time that extensive use was made of computers to construct portfolios in a way that maximized returns by keeping portfolio switches and costs to a minimum.

The other types of quant management involve active strategies. *Rocket science* began in the mid 1980s when US investment banks began to use mathematicians and physicists to develop option pricing models. Later their services were employed to design computer forecasting models that used sophisticated maths (such as chaos theory and neural networks (see Chapter 18)) to predict share price movements. The predictions cover a very short time horizon, typically no more than a few days ahead and are not based on any notion of fundamental value. In other words, rocket science is a highly mathematical version of technical analysis.

The most recent innovation is *value-based quant*. The objective here is to increase portfolio returns by changing the asset allocation or the stock selection in response to a perceived over- or undervaluation of a particular market or security. One example is tactical asset allocation (TAA). Suppose that it is believed that the UK stock market is overvalued relative to the US. A value-based quant would sell UK stock index futures contracts and buy US stock index futures to take advantage of this relative misvaluation. The assessment about whether a market is over- or undervalued is based on an econometric forecasting model involving the factors believed to influence the behaviour of the particular market, such as nominal and real dividend yields, trade flows and liquidity conditions. In order to be included in the forecasting model, the factors must satisfy a clearly defined and objective set of rules. For example, the factors must behave in an economically sensible manner and their relationship to subsequent future returns must be highly statistically significant (in other words have good predictive power). A high dividend yield, for instance, implies that a market is undervalued and so should be associated with subsequent above-average performance. If this is the case, the dividend yield will be included as a factor in the model. Another example of value-based quant is a stock selection technique called *advanced active* which involves the construction of *tilt portfolios*. Large numbers of shares are analyzed in terms of about 20 factors such as price earnings ratios, market-to-book, dividend yield, price to sales and operating profits to sales. The idea is to identify inefficiencies that can be exploited to generate market outperformance. For instance, it might be discovered that high-yield shares tend to outperform low-yield shares. Hence the portfolio would be tilted towards high-yield shares. It is essential to have large numbers of shares in the portfolio, because the portfolios are designed to generate outperformance by aggregating over large numbers of small gains, while keeping diversifiable risk to a minimum.

Value-based quants will always base their portfolio decisions on the predictions from their models and will update their models each time they make a forecast. This contrasts with traditional fund managers who, while also examining the same market information as the quants, have the power to override the analysis. Quants argue that this override is too often based on emotion, e.g. overconfidence during a boom or fear during a slump. Also traditional managers, because they do not analyze all the information available objectively, have to decide on a subjective basis which information to use and what weight this information is given. They therefore risk giving excessive weight to irrelevant information and inadequate weight to information with strong predictive power. They will also tend to place excessive weight on factors which happen to be currently the most fashionable in the market.

## 14.7   Recent innovations: hedge funds and bear funds

It has been said that if the world's financial markets are viewed as a global casino, then *hedge funds* are the biggest gamblers in town. Hedge funds have nothing to do with hedging risks; instead they make massive highly geared speculative bets worth billions of dollars on movements in the world's interest rates, exchange rates and share prices. They are formed either as off-shore companies or private investment partnerships which because they have fewer than 100 partners do not have to disclose their activities. Investors in hedge funds typically have to have net worth of at least $1m and invest between $250,000 and $10m in their funds. The managers of the funds take a fee of 1 per cent of the fund value and between 15 and 25 per cent of profits. Investors can withdraw only after the first year and thereafter only once every quarter. The investors' capital is deposited with a bank and used as collateral for an overdraft of between 10 and 100 times the capital deposited. The overdraft is then used to finance positions in derivatives markets, especially in futures contracts. This implies that there is gearing on top of gearing since futures contracts are already heavily geared. For example, with the margin on gilt futures at 2 per cent, each £1 of hedge fund capital when magnified by both the overdraft and the futures margining, could buy between £500 and £5000 nominal of gilt futures contracts. If bond prices rise, a huge profit accrues to hedge fund investors. On the other hand, if bond prices fall, the hedge fund has to find extra capital to finance the margin calls or to unwind its position at a loss by selling futures contracts.

Some observers have argued that the actions of hedge funds in selling futures contracts when the price of the underlying security is already falling can lead to further downward pressure on security prices and hence help to destabilize financial markets on a global basis. This has certainly caused concern amongst the world's financial regulators, especially the central banks who are responsible for preventing a systemic collapse of the banking system. Hedge funds have been blamed for the collapse of the European Exchange Rate Mechanism in September 1992, the fall in global bond prices in February 1994 following the hike in interest rates by the US Federal Reserve, and the collapse in the Far Eastern stock markets in October 1997. Regulators have been unable to design mechanisms to prevent this increase in the volatility of financial markets.

It has been estimated that at the end of 1993, there were about 800 hedge funds with capital of about $75bn (£50bn). They began to take off after the 1987 crash. The ten largest funds in 1993 are listed in Table 14.2. The largest is the Quantum Fund run by George Soros, the man reputed to have made $1bn from selling sterling short and causing its exit from the ERM in 1992. Soros started the Soros Fund in 1973 with $4.8m, changing its name to the Quantum Fund in 1979. He claims to have

**Table 14.2** Top ten hedge funds in 1993

| Principal(s) | Fund name | Assets under management ($bn) | Gross returns (%) | Estimated fee income ($m) |
|---|---|---|---|---|
| Grorge Soros | Quantum | 11.0 | 67 | 625 |
| Julian Robertson | Tiger | 7.0 | 68 | 525 |
| Michael Steinhardt | Steinhardt Partners | 4.8 | 57 | 300 |
| Bruce Kovner | Caxton | 2.5 | 45 | 250 |
| Leon Levy & Jack Nash | Odyssey Partners | 2.8 | 40 | 184 |
| Louis Bacon | Moore Capital | 1.9 | 46 | 166 |
| Leon Cooperman | Omega Partners | 2.0 | 68 | 100 |
| Philip Hempleman | Ardsley Partners | 3.2 | 32 | 86 |
| John Henry | John W Henry | 1.1 | 36 | 72 |
| Jeffrey Susskind & Mark Strome | Strome-Susskind | 0.8 | 143 | 40 |

earned investors an annual return of 35 per cent since 1973. However, things have not always gone Soros' way. On 14 February 1994, the Quantum Fund lost $600m on a bet that the yen would fall against the dollar, whereas it rose instead; this loss has been dubbed the St Valentine's Day Massacre! An even bigger disaster occurred in 1998 when Long Term Capital Management, a hedge fund founded by John Meriwether of *Liar's Poker* fame (Lewis (1989)) and with two Nobel prize winners (Myron Scholes and Robert Merton) on the board of directors, had to be saved from insolvency following the collapse of the Russian stock market. LTCM had taken out a huge bet that the spread between US Treasury bonds and US corporate bonds would narrow. It had purchased $120bn of US corporate bonds financed by the short sale of an equivalent amount of US Treasury bonds (using the repo market) in the expectation that the corporate bonds would rise in value relative to the Treasury bonds. The bet was backed by just $2.3bn in shareholders' funds. But the crisis in Russia led to a global 'flight to quality' with Treasury bonds rising sharply in value and corporate bonds falling in value. The huge bet had gone terribly wrong and LTCM had to be rescued by Merrill Lynch, Goldman Sachs, J.P. Morgan and other leading investment banks.

Another recent innovation is *bear funds*. These are funds that speculate only on falling markets because when markets do fall, they fall very rapidly (in contrast, bull markets tend to rise much more slowly). The first major bear funds were Japanese bear funds which bet on falls in the Nikkei index. Examples are the Govett MIS Japanese Bear Fund (which was launched in 1991) and the Mercury WT Japanese Equity Bear Fund. A variation is *bear tracker funds* which track falls in a stock market index: the cash investment in such a fund is used to maintain short positions in stock index futures contracts. An example is the fund operated by AIB Govett Asset Management which tracks falls in the FTSE 100 index. Bear funds differ from hedge funds because they tend not to be so heavily geared.

# Appendix: Investment-objectives questionnaire

1 *How would you describe your outlook for the economy over the next 5 years?*

a) Very positive.                    d) Somewhat negative.

b) Somewhat positive.                e) Very negative.

c) Neither positive nor negative.    f) I am undecided.

2 *How do you feel about investigating in common stocks in general?*

a) I think stocks are very attractive and should occupy a dominant position in our portfolio.

b) Common stocks should have a place in our investment portfolio.

c) I think stocks are relatively risky and their use should be limited.

d) I think stocks should be used very sparingly, if at all.

3 *How would you generally categorize your investment objectives?*

a) Growth — maximum growth of capital with little or no income considerations.

b) Growth with income — primary emphasis on capital growth of the fund with some focus on income.

c) Income.

4 *Does the portfolio have current income objectives (interest plus dividends)?*

a) No income objective.

b) 3%

c) 4%

d) 5%

e) 6%

f) 7%

g) Other. If other please describe.

5 *Some plans have a need for growing investment 'income' (i.e. dividends and interest) over time. Do the plan's assets have a need for growth in 'income'?* (Yes/No.)

6 *If your investment manager is very positive on the outlook for common stocks, what is the maximum percentage of your portfolio you would allow to be invested in common stocks?*

a) 0%

b) 20%

c) 40%

d) 60%

e) 80%

f) 100%

*In bonds?*

a) 0%

b) 20%

c) 40%

d) 60%

e) 80%

f) 100%

7 *If your investment manager is very negative on the outlook for common stocks, what is the minimum percentage of your portfolio you would allow to be invested in common stocks?*

    a)   0%
    b)   20%
    c)   40%
    d)   60%
    e)   80%
    f)   100%

*In bonds?*

    a)   0%
    b)   20%
    c)   40%
    d)   60%
    e)   80%
    f)   100%

8 *What average annual 'absolute' rate of return (as opposed to return 'relative' to a market index) do you consider to be the investment objective for a fund, on a long-term basis?*

    a)   12–14% p.a.
    b)   10–11.9% p.a.
    c)   8–9.9% p.a.
    d)   6–7.9% p.a.
    e)   Other.

9 *An increase in investment return is usually associated with an increase in the acceptable level of fluctuation of the portfolio value cycle to market cycle. Would you be willing to accept a wider possible range of fluctuation in an attempt to achieve a higher return?* (Yes/No.)

10 *If a target rate of return over and above the inflation rate has been established, please specify.*

    a)   Not determined.
    b)   Keep pace with inflation.
    c)   1% above inflation.
    d)   2% above inflation.
    e)   3% above inflation.
    f)   3-4% above inflation.
    g)   Other. If other, please describe.

11 *Plan 'risk' can be defined in different ways. Please indicate below the single item that best describes how you tend to view risk.*

    a)   The possibility of not meeting the actuarial assumption (if a pension plan).
    b)   The possibility of not achieving an established larger rate of return.
    c)   Not at least equalling the rate of inflation.
    d)   High degree of fluctuation in the value of the portfolio within a market cycle.
    e)   The chance of a great loss in the value of an individual security regardless of how well the overall portfolio might perform.
    f)   Other. If other, please specify.

12 *The primary emphasis in examining the investment performance for the account should be on:*

    a)    Comparing actual returns to an 'absolute' per cent return target.

    b)    'Relative' comparison. That is, comparing the actual account returns to various market indexes.

    c)    Using both 'absolute' and 'relative' measures.

    d)    I have no real preferences.

13 *Bond interest varies with quality and length of maturity of the bond. What bond quality do you feel is appropriate for the portfolio?*

    a)    All AAA rated.

    b)    None lower than AA.

    c)    None lower than A.

    d)    None lower than BAA.

14 *The time period used in evaluating investment return has a significant impact on the probability of realizing the stated return objective. The longer used, the better chance that up and down market cycles will average out to your desired return. What investment time horizon seems most appropriate for the account?*

    a)    Ten years or more.

    b)    Five years.

    c)    Three years.

    d)    A complete market cycle.

    e)    I do not know.

15 *What regularity of direct contact with your adviser is preferable?*

  *Meetings:*

    a)    Annually.

    b)    Semiannually.

    c)    Quarterly.

    d)    When deemed necessary by either the investment manager or client.

  *Written or oral communication:*

    a)    Quarterly.

    b)    More frequently than quarterly.

    c)    When deemed necessary by investment manager or client.

16 *Is geographical location of your manager important to you?* (Yes/No.)

  *Comment.*

17 *Would you consider investing a portion of the assets in tangible vehicles?* (Yes/No.)

  *If yes, which of the following?* Real estate; oil and gas; precious metals; other.

18 *Would you be inclined to consider the use of put and call option strategies to increase portfolio income and/or reduce volatility?* (Yes/No.)

(Source: Shearson Lehman Brothers, Consulting Group Institutional Services, 1991.)

## Selected references

Arnott, R. and Fabozzi, F. (1992), *Active Asset Allocation*, McGraw-Hill, Maidenhead.

Belchamber, C. (1988), *The UK Government Bond Market*, Credit Suisse First Boston, London. (Chapter: 'Two Bond Comparisons'.)

Bitner, J. and Goddard, J. (1992), *Successful Bank Asset-Liability Management*, Wiley, New York.

Elton, E.J. and Gruber, M.J. (1978), 'Optimum Portfolios from Simple Ranking Devices', *Journal of Portfolio Management*, Spring, 15–19.

Elton, E.J. and Gruber, M.J. (1995), *Modern Portfolio Theory and Investment Analysis*, John Wiley, New York. (Chapters 21 and 26.)

Fabozzi, F. (1997), *Managing Fixed Income Portfolios*, FJF Publishing, New Hope, Penn.

Fabozzi, F. (1996), *Bond Portfolio Management*, FJF Publishing, New Hope, Penn.

Fabozzi, F. (ed.)(1990), *Pension Fund Investment Management*, McGraw-Hill, London.

Fabozzi, F. and Fong, G. (1994), *Advanced Fixed Income Portfolio Management*, Probus, Chicago.

Fabozzi, F. and Konishi, A. (eds.)(1991), *Asset-Liability Management*, Probus, Chicago.

Farrell, J. (1997), *Portfolio Management*, McGraw Hill, New York.

Fischer, R.E. and Jordan, R.J. (1987), *Security Analysis and Portfolio Management*, Prentice-Hall, Englewood Cliffs, NJ. (Chapters 13, 19 and 21.)

Fong, H.G. and Fabozzi, F.J. (1985), *Fixed Income Portfolio Management*, Dow Jones-Irwin, Homewood, Ill.

Frost, A.J. and Hager, D.P. (1986), *A General Introduction to Institutional Investment*, Heinemann, London.

Lewis, M. (1989), *Liar's Poker*, Hodder and Stoughton, London.

Lofthouse, S. (1994), *Equity Investment Management*, Wiley, Chichester.

Redington, F.M. (1952), 'Review of the Principles of Life Office Valuations', *Journal of the Institute of Actuaries*, 18, 286–315.

Rutterford, J. (1993), *Introduction to Stock Exchange Investment*, Macmillan, London. (Chapter 13.)

Sharpe, W.F., Alexander, G., and Bailey, J. (1995), *Investments*, Prentice-Hall, Englewood Cliffs, NJ. (Chapter 24.)

Shepherd, A.G. (ed.)(1987), *Pension Fund Investment*, Woodhead-Faulkner, Cambridge. (Chapters 9, 12 and 14.)

Watsham, T. (1992), *Options and Futures in International Portfolio Management*, Chapman Hall, London.

**Exercises**

1  What are the main functions of a fund manager?

2  Distinguish between the following different fund management styles:

   a)  balanced management;

   b)  specialist management;

   c)  split funding.

3  Analyze the differing investment requirements of

   a)  an investor with positive net worth;

   b)  an investor with zero net worth.

4  What features of the securities markets justify passive portfolio management?

5  How would you go about determining an investor's degree of risk tolerance?

6  You are given the following information:

   | | |
   |---|---|
   | Expected return on shares | = 18% |
   | Expected return on bonds | = 12% |
   | Standard deviation of the return on shares | = 30% |
   | Standard deviation of the return on bonds | = 20% |
   | Correlation between the returns on shares and bonds | = 40% |

   Determine the optimal share-bond mix for the following investors:

   a)  an investor with a degree of risk tolerance of 0.0;

   b)  an investor with a degree of risk tolerance of 1.5;

   c)  an investor with a degree of risk tolerance of 3.0.

7  Explain the roles and significance of asset allocation, security selection and market timing in portfolio management.

8  Discuss the advantages and disadvantages of both active and passive portfolio management.

9  The secret of successful active share portfolio management is finding positive alphas. Discuss.

10  The capital asset pricing model suggests that passive investment strategies are superior to active strategies. Discuss.

11  Using the following bonds:

   | Bond | Duration |
   |------|----------|
   | A | 4 |
   | B | 11 |
   | C | 15 |

   construct three different portfolios of the three bonds with a duration of ten years.

12 Discuss how a fund manager can use stock index and bond futures contracts to aid his market timing strategies.

13 The rapid growth in index funds and passive portfolio strategies will eventually lead to substantial mispricings of securities, thereby increasing the ability to increase returns through active management. Discuss.

14 Government bonds are riskless and should not be included in a risk portfolio. Discuss.

15 Explain how the following factors might influence portfolio planning for the private investor:

    a) liquidity;

    b) responsibilities and commitments;

    c) income and tax considerations;

    d) attitudes to risk;

    e) legal constraints;

    f) age.

16 The principles of portfolio management for a rich individual investor differ from those of an institutional investor. Discuss.

17 No rational investor should include fixed-interest securities in his portfolio during a period of inflation. Discuss.

18 One of the best ways for a fund manager to enhance portfolio returns is to write options against his cash portfolio. Discuss.

19 'Buying cheap and selling dear' has always been and will always be the most profitable investment rule. Critically appraise this investment rule.

20 Explain and analyze the main types of bond-switching strategies that can be used to enhance the returns to a fixed-interest portfolio.

21 Yield curve analysis is the most important input in trading a portfolio of gilt-edged securities. Discuss.

22 Duration is the single most important concept for a bond portfolio manager. Discuss.

23 a) What are the main differences between:

    i) an expected utility-maximizing investor and

    ii) a safety-first investor?

   b) What are the implications for portfolio structuring?

24 What are the main ways of constructing an index fund?

25 Why do index funds generally underperform in the market?

26 How would you immunize a bond portfolio?

27 Examine the main ways of dedicating a portfolio.

28 An immunized portfolio has to be rebalanced periodically, whereas cash flow matching requires no rebalancing at all. Immunization is therefore not a true passive portfolio management strategy. The only pure passive strategy is cash flow matching. Discuss.

29 An immunized portfolio has to be rebalanced too frequently, whereas exact cash flow matching is almost impossible to achieve. Horizon matching provides an acceptable middle course between these alternative strategies. Discuss this view of passive portfolio management strategies.

30 In terms of performance, selecting the best-performing asset category is more important than selecting the best-performing securities from each asset category. Discuss.

31 You are given the following information about three securities:

| Security | Return | Beta |
|----------|--------|------|
| A | 19% | 1.3 |
| B | 24% | 2.0 |
| C | 12% | 0.4 |

If the return on the market is 16 per cent and the riskless interest rate is 9 per cent, determine the alphas for each security and recommend whether to buy, sell or hold each security.

32 Explain the 'quest for alpha'.

33 In what sense can an active portfolio be viewed as a set of side bets against the market?

34 Examine the similarities and differences between the way in which equity, bond and treasury portfolios are actively managed.

35 a) Calculate the durations of the following annual coupon bonds (assuming that a coupon has just been paid):

| Bond | Coupon (%) | Maturity (years) | Price (£) | Yield to maturity (%) |
|------|-----------|-------------------|-----------|------------------------|
| A | 8 | 6 | 90 | 9.5 |
| B | 12 | 5 | 110 | 10.5 |
| C | 9 | 20 | 98 | 9.7 |
| D | 5 | 1 | 96 | 9.4 |

b) Using these bonds, construct an immunized bullet portfolio and an immunized barbell portfolio for an investor with a five-year investment horizon. Which portfolio is likely to need less frequent rebalancing?

36 Using the following annual coupon bonds:

| Bond | Coupon (%) | Price (£) | Maturity years |
|------|-----------|-----------|-----------------|
| A | 10 | 99 | 1 |
| B | 8 | 92 | 2 |
| C | 15 | 116 | 2 |
| D | 12 | 108 | 3 |
| E | 14 | 115 | 3 |
| F | 7 | 90 | 4 |
| G | 9 | 98 | 4 |
| H | 10 | 99 | 5 |

construct the least-cost portfolio to suit an investor with the following year-end cash flow commitments:

| Year | Cash flow commitment (£) |
|------|--------------------------|
| 1 | 1,000,000 |
| 2 | 1,100,000 |
| 3 | 1,210,000 |
| 4 | 1,331,000 |

37  An important implication of the capital asset pricing model is that portfolios should be managed passively. What justifies the active management of a portfolio?

38  How would you construct an optimal active portfolio of securities?

39  You are given the following information on four securities:

| Security | Expected return (%) | Beta | Specific risk (%) |
|----------|---------------------|------|-------------------|
| A | 20 | 1.5 | 30 |
| B | 16 | 1.2 | 20 |
| C | 14 | 0.9 | 25 |
| D | 12 | 0.8 | 15 |

If the riskless interest rate is 10 per cent and market risk is 25 per cent, calculate the optimal proportion of each security in a risky portfolio (assuming short sales are not allowed). If the market proportions are:

| Security | Market proportions (%) |
|----------|------------------------|
| A | 30 |
| B | 20 |
| C | 40 |
| D | 10 |

calculate the side bets against the market for this portfolio.

40  Examine the different market timing strategies available to:

   a) a share portfolio manager, and

   b) a bond portfolio manager.

41  How can a corporate treasurer engage in active portfolio management?

42  What are:

   a) anomaly switches?

   b) policy switches?

Provide *two* examples of each type of switch.

43  Describe some mixed active-passive portfolio management strategies. What advantages and disadvantages do they have over pure active or pure passive strategies?

44 An investor with £100,000 in cash observes that FTSE 100 index futures on LIFFE are trading at 6260.7 (expiry in 3 months) and that deposits in a futures margin account earn 6 per cent. The initial margin on a FTSE 100 index futures contract is £1000.

   a) How could the investor construct a synthetic equity index fund?

   b) What would be the annualized rate of return on the fund if in three months' time the spot FTSE 100 index stood at 6542.8?

   c) What other factors would the investor have to take into account?

# Chapter 15

# Portfolio performance measurement

In the last chapter, we examined two of the three functions of a portfolio manager: portfolio structuring and analysis, and portfolio adjustment. In this chapter, we shall consider the third function: portfolio performance measurement. Sometimes this function is performed by the portfolio manager himself; sometimes it is performed by an independent performance measurement service. Figure 15.1 provides an example of a typical performance evaluation summary that might be prepared for a fund manager.

## 15.1   The components of portfolio performance measurement

The questions that are important for assessing how well a fund manager performs are:

- How do we measure the *ex post* returns on his portfolio?

- How do we measure the risk-adjusted returns on his portfolio?

- How do we assess these risk-adjusted returns?

To answer these questions, we need to examine returns, risks and benchmarks of comparison.

### 15.1.1   *Ex post* returns

There are two ways in which *ex post* returns on the fund can be measured: *time-weighted rates of return* (or geometric mean), and *money-weighted* (or *value-weighted*) *rates of return* (or internal rate of return). The simplest method is the money-weighted rate of return, but the preferred method is the time-weighted rate of return, since it accounts for cash inflows and outflows that are beyond the control of the fund manager. However, the time-weighted rate of return has the disadvantage of requiring that the fund be valued every time there is a cash flow.

Consider the following table on the value $(V)$ of and cash flow $(CF)$ from a fund over the course of a year:

**Figure 15.1** Fund manager performance evaluation summary

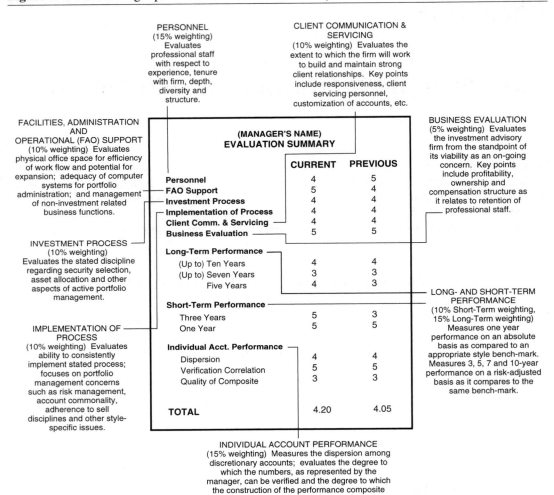

PERSONNEL
(15% weighting)
Evaluates
professional staff
with respect to
experience, tenure
with firm, depth,
diversity and
structure.

CLIENT COMMUNICATION &
SERVICING
(10% weighting) Evaluates the
extent to which the firm will work
to build and maintain strong
client relationships. Key points
include responsiveness, client
servicing personnel,
customization of accounts, etc.

FACILITIES, ADMINISTRATION
AND
OPERATIONAL (FAO) SUPPORT
(10% weighting) Evaluates
physical office space for efficiency
of work flow and potential for
expansion; adequacy of computer
systems for portfolio
administration; and management
of non-investment related
business functions.

BUSINESS EVALUATION
(5% weighting) Evaluates
the investment advisory
firm from the standpoint of
its viability as an on-going
concern. Key points
include profitability,
ownership and
compensation structure as
it relates to retention of
professional staff.

INVESTMENT PROCESS
(10% weighting)
Evaluates the stated discipline
regarding security selection,
asset allocation and other
aspects of active portfolio
management.

IMPLEMENTATION OF
PROCESS
(10% weighting) Evaluates
ability to consistently
implement stated process;
focuses on portfolio
management concerns
such as risk management,
account commonality,
adherence to sell
disciplines and other style-
specific issues.

LONG- AND SHORT-TERM
PERFORMANCE
(10% Short-Term weighting,
15% Long-Term weighting)
Measures one year
performance on an absolute
basis as compared to an
appropriate style bench-mark.
Measures 3, 5, 7 and 10-year
performance on a risk-adjusted
basis as it compares to the
same bench-mark.

INDIVIDUAL ACCOUNT PERFORMANCE
(15% weighting) Measures the dispersion among
discretionary accounts; evaluates the degree to
which the numbers, as represented by the
manager, can be verified and the degree to which
the construction of the performance composite
complies with industry standards.

**(MANAGER'S NAME)
EVALUATION SUMMARY**

|  | CURRENT | PREVIOUS |
|---|---|---|
| **Personnel** | 4 | 5 |
| **FAO Support** | 5 | 4 |
| **Investment Process** | 4 | 4 |
| **Implementation of Process** | 4 | 4 |
| **Client Comm. & Servicing** | 4 | 4 |
| **Business Evaluation** | 5 | 5 |
| **Long-Term Performance** |  |  |
| (Up to) Ten Years | 4 | 4 |
| (Up to) Seven Years | 3 | 3 |
| Five Years | 4 | 3 |
| **Short-Term Performance** |  |  |
| Three Years | 5 | 3 |
| One Year | 5 | 5 |
| **Individual Acct. Performance** |  |  |
| Dispersion | 4 | 4 |
| Verification Correlation | 5 | 5 |
| Quality of Composite | 3 | 3 |
| **TOTAL** | 4.20 | 4.05 |

*Source:* Shearson Lehman Brothers Consulting Group Institutional Services, 1991

| Time | 0 | 6 months | 1 year |
|---|---|---|---|
| Value of fund | $V_0$ | $V_1$ | $V_2$ |
| Cash flow | – | $CF$ | – |

The money-weighted rate of return is the solution to (assuming compound interest):

$$V_2 = V_0(1+r) + CF(1+r)^{\frac{1}{2}}, \tag{15.1}$$

or to (assuming simple interest):

$$V_2 = V_0(1+r) + CF\left(1+\frac{r}{2}\right). \tag{15.2}$$

In the latter case, this implies that:

$$\text{Money-weighted rate of return} = \frac{V_2 - (V_0 + CF)}{V_0 + \frac{1}{2}CF}. \tag{15.3}$$

The time-weighted rate of return is defined as:

$$\text{Time-weighted rate of return} = \frac{V_1}{V_0} \cdot \frac{V_2}{V_1 + CF} - 1. \tag{15.4}$$

If the semi-annual rate of return on the portfolio equals $r_1$ for the first six months and $r_2$ for the second six months, then we have:

$$V_1 = V_0(1+r_1), \tag{15.5}$$

and:

$$\begin{aligned} V_2 &= (V_1 + CF)(1+r_2) \\ &= [V_0(1+r_1) + CF](1+r_2). \end{aligned} \tag{15.6}$$

Substituting (15.5) and (15.6) into (15.4) gives:

$$\begin{aligned} \text{Time-weighted rate of return} &= \frac{V_0(1+r_1)}{V_0}\left[\frac{[V_0(1+r_1)+CF](1+r_2)}{V_0(1+r_1)+CF}\right] - 1 \\ &= (1+r_1)(1+r_2) - 1, \end{aligned} \tag{15.7}$$

which is a chain-linking of returns between cash flows.

It is clear that the time-weighted rate of return reflects accurately the rate of return realized on the portfolio. This is because both cash inflows and outflows are beyond the control of the fund manager, and their effects should be excluded from influencing the performance of the fund. This is the case for the time-weighted rate of return ($CF$ does not appear in the second line of (15.7)), but not the money-weighted rate of return.

We can illustrate this using the following example where the initial value of two funds is £100:

| Time | 0 | 6 months | 1 year |
|---|---|---|---|
| Share price index | 1.0 | 0.8 | 1.2 |
| Cash flow into fund A | 20 | — | — |
| Value of fund A including cash flow | 120 | 96 | 144 |
| Cash flow into fund B | 10 | 10 | — |
| Value of fund B including cash flow | 110 | 98 | 147 |

Both funds have an initial value of £100 and both funds receive £20 during the year, but the timing of the cash flows is different: fund B receives cash at a time when shares are relatively cheap and subsequently perform well.

Assuming simple interest, the money-weighted rate of return can be calculated as follows:

$$\text{Money-weighted rate of return of fund A} = \frac{V_2}{V_0 + CF_0} - 1$$

$$= \frac{144}{120} - 1 = 0.20 \quad (20\%);$$

$$\text{Money-weighted rate of return of fund B} = \frac{V_2 - (V_0 + CF_1 + CF_2)}{V_0 + CF_1 + \frac{1}{2}CF_2}$$

$$= \frac{147 - 120}{115} = 0.2348 \quad (23.48\%).$$

So the fund B manager is performing better than the fund A manager according to the money-weighted rate-of-return measure. (Assuming compound interest, the money-weighted rate of return for fund B would be even higher at 23.53 per cent.)

The time-weighted rate of return is calculated as follows:

$$\text{Time-weighted rate of return of fund A} = \frac{V_1}{V_0 + CF_0} \cdot \frac{V_2}{V_1 + CF_1} - 1$$

$$= \frac{96}{120} \frac{144}{96} - 1 = 0.20 \quad (20\%);$$

$$\text{Time-weighted rate of return of fund B} = \frac{V_1}{V_0 + CF_0} \cdot \frac{V_2}{V_1 + CF_1} - 1$$

$$= \frac{88}{110} \frac{147}{98} - 1 = 0.20 \quad (20\%).$$

The time-weighted rate of return of 20 per cent is the same in both cases. This reflects the true performance of both funds over the period, since both funds are invested in the same portfolio of shares and shares increased by 20 per cent during the year.

### 15.1.2  Adjusting for risk

The *ex post* rate of return has to be adjusted for the fund's exposure to risk. The appropriate measure of risk depends on whether the beneficiary of the fund's investments has other well diversified investments or whether this is his only set of investments. In the first case, the *market risk* (beta) of the fund is the best measure of risk. In the second case, the *total risk* or volatility (standard deviation) of the fund is best. If the portfolio is a bond portfolio, then the appropriate measure of market risk is *relative duration*.

### 15.1.3  Benchmarks of comparison

In order to assess how well a fund manager is performing, we need a benchmark of comparison. Once we have determined an appropriate benchmark, we can then compare whether the fund manager outperformed, matched or underperformed the benchmark on a risk-adjusted basis.

The appropriate benchmark is one that is consistent with the preferences of the fund's trustees and the fund's tax status. For example, a different benchmark is appropriate if the fund is a *gross fund* (and does not pay income or capital gains tax, such as a pension fund) than if it is a *net fund* (and so does pay income and capital gains tax, such as the fund of a general insurance company). Similarly, the general market index will not be appropriate as a benchmark if the trustee has a preference for high-income securities and an aversion to shares in rival companies or, for moral reasons, the shares in tobacco companies, say. Yet again, the FTSE-A All Share Index would not be an appropriate benchmark if half the securities were held overseas.

There will therefore be different benchmarks for different funds and different fund managers. For example, consistent with the asset allocation decision, there will be a share benchmark for the share portfolio manager and a bond benchmark for the bond portfolio manager.

So the benchmark will be an index of one kind or another. It is important to understand the structure of the relevant index. We can distinguish between *absolute* and *relative* indices, between *price-weighted* and *value-weighted* indices, and between *arithmetic* and *geometric* indices. These can be explained using the following table, which contains the input to an index containing four shares:

|  | Share no. | Price (£) | No. of shares (m) | Capitalization (£m) |
|---|---|---|---|---|
| **Day 1** | 1 | 0.65 | 50 | 32.50 |
|  | 2 | 0.82 | 50 | 41.00 |
|  | 3 | 1.15 | 75 | 86.25 |
|  | 4 | 0.25 | 100 | 25.00 |
|  |  | 2.87 |  | 184.75 |
| **Day 2** | 1 | 0.70 | 50 | 35.00 |
|  | 2 | 0.78 | 50 | 39.00 |
|  | 3 | 1.23 | 75 | 92.25 |
|  | 4 | 0.21 | 100 | 21.00 |
|  |  | 2.92 |  | 187.25 |

If day 1 is the base date, then the base price-weighted absolute index is given by:

$$\text{Index} = \frac{2.87}{0.0287} = 100,$$

and the base value-weighted absolute index is given by:

$$\text{Index} = \frac{184.75}{1.8475} = 100.$$

One day 2, the *price-weighted arithmetic absolute index* is:

$$\text{Index} = \frac{2.92}{0.0287} = 101.74,$$

while the *value-weighted arithmetic absolute index* is:

$$\text{Index} = \frac{187.25}{1.8475} = 101.35.$$

The day 2 to day 1 price relatives for the four shares are given by:

| Share no. | Price relative | | |
|:---:|:---:|:---:|:---:|
| 1 | (0.70/0.65) | = | 1.0769 |
| 2 | (0.78/0.82) | = | 0.9512 |
| 3 | (1.23/1.15) | = | 1.0696 |
| 4 | (0.21/0.25) | = | 0.8400 |

The *equal-weighted arithmetic relative index* for day 2 is:

$$\text{Index} \quad = \quad \frac{1.0769 + 0.9512 + 1.0696 + 0.8400}{4} \cdot 100 \quad = \quad 98.44 \,.$$

The *equal-weighted geometric relative index* for day 2 is:

$$\text{Index} \quad = \quad [(1.0769)(0.9512)(1.0696)(0.8400)]^{\frac{1}{4}} \cdot 100 \quad = \quad 97.95 \,.$$

It can be seen that the four indices give quite different results even across just one day's price movements. So it is important that the returns on the portfolio are constructed in the same way as the benchmark index.

For example, the FTSE-A All Share and the FTSE 100 Indices are value-weighted arithmetic absolute, whereas the FT 30 Index and the FT Government Securities Index are equal-weighted geometric relative.

## 15.2   Measures of portfolio performance

### 15.2.1   Performance measures based on risk-adjusted excess returns

There are three performance measures based on risk-adjusted excess returns, each one distinguished by the risk measure used. The first is the *excess return to volatility measure*, also known as the *Sharpe measure* (Sharpe (1966)). This uses the total risk measure:

$$\text{Excess return to volatility (Sharpe)} \quad = \quad \frac{r_p - r_f}{\sigma_p} \,, \tag{15.8}$$

where:

$r_p$ = average return on the portfolio (usually geometric mean) over an interval (typically the last 20 quarters);

$\sigma_p$ = standard deviation of the return on the portfolio (calculated over the last 20 quarters) (Note: the geometric mean is used to construct the average return, but the arithmetic mean is used to construct the standard deviation);

$r_f$ = average risk-free return (usually geometric mean) over the same interval.

The Sharpe measure is illustrated in Figure 15.2. BM is the benchmark portfolio (it could be the market portfolio). A, B, C and D are four portfolios. Portfolios A and B beat the benchmark on a risk-adjusted basis, while C and D underperform the benchmark. Portfolio A is the best (i.e. is ranked highest according to the Sharpe measure) and D is the worst. Sometimes (15.8) is known as the *information ratio*, since it shows the amount of excess return that was generated per unit of risk taken on, or the amount of 'bang per buck'.

**Figure 15.2** Excess return to volatility

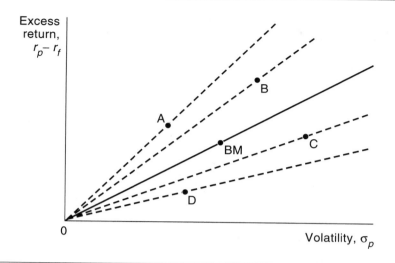

The second is the *excess return to beta measure*, also known as the *Treynor measure* (Treynor (1965)). This uses the systematic risk measure:

$$\text{Excess return to beta (Treynor)} \quad = \quad \frac{r_p - r_f}{\beta_p}, \tag{15.9}$$

where $\beta_p$ is the beta of the portfolio (calculated over the last 20 quarters). This is illustrated in Figure 15.3.

The third is the *excess return to relative duration measure*, a measure suitable for bond portfolios:

$$\text{Excess return to relative duration} \quad = \quad \frac{r_p - r_f}{D_p / D_m}, \tag{15.10}$$

where $D_p / D_m$ is the duration of bond portfolio relative to duration of the market. This is illustrated in Figure 15.4.

How should these measures be interpreted? Let us compare the Sharpe and Treynor measures. Suppose that for an individual and for the market they are as follows:

|        | *Individual* | *Market* |
|--------|--------------|----------|
| Sharpe | 1.3          | 1.6      |
| Treynor| 5.0          | 4.0      |

Comparing Treynor measures, the individual is good at market timing, but, comparing Sharpe measures, he is less good at security selection: he has taken on a lot of specific risk (which could have been diversified away) and has not been adequately rewarded for doing so. The Sharpe measure is suitable for an individual with a portfolio that is not well diversified. The Treynor measure is suitable for an individual with a well-diversified portfolio.

**Figure 15.3** Excess return to beta

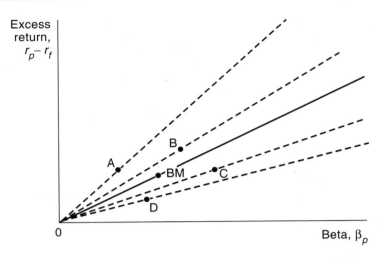

**Figure 15.4** Excess return to relative duration

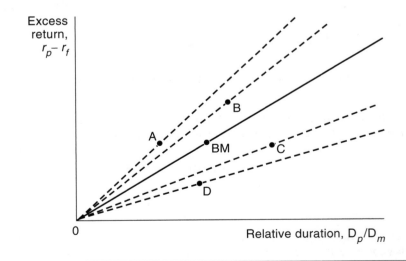

Ranking portfolios according to their excess return to risk measure is very useful, but there are problems with interpreting the numbers. One problem is that it is not possible to borrow at the riskless rate. This is illustrated in Figure 15.5. A' dominates B only if it is possible to borrow and lend at the same riskless rate (A' is a combination of A and borrowing at $r_f$). Otherwise, the borrowing line is $r_bAC$ and B dominates A'', which is a combination of A and borrowing at $r_b$. Another problem is that these ranking measures do not take account of risk aversion. We cannot really say that one portfolio is preferred to another without taking risk aversion into account.

**Figure 15.5** Excess return to volatility with different borrowing and lending rates

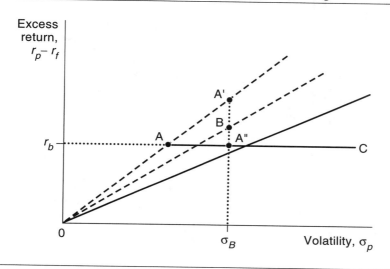

## 15.2.2 Performance measures based on alpha values

As an alternative to ranking portfolios according to their risk-adjusted returns in excess of the riskless rate, it is possible to rank them according to their alpha values. Again, three different performance measures are available depending on the risk measure used.

If the risk measure is total risk, the appropriate alpha value is defined with respect to the capital market line:

$$\bar{r}_p = r_f + \left(\frac{\bar{r}_m - r_f}{\sigma_m}\right)\sigma_p,$$  (15.11)

where:

$$
\begin{array}{rcl}
\bar{r}_p & = & \text{expected return on the portfolio;} \\
\bar{r}_m & = & \text{expected return on the market;} \\
\sigma_p & = & \text{standard deviation of the return on the portfolio;} \\
\sigma_m & = & \text{standard deviation of the return on the market.}
\end{array}
$$

The corresponding alpha value is:

$$\alpha_\sigma \ = \ r_p - \bar{r}_p.$$

(15.12)

This is shown in Figure 15.6. The best-performing fund is the one with the largest alpha.

---

**Figure 15.6** Alpha values and the capital market line

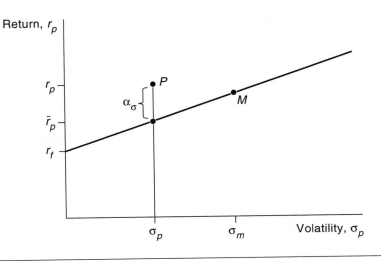

---

If the risk measure is systematic risk, the relevant alpha value is defined with respect to the security market line:

$$\bar{r}_p \ = \ r_f + (\bar{r}_m - r_f)\beta_p.$$

(15.13)

The corresponding alpha value is:

$$\alpha_\beta \ = \ r_p - \bar{r}_p.$$

(15.14)

This is known as the *Jensen differential performance index* (Jensen (1969)). It is illustrated in Figure 15.7.

If the risk measure is relative duration, the relevant alpha value is defined with respect to the bond market line:

$$\bar{r}_p \ = \ r_f + (\bar{r}_m - r_f)\frac{D_p}{D_m}.$$

(15.15)

The corresponding alpha value is:

$$\alpha_D \ = \ r_p - \bar{r}_p.$$

(15.16)

This is illustrated in Figure 15.8.

**Figure 15.7** Alpha values and the security market line

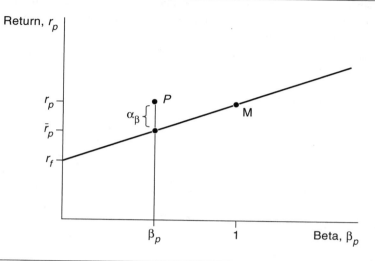

**Figure 15.8** Alpha values and the bond market line

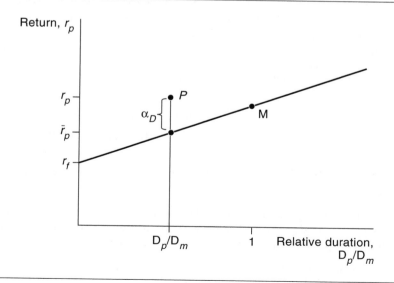

## 15.3   The decomposition of total return

Having discussed various measures of the performance of a fund, the next task is to identify the sources of that performance, an exercise that is sometimes known as *performance attribution*. This involves breaking down the total return into various components. One way of doing this is known as the *Fama decomposition of total return* (after Fama (1972)).

**Figure 15.9** Fama decomposition of total return

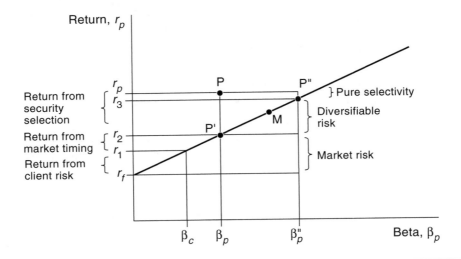

The Fama decomposition is shown in Figure 15.9, in the case where the relevant measure of risk is systematic risk, beta. Suppose that fund $P$ generates a return $r_p$ and has a beta of $\beta_p$. The fund has performed well over the period being considered. Using the Jensen performance measure, it has a positive alpha value, equal to $(r_p - r_2)$. The total return $r_p$ can be broken down into four components:

$$
\begin{aligned}
\text{Return on the portfolio} \quad = \quad & \text{Riskless rate} \\
& + \text{Return from client's risk} \\
& + \text{Return from market timing} \\
& + \text{Return from security selection.} \qquad (15.17)
\end{aligned}
$$

The first component of the return on the portfolio is the riskless rate, $r_f$: all fund managers expect to earn the riskless rate.

The second component of portfolio return is the *return from the client's risk*. The fund manager will have assessed the client's degree of risk tolerance to be measured by $\beta_c$, say. The client is therefore expecting a return on the portfolio of at least $r_1$. The return from the client's risk is therefore $(r_1 - r_f)$.

The third component is the *return from market timing*. This is also known as the return from the fund manager's risk. This is because the manager has chosen (or at least ended up with) a portfolio with a beta of $\beta_p$ which differs from that expected by the client. The fund manager has implicitly taken a more bullish view of the market than the client. He has consequently decided to raise the beta of the portfolio above that expected by the client. He has done this by selecting a portfolio with a larger proportion invested in the market portfolio and a smaller proportion invested in the riskless asset than the client would have selected. In other words, the fund manager has engaged in market timing. With a portfolio beta of $\beta_p$, the expected return is $r_2$, so that the return to market timing is $(r_2 - r_1)$.

**Figure 15.10** Successful market timing

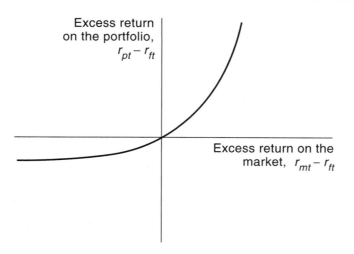

An alternative test for successful market timing is shown in Figure 15.10. A successful market timer increases the beta of his portfolio prior to market rises and lowers the beta of his portfolio prior to market falls. Over time, a successful market timer will therefore have the excess returns of his portfolio over the market plot along the curved line in Figure 15.10. To test this, the following quadratic curve is fitted using historical data on excess returns on the portfolio and the market (see, e.g., Treynor and Mazuy (1966)):

$$(r_{pt} - r_{ft}) = a + b(r_{mt} - r_{ft}) + c(r_{mt} - r_{ft})^2, \qquad (15.18)$$

where both $b$ and $c$ are positive for a successful market timer.

The fourth component is the *return from security selection* or the *return to selectivity*. This is equal to $(r_p - r_2)$ and is known as the return to selectivity for the following reason. Consider portfolios $P$ and $P'$ in Figure 15.9. They both have the same amount of market risk, because they both have the same beta, $\beta_p$. However, they have different total risks. Portfolio $P'$ contains no diversifiable risk since it lies on the security market line. Portfolio $P$, however, lies above the SML. It is therefore not a linear combination of the market portfolio and the riskless asset. (Only portfolios along the SML are.) It must contain an active portfolio of risky assets that differs from the market portfolio by a set of side bets. In other words, $P$ differs from $P'$ because P's manager has engaged in active security selection. This has resulted in portfolio $P$ earning an additional return, but the fund manager has had to take on diversifiable risk to do so.

Is the extra return worth the risk? To answer this question, we need to compare portfolio $P$ with another portfolio which lies on the SML and which has the same total risk. Suppose that this other portfolio is $P''$. $P''$ is found as follows. Suppose that the total risk of both $P$ and $P''$ is $\sigma_p^2 = 30$. Since

$P''$ lies on the SML, we know that all the risk of $P''$ is undiversifiable and that this is equal to $(\beta_p'')^2 \sigma_m^2$. If $\sigma_m^2 = 25$, it follows that:

$$\beta_p'' = \frac{\sigma_p}{\sigma_m} = \left(\frac{30}{25}\right)^{\frac{1}{2}} = 1.1.$$

The return on $P''$ is $r_3$ (given that the beta of $P''$ is $\beta_p''$), while the return on $P$ is $r_p$. Since $r_p$ is greater than $r_3$, it means that the risk in selecting $P$ was worthwhile. The additional *return from taking on additional diversifiable risk* is $(r_3 - r_2)$. But the $P$ fund manager has done even better than this, and earned an additional return $(r_p - r_3)$, known as the *return to pure selectivity*.

Figure 15.9 can also be used to show a different decomposition from that given in (15.17). The return $(r_2 - r_f)$ is the return from taking on market risk: it is equal to the sum of the returns from the client's risk and the manager's risk. Similarly, the return from security selection can be broken down into the return from diversifiable risk and the return from pure selectivity. Therefore an alternative decomposition to (15.17) is:

$$
\begin{aligned}
\text{Return on the portfolio} \quad = \quad & \text{Riskless rate} \\
& + \text{Return from market risk} \\
& + \text{Return from diversifiable risk} \\
& + \text{Return from pure selectivity.} \qquad (15.19)
\end{aligned}
$$

The original Fama decomposition was done in terms of beta and is therefore important for share portfolios. It is possible to perform a similar decomposition in terms of bond portfolios using relative duration (see, e.g., Fong, Pearson and Vasicek (1983)).

**Example 15.1 (Fama decomposition)** *We can illustrate the Fama decomposition using the following data on a fund based on the previous 20 quarters:*

$$
\begin{aligned}
r_p &= 20\% & r_m &= 16\% \\
\sigma_p &= 15\% & \sigma_m &= 12\% \\
\beta_p &= 0.9 & r_f &= 10\%.
\end{aligned}
$$

*The client's desired beta is given as $\beta_c = 0.8$. Using this, we can calculate the expected return on the client's desired portfolio. A beta of 0.8 implies a portfolio that is 80 per cent invested in the market and 20 per cent invested in the riskless asset. Therefore:*

$$r_1 = 0.2(10) + 0.8(16) = 14.8\%.$$

*This means a return from client's risk of:*

$$r_1 - r_f = 14.8 - 10.0 = 4.8\%.$$

*However, the actual beta of the portfolio is 0.9, implying that it is 90 per cent invested in the market and 10 per cent invested in the riskless asset. This in turn implies an expected return on the actual portfolio of:*

$$r_2 = 0.1(10) + 0.9(16) = 15.4\%.$$

*This gives a return from market timing of:*

$$r_2 - r_1 \quad = \quad 15.4 - 14.8 \quad = \quad 0.6\%.$$

*The next step is to find the portfolio P'' with the same total risk as our portfolio P. This portfolio has a beta of:*

$$\beta_p'' \quad = \quad \frac{\sigma_p}{\sigma_m} \quad = \quad \frac{15}{12} \quad = \quad 1.25.$$

*Portfolio P'' is invested 125 per cent in the market and −25 per cent in the riskless asset. The expected return on this portfolio is:*

$$r_3 \quad = \quad -0.25(10) + 1.25(16) \quad = \quad 17.5\%.$$

*Therefore the return from diversifiable risk is:*

$$r_3 - r_2 \quad = \quad 17.5 - 15.4 \quad = \quad 2.1\%.$$

*This leaves the return to pure selectivity as:*

$$r_p - r_3 \quad = \quad 20.0 - 17.5 \quad = \quad 2.5\%.$$

The decomposition of total return can be used to identify the different skills involved in active fund management. For example, one fund manager might be good at market timing but poor at stock selection. The evidence for this would be that his $(r_2 - r_1)$ was positive but his $(r_p - r_2)$ was negative; he should therefore be recommended to invest in an index fund but be allowed to select his own combination of the index fund and the riskless asset. Another manager might be good at stock selection but poor at market timing; he should be allowed to choose his own securities, but someone else should choose the combination of the resulting portfolio of risky securities and the riskless asset.

An alternative decomposition to that of Fama is due to Brinson and Fachler (1986) and Brinson, Hood and Beebower (1986). Let:

$$
\begin{array}{rcl}
N & = & \text{number of securities in the portfolio;} \\
\theta_i & = & \text{actual weight of } i\text{th security in total portfolio;} \\
r_i & = & \text{actual return on } i\text{th security;} \\
\theta_i^* & = & \text{strategic weight of } i\text{th security in total portfolio;} \\
r_i^* & = & \text{strategic return on } i\text{th security.}
\end{array}
$$

The decomposition of the total return on the portfolio is then:

$$
\begin{aligned}
r_p & = \sum_{i=1}^{N} \theta_i r_i \\
& = \sum_{i=1}^{N} \theta_i^* r_i^* + \sum_{i=1}^{N} (\theta_i - \theta_i^*) r_i^* + \sum_{i=1}^{N} \theta_i^* (r_i - r_i^*) + \sum_{i=1}^{N} (\theta_i - \theta_i^*)(r_i - r_i^*) \\
& = \text{Strategic return} \\
& \quad + \text{Return from market timing} \\
& \quad + \text{Return from security selection} \\
& \quad + \text{Residual return.}
\end{aligned}
$$

$$(15.20)$$

The *strategic return* is the return from the strategic asset allocation agreed at the start of the year between the fund manager and the client. It is also known as the *benchmark return*, since it is the benchmark against which the fund manager's performance will be compared: $r_i^*$ is the pre-agreed benchmark return on the $i$th security. The return from market timing, also called the *return from tactical asset allocation*, is the return resulting from the fund manager changing the actual weights of portfolio away from the strategic weights in an attempt to time the market, increasing the weight in asset categories that the fund manager believes will go up in value and reducing the weight in asset categories that the fund manager believes will go down in value. The return from security selection is the return from the fund manager's ability to pick securities that outperform the benchmark return for those securities. Finally we have the residual return, which ideally should be small relative to the return from market timing or security selection.

## 15.4   Treasury performance measurement

Treasury performance measurement deals with the effectiveness of the treasury department's cash (including working capital) management, interest exposure management and currency exposure management. Typical corporate objectives and performance measures are given in Table 15.1. The performance benchmarks against which treasury activities are measured should satisfy the following criteria:

1  They should be consistent with both the specified corporate objective and the company's attitude to risk;

2  The time horizon of the benchmark should be appropriate for the activity being measured (e.g. 3 month interest rates would not be as appropriate for assessing the effectiveness of long-term funding as, say, seven year rates);

3  They must be capable of being achieved;

4  They must be mutually acceptable to both the corporate treasurer and finance director.

## 15.5   Asset-liability managed portfolios

In this section, we analyze performance measurement and attribution in the case of asset-liability managed (ALM) portfolios. These are portfolios whose investment strategy is driven by the nature of the investing client's liabilities. The principal examples are pension funds and insurance companies. A *liability-driven performance attribution* (LDPA) framework has been derived by Plantinga and van der Meer (1995).

We can illustrate the LDPA framework using the following balance sheet for an asset-liability managed portfolio:

| *Assets* | | *Liabilities* | |
|---|---|---|---|
| Liability-driven assets | $V_b$ | Liabilities | $V_l$ |
| General assets | $V_s$ | Net worth | $W$ |

**Table 15.1** Treasury performance measurement

| Treasury department activity | Corporate objective | Performance measures |
|---|---|---|
| **Cash mangement** | Assist effective decision-making by accurate cashflow forecast | Maximum acceptable percentage error in actual against forecast cashflow, in total and by business unit |
| | Minimize idle balances | Maximum acceptable incidence of and value of credit balances |
| | Minimize bank charges | Alternative measures are: 1. Total costs for a year 2. Per item transmission or handling costs |
| **Short-term interest rate management** | Achieve budget interest rate | Budget interest rate based on market rates available at budget setting dates (NB: the variance due to poor forecasts would need to be identified) |
| | *or* Outperform market rates | Benchmark rate such as one-month LIBOR for borrowings, one-month LIBID for investments |
| | *or* Minimize interest costs/maximize interest returns subject to achievement of pre-specified rate (based on budget rate) | 1. Target rate drawn up at start of budget period based on forecast rates 2. Worst-case rate, being budget rate as above but with an allowance of, say, $\frac{1}{2}\%$ on for borrowings, $\frac{1}{2}\%$ off for deposits to allow for the additional risk deliberately adopted |
| **Currency exposure management** | Minimize adverse effect of exchange rate movements on the business by hedging as soon as committed payable or receivable in currency is identified | 1. Forward rate at a time commitment is identified, for known certain transactions 2. Forward rate adjusted by option premium for any uncertain part of a transaction |

*Source: Corporate Finance* (September 1988).

Suppose that the liabilities $(V_l)$ generate a predetermined set of future cash outflows. The manager can meet these cash outflows by investing in fixed interest bonds $(V_b)$ with the same pattern of cash flows; these bonds constitute the *liability-driven assets* (LDAs) in the balance sheet above. Suppose that the net worth of the investor $(W)$ is invested in general assets $(V_s)$ other than bonds (e.g. shares): net worth is defined as assets $(V_s + V_b)$ *minus* liabilities $(V_l)$. The return on net worth (i.e. net income to the investor) is defined as:

$$r_w W = r_s V_s + r_b V_b - r_l V_l,\tag{15.21}$$

where:

$$
\begin{aligned}
r_w &= \text{return on net worth;}\\
r_s &= \text{return on general assets;}\\
r_b &= \text{return on liability-driven assets (bonds);}\\
r_l &= \text{payout rate on liabilities.}
\end{aligned}
$$

Assuming that interest rate risk is the only source of risk to this portfolio, we can use equation (15.21) to derive a decomposition of portfolio performance as follows. First we rewrite the income generated by the general assets as:

$$r_s V_s = r_s W + r_s (V_s - W),\tag{15.22}$$

and the income generated by the bond portfolio as:

$$r_b V_b = r_b V_l + r_b (V_b - V_l).\tag{15.23}$$

Then we can divide each side of (15.21) by $W$ and substitute (15.22) and (15.23) to get the LDPA:

$$
\begin{aligned}
r_w &= \frac{r_s W + r_s (V_s - W)}{W} + \frac{r_b V_l + r_b (V_b - V_l)}{W} - r_l \cdot \frac{V_l}{W}\\
&= r_s + \lambda (r_b - r_l) + \gamma (r_s - r_b)\\
&= r_s + \lambda (r_b - \bar{r}_b) + \lambda (\bar{r}_b - r_l) + \gamma (r_s - r_b),
\end{aligned}\tag{15.24}
$$

or:

$$
\begin{aligned}
\text{Return on net worth} =\ & \text{Return on general assets}\\
& + \text{Return on LDAs due to security selection}\\
& + \text{Return on LDAs due to market timing}\\
& + \text{Return from funding mismatch}
\end{aligned}\tag{15.25}
$$

where:

$$
\begin{aligned}
\lambda &= V_l/W = \text{financial leverage ratio;}\\
\gamma &= (V_l - V_b)/W = (V_s - W)/W = \text{funding mismatch ratio;}\\
\bar{r}_b &= \text{expected return on bonds when bonds are theoretically priced on the}\\
&\quad \text{basis of the spot yield curve.}
\end{aligned}
$$

The four components of the LDPA in (15.25) can be explained as follows:

1 The *return on general assets* $(r_s)$. This can be analyzed using the Fama decomposition or one of the other decompositions listed in section 15.3 above;

2 The *return on liability-driven assets due to security selection* in terms of say credit quality management or sector management. This follows because $r_b$ is the actual return on the bonds chosen by the fund manager, whereas $\bar{r}_b$ is the benchmark return on the bonds if they were correctly priced according to the yield curve: $(r_b - \bar{r}_b)$ has a similar interpretation to $\alpha_D$ in (15.16) above;

3 The *return on liability-driven assets due to market timing*, that is, from choosing a portfolio of bonds with a maturity structure that differs from that of the underlying liabilities;

4 The *return from funding mismatch*, that is, from active management of the liability-driven assets such that part of this category is invested in general assets such as shares.

We can illustrate the LDPA using an example. Suppose that an investor has the following balance sheet at the start and end of the year:

| | Assets | | | Liabilities | |
|---|---|---|---|---|---|
| | *Start year* | *End year* | | *Start year* | *End year* |
| Liability-driven assets $(V_b)$ | 850 | 950 | Liabilities $(V_l)$ | 900 | 990 |
| General assets $(V_s)$ | 150 | 180 | Net worth $(W)$ | 100 | 140 |
| | 1000 | 1130 | | 1000 | 1130 |

We will assume that the liability-driven assets are bonds, while the general assets are shares (and that shares have no yield curve effect). The value of the liabilities is calculated as the present value of the liability cash flows using appropriate spot yields. We have the following returns on the components of the balance sheet:

| Component | Actual return | Benchmark return |
|---|---|---|
| Bonds | $r_b = 11.76\%$ | $\bar{r}_b = 12.50\%$ |
| Shares | $r_s = 20.00\%$ | $\bar{r}_s = 17.50\%$ |
| Liabilities | $r_l = 10.00\%$ | |

The actual returns are found by taking the difference between the end-of-year to start-of-year values as a ratio of the start-of-year values. The benchmark return on bonds is calculated in a similar way but based on start- and end-year present values of coupon payments using appropriate spot yields. The benchmark return on shares is simply the return on a relevant index, e.g. FTSE 100 index.

Using equation (15.24) with $\lambda = V_l/W = 9$ and $\gamma = (V_l - V_b)/W = 0.5$ (using start-of-year values), the LDPA is determined as follows:

| | Component | Return (%) |
|---|---|---|
| 1 | General assets $[r_s]$ | 20.00 |
| 2 | Security selection $[\lambda(r_b - \bar{r}_b)]$ | −6.66 |
| 3 | Market timing $[\lambda(\bar{r}_b - r_l)]$ | 22.50 |
| 4 | Funding mismatch $[\gamma(r_s - r_b)]$ | 4.12 |
| | Total | 39.96 |

The total return on net worth of 39.96 per cent is made up of 20.00 per cent from the performance of general assets, 22.50 per cent from successful market timing of the bond portfolio, 4.12 per cent from a successful funding mismatch, and a loss of 6.66 per cent from unsuccessful security selection. The security selection and market timing effects are magnified by a high leverage ratio ($\lambda$) of 9, while the funding mismatch effect is reduced by a small funding mismatch ratio ($\gamma$) of 0.5.

## 15.6  Portfolios containing financial futures and options contracts

In 1992, LIFFE recommended that an industry standard be adopted for both the reporting and performance measurement of financial futures and options in investment portfolios. The following draws heavily on the LIFFE report containing these recommendations (LIFFE (1992)). One of the most striking aspects of these recommendations is that they do not deal with risk-adjusted performance measurement. LIFFE considered the issue but concluded that 'risk-adjusted performance measurement has never really been adopted in the UK, and currently forms no part of conventional performance measurement reports. We believe very strongly that it should not be employed solely for derivatives, which would only reinforce the misconception that they are inherently more risky than securities' (p.6).

### 15.6.1  Individual treatment of futures

**Reporting.** *All futures positions should be individually listed under the relevant asset class. All futures positions should be shown at market value. The holdings of cash assets in the portfolio should be shown separately from futures positions.* Margin payments should simply be aggregated into the appropriate asset class for summary purposes. The general principle is that *where the exposure of the portfolio to different asset classes has been changed through the use of futures this should be both recognized and explicit.* Thus in the reporting process, the true level of exposure, the *associated economic exposure of the portfolio after adjustment for the futures positions*, should be shown.

A futures contract represents a transaction with delayed settlement. Thus a long futures position is equivalent to purchasing the underlying asset with delayed or borrowed payment. Therefore, a long FTSE 100 futures position together with a holding in cash creates an asset which behaves like the FTSE 100 index. An explicit adjustment should be shown in the portfolio valuation to recognize this. In this case, the adjustment is made by increasing the UK equity exposure and reducing the cash exposure of the portfolio by the associated economic exposure of the futures position. Similarly, a short futures position is equivalent to selling the underlying asset with delayed receipt. Thus holding the stocks comprising the FTSE 100 index together with a short FTSE 100 futures position creates an asset which behaves like cash. Here the adjustment required is to reduce the UK equity exposure and increase the cash exposure of the portfolio, again by the associated economic exposure of the futures position. *In producing a central summary of the portfolio, futures positions should be treated as creating exposure to the underlying asset of value equal to the market value of the futures.*

Where there is insufficient cash to back a long futures position, the portfolio has geared its exposure to the underlying assets. *The same reporting procedure must be followed in such cases.* This will show that the cash position is effectively overdrawn, making the nature of the gearing clear to the reader.

*Associated economic exposure is in all cases calculated by reference to the market price of the futures contract.* (LIFFE (1992), S4–S7).

**Performance measurement.** The true asset allocation of the portfolio, including the associated economic exposure of the futures position, should be used in the measurement calculations. It is therefore necessary to adjust the components of return within individual asset classes to reflect this modified exposure.

LIFFE therefore recommends that *the capital gain on the futures contracts should be allocated to the underlying asset class. Interest earned on the cash backing the futures should be transferred between the cash sector and the underlying asset class.* For a long futures positions interest would be transferred from the *cash sector* to the *underlying asset class.* For a short futures position the transfer would be from the *underlying asset class* to the *cash sector* (LIFFE (1992) S8–S7).

While the futures themselves will not generate any cash return, they should be credited with a return either at the same rate actually earned on the cash backing the futures position or at a notional rate equal to the interest rate earned on the cash assets in the portfolio or at some suitable benchmark rate.

## 15.6.2 Individual treatment of options

**Reporting.** *All options positions should be individually listed under the relevant asset class. All options positions should be shown at market value and the book cost of the purchase price should also be shown. The holdings of cash assets in the portfolio should be shown separately from options positions.* Margin payments should simply be aggregated into the appropriate asset class for summary purposes.

Options contracts can be used for a wide variety of strategies, and the behaviour of the contracts themselves will not be the same for positive and negative price movements. It is, therefore, not possible to produce a single statement of exposure which accurately reflects the true position of the portfolio. Nevertheless the central summary of the portfolio should value any options positions at their market value and *options positions should be treated as creating exposure to the underlying asset of value equal to the market value of the options.* However, because this is not fully informative it should be supplemented in two ways: written explanation of the strategies being employed should be given, and, where the use of options is material, there should be a subsidiary analysis showing the sensitivity of the options and the asset underlying the options to market movements. The depth of this analysis should reflect the specific needs of the audience to whom the report is addressed.

For externally managed funds such as pension funds, the only requirement is that the sensitivity of the portfolio to a large positive and a large negative market movement is shown. This could be supplemented with intermediate reports if either the managers or their trustees wish to do so. On the other hand, internally managed funds with different risk profiles can adopt more complex and wide ranging formats if they wish.

It has been necessary to develop a test to establish whether the use of options is material. This is done by assessing the size of *all* options positions, irrespective of whether they are long or short, against the total portfolio. Where this ratio exceeds a certain amount, a supplementary reporting process is triggered (LIFFE (1992), S10–S14). LIFFE recommends the following *test of materiality.* LIFFE defines the *options position ratio* (OPR) as:

$$\text{Options position ratio} = \frac{\text{Aggregate exercise value of all options positions}}{\text{Total value of portfolio}}, \tag{15.26}$$

where:

$$\text{Exercise value of an option} = \text{Exercise price} \times \text{Number of shares in option contract}. \quad (15.27)$$

LIFFE recommends that bought and written options positions be shown separately and also that if the OPR exceeds 4 per cent of the total value of the portfolio, then this should trigger a supplementary report. The purpose of any supplementary report is to indicate to the reader the impact on the portfolio of the exposure to options. In particular, it should provide:

1  A sensitivity analysis describing the impact of the options (both individually and in aggregate) on the behaviour of the portfolio if the underlying securities rise or fall in value by 50 per cent;

2  A list of all short positions that are not offset by a related long position; and

3  An analysis of the aggregate exposure of all short put positions against the total cash available to cover them.

**Performance measurement.**    The capital gain (or loss) on the options position should be determined on a market value basis and should be allocated to the asset class underlying the option (LIFFE (1992), S15).

## 15.6.3  A worked example

This worked example of reporting and performance measurement with futures and options is taken from LIFFE (1992), Appendix A.

### 1  Valuation report

Consider a portfolio consisting of the following at the beginning of a quarter:

| *Holding* | *Security description* | *Current price* | *Market value (£,000)* |
|---|---|---|---|
| 100,000 | ICI ordinary | 1,060p | 1,060 |
| (10,000) | ICI call options: July 1050 | 90p | (9) |
| 2,000,000 | Unilever ordinary | 747p | 14,940 |
| 100,000 | Unilever call options: July 700 | 67p | 67 |
| 75 | FTSE 100 June futures contracts (Index × £10) | 2,400 | 1,800 |
| | Cash (including margin) | | 4,000 |

In other words, the fund has sold call options on 10,000 ICI shares, bought call options on 100,000 Unilever shares and bought 75 FTSE 100 futures contracts.

The main valuation summary takes the following form:

| Asset class | Actual holding (£,000) | Associated economic exposure of futures (£,000) | Adjustment for options (£,000) | Aggregate holding (£,000) | Percentage of portfolio (%) |
|---|---|---|---|---|---|
| Equities | 16,000[1] | +1,800[2] | +58 | 17,858 | 89.0 |
| Options | 58[3] | — | (58) | — | — |
| Cash | 4,000 | (1,800) | — | 2,200 | 11.0 |
| | 20,058 | 0 | 0 | 20,058 | 100.0 |

| | |
|---|---|
| OPR for bought options | 3.49% |
| OPR for written options | 0.52% |
| Total OPR[4] | 4.01% |

The amounts numbered are calculated as follows:

1 The sum of the value of the equity holdings:

$$£1,060,000 + £14,940,000 = £16,000,000.$$

2 As shown in the portfolio listing, this is calculated as:

$$75 \times 2,400 \times £10 = £1,800,000.$$

3 The sum of the value of the two options positions:

$$£67,000 - £9,000 = £58,000.$$

4 The exercise value of the options positions would be:

| | | | |
|---|---|---|---|
| ICI | $10,000 \times £10.50$ | = | £105,000 |
| Unilever | $100,000 \times £7.00$ | = | £700,000 |
| | | | £805,000, |

and the OPR would be:

| | | | |
|---|---|---|---|
| Bought options | $\dfrac{£700,000}{£20,058,000}$ | = | 3.49% |
| Written options | $\dfrac{£105,000}{£20,058,000}$ | = | 0.52% |
| | | | 4.01%. |

Since the OPR exceeds the materiality threshold of 4 per cent, the supplementary reporting process takes place. The **Supplementary Report** covering the options positions would be as follows:

### A. Effect of options

*Overall summary.* Percentage change in value if market moves by:

| | −50% | 0 | +50% |
|---|---|---|---|
| Equities | −50.2[1] | 0 | +51.7[2] |

*Individual holdings.* Value in £,000 if share price moves by:

|  |  | −50% | 0 | +50% |
|---|---|---|---|---|
| **Holdings in ICI** | ICI shares | 530[3] | 1,060 | 1,590[4] |
|  | ICI options | 0[5] | (9) | (54)[6] |
|  |  | 530 | 1,051 | 1,536 |
| **Holdings in Unilever** | Unilever shares | 7,470[7] | 14,940 | 22,410[8] |
|  | Unilever options | 0[5] | 67 | 421[9] |
|  |  | 7,470 | 15,007 | 22,831 |

## B.  Short options positions

| Holding | Stock | Type of option | Strike price | Current price of underlying |
|---|---|---|---|---|
| 10,000 | ICI | July Call | 1050p | 1060p |

## C.  Cash required for short put positions

There are no short put positions.

The amounts numbered are calculated as follows:

1  The total value of the equities and equity options (ignoring time value) under this scenario is:

$$£530,000 + £7,470,000 \ = \ £8,000,000.$$

Compared with an initial value of £16,058,000 this represents a net fall of 50.2%.

2  The total value of the equities and equity options (ignoring time value) under this scenario is:

$$£1,536,000 + £22,831,000 \ = \ £24,367,000.$$

Compared with an initial value of £16,058,000 this represents a net increase of 51.7%.

3  Under this scenario, the price of ICI goes to 530p. The value of the ICI shares is then:

$$100,000 \times £5.30 \ = \ £530,000.$$

4  Under this scenario, the price of ICI goes to 1590p. The value of the ICI shares is then:

$$100,000 \times £15.90 \ = \ £1,590,000.$$

5  When the share price halves, the calls are both assumed to be worthless.

6  With the price of ICI at 1590p, the intrinsic value of the call option becomes:

$$£15.90 - £10.50 \ = \ £5.40,$$

and the value of the fund's short position is:

$$-10,000 \times £5.40 \ = \ -£53,000.$$

7 Under this scenario, the price of Unilever goes to 373.5p. The value of Unilever shares is:

$$2,000,000 \times £3.735 \ = \ £7,470,000.$$

8 Under this scenario, the price of Unilever goes to 1120.5p. The value of the Unilever shares is then:

$$2,000,000 \times £11.205 \ = \ £22,410,000.$$

9 With the price of Unilever at 1120.5p the intrinsic value of the call option is:

$$£11.205 - £7.00 \ = \ £4.205,$$

and the value of the long call position held is:

$$100,000 \times £4.205 \ = \ £420,500.$$

## 2   Performance measurement

Suppose the portfolio is held until the end of the quarter, there are no contributions or withdrawals over the quarter and that all investment income is retained as cash. At the end of the quarter the following price movements have taken place:

| | | |
|---|---|---|
| ICI | — | 10% increase to 1.166p. Dividend payment of 21p per share. |
| ICI call option | — | Increase to 120p per option. |
| Unilever | — | 7% increase to 799p. No dividend payment. |
| Unilever call option | — | Increase to 105p per option. |
| FTSE 100 future | — | 4% increase to 2496.   The portfolio therefore has profited by £72,000 which, as variation margin, has already been transferred to the cash sector (see note 2 below). |
| Cash | — | Interest of £121,395 including interest on the variation margin and on the dividend income received (see note 3 below). |

This information can be represented in the following manner:

| Asset | Market value at start of quarter (£,000) | Capital gain (£,000) | Investment income (£,000) | Net transfer into sector (£,000) | Market value at end of quarter (£,000) |
|---|---|---|---|---|---|
| ICI | 1,060 | 106 | 21[1] | (21) | 1,166 |
| ICI options | (9) | (3) | — | — | (12) |
| Unilever | 14,940 | 1,040 | — | — | 15,980 |
| Unilever options | 67 | 38 | — | — | 105 |
| FTSE futures | — | 72[2] | — | (72) | — |
| Cash | 4,000 | — | 121[3] | 93[4] | 4,214 |
| | 20,058 | 1,253 | 142 | 0 | 21,453 |

The amounts numbered are calculated as follows:

1  This represents the dividends received of:

$$100,000 \times £0.21 \;=\; £21,000.$$

2  The gain on the futures contracts is:

$$(2496 - 2400) \times £10 \times 75 \;=\; £72,000.$$

3  The interest can be reconciled as:

$$0.03 \times £4,000,000 + 0.15 \times £93,000 \;=\; £121,395.$$

4  This is the total cash received, being variation margin *plus* investment income:

$$£21,000 + £72,000 \;=\; £93,000.$$

The performance of the fund can then be measured as:

| | Market value at start of quarter (£,000) | Capital gain (£,000) | Investment income (£,000) | Net transfer into sector (£,000) | Market value at end of quarter (£,000) | Percentage return[1] (%) |
|---|---|---|---|---|---|---|
| ***Before adjustment*** | | | | | | |
| Equities | 16,000 | 1,146 | 21 | (21) | 17,146 | 7.3 |
| Options | 58 | $35^2$ | — | — | 93 | — |
| Cash | 4,000 | — | 121 | 93 | 4,214 | 3.0 |
| Futures | — | 72 | — | (72) | — | — |
| | 20,058 | 1,253 | 142 | 0 | 21,453 | 7.0 |
| | | | | | | |
| ***Impact on futures*** | | | | | | |
| Synthetic equities | $1,800^3$ | $72^4$ | $54^5$ | $(54)^6$ | $1,872^7$ | 7.1 |
| Cash | $(1,800)^8$ | — | $54^9$ | $(18)^{10}$ | $(1,872)^{11}$ | 3.0 |
| Total $^{12}$ | 0 | 72 | 0 | (72) | 0 | |
| | | | | | | |
| ***After adjustment*** | | | | | | |
| Equities $^{13}$ | 17,858 | 1,253 | 75 | (75) | 19,111 | 7.5 |
| Cash $^{14}$ | 2,200 | — | 67 | $75^{15}$ | 2,342 | 3.0 |
| | 20,058 | 1,253 | 142 | 0 | 21,453 | 7.0 |

The amounts numbered are calculated as follows:

1  All return figures are calculated using the approximate formula for the return:

$$r \;=\; \frac{V_1 - V_0 - CF}{V_0 + CF/2},$$

where:

$$V_1 = \text{market value at end of quarter;}$$
$$V_0 = \text{market value at beginning of quarter;}$$
$$CF = \text{net transfer into sector.}$$

2  The sum of the capital gains on each option position is:

$$£38,000 - £3,000 = £35,000.$$

3  The associated economic exposure of the futures position.

4  The capital gain on the futures position.

5  It is assumed that the interest received on the cash backing the futures contracts cannot be separately identified and therefore the average rate earned of 3.0% is used. It should be noted that the associated economic exposure of the futures positions increased over the quarter as the contract price rose. This increase in the exposure is matched by the positive variation margin flows. It is allowed for by including the interest earned (actually or notionally) on the variation margin. Therefore the investment income that should be allocated is:

$$£1,800,000 \times 0.03 + £72,000 \times 0.015 = £55,080.$$

However, this figure needs to be adjusted to reflect the fact that the performance calculation in (1) assumes income is received mid-quarter. This is done by reducing the allocated amount by half a quarter's interest:

$$\frac{£55.080}{1.015} = £54,266.$$

6  The transfer out balances the investment income credited in (5).

7  The sum of the preceding items in the line. It can also be reached as:

$$75 \times 2496 \times £10 = £1872,000.$$

8  The complementary exposure to (3).

9  The complementary income to (5).

10  There are two elements to transfer. The investment income credited to the futures position must be transferred into the cash sector by analogy with actual dividend income received. In the opposite direction the variation margin which has already been transferred into the cash sector must be reallocated to the synthetic equity position. Thus the net transfer on the cash backing the futures contract is:

$$£54,266 - £72,000 = -£17,734.$$

11  The complementary exposure to (7).

12  Note that these sums mirror the entry for futures in the first table.

13  This line represents the sum of the UK equities, options and synthetic equities lines above.

14  This line represents the sum of the two cash lines above.

15  Thus the transfer into the cash sector, assumed to occur mid-way through the period, is the investment income on the equity position (actual dividends on the ICI shares and notional income on the futures position).

## 15.7  Performance measurement with multiple fund managers

It is inevitable that large funds (those with assets in excess of around £500m) will have more than one fund manager running them; indeed very large funds might have more than 50 managers. This is because no single manager can possibly be an expert on all the securities traded on all the financial markets of the world. Fund managers will be appointed for their different specialities (e.g. large cap stocks, small cap stocks, growth stocks, value stocks, bonds, cash, managed futures, established overseas markets and emerging markets). But the use of multiple managers increases the costs of fund management and, in particular, introduces coordination problems between fund managers. So the sponsor of any investment fund (such as the trustees of a pension scheme) faces a trade-off between the additional costs and the additional perceived benefits of multiple management.

This trade-off has long been recognized in the US where the appointment of managers with a specialist mandate (e.g. in US large cap stocks) is common. For example, with US pension funds, the trustees, using pension consultants, will decide the strategic asset allocation and then set specialist mandates for managers. The consultants are aware that they are sacrificing control to obtain informational advantage from specialist managers (see, e.g., Rudd and Clasing (1982, Chapter 6)). However, the trade-off is also present in the UK context where balanced management dominates. This is because large funds will often appoint a number of balanced fund managers and even within the same balanced fund management house, there will be a specialist equity manager and a specialist bond manager each of whom will not necessarily know precisely what the other is doing at least on a day-to-day basis.

The excess return earned by the fund as a whole will be the weighted average of the excess returns earned by each of the appointed fund managers. But these excess returns are the outcome of the sponsor's own selection process, and the sponsor's ability in identifying good managers. Able sponsors will select able managers, while substandard sponsors will choose substandard managers.

The benefit from multiple management is the increase in alpha which the fund as a whole generates above that achieved by a single manager alone. The increase in alpha should exceed the additional costs of multiple management in the form of additional fees paid to multiple managers, additional trading costs incurred by multiple managers and any increase in residual risk resulting from inadequate coordination between managers. One important measure of skill is the *information ratio* (see equation (15.8)). This can be used in both the selection and appraisal processes. Managers should be appointed or removed if this leads to an improvement in the overall portfolio's information ratio. However, fund managers should be given sufficient time to demonstrate their superior abilities, e.g. at least three years. Consultants now realize that there are different variabilities of performance between, say, value and growth styles of management in the short term.

Figure 15.11 shows the typical effect of multiple managers on total risk. Total risk can be reduced by around 20%, but systematic risk is *not* reduced at all by the appointment of multiple managers. This is because the appointment of more managers *cannot* lead to greater diversification. Greater diversification can be achieved only by placing a larger proportion of the portfolio in an index fund. The effect of multiple managers can be to diversify away specific risk however. Specific risk has three components: stock selection, market timing and exposure to common factors (i.e. where managers have the same relative bias, e.g. a growth stock bias in the 1970s, a small-cap bias in the 1980s, an emerging markets bias in the 1990s). The stock selection component of specific risk is generally reduced the most by having multiple managers, since stock selection skills are likely to be the least correlated between fund managers. Market timing and exposure to common factors are likely to be more highly correlated and so will be reduced less. However, the effect of successful multiple management is to increase the relative proportion of systematic risk in the total risk of the portfolio.

**Figure 15.11** The effect on total risk of multiple managers

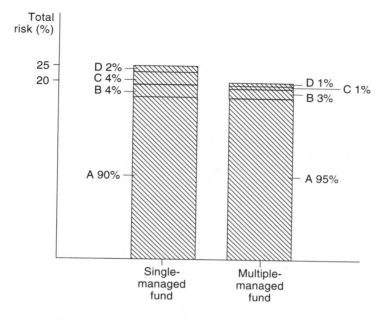

*Source:* Rudd and Clasing (1982)

The greatest risk incurred by the sponsor of a multi-managed fund is exposure to common factors. A number of the managers could have the same exposure, leading to the aggregate portfolio having an excessive concentration in a particular sector. To avoid this, the sponsor has to understand fully the investment styles of each of his managers and control the distribution of funds to the different managers accordingly. This must be done in a way that ensures that the sum of the normal weights of the individual managers equates to the sponsor's own normal weights for the whole portfolio (i.e. to the portfolio strategic asset allocation). This is the only way to avoid exposure to common factors, and only the sponsor, as central co-ordinator, can do this. There are two main ways of dealing with exposure to common factors: a *completeness fund* or a *compensating core*.

With a completeness fund, the sponsor specifies normal portfolio weights, e.g. a market-weighted portfolio of all quoted shares in the economy. The sponsor then appoints two managers say: one specializing in the largest 100 companies, the other specializing in small-cap stocks. The sponsor is therefore going to be under-weight in medium-sized companies, and so builds up a passive completeness fund in such companies. Each manager is allowed to specify his own universe of shares and is set the target of out-performing the value-weighted index comprising this universe. This is the only target that is relevant, since it allows managers to be judged exclusively on the basis of their declared skills (as specified by the universe they select). The managers do, however, have an incentive to include in their specified universe as many underperforming stocks (or *dogs*) as possible, since this makes it easier to beat the index.

With a compensating core, the intention is to construct a passive core fund that counteracts any undesired exposures and leaves the active fund facing only the exposures desired by the active fund manager. For example, the fund manager might prefer computer software companies, but choosing these also gives an undesired exposure to a small-cap factor and a Californian factor. The compensating core would be constructed in such a way to minimize the portfolio's overall exposure to undesirable factors.

Sponsors of active funds can help to reduce transactions costs by establishing an *inventory index fund*. Active fund managers can sell shares to the inventory fund and buy shares from the fund if it has them in stock. These trades are done at the last quoted price on the official market, but the active fund managers are not charged brokerage commissions or spreads.

We argued above that managers should be appointed and removed on the basis of their information ratios. But the information ratio itself can lead to a conflict between the sponsor and the manager. The sponsor wants to see an increase in the information ratio. The manager could attempt to do this by increasing the alpha of the portfolio, but this involves some risk and the alpha could end up being negative, which is likely to lead to the manager being fired. An alternative is for the manager to reduce specific risk by running a closet index fund, on the grounds that the best way to keep your client is never to come last. But then the danger is that the manager does not generate sufficient additional return to finance his active fee.

In summary, managers should be appointed to increase the total portfolio alpha, not to increase diversification; individual active fund managers should attempt to beat their individually agreed benchmark targets, but the sponsor should be concerned about the individual fund managers' contributions to the total portfolio return; the sponsor should also deal with undesired exposure to common factors by ensuring that they are hedged by use of a completeness fund or a compensating core, and that the aggregate normal asset holdings of individual fund managers do not get out of line with the fund's intended strategic asset allocation.

## 15.8   The Roll critique of performance measurement

The evaluation of performance measurement outlined above, which is based on the capital asset pricing model and the security market line, has been criticized by Roll (1977). His main criticisms are that:

1 The market portfolio must include all assets, both marketable and non-marketable (e.g. human capital, land, paintings, homes); it is therefore impossible to observe the market portfolio in practice;

2 The market portfolio has to be mean-variance-efficient if the CAPM is valid; this makes the efficiency of the market portfolio and the validity of the CAPM joint hypotheses which are virtually impossible to test because of the problem of measuring the true market portfolio;

3 If an *ex post* inefficient benchmark index is used, then any ranking of portfolio performance is possible depending on which inefficient benchmark is used; this means that the CAPM cannot be meaningfully used to decompose portfolio performance.

## 15.9   Evidence on the performance of fund managers

A number of studies have investigated the performance of fund managers; most of them have involved an examination of the performance of US institutional managers of unit trusts (mutual funds in the US) and pension funds. They have examined the managers' abilities in security selection, market timing and persistence of performance over time.

Studies to determine the ability of fund managers to pick securities generally analyze the (Jensen version of the) alpha values of the funds (see equation (15.14)). For example, Elton et al. (1993), using data from 1965 to 1984 on 143 equity mutual funds, found that the average *ex post* alpha value was negative (at –0.8 per cent per annum) and that only 44 (31 per cent) of the funds had positive alphas; while Shukla and Trzcinka (1992), using a larger and more recent data set from 1979 to 1989 on 257 equity mutual funds, also found a negative average *ex post* alpha value (–0.74 per cent per annum) and that only 115 funds (45 per cent) had positive alphas. Similar results were found for US pension funds by Lakonishok et al. (1992): using data on 769 all-equity pension funds between 1983 and 1989, they found that the average fund had a negative *ex post* alpha value of –2.6 per cent per year. These results suggest that a typical fund manager has not been able to select shares that on average subsequently outperform the market, i.e. a buy-and-hold strategy with the same overall beta as the typical fund manager.

However, these results have to be modified when shares are separated into types according to investment style: *value strategies* invest only in *value shares* (shares which have low market-to-book rates) and *growth strategies* invest only in *growth shares* (shares which have high market-to-book ratios). Fama and French (1992), using data on US shares between 1963 and 1990, found a strong negative relationship between these shares' performance and their market-to-book ratios, suggesting that value strategies might outperform growth strategies. Coggin et al. (1993), using data on 71 all-equity pension funds between 1983 and 1990, also found that this was the case: the average value strategy generated an *ex post* alpha value of 2.1 per cent per annum, while the average growth strategy produced an *ex post* alpha value of –0.96 per cent per annum.

The market timing skills of fund managers have been examined in studies by Treynor and Mazuy (1966), Shukla and Trzcinka (op.cit.) and Coggin et al. (op.cit.). Treynor and Mazuy examined 57 US mutual funds between 1953 and 1962 and found that only one had any significant timing ability. The later study of 257 mutual funds by Shukla and Trzcinka found that the average fund had negative timing ability, indicating that the average fund manager would have done better by executing the opposite set of trades. A similar result was identified in the study of 71 pension funds by Coggin et al. This study found an overall market timing ability (i.e. the estimate of $c$ in (15.18)) of –0.28, with growth strategies and value strategies generating market timing coefficients of 0.01 and –0.18, respectively, indicating that managers following growth strategies showed negligible market timing skills and managers following value strategies had negative market timing skills.

Hendricks et al. (1993) examined 165 US mutual funds between 1974 and 1988 for persistence of performance over time, i.e. whether good (or bad) performance in one period was associated with good (or bad) performance in subsequent periods. They found that the top quartile of funds with the best performance over a two-year period subsequently had an average 6.5% p.a. superior return over the subsequent two-year period compared with the bottom quartile of funds with the worst performance over the same two-year period. But this was the average superior performance, and individual funds' performance can differ significantly from the average. This is shown clearly in a study by Bogle (1992) who examined the subsequent performance of the top 20 funds every year between 1982 and 1992. He found that the average position of the top 20 funds in the following year was only 284th out of 681, not very far in ranking from the median fund in 341st position.

Similar results have been found for the UK. For example, Blake, Lehmann and Timmermann (1998, 1999), in a study of 364 UK pension funds between 1986 and 1994, found that the average return over the sample period was 12.034 per cent per annum. Using the decomposition of Brinson and Fachler (1986) and Brinson, Hood and Beebower (1986) (i.e., (15.20)), this total return could be decomposed as follows:

| | |
|---|---|
| Strategic return | 12.373% |
| Return from market timing | -0.333% |
| Return from security selection | -0.058% |
| Residual return | 0.052% |
| | 12.034% |

These results demonstrate that the bulk of the return generated by UK pension funds comes from the passive strategic asset allocation, while the returns to both market timing and security selection are negative. This study also found that there was some short-term persistence in performance. The top quartile of funds in one year generated an average superior return of 0.4 per cent the following year compared with the bottom quartile of funds for the same year. However, this superior performance did not extend over a three-year investment horizon.

All these results indicate that fund managers are, on average, not especially successful at active portfolio management, either in the form of security selection or in market timing; although there does appear to be a negative correlation between selection and timing skills. However there does appear to be some evidence of consistency of performance, at least over short periods; but as the saying goes: past performance is not necessarily a good indicator of future performance.

## Appendix: A note on the different uses of the geometric mean and the arithmetic mean

It is generally the case that the geometric mean should be used to determine *past* performance but that the arithmetic mean is a better indicator of likely *future* performance. This can be demonstrated very simply using an example.

Suppose that over a two-year period a share with an initial value of £1 doubles in value in the first year (i.e. $r_1 = 100$ per cent) and then halves in value in the second year (i.e. $r_2 = -50$ per cent). The share price therefore ends up at £1 where it started two years before and so the average return over the period is zero. The geometric mean return for years 1 and 2 generates this result as follows:

$$
\begin{aligned}
\bar{r}_g &= [(1+r_1)(1+r_2)]^{\frac{1}{2}} - 1 \\
&= [(1+1)(1-0.5)]^{\frac{1}{2}} - 1 \\
&= 0.
\end{aligned}
$$

However the expected return in the third year is not zero if it is believed that the distribution of returns in the third year is the same as in the first two years. In this case there is a 50 per cent chance that a share valued at £1 at the end of year 2 will increase by £1 by the end of year 3 (i.e., when $r_3 = 100$ per cent) and a 50 per cent chance that it will fall by £0.50 by the end of year 3 (i.e. when $r_3 = -50$ per cent). The expected return is simply the average of the two returns in the two states of the world, i.e. $(£1 + (-£0.50))/2 = £0.25$, which equates to a 25 per cent expected rate of return on an initial investment of £1. The arithmetic mean return for years 1 and 2 gives us this result as follows:

$$\bar{r}_a = \frac{r_1 + r_2}{2}$$
$$= \frac{1 + (-0.5)}{2}$$
$$= 0.25 \quad (25\%).$$

A related issue concerns the use of the geometric mean and arithmetic mean in performance evaluation. A geometric index will always 'underperform' in comparison with an arithmetic index. It is therefore sensible for a fund manager to try to persuade the client to agree to a benchmark based on a geometric index which is easier to 'beat'. This can be demonstrated very easily using Jensen's inequality. Consider two securities with *ex post* returns $r_1$ and $r_2$. Jensen's inequality states that:

$$\left[ (r_1)^{\frac{1}{2}} - (r_2)^{\frac{1}{2}} \right]^2 = r_1 + r_2 - 2(r_1)^{\frac{1}{2}}(r_2)^{\frac{1}{2}} > 0.$$

This, in turn, implies that:

$$r_1 + r_2 > 2(r_1)^{\frac{1}{2}}(r_2)^{\frac{1}{2}},$$

or:

$$\frac{r_1 + r_2}{2} > (r_1 r_2)^{\frac{1}{2}},$$

that is, arithmetic mean $(\bar{r}_a) >$ geometric mean $(\bar{r}_g)$.

## Selected references

Belchamber, C. (1988), *The UK Government Bond Market*, Credit Suisse First Boston, London. (Chapter: 'Indices and Investment Performance'.)

Blake, D., Lehmann, B.N. and Timmermann, A. (1998), 'Performance Clustering and Incentives in the UK Pension Fund Industry', Discussion Paper 294, Financial Markets Group London School of Economics.

Blake, D., Lehmann, B.N., and Timmermann, A. (1999), 'Asset Allocation Dynamics and Pension Fund Performance', *Journal of Business*, 72, 429–62.

Bogle, J. (1992), 'Selecting Equity Mutual Funds', *Journal of Portfolio Management*, Winter, 94–100.

Brinson, G. and Fachler, N. (1986), 'Measuring Non-US Equity Portfolio Performance', *Journal of Portfolio Management*, Spring, 73–76.

Brinson, G., Hood, L. and Beebower, G. (1986), 'Determinants of Portfolio Performance', *Financial Analysts Journal*, July-August, 39–48.

Coggin, T., Fabozzi, F. and Rahman, S. (1992), 'The Investment Performance of US Equity Pension Fund Managers: An Empirical Investigation', *Journal of Finance*, 48, 1039–55.

Cooper, I. and Franks, J. (1987), 'Treasury Performance Measurement', *Midland Corporate Financial Journal*, 4, 29–43.

Elton, E.J. and Gruber, M.J. (1995), *Modern Portfolio Theory and Investment Analysis*, John Wiley, New York. (Chapter 24.)

Elton, E., Gruber, M., Das, S. and Hlavka, M. (1993), 'Efficiency with Costly Information: A Reinterpretation of Evidence from Managed Funds', *Review of Financial Studies*, 6, 1–22.

Fama, E. (1972), 'Components of Investment Performance', *Journal of Finance*, 27, 551–67.

Fama, E. and French, K. (1992), 'The Cross-Section of Expected Returns', *Journal of Finance*, 47, 427–65.

Francis, J.C. (1995), *Investments*, McGraw-Hill, Singapore. (Chapter 21.)

Fong, H.G. and Fabozzi, F.J. (1985), *Fixed Income Portfolio Management*, Dow Jones-Irwin, Homewood, Ill. (Chapter 7.)

Fong, H.G., Pearson, C. and Vasicek, O. (1983), 'Bond Performance: Analyzing Sources of Returns', *Journal of Portfolio Management*, Spring, 46–50.

Hendricks, D., Patel, J. and Zeckhauser, R. (1993), 'Hot Hands in Mutual Funds: Short-Run Persistence of Relative Performance', *Journal of Finance*, 48, 93–130.

Jensen, M. (1969), 'Risk, the Pricing of Capital Assets and the Evaluation of Investment Portfolios', *Journal of Business*, 42, 167–247.

Lakonishok, J., Shleifer, A. and Vishny, R. (1992), 'The Structure and Performance of the Money Management Industry', *Brookings Papers on Economic Activity: Microeconomics*, 339–379.

LIFFE (1992), *The Reporting and Performance Measurement of Financial Futures and Options in Investment Portfolios*, London International Financial Futures and Options Exchange, London, January.

Plantinga, A. and van der Meer, R. (1995), 'Liability-Driven Performance Attribution', *Geneva Papers on Risk and Insurance*, 20, 16–29.

Roll, R. (1977), 'A Critique of the Asset Pricing Theory's Tests', *Journal of Financial Economics*, 4, 129–76.

Rudd, A. and Clasing, H.K. (1982), *Modern Portfolio Theory: The Principles of Investment Management*, Dow Jones-Irwin, Homewood, Ill.

Rutterford, J. (1993), *Introduction to Stock Exchange Investment*, Macmillan, London. (Chapter 13.)

Sharpe, W.F. (1966), 'Mutual Fund Performance', *Journal of Business*, 39, 119–38.

Sharpe, W.F., Alexander, G. and Bailey, J. (1995), *Investments*, Prentice-Hall, Englewood Cliffs, NJ. (Chapter 25.)

Shukla, R. and Trzcinka, C. (1992), 'Performance Measurement of Managed Portfolios', *Financial Markets, Institutions and Instruments*, 1.

Treynor, J. (1965), 'How to Rate Management of Investment Funds', *Harvard Business Review*, January-February, 63–75.

Treynor, J. and Mazuy, K. (1966), 'Can Mutual Funds Outguess the Market?', *Harvard Business Review*, July-August, 131–36.

## Exercises

1 Distinguish between the time-weighted rate of return and the money-weighted rate of return on a portfolio.

2 The performance of five portfolios last year was as follows:

| Portfolio | Return (%) | Standard deviation of returns (%) | Beta |
|---|---|---|---|
| A | 25 | 10 | 1.5 |
| B | 15 | 8 | 0.8 |
| C | 20 | 6 | 1.1 |
| D | 19 | 7 | 0.9 |
| E | 20 | 5 | 1.5 |

The riskless interest rate during the year was 10 per cent and the return on the market was 19 per cent.

   a) Rank the portfolios using Sharpe's measure.

   b) Rank the portfolios using Treynor's measure.

   c) Rank the portfolios using Jensen's measure.

   d) With reference to your calculations, how well was portfolio E managed?

3 Discuss the difference between the Sharpe and Treynor measures of portfolio performance measurement.

4 Explain the Fama decomposition of portfolio returns.

5 The Treynor measure is the best way of assessing portfolio performance. Do you agree?

6 Explain how you would analyze the performance of

   a) a treasury portfolio;

   b) a bond portfolio;

   c) a share portfolio.

7 You are given the following data on the annual returns generated by a fund manager and by the market portfolio:

| Year | Fund manager (%) | Market portfolio (%) |
|------|------------------|----------------------|
| 1 | +10 | +8 |
| 2 | +30 | +15 |
| 3 | 0 | +10 |
| 4 | −15 | −9 |
| 5 | +12 | +7 |

Calculate and analyze the excess return earned by the fund manager during the period, assuming that the average value of the riskless rate of interest was 4 per cent.

8 Is the following statement true or false? The money-weighted rate of return is the same as the internal rate of return, whereas the time-weighted rate of return is the same as the geometric mean return.

9 You are given the following information about a fund:

| Time | 0 | 6 mos. | 1 yr. | 18 mos. | 2 yrs |
|------|---|--------|-------|---------|-------|
| Cash flow | 20 | −30 | 60 | −50 | 0 |
| Value of fund (excl. cash flow) | 100 | 135 | 120 | 190 | 150 |

Calculate (a) the two-year money-weighted rate of return; (b) the two-year time-weighted rate of return. Comment on your results.

10 Suppose that you are a fund manager. If you were given the choice, what kind of benchmark portfolio would you like your performance to be measured against? Is it likely that your preferred benchmark portfolio would differ from that preferred by your client?

11 You are given the following data on the annual return generated by the riskless security, by a fund manager and by the market portfolio:

| Year | Riskless security (%) | Fund manager (%) | Market portfolio (%) |
|------|-----------------------|------------------|----------------------|
| 1 | +4 | +10 | +8 |
| 2 | +5 | +30 | +15 |
| 3 | +4 | 0 | +10 |
| 4 | +3 | −15 | −9 |
| 5 | +4 | +12 | +7 |

How well did the fund manager perform against the market using (a) Sharpe's measure, (b) Treynor's measure, and (c) Jensen's measure?

12 You are given the following information on a bond portfolio:

| Bond | Proportion of portfolio (%) | Return (%) | Specific risk (%) | Duration (years) |
|------|-----------------------------|------------|-------------------|------------------|
| A | 20 | 9 | 12 | 5 |
| B | 25 | 10 | 10 | 7 |
| C | 35 | 11 | 11 | 9 |
| D | 20 | 12 | 13 | 11 |

If the riskless rate of interest is 7 per cent and the return, total risk and duration of the market portfolio of bonds are respectively 10 per cent, 12 per cent and 10 years, assess the performance of the manager of the bond portfolio.

13  What are the main problems with presenting measures of portfolio performance, such as the Sharpe and Treynor measures?

14  You are given the following data on the performance of a fund and on the market:

| | |
|---|---|
| Return on the portfolio | 22% |
| Total risk of the portfolio | 26% |
| Beta of the portfolio | 1.2 |
| Return on the market | 17% |
| Total risk of the market | 20% |
| Riskless interest rate | 9% |

Using Fama's decomposition, identify the sources of the fund manager's performance.

# Chapter 16

# Hedging and efficient portfolio management

In this chapter, we consider the important function of hedging or managing risks, and the role of futures, options and swaps and other derivatives in performing this function. We also examine a recent hedging innovation, portfolio insurance. We conclude with a discussion of the use of derivatives in efficient portfolio management.

## 16.1   The objective of hedging

The objective of *hedging* (or *risk management*) is to transfer risk from one individual or corporation to another individual or corporation. The person off-loading the risk is the *hedger*, the person taking on the risk is the *speculator* or *trader*.

The hedger is concerned with adverse movements in security prices or with increases in volatility which increase the overall riskiness of his position. For example, if an individual has a long position (net asset position) in cash market securities, he will be concerned about the prices of those securities falling and may want to protect against this possibility. Alternatively, if an individual has a short position (net liability position) in cash market securities, he will be concerned about rising prices and may want to protect against this possibility.

In order to hedge successfully and so transfer all (or at least most) risk, the hedger will have to select a suitable hedging instrument, i.e. one whose price movements mirror closely those of the underlying cash market securities. The two most suitable hedging instruments will therefore be instruments that are derivative upon cash market securities, namely financial futures and options. Figure 16.1 shows the effect of hedging on the distribution of security prices. A *perfect hedge* is one in which the hedging instrument is established in such a way that its price movements are *perfectly negatively correlated* with those of the underlying cash security. In this case, the price distribution of the hedged position is said to be *degenerate*. In many cases, however, it is not possible to create a perfect hedge because a perfectly correlated hedging instrument is not available. In such cases, only a partial hedge can be established, but this is often better than no hedge at all. An *anticipatory hedge* is one that hedges an anticipated future or contingent exposure.

**Figure 16.1** The effect of hedging on the distribution of security prices

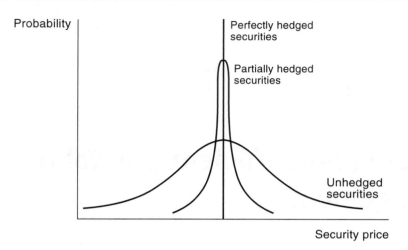

Financial futures and options were first introduced in the 1970s in response to the huge increase in interest rate and exchange rate volatility that resulted from the ending of the Bretton Woods system of fixed exchange rates and the consequential increased volatility in global interest rates. The first hedging instruments were therefore designed to hedge against adverse movements in interest rates and exchange rates. Later, the introduction of (exchange-traded) options on individual shares and options and futures on stock indices allowed share price movements to be hedged as well.

Before deciding which hedging instruments to use, it is necessary to determine the level of risk exposure. Sometimes there is only a single asset or liability that needs to be hedged. But if the hedger has both assets and liabilities on his balance sheet, then the overall level of risk exposure can be reduced by the *natural hedges* within the balance sheet.

We can consider, for example, a bank with the following balance sheet, categorized by maturity of assets and liabilities:

| *Maturity* | *Assets* | *Liabilities* | *Net exposed balance before hedging* | *Net exposed balance after hedging* |
|---|---|---|---|---|
| *(days)* | *(£m)* | *(£m)* | *(£m)* | *(£m)* |
| 0–90 | 100 | 500 | (400) | 0 |
| 91–180 | 200 | 0 | 200 | 0 |
| 181–270 | 200 | 0 | 200 | 200 |
| 271–365 | 200 | 0 | 200 | 200 |
| Perpetual or interest-rate insensitive | 300 | 500 | (200) | (200) |

The assets comprise Treasury bills, loans and property. The liabilities comprise non-interest bearing current accounts, interest-bearing deposit accounts and certificates of deposit, and the bank's equity. The bank has net liabilities (net negative exposure) over the first 90 days and net assets (net positive exposure) over the next 90 days. The bank is therefore concerned that there might be an adverse shift in the yield curve, with three-month interest rates rising and six-month interest rates falling. To protect against this risk, the bank might hedge both the 90-day and 180-day positions, leaving a zero net exposed balance, as shown in the last column of the above table. Precisely what types of hedges might be put on will be discussed later, but in the meantime it is instructive to note the difference between the behaviour considered here and the behaviour considered in Chapter 14. There, when discussing active treasury portfolio management, the treasurer deliberately selected a maturity mismatched balance sheet in order to enhance return. In the present case, the bank is eliminating its maturity mismatching through hedging in order to reduce its exposure to interest rate risk.

## 16.2   Money market hedges

A *money market hedge* (sometimes called a *forward-forward hedge*) works by taking out money market loans and deposits of different maturities, thereby locking in current rates at different maturities along the yield curve.

Suppose that a corporate treasurer wishes to take out a three-month loan of $10m to begin in three month's time and is concerned that interest rates will rise over the next three months. Suppose also that the following eurodollar rates are currently available:

| *Maturity* | *Eurodollar rates* |
|---|---|
| 1 month | 6–6.125 |
| 2 months | 6–6.125 |
| 3 months | 6.125–6.25 |
| 6 months | 6.25–6.375 |

To hedge this risk, the treasurer could borrow $10m now for six months at the current six-month eurodollar offer rate (6.375 per cent) and simultaneously deposit the money for three months at the three-month eurodollar bid rate (6.125 per cent). This means that, in effect, the treasurer is only borrowing three-month money beginning in three months' time:

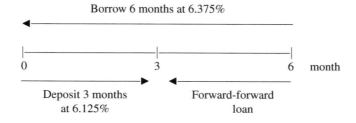

The effective forward-forward borrowing rate is found as follows:

$$\left(6.375 \cdot \frac{180}{360}\right) - \left(6.125 \cdot \frac{90}{360}\right) \quad = \quad 3.1875 - 1.53125$$
$$= \quad 1.65625\%.$$

This is a quarterly rate and has to be annualised:

$$1.65625 \cdot \frac{360}{90} \quad = \quad 6.625\%.$$

Further this rate applies from the third month and has to be discounted back to the current date using the current three-month borrowing rate:

$$\frac{6.625}{1 + [0.0625(90/360)]} = 6.52\%.$$

So the corporate treasurer is locking in a borrowing rate of 6.52% on $10m for three months beginning in three months' time.

The formula for calculating the forward-forward rate directly is as follows:

$$_1rf_2 = \frac{N}{N_2 - N_1} \cdot \frac{\left(rs_2 \cdot \dfrac{N_2}{N}\right) - \left(rs_1 \cdot \dfrac{N_1}{N}\right)}{1 + \left(rs_1 \cdot \dfrac{N_1}{N}\right)}, \tag{16.1}$$

where:

$$
\begin{array}{rcl}
rs_1 & = & \text{spot rate over shorter period;} \\
rs_2 & = & \text{spot rate over longer period;} \\
N_1 & = & \text{number of days in shorter period;} \\
N_2 & = & \text{number of days in longer period;} \\
N & = & \text{number of days in year.}
\end{array}
$$

As another example, suppose that another corporate treasurer, observing the same rates as above, wishes to lock in a three-month deposit rate in three months' time because he fears that interest rates are about to fall and he has dollar funds coming in in three months' time. He can lock in this deposit rate by borrowing money for three months at the current three-month eurodollar offer rate (6.25 per cent) and placing the money on deposit for six months at the current six-month eurodollar bid rate (6.25 per cent). In effect, the treasurer is only taking out a deposit of three months beginning in three months' time:

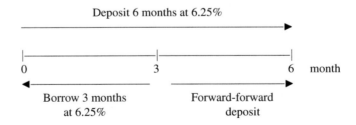

The effective forward-forward deposit rate is found as follows:

$$\left(6.25 \cdot \frac{180}{360}\right) - \left(6.25 \cdot \frac{90}{360}\right) = 3.125 - 1.5625$$

$$= 1.5625.$$

This is a quarterly rate and has to be annualised:

$$1.5625 \cdot \frac{360}{90} = 6.25\%.$$

Again this rate applies from the third month and has to be discounted back to the current date using the current three-month deposit rate:

$$\frac{6.25}{1 + [0.0625 \cdot (90/360)]} = 6.15\%.$$

So the corporate treasurer is locking in a deposit rate of 6.15 per cent on the funds that he expects to receive in three months' time whatever subsequently happens to interest rate levels.

Money market hedges are relatively straightforward to implement but they have certain costs. It is impossible to unwind the hedge once it has been implemented since the money market deposits and loans are of fixed term and non-negotiable. They also involve an expansion of the balance sheet, e.g. the company has to take out debt in order to hedge the future return on the deposit and this may adversely affect the company's gearing level. Finally, money market hedges are generally much more expensive to implement than futures hedges which also remain off-balance sheet. We now turn to an examination of futures hedges.

## 16.3 Hedging using futures

Futures contracts can be used to hedge interest rate risk (both short-term and long-term), market risk and exchange rate risk.

### 16.3.1 Hedging with short-term interest rate futures contracts

We can consider two very simple hedges: a long hedge and a short hedge.

Suppose a company is expecting a cash inflow of £2 million in two months' time which will be invested in a short-term deposit account. The company is concerned that short-term interest rates are going to decline between now and then and decides to hedge this risk by buying four three-month short sterling interest rate futures contracts. In other words, the company puts on a *long hedge*. The outcome is as follows:

| *Date* | *Cash market* | *Futures market* |
|--------|---------------|------------------|
| 15 Apr | Deposit rate $= 11\%$ | Purchase $4 \times £500,000$ June 3-month interest rate futures contracts at 88.5 (i.e. $100 - 11.5\%$) |
| 15 Jun | Invest £2m in 3-month sterling deposit at deposit rate of 9% | Sell $4 \times £500,000$ June contracts at 90.5 (i.e. $100 - 9.5\%$) |
| | Loss in interest: $£2,000,000 \cdot \dfrac{0.11 - 0.09}{4}$ $= £10,000$ | Profit on contracts: $4 \text{ contracts} \times 200 \text{ ticks} \times £12.50 \text{ per tick}$ $= £10,000$ |

This is a perfect hedge. As anticipated, interest rates fell by 2 per cent and this resulted in interest payments being £10,000 lower than expected. However, the futures price and the cash price moved together, and the futures position showed a profit of £10,000, completely compensating for the loss in the cash market. So whatever happens to interest rates subsequently, we are locking in a deposit rate of 11 per cent on 15 April.

As another example, suppose that a company has a £10 million bank loan at 1 per cent above the three-month sterling deposit rate with quarterly rollovers. At the next rollover date in a month's time, the interest rate is expected to be higher, so the company decides to hedge this risk by selling 20 three-month short sterling interest rate futures contracts. In other words, the company puts on a *short hedge*. The outcome is as follows:

| *Date* | *Cash market* | *Futures market* |
|---|---|---|
| 10 Feb | Borrowing rate = 13%  (12% + 1%) | Sell 20 × £500,000 March 3-month interest rate futures contracts at 87.75 (i.e. 100 − 12.25%) |
| 10 Mar | Firm borrows £10m for 3 months at 14%  (13% + 1%) | Purchase 20 × £500,000 March contracts at 86.75 (i.e. 100 − 13.25%) |
|  | Additional interest: $£10,000,000 \cdot \dfrac{0.14 - 0.13}{4}$ $= £25,000$ | Profit on contracts: 20 contracts × 100 ticks × £12.50 per tick $= £25,000$ |

Again, we have a perfect hedge: the additional interest on the loan is exactly matched by the profit on the futures position, thereby locking in a borrowing rate of 13 per cent on 10 February.

So we have the following simple rules for hedging with futures:

1  If *short cash* (i.e. expecting a cash inflow and worried that prices will rise or interest rates will fall), then *buy futures* (i.e. put on a *long hedge*).

2  If *long cash* (i.e. holding cash or securities and worried that prices will fall or interest rates will rise), then *sell futures* (i.e. put on a *short hedge*).

The number of futures contracts required to hedge a cash position is determined as follows. We construct a *hedge portfolio* from a long position in the cash security and a short position in $h$ units of the corresponding futures contract (where $h$ is the *hedge ratio*). (If the initial cash position is a short one, then the hedge portfolio involves a long position in $h$ units of the futures contract.) The value of the hedge portfolio ($V^h$) is given by:

$$V^h = P^s - hP^f, \tag{16.2}$$

where $P^s$ is the value of the cash security and $P^f$ is the value of the futures contract. The optimal hedge ratio is determined to ensure that the hedge portfolio is riskless, or, in other words, has a constant value independent of whether the value of the cash security rises or falls. This requires:

$$\Delta V^h = \Delta P^s - h\Delta P^f = 0, \tag{16.3}$$

(where $\Delta$ denotes a change in value), so that the hedge ratio is determined as:[1]

$$h = \frac{\Delta P^s}{\Delta P^f}. \tag{16.4}$$

---

[1] An alternative definition of the optimal hedge ratio is one that minimizes the variance of the hedge portfolio:

$$\sigma_h^2 = \sigma_s^2 + h^2\sigma_f^2 - 2h\rho\sigma_s\sigma_f.$$

The number of futures contracts necessary to hedge a cash security is given by:

$$\text{Number of contracts} = \frac{\text{Face value of cash exposure}}{\text{Face value of futures contract}} \times h; \qquad (16.5)$$

that is, the number of contracts equals the hedge ratio scaled up by the ratio of the face value of the cash exposure to the face value of the futures contracts. (Note that, in the case of the interest rate contracts just discussed, $h = 1$; i.e., the futures price moved exactly in line with the price of the underlying cash market security.) With the number of contracts determined in this way, the hedge will be perfect (i.e. completely riskless for small changes in security prices). However, in practice, and for reasons discussed below, it may not be possible to put on a perfect hedge, and so the underlying cash position may only be partially hedged (see Figure 16.1).

So far, we have considered hedging using hedging instruments that are perfectly correlated with the underlying cash securities and also have the same maturity. A hedge in which the hedging instrument involves the same underlying security as the security being hedged is called a *direct hedge*. In practice, it may not be possible to hedge using a hedging instrument that is perfectly correlated with, and has the same maturity as, the cash security. A hedge in which the hedging instrument involves a different (and therefore less than perfectly correlated) underlying security to the security being hedged is called a *cross hedge*. In this case, a number of modifications to the hedge ratio have to be made.

With these modifications, the number of contracts is determined by the following formula:

$$\begin{aligned}\text{Number of contracts} = \;&\frac{\text{Face value of cash exposure}}{\text{Face value of futures contract}}\\ &\times \text{Money equivalent ratio}\\ &\times \text{Regression coefficient}, \qquad (16.6)\end{aligned}$$

so that the hedge ratio, $h$, is equal to the product of the money equivalent ratio and the regression coefficient.

The *money equivalent value* measures the change in the price of a futures contract or a cash security in response to a given change in interest rates. This varies with term to maturity. For example, the money equivalent value of 0.01 per cent interest for a contract size of £500,000 is:

|  | Money equivalent value (£) |
|---|---|
| One year | 50.00 |
| Nine months | 37.50 |
| Six months | 25.00 |
| Three months | 12.50 |
| One month | 4.17 |

Differentiating with respect to $h$ gives:

$$\frac{\partial \sigma_h^2}{\partial h} = 2h\sigma_f^2 - 2\rho\sigma_s\sigma_f.$$

Setting this to zero and solving for $h$ gives:

$$h = \rho\frac{\sigma_s}{\sigma_f}.$$

Since $\partial^2\sigma_h^2/\partial h^2 > 0$, we know that this is the hedge ratio that minimizes the variance of the hedge portfolio. The optimal hedge ratio increases with the correlation between the hedging instrument and the underlying security ($\rho$) and with the relative volatility of the underlying security to the hedging instrument.

The *money equivalent ratio* is the ratio of two money equivalent values. For example, in order to hedge a six-month cash security with a three month futures contract, the money equivalent ratio will be 2 (i.e. 25.00/12.50); i.e., two futures contracts will be needed for each cash security because the six-month security is twice as responsive to a given interest rate change as the three-month futures contract.

The *regression coefficient* measures the responsiveness of the cash price to the futures price. Suppose, for example, we are proposing to hedge six-month certificates of deposit with three-month interest rate futures, and further suppose that the regression of the CD rate on the future rate yields:

$$\text{6-month CD rate} = 0.12 + 0.95 \times (\text{3-month deposit futures rate})$$

with a correlation coefficient $R^2 = 0.93$. This means that if the futures rate rises by 1 per cent, the CD rate rises by 0.95 per cent, implying that six-month CDs are slightly less responsive to interest rate changes than three-month deposit futures (i.e., $h = (\Delta$ 6-month CD rate$)/(\Delta$ 3-month deposit rate$) = 0.95$). So although six-month CDs are twice as responsive as three-month futures if there is a parallel shift in the yield curve (and interest rates change by the same amount), in reality, the yield curve movements are not parallel since the six-month rate moves by only 95 per cent of the three-month rate and this will tend to reduce the number of contracts required for hedging.

Using this information, and assuming that the aim is to hedge £10 million of six-month CDs with three-month sterling interest rate futures, we can derive the optimal hedge as follows:

$$\text{Number of contracts} = \frac{£10,000,000}{£500,000} \cdot \frac{25.00}{12.50} \cdot 0.95 = 38.$$

Therefore 38 contracts will be needed to hedge the position.

### 16.3.2   Hedging with stock index futures contracts

Stock index futures contracts (such as the FTSE 100 contract on LIFFE) can be used to hedge the market risk arising from holding equity portfolios.

Suppose that on 1 April a pension fund manager is uncertain about where the market is going over the next three months and wishes to hedge £1 million of his equity portfolio which has a beta of 1.15. On 1 April, the FTSE 100 index is standing at 2204.1 and the value of the June contract on LIFFE is 2300.0. Because the fund manager is long in the cash market, he will need to be short in the futures market to hedge the portfolio. The fund manager has to calculate the number of futures contracts that have to be sold in order to hedge the portfolio. He has to calculate the cost of putting on the hedge, and he also has to calculate the value of the portfolio that he is locking in.

Since the value of each one-point movement (tick) in the LIFFE FTSE 100 contract is worth £10, the fund manager will need to sell futures contracts according to the following formula:

$$\text{Number of contracts} = \frac{\text{Face value of cash exposure}}{\text{Face value of futures contract}} \times \beta_p$$

$$= \frac{\text{Face value of cash exposure}}{\text{Value per index point} \times \text{Futures price}} \times \beta_p, \qquad (16.7)$$

where $\beta_p$, the beta of the portfolio, is the hedge ratio. Using the data in the example, this means that the fund manager needs to sell:

$$\text{Number of contracts} = \frac{£1,000,000}{£10 \times 2300.0} \times 1.15$$

$$= 50 \text{ June contracts}$$

to hedge the portfolio exactly. (A hedge using only the nearest contracts is called a *spot hedge*.) Because the portfolio beta exceeds unity, more contracts will be needed for a perfect hedge than if the portfolio exactly matched the market index and had a beta of unity. The initial margin for the LIFFE FTSE 100 contract is £1000, so the total initial cost of selling the contracts would be £50,000 (i.e. 50 × £1000).

The portfolio value that the fund manager is locking in is based on the index value of the June contract, namely 2300.0 (as long as the futures contracts are held to expiry). The fund manager knows that, whatever happens to the cash market index between 1 April and 30 June, his hedged portfolio will have a value on 30 June determined by:

$$\text{Terminal value of hedged fund} = \text{Initial value of hedged fund}$$

$$\times \left[ 1 + \left( \frac{P^f_{(1 \text{ April})} - P^s_{(1 \text{ April})}}{P^s_{(1 \text{ April})}} \times \beta_p \right) \right], \qquad (16.8)$$

where:

$$P^f = \text{futures index or price;}$$
$$P^s = \text{cash index or price.}$$

That is:

$$\text{Terminal value of hedged fund} = £1,000,000 \times \left[ 1 + \left( \frac{2300.0 - 2204.1}{2204.1} \right) \times 1.15 \right]$$

$$= £1,050,036.30.$$

The fund manager cannot use futures contracts to lock in the current value (as of 1 April) of the cash index; he can only lock in the current value (as of 1 April) of the futures index for 30 June, see Figure 16.2. In addition, since the beta of the portfolio exceeds unity, the terminal value of the portfolio will be more volatile than the underlying cash index: in this case the terminal value of the index is 4.35 per cent above the initial value, whereas the portfolio itself is 5.00 per cent higher.

The reason that the portfolio value is fixed for 30 June is that the cash and futures market positions are exactly offsetting. If the index rises between 1 April and 30 June, the value of the cash portfolio rises by an amount that exactly offsets the fall in the value of the futures contract. The opposite holds for a fall in the index over the period.

This can be seen by looking at the outcome on 30 June under two different scenarios for the index: (1) a rise in the index to 2700.0, and (2) a fall in the index to 1700.0. Under scenario 1 the cash

**Figure 16.2** Terminal value of a hedged fund

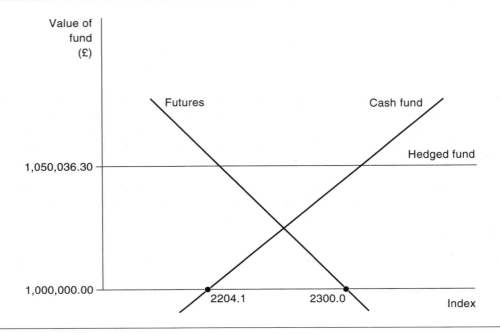

portfolio will have risen in value to:

$$\text{Terminal value of cash fund} \;=\; \text{Initial value of cash fund}$$
$$\times \left[ 1 + \left( \frac{P^s_{(30\,\text{June})} - P^s_{(1\,\text{April})}}{P^s_{(1\,\text{April})}} \times \beta_p \right) \right]$$
$$\approx\; \text{Initial value of cash fund}$$
$$\times \left[ 1 + \left( \frac{P^f_{(1\,\text{April})} - P^s_{(1\,\text{April})}}{P^s_{(1\,\text{April})}} \times \beta_p \right) \right.$$
$$\left. + \left( \frac{P^s_{(30\,\text{June})} - P^f_{(1\,\text{April})}}{P^f_{(1\,\text{April})}} \times \beta_p \right) \right]; \qquad (16.9)$$

that is,

$$\text{Terminal value of cash fund} \;=\; £1,000,000$$
$$\times \left[ 1 + \left( \frac{2300.0 - 2204.1}{2204.1} \times 1.15 \right) \right.$$
$$\left. + \left( \frac{2700.0 - 2300.0}{2300.0} \times 1.15 \right) \right]$$
$$=\; £1,250,036.30.$$

The formula in (16.9) decomposes the total change in the value of the cash portfolio into the difference between the initial cash index and the initial futures index, and the difference between the initial futures index and the final cash index. The decomposition is approximate and uses the result that:

$$\frac{C-A}{A} \approx \ln C - \ln A$$

$$= \ln C - \ln B + (\ln B - \ln A)$$

$$\approx \frac{C-B}{B} + \frac{B-A}{A}.$$

The approximation is fairly good if $A$, $B$ and $C$ are all close together and the usefulness of this decomposition will be seen shortly.

The futures position, because it is a short position, will be showing a loss equal to:

$$\text{Loss on futures position} = - \begin{array}{c} \text{Number of} \\ \text{contracts} \end{array} \times \begin{array}{c} \text{Value per} \\ \text{index point} \end{array} \times \left( P^s_{(30 \text{ June})} - P^f_{(1 \text{ April})} \right)$$

$$= - \frac{\text{Initial value of cash fund}}{\text{Value per index point} \times P^f_{(1 \text{ April})}} \times \beta_p \times \text{Value per index point}$$

$$\times \left( P^s_{(30 \text{ June})} - P^f_{(1 \text{ April})} \right)$$

$$= - \text{Initial value of cash fund}$$

$$\times \left( \frac{P^s_{(30 \text{ June})} - P^f_{(1 \text{ April})}}{P^f_{(1 \text{ April})}} \times \beta_p \right) ; \qquad (16.10)$$

that is (using the first line of (16.10)):

$$\text{Loss on futures position} = - [50 \times £10 \times (2700.0 - 2300.0)]$$

$$= - £200,000.$$

The terminal value of the hedged portfolio on 30 June is therefore given by adding (16.9) and (16.10) together. As expected this equals (16.8):

$$\text{Terminal value of hedged fund} = £1,250,036.30 - £200,000$$

$$= £1,050,036.30.$$

Under scenario 2, the cash portfolio will have fallen in value to (using (16.9)):

$$\text{Terminal value of cash fund} = £1,000,000$$

$$\times \left[ 1 + \left( \frac{2300.0 - 2204.1}{2204.1} \times 1.15 \right) \right.$$

$$\left. + \left( \frac{1700.0 - 2300.0}{2300.0} \times 1.15 \right) \right]$$

$$= £750,036.30,$$

but the futures position will now be showing a profit equal to (using the first line of (16.10)):

$$\text{Profit on futures position} = - [50 \times £10 \times (1700.0 - 2300.0)]$$

$$= £300,000.$$

The terminal value of the hedged portfolio on 30 June is therefore £1,050,036.30 (i.e. £750,036.30 + £300,000), again as expected.

So under both scenarios, the availability of stock index futures contracts allows the fund manager on 1 April to lock in the value of his portfolio on 30 June. The hedge was perfect. This followed because the terminal value of the hedged portfolio did not depend on the final value of the cash index on 30 June. This in turn followed because, when (16.9) and (16.10) were added together to get (16.8), the terms involving the final value of the cash index on 30 June cancelled out. The terminal value of the hedged portfolio was known on 1 April because it depended only on factors that were observable on 1 April (see (16.8)).

However, while the hedge was perfect so that the terminal value of the fund was known with certainty on 1 April irrespective of what eventually happened to the cash index, this does not mean that the fund manager himself is indifferent to where the cash index ends up. Under scenario 1, he would wish that he had not bothered to hedge the portfolio because the hedge lost money for the portfolio and he is likely to incur the displeasure of his clients for being so reckless. Under scenario 2, the hedge made a profit, and the clients are likely to be pleased with the astuteness of their fund manager.

The efficiency of a hedge can be measured as follows:

$$\text{Hedge efficiency} \;=\; \frac{\text{Gain (loss) on futures position}}{\text{Gain (loss) on cash exposure}}. \qquad (16.11)$$

Under scenario 1, we have:

$$\begin{aligned}\text{Hedge efficiency} \;&=\; \frac{£200,000}{£250,036.30} \\ &=\; 80\%,\end{aligned}$$

while under scenario 2, we have:

$$\begin{aligned}\text{Hedge efficiency} \;&=\; \frac{£300,000}{£249,963.70} \\ &=\; 120\%.\end{aligned}$$

So while both hedges were perfect, their efficiencies differ.

However, the fund manager may find it difficult in practice to hedge his portfolio exactly. There are four main reasons for this.

The first results from the approximation used to derive (16.9). Without the approximation, the terminal value of the hedged portfolio is not independent of the terminal value of the cash portfolio. Therefore the terminal value of the hedged portfolio cannot be known on 1 April, so the hedge cannot in practice be perfect. For example, under scenario 1, the true terminal value of the cash portfolio is £1,258,738.21 (not £1,250,036.30), and this reduces the hedge efficiency from 80 to 77 per cent. Nevertheless, the approximation is useful for demonstrating the purpose of hedging: namely, to eliminate the effect that the terminal value of the cash portfolio has on the terminal value of the hedged portfolio.

The second reason arises from the indivisibility of futures contracts. In the above example, the fund manager could create a perfect hedge using exactly 50 contracts. But if the beta of his cash portfolio had been 1.14 rather than 1.15, then he would have needed to have sold 49.5 contracts rather than 50. Since fractional contracts do not exist, the fund manager could not create a perfect hedge. If he had sold 49 contracts he would have been partially underhedged, while if he had sold 50 contracts he would have been partially overhedged.

The third reason concerns the interest on the initial and variation margin payments which have not been taken into account in the above calculations. If margin payments are received, the fund manager can earn money market interest rates on those payments, but if margin payments have to be made, they will have to be financed at money market rates. This implies that if the fund manager is making profits he is making too much for the hedge to be perfect, while if he is making losses he is losing too much for the hedge to be perfect. The solution therefore is to trade slightly fewer contracts. Assuming linear accrual of profits or losses over the life time of the hedge, an interest rate factor is used to adjust the number of contracts:

$$\text{Interest rate factor} = 1 + r\left(\frac{1}{2} \cdot \frac{N}{365}\right),$$

where $r$ is the money market rate of interest and $N$ is the number of days' duration of the hedge. For example, if $r = 10$ per cent and the hedge exposure is 350 days, then with the interest rate adjustment, the fund manager needs to sell only

$$50 \left/ \left(1 + 0.1 \cdot \frac{1}{2} \cdot \frac{350}{365}\right)\right. = 48$$

contracts rather than 50 in order to fully hedge his portfolio.

The fourth reason concerns the duration of the hedge. On 1 April, the fund manager knows for certain only what the value of his portfolio will be on 30 June, the delivery day of the June contract. This is because on that day, and only on that day, the cash and futures prices converge. Before 30 June, the futures price will generally be higher than the cash market price (because of the positive cost-of-carry; see Chapter 8). But the questions of interest to the fund manager are 'How much higher?' and 'Will the path to convergence on 30 June be a smooth one?'

If the fund manager wishes to hedge only until 1 June and not 30 June, then there is some risk that the futures price will not move in line with the cash price. Since the fund manager is long cash and short futures, he is worried that the cash price will fall and the futures price will rise, so that he loses on both sides of the hedge. The risk of this happening is known as *basis risk*, where the *basis* is defined as:

$$\begin{aligned} \text{Basis} &= \text{Futures price} - \text{Cash price} \qquad\qquad (16.12)\\ &= P^f - P^s. \end{aligned}$$

Basis risk arises because of changes in dividend yields, interest rates, government or corporate policy announcements.

The basis will be zero on 30 June and it will be positive before then. If the convergence of the cash and futures prices is smooth and linear, then the fund manager can estimate the basis on 1 June by linear interpolation using the cash and futures prices on 1 April:

$$\begin{aligned} \text{Estimated basis (1 June)} &= \frac{\text{No. of days 1 June} - 30 \text{ June}}{\text{No. of days 1 April} - 30 \text{ June}} \cdot \left[P^f_{(1 \text{ April})} - P^s_{(1 \text{ April})}\right]\\ &= \frac{30}{91} \cdot (2300.0 - 2204.1)\\ &= 31.6. \end{aligned}$$

So under these assumptions, the fund manager might expect to lock in an index value of 2235.7 (i.e. 2204.1 + 31.6) on 1 June by selling the 50 contracts (see Figure 16.3). This implies that the hedged portfolio has an estimated value on 1 June of (cf. (16.9) and (16.10)):

$$\text{Value of hedged portfolio (1 June)} = \text{Initial value of cash fund}$$

$$\times \left[ 1 + \left( \frac{P^f_{(1\,\text{April})} - P^s_{(1\,\text{April})}}{P^s_{(1\,\text{April})}} \times \beta_p \right) \right.$$

$$+ \left( \frac{P^s_{(1\,\text{June})} - P^f_{(1\,\text{April})}}{P^f_{(1\,\text{April})}} \times \beta_p \right)$$

$$\left. - \left( \frac{P^s_{(1\,\text{June})} + \text{Basis}_{(1\,\text{June})} - P^f_{(1\,\text{April})}}{P^f_{(1\,\text{April})}} \times \beta_p \right) \right]$$

$$= \text{Initial value of cash fund}$$

$$\times \left[ 1 + \left( \frac{P^f_{(1\,\text{April})} - P^s_{(1\,\text{April})}}{P^s_{(1\,\text{April})}} \times \beta_p \right) \right.$$

$$\left. - \left( \frac{\text{Basis}_{(1\,\text{June})}}{P^f_{(1\,\text{April})}} \times \beta_p \right) \right], \tag{16.13}$$

that is:

$$\text{Value of hedged portfolio (1 June)} = £1,000,000$$

$$\times \left[ 1 + \left( \frac{2300.0 - 2204.1}{2204.1} \times 1.15 \right) \right.$$

$$\left. - \left( \frac{31.6}{2300.0} \times 1.15 \right) \right]$$

$$= £1,034,236.30.$$

Suppose that on 1 June, the cash index had fallen to 1900.0 and the futures index had fallen to 1950.0. The basis on 1 June is therefore 50.0 (i.e. 1950.0 − 1900.0). Substituting this into (16.13) gives a value for the hedged portfolio on 1 June of £1,025,036.30. This is £9200 less than anticipated, but it is still better than not hedging at all.

In this example the basis has moved against the fund manager. This happened because the fund manager is a *short hedger*. He is long cash and short futures and is therefore said to be *short the basis*. This means that he loses when the basis increases (or becomes less negative) and gains when the basis declines (or becomes more negative). In this example, the spread between the futures and cash prices was expected to be 31.6 points on 1 June, but turned out to be wider than this at 50.0 points, and so the hedged portfolio's value was lower than expected. (A *long hedger* is short cash and long futures and consequently *long the basis*; this means that he gains when the basis increases and loses when the basis narrows.)

**Figure 16.3** Estimating the basis by linear interpolation

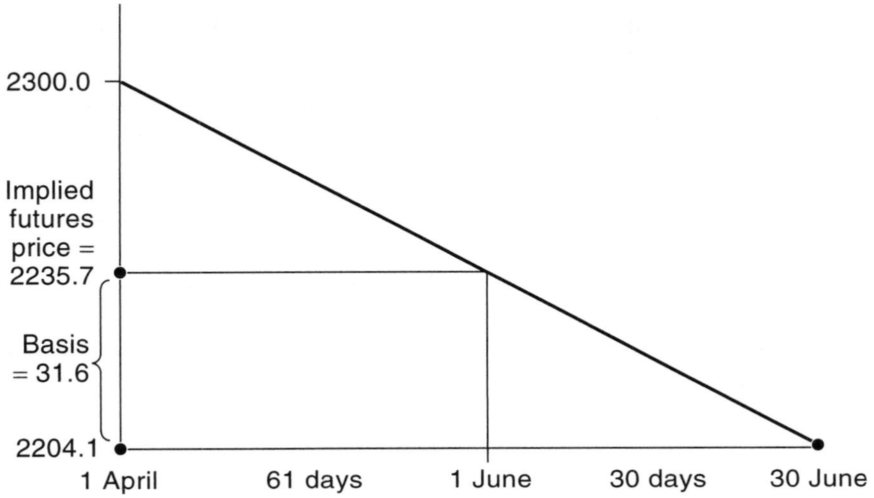

We can see that hedging with futures contracts does not eliminate risk entirely, unless the contracts are held to expiry. If the futures position is closed before expiry, the fund manager has substituted market risk for basis risk.

It is possible to hedge basis risk (at least partially), but to do this the fund manager will need to use more than one maturity of futures contract. Depending on which contracts are used, such hedges are known as *interpolative hedges* or *extrapolative hedges*. Interpolative hedges are used whenever the exposure date of the hedge lies between two trading contracts. Extrapolative hedges are used whenever the exposure date lies beyond the most distant trading contract.

As an example of an interpolative hedge, suppose that on 1 April, a fund manager wishes to put a hedge on his portfolio for 1 August, a date that lies between the June contract and the September contract. On 1 April, the June contract is trading at 2300.0, the September contract is trading at 2365.0 and the December contract is trading at 2420.0. Using linear interpolation, this implies a futures price on 1 August of:

$$\frac{60}{92} \cdot 2300.0 + \frac{32}{92} \cdot 2365.0 = 2322.6.$$

In order to hedge a £1 million, 1.15 beta portfolio on 1 April, when the cash index stands at 2204.1, the fund manager will still need to sell 50 contracts, but 33 (i.e. 50 × (60/92)) will be June contracts and 17 (i.e. 50 × (32/92)) will be September contracts.

There will be no basis risk in this hedge because any change in the basis is exactly matched by an identical offsetting change in the spread between the June and September futures prices (i.e. $\Delta$(June index − cash index) = −$\Delta$(September index − June index)). But the problem is that the June contracts expire on 30 June and the hedge changes from an interpolative hedge to a spot hedge, which does have basis risk. The basis risk from 30 June to 1 August can be partially hedged on 30 June by buying back 33 × June contracts, selling 33 × September contracts and buying 33 × September–December spreads.

Any change in the basis will now be partially offset by an opposite change in the September–December spread. On 1 August, the hedge is unwound.

The entire strategy for an interpolative hedge of a £1 million portfolio with an exposure date of 1 August is summarized in Table 16.1.

On 1 April, on the basis of the linear interpolation, the fund manager expected the futures price to be 2322.6 on 1 August. This implies that the value of the hedged portfolio is expected to be (cf. (16.8)):

$$£1,000,000 \cdot \left[ 1 + \left( \frac{2322.6 - 2204.1}{2204.1} \cdot 1.15 \right) \right] = £1,061,827.96.$$

How does this compare with the actual outcome on 1 August? We can use the data in Table 16.1 to answer this question.

---

**Table 16.1** Strategy for an interpolative hedge

|  |  |  |  |  |
|---|---|---|---|---|
| ***April 1*** |  | Sell<br>Sell | 33 June contracts<br>17 September contracts | interpolative<br>hedge |
| Cash index | = 2204.1 |  |  |  |
| June index | = 2300.0 |  |  |  |
| September index | = 2365.0 |  |  |  |
| December index | = 2420.0 |  |  |  |
| ***June 30*** |  | Buy<br>Sell | 33 June contracts<br>33 September contracts | spot<br>hedge |
| Cash index | = 1700.0 |  |  |  |
| June index | = 1700.0 |  |  |  |
|  |  | Sell<br>Buy | 33 September contracts<br>33 December contracts | basis risk<br>hedge |
| September index | = 1740.0 |  |  |  |
| December index | = 1800.0 |  |  |  |
| ***August 1*** |  | Buy<br>Sell | 83 September contracts<br>33 December contracts | unwind<br>hedge |
| Cash index | = 1790.0 |  |  |  |
| September index | = 1825.0 |  |  |  |
| December index | = 1870.0 |  |  |  |

---

On 30 June, when the June contracts expire, the profit that is locked away on the 33 short June contracts is:

$$- [33 \cdot £10 \cdot (1700.0 - 2300.0)] = £198,000.$$

On 1 August, when the hedge is unwound, the value of the cash portfolio is:

$$£1,000,000 \cdot \left[ 1 + \left( \frac{2322.6 - 2204.1}{2204.1} \cdot 1.15 \right) + \left( \frac{1790.0 - 2322.6}{2322.6} \cdot 1.15 \right) \right] = £798,119.18;$$

the profit on the $17 \times$ September contracts sold on 1 April is:

$$-[17 \cdot £10 \cdot (1825.0 - 2365.0)] = £91,800;$$

the loss on the $66 \times$ September contracts sold on 30 June is:

$$-[66 \cdot £10 \cdot (1825.0 - 1740.0)] = -£56,100;$$

and the profit on the $33 \times$ December contracts bought on 30 June is:

$$[33 \cdot £10 \cdot (1870.0 - 1800.0)] = £23,100.$$

The total value of the hedged portfolio on 1 August is therefore £1,054,919.18. This is £6,908.78 less than the value expected on 1 April, so the basis risk hedge was not perfect. This is because, while the September basis fell between 30 June and 1 August (from 40 to 35), the September–December spread fell by more (from 60 to 45). While the fund manager was short the basis, he was long the spread, and so lost more on the spread than he gained on the basis.

The extrapolative hedge is used when the exposure date of the portfolio lies beyond the most distant trading contract. Suppose again that it is 1 April and that the exposure date is 31 December but that the December contract is not trading. If the fund manager wished to hedge his £1 million, 1.15 beta portfolio on 1 April, he could use an extrapolative hedge as follows. He could sell $50 \times$ September contracts to hedge the 31 December exposure, but this leaves basis risk between September and December which he would like to hedge by buying $50 \times$ September–December spreads. However, the December contract is unavailable, so he hedges the basis risk by selling $50 \times$ June–September spreads. In total, therefore, he buys $50 \times$ June contracts and sells $100 \times$ September contracts.

So far we have considered the case of a pension fund manager who has a long cash portfolio, and is worried that equity prices will fall; he therefore sells futures. Another pension fund manager might be expecting a cash inflow into his fund in the near future and is concerned that equity prices will rise. He is therefore said to be short cash and will want to hedge this position by buying futures contracts.

### 16.3.3   Hedging with long-term interest rate futures contracts

Bond futures contracts (such as the long gilt contract on LIFFE) can be used to hedge the market risk arising from holding bond portfolios.

The market risk facing fund managers with bond portfolios is interest rate risk. Suppose that a fund manager believes that interest rates will rise and that, as a consequence, the value of his bond portfolio will fall. One alternative would be to dispose of the bonds and repurchase them after interest rates have risen. But this would involve transaction costs and there is no guarantee of being able to repurchase the same portfolio of bonds. A much cheaper alternative is for the fund manager to use the long-gilt futures contract to temporarily 'step outside' his portfolio.

We know that the futures contract is priced off the cheapest-to-deliver (CTD) bond. If the price of the CTD bond changes, so does the futures price, and in the same direction. Ignoring cost-of-carry terms, the relationship between changes in the futures price and the price of the CTD bond is given by:

$$\Delta P^f = \frac{1}{PF_{CTD}} \cdot \Delta P_{CTD}, \tag{16.14}$$

where:

$$\Delta P^f \quad = \quad \text{change in the price of the long gilt future;}$$
$$\Delta P_{CTD} \quad = \quad \text{change in the price of the CTD bond;}$$
$$PF_{CTD} \quad = \quad \text{price factor for the CTD bond.}$$

It follows from (16.14) that the futures price moves by less than the cash bond if the price factor ($PF_{CTD}$) exceeds unity and by more otherwise. This relationship can be used to hedge the CTD bonds. However, it should be remembered that the relationship is approximate because it excludes any allowance for accrued interest, etc. The relationship given in (16.14) is sometimes expressed in the form:

$$BPV_f \quad = \quad \frac{1}{PF_{CTD}} \cdot BPV_{CTD}, \tag{16.15}$$

where:

$$BPV_f \quad = \quad \text{basis point value of future (change in price of future in response to a}$$
$$\text{one basis point change in interest rates);}$$
$$BPV_{CTD} \quad = \quad \text{basis point value of cheapest-to-deliver (change in price of cheapest-to-}$$
$$\text{deliver in response to a one basis point change in interest rates).}$$

Suppose that on 1 April a pension fund manager is expecting a cash inflow of about £1.20 million in two months' time, which he intends investing in the CTD bond (which we suppose to be Treasury 10.5% 2013–15 with a price factor of 1.3032131 and currently trading at £118 per £100 nominal). He is concerned that yields will fall and gilt prices will rise against him. Because he is short cash, he decides to hedge his exposure by purchasing futures contract. To do this, he buys June contracts according to the following formula:

$$\text{Number of contracts} \quad = \quad \frac{\text{Face value of cash exposure}}{\text{Face value of futures contracts}} \times PF_{CTD}, \tag{16.16}$$

where $h = PF_{CTD}$ is the hedge ratio, and where:

$$\text{Face value of cash exposure} \quad = \quad \frac{\text{Market value of cash exposure}}{P_{CTD}},$$

where $P_{CTD}$ is the price of the CTD bond. That is:

$$\text{Number of contracts} \quad = \quad \frac{£1,000,000}{£100,000} \cdot 1.3032131 \approx 13.$$

The first point to note about (16.16) is that the number of contracts depends on the face value of the futures contract *and* the face value of the cash exposure. Since $P_{CTD}$ is £118 per £100 nominal, a market exposure of around £1.2 million is equivalent to a nominal exposure of around £1 million (i.e., £1m ≈ £1.2m/1.18).

Second, because $PF_{CTD}$ exceeds unity, the futures price will be less volatile than the cash bond price. In order to hedge adequately his exposure, the fund manager must buy 13 contracts, three more than would be necessary if the futures price and the cash bond moved exactly in line. The price factor plays the same role in long-term hedges that the regression coefficient plays in short-term hedges (cf. equation (16.6)).

On 1 June, the cash inflow arrives, and the fund manager sells 13 contracts. His position is well hedged, as the following calculations show.

On 1 April, the futures price is 91.66 and the price of the Treasury gilt is £118.00 with a price factor of 1.3032131. The fund manager's fears about adverse movements in the bond price over the next two months are confirmed, and the price of the CTD gilt increases to £120.125. The futures price is 93.3259. The cost of purchasing £1 million nominal of the Treasury gilt is £1,201,250, an increase of £21,250 (i.e. £1,201,250 – £1,180,000) over the 1 April cost. However, the futures contracts are showing a profit:

$$\text{Profit on futures position} \; = \; \left[ \begin{array}{c} \text{Number of} \\ \text{contracts} \end{array} \times \begin{array}{c} \text{Tick} \\ \text{value} \end{array} \times \left( P^f_{(1\,\text{June})} - P^f_{(1\,\text{April})} \right) \right], \qquad (16.17)$$

that is:

$$\text{Profit on futures position} \; = \; [13 \cdot £1000 \cdot (93.3259 - 91.66)] \; = \; £21,656.70,$$

where the tick value on the long gilt future is £1000 per £1 change in the futures price (or £10 per £0.01 change).

So the hedge was almost perfect: there was actually a small net profit of £406.70 (i.e. £21,656.70 – £21,250). The hedge efficiency was therefore 101.91 per cent (i.e. £21,656.70/£21,250).

We have seen how it is possible to use futures contracts to hedge an individual bond. The next questions to ask are 'How can the fund manager use futures contracts to hedge individual bonds other than the CTD?' and 'How can he use futures contracts to hedge a portfolio of bonds?'

There are two ways of hedging a bond other than the CTD. One is known as a *perturbation-based hedge*, the other is a *duration-based hedge*. Suppose that the fund manager wishes to hedge the Treasury 11.5 per cent 2014–18 bond, which has a price factor of 1.3914412 and which was trading at £126.25 on 1 April.

The aim of perturbation analysis is to calculate the change in the price of a bond following a small change in interest rates. Suppose that we find that, when interest rates rise by half a percentage point, the price of the CTD bond falls by £2 and the price of the bond to be hedged falls by £2.50. This information can be used to derive a modified hedging formula:

$$\text{Number of contracts} \; = \; \frac{\text{Face value of cash exposure}}{\text{Face value of futures contract}} \times PF_{CTD} \times PHR, \qquad (16.18)$$

where:

$$
\begin{aligned}
PHR \;&=\; \text{perturbation hedge ratio for bond to be hedged} \; = \; \Delta P_H / \Delta P_{CTD}; \\
\Delta P_{CTD} \;&=\; \text{(absolute) change in the price of the CTD bond following a one-half} \\
&\quad\; \text{percentage point (i.e. 50 basis point) change in interest rates;} \\
\Delta P_H \;&=\; \text{(absolute) change in the price of the bond to be hedged following a} \\
&\quad\; \text{one-half percentage point (i.e. 50 basis point) change in interest rates.}
\end{aligned}
$$

Using the information given, we need the following number of contracts to hedge a nominal cash position in the Treasury 11.5 per cent 2014–18 bond of £1 million:

$$\text{Number of contracts} \; = \; \frac{£1,000,000}{£100,000} \cdot 1.3032131 \cdot \left( \frac{2.5}{2.0} \right) \; \approx \; 16.$$

The perturbation hedge ratio shows that the Treasury 11.5 per cent 2014–18 bond is equivalent to 1.25 (i.e. 2.5/2.0) CTD bonds.  Because the bond is more volatile than the CTD bond (25 per cent more volatile), the fund manager needs more contracts to hedge this bond than the CTD bond (three more contracts).

The problem with perturbation analysis is that the response of the bond price to changes in interest rates is not linear: the change in the bond price for a 100-basis-point change in interest rates will not be twice the change in the bond price for a 50-basis-point change. It is for this reason that duration-based hedging is generally the preferred method.

Duration is defined from the relationship (see Chapter 5):

$$\Delta P = -D \cdot P \cdot \frac{\Delta rm}{1 + rm}, \tag{16.19}$$

where:

$$
\begin{aligned}
D  &= \quad \text{duration of a bond;} \\
P  &= \quad \text{price of a bond;} \\
rm &= \quad \text{yield to maturity on a bond.}
\end{aligned}
$$

This relationship can be used to calculate the duration hedge ratio (DHR) for the Treasury 11.5 per cent 2014–18 bond (denoted by subscript $H$ below):

$$DHR = \frac{\Delta P_H}{\Delta P_{CTD}} = \frac{D_H \cdot P_H \cdot \Delta rm_H \cdot (1 + rm_{CTD})}{D_{CTD} \cdot P_{CTD} \cdot \Delta rm_{CTD} \cdot (1 + rm_H)}. \tag{16.20}$$

This ratio can be simplified if we assume parallel yield curve movements (i.e. $\Delta rm_{CTD} = \Delta rm_H$):

$$DHR = \frac{\Delta P_H}{\Delta P_{CTD}} = \frac{D_H \cdot P_H \cdot (1 + rm_{CTD})}{D_{CTD} \cdot P_{CTD} \cdot (1 + rm_H)}. \tag{16.21}$$

It can be simplified even further if we assume parallel percentage yield curve movements (i.e. $\Delta rm_{CTD}/(1 + rm_{CTD}) = \Delta rm_H/(1 + rm_H)$):

$$DHR = \frac{\Delta P_H}{\Delta P_{CTD}} = \frac{D_H \cdot P_H}{D_{CTD} \cdot P_{CTD}}. \tag{16.22}$$

Using (16.22), and assuming that $D_{CTD} = 11.6$ years and $D_H = 13$ years, then:

$$DHR = \frac{13 \cdot 126.25}{11.6 \cdot 118.00} = 1.199.$$

In terms of duration, the Treasury 11.5 per cent 2014–18 bond is equivalent to 1.2 CTD bonds in the sense that it is about 20 per cent more volatile than the CTD bond. This suggests that the appropriate number of contracts required to hedge this bond is given by:

$$\text{Number of contracts} = \frac{\text{Face value of cash exposure}}{\text{Face value of futures contract}} \times PF_{CTD} \times DHR, \tag{16.23}$$

that is (assuming again a nominal exposure of £1 million):

$$\text{Number of contracts} = \frac{£1,000,000}{£100,000} \cdot 1.3032131 \cdot 1.199 \approx 16.$$

In terms of hedging bond portfolios, again it is possible to use perturbation analysis as with a single bond. However, the nonlinearity and non-additivity of individual bond perturbations (with respect to interest rate changes) render this method impractical. On the other hand, using the duration of the bond portfolio in order to hedge the portfolio is extremely easy. Suppose that the duration of the portfolio (which is the value-weighted average of the durations of the individual bonds) is 14.2 years and the value-weighted average price (per £100 nominal) of the bonds in the portfolio is £110.125. Then the appropriate duration hedge ratio for the portfolio is:

$$DHR_p = \frac{D_p \cdot P_p}{D_{CTD} \cdot P_{CTD}},$$  (16.24)

where:

$$
\begin{aligned}
D_p &= \text{duration of the portfolio;} \\
P_p &= \text{value-weighted average price of the bonds in the portfolio;}
\end{aligned}
$$

this is:

$$DHR_p = \frac{14.2 \cdot 110.125}{11.6 \cdot 118.00} = 1.142.$$

The number of futures contracts necessary to hedge a £10 million bond portfolio is given by:

$$\text{Number of contracts} = \frac{\text{Face value of cash exposure}}{\text{Face value of futures contract}} \times PF_{CTD} \times DHR_p$$

$$= \frac{£10,000,000}{£100,000} \cdot 1.3032131 \cdot 1.142 \approx 149.$$

## 16.3.4 Hedging with currency futures contracts

Hedging exchange rate risk with currency futures contracts is an alternative to hedging with forward contracts.

To illustrate the use of currency futures, we can consider the case of a fund manager who is expecting dividend payments on his US investments of $3 million. It is now 1 April and the dividend payments are due on 1 June. They will be repatriated immediately, and the fund manager is concerned that sterling will rise against the dollar between 1 April and 1 June. To hedge against this risk, he decides to buy sterling currency futures contracts. (In other words, the fund manager is short cash sterling and therefore needs to be long in sterling contracts to hedge the exposure.)

Suppose that on 1 April the spot exchange rate is $1.75 per £, and the June CME futures price is $1.77. At the spot exchange rate, the dividend payments are valued at £1,714,285.71 (i.e. $3,000,000/$1.75) in sterling. The number of sterling contracts necessary to hedge this exposure is determined as follows:

$$\text{Number of contracts} = \frac{\text{Face value of cash exposure (sterling)}}{\text{Face value of futures contract (sterling)}},$$  (16.25)

that is:

$$\text{Number of contracts} = \frac{£1,714,285.71}{£62,500} \approx 27.$$

So a short exposure of £1,714,285.71 can be hedged by buying 27 sterling contracts. The contracts have a sterling value of £1,687,500 (i.e. 27 × £62,500) and a dollar value of $2,986,875 (i.e. £1,687,500 × $1.77). On 1 June the spot rate has risen to $1.82 and the futures price has risen to £1.83. The fund manager receives $3 million in dividend payments, exchanges this sum into sterling, and sells 27 sterling futures contracts.

The dividends have a sterling value on 1 June of £1,648,351.65 (i.e. $3,000,000/$1.82), representing a cash loss over their expected value on 1 April of:

$$\text{Loss on cash position} \quad = \quad £1,714,285.71 - £1,648,351.65$$
$$= \quad £65,934.06.$$

The futures position, on the other hand, is showing a gain of:

$$\text{Gain on futures position} \quad = \quad 27 \text{ contracts} \times \$12.50 \text{ per tick} \times \frac{\$1.83 - \$1.77}{0.0002 \text{ ticks}}$$
$$= \quad 27 \text{ contracts} \times \$12.50 \text{ per tick} \times 300 \text{ ticks} \quad = \quad \$101,250$$
$$= \quad £55,631.87 \quad (\text{i.e. } \$101,250/\$1.82).$$

This implies a hedge efficiency of:

$$\text{Hedge efficiency} \quad = \quad \frac{£55,631.87}{£65,934.06} \quad = \quad 84.4\%.$$

So the futures hedge made money, but not enough to compensate for the loss on the cash position. There are two reasons for this. First, it is not possible with the futures contracts to hedge the exact value of the cash exposure. Ideally, the fund manager would have wanted to use 27.43 contracts, but was obliged to use 27. In other words, he was slight underhedged. Second, and more important, the fund manager faced basis risk which went against him. The fund manager is long futures and therefore long the basis: he therefore loses if the basis narrows. On 1 April the basis was 100 ticks (i.e. ($1.77 − $1.75)/0.0002). On 1 June the basis had fallen to 50 ticks (i.e. ($1.83 − £1.82)/0.0002).

It is possible to compare the position using futures contracts with that using forward contracts. Forward contracts have the advantage of being tailored to meet the precise terms of the exposure of the hedger in terms of size and duration (in the above example, $3 million for two months). Also, they do not incur transaction costs or have to be marked to market as with futures contracts. However, forward contracts are not as liquid as futures contracts and they use up credit lines with banks which futures contracts do not.

In order to compare futures with forwards, the futures rate has to be adjusted for transaction costs and the fall in the basis is as follows:

|   | | |
|---|---|---|
| | $3,000,000 at $1.83 per £ | = | £1,639,344.26 |
| − | Transaction costs at £50 per contract 27 × 50 | = | (£1,350.00) |
| + | Gain on futures | = | £55,631.87 |
| | Net sterling position | | £1,693,626.13 |

$$\text{Adjusted futures exchange rate} \quad = \quad \frac{\$3,000,000}{£1,693,626.13} \quad = \quad \$1.7713 \text{ per } £.$$

If, on 1 April, the two-month forward rate was less than $1.7713, then it would have been preferable to have used the forward rate and vice versa, although this could not have been known at the time.

Sometimes an investor faces both interest rate and exchange rate risk. It is possible to hedge against both types of risk by using a combination of interest rate and exchange rate contracts.

Suppose, for example, that an investor plans to invest in the USA in the near future and is concerned that sterling will fall against the dollar (say, because UK interest rates are expected to fall more than US interest rates). To hedge against these risks, the investor decides to sell sterling currency futures contracts and buy eurodollar interest rate futures contracts. (That is, the investor is long cash sterling and therefore needs to be short sterling currency contracts to hedge the exchange rate exposure; and he is short US dollar deposits and therefore needs to be long eurodollar futures contracts to hedge the interest rate exposure.)

To illustrate, we will consider the case of an investor who plans to invest £4 million in the USA on 20 September. It is now 22 June, and the following rates are available (note September contracts expire on September 20):

|  | *Spot* | *September future* |
| --- | --- | --- |
| Sterling exchange rate ($/£) | 1.78 | 1.75 |
| 3-month eurodollar interest rate (%) | 8.00 | 7.25 |
| 100 − interest rate | 92.00 | 92.75 |

These rates suggest that sterling is expected to depreciate against the dollar by:

$$\text{Implied sterling depreciation} = \frac{1.75 - 1.78}{1.78} \cdot \frac{365}{90}$$

$$= -0.0684 \quad (-6.84\%)$$

between 22 June and 20 September (i.e. over 90 days on an annualized basis). Similarly, US interest rates are expected to fall from 8.00 to 7.25 per cent over the same period.

In order to hedge the exchange rate risk, the investor sells CME September sterling currency futures contracts according to the formula given by (16.25); that is:

$$\text{Number of contracts} = \frac{£4,000,000}{£62,500} = 64.$$

The contracts have a dollar value of $7 million (i.e. £4,000,000 × $1.75). In order to hedge the interest rate risk, the investor buys CME September eurodollar interest rate futures contracts according to the formula:

$$\text{Number of contracts} = \frac{\text{Face value of cash exposure}}{\text{Face value of futures contract}}$$

$$= \frac{\$7,000,000}{\$1,000,000} = 7.$$

By taking out these hedges, the investor is locking in an interest rate over three months of 7.25 per cent on $7 million of funds, thereby generating interest of $126,875 (i.e. $7,000,000 × 0.0725 × (90/360)). This can be seen as follows.

Suppose that on 20 September, when the investor's £4 million becomes available and the contracts expire, the spot exchange rate is $1.70 and the three-month eurodollar interest rate is 6.5 per cent (giving a eurodollar deposit price equivalent of 93.50). The £4 million cash position has a dollar value of $6.8 million (i.e. £4,000,000 × $1.70), which can be invested for three months to generate:

$$\text{Interest on cash investment} \quad = \quad \$6,800,000 \cdot 0.065 \cdot \frac{90}{360} \quad = \quad \$110,500.$$

The sterling currency futures are showing a profit of:

$$\text{Profit on currency futures} \quad = \quad -64 \text{ contracts} \times \$12.50 \text{ tick value} \times \frac{\$1.70 - \$1.75}{0.0002 \text{ ticks}}$$

$$= \quad \$200,000.$$

This profit exactly offsets the fall in the dollar value of the £4 million sterling investment between 22 June and 20 September from $7 million to $6.8 million. This profit can also be invested for three months to generate:

$$\text{Interest on currency futures profit} \quad = \quad \$200,000 \cdot 0.065 \cdot \frac{90}{360} \quad = \quad \$3250.$$

The eurodollar deposit futures are showing a profit of:

$$\text{Profit on interest rate futures} \quad = \quad 7 \text{ contracts} \times \$25,000 \text{ tick value} \times \frac{93.50 - 92.75}{0.01 \text{ ticks}}$$

$$= \quad \$13,125.$$

This profit exactly offsets the interest lost as a result of the interest rate falling from 7.25 to 6.50 per cent (i.e. $13,125 = $7,000,000 × (0.0725 – 0.0650) × (90/360)).

The total amount of interest earned by the investor is:

$$\text{Total interest} \quad = \quad \text{Interest on cash investment}$$
$$+ \text{ Interest on currency futures profit}$$
$$+ \text{ Profit on interest rate futures}$$
$$= \quad \$110,500 + \$3250 + \$13,125 \quad = \quad \$126,875,$$

as expected.

As always, it must be remembered that we can only lock in prices and interest rates implied by the futures rates, not the spot rates on the day that the hedge was taken out. The spot rates on 22 June implied a dollar value for the £4 million investment of $7.12 million (i.e. £4,000,000 × $1.78) and an interest amount of $142,400 (i.e. $7,120,000 × 0.08 × (90/360)). These sums could be guaranteed only by making the transaction on 22 June, but the investor's funds were not available until 20 September.

## 16.4   Hedging using options

Hedging using options can be a more flexible alternative to hedging using futures. Futures are used when the amount and timing of the exposure are known with certainty: a futures contract locks in the price of a specific amount of an asset at a specific future date. Options can be used when either the amount or the timing of the exposure is not known with certainty. Options can also be used when the hedger wants to protect against adverse price movements but would like to benefit from favourable price movements; with futures, he gains when prices move in one direction but loses when prices move in the opposite direction. In addition to being able to hedge interest rate risk, market risk and exchange rate risk, it is also possible to use options contracts to hedge the specific risks of individual securities (a hedging possibility not generally available using futures).

## 16.4.1 Hedging with individual stock options contracts

The simplest way for a fund manager to hedge a long position in ABC shares is to purchase an at-the-money put option. Figure 16.4 shows the profit and loss profile for this combination when the put costs 10p and the share price is trading at 115p (shown by the broken line). The fund manager is protected (at the cost of the premium on the put) if the share price falls below 115p and keeps the gains he would make if the share price rises above 115p. But this profit and loss profile is exactly the same as that of a long call option. In other words, the combination of a long share and a long put is equivalent to a synthetic long call.

**Figure 16.4** A fixed hedge using a long at-the-money put

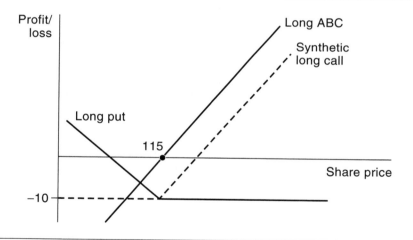

The fund manager has a number of alternatives to hedge a portfolio of ABC shares. He could hold on to ABC and buy an at-the-money put. Alternatively, he could sell ABC and buy an at-the-money call. Obviously, he will do whatever is cheaper, taking into account the cost-of-carry. Suppose that on 1 April, with ABC trading at 115p, the June 115p call is trading at 12p and the June 115p put at 10p. The riskless rate of interest is 10 per cent, and ABC has annual dividends of 6 per cent (assuming quarterly dividends are paid at the end of each quarter. We can consider two hedging alternatives.

The first alternative involves holding on to ABC, earning the dividends and buying the put option. The net cash flow per share from this position as of 30 June is as follows:

| | | |
|---|---|---|
| Purchase of 115p put option on 1 April × interest factor | $-10[1+0.1(91/365)]$ | $-10.25p$ |
| Dividends on ABC on 30 June | $115[0.06(91/365)]$ | $\underline{1.72p}$ |
| | | $-8.53p$ |

The second alternative involves selling ABC, investing the proceeds at 10 per cent, and buying the call option. The net cash flow per share from this position as of 30 June is as follows:

| | | |
|---|---|---|
| Interest on ABC sale | $115[0.1(91/365)]$ | $2.87p$ |
| Purchase of 115p call option on 1 April × interest factor | $-12[1+0.1(91/365)]$ | $\underline{-12.30p}$ |
| | | $-9.43p$ |

So the first alternative is less expensive than the second: it is better to hold on to ABC and buy the put. This solution is likely to be reinforced when transaction costs are taken into account. The second alternative involves a sale and a purchase and so incurs two sets of transaction costs involving both spreads and commissions. The first alternative involves only one set of transaction costs. A further disadvantage of the second alternative is the risk of not being able to buy back the ABC shares at the end of June, especially if a large block had been sold on 1 April. At the end of June, the market for ABC stock may be quite thin and a large block of shares may not be available on the market to be repurchased.

To avoid the costs and the risks associated with selling the underlying security, there is a hedging alternative to selling the security and buying call options, and this is to retain the security and write call options. This is illustrated in Figure 16.5. The combination is a synthetic short put, and the hedger is protected from a limited decline in the price of ABC shares because of the premium earned from writing the call option. The premium on the June call option is 12p, and this protects the hedger from a 12p fall in the share price.

**Figure 16.5** A fixed hedge using a short at-the-money call

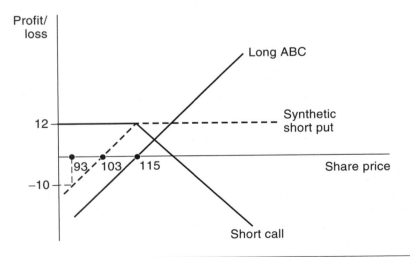

Comparing Figures 16.4 and 16.5, it is clear that the share price would have to fall to less than 93p before hedging with a short call leads to larger losses than hedging with a long put. Nevertheless, the

long put (Figure 16.4) gives complete downside protection, whatever the fall in the share price, and has better upside potential in the event of the share price rising rather than falling. Again comparing Figures 16.4 and 16.5, we can see that the profit on the short call (Figure 16.5) is limited to 12p whatever the rise in the share price, whereas, with the long put (Figure 16.4), the upside potential is unlimited.

So we have the following simple rules for hedging with options:

1 If the cash position is adversely affected by *falling* prices, then *buy puts* or *sell calls.*

2 If the cash position is adversely affected by *rising* prices, then *sell puts* or *buy calls.*

But when should we use options in preference to futures? The answer depends (1) on whether the exposure in terms of amount or timing is certain or uncertain, and (2) on whether the exposure is symmetrical or asymmetrical.

The exposure is *certain* (both in amount and in timing), for example, for an exporter planning to export goods invoiced in dollars on a given future date and wishing to guarantee the sterling value of the exports. In this case, a currency futures or forward contract is the appropriate hedging instrument. On the other hand, a fund manager wanting to reduce the volatility of his portfolio's value through a partial hedge faces an *uncertain* exposure over an *uncertain* time interval. In this case an options contract is the appropriate hedging instrument.

The exposure is *symmetrical* when it is equally responsive to a rise or a fall in the underlying security price. This means that a price move in one direction benefits the cash position, while a price move in the opposite direction damages the cash position, and the hedger wishes to protect against the second possibility. In this case, a futures contract is the appropriate hedging instrument. The exposure is *asymmetrical* when the cash position is damaged by a price move in one direction, but does not benefit from a price move in the opposite direction. An example of this is a bank that has provided an interest rate cap guarantee to a borrower: the bank loses if interest rates fall, but does not benefit if interest rates rise. In this case, an options contract is the appropriate hedging instrument.

Once an options hedge has been chosen, the next step is to decide whether to use a fixed hedge or a ratio hedge.

A *fixed hedge* is a one-off options hedge designed to limit the maximum loss on the hedged position, but to benefit from any upside potential. In other words, a fixed options hedge is rather like an insurance policy: in return for a premium, the minimum value of a cash position is guaranteed. A fixed hedge hedges the full amount of the actual or expected exposure, and the hedge is maintained until the exposure is eliminated, at which point the options are either sold or exercised. The hedges illustrated in Figures 16.4 and 16.5 were examples of fixed hedges.

A *ratio* (or *delta-neutral*) *hedge* is designed to establish and preserve a combined cash and options position that is delta-neutral over time. Since delta is the inverse of the hedge ratio (see Chapter 9), a delta-neutral hedge is one in which the ratio between the number of options and the number of the securities being hedged is always kept equal to the inverse of the option delta. This implies that a ratio hedge has to be rebalanced whenever the option delta changes.

To illustrate, we will consider a ratio hedge involving a combination of a long position in ABC shares and a long position in put options. The number of put option contracts necessary to hedge the

ABC shares is determined as follows:

$$\text{Number of contracts} = \frac{\text{Number of shares}}{\text{Delta of the option} \times 1000}. \qquad (16.26)$$

Since the standard options contract size is for 1000 shares (in the UK), this implies that we must divide the number of shares by 1000. In addition, because the delta of an option is always less than unity, more options contracts will be required to construct a ratio hedge than a fixed hedge. For example, if the delta of the put option used to hedge 30,000 ABC shares is 0.75, then the number of put options required to construct the ratio hedge is given by:

$$\text{Number of contracts} = \frac{30,000}{0.75 \cdot 1000} = 40,$$

equivalent to 1.33 (i.e. 1/0.75) contracts per 1000 shares (cf. a fixed hedge, which uses 1 contract per 1000 shares).

Figure 16.6 illustrates a ratio hedge using 1.33 long at-the-money puts per 1000 ABC shares. It shows both the short-term profit and loss profile and the profit and loss profile at expiration. In the short-term, the hedge is both delta-neutral and gamma-positive, so that it shows a short-term profit whether the price of ABC shares rises or falls.

**Figure 16.6** A ratio hedge using at-the-money puts

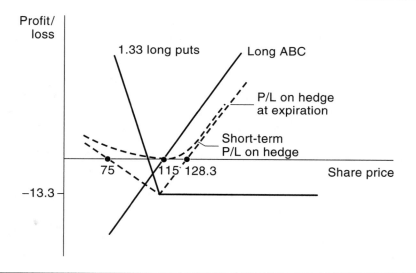

But any long position in options suffers from the negative effect of time and volatility on option values: theta and kappa always damage long positions in options. We can use Figure 16.6 to show the effect of time on option values. Suppose that the put option costs 10p, so that 1.33 puts cost 13.3p to set up. In this case, the price of ABC shares would have to fall below 75p (i.e., 115 − 13.3/0.33) or rise above 128.3p (i.e., 115 + 13.3) before the hedge made a profit at expiry. Similarly, it is possible for a sharp decline in implied volatility to reduce the value of the put option, even if the underlying share price does not change at all, causing the hedge to make a loss even in the short run.

**Figure 16.7** Ratio hedge management

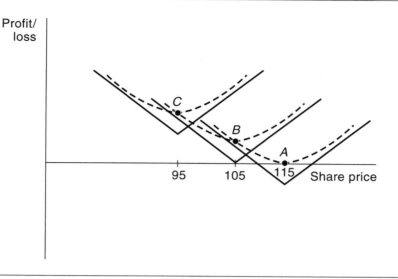

As the share price changes, the ratio hedge will have to be rebalanced. The process of ratio hedge management is illustrated in Figure 16.7. The initial position is at $A$. Suppose that at the end of several weeks the share price has fallen to 105p, so that the hedger is sitting on a profit. He will want to lock in this profit because, as we have seen, it is not guaranteed. The hedger will therefore want to lock in the profit by rebalancing the hedge at $B$ with respect to the new option delta. If the delta of the 115p puts has risen to 0.88, the number of contracts would be reduced to 34 (using (16.26)). The hedge could also be rebalanced with respect to the new exercise price of 105p. If the delta of the 105 options is 0.6, then the 34 × 115 puts are sold and 50 × 105 puts are purchased (again using (16.26)). The hedge is again rebalanced at $C$ when the share price falls to 95p, and a further profit is locked in. The principle of ratio hedge management is simple: as the option delta rises, options are sold, and as the delta falls, more options are purchased.

Because frequent rebalancing will be an expensive process, it is advisable to use a ratio hedge only when a cheaper alternative is not available, that is, when it is desired to hedge a cash position continuously over time rather than for a specific date. When a specific sum is going to be hedged for a specific date, then a fixed options hedge or even a futures hedge should be used.

We can now consider a couple of fairly sophisticated hedging strategies where the broad direction of the market movement is clear but there is a zone of ignorance about precisely what is going to happen to the share price in the short term. It is possible for the fund manager to earn premium income in this zone of ignorance. One strategy is designed for a bull market and the other for a bear market.

The *rotated vertical bull hedge* is designed to profit from a zone of ignorance in an otherwise bullish market. If ABC shares are held in the portfolio and are trading at 115p on 1 April, and a 105p June call option is sold while a 125p June call option is purchased, the profit and loss profile from such a combination is shown in Figure 16.8. In the zone of ignorance between $A$ and $B$, some premium income is earned from the sale of the call option and the position is protected from a surprise fall in the market, but otherwise the profit and loss profile is exactly the same as that of a long position in the underlying asset.

**Figure 16.8** A rotated vertical bull hedge

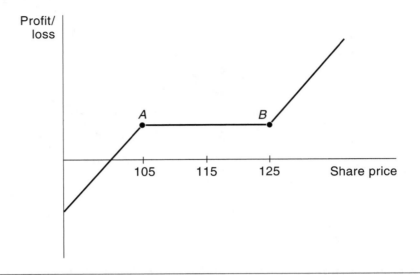

**Figure 16.9** A rotated vertical bear hedge

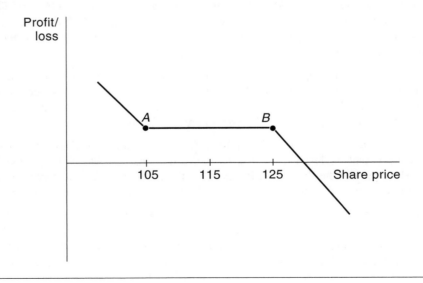

A *rotated vertical bear hedge*, on the other hand, is designed to profit from a zone of ignorance in an otherwise bearish market. The hedge is constructed from a long position in the underlying ABC shares (again trading at 115p), the purchase of two 105p June put options, the sale of one 105p June call option and the sale of one 125p June call option. The resulting profit and loss profile is shown in Figure 16.9. Again, premium income is earned from the sale of the call options in the zone of ignorance between $A$ and $B$ and the position is protected from a surprise rise in the market; otherwise the profit and loss profile is exactly the same as that of a short position in the underlying security.

Another type of hedge commonly used in bull markets is known as the *Zeus hedge* or *naked blue lightning bolt*, for reasons that are obvious from an examination of Figure 16.10. This hedge protects against falls in a bull market by using some of the profits from the increase in value of the security to purchase put options. In Figure 16.10, puts are purchased at $T_1$ and $T_2$. They both expire worthless, but they nevertheless provided some protection against the onset of a bear market.

**Figure 16.10** A naked blue lightning bolt hedge

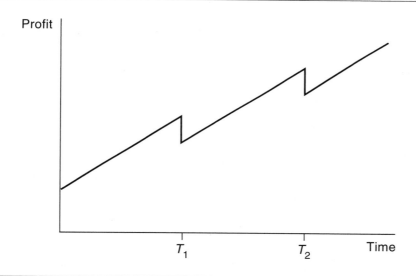

## 16.4.2 Hedging with stock index options contracts

The aim of hedging with individual stock options is to hedge the specific (or non-systematic) risks of individual shares. The aim of hedging with stock index options, on the other hand, is to hedge the market (or systematic) risk of a portfolio of shares. We must therefore take into account the beta of the portfolio being hedged. The specific risks attached to the individual shares in the portfolio remain unhedged by this strategy.

Another factor that must be taken into account is that it is possible to hedge a share portfolio using either an option on the cash index or an option on the futures index. For example, LIFFE trades options contracts on the FTSE 100 cash index. The contract is valued at £10 per index point, so that if the cash index is currently valued at 1825.0, the contract has a value of £18,250. The premium on the contract is quoted in index points, so that if the November 1850 put is quoted at 51, the total premium on the option is £510 (i.e. £10 × 51).

The number of contracts needed to hedge a portfolio of shares is determined as follows. For a fixed hedge,

$$\text{Number of contracts} \ = \ \frac{\text{Face value of cash exposure}}{\text{Face value of index}} \times \beta_p. \qquad (16.27)$$

For a ratio hedge,

$$\text{Number of contracts} \ = \ \frac{\text{Face value of cash exposure}}{\text{Face value of index}} \times \frac{\beta_p}{|\text{Option delta}|}. \qquad (16.28)$$

To illustrate, we will suppose that on 15 July a fund manager has a £5 million portfolio with a beta of 1.15 which he intends to hedge by buying LIFFE November 1850 put options on the FTSE 100 index. The closing index on 15 July is 1825.0, and the fund manager intends employing a fixed hedge. The number of contracts to hedge the portfolio is found using (16.27):

$$\text{Number of contracts} \ = \ \frac{£5,000,000}{£10 \cdot 1825.0} \cdot 1.15 \ = \ 315.$$

If the November 1850 puts are priced at 51, then the cost of the hedge is:

$$\text{Cost of hedge} \ = \ 315 \text{ contracts} \times £10 \times 51 \ = \ £160,650,$$

around 3.2 per cent of the value of the portfolio.

The advantage of this type of hedge is that it protects against downside risk while preserving any upside potential, but it is an expensive form of insurance. A cheaper alternative is to create a synthetic short position in the index. This is achieved by buying 315 November 1850 puts and selling 315 November 1850 calls. If the calls are quoted at 38, then the net cost of the hedge is reduced to:

$$\text{Net cost of hedge} \ = \ 315 \text{ contracts} \times £10 \times (51 - 38) \ = \ £40,950,$$

only 0.8 per cent of the value of the portfolio. However, this strategy takes away the upside potential of the portfolio as well as the downside risk. This is because it creates a synthetic short future at 1850 (see Figure 16.11).

We can check the effectiveness of the last hedge by examining the position on 30 November when the options expire. Suppose that the FTSE 100 index has fallen by 20 per cent and the portfolio has fallen by 23 per cent (i.e. 20 per cent × 1.15). This means that the FTSE 100 index on 30 November is 1460.0 while the value of the cash portfolio is £3,850,000. The call options expire worthless (so that the fund manager retains the entire amount of premium income of 38), while the put options expire with a premium of 390 (i.e. 1850 − 1460). The profit on the options position is therefore:

$$
\begin{aligned}
\text{Net profit on options position} \ &= \ \text{Net profit on puts} + \text{Net profit on calls} \\
&= \ [315 \text{ put contracts } \times £10 \times (390 - 51)] \\
&\quad + [315 \text{ call contracts } \times £10 \times (38 - 0)] \\
&= \ £1,187,550.
\end{aligned}
$$

The terminal value of the hedged portfolio is therefore £5,037,550 (i.e. £3,850,000 + £1,187,550). The hedge therefore makes an overall profit of £37,550.

**Figure 16.11** A fixed hedge using long puts and short calls

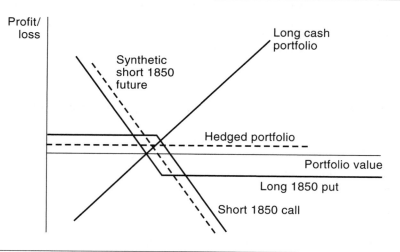

This result followed because the cash portfolio moved exactly in line with the market (adjusted for the portfolio's beta). Suppose instead that the non-systematic risk in the portfolio caused an even larger fall, say a 30 per cent fall to £3,500,000. In this case the terminal value of the hedged portfolio would be £4,687,550 (i.e. £3,500,000 + £1,187,550). The hedged portfolio is showing a loss of £312,450, but this is still nearly £1.2 million better than if the hedge had not been put on.

This example demonstrates the difference between hedging market risk and hedging specific risk:

1  It is possible to hedge the market risk but *not* specific risk within a portfolio of shares by using any of the following:

- a short stock index futures position;
- a synthetic short stock index futures position created from a long stock index put and a short stock index call;
- a short stock index call;
- a long stock index put.

In the latter case, the upside potential of the portfolio is preserved (but at some cost).

2  It is possible to hedge both the market risk *and* the specific risk within a portfolio of shares by using any of the following:

- a synthetic short futures position in *every* share in the portfolio created from a long individual stock put option and a short individual stock call option;
- a short individual stock call option on *every* share in the portfolio;
- a long individual stock put option on *every* share in the portfolio.

In the latter case the upside potential of the portfolio is preserved (but at some cost).

So hedging with individual stock options eliminates all risks, while hedging with stock index options eliminates only market risk. A fund manager who hedges the market risk in his portfolio using any of the methods listed in 1 above is therefore taking on a *relative performance bet* against the market. He is eliminating the market risk in his portfolio but leaving it exposed to specific risk, which, if he is good at security selection, he will be very pleased to do. In short, he is hoping to beat the market, having eliminated market risk.

### 16.4.3   Hedging with short-term interest rate options contracts

The only short-term interest rate options contracts that are available in the UK are those on the futures contracts traded on LIFFE: e.g. the option on the three-month short sterling interest rate future. LIFFE no longer trades a eurodollar contract but the CME offers an option on its three-month eurodollar interest rate future that is almost identical to that formerly offered by LIFFE.

The rules for hedging interest rate risk are as follows:

1  If the cash position will be worsened by *higher* interest rates, *buy* interest rate *put options* or *sell* interest rate *call options*.

2  If the cash position will be worsened by *lower* interest rates, *sell* interest rate *put options* or *buy* interest rate *call options*.

To illustrate the use of short-term interest rate options, we will assume that a company intends to borrow £2 million on 16 June. It is now 1 March and the company is concerned that interest rates will rise between now and June. The company therefore decides to hedge this risk by buying put options on the June three-month sterling interest rate futures contract. The current three-month interest rate is 10 per cent (implying a price equivalent of 90.00, i.e. 100.00 – 10.00), while the current price of the June futures contract is 89.00. The following June put options are available:

| Exercise price | Premium |
|---|---|
| 88.75 | 0.20 |
| 89.00 | 0.50 |
| 89.25 | 0.75 |

The premium is quoted in percentages, so that, for example, the premium on the 89.00 put is 0.50 per cent or 50 basis points. Since the three-month sterling futures contract has a face value of £500,000, each basis point price change has a value of £12.50 (i.e. £500,000 × 0.0001 × (3/12)). The total cost of the 89.00 put is therefore £625 (i.e. £12.50 × 50).

The company could use any of the above put options to hedge the £2 million borrowing require-, ment. The 89.25 put locks in the most favourable interest rate for 16 June (i.e. 10.75 per cent) but costs 75 basis points or £937.50 to buy. The 88.75 put locks in the least favourable interest rate (i.e. 11.25 per cent) but costs only 20 basis points or £250.00 to buy.

Suppose that the company decides to put on a fixed hedge using the 89.25 put options. In order to hedge £2 million, four (i.e. £2,000,000/£500,000) put options will have to be purchased at a cost of £3750 (i.e. 4 contracts × £12.50 tick value × 75 ticks).

Suppose that on 16 June, when the company borrows the funds and the options contracts expire, the futures price has fallen to 88.00 (from 89.00), implying an annual interest rate of 12 per cent. The company exercises its options and establishes a short futures position at an effective price of 89.25 which is marked to market at 88.00. The futures position is showing a profit of:

$$\text{Profit on futures position} = 4 \text{ contracts} \times £12.50 \text{ tick value} \times \frac{89.25 - 88.00}{0.01 \text{ ticks}}$$
$$= £6250.$$

The cost of the options was £3750, so that the net profit on the hedge is £2500 (i.e. £6250 – £3750). The additional cost of borrowing over the three months from 16 June to 16 September is:

$$\text{Additional borrowing cost} = £2,000,000 \cdot (0.12 - 0.1075) \cdot \frac{3}{12} = £6250,$$

which, as expected, is equal to the gross profit on the futures position. However, the cost of the options raises the effective borrowing rate from 10.75 per cent to:

$$\text{Effective borrowing rate} = 0.1075 + \frac{3750 \cdot (12/3)}{2,000,000} = 0.1150 \quad (11.50\%).$$

Suppose instead that the company decided to put on a fixed hedge using the 88.75 puts. Again, four put options have to be purchased, but the cost falls to £1000 (i.e. 4 contracts × £12.50 tick value × 20 ticks). On 16 June, when the options are exercised, a short futures positions is established at an effective price of 88.75, which is marked to market at 88.00. The futures position is showing a profit of:

$$\text{Profit on futures position} = 4 \text{ contracts} \times £12.50 \text{ tick value} \times \frac{88.75 - 88.00}{0.01 \text{ ticks}}$$
$$= £3750.$$

The net profit on the hedge is £2750 (i.e. £3750 – £1000). The additional cost of borrowing over the three months from 16 June to 16 September is:

$$\text{Additional borrowing cost} = £2,000,000 \cdot (0.12 - 0.1125) \cdot \frac{3}{12} = £3750,$$

again equal to the gross profit on the futures position. But again, the cost of the options raises the effective borrowing rate, this time from 11.25 per cent to:

$$\text{Effective borrowing rate} = 0.1125 + \frac{1000 \cdot (12/3)}{2,000,000} = 0.1145 \quad (11.45\%).$$

Now the effective borrowing rate with the 88.75 put is less than with the 89.25 put, so it would have been better to have hedged with the cheaper 88.75 put. This result is reinforced when we consider the case of interest rates falling rather than rising. Both options would have expired worthless, but a smaller premium was paid on the 88.75 put than the 89.25 put.

## 16.4.4 Hedging with long-term interest rate options contracts

It is possible to hedge long-term interest rate risk using either options on a cash bond or options on bond futures. In London, only options on bond futures are available.

To hedge long-term interest risk using options on bond futures, the following rules apply:

1  Calculate the best futures hedge (using duration, say).

2  For a fixed hedge, replace the futures hedge with the same number of options contracts.

3  For a ratio hedge:

$$\text{Number of contracts} \ = \ \frac{\text{Number of contracts in futures hedge}}{\text{Option delta}}. \qquad (16.29)$$

This can be illustrated using the earlier example of long gilt futures contracts traded on LIFFE. The futures contract is priced off the CTD bond, which was the Treasury 10.5 per cent 2013–15 with a price factor ($PF_{CTD}$) of 1.3032131, a duration ($D_{CTD}$) of 11.6 years, and a current price ($P_{CTD}$) (1 April) of £118.00 per £100 nominal. The bond portfolio being hedged has a face value of £10 million, a duration ($D_p$) of 14.2 years, and a weighted average current price ($P_p$) of £110.125 per £100 nominal. The number of futures contracts to hedge the portfolio is given by (cf. (16.23)):

$$\text{Number of contracts} \ = \ \frac{\text{Face value of cash exposure}}{\text{Face value of futures contract}} \times PF_{CTD} \times DHR_p, \qquad (16.30)$$

where $DHR_p$, the duration hedge ratio for the portfolio, is calculated using (16.24):

$$\begin{aligned} DHR_p \ &= \ \frac{D_p \cdot P_p}{D_{CTD} \cdot P_{CTD}} \\ &= \ \frac{14.2 \cdot 110.125}{11.6 \cdot 118.00} \ = \ 1.142. \end{aligned}$$

Therefore the number of futures contracts is:

$$\text{Number of contracts} \ = \ \frac{£10,000,000}{£100,000} \cdot 1.3032131 \times 1.142 \ \approx \ 149.$$

This is also the same number of put options on the long gilt futures contract that must be purchased to create a fixed options hedge.

On 1 April, the June futures price is 91.21 and the June 90 put costs 0.59 (i.e. £0.59 per £100 nominal) or £590 (i.e. $1000 \times £0.59$) per £100,000 contract. The total cost of 149 contracts is therefore £87,910 (i.e. $149 \times £590$), or 0.8 per cent of the market value of the bonds of £11,012,500 (where the market value is the nominal value (£10,000,000) multiplied by the weighted average price (£110.125)).

Suppose that by 1 June the price of the bonds had risen rather than fallen. The rise is 1.781 per cent. The market value of the bonds is £11,208,633, the futures price is 92.00, and the premium on the puts has fallen to 0.17 (i.e. £0.17 per £100 nominal or £170 per £100,000 contract). The hedge is closed out by selling 149 put options, generating an income of £25,330. The loss on the options is £62,580 (i.e. £87,910 – £25,330). The increase in the value of the cash portfolio is £196,122. So even though the options lost money, overall the portfolio increases in value by more than £133,000. Nevertheless, this is by less than if the portfolio had not been hedged at all.

## 16.4.5   Hedging with currency options contracts

As with other types of options hedges, hedging with currency options is useful when the hedger wants to insure against downside exchange rate risk, but also wants to preserve some of the benefits of favourable exchange rate movements. There are no currency options trading on LIFFE, but it is possible to use options contracts trading on other exchanges, such as the Philadelphia Stock Exchange, where a £31,250 sterling currency option is traded with a tick size of 0.01 cents per £ and a tick value of $3.125.

To illustrate, we will consider a UK fund manager with a US portfolio valued at $1 million on 1 April when the current exchange rate is $1.59 and the three-month forward rate is $1.65 per £. Suppose that he decides to hedge half the portfolio against a rise in sterling over the next three months. (The fund manager is short sterling cash and therefore needs to be long call options and/or short put options; if he is both long calls and short puts, he has created synthetic long futures.) A fixed hedge using cash options could involve the purchase of the following number of PSE June 160 sterling call options contracts:

$$\text{Number of contracts} = \frac{\text{Face value of cash exposure (sterling)}}{\text{Face value of option contract (sterling)}}, \tag{16.31}$$

that is:

$$\text{Number of contracts} = \frac{\$500,000/\$1.59}{£31,250} = \frac{£314,465.41}{£31,250} \approx 10.$$

If the option premium is 3.5 cents per £, then the total cost of the contracts is $10,937.50 (i.e. 10 contracts × $0.035 premium × £31,250). If, instead, a ratio hedge is used and the option delta is 0.455, then 22 contracts (i.e. 10/0.455) will have to be purchased, and this will raise the cost of the hedge to $24,062.50. The cost of the options therefore lies between 2.19 per cent (i.e. $10,937.50/$500,000) and 4.81 per cent (i.e. $24,062/$500,000) of the fund being hedged. Since this is usually much greater than the cost of forward cover (about 0.5 per cent of the value of the exposure), options are generally less favoured than forward cover. Because of the options premium, the effective exchange rate locked in by the option is $1.635 (i.e. $1.60 + $0.035).

Suppose that, when the options expire in June, the spot exchange rate is $1.80. The value of the $1 million portfolio is £555,555.56 in sterling, representing a sterling loss of £73,375.26 (i.e. [$1,000,000/$1.80] − [$1,000,000/$1.59]) over three months. When the options are exercised, they show a profit of (in the case of the fixed hedge):

$$\begin{aligned} \text{Profit on options} &= 10 \text{ contracts} \times (\$1.80 - \$1.60 - \$0.035) \text{ profit per £} \times £31,250 \\ &= \$51,562.50, \end{aligned}$$

or £28,645.83 (i.e. $51,562.50/$1.80). Therefore the portfolio made a net loss of £44,729.43 (i.e. £73,375.26 − £28,645.83) in sterling terms. The size of the loss is partly the result of hedging only half the portfolio, but even a full hedge would have lost money in this case.

## 16.5 Hedging with swaps and swaptions

Swaps provide an alternative to futures and options as hedging instruments. For example, a company with fixed-rate debt that expected interest rates to fall could execute an interest rate swap, convert its debt to floating rate, and hence benefit from any falls in interest rates. Alternatively, a company with floating-rate debt which expected interest rates to rise could also execute an interest rate swap and hence secure a low fixed rate for its debt funding, if its expectations were fulfilled. Corporate treasurers tend to use interest swaps for the two- to ten-year period which greatly exceeds the maturities available on the futures or options markets. Similarly, a fund manager with fixed coupon bonds in his portfolio who expected rates to rise could execute an asset swap and hence earn a return related to market rates.

This can be illustrated as follows. Suppose that a fund manager holds £50m nominal of bonds trading at par with a coupon of £10 per £100 nominal. He executes an asset swap with a bank whereby he retains ownership of the bonds, but makes fixed-rate payments to the bank of 9.75 per cent of the notional sum of £50m, and in return receives floating-rate payments from the bank equal to LIBOR. The cash flows involved in this transaction from the fund's point of view are as follows. The fund:

| | |
|---|---:|
| Earns from the fixed coupon bonds | 10% |
| Pays to the bank | (9.75%) |
| Receives from the bank | LIBOR |
| | LIBOR + 0.25% |

and so receives floating-rate payments on £50m of LIBOR plus 0.25 per cent. In other words, the fund has transformed its fixed-coupon bonds into synthetic floating-rate notes (FRNs) yielding LIBOR plus 0.25 per cent.

If at the time of the swap LIBOR was 9.50 per cent, then the synthetic FRNs would yield 9.75 per cent, which is less than the yield on the fixed-coupon bonds. If, however, immediately after the swap had taken place LIBOR rose to 10.50 per cent, then the synthetic FRNs would yield 10.75 per cent. This is a yield that is 0.75 per cent higher than that on the fixed-coupon bonds, equivalent to £375,000 p.a. on £50m. The increase in yield would reduce the value of the underlying bonds, of course, but the fund manager believes that the increase in interest rates is only temporary, say, because the government has imposed a temporary credit squeeze. If this squeeze is expected to last about a year, after which interest rates are expected to return to their original level, the fund manager could then unwind the swap. Bond prices would return to their original level and the fund manager would have saved the costs involved in selling the bonds before rates rose and repurchasing them before rates subsequently fall again; this was the only procedure available to fund managers to protect themselves against rising interest rates before the introduction of swaps, futures, and options.

The bank, as floating rate payer, is exposed to increases in interest rates over the period of the swap and might wish to hedge this exposure using short sterling interest rate futures contracts. Suppose that the terms of the swap are such that the floating rate payments are equal to three-month LIBOR, with the three-month rollover dates coinciding with the expiry dates of the short sterling futures contracts. If the swap started on December 14 with LIBOR at 9.50 per cent and lasts one year, the bank could hedge its exposure by selling a *futures strip* of March, June and September short-sterling futures contracts at the following prices:

| | |
|---|---|
| March futures price | 90.25 |
| June futures price | 90.00 |
| September futures price | 89.75 |

The implied futures interest rates are 9.75 per cent (14 March to 13 June), 10.00 per cent (14 June to 13 September) and 10.25 per cent (14 September to 13 December). These are deposit rates and 0.125 per cent has to be added to get the implied LIBOR rates. The one-year *futures strip rate* is the solution to:

$$(1+r_f) = \left(1+0.095\cdot\tfrac{90}{365}\right)\left(1+0.09875\cdot\tfrac{92}{365}\right)\left(1+0.10125\cdot\tfrac{92}{365}\right)\left(1+0.10375\cdot\tfrac{91}{365}\right)$$

that is, $r_f = 10.35$ per cent. This is the average rate of LIBOR that the bank can expect to pay out on its leg of the swap on the basis of futures prices ruling in December when the swap was initiated. The bank decides to hedge its position by selling 100 each of the March, June and September short sterling futures contracts. (Note, the period prior to the start of the first futures contract (namely 14 December to 13 March) is known as the *stub*.)

Suppose that the bank achieves the following outcome:

**March 13**

| | | |
|---|---|---|
| March futures EDSP | = | 89.50 |
| Three-month LIBOR | = | 10.625% (i.e., 100.00 – 89.50 + 0.125) |
| March contract profit | = | 0.75% (i.e., 90.25 – 89.50) |
| Effective rate | = | Three-month LIBOR – Futures profit |
| | = | 9.875% (i.e., 10.625 – 0.75) |

**June 14**

| | | |
|---|---|---|
| June futures EDSP | = | 89.20 |
| Three-month LIBOR | = | 10.925% (i.e., 100.00 – 89.20 + 0.125) |
| June contract profit | = | 0.80% (i.e., 90.00 – 89.20) |
| Effective rate | = | Three-month LIBOR – Futures profit |
| | = | 10.125% (i.e., 10.925 – 0.80) |

**September 14**

| | | |
|---|---|---|
| September futures EDSP | = | 89.50 |
| Three-month LIBOR | = | 10.625% (i.e., 100.00 – 89.50 + 0.125) |
| September contract profit | = | 0.25% (i.e., 89.75 – 89.50) |
| Effective rate | = | Three-month LIBOR – Futures profit |
| | = | 10.375% (i.e., 10.625 – 0.25) |

The futures strip hedge has been perfect and the bank has managed to achieve precisely the 10.35 per cent strip rate over the one-year hedge period.

Another example is a *forward interest rate swap* which locks in today the fixed rate payments on an interest rate swap that will take place at some date in the future. A company might take out such a swap if it had a floating rate liability and it believed interest rates were going to rise at some date in the future. When this future date arrived, the swap would come into effect and the company would pay the fixed rate to the counterparty which, in turn, would pay the floating rate payments on the company's liability. The fixed rate quoted would be related to today's forward yield curve, so that if the yield curve was upward sloping, the forward fixed rate quoted would be higher than the fixed rate on a swap taken out today.

As another example, we can consider hedging using a *swaption*. Suppose that a company has issued a five-year bond with a coupon of 9 per cent and that the bond is callable after three years. The bond would be called in three years' time if, at the time, six-month LIBOR is below 9 per cent. Suppose that the company also sells a three-year option on a two-year swap to a bank with an exercise price of 9 per cent for a premium of 0.5 per cent amortized over the two-year life of the swap. The swaption would be exercised in three years' time if, at the time, six-month LIBOR is below 9 per cent.

But whatever happens to LIBOR in three years' time, the company will be locking in a fixed borrowing cost of 8.50 per cent over the next two years. This can be seen as follows. Suppose that six-month LIBOR is below 9 per cent in three years' time. The company will call the bond and borrow for two years at LIBOR. The bank will exercise the swaption and pay the company LIBOR while receiving 9 per cent from the company. The company receives the premium of 0.5 per cent. The company therefore:

| | |
|---|---:|
| Pays floating | LIBOR |
| Receives swaption premium | (0.50%) |
| Pays to bank holding swaption | 9% |
| Receives from bank holding swaption | (LIBOR) |
| | 8.50% |

and so pays a fixed rate of 8.50 per cent over the next two years. Suppose instead that six-month LIBOR is above 9 per cent in three years' time. The bond will not be called and the swaption will not be exercised. In this case, the company:

| | |
|---|---:|
| Pays fixed to bondholders | 9% |
| Receives swaption premium | (0.50%) |
| | 8.50% |

and so also pays a fixed rate of 8.50 per cent over the next two years. So the effect of the swaption when combined with the callable bond is to reduce the company's funding costs by the amount of the swaption premium between years three and five.

As a more sophisticated example, we can consider a *reversal swaption*. This is a sequence of two swaptions (both having the same maturity date, but the second starting later than the first) with the effect of the second swaption (if exercised) being to reverse the effect of the first swaption (if it is exercised). Suppose that a company with floating-rate borrowings believes that interest rates could rise over the next six months, but then fall back over the following six months. The company could take out one swaption with its bank whereby it pays a fixed rate and receives a floating rate over the next twelve months if it exercises the swaption. The company could simultaneously take out a second swaption with the bank which begins in six months' time and ends in twelve months' time and which, if exercised, enables the company to pay a floating rate and receive a fixed rate over the second six months. The effect of the first swaption is to enable the company to place a limit on its borrowing costs if short term interest rates do rise in the way it predicts. The effect of the second swaption is to enable the bank to return to low-cost floating rate borrowing if interest rates do fall over the second half of the year to below the fixed rate on the first swaption.

Just as it is possible to hedge a cash market exposure using a swap, so it is possible to hedge a swap exposure with a cash market instrument. For example, a swap bank might have become the fixed-rate payer on an interest rate swap and is waiting to match this with another swap. In the interim, it can hedge its swap exposure by buying an equivalent amount of fixed-interest government bonds with the same maturity as the swap, using funds borrowed at a floating rate. The government bonds provide a hedge against a capital loss on the swap if long term interest rates change, while also providing fixed-rate income to match the fixed-rate payments on the swap. Similarly, the floating-rate receipts from the swap hedge the floating-rate cost of financing the bond purchase. However, the disadvantage of this strategy is that both the bonds and the floating-rate loan appear on the swap bank's balance sheet and hence tie up capital. It is for this reason that swaps with maturities below two years are generally hedged using interest rate futures rather than cash market instruments, thereby avoiding a balance sheet exposure.

## 16.6  Hedging with FRAs

Corporate treasurers frequently use forward rate agreements to hedge for periods up to two years ahead. As we said in chapter 10, FRAs are synthetic forward interest rate swap contracts. The buyer of an FRA locks in a fixed rate of interest, while the seller locks in a floating rate of interest.

For example, suppose that on April 1 a corporate treasurer believes that borrowing costs are going to rise in the near future. He therefore buys an FRA from a bank for 3-6s (i.e. three-month LIBOR in three months' time) on a notional sum of £5 million at an agreed interest rate of 9 per cent. The settlement date of the agreement is 1 July and the term to maturity of the FRA is 92 days. Suppose that on 1 July, three-month LIBOR is 10 per cent, so the bank makes the following payment to the corporate treasurer:

$$\text{Payment made} = \frac{(0.10 - 0.09) \cdot (92/365) \cdot £5{,}000{,}000}{1 + 0.10(92/365)} = £12{,}292.89.$$

The treasurer was therefore fully hedged for any rise in interest rates above 9 per cent.

However, the bank faced the risk that interest rates were going to rise. The bank could hedge this risk by selling short-term interest rate futures contracts. The FRA will in any case be priced off the nearest relevant futures contract: if futures prices fall, FRA rates will increase. Suppose that on April 1, the June short sterling future is trading at 91.10. This implies a three-month forward interest rate of 8.9 per cent and a corresponding spread against the FRA rate of 0.1 per cent. Given that the FRA was for a notional sum of £5 million, the bank sells 10 June sterling short futures (i.e. £5,000,000/£500,000 short sterling futures contract size).

Suppose that when the futures contracts expire at the end of June, the EDSP on the futures is 90.12, implying a settlement interest rate of 9.88 per cent. The profit on the future is 98 ticks per contract or

$$\text{Total profit} = 10 \text{ contracts} \times 98 \text{ ticks} \times £12.50 \text{ per tick} = £12{,}250,$$

which almost exactly matches the payment made on the FRA.

## 16.7  Hedging with caps, floors and collars

Companies can use interest rate caps to hedge their floating-rate borrowings against a rise in interest rates. They can use interest rate floors to hedge their floating rate deposits against a fall in interest rates.

To illustrate, we will consider a company which buys a £10m cap from a bank to hedge £10m of floating rate borrowing costs. The cap has the following specification:

| | |
|---|---|
| Term: | 2 years |
| Index: | 3 month LIBOR |
| Strike: | 10% |
| Premium: | 0.15 – 0.35% (amortized) |

The premium indicates that the bank will sell a cap to a customer at 0.35 per cent and buy it back at 0.15 per cent. At the time LIBOR is 9 per cent. Suppose that a year later, LIBOR rises to 11 per cent. The company has the choice of either exercizing the cap or selling it back to the bank at 1.25 per cent amortized (the cap is in the money, so the bank is willing to pay more to buy it back). If it exercises the cap, it will pay an effective interest rate on its borrowings of 10.35 per cent (i.e. the strike rate (10 per cent) *plus* the annual premium of 0.35 per cent). If the company sells the cap back to the bank, it pays an effective rate on its borrowings of only 10.10 per cent (i.e. the current LIBOR rate (11 per cent) *plus* the annual premium (0.35 per cent) *minus* the price paid by the bank (1.25 per cent)). However, the company now faces the risk of even higher interest rates. If LIBOR rises to 12 per cent, the company's borrowing costs rise to 11.10 per cent, whereas they would be contained at 10.35 per cent if the company had exercised rather than sold the cap. The breakeven interest rate is 11.25 per cent (i.e. the strike price (10 per cent) *plus* the buy-back price paid by the bank (1.25 per cent)).

An alternative to selling the cap would be to keep the cap and, in addition, sell a floor. Suppose that a floor is available with the following specification when LIBOR is 11 per cent:

| | |
|---|---|
| Term: | 1 year |
| Index: | 3 month LIBOR |
| Strike: | 11% |
| Premium: | 0.60 – 0.80% (amortized) |

If the company sells this floor to the bank at 0.60 per cent, it is in effect buying a *reverse collar* (since the strike price on the floor is higher than the strike price on the cap). The consequence of the floor is to reduce borrowing costs to 9.75 per cent (i.e., effective rate from holding the cap (10.35 per cent) *minus* the premium from selling the floor (0.60 per cent)) as long as interest rates remained at 11 per cent or above. However, if interest rates fell back to 9 per cent, the company's borrowing cost would rise to 10.75 per cent since the sold floor would then be in-the-money (i.e. the current LIBOR rate (9 per cent) *plus* the premium on the cap bought (0.35 per cent) *minus* the premium on the floor sold (0.60 per cent) *plus* the intrinsic value of the floor (i.e. $(11 - 9)$ per cent)).

To illustrate the more conventional use of the floor, we will consider a company which buys a £5m floor from a bank to hedge a £5m floating-rate deposit. The floor has the following specification when LIBOR is 9 per cent:

| | |
|---|---|
| Term: | 2 years |
| Index: | 6 month LIBOR |
| Strike: | 8% |
| Premium: | 0.2 – 0.4% p.a. (amortized) |

Suppose that a year later, LIBOR falls to 7 per cent. The company exercises the floor and locks in an effective deposit rate of 7.6 per cent (i.e., the strike rate (8%) *minus* the premium (0.4%)).

## 16.8   Portfolio insurance

In this section, we will consider a particular hedging strategy that has become important in the 1980s, namely *portfolio insurance* Portfolio insurance is a method of risk hedging that attempts to replicate the outcome of a put option on a portfolio of securities. This means that the portfolio investor maintains any upside potential but limits downside risk. There are four ways of 'insuring' a portfolio.

The first way is simply to buy a *protective put option* on the underlying portfolio. The effect of this is illustrated in Figure 16.12. Suppose that an investor has a portfolio valued at £100,000 which he wishes to insure over the next year. The line $OB'C'$ represents the net value of the portfolio in the absence of portfolio insurance: the gross and net values will be the same. The curve $ADE$ shows the payoffs to the buyer of the put option, assuming an exercise price of £100,000, a premium of £5000 and a year to expiry. The payoffs for the combined position are given by the curve $ABC$. Some upside potential is lost (the line segment $B'C'$ is always higher than the line segment $BC$), but all downside risk to the portfolio below £95,000 is avoided: this is why the put is known as a protective put. The put will be exercised if, at the end of the year, the gross portfolio value is less than £100,000; the put will expire worthless if, at the end of the year, the gross portfolio value exceeds £100,000.

The second way is to buy an insurance policy from an investment bank or insurance company in return for an insurance premium. Suppose again that the investor has a portfolio valued at £100,000. In return for a premium of £5000 (i.e. 5 per cent of the current portfolio value), an investment bank might be willing to insure the portfolio for a year at its current level. If at the end of the year, the portfolio is worth only £90,000, the investment bank pays out £10,000. If, however, it is worth £110,000, the bank pays out nothing. Figure 16.13 illustrates the outcome. The line $OB'C'$ represents the net value of the portfolio in the absence of portfolio insurance. The line $ABC$ represents the net value of the portfolio with an insurance policy. As with the put option, some upside potential is lost, but all risk to the portfolio below £95,000 is avoided.

The main problem with buying an insurance policy is that few investment banks or insurance companies are willing to sell insurance policies on portfolios. One problem with buying a protective put option is that it may not be possible to buy put options on all the underlying securities in the portfolio. An alternative to this would be to buy a stock index put option. However, the main problem with traded options is that they are really liquid only in near-maturing contracts; it would not be feasible to buy puts maturing in a year's time. In addition, traded options are subject to position limits which make it difficult to handle large portfolios.

For these reasons, two alternative strategies for insuring a portfolio were designed. Both are known as *dynamic asset allocation* strategies. Both aim to replicate the payoff pattern that results from combining a portfolio of risky securities and a put option. One strategy seeks to achieve this using the cash market, by altering the allocation of funds between the underlying portfolio of risky securities and a riskless security (such as Treasury bills) as the value of the portfolio changes. The other strategy uses the futures market by holding the cash portfolio fixed and reallocating between futures and the riskless asset. Dynamic asset allocation strategies are feasible only if the reallocations can be made sufficiently frequently (technically, this requires the continuity of security price movements) and if transaction costs are very low. Since transaction costs are usually lower in futures markets than in cash markets, the strategy is generally implemented using futures.

We can illustrate a dynamic asset allocation strategy using reallocations between cash securities and the riskless asset (see Rubinstein and Leland, 1981). This was the first type of dynamic asset allocation strategy devised and the only one that is feasible in the absence of futures markets. In order to simplify matters, we will assume that security price movements are continuous (i.e. they do not jump) and that transaction costs are zero.

Suppose again that an investor has a portfolio valued at £100,000 and that he wishes to protect it from falling below this value, but does not want to forgo the chance of benefiting if the portfolio rises above this level. How can this result be achieved over the course of the next year? Suppose we know that after six months the portfolio could have risen in value to £110,000 or fallen in value to £90,000.

**Figure 16.12** Portfolio insurance: buying a protective put option

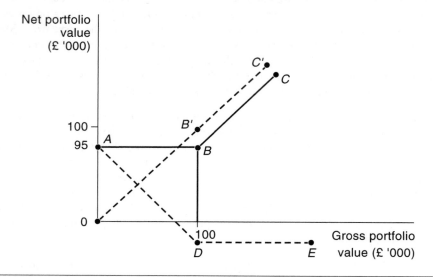

**Figure 16.13** Portfolio insurance: buying an insurance policy

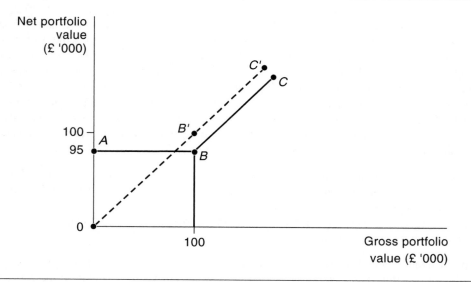

Also, suppose that if it had risen to £110,000, then after a further six months, the portfolio could have risen to £120,000 or fallen to £100,000; while if it had fallen to £90,000 after six months, then by the end of the year, it could have risen to £100,000 or fallen to £80,000. (Such behaviour is consistent with a random walk theory of security prices.) These outcomes (or *states of the world*) are shown below, together with the desired portfolio values at the end of the year in different states:

| *Time* | *Portfolio values in different states of the world* | | | |
|---|---|---|---|---|
| | (A) | | | |
| Beginning of year | 100,000 | | | |
| | (B) | | (C) | |
| Mid-year | 90,000 | | 110,000 | |
| | (D) | (E) | (F) | (G) |
| End of year:  Actual | 80,000 | 100,000 | 100,000 | 120,000 |
| Desired | 100,000 | 100,000 | 100,000 | 120,000 |

In order to achieve the desired (i.e. insured) year-end values of the portfolio, it is necessary to work backwards from the actual (i.e. uninsured) year-end values of the portfolio, through the mid-year values to the initial values, to determine, at each stage, the optimal allocation of the portfolio between risky securities and the riskless security that will deliver the desired portfolio values at the next stage and ultimately at the end of the year. This procedure is known as *dynamic programming*.

We will take the mid-year asset allocation decision first. If the state of the world after six months is C, then the investor will need to have a mid-year portfolio allocation that guarantees to deliver £100,000 if, at the end of the year, the state of the world is F and £120,000 if the state of the world is G. From the above table, it is clear that only a portfolio entirely invested in risky securities (with nothing in the riskless security) will deliver these outcomes. This implies that, working backwards, we must have a beginning-of-year portfolio allocation that delivers a portfolio value of £110,000 if state of the world C arises after six months.

If, however, the state of the world after six months is B, then the investor will need to have a mid-year portfolio allocation that guarantees to deliver £100,000 at the end of the year, whether the state of the world at that time is D or E. Only a portfolio entirely invested in the riskless security (and with nothing in risky securities) will deliver the same outcome regardless of the state of the world. Suppose that the riskless security has a semi-annual interest rate of 5 per cent; then a mid-year investment of £95,238 (i.e. £100,000/1.05) will deliver £100,000 at the end of the year if either state D or E arises. This implies that, again working backwards, we must have a beginning-of-year portfolio allocation that delivers a portfolio value of £95,238 if state of the world B arises after six months.

We now have to determine the beginning-of-year portfolio allocation that delivers £110,000 if state C arises and £95,238 if state B arises. A beginning-of-year investment of £$S$ in risky securities will grow to £$(1.1)S$ if state C arises, while a similar investment of £$B$ in the riskless security will grow to £$(1.05)B$. We require £110,000 if state C arises, and this can be achieved with the following combination of risky and riskless securities:

$$(1.1)S + (1.05)B = 110,000. \tag{16.32}$$

A beginning-of-year investment of £$S$ in risky securities will fall to £$(0.9)S$ if state B arises, while a similar investment of £$B$ in the riskless security will grow to £$(1.05)B$. We require £95,238 in state B arises, and this can be achieved with the following combination of risky and riskless securities:

$$(0.9)S + (1.05)B = 95,238. \tag{16.33}$$

Equations (16.32) and (16.33) must both hold simultaneously, and this allows us to solve for the required initial investment in risky securities (S) and the riskless security (B). The solution is to invest £73,810 in risky securities and £27,437 in the riskless security at the beginning of the year. The total initial investment is therefore £101,247.

An initial investment of £101,247, allocated £73,810 to risky securities and £27,437 to the riskless security, will deliver £95,238 if state B arises and £110,000 if state C arises after six months. At that time, the entire portfolio is invested in the riskless security if state B has occurred, while if state C has occurred, the entire portfolio is invested in risky securities. By reallocating the portfolio in this way, the desired year-end portfolio values will be achieved. This is shown as follows:

| *Time* | *Portfolio values in different states of the world* | | | |
|---|---|---|---|---|
| | (A) | | | |
| Beginning of year | S:   73,810 | | | |
| | B:   27,437 | | | |
| | Total:  101,247 | | | |
| | (B) | | (C) | |
| Mid-year | S:      0 | | S:  110,000 | |
| | B:  95,238 | | B:      0 | |
| | Total:  95,238 | | Total:  110,000 | |
| | (D) | (E) | (F) | (G) |
| End of year | 100,000 | 100,000 | 100,000 | 120,000 |

The year-end portfolio values replicate the outcome of a put option in the four states of the world. Thus, this type of portfolio insurance is equivalent to investing £100,000 in a portfolio of risky securities and buying a protective put option for £1247.

The desired year-end outcomes are achieved not by a static buy-and-hold strategy but by a dynamic strategy of reallocating between risky securities and the riskless security as the prices of risky securities change. The procedure involves:

1 *buying* risky securities as prices *rise*;

2 *selling* risky securities as prices *fall*.

In reality, two factors complicate matters. These are transaction costs and price discontinuities. The transaction costs involved in buying and selling securities will reduce the returns associated with the dynamic strategy; alternatively, a larger initial investment will be required to deliver a given final outcome. Normally, security price movements are smooth and continuous, but occasionally security prices exhibit jumps. At such times, it becomes difficult if not impossible to make the required portfolio reallocations. These two factors make dynamic asset allocation an approximate rather than an exact method of achieving portfolio insurance.

Because transaction costs are generally lower in futures markets than cash markets, the dynamic asset allocation strategy is usually implemented using futures, with the cash market portfolio held fixed. The strategy involves:

1 *buying* stock index futures as prices *rise*;

2 *selling* stock index futures as prices *fall*.

With this strategy, the part of the portfolio of risky securities covered by short positions in futures corresponds exactly, in the case of the last strategy, to the part of the portfolio invested in the riskless security.

Finally, we can ask: 'Who should use portfolio insurance?' The answer depends on the investor's degree of risk aversion. We can divide investors into three groups: those who buy portfolio insurance, those who sell portfolio insurance (clearly, if someone buys insurance, someone else must sell the insurance), and those who do not insure at all. Investors with an average degree of risk aversion should not use portfolio insurance at all: in an efficient market, the benefits are not sufficiently large. Investors who are extremely risk-averse should buy portfolio insurance, while investors who exhibit little risk aversion should sell portfolio insurance.

## 16.9 Efficient portfolio management

*Efficient portfolio management* (EPM) is the name given to the management of a portfolio that involves the use of futures and options in certain specified ways.

For some types of institution, the use of futures and options is strictly controlled. Authorized unit trusts (AUTs), for example, are able to use futures and options for the purpose of EPM, but their use is subject to two constraints as laid down in the Financial Services (Regulated Schemes) Regulations 1991. First, the use of futures or options transactions must be deemed to be *economically appropriate*. Second, futures or options transactions must be *fully covered* by the appropriate amount of cash or securities in case the futures go to delivery or the options are exercised; futures and options cannot be used for speculative purposes. To be considered as economically appropriate, futures and options must be used for only one of three purposes:

1  reduction of risk, i.e. for the purpose of hedging current exposures or as anticipatory hedges to cover exposures that are *certain* to arise in the future but are *anticipated* to arise no further ahead than one month;

2  reduction of cost, such as prepositioning using futures or options prior to a certain cash market purchase or sale; however asset allocation overlays or the creation of synthetic funds which require the long-term maintenance of futures and options positions are not permitted;

3  generation of additional capital or income by writing options or engaging in arbitrages; written options positions must be fully covered.

Other institutional investors can also use futures and options in EPM, but may be subject to a different set of restrictions on their use, either more or less stringent. We can consider some examples of how they are used in EPM.

Futures contracts, for instance, can be used to implement the following active portfolio strategies: changing asset allocation, market timing and security selection. Such strategies can be implemented more cheaply than can be done in the cash market.

A cheap and simple way of changing the asset allocation of the portfolio between shares, bonds and money market securities is by buying or selling futures contracts. Suppose, for example, that a fund manager wanted to increase the proportion of shares in the portfolio. He could do this by first buying stock index futures contracts. This locks in the prices of shares prior to buying them in the market. This strategy is also known as *pre-positioning*.

Market timing with an equity portfolio is equivalent to beta trading, i.e. trading in and out of high beta stocks depending on whether the fund manager's views are bullish or bearish. This strategy is expensive in terms of transaction costs, however, and identical results can be achieved much more cheaply using stock index futures contracts. This can be seen from the perfect hedge example in section 16.3.2 above. The £1 million 1.15-beta portfolio, which was fully hedged by selling 50 futures contracts, was entirely unresponsive to market movements and so had a beta of zero, exactly the same as the riskless asset. But any portfolio beta can be achieved with appropriate use of futures contracts. The portfolio beta with futures ($\beta_{pf}$) is given by:

$$\beta_{pf} = \beta_p + \theta_f \beta_f, \tag{16.34}$$

where $\beta_f$ is the beta for the futures contract; normally we would set $\beta_f = 1$, but in practice stock index futures contracts are slightly more volatile than the underlying index, implying $\beta_f = 1.1$. In (16.34):

$$\theta_f = \beta_p \cdot \frac{N_f}{N_0}, \tag{16.35}$$

where $N_0$ is the number of futures contracts needed to ensure $\beta_{pf} = 0$ ($N_0 = 50$ in the above example) and $N_f$ is the number of futures contracts needed to give the desired $\beta_{pf}$. Substituting (16.35) into (16.34) and rearranging gives (if we also set $\beta_f = 1$):

$$N_f = \frac{\beta_{pf} - \beta_p}{\beta_p} \cdot N_0. \tag{16.36}$$

So for example, a portfolio beta of 0.8 could be achieved by selling 15 futures contracts (i.e. $N_f \approx -15$), while a portfolio beta of 2.0 could be achieved by buying 37 contracts (i.e. $N_f \approx +37$). Market timing strategies using futures contracts are also known as *overlay* strategies, since there is a temporary futures overlay on an underlying strategic asset allocation.

A third active strategy is security selection. Stock index futures allow the fund manager who is skilled at security selection to separate this activity from market timing. By holding a long position in shares and an appropriate short position in stock index futures, the fund manager can remove any market risk from holding the shares but retain the specific risk. He will do this if he believes the particular shares are underpriced relative to the market. In other words, he is taken on a *relative performance bet* and has constructed a *relative performance portfolio*. If he is correct he will earn a return appropriate to security selection. With stock index futures contracts, it is possible to hedge the market risk of an equity portfolio but not the specific risk in the individual equities in the portfolio. In order to hedge this non-systematic risk, it is necessary to use traded options.

In a similar way, gilt futures provide a relatively inexpensive vehicle for engaging in active bond portfolio management. Take, for example, market timing. With a bond portfolio, market timing is equivalent to duration trading. At the onset of a bear market, the bond manager might trade out of high-duration bonds into low-duration bonds. This is expensive in terms of transaction costs. A much cheaper alternative is to use futures contracts to hedge the portfolio. In this way, any desired bond portfolio duration target can be achieved. For example, a perfect hedge consisting of a long cash bonds and (the appropriate number of) short contracts in gilt futures will have a zero net change in capital value, whatever happens to underlying interest rates. The duration of the hedge will be zero. Any desired bond portfolio duration can be achieved using:

$$D_{pf} = D_p + \theta_f D_f, \tag{16.37}$$

where $D_{pf}$ is the duration of the portfolio hedged with futures, $D_f$ is the duration of the futures contract and:

$$\theta_f = D_p \cdot \frac{N_f}{N_0}, \tag{16.38}$$

where $N_0$ is the number of futures contracts needed to ensure $D_{pf} = 0$ and $N_f$ is the number of futures contracts needed to give the desired $D_{pf}$.

Futures can be used to adjust the bond portfolio's duration while keeping the underlying cash bond portfolio fixed. If the fund manager thinks that interest rates are going to fall, he buys futures: if he thinks that they are going to rise, he sells futures.

Another activist strategy using futures contracts is *pre-positioning*, i.e. locking in prices prior to buying or selling a bond. Suppose that a fund manager wishes to purchase a substantial amount of a particular gilt (say £200 million). If he attempted to do this in a single tranche, the GEMMs would exploit this by hiking up the price against him. On the other hand, if he attempted to purchase the required amount in £20 million tranches over two or three days, general market prices might move suddenly against him. The solution is for the fund manager to pre-position using futures contracts and then to purchase the bond in tranches when they become available on the market. In order to pre-position £200 million of the bond, the fund manager would purchase 2000 futures contracts. He would then purchase the bond in tranches and simultaneously sell an equivalent number of futures contracts. This strategy fully protects the fund manager against falls in interest rates. Similarly, if the fund manager wished to sell a substantial amount of a particular gilt, he could pre-position by first selling an equivalent number of futures contracts and then buying them back as the cash bond was sold. Pre-positioning is a particularly effective strategy when the futures market is more liquid than the cash market.

Futures can also be used to aid another activist strategy, bond selection. Suppose that an analysis of the (zero-coupon) yield curve suggests that the Treasury 8 per cent 2019 is relatively underpriced. The fund manager would like to remove any market risk and trade only what he believes to be the relative mispricing of this bond; in other words, he would like to place a *relative performance bet* against the market. With equities this is easy, because the stock index futures contract involves a market index. With bonds, on the other hand, the relative performance bet is against the CTD bond not a bond market index. This is because the bond futures contract is priced off the CTD bond rather than an index. So a bond relative performance bet cannot entirely remove market risk. Nevertheless, the procedure for placing the bet is simple. Because the Treasury 8 per cent 2019 bond is underpriced, the fund manager buys the gilt and sells an equivalent number of futures contracts. Had the gilt been relatively overpriced rather than underpriced, it is necessary to short the bond in the repurchase market. This is achieved by *reversing* the bond into the repurchase market and buying futures contracts against the reverse position. Once the relative mispricing has been corrected, the bond would be *repoed* out of the repurchase market and the futures contracts sold.

Another example of EPM is *income enhancement* using options. Investors who already own securities can generate additional income by writing out-of-the-money call options against these holdings. This procedure is known as *covered call option writing*. While writing call options can lead to the underlying securities being sold if the writer is exercised against, the main objective of the strategy is income enhancement. The writer receives the option premium, thereby enhancing the performance of his portfolio in an otherwise flat or bearish market. However if the investor's view concerning market direction is wrong, and prices rise rather than fall, the investor loses all gains above the exercise price of the security, since he will be exercised against and so be obliged to deliver securities for a lower price than they are worth in the market place.

To illustrate, suppose that ABC shares are trading at 115p and December 125 calls are trading at 5p. An investor with 50,000 ABC shares could write 50 December 125 call options against his holding and receive premium income of:

$$\text{Premium income} \quad = \quad 50 \text{ contracts} \times 1000 \text{ shares} \times 5\text{p premium} \quad = \quad \pounds 2,500.$$

If, when the December contracts expire, ABC shares are trading below 125p, the investor retains the entire premium income of £2,500. The value of the investor's shares are capped at 130p (i.e. 125p exercise price + 5p premium); if, when the options expire, ABC is trading above 130p, the investor will regret having implemented the strategy.

Investors with large cash holdings can generate additional income, by writing out-of-the-money put options against these cash holdings. This procedure is known as *covered put option writing*. Again the main purpose of this strategy is income enhancement, although the investor must be prepared to buy the underlying security if he is exercised against. However he does have the cash to pay for the securities if the exercise occurs. The strategy is therefore suited to a flat or bullish market.

To illustrate, consider an investor with £30,000 in cash who writes 30 September 105 puts on ABC shares when ABC is trading at 115p; the premium on the puts is 11p. The total premium income received is:

$$\text{Premium income} \quad = \quad 30 \text{ contracts} \times 1000 \text{ shares} \times 11\text{p premium} \quad = \quad \pounds 3,300.$$

If, when the September contract expires, ABC shares are trading above 105p, the investor retains the entire premium income of £3,300. The breakeven on the strategy occurs with a share price of 94p (i.e. 105p exercise price - 11p premium). If, when the options expire, ABC is trading below 94p, the investor will regret having undertaken the strategy.

As a final example of their use in EPM, futures and options can be used to separate currency risk from investment risk. They enable investors to achieve exposure to overseas share and bond markets via equity index and bond futures and options without taking on the risk associated with the currency of the overseas markets. This is because trading futures and options requires only the payment of initial margin in the case of futures and the premium in the case of options, together with any variation margin payments. The funds that would otherwise have to be used to pay for overseas shares and bonds can be put on deposit in the domestic currency. So a portfolio can have full exposure to overseas equity and bond markets, with only negligible funds actually held in foreign currency. It is even possible to use domestic assets as collateral for margin payments.

**Selected references**

Eales, B. (1995), *Financial Risk Management*, McGraw-Hill, London.

Epstein, C. (ed.)(1992), *Managed Futures in the Institutional Portfolio*, Wiley, New York.

Fitzgerald, M.D. (1983), *Financial Futures,* Euromoney Publications, London. (Chapters 4 and 5.)

Fitzgerald, M.D. (1987), *Financial Options*, Euromoney Publications, London. (Chapter 5.)

Fong, H.G. and Fabozzi, F.J. (1985), *Fixed Income Portfolio Management*, Dow Jones-Irwin, Homewood, Ill. (Chapter 8.)

Ray, C. (1993), *The Bond Market: Trading and Risk Management*, Business One, Irwin, Homewood, Ill.

Redhead, K. and Hughes, S. (1988), *Financial Risk Management*, Gower, London.

Rubinstein, M. and Leland, H.E. (1981), 'Replicating Options with Positions in Stock and Cash', *Financial Analysts Journal*, July-August, 63–72.

Schwarz, E.W., Hill, J.M., and Schneeweis, T. (1986), *Financial Futures*, Irwin, Homewood, Ill. (Chapters 7 and 11.)

Watsham, T. (1992), *Options and Futures in International Portfolio Management*, Chapman and Hall, London.

**Exercises**

1 What are the differences between buying put options and selling call options to hedge an underlying long position in a security? Which is riskier? Use options diagrams to illustrate your answer.

2 Discuss the roles played by futures and options in hedging interest rate and exchange rate risk.

3 Discuss *three* ways of implementing 'portfolio insurance'.

4 You are a borrower wishing to hedge a six-month eurodollar interest rate exposure beginning on 1 August. What rate can you lock in by hedging with the following eurodollar futures contracts?

| *Futures prices* | | |
|---|---|---|
| June | September | December |
| 93.20 | 93.00 | 92.80 |

5 Illustrate a duration-based hedge for a portfolio of government bonds.

6 Explain the ideas behind relative performance portfolios.

7 How would you calculate the number of sterling interest rate futures contracts to hedge a six-month sterling interest rate exposure?

8  What is basis risk? How would you hedge against it?

9  What is the difference between hedging and speculation?

10  List some of the characteristics of a good hedging instrument.

11  What are 'natural hedges'? How do they limit the overall level of risk exposure?

12  Explain how you would implement a cross-hedge. Illustrate your answer with an example.

13  Since it is always possible to construct a riskless hedge, this means that it is possible to entirely eliminate risk from the economy. Discuss.

14  Determine the number of December futures contracts on the FTSE 100 index needed to hedge an equity portfolio currently valued at £2,659,495, with a beta of 0.95. The current value of the FTSE 100 index is 6180.7, while the December contract is quoted as 6316.3.

15  What are the differences between:

   a) a spot hedge,

   b) an interpolative hedge, and

   c) an extrapolative hedge?

16  A fund manager is concerned that share prices are going to fall and he wishes to hedge his £50 million, 1.2 beta portfolio against this possibility. It is 28 May, the current FTSE 100 index is standing at 5909.0, and the following FTSE 100 futures contracts are available:

| Contract | Price | Open interest |
|---|---|---|
| June | 5926.0 | 34,361 |
| September | 5997.0 | 28,970 |
| December | 6088.0 | 2,127 |

Design a suitable hedge for the fund manager. Calculate the difference between the value of the hedged portfolio and the value of the portfolio assuming it had remained unhedged if, on the expiry date of your selected contract, the FTSE 100 index is standing at 5572.0. How efficient was the hedge?

17  Explain what it means to be 'long the basis'.

18  What is pre-positioning? Illustrate your answer with *two* examples of pre-positioning.

19  Explain how futures contracts can be used by a fund manager to engage in market timing.

20  If the beta of an equity portfolio is 0.75, explain how you would use stock index futures contracts (a) to increase the beta of the portfolio to equal that of the market, and (b) to reduce the beta to equal half that of the market.

21  What is the cheapest-to-deliver security? What role does it play in risk management?

22  What is a price factor? What role does it play in risk management?

23 A fund manager has a portfolio of bonds with a face value of £15 million, an average duration of 11.2 years, and an average price of £96.50 per £100 nominal. The cheapest-to-deliver gilt for the June long-gilt contract has a duration of 10.75 years, a price of £101.75 per £100 nominal and a price factor of 1.0267198. How many June contracts have to be sold to hedge this portfolio fully?

24 Compare and contrast duration-based hedging and perturbation-based hedging.

25 Discuss the advantages and disadvantages of using futures and options as hedging instruments.

26 It is 30 September. You are holding a long position in DEF shares currently valued at 315p and you are concerned that share prices might fall over the next few months. You observe the following options prices quoted on LIFFE:

|  | *January* | |
| --- | --- | --- |
| *Exercise price* | *Calls* | *Puts* |
| 300 | 26 | 12 |
| 330 | 10 | 30 |

(Expiry date is 30 January)

Design *two* ways of hedging against the risk of falling share prices. Assuming that four-month interest rates are $10 - 10.125$, calculate the net values of your two hedged portfolios if, on the expiry date of the options, DEF shares are trading at:

a) 250p;

b) 315p;

c) 350p.

Comment on your results.

27 What is the difference between a fixed hedge and a ratio hedge? Which is cheaper to implement?

28 What are the objectives of ratio hedge management?

29 Compare and contrast the LIFFE FTSE 100 option and the LIFFE FTSE 100 future as hedging instruments.

30 You are observe the following information on 1 November:

| Market value of portfolio | | = £3m |
| --- | --- | --- |
| Beta of portfolio | | = 1.09 |
| Spot FTSE 100 index | | = 6920.0 |
| LIFFE March 6950 put: | premium | = 53 |
| | delta | = $-0.45$ |

Calculate the number of contracts and the cost of putting on a fixed hedge and a ratio hedge using the LIFFE options.

31 a) You want to hedge both the market risk and the specific risk in a portfolio of shares. How can you do this?

b) You want to hedge only the market risk in a portfolio of shares. How can you do this?

32  You are a UK corporate treasurer expecting to receive surplus funds of £2.5 million at the end of June. You intend to place the funds temporarily on deposit for three months. You are concerned that interest rates will fall over the next few months, although you are aware of the possibility that short-term interest rates might actually rise. It is now 1 April and you observe the following LIFFE contracts trading:

| | | |  |  |
|---|---|---|---|---|
| June 3-month short sterling future: | | 89.75 | | |
| June 3-month short sterling futures options: | *Exercise price* | *Calls* | *Puts* | |
| | 89.50 | 0.75 | 0.15 | |
| | 89.75 | 0.35 | 0.30 | |
| | 90.00 | 0.10 | 0.60 | |

Design *two* hedging strategies consistent with your concerns. Calculate the profit or loss on your hedged position if current interest rates are 10 per cent and if, on 30 June, three-month interest rates equal:

a) 8.0 per cent;

b) 12.0 per cent.

(Assume the expiry date for all contracts is 30 June.)

33  It is 30 April. A UK importer has bought equipment invoiced in US dollars from a US supplier and he does not have to pay for the equipment for two months. What risks does the exporter face? How could he manage those risks if he observes the following?

| | |
|---|---|
| UK spot 2-month interest rate | $11 - 11.125$ |
| US spot 2-month interest rate | $7 - 7.125$ |
| Spot exchange rate | $1.65 |
| CME June sterling future (initial margin = $1000) | $1.61 |
| PSE June sterling options:    165 call | $0.03 |
| 165 put | $0.07 |

34  Share prices move according to the following (binomial) process: during any six-month period, there is a 50 per cent chance that share prices will rise by 8 percentage points and a 50 per cent chance that share prices will fall by 8 percentage points. On the other hand, Treasury bills (TBs) generate a safe return of 4 per cent during any six-month period. Design a minimum-cost portfolio strategy that guarantees a year-end portfolio value of £1 million whatever happens to share prices, but which takes advantage of favourable share price movements.

35  How can swaps be used as hedging instruments?

36  What is the difference between speculation and hedging?

37  A company has £5m on deposit which it rolls over on a three-month basis and it has just rolled over the deposits again. While the yield curve is currently upward sloping over the next twelve months, the company treasurer believes that interest rates will fall over this period. The following FRA is available:

3–6 months        $8.50 - 8.55\%$

a) Should the company buy or sell this FRA to hedge its view on interest rate movements and at what price will it deal?

b) Suppose that the company took out the FRA and that three months later the company rolls over the deposit for another three months (91 days) at 7.50 per cent. The settlement rate for the FRA was 7.55 per cent. What was the effective return on the company's deposits during this three month period?

38 A company wishes to take out a £1m six month loan in six months' time and notes that the following interbank rates are currently being quoted:

| Maturity | Interbank rates |
|----------|-----------------|
| 6 months | 8.125 – 8.375 |
| 12 months | 8.625 – 8.875 |

The company can access the money markets on terms that are 0.125 less favourable than the rates quoted here. The company is concerned that interest rates will rise over the course of the next six months.

a) How can the company hedge this risk?

b) What rate of interest can be locked in today by taking out this hedge?

c) What are the cost savings from this strategy if in 6 months' time, the 6 month interbank rate is 9.625 – 9.875?

d) What are the disadvantages of this strategy?

39 A company raises funds in the sterling commercial paper market at 3 month LIBOR + 0.15 per cent. Current 3 month LIBOR is 8 per cent. It is concerned that interest rates will rise shortly. The following cap is available:

| | |
|---|---|
| Term: | 2 years |
| Index: | 3 month LIBOR |
| Strike: | 9% |
| Premium: | 0.20 – 0.40% p.a. (amortized) |

The company buys the cap and six months later, 3 month LIBOR has risen to 10 per cent and the premium on the cap has risen to 1.35 – 1.55 per cent p.a.

a) What is the effective interest rate paid by the company if it exercises the cap?

b) What is the effective interest rate paid by the company if it sells the cap back to the bank?

c) What factors should be taken into account by the company when it makes one of the above decisions?

40 The following spot yields are available:

| Term (years) | Spot yield (%) |
|--------------|----------------|
| 1 | 9 |
| 2 | 9.25 |
| 3 | 9.75 |

A bank is asked by a company for a quote on a two-year forward interest rate swap beginning in one year's time. The bank's quote for the fixed rate on the swap contains a premium of 50 b.p. above the relevant forward rate. What quote does the company receive?

41  The following two-year LIBOR caps and collars are available:

|  |  |  | Premium (%, amortized) |
| --- | --- | --- | --- |
| Cap 11% |  |  | 0.25 |
| Cap 9% |  |  | 0.50 |
| Collar: | cap | 11% | 0 |
|  | floor | 5% |  |
| Collar: | cap | 9% | 0 |
|  | floor | 6% |  |

The collars are zero-cost collars with the premium on the floor exactly offsetting the premium on the cap.

a) Calculate the effective rate of interest payable on each of these instruments when LIBOR is 3%, 4%, 5%, ..., 12%, 13%.

b) Over what range of interest rates does each of these instruments provide the lowest effective borrowing costs?

42  Current 3 month LIBOR is 9 per cent. A cap is available with the following specification:

| Term: | 2 years |
| --- | --- |
| Index: | 3 month LIBOR |
| Strike: | 12% |
| Premium: | $0.25 - 0.50\%$ p.a. (amortized) |

An American swaption is available with the following specification:

| Term: | 2 years |
| --- | --- |
| Floating rate index: | 3 month LIBOR |
| Fixed rate: | 10% |
| Premium: | $1.35 - 1.55\%$ p.a. (amortized) |

a) Over what LIBOR range does each of these instruments provide the lowest effective interest rate? Calculate the breakeven rate.

b) Compare and contrast the two instruments as hedges of interest rate exposure.

43  A UK corporate with revenues predominantly in sterling has issued a Japanese yen bond with 5 years to maturity. It anticipates sterling will depreciate against the yen and UK interest rates will fall over the next five years. Design a swap transaction to hedge this risk exposure.

44  A US corporate with revenues predominantly in dollars has issued a euro bond with 4 years to maturity. It anticipates the euro will appreciate and that US interest rates will rise over the next four years. Design a swap transaction to hedge this risk exposure.

45  A UK pension fund holds US dollar bonds which have some 6 years remaining to maturity. It now expects the dollar to depreciate against sterling and sterling to depreciate against the euro over the period to maturity. The pension fund decides to shift its currency exposure from dollars into euros. However, euro interest rates are anticipated to rise sharply over the next six years. Design a swap transaction to hedge this risk exposure.

46  A UK company has issued a euro bond which has 3 years to maturity. It now anticipates that the euro will depreciate against sterling and that euro interest rates will fall over the period. Design a swap transaction to hedge this risk exposure.

47  It is currently 1 April, and on 15 June a corporate treasurer is going to borrow £10m for a six month period and is concerned that interest rates will rise between now and June. The following put options on the short sterling futures contract are available:

| Month | Exercise price | Premium |
|-------|----------------|---------|
| June | 91.00 | 0.33 |
| September | 91.00 | 0.69 |

(Assume the June contract expires on 15 June)

a)  Design a six-month interest rate cap using the two put options.

b)  What is the maximum effective six-month borrowing rate on the cap?

c)  What is the effective borrowing rate on 15 June if the 6-month interest rate is 9.45% and the September put is trading at 0.95?

48  Suppose that a fund manager has a £100m portfolio invested in UK equities, long-dated gilts and cash in the ratio 60:30:10. The fund manager wishes to change the asset allocation to 50:40:10. Suppose that the cheapest-to-deliver gilt on the nearest gilt futures contract is the Treasury 8.5% 2020 with a price factor of 1.105001, while the nearest FTSE 100 futures contract is trading at 6478.3.

a)  Discuss two ways in which the fund manager can achieve the desired change in asset allocation, specifying in each case the nature and number of transactions involved.

b)  What are the advantages and disadvantages of each strategy?

# Part IV

# POSTSCRIPT

In this final section, we examine first the causes of failure in financial markets. Financial markets fail very infrequently - only once every fifty years or so in economies with advanced financial systems. But when it happens, the failure can be extremely dramatic and the consequences can be very severe. Then in the last chapter, we investigate some of the most important recent developments in financial market analysis.

# Chapter 17

# The failure of financial markets

This chapter examines what happens when financial markets fail. We consider what failure involves. We also examine the causes and consequences of failure.

We should remember that financial markets fail in a serious way very infrequently — only once every fifty years or so in economies with advanced financial systems. But when it happens, the failure itself can be extremely dramatic, and the consequences of failure can be very severe.

This analysis will be illustrated by an examination of the famous crash of October 1987.

## 17.1   The anatomy of the crash

On *Black Monday*, 19 October 1987, the world experienced its most several financial failure. The only earlier experience of a financial failure on this scale was the crash that began on *Black Tuesday*, 28 October 1929, almost exactly 58 years earlier. The 1929 crash presaged the Great Depression of the 1930s. Would the 1987 crash lead to an even greater recession in the 1990s? Fortunately, the authorities (especially the monetary authorities) had learnt some important lessons from the experience of the 1930s. But before considering those lessons, let us examine what happened in 1987.

Figure 17.1 provides some financial information about the world's principal financial centres for 1987 and 1988. At the beginning of 1987, the UK had been in a bull market for 12 years. Half a generation of players in the UK financial markets had never experienced a bear market. Virtually everyone was making very easy money, either with very little effort or with very little skill. By the time of the crash, the stock exchange index had increased by 75 per cent of its beginning-of-year value. The average daily turnover of shares reached a record 800 million. New issues were also at a record during 1987: in excess of £4 billion in July.

In New York, the index was about a third higher in October than it had been in January 1987. Turnover of shares reached a peak just prior to the crash. Similarly, new issues were at an all-time high in 1987. Similar patterns were experienced in all other financial centres, including Hong Kong and Frankfurt. The bull market was truly a global phenomenon. As the figure shows, the world index during 1987 peaked 40 per cent above the beginning-of-year value. Just prior to the crash, therefore,

**Figure 17.1** Summary information: world financial centres, 1987–1988

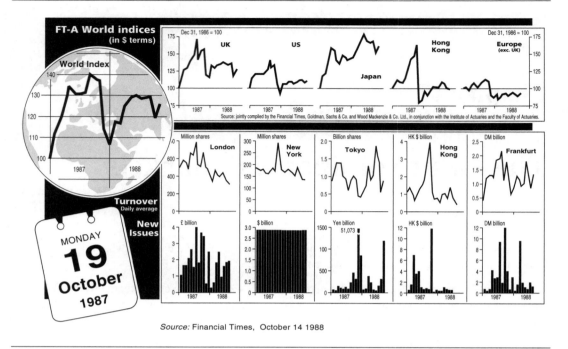

*Source:* Financial Times,  October 14 1988

the financial markets were valuing the world's capital stock at 40 per cent more than they were valuing it at the start of the year.

Then came the crash. In a matter of hours, the bull market was over in every major financial centre except one.

In the UK, the index fell by one-third in three days, wiping out most of the gains of the year (see Figure 17.1). While it recovered somewhat during November and December, it nevertheless remained very flat during 1988. Trading in shares also fell sharply, with average daily turnover down by one-third in 1988 compared with 1987. Similarly, new equity issues were substantially lower in 1988 compared with 1987.

The deregulation of the UK securities industry (the Big Bang) had taken place one year earlier. This had led to a huge increase in competition as many UK and overseas banks either acquired or introduced broking and market-making facilities. The full adjustment of the industry to the deregulation was far from complete by the time the crash came. In particular, there were high costs and excess capacity in a number of activities, and management controls for dealing with the expansion of activities were not fully operational. For example, the banks had paid huge sums to acquire broking and market-making facilities; the subsequent running costs were also very high, as a result of the salaries and bonuses demanded by the brokers and market-makers whose firms were being bought out. Also, there was inadequate monitoring of the position risk exposures of individual traders and clients, especially in relation to traded options and futures. Similarly, the cost accounting systems being used were largely inadequate; this made it very difficult to price activities and to determine which were profitable and which were not, as the extremely brief incursions by a number of banks into private client discount broking indicated.

In the USA, the index also fell by one-third (wiping $1 trillion off the market value of US securities), and, because it had not risen as far during 1987 as the UK index had done, the US index fell below the beginning-of-year level during October, although it did end the year higher than at the start (Figure 17.1). As in the UK, the US index remained very flat during 1988. Similarly, the volume of shares traded and the volume of new issues (both equity and debt) were much lower in 1988 compared with 1987.

Other financial centres faired even worse. For example, in Europe (excluding the UK), the rise in the index during 1987 had been very modest compared with that in other centres (see Figure 17.1). But the percentage fall in the index during the crash was very similar to that elsewhere, and the index languished at its post-crash level for the whole of 1988. Using the Frankfurt Stock Exchange for illustration, turnover was slightly lower following the crash than before, but the volume of new issues was substantially lower.

Even worse than Europe was Hong Kong. This was the only financial centre with international significance that actually closed during the crash (from Tuesday 20 October to Friday 23 October). During 1987 the Hong Kong index had risen by 70 per cent. During the crash, the index fell by 50 per cent in total, with a 10 per cent fall on Monday 19 October and a 33 per cent fall on Monday 26 October, the day the market reopened. The collapse of the Hong Kong futures market was even more dramatic. Futures trading was suspended for a whole week and the futures market needed to be rescued with a HK$2 billion government-backed lifeboat operation as a result of the massive default on obligations. There were also allegations of serious corruption, and soon after the crash, the chairmen of both the Hong Kong Stock Exchange and the Hong Kong Futures Exchange were fired. A new Securities and Futures Commission was established to improve the regulation of both exchanges.

Only one world financial centre escaped the worst of the crash, and that was Tokyo. The Tokyo market had for some considerable time been regarded as being overvalued. This was especially so when, during 1987, the market capitalization of the Tokyo exchange exceeded that of New York for the first time. A long overdue correction was anticipated. Well, a correction did take place, but not in the way that was expected. A year after the crash, the Tokyo market was 50 per cent larger than that in New York. The Japanese index fell very little during the crash and was much higher in 1988 than in 1987 (see Figure 17.1). Similarly, the volume of shares traded was significantly higher in 1988 than in 1987, while the volume of new equity issues was about the same. In short, the crash had no real effect on the Japanese market. Instead, it signalled a transfer of financial power to Japan from the USA, although this was subsequently amd dramatically reversed during the 1990s.

So while the crash was a truly global phenomenon, there were significant differences in the behaviour of different financial centres during the crash.

## 17.2 The consequences of the crash

There are several reasons why Japan escaped the worst effects of the crash. One immediate reason is the system of price limits that operates on the Tokyo market. If the index falls by more than 15 per cent in any one trading day, the exchange closes limit down. Despite imposing temporary but complete illiquidity, the system of price limits helps to provide a breathing space to calm investors' nerves. Another reason is that there was a co-ordinated attempt to stabilize the market by the Ministry of Finance and the major Japanese stockbrokers. The major brokers were induced to make massive purchases of shares for their own account, thereby resuscitating a market that was paralyzed by the absence of any other buyers. They were able to do this because of their massive balance sheets. These balance sheets had arisen for two reasons. First, Japan had accumulated huge reserves as a result of her export surpluses. Second, Japanese individuals have the world's highest savings ratio (20 per cent of income for the average individual). These funds are channelled through the banking system to the brokers who in the event were able to use them to save Japan from the crash. The Ministry of Finance's justification for initiating this rescue operation was that the stock market serves the whole economy, and that ensuring that it continues to do this is more important than having to face charges that the Ministry was engaged in market manipulation. The consequences of the crash for other financial centres were far less attractive, however.

In the UK, for example, the sharp cutback in the volume of securities trading following the crash led to a period of retrenchment. Commission income from institutional clients fell by 32 per cent. Many major activities, such as agency broking, sales, marketing and research, were hardly breaking even in 1988. The opportunity of the crash was used by banks to cut back on the excess capacity (especially in respect of market-making) that resulted from Big Bang. The result was a substantial number of staff layoffs, about 10,000 in the year following the crash. The staff layoffs, together with an improvement in revenues from market-making because of the widening of spreads following the crash, led to an increase in profitability in market-making, virtually the only major activity that managed to cover costs in 1988.

In the USA, securities firms experienced their largest ever losses at $2.2 billion during the fourth quarter of 1987. Costs were cut by nearly 7 per cent during 1988, as a result of a combination of staff layoffs and cuts in bonuses. This led to a slight recovery of profits during 1988. Nevertheless, the 20 per cent fall in the volume of share trading and the 50 per cent fall in the volume of futures trading meant that profits were lower in 1988 than in any year (with the exception of 1987) since 1984. The main activities that did make money in 1988 were corporate finance (especially mergers and acquisitions), bonds and swaps.

Another casualty of the crash was the global equities market, the continuous 24-hour market in the world's leading equities, with trading moving around the world between Tokyo, London and New York. This market cooled down substantially during 1988.

Related to this was the collapse of cross-border portfolio investment following the crash. Institutional investors unloaded their holdings of overseas securities even more substantially than they unloaded their domestic security holdings. Table 17.1 shows the effect of this in the fourth quarter of 1987. In 1986 total cross-border portfolio investment was $30 billion; but in 1987 (IV) cross-border disinvestment reached $30.83 billion. The UK was the largest disinvestor, with $11.24 billion of funds repatriated, mainly from the USA and Japan. The USA was also a net disinvestor, but on a much smaller scale, with $3.71 billion of funds repatriated, mainly from Japan. Japan received the brunt of the disinvestment, with $21.54 billion of funds repatriated from that country (i.e. 70 per cent of the total). Given the subsequent performance of the Japanese market in 1988, this was an extremely poor investment decision by international investors. In 1988 overseas investors accounted for only 4 per cent of the market capitalization of the Japanese market. Japan itself was a net investor overseas during this period, with $3.35 billion of funds invested. The UK was one of the few net beneficiaries of overseas investment, with $1.25 billion in net inflows, although this was due mainly to the international tranche of the British Petroleum privatization issue.

The October 1987 crash was the worst experienced by the world's main financial centres (with the exception of Tokyo) since 1929. As a consequence of the 1929 crash, the world entered a deep depression which lasted for a whole decade. The consequences of the 1987 crash could not have been more different. Instead of facing a collapse in economic growth, the growth rate in GDP in the

**Table 17.1** International net equity flows ($bn): 4th quarter 1987

| Market to | Investor from | | | | | |
|---|---|---|---|---|---|---|
| | USA | UK | Continental Europe | Japan | Rest of world[a] | Market total |
| USA | – | (4.99) | (2.97) | 1.85 | (1.12) | (7.23) |
| UK | 0.50 | – | 0.23 | 0.50 | 0.02 | 1.25[b] |
| Continental Europe | (1.59) | (3.42) | (2.92) | 0.37 | 1.55 | (6.01) |
| Japan | (2.76) | (4.00) | (3.19) | – | (11.59) | (21.54) |
| Rest of world | 0.14 | 1.17 | 1.64 | 0.63 | (0.88) | 2.70 |
| Investor total | (3.71) | (11.24) | (7.21) | 3.35 | (12.02) | (30.83) |

[a]Includes 'offshore' fund managers.
[b]Includes $1.8bn from international tranche of BP issue.

*Source:* Salomon Brothers, *Financial Times*, 14 October 1988.

advanced industrial countries was higher in 1988 than in any year of the decade except 1984. The world economy was in a very strong position at the time of the crash. The oil price collapse in 1985-6 had reduced corporate costs and raised profitability. Corporate liquidity had been improved because of the success in controlling inflation. These factors in turn had increased confidence and raised investment expenditure. In addition, the authorities responded to the crash in a more appropriate way than they did in 1929. In 1929 the authorities especially in the USA, tightened both monetary and fiscal policy. This compounded the contraction that was already taking place as a result of the collapse of the banking system and the consequent contraction of liquidity, again especially in the USA. By 1987, the lessons of the 1930s had been well and truly learnt. The authorities co-ordinated their response on a world-wide basis. Monetary policy was eased and interest rates lowered in order to provide liquidity to the banking system. (The excess liquidity was subsequently reabsorbed during 1988 once it was recognized that the crash had been successfully managed, although in the UK this reabsorption took place too slowly, as the successive increases in inflation and interest rates during 1988 and 1989 indicated). In addition, fiscal policy was eased, especially in Japan and West Germany. These actions, together with the buoyancy of investment, proved to be more than sufficient to counteract the contractionary effect of reduced consumption expenditure as a result of the dramatic fall in the value of financial wealth during the crash.

Thus, while the 1987 crash had severe consequences for the securities industry itself, it had remarkably little effect on the real economy.

# 17.3 The causes of the crash

Was the crash of 1987 a rational response to events, or was it the outcome of an irrational attack of panic? In this section we will examine both of these possible explanations.

It could simply be the case that the crash was merely the bursting of a speculative bubble. There have been many examples of such bubbles throughout history. Malkiel (1996) cites a number of examples: the Tulip Bulb Craze of the 1630s, the South Sea Bubble in the 1720s, the Florida Real Estate Craze in the 1920s, the Great Crash of 1929, the Growth Stock/New Issue Craze in the early

1960s, the Concept Stocks Craze in the mid-1960s, the Conglomerate Boom in the late 1960s and the Gambling Stock Craze in the late 1970s. He also has an explanation for the behaviour that leads to a bubble. He calls it the *greater fool theory*. Prices of securities can be rising very rapidly. Many investors continue to buy, knowing that securities are grossly overvalued, because they believe that they can sell at a huge profit to other investors (i.e. to greater fools). Then suddenly, and for no apparent reason, the bubble bursts. There are no more fools around willing to buy. There is mass panic and everybody tries to unload their holdings of securities. Prices drop like a stone until they are in line with intrinsic values. When this happens the speculative bubble is over.

Many people have argued that the 1987 crash could be explained in these terms. For example, Alan Greenspan, the chairman of the Federal Reserve Board, said that the crash was 'an accident waiting to happen. ... Stock prices finally reached levels which stretched to incredulity expectations of rising real earnings and falling discount factors. Something had to snap. If it didn't happen in October, it would have happened soon thereafter. The immediate cause of the break was incidental.' Similarly, Nicholas Goodison, the chairman of the London Stock Exchange, said that 'many of us were arguing during those buoyant months that, on fundamental grounds, world equity markets were valued too optimistically'.

While it is possible to argue, as these quotations do, that the crash was the result of irrational behaviour by investors, other explanations for the crash have been put forward. These are consistent with *rational* behaviour by investors. They were put forward by supporters of the efficient markets hypothesis. Such people do not like the argument that financial markets are rational 'most of the time', but that 'occasionally' (i.e. once every half-century) investors go mad and behave in an entirely irrational way. They believe that investors are rational 'at all times' and so prefer explanations of the crash that are consistent with this. Leland (1987) considers three theories of the crash that are consistent with rational behaviour by investors.

The first is known as the *bad news theory*. It is entirely consistent with the efficient markets hypothesis, which says that security prices immediately and fully reflect all available information. Proponents of the bad news theory argue that sufficient adverse news accumulated over the weekend of 17–18 October to explain the decline in share prices on Monday 19 October. All information available before the weekend would have been incorporated into security prices as of the close of business on Friday 16 October.

During that weekend, bad economic and political news (especially from the USA) continued to pour in: the twin US trade and budget deficits, the falling value of the dollar, the political problems of the US president over confirming Supreme Court judge Robert Bork, the Iran-Contra affair, the Gulf War, the tightening of German monetary policy. But most of these issues were known in the market before the weekend, so it is extremely unlikely that the additional information acquired over the weekend could have reduced expected prices to an extent that justified the actual fall in prices witnessed on Monday.

However, the news that accumulated over the weekend, together with the information that was collected over the previous week, could have changed investors' views during the week prior to 19 October about market *volatility*. The New York Stock Exchange fell by nearly 10 per cent during the week prior to 19 October; there was a record one-day fall on Friday 16 October alone, and John Phelan, President of the NYSE, warned about possible 'market meltdown'. As Leland (1987) argued, 'it is not unreasonable that many investors concluded over the weekend that market volatility had indeed reached unprecedented levels'.

It has been estimated that, in the USA, volatility (as measured by the standard deviation of the market portfolio) rose from about 20 per cent (the long-run average for the USA) to about 25 per cent over the course of the weekend. Now the market price of risk is measured by (see equation (13.55)):

$$\pi = \frac{\bar{r}_m - r_f}{\sigma_m^2},$$ (17.1)

where:

$r_f$ = riskless rate of return;
$\bar{r}_m$ = expected return on the market portfolio;
$\sigma_m^2$ = variance of the return on the market portfolio (i.e. the square of volatility).

In equilibrium, the market price of risk $\pi$ is constant, so that if market volatility increases then so must $(\bar{r}_m - r_f)$, the market risk premium on equities. If $\sigma_m^2$ increases from 0.04 (i.e. $(0.2)^2$) to 0.0625 (i.e. $(0.25)^2$), that is, by about 50 per cent, then $(\bar{r}_m - r_f)$ must also increase by about 50 per cent. Since the long-run market risk premium in the USA is 6 per cent, the increase in market volatility suggests that the market risk premium must rise by 50 per cent from 6 to 9 per cent. Given the riskless rate of interest in the USA at the time of the crash was 6 per cent, this implies that the expected return on equities would have to rise from 12 per cent (i.e. $r_f(6\%) + (\bar{r}_m - r_f)(6\%)$) to 15 per cent (i.e. $r_f(6\%) + (\bar{r}_m - r_f)(9\%)$) to compensate investors for the increase in risk. This increase in required return would lead to equity prices falling by 20 per cent (i.e. $(0.12 - 0.15)/0.15$) if dividends on shares are not expected to change. Now the fall in share prices on Monday 19 October was almost exactly 20 per cent. So the crash could be explained by a perceived increase in market volatility brought about by an accumulation of bad news over the weekend of the 17–18 October.

The second rational theory of the crash that has been suggested is called the *fear of market failure theory*. With this theory, investors (especially in the USA) feared that the market mechanism itself would fail, with market-makers unable to maintain open, orderly markets. Because of this fear, investors attempted to unload securities before the market mechanism collapsed, and in doing so induced the failure they so much feared. Thus, this theory is another example of a self-fulfilling prophecy, and, as it happened, it turned out to be a perfectly rational belief for investors to have.

There were two reasons why investors (especially in the USA) became concerned about the ability of the market mechanism to sustain an open and orderly market. First, there was concern that market-makers in both equities and futures might have inadequate capital to bridge selling and buying and hence to stabilize a collapsing market. (In the USA, market-makers are obliged to attempt to stabilize the market.) This concern was magnified by remarks by David Ruder, chairman of the US Securities and Exchange Commission, that markets might have to be closed. As prices fell, rumours of insolvency among market-makers, specialists and brokers on the NYSE began to grow, and this induced investors to attempt to liquidate their portfolios. Second, there was a complete failure of the computerized Designated Order Turnaround list-processing system called Super-DOT. This system was designed to execute small orders automatically, and when it became overloaded with sell orders it failed. As news of the failure became public, the prospect of the NYSE itself collapsing led to complete panic among investors.

So the combination of capital inadequacy and computer failure led to a fear of market failure by investors that in fact resulted in market failure. This fear, although it was valid among US investors, was soon dispelled among Japanese investors; this was because the Japanese securities industry applied sufficient resources to stabilize the Tokyo market and, in addition, did not have a computerized trading system that collapsed under the strain.

The third rational theory of the crash is called the *excess hedging theory* and concerns the role of hedging strategies such as portfolio insurance in magnifying the extent of the crash. While portfolio insurance itself accounted for only 10 per cent of the volume of trading on the NYSE on Monday 19 October, it is believed that many more investors used less formal methods of hedging. So we can accept that trading by hedgers on Black Monday was substantial, at least in the USA. But the real question is: did these hedging trades cause the crash? Leland (1987) developed a model that suggests that hedging trades could have been responsible for the crash.

Leland's model distinguishes between two types of investor: information-motivated investors and information-free investors. *Information-motivated investors* base their market demands for securities on both the price of securities and the information they have about securities:

$$D^I = D^I(P, \Omega),  \tag{17.2}$$

where:

$$
\begin{array}{rcl}
D^I & = & \text{demand for risky securities by information-motivated investors;} \\
P & = & \text{price of risky securities;} \\
\Omega & = & \text{information set.}
\end{array}
$$

We will suppose that the information set can be represented by a single variable $\Omega$, where increases in $\Omega$ represent good news and so lead to an increase in demand, while falls in $\Omega$ correspond to bad news and so lead to a fall in demand. Also, demand responds negatively to changes in the price of securities.

If the supply of securities, $S$, is fixed, then market equilibrium with only information-motivated investors is determined by solving

$$D^I(P, \Omega) = S  \tag{17.3}$$

to give the equilibrium price as a continuous and increasing function of $\Omega$:

$$P = P(\Omega).  \tag{17.4}$$

Figure 17.2 depicts market equilibrium for different levels of information when there are only information-motivated investors. Figure 17.3 shows the equilibrium price as a continuous and increasing function of $\Omega$.

*Information-free investors* are not concerned about information. They adjust their portfolios only in response to changes in the level of security prices. There are two main types of information-free investor: *portfolio insurers* and other hedgers, who *sell* securities as prices *fall*; and *portfolio rebalancers*, who wish to preserve a constant ratio between asset categories (e.g. between shares and bonds) and hence *buy* securities as prices *fall*.

The net demand of information-free investors at different prices consists of the planned purchases by rebalancers less the planned sales by hedgers at different prices. If there is a substantial number of hedgers operating in the market, the net demand of information-free investors will be both negative and an increasing function of price:

$$D^H = D^H(P),  \tag{17.5}$$

where $D^H$ is the net demand for risky securities by information-free investors (i.e. net hedging demand).

**Figure 17.2** Market equilibrium with only information-motivated investors

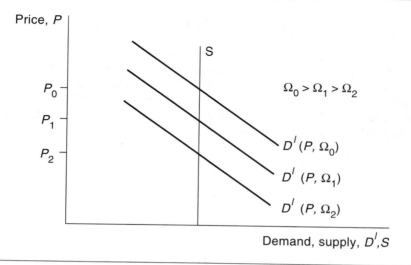

**Figure 17.3** Market price with only information-motivated investors

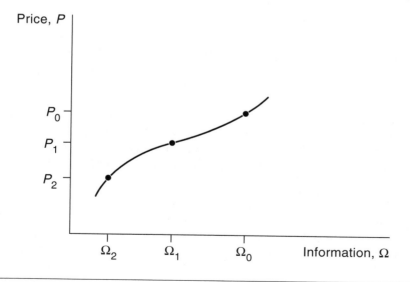

Figure 17.4 shows net hedging demand for the case in which net hedging demand is negative below $P_0$ and an increasing function of price (i.e. net hedging demand becomes more negative as price falls). Total demand, $D$, is given by the sum of the demand by information-motivated investors and net hedging demand:

$$D(P,\Omega) \;=\; D^I(P,\Omega) + D^H(P). \tag{17.6}$$

Figure 17.5 depicts market equilibrium for different levels of information when there is substantial net hedging demand in addition to the conventional demand of information-motivated investors. The effect of the net hedging demand is to cause the total demand curve to be *backward-bending* (i.e. upward-sloping) between $P_0'$ and $P_2$. This backward-bending segment of the total demand curve arises only if net hedging demand is sufficiently large. If there are only a few hedgers at every price level, their negative hedging demands are not sufficient to generate the upward-sloping segment in Figure 17.5.

**Figure 17.4** Net hedging demand

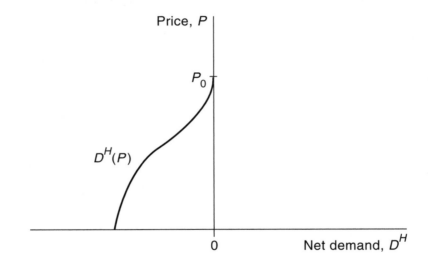

It is the backward-bending segment that is the key to explaining the crash. We will begin at the peak of the market (which in the USA occurred on 25 August). The market stood at $P_1$ with information level $\Omega_1$. At this historically high level of the market, many investors decided to purchase portfolio insurance and other hedging programmes. Total demand is given by $D(P,\Omega_1)$ in Figure 17.5.

Over the next two months, news (both economic and political) became less favourable. The demand curve shifted to the left and security prices fell, but in a continuous manner. By 16 October, the information level was $\Omega_2$ and the market was at $P_2$ with total demand given by $D(P,\Omega_2)$. Then over the weekend of 17–18 October, some more bad news emerged. In itself, it was not particularly significant (and certainly not earth-shattering), but it was all that was needed to induce the crash. This is because the news reduced the information level below $\Omega_2$. As can be seen from Figure 17.5, this caused portfolio insurers to begin selling securities in a massive way. The selling dominated the buying by information-motivated investors. Prices fell from $P_2$ to $P_2'$, at which level a new stable equilibrium was established. Despite the fact that the change in information was continuous, the change in price

**Figure 17.5** Market equilibrium with substantial net hedging demand

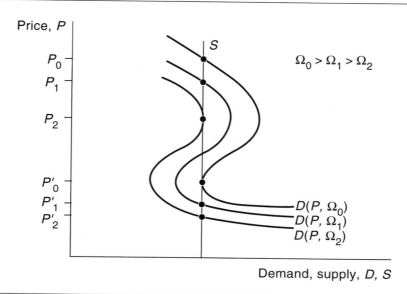

was markedly discontinuous. Thus, we have explained the crash in terms of an excessive number of hedgers unloading securities as prices fell.

But if it is possible for a small piece of unfavourable information to cause a crash, is it possible for a small piece of favourable information to reverse the crash and for prices to jump back to pre-crash levels? Unfortunately, the answer is no, as can be seen from Figure 17.6. This figure shows the equilibrium price of securities as a positive but discontinuous function of $\Omega$. For every information level between $\Omega_0$ and $\Omega_2$, there are two sets of equilibrium price levels: a set of locally continuous high prices and a set of locally continuous low prices. If the information level falls below $\Omega_2$, equilibrium prices will fall from a high level at $P_2$ to a low level at $P_2'$. Once prices have fallen, small favourable changes in information will not be sufficient to reverse the price fall. Prices will remain at a low level until information reaches level $\Omega_0$. At this level, the demand curve has moved to the right to $D(P, \Omega_0)$ as shown in Figure 17.5. Any good news that shifts $\Omega$ above $\Omega_0$ will cause portfolio insurers and other hedgers to unwind their hedges and will lead to a jump in prices from $P_0'$ to $P_0$. Because the crash is not immediately reversible, it is known technically as a *catastrophe*, and the model used to explain the crash is simply an application of *catastrophe theory*.

## 17.4 Conclusion

In this chapter we have examined the failure of financial markets, with particular emphasis on the crash of October 1987. We looked at a number of explanations for the crash, some based on irrational behaviour and others based on rational behaviour. The irrational explanation is based on speculative bubbles and so makes the crash of 1987 just another example of the bursting of a speculative bubble that has taken place in financial markets throughout the centuries. The three explanations based on rational behaviour were: the bad news theory, in which bad news led to an increase in perceived

**Figure 17.6** Equilibrium price with substantial net hedging demand

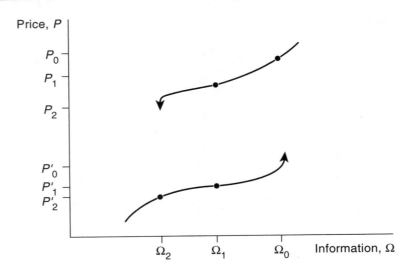

market volatility which reduced security prices; the fear of market failure theory, in which inadequately capitalized market-makers were unable to stabilize a volatile market; and the excess hedging theory, in which the mechanical selling behaviour of portfolio insurers induced the crash.

Which (if any) of these theories is true? Although the crash occurred simultaneously in all the main financial centres, it is possible that the cause of the failure was different in different centres. It is likely, for example, that the excess hedging theory is valid for the USA, where many institutional investors were using portfolio insurance. It is a less plausible explanation in other financial centres, where portfolio insurance did not play such an important role. In Hong Kong, the fear of market failure theory appears to provide the most plausible explanation, given that the market did in fact close for four days. In Japan, on the other hand, any fear of market failure was quickly dispelled as government brokers and market-makers collaborated to stabilize the market. The bad news theory appears to be more an *ex post* rationalization of events than a plausible explanation of the crash; it seems implausible that the bad news that accumulated during the weekend prior to the crash could have increased perceived volatility to the extent that justified the fall on Monday 19 October. And the bursting of a speculative bubble? Perhaps that is the best explanation for the crash in London!

Finally, what lessons can be learnt from the crash? Is it possible to eliminate crashes or at least reduce the probability of them occurring?

It is clearly not possible to legislate against speculative bubbles occurring, even when they are caused by sophisticated institutional investors. Similarly, it is not possible to legislate against the panic that ensues, even among institutional investors, when the bubble bursts. But there are lessons to be learnt from the rational explanations of the crash, as has been suggested by Rubinstein (1988). First, it is desirable for market-makers to be adequately capitalized in order to have the capacity to stabilize a volatile, or even worse, a collapsing market. Second, it may be necessary to reduce excessive volatility of the market by introducing such regulatory changes as price limits, increased margins for speculators or reduced margins for hedgers. Third, it is desirable to improve the quality of information that reaches the market. One important example of this would be to distinguish information-motivated transactions from information-free transactions. This could be achieved by portfolio insurers and other information-free traders being required to publish their trading intentions and to execute the trade if the stated conditions were met. (This is known as *sunshine trading*.) In this way an orderly market could be maintained, since prior publication of trading intentions will enhance liquidity compared with the alternative of a large order surprising the market.

**Selected references**

Bank of England (1988), 'The Equity Market Crash', *Bank of England Quarterly Bulletin,* February, 51–8.

Financial Times Survey (1988), 'A Day to Remember', *Financial Times*, 14 October.

Leland, H.E. (1987), 'On the Stock Market Crash and Portfolio Insurance', University of California, Berkeley.

Malkiel, B.G. (1996), *A Random Walk Down Wall Street*, W.W. Norton, New York.

Rubinstein, M. (1988), 'Portfolio Insurance and the Market Crash', *Financial Analysts Journal*, January-February, 38–47.

Rubinstein, M. and Leland, H. (1981), 'Replicating Options with Positions in Stock and Cash', *Financial Analysts Journal*, July-August, 63–72.

**Exercises**

1 Examine and analyze the main events surrounding the October 1987 crash.

2 What caused the October 1987 crash?

3 Compare and contrast the causes and consequences of the crashes of 1929 and 1987.

# Chapter 18

# Recent developments in financial market analysis

Just as the financial markets themselves are in a constant state of flux, so is the analysis of financial markets. There are always new ideas and techniques coming into fashion. Some stay, while others just as rapidly go out of fashion. In this final chapter, we examine some of the more important recent developments in the analysis of financial markets: value-at-risk analysis, speculative bubbles, volatility clustering, volatility asymmetry, volatility spillovers, chaos and neural networks. In order to understand this chapter fully, the reader will also require some understanding of recent developments in financial econometrics (see, e.g., Mills (1993)).

## 18.1 Value-at-risk analysis

In 1988, the Bank for International Settlements (BIS) established a common framework of prudential controls for the world's banking system. This framework is known as the *Basle Accord*. The new system required that banks have sufficient capital to cover the *specific risks* (i.e. credit risk) that they face on the asset side of their balance sheet. Bank assets are risk-weighted to reflect their inherent riskiness. For example, cash held in bank tills has a zero risk weight and banks need have no capital to support this asset. However, government bonds with less than one year to maturity have a 10% risk weight, government bonds with maturities in excess of one year have a 20% risk weight, loans for house purchase have a 50% risk weight and loans to the non-bank private sector have a 100% risk weight. Each asset is multiplied by its risk weight and then summed to give *risk-weighted assets*. Banks then face an 8% *risk assets ratio*, i.e. there must be £8 of shareholders' funds for every £100 of risk-adjusted assets.

While the Basle Accord dealt with credit risk, it did not deal with the *market risk* on assets held by banks and other financial institutions. Market risk is the risk coming from unanticipated changes in interest rates and exchange rates etc. that adversely affect the net position of banks' and securities houses' trading books, even when there is no risk of counterparty default. In January 1996, the European Union introduced the *Capital Adequacy Directive* (CAD) which imposed a common set of capital requirements for the securities trading books of banks and securities houses operating within the European Financial Area. In addition, the internal risk management systems adopted by banks required authorization. The most frequently used of these is based on *value-at-risk* (VaR) *analysis*.

The objective of VaR analysis is to estimate the capital loss on a portfolio over a given period (typically 24 hours) that will be exceeded with a given frequency (e.g. 1 per cent or 5 per cent of the time). There are two types of VaR model that have been used in practice: parametric models and non-parametric models.

*Parametric VaR models* (sometimes also called *variance-covariance models*) assume that the returns on securities follow a particular statistical distribution, typically that the returns are stationary, multivariate normal and independent over time. Using estimates of the expected returns, variances of the returns and covariances between the returns, it is possible to estimate the daily capital loss that will be exceeded with the given probability. Estimated means and variances are based on historical data on returns:

$$\bar{r}_t = \frac{1}{T} \sum_{i=1}^{T} r_{t-i+1}, \tag{18.1}$$

$$\sigma_t^2 = \frac{1}{T-1} \sum_{i=1}^{T} \lambda_i \left( r_{t-i+1} - \bar{r}_t \right)^2, \tag{18.2}$$

where:

$r_t$ = holding period return on security at time $t$;

$\bar{r}_t$ = expected return on security at time $t$;

$\sigma_t^2$ = variance of return on security at time $t$;

$\lambda_i$ = weighting scheme used in estimating variance, such that $0 \le \lambda_i \le 1$ and $\sum_{i=1}^{T} \lambda_i = 1$ (the standard variance sets $\lambda_i = 1$).

The VaR analyst has to determine $T$, the appropriate length of the lagged data window, and $\lambda_i$, the weighting scheme used in estimating the variance. The most common procedure for determining $T$ is to find the value that minimizes the *mean absolute forecast error*:

$$\text{MAFE} = \frac{1}{T} \sum_{t=1}^{T} \left| (r_t - \bar{r}_t)^2 - \sigma_t^2 \right|. \tag{18.3}$$

A common procedure for choosing $\lambda_i$ is to assume that the weights decay exponentially over time:

$$\lambda_i = \frac{1-\lambda}{1-\lambda^{T-1}} \cdot \lambda^{i-1} \qquad i = 1, \dots, T. \tag{18.4}$$

Again $\lambda$ (where $0 \le \lambda \le 1$) can be chosen to minimize the mean absolute forecast error.

If asset returns are assumed to be normally distributed, then with parametric VaR modelling, it is possible to determine a critical rate of capital loss on a trading book during the next period, such that the actual rate of capital loss exceeds the critical rate with a given probability (e.g. 1 per cent). This is found by solving the following equation for $\gamma_t$:

$$\Pr\left( \sum_{i=1}^{N} \theta_{i,t} r_{i,t} < -\gamma_t \mid r_t, \sigma_t^2 \right) = 0.01, \tag{18.5}$$

where:

$\theta_{i,t}$ = proportion of the investment portfolio in the $i$th security at time $t$;

$\gamma_t$ = critical rate of capital loss.

The solution for $\gamma_t$ is given by:

$$
\begin{aligned}
\gamma_t &= -\bar{r}_t - N^{-1}(0.01)\sigma_t \\
&= -\bar{r}_t - 2.33\sigma_t,
\end{aligned}
\tag{18.6}
$$

where $N(\ )$ is the cumulative distribution function for a standard normal variate. Figure 18.1 shows that the trading institution will need capital of $\gamma_t K_t$ to cover daily trading losses no greater than 1 per cent (where $K_t$ is the value of the trading book).

---

**Figure 18.1** Determining the critical rate of capital loss in a VaR analysis

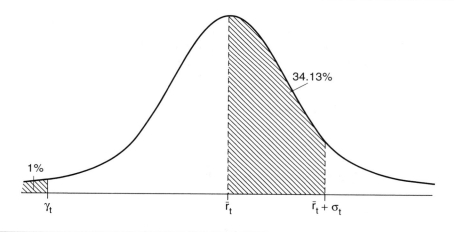

---

In *non-parametric VaR models* (sometimes also called *simulation* or *back-testing models*), a long historical run of daily data on security returns is used to determine the frequency with which a capital loss of a given size occurs; it is called a non-parametric approach because it makes no assumptions about the underlying distribution of security returns. For example if from a run of 1000 daily returns, 12 returns were less than $-3$ per cent, then the probability that the capital loss on a portfolio would exceed 3 per cent in any one trading day is 1.2 per cent.

Evidence presented by Jackson et al. (1997) indicates that non-parametric VaR modelling generates more accurate estimates of the critical rates of capital loss $\gamma_t$, since in practice the distributions of security returns exhibit *leptokurtosis* (fat distribution tails) relative to the normal. This means that there is a higher probability of securities generating both much larger and much smaller returns than implied by the normal distribution. This, in turn, implies that the true loss $\gamma_t$ is larger than indicated by the normal distribution and so more capital needs to be in place to cover this potential loss than indicated by the normal distribution.

Despite this, parametric VaR models are widely used, and one of the best known of these is *Risk-Metrics* designed by the investment bank J.P. Morgan of New York.

## 18.2   Speculative bubbles

In section 6.3, when we discussed the fair pricing of shares based on expected dividends, we ruled out the possibility of speculative bubbles developing. In this section, we consider some recent develop-ments in the theory of *speculative bubbles.*

The fair pricing model for shares (also sometimes called the *efficient market* or *no-arbitrage model*) is:

$$P_0 = \frac{E(d_1)}{1+r} + \frac{E(P_1)}{1+r}$$

$$= \sum_{t=1}^{T} \frac{E(d_t)}{(1+r)^t} + \frac{E(P_T)}{(1+r)^T}, \tag{18.7}$$

where:

$$
\begin{aligned}
P_0 &= \text{fair price of the share;} \\
E(d_t) &= \text{expected annual dividend per share at the end of year } t; \\
E(P_t) &= \text{expected price of the share at the end of year } t; \\
r &= \text{market-determined discount rate on a firm with this risk class.}
\end{aligned}
$$

When the *terminal* or *transversality condition*:

$$\lim_{T \to \infty} \frac{E(P_T)}{(1+r)^T} = 0 \tag{18.8}$$

is imposed and the growth rate of dividends is less than the discount rate, then (18.7) has a unique finite solution:

$$P_0 = \sum_{t=1}^{\infty} \frac{E(d_t)}{(1+r)^t}. \tag{18.9}$$

However, if the transversality condition (18.8) does not hold, then (18.7) has an infinite number of solutions. One of these can take the form:

$$P_t = P_0 + b_t, \tag{18.10}$$

where $b_t$ is known as the *rational speculative bubble* component of the share price satisfying:

$$E(b_{t+1}) = (1+r)b_t, \tag{18.11}$$

i.e., the market expects the bubble component to grow at the same rate as the discount rate. There are an infinite number of bubbles satisfying (18.11), each one having a different initial condition $b_0$. According to West (1988, p.648), 'a rational bubble [is] an extraneous event that affects stock prices because everyone expects it to do so. The term bubble refers to the explosive process $b_t$ and not to any deviation from fundamentals induced by speculation.' In other words, a rational bubble is a self-fulfilling belief even though it is still a solution to the no-arbitrage model.

The bubble component $b_t$ can take a number of forms. The simplest is the *deterministic bubble*:

$$b_{t+1} = (1+r)b_t, \tag{18.12}$$

which develops along a constant growth trend. Tirole (1982, 1985) argued that such a bubble might develop because each generation of investors is willing to pay more for a share so long as the following generation is also willing. The problem with (18.12) is that this bubble will never burst. To account for bubbles bursting we have to have *stochastic bubbles*. There are several types.

West (1987) developed a model of *collapsing bubbles*:

$$b_{t+1} = (b_t - b^*)/\pi \quad \text{with probability } \pi, \tag{18.13}$$

and:

$$b_{t+1} = b^*/(1-\pi) \quad \text{with probability } 1-\pi, \tag{18.14}$$

where $b^* > 0$ and $0 < \pi < 1$. In this model, the bubble continues with probability $\pi$ each period and an expected life of $1/(1-\pi)$ years, and collapses with probability $(1-\pi)$ each period.

Evans (1989) developed a model of *periodically collapsing and regenerating bubbles*:

$$b_{t+1} = \alpha b_t \varepsilon_{t+1} \quad \text{if } b_t \le \beta, \tag{18.15}$$

and:

$$b_{t+1} = [\gamma + \delta(b_t - \gamma/\delta)\theta_{t+1}/\pi]\varepsilon_{t+1} \quad \text{if } b_t > \beta, \tag{18.16}$$

where $0 < \gamma < \beta\delta$, $\varepsilon_{t+1}$ is a positive exogenous random variable satisfying $E(\varepsilon_{t+1}) = 1$ and $\theta_{t+1}$ is a Bernoulli process taking the value 1 with probability $\pi$ and 0 with probability $(1-\pi)$. The bubble grows at an average rate of $\alpha$ until $b_t > \beta$, at which point this erupts into a phase of explosive growth which averages $\delta/\pi$ so long as the bubble continues, but which collapses with a probability of $(1-\pi)$ per period. When the bubble collapses (i.e. when $\theta_{t+1}$ takes the value 0), $b_t$ declines to a mean value of $\gamma$ and the process starts again.

Diba and Grossman (1987) developed a model of a *periodically shrinking bubble*:

$$b_{t+1} = \alpha b_t + \varepsilon_{t+1} \quad \text{with probability } \pi, \tag{18.17}$$

and:

$$b_{t+1} = \frac{(\gamma - \alpha\pi)}{1-\pi} b_t + \varepsilon_{t+1} \quad \text{with probability } 1-\pi, \tag{18.18}$$

where $E(\varepsilon_{t+1}) = 0$.

Several studies have tested for the existence of speculative bubbles. For example, Diba and Grossman (1988) tested whether stock prices were more explosive than dividends. They concluded that 'stock prices did not contain explosive rational bubbles'. Diba and Grossman (1987) also argued on theoretical grounds that if a rational speculative bubble is present in a security it would have been present from the time that the security first began to be traded. This is because if $E(b_{t+1}) = (1+r)b_t > 0$, then this must be because $b_t > 0$, which in turn implies $b_0 > 0$. By the same argument, if $b_0 = 0$ then $E(b_{t+1}) = 0$. Similarly if a bubble were ever to burst, it could never start up again. However, this argument does not apply to periodically collapsing and regenerating bubbles. Nevertheless, Evans (1989) could not find evidence of periodically collapsing bubbles; he only demonstrated that such a bubble is theoretically possible. Blackburn and Sola (1996) suggest that it is possible to test for the presence of bubbles by examining the residuals from a regression of the price of a security on fundamental variables determining the price. They argue that 'If the residuals cannot be made integrated of order zero after any order of differencing, then there is evidence of a deterministic bubble. If the residuals can be made integrated of order zero after some order of differencing and there are no signs of structural breaks, then there is evidence against any type of bubble. And if the residuals can be made integrated of order zero after some order of differencing and there are signs of structural breaks, then there is evidence consistent with a periodically collapsing bubble.' Blackburn and Sola's procedure attempts to bypass the two principal problems associated with testing for bubbles. The first is the problem of differentiating between a bubble and an anticipated change in fundamentals. The second is the difficulty of detecting a periodically collapsing bubble when the residuals are integrated and hence have an infinite unconditional variance.

## 18.3  Volatility effects in financial markets

The efficient markets hypothesis predicts that returns on securities are not correlated over time: knowing the return on a security today is of no help in predicting the security's return tomorrow. However, what was discovered during the 1980s was that the squares of the returns on securities were correlated over time. This implied that a large return on one day (whether positive or negative) was likely to be followed by a large return the next day (which could also be either positive or negative), even if it was not possible to predict the sign of the return. This in turn suggested that volatility runs in trends or that returns on securities exhibited *volatility clustering*, that is, periods when volatility is high followed by periods when volatility is low. One of the most popular tools used to explain volatility clustering is the *autoregressive conditional heteroscedasticity* (ARCH) class of models.

In order to explain ARCH processes, it is necessary to review some basic statistical concepts. The *unconditional mean*, $\mu$, of a random variable, $z_t$, is the mathematical expectation, $E$, of that variable:

$$\mu = E(z_t). \tag{18.19}$$

The *conditional mean*, $m_t$, of a random variable at time $t$ is the mean conditional on knowledge of a set of random variables contained in an information set, $\Omega_{t-1}$, dated at an earlier period. This is written:

$$m_t \equiv E(z_t \mid \Omega_{t-1}) \equiv E_{t-1}(z_t). \tag{18.20}$$

Whereas the unconditional mean is not a random variable, the conditional mean is a random variable that depends on the information set.

The *unconditional variance* of a random variable is defined as:

$$\sigma^2 = E(z_t - \mu)^2. \tag{18.21}$$

The *conditional variance* is defined as:

$$h_t \equiv E\left[(z_t - m_t)^2 \mid \Omega_{t-1}\right] \equiv E_{t-1}(z_t - m_t)^2. \tag{18.22}$$

Forecasts made using conditional means and variances are generally more reliable than forecasts based on unconditional means and variances.

An *autoregressive process* is one which depends on its own lagged values. For example, if $z_t$ follows an autoregressive process of order $p$ (i.e. $AR(p)$), we have:

$$z_t = \sum_{i=1}^{p} \theta_i z_{t-i}. \tag{18.23}$$

A random variable is said to be *homoscedastic* if its variance is constant over time:

$$E(z_t - \mu)^2 = \sigma^2. \tag{18.24}$$

A random variable is said to be *heteroscedastic* over time if its variance is time varying:

$$E(z_t - \mu)^2 = \sigma_t^2. \tag{18.25}$$

Figures 18.2 and 18.3 show examples of homoscedastic and heteroscedastic variables respectively.

We can now consider ARCH processes in the context of the following regression equation:

$$y_t = \beta x_t + u_t, \tag{18.26}$$

where $y_t$ is the dependent variable, $x_t$ is the independent variable, and $u_t$ is a random error or residual. We will assume that the unconditional mean of $u_t$ is zero, that the unconditional variance of $u_t$ is constant, so that $u_t$ is unconditionally homoscedastic, and that $u_t$ is generated by a normal distribution:

$$E(u_t) = 0, \tag{18.27}$$

$$E(u_t^2) = \sigma^2, \tag{18.28}$$

$$u_t \sim N(0, \sigma^2). \tag{18.29}$$

However, we will also assume that given the information set $\Omega_{t-1} = \{x_{t-1}, x_{t-2}, x_{t-3}, \dots\}$, the conditional variance of $u_t$ is an autoregressive process of order $p$:

$$E\left(u_t^2 \mid \Omega_{t-1}\right) = h_t$$

$$= \theta_0 + \sum_{i=1}^{p} \theta_i u_{t-i}^2. \tag{18.30}$$

This implies that the squared error $u_t^2$ follows an ARCH($p$) process: *conditional* on the information set, the process $u_t$ is *heteroscedastic* since the conditional variance follows an *autoregressive process* of order $p$. In addition, since the unconditional distribution of $u_t$ is normal, so the conditional distribution of $u_t$ will also be normal:

$$u_t \mid \Omega_{t-1} \sim N(0, h_t). \tag{18.31}$$

The ARCH model was invented by Engle (1982). A special case of (18.30) is $\theta_0 = 0$ and $\theta_i = 1/p$ which makes the forecast of the variance at time $t$ equal to the sample variance of the previous $p$ observations on $u_t$. Practitioners frequently use this special case to model volatility. However, the ARCH model is more flexible than this special case, since it allows, for example, more recent observations to be given a larger weight in the forecast of current volatility (as in (18.2) above). An example of an ARCH model is taken from Blake (1996) who showed that the rate of return on interest-bearing accounts ($r_t$) in the UK over the period 1946–1991 was generated by the following process:

$$r_t = 0.2268 + r_{t-1} - 0.0410 r_{B,t-1} + u_t, \tag{18.32}$$

$$h_t = 0.5009 + 0.8331 u_{t-1}^2, \tag{18.33}$$

where $r_{B,t}$ is the rate of return on government bonds. These equations show the return on interest-bearing accounts follows a random walk with positive drift (reflecting the gradual rise in nominal

**Figure 18.2** Homoscedastic variable

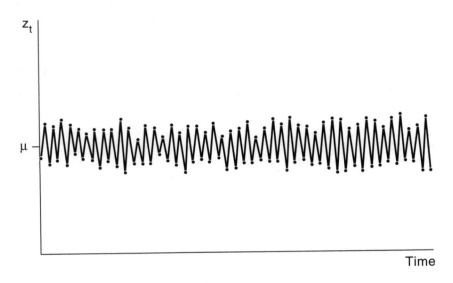

**Figure 18.3** Heteroscedastic variable

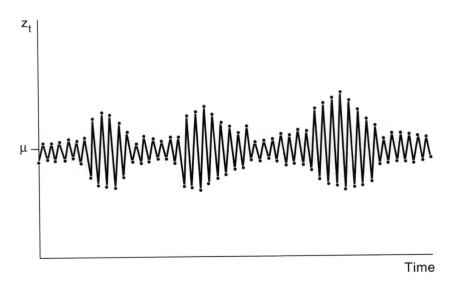

interest rates over the post-war period) together with a small negative spillover effect from the bond market in the previous year. The errors on this equation follow an ARCH(1) process with zero mean and conditional variance given by $h_t$ in (18.33).

Over the years there has been a number of extensions to the basic ARCH model. The most important of these is the *generalized ARCH* (or GARCH) model developed by Bollerslev (1986) which includes lagged values of the conditional variance in equation (18.30). The GARCH$(p,q)$ model is:

$$h_t = \theta_0 + \sum_{i=1}^{p} \theta_i u_{t-i}^2 + \sum_{i=1}^{q} \phi_i h_{t-i}. \tag{18.34}$$

The advantage of this specification is that it often allows for a more parsimonious representation for the conditional variance than the ARCH model. In other words, a low-order GARCH process (e.g. GARCH(1,1)) can explain conditional variance just as well as a high-order ARCH process. For example, Mills (1993, Example 4.2) reports that the conditional variance of the sterling-dollar exchange rate follows a GARCH(1,1) process:

$$h_t = 0.054 u_{t-1}^2 + 0.946 h_{t-1}. \tag{18.35}$$

Bollerslev et al. (1992) have shown that a wide range of financial time series follow GARCH(1,1) models.

Another use of ARCH-type models is to model *volatility asymmetry*, the differential effects of positive and negative shocks on volatility. One method of modelling this is the *exponential GARCH* (EGARCH) model of Nelson (1991):

$$\ln h_t = \theta_0 + \sum_{i=1}^{p} \phi_i \ln h_{t-i} + \sum_{i=1}^{p} \theta_i \frac{|u_{t-i}|}{\sqrt{h_{t-i}}} + \sum_{i=1}^{p} \frac{\gamma_i u_{t-i}}{\sqrt{h_{t-i}}}, \tag{18.36}$$

where $|u_t|$ is the absolute value of $u_t$. Positive and negative values of $u_t$ are allowed to have different effects on volatility. In addition, the use of logarithms implies that the coefficients in (18.36) can be negative without the variance being negative.

An even simpler model is the *dummy GARCH* (DGARCH) model of Glosten et al. (1993):

$$h_t = \theta_0 + \theta_1 u_{t-1}^2 + \phi_1 h_{t-1} + \gamma D_{t-1} u_{t-1}^2, \tag{18.37}$$

where $D_t$ is a dummy variable which takes the value 1 if $u_t < 0$ and zero otherwise. If volatility responds to good and bad news in different ways, then we would expect $\gamma > 0$. Engle and Ng (1991) found that the DGARCH model was the preferred one for characterizing the asymmetry of the volatility response to news, using a data set based on daily Japanese stock return data.

Bae and Cheung (1993) used the DGARCH model to test for *international spillovers* in volatility and also to test whether such spillovers are symmetric or asymmetric. Two questions are being asked here: (1) Does good news (or bad news) in the stock market of one country affect the volatility of the stock market of another country? and (2) If so, does the spillover of volatility go both ways (is it symmetric?) or only one way (is it asymmetric?)? Bae and Cheung addressed these questions using intraday data on the Standard and Poors 500 index for the US and the Hang Seng index for Hong Kong between April 1986 and October 1990. They found the following model for conditional volatility in Hong Kong (with t-ratios in parenthesis):

$$h_t = \underset{(6.11)}{0.0889} + \underset{(2.89)}{0.0907 \, u_{t-1}^2} + \underset{(22.91)}{0.7386 h_{t-1}}$$

$$+ \underset{(2.36)}{0.0894 D_{t-1} u_{t-1}^2} - \underset{(1.19)}{0.0241 \varepsilon_t^2} + \underset{(5.05)}{0.1108 \, F_t \varepsilon_t^2}, \tag{18.38}$$

where $\varepsilon_t$ is the shock in the US market and $F_t$ is a dummy variable that takes the value 1 if $\varepsilon_t < 0$ and zero otherwise. This specification shows that bad news from the US has a larger effect in increasing stock market volatility in Hong Kong than bad news about Hong Kong from the previous day (i.e. $0.1108 > 0.0894$). It also shows that good news from the US has a small but not statistically significant effect in reducing volatility in Hong Kong. In contrast, Bae and Cheung found that the Hong Kong market has no effect on the volatility of the US market.

Another generalization is the *ARCH-in-mean* (ARCH-M) model which involves expanding the regression equation (18.26) to include the conditional variance term $h_t$ :

$$y_t = \beta x_t + \alpha h_t + u_t. \tag{18.39}$$

By doing this, we allow the conditional variance of the error term, $u_t$, to influence the conditional mean of $y_t$. The model therefore allows us to investigate the effects of volatility on, say, the expected returns on securities. For example, Engle et al. (1987) used an ARCH-M framework to estimate a model of the term structure of interest rates in which a time-varying risk premium is used to influence the rate of return on Treasury bills (t-ratios in parenthesis):

$$r_t = \underset{(4.38)}{0.355} + \underset{(3.36)}{0.068} \ln h_t + u_t, \tag{18.40}$$

$$h_t = \underset{(2.22)}{0.055} + \underset{(5.56)}{0.148} \sum_{i=1}^{4} (5-i) u_{t-i}^2. \tag{18.41}$$

## 18.4   Chaos

*Chaos* (sometimes called *deterministic chaos*) refers to the case of a variable whose behaviour over time appears to be quite random but is, in fact, perfectly predictable because the dynamic behaviour of the variable is defined by a *deterministic, non-linear difference equation*.

To illustrate chaotic behaviour we can consider a model developed by Day and Huang (1990). This model attempts to explain how bull markets suddenly switch into bear markets and vice versa in an apparently random fashion. The model has two types of investor. The first type (denoted $\alpha$-investors) are sophisticated *informed investors* (akin to Black's (1986) *information traders*) who devote considerable resources to determine the *fair value* ($P_0$) of a particular security. Their excess demand for the security is assumed to be determined as follows:

$$\alpha(P_t) = \begin{cases} a(P_0 - P_t)\pi(P_t), & P_t \in [m, M], \\ 0 & \text{otherwise}, \end{cases} \tag{18.42}$$

where $m$ and $M$ are respectively the lowest and highest possible prices for the security, and $a$ is a positive coefficient. In other words, their excess demand is an increasing function of the deviation between the fair value ($P_0$) and the actual price ($P_t$), scaled by $\pi(P_t)$ which measures the probability of a lost opportunity, namely the failure to buy when the market is low and the failure to sell when the market is high. Day and Huang assume $\pi(P_t)$ takes the form:

$$\pi(P_t) = \left[ \frac{1}{(P_t - m + 0.01)(M - P_t + 0.01)} \right]^{0.5}. \tag{18.43}$$

This function is illustrated in Figure 18.4. When $P_t$ is close to $M$, the probability of losing a capital gain and of suffering a capital loss is high. When $P_t$ is close to $P_0$ the probability of a capital gain or loss is small. The excess demand for the security by $\alpha$-investors $\alpha(P_t)$ is shown in Figure 18.5. It is positive and high, when $P_t$ is close to $m$; it is negative and low when $P_t$ is close to $M$; it is zero when $P_t = P_0$.

The second type of investor (denoted $\beta$-investors) do not engage in costly research about a company's prospects, unlike $\alpha$-investors. They form estimates of next period's price in an extrapolative manner based on the difference between the current market price $(P_t)$ and the fair price $(P_0)$, as revealed to them by $\alpha$-investors:

$$P^\beta_{t+1} = P_t + \sigma(P_t - P_0),\tag{18.44}$$

where:

$$
\begin{aligned}
P^\beta_{t+1} &= \quad \text{estimate of next period's price;}\\
\sigma &= \quad \text{a positive coefficient.}
\end{aligned}
$$

If $P_t$ falls below $P_0$, $\beta$-investors will forecast a fall in the price of the security next period, since, in their view, 'the market as represented by $P_t$ is signalling that the current fair price won't hold up in the future.' If the current price fluctuates, the behaviour of $\beta$-investors will be like that of Black's (1986) *noise traders* or Shiller's (1989) *trend chasers* whose actions are based on erratic changes 'as if it were information'. Day and Huang call them *market sheep*. They buy when prices have risen because they expect them to continue to rise and they sell when prices have fallen because they expect them to continue to fall. As a consequence, $\beta$-investors chase prices up and down causing bull and bear markets. They, unlike $\alpha$-investors, do not take into account the probability of the lost opportunity from not selling when prices are close to $M$ or from not buying when prices are close to $m$. As a result their excess demand function for the security is given by:

$$
\begin{aligned}
\beta(P_t) &= \delta\left(P^\beta_{t+1} - P_t\right)\\
&= b(P_t - P_0),\tag{18.45}
\end{aligned}
$$

where $b = \sigma\delta$ is a positive coefficient.

The model also contains market-makers whose role is to accommodate the aggregate excess demand (supply) of $\alpha$- and $\beta$-investors through an accumulation (decumulation) of their inventory of securities:

$$
\begin{aligned}
Q_{t+1} - Q_t &= \alpha(P_t) + \beta(P_t)\\
&= ED(P_t),\tag{18.46}
\end{aligned}
$$

where $Q_t$ is the market-makers' inventory of the security at time $t$ and $ED(P_t)$ is aggregate excess demand. At unchanged prices, excess demand will exhaust the market-makers' inventory, while excess supply will exhaust their resources. Market-makers will therefore have to adjust the market price over time in response to the excess demand or supply, but they will want to do so in a way that does not create a disorderly market. Day and Huang assume that the price adjustment is proportional to the level of excess demand:

$$
\begin{aligned}
P_{t+1} - P_t &= cED(P_t)\\
&= c(P_0 - P_t)[a\pi(P_t) - b],\tag{18.47}
\end{aligned}
$$

**Figure 18.4** Probability of a lost opportunity

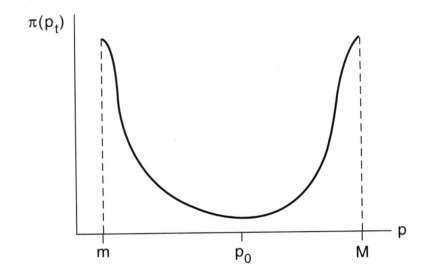

**Figure 18.5** Excess demand by $\alpha$-investors

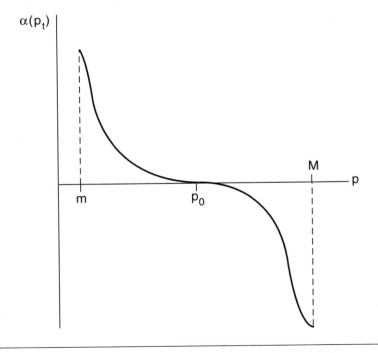

where $c$ is a positive price adjustment coefficient. This is a deterministic, non-linear difference equation in prices. It is non-linear by virtue of the functional form for $\pi(P_t)$, and it is deterministic, since it has no stochastic or random components.

Day and Huang simulate the dynamic path of prices based on equation (18.47), on the assumption that $a = 0.2$, $b = 0.88$, $c = 1$, $P_0 = 0.5$, $m = 0$ and $M = 1$. The *phase space diagram* with this set of assumptions concerning coefficients is shown in Figure 18.6. The curved line is the graph of the price adjustment function $P_{t+1} = P_t + cED(P_t)$; while the straight line is the 45° line along which

**Figure 18.6** Switching bear and bull markets

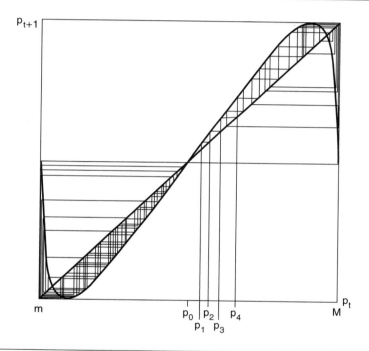

$P_{t+1} = P_t$. Any intersection between the price adjustment function and the 45° line represents a stationary equilibrium. These are three such equilibria in Figure 18.6: a low price equilibrium, a high price equilibrium, and an equilibrium where the price is always equal to the fair value, $P_t = P_0$. If the actual price of the security happened to equal one of these three equilibrium values, it would have no tendency to depart from this value. However if the price happened to take any other value, it would subsequently exhibit a dynamic pattern that appeared to be completely chaotic with no tendency to converge to one of the three equilibria. This is shown in Figure 18.7. In Figure 18.7, the initial market price ($P_1$) exceeds the fair value ($P_0$), so that β-investors enter the market. This creates an excess demand, to which the market-maker responds by selling some inventory and marking up the price. This encourages even more bullish behaviour by β-investors, which drives the price up even further, until α-investors, recognizing that the price is now too high, start to sell in sufficient amounts that an excess supply is created. The price then begins to fall back and suddenly and apparently randomly, a bull market has turned into a bear market. The model exhibits a dynamic behaviour that is aperiodic and irregular as excess demand switches to excess supply. The price dynamics in Figure 18.7 appear

**Figure 18.7** A stock price series generated by the Day and Huang model

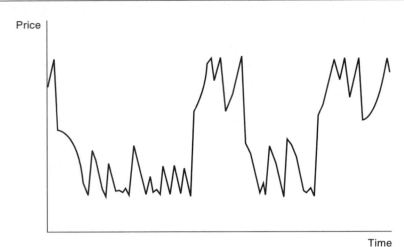

to be random, but they are in fact perfectly predictable (although the pattern *never* repeats), once we know the coefficients of the model and the initial conditions for the model's dynamic process (namely the initial price).

The curved line in Figure 18.6 is called the *strange attractor* of the system. It is known as an attractor because every price $P_t$ always maps onto the curved line, but it is strange in the sense that the resulting series of prices $P_t$ forms an aperiodic, irregular, never-repeating series. This contrasts with standard attractors, such as that generated by the following *logistic equation*:

$$P_{t+1} = 3.2P_t(1 - P_t). \tag{18.48}$$

Whatever the initial value $P_0$, the dynamic system settles down into a regular two-period *limit cycle* as shown in Figures 18.8 and 18.9. The attractor in this case is the two-period cycle. A chaotic system never exhibits a regular cyclical pattern like this. An even simpler example is the logistic equation:

$$P_{t+1} = 2.5P_t(1 - P_t). \tag{18.49}$$

Whatever the starting value $P_0$, the dynamic system settles down to a single fixed point $P_\infty = 0.6$ (i.e. $\lim_{t \to \infty} P_t = 0.6$). In this case we have a *point attractor*.

A number of tests have been developed to identify chaotic systems. One test is based on the size of *Lyapunov exponents*. There is a different exponent for each *Euclidean dimension* of the system. For example, a system involving $P_{t+1}$ and $P_t$ has two Euclidean dimensions, and can be represented by a two-dimensional phase space diagram; while a system involving $P_{t+1}$, $P_t$ and $P_{t-1}$ has three Euclidean dimensions and can be represented by a three-dimensional phase space diagram. The $i$th Lyapunov exponent ($\lambda_i$) measures the exponential growth rate of the system in the $i$th dimension, i.e. $e^{\lambda_i t}$. A positive Lyapunov exponent in any dimension indicates divergence in that dimension: any perturbation or shock to the system will cause the dynamics of the system to diverge completely from the current trajectory. For example, if in a three-dimensional system, $\lambda_1 = 0.2$, all predictive power based on forecasts from the original system will be lost in 5 (i.e. $1/0.2$) periods. The system will start as

**Figure 18.8** Limit cycle

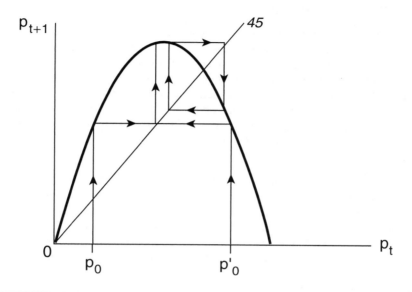

**Figure 18.9** Price pattern with a limit cycle

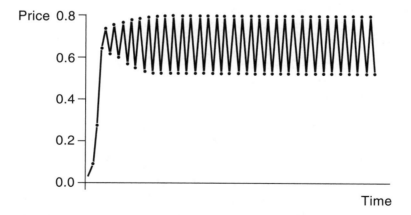

a sphere of neighbouring points representing slightly different initial conditions. Over time, the sphere will be stretched into an ellipsoid along the first dimension. A negative Lyapunov exponent in any dimension indicates convergence in that dimension. For example, if $\lambda_1 = -0.1$, the system will return to its attractor in 10 (i.e. 1/0.1) periods. A Lyapunov exponent of zero in one dimension indicates no change in the relative state of the system in that dimension.

A system cannot be chaotic unless it has at least one positive Lyapunov exponent. A three-dimensional system with three negative exponents $(-, -, -)$ will always converge to a point attractor. A three-dimensional system with two negative and one zero exponent $(-, -, 0)$ will converge to a limit cycle: two dimensions converge into one and there is no change in the relative position of the points in the third dimension. Strange attractors and chaotic systems have one positive, one negative and one zero exponent $(+, -, 0)$. The positive exponent leads to divergence as initial conditions change. The negative exponent ensures the diverging system remains within the range of the attractor and is brought back within range if it diverges too far. A chaotic system will therefore stretch and fold back in endless irregular patterns.

Another test involves calculating the *fractal dimension* of the system. Consider again Figures 18.6 and 18.7. Figure 18.7 shows that the pattern of prices over time appears to be random. But Figure 18.6 shows that the relationship between consecutive prices is not at all random. Consecutive pairs of prices will always plot on the one-dimensional curved line (i.e. the attractor) in the two-dimensional space characterized by Figure 18.6. In contrast, if there was a purely random relationship between prices, we would observe a plot between consecutive pairs of prices that looked like Figure 18.10. A purely random process 'fills out' the whole of two-dimensional space, whereas a chaotic system 'leaves holes' in two dimensional space. A stochastic process, such as a random walk, will have a fractal dimension of 2, whereas a chaotic process, such as the Day and Huang model in (18.47), will have a fractal dimension of less than 2.

An analogy that is commonly used to explain fractal dimensions is a piece of paper with different degrees of crumpledness. When the piece of paper is lying flat on a table, it has a fractal dimension of 2. If the piece of paper is crumpled a little, it now has a fractal dimension above 2 but below 3: the piece of paper is more than a plane but less than a cube, since it does not fill 3-dimensional space. The more the paper is crumpled up, the greater its fractal dimension, but it will always be less than 3 because of the holes in the space between the crumpled parts of the sheet. Another analogy involves the coast line of an island such as Great Britain. The coastline of Great Britain has a fractal dimension of 1.3, which indicates that it is more than a one-dimensional straight line, but less than a two-dimensional plane.

There are two key features of fractal objects. The first is *self-similarity*: the shape of a fractal object is similar whatever the degree of magnification through which it is observed. The same is not true with non-fractal objects. Take for example a non-fractal object such as a circle: the closer we focus in on the curve of a circle, the more the curve begins to look like a straight line. Figure 18.11 shows a plot of the Dow Jones industrial average index annually over the period 1897 to 1993. It also shows a plot of the same index on a monthly, weekly, daily and hourly basis. The striking feature is the similarity between the plots whatever the frequency with which the index is observed.

The second feature is the *high degree of correlation* between neighbouring points in a fractal object. This is because neighbouring points are related through a nonlinear deterministic equation. In Figure 18.10, there is no correlation between neighbouring points because this plot was generated purely randomly. In contrast, in Figure 18.6, neighbouring points on the attractor and also neighbouring points on the corresponding time series plot in Figure 18.7 are highly correlated because they are generated by the nonlinear, deterministic difference equation (18.47).

**Figure 18.10** A purely random relationship between prices

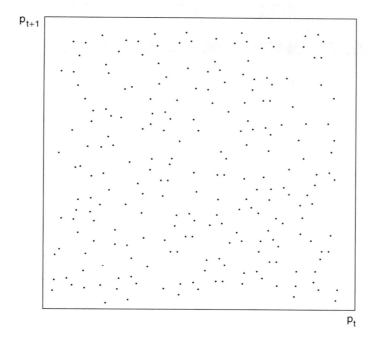

One method of finding the fractal dimension of a fractal object such as a jagged line is to superimpose a series of touching circles of the same diameter on top of the line as in Figure 18.12. The fractal dimension is then given by:

$$MD^{FD} = 1,$$ (18.50)

or:

$$FD = -\frac{\ln M}{\ln D},$$ (18.51)

where:

$$
\begin{aligned}
M &= \text{number of circles;} \\
D &= \text{diameter of circle;} \\
FD &= \text{fractal dimension.}
\end{aligned}
$$

In the case of the jagged line in Figure 18.12, the fractal dimension is:

$$FD = -\frac{\ln(4)}{\ln(0.3)} = 1.26.$$

It is clearly quite cumbersome to calculate the fractal dimension in this way. A more practical procedure is to calculate an approximation to the fractal dimension, called the *correlation dimension*

**Figure 18.11** Dow Jones Industrial Average Index, end period

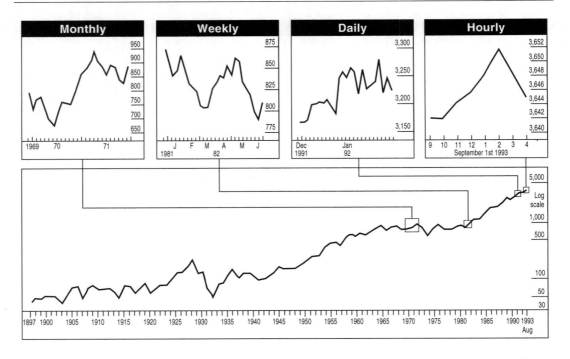

*Source:* Economist October 9, 1993

**Figure 18.12** Calculating the fractal dimension

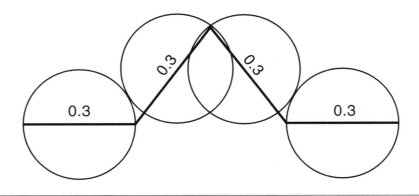

which is based on the *correlation integral*. The correlation integral measures the probability that sets of data points lie within a distance $D$ of one another. The number of data points in each set is known as the *embedding dimension*. (The embedding dimension should be at least as large as the Euclidean dimension of the system.) If the embedding dimension is $N$, then sets of $N$ consecutive observations (known as *N-histories*) can be constructed: $P_t^N = (P_t, P_{t+1}, \ldots, P_{t+N-1})$. Pairs of $N$-histories can then be compared to see if they lie within a distance $\varepsilon$ of each other:

$$|P_{t+i} - P_{s+i}| \ < \ \varepsilon, \quad i = 0, 1, \ldots, N-1. \tag{18.52}$$

If this condition is satisfied for all $i$, then an indicator function of the event $I\left(P_t^N, P_s^N, \varepsilon\right)$ takes the value 1, otherwise the indicator function takes the value 0 (technically this indicator function is known as a heaviside function). The correlation integral for dimension $N$ and distance $\varepsilon$ is defined by:

$$C(N, \varepsilon) \ = \ \frac{1}{T_N(T_N - 1)} \sum_{\substack{t=1 \\ t \neq s}}^{T_N} \sum_{s=1}^{T_N} I\left(P_t^N, P_s^N, \varepsilon\right), \tag{18.53}$$

where $T_N = T - N + 1$. The correlation dimension can be interpreted as the elasticity of the correlation integral with respect to $\varepsilon$. In other words, it measures the percentage increase in new neighbours for a typical $N$-history when the distance $\varepsilon$ increases by 1 per cent. Thus we have:

$$C(N, \varepsilon) \ = \ \varepsilon^N, \tag{18.54}$$

or:

$$N \ = \ \frac{\ln C(N, \varepsilon)}{\ln \varepsilon}. \tag{18.55}$$

This relationship can be used to differentiate a deterministic system from a stochastic system. This can be seen by examining again Figure 18.6 (the phase space diagram for a two-dimensional deterministic, chaotic system) and Figure 18.10 (the phase space diagram for a two-dimensional stochastic system). Suppose both figures are covered in small squares and the average number of points in each square is calculated. If the length of the square is doubled (i.e. the area is quadrupled), the average number of points in the squares in Figure 18.6 will double, while the average number of points in the squares in Figure 18.10 will quadruple. The elasticity is therefore 1 (i.e. the correlation dimension is 1) for the chaotic system and 2 for the stochastic system (i.e. the correlation dimension is equal to the Euclidean dimension of the system for the stochastic system). A similar analysis applies to a three-dimensional system, where cubes rather than squares are used to fill the phase space. With a chaotic system the elasticity is again 1 (doubling the sides of the cubes would double the average number of points included). With a stochastic system, the elasticity is 3 (the correlation dimension is again equal to the Euclidean dimension of the system). So long as the embedding dimension exceeds the fractal dimension, the correlation integral will provide a good estimate of the fractal dimension.

A further test for chaos is based on the *Hurst exponent* and *rescaled range analysis* (or R/S analysis). Consider a series of observations, $x_t$ ($t = 1, T$). Define $X_{s,T}$ as the cumulative deviation at time $s$ ($1 < s < T$) from the mean $\bar{x}$, estimated over all $T$ observations:

$$X_{s,T} \ = \ \sum_{t=1}^{s} (x_t - \bar{x}), \quad s = 2, T - 1. \tag{18.56}$$

The *range* $(R)$ is defined as the difference between the maximum and minimum values of $X_{s,T}$:

$$R = \max(X_{s,T}) - \min(X_{s,T}). \tag{18.57}$$

The *rescaled range* (R/S) is the range divided by the standard deviation of the $x_t$ and is related to the Hurst exponent as follows:

$$\text{R/S} = aT^H, \tag{18.58}$$

where $a$ is a positive coefficient and $H$ is the Hurst exponent. R/S should increase with time. For a random walk, it can be shown that $H = 0.5$, so that R/S increases with the square root of time. When $H = 0.5$, observations are uncorrelated over time. The Hurst exponent is related to the autocorrelation coefficient as follows:

$$\rho = 2^{(2H-1)} - 1. \tag{18.59}$$

When $H = 0.5$, then $\rho = 0$. When $0 \le H < 0.5$, then $\rho < 0$. In this case, a time series is said to be *ergodic*, *mean-reverting* or *antipersistent*: if a time series with a Hurst exponent less than 0.5 experiences a shock, it rapidly returns to equilibrium. When $0.5 < H < 1$, then $\rho > 0$. In this case, a time series is said to be a *long memory process*, *trend-reinforcing* or *persistent*: if a time series with a Hurst exponent above 0.5 experiences a shock, the effect of the shock persists, it never dies away, it never forgets. Persistent series are also known as *fractional brownian motion* or *biased random walks* (i.e. they are trended random walks). Furthermore, time series exhibit chaos if they have Hurst exponents above 0.5. This is because it can be shown that the fractal dimension of a series is equal to the inverse of $H$. The value of the Hurst exponent can be found as the slope coefficient in a graph of $\ln(\text{R/S})$ on $\ln(T)$, since from (18.58):

$$\ln(\text{R/S}) = \ln a + H \ln T. \tag{18.60}$$

It is actually very difficult to prove that a chaotic system exists, both theoretically and empirically. On theoretical grounds, it is necessary to know the *exact* values of a chaotic model's coefficients and the *exact* starting values for all the variables in the model; approximations (however close) will never be good enough. This is because it can be shown that a very small change in the starting values (even in a model with identical coefficients) will eventually lead to a very different pattern of dynamic behaviour in a chaotic model, even if the dynamic behaviour of the variables starts out being very similar. This has been called *sensitive dependence on initial conditions* or the *butterfly effect*: the flapping of a butterfly's wings in Australia could initiate a chain of events that eventually causes a storm in the UK, a storm that would not have occurred if the butterfly had not flapped its wings. As another example, consider the tossing of a coin. The outcome is usually regarded a random event. But in fact it is not. If we could replicate *exactly* the force of the toss, the motion of the surrounding air currents when the toss is taking place, the weight of the coin etc., then we could predict the outcome *every time*. In practice, of course, we cannot do this and so the outcome of tossing a coin is indistinguishable from a random event.

Empirically, it has proved very difficult to find evidence of chaotic systems in the financial markets, at least if large data sets are used. Using very large data sets on the foreign exchange and stock markets, Tata and Vassilicos (1991) could find no evidence of chaos in these markets. In particular, they examined tick-by-tick data on the US dollar-Deutschmark and US dollar-Swiss franc exchange rates over the one-week period 9 April 1989 to 15 April 1989 (giving 20,408 observations) and also daily data on the US S&P 500 stock index between February 1895 to December 1988 (giving 29,137 observations). In no case could they find a positive Lyapunov exponent and they therefore concluded that there was little evidence of chaos in financial markets.

Peters (1996) argued that a typical stock index has a fractal dimension between 2 and 3 (the S&P 500 has a fractal dimension of 2.33, while the MSCI UK index has a fractal dimension of 2.94). This implies that the dynamic behaviour of a stock index, if it is chaotic, is determined by at most three variables. The problem is finding the three variables and also finding the *exact* values of coefficients that link the three variables to the underlying index. It is the *de facto* impossibility of doing this that probably makes chaos more useful as a description of financial markets than a means of predicting them. Lo (1991) used rescaled range analysis to test for long-memory processes in US stock returns derived from the value-weighted and equal-weighted CRSP (Center for Research in Security Prices) indices. He could find no evidence of long memory and hence of chaotic dynamics, once account was taken of short term dependence (or *short memory* or *Markovian effects*) and conditional heteroscedasticity (see section 18.3 above).

## 18.5  Neural networks

A *neural network* is a data-processing tool in the form of a computer program that is capable of recognizing patterns in a set of data; in short, it 'learns' to recognize patterns. A neural network operates in a similar manner to the human brain using a network of parallel processes.

The basic operating unit is a *neuron* (or processing cell) which generates a single *output* signal depending on the intensity of a range of *input* signals (also known as input *nodes*). The inputs are weighted, summed and passed through a *transfer function*, and if the resulting value exceeds a particular threshold level then the neuron produces an output signal, otherwise no signal is produced. The weights are also known as *free parameters*. The neurons are connected together in a network.

Neural networks can be 'trained' to recognize patterns in, say, share price movements (inputs) and can then be used to predict future movements in prices (outputs). The network is trained by being given input examples and expected output results. As the input signals feed through the network, the neurons calculate the weights and output signals are sent to the next stage in the network, and so on until the final output stage is reached. The final results are compared with the expected results (called *targets*). If they do not correspond, then the weights have to be adjusted in an iterative fashion until they do. Typically thousands of examples have to be used before the network produces consistent results. This procedure is known as *supervised learning* or *supervised training*. The advantage of neural networks, however, is that they have the capacity to generalize, so that a previously unseen input pattern can also be processed.

Neural networks perform four tasks:

1. *classification*: selecting the category of an input pattern;

2. *association*: identifying an output given part of its input;

3. *encoding*: transforming a range of input signals into an output signal of lower dimension;

4. *simulations*: generating an output given an input signal, with the network having been trained to identify different input patterns.

Forecasting share prices using neural networks involves all these tasks.

The most popular modelling framework in this area is the *multilayer perceptron* (MLP) neural network and the *backpropagation* training algorithm. A typical MLP network consists of three layers of cells with interconnections between the three layers, but no interconnections between cells within a single layer. This is shown in Figure 18.13. The first layer is called the *input layer*. These nodes contain the *input vector* of data. A vast number of different input vectors is used to train the network. The second and third layers contain processing cells or *neurons*. The third layer is called the *output layer*.

**Figure 18.13** Multilayer perceptron neural network

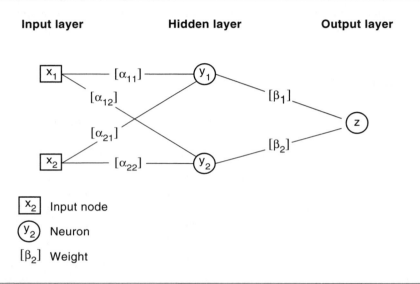

The transfer and processing of data from the first to the third layer is known as a *forward pass* or *cycle*. The second layer, which lies between the input and output layers, is known as the *hidden layer*. The interconnecting lines between the layers are shown with *weights* or *free parameters* in parentheses. The initial set of weights are chosen randomly in the range $[-1, 1]$. The weights are adjusted iteratively during the supervized training stage so that a desired *output target* (e.g. next period's exchange rate) is achieved from a given input vector. The weighted value of the input data is then passed through a *transfer function* and the result corresponds to the neuron's output value. The transfer function (which is sometimes also called a *squashing function*) can be linear but is generally a nonlinear function such as a *sigmoid function* which constrains (or squashes) the neuron output to lie in the range $[0, 1]$, see Figure 18.14.

For example, if the $i$th element of the input vector of $N$ inputs is $x_i$, if the $j$th element of the $M$ ($\leq N$) intermediate outputs in the hidden layer is $y_j$, and if the weights linking connections between the input and hidden layers are $\alpha_{ij}$, then the $j$th intermediate output is given by:

$$y_j = f[h_j(\alpha)], \tag{18.61}$$

**Figure 18.14** Sigmoid transfer function

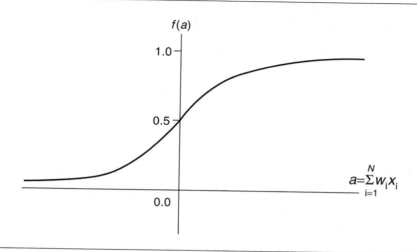

where:

$$h_j(\alpha) = \sum_{i=1}^{N} \alpha_{ij}x_i \qquad (18.62)$$

is the input to the transfer function $f[\ ]$. If the transfer function is sigmoid then:

$$f[h_j(\alpha)] = \frac{1}{1+e^{-h_j(\alpha)}} . \qquad (18.63)$$

One of the input nodes is called the *bias node*. It has a fixed value of 1, but has adjustable weights. It is used to represent the threshold level in the transfer function's inputs.

There is a similar relationship between the hidden layer and the output layer. The intermediate outputs $y_j$ become inputs in the process generating the single output $z$. If the weights linking the connections between the hidden and output layers are $\beta_j$, then the (final) output is given by:

$$z = g[o(\beta)] , \qquad (18.64)$$

where:

$$o(\beta) = \sum_{j=1}^{M} \beta_j y_j \qquad (18.65)$$

is the input into the transfer function $g[\ ]$. If the transfer function at this stage is linear then:

$$z = \sum_{j=1}^{M} \beta_j y_j . \qquad (18.66)$$

The MLP is trained using a supervised training technique called *back-propagation*. This involves sending the *output errors* (defined as the difference between the actual and target output values) in reverse order through the network in order to make adjustments to the weights. The forward and backward passes through the network constitute an *iteration* or a complete *presentation cycle*. The set of presentation cycles for all the training vectors is called an *epoch*.

We can illustrate briefly the procedure involved as follows. First we define a quadratic *cost function*:

$$c(\alpha, \beta) = \tfrac{1}{2}[\bar{z} - z(\alpha, \beta)]^2, \tag{18.67}$$

where $\bar{z}$ is the target and $z(\alpha, \beta)$ is the actual output based on the vectors of weights connecting respectively the input and hidden layers and the hidden and output layers, $\alpha = \{\alpha_{ij}, \ i = 1, N, \ j = 1, M\}$, $\beta = \{\beta_j, \ j = 1, M\}$. Starting with initial vectors of weights $\alpha^0$ and $\beta^0$, we can propagate the input vector forward through the network to generate the initial output vector $z(\alpha^0, \beta^0)$. This is compared with the target $\bar{z}$ and the cost function $c(\alpha^0, \beta^0)$ is calculated. The cost function is minimized by appropriate adjustment to the weights. A common procedure for achieving this is known as *gradient descent*. This involves calculating the response (or *gradient*) of the cost function to a change in the (final) output level caused by adjusting the weights connecting the hidden and output layers:

$$
\begin{aligned}
\Delta_j &= \frac{\partial c}{\partial z} \cdot \frac{\partial z}{\partial \beta_j} \\
&= -[\bar{z} - z(\alpha^0, \beta^0)] y_j.
\end{aligned}
\tag{18.68}
$$

The resulting $\Delta_j$ are then backpropagated through the network to the preceding hidden layer of neurons. The optimal change in the $j$th weight $(\Delta\beta_j)$ is found by subtracting $\eta\Delta_j$ from the initial weight:

$$
\begin{aligned}
\beta_j^1 &= \beta_j^0 - \Delta\beta_j \\
&= \beta_j^0 - \eta\Delta_j,
\end{aligned}
\tag{18.69}
$$

where $\eta$ is the *learning parameter* $(0 < \eta \leq 1)$. The weight change $(\Delta\beta_j)$ is subtracted, since our objective is to minimize the cost function (i.e. to reduce the gradient to zero).

This process is continued backwards from the hidden layer to the input layer. The response of the cost function to a change in the (final) output level caused by adjusting the weights connecting the input and hidden layers is:

$$
\begin{aligned}
\Delta_{ij} &= \frac{\partial c}{\partial z} \cdot \frac{\partial z}{\partial y_j} \cdot \frac{\partial y_j}{\partial \alpha_{ij}} \\
&= -[\bar{z} - z(\alpha^0, \beta^1)] \beta_j^1 f'[h_j(\alpha^0)] \cdot \frac{\partial h_j(\alpha)}{\partial \alpha_{ij}} \\
&= -[\bar{z} - z(\alpha^0, \beta^1)] \beta_j^1 \cdot \frac{e^{-h_j(\alpha^0)}}{\left[1 + e^{-h_j(\alpha^0)}\right]^2} \cdot x_k.
\end{aligned}
\tag{18.70}
$$

Again, the optimal change in the weight connecting the $i$th input and the $j$th intermediate output $(\Delta\alpha_{ij})$ is found by subtracting $\eta\Delta_{ij}$ from the initial weight:

$$
\begin{aligned}
\alpha_{ij}^1 &= \alpha_{ij}^0 - \Delta\alpha_{ij} \\
&= \alpha_{ij}^0 - \eta\Delta_{ij}.
\end{aligned}
\tag{18.71}
$$

The updated set of weights ($\alpha_{ij}^1$ and $\beta_j^1$) are such that the cost is minimized for this training vector. The whole process is repeated for all the training vectors in the epoch. The *root mean square output error* across all training vectors is calculated as:

$$\text{RMSOE} = \sqrt{\frac{\sum\limits_{k=1}^{K} [\bar{z}_k - z_k(\alpha^1, \beta^1)]^2}{K}}, \tag{18.72}$$

where $K$ is the number of training vectors in the epoch. If this is below an acceptable tolerance level, the network has converged and training stops. Otherwise a new epoch of training vectors is used and this process continues until convergence is achieved. The neural network is now ready to use as it was trained to do.

Neural networks are nonlinear models that have been trained to identify patterns in a time series of data. Azoff (1994) describes neural networks as a 'multivariate, nonlinear, nonparametric inference technique that is data driven and model free'. He embellishes this description thus: '*Multivariate* refers to the neural network input comprising many different variables whose interdependencies and causative influences are exploited in predicting future behaviour of a temporal sequence. *Nonparametric, model free* is a consequence of the lack of any presumptions regarding the relation between input variables and extrapolations into the future. Rather the network is trained by adaptation of *free parameters* to discover any possible relationships, devoid of model constraints, driven and shaped solely by the input data. Here nonparametric, in a statistical model sense, describes the fact that no predetermined parameters are required to specify the mapping model, which leads to the most general approach in processing data' (pp.1–2).

In fact, neural networks are equivalent to nonlinear regression models. This can be seen by combining equations (18.61) to (18.66) above and adding a residual term $u$:

$$z = \sum_{j=1}^{M} \frac{\beta_j}{1 - \exp\left(-\sum\limits_{i=1}^{N} \alpha_{ij} x_i\right)} + u. \tag{18.73}$$

This is a standard nonlinear regression between $z$ and the $x_i$ and the parameters of the regression ($\beta_j, \alpha_{ij}$) can be found using the standard technique of minimizing the residual sum of squares.

A number of studies have attempted to use neural networks to predict security prices. Early studies (e.g. White (1988)) indicated that neural network forecasting was unsuccessful. However later studies indicated greater success. For example, Weigend et al. (1992) were able to predict foreign exchange rates using a neural network consisting of two output signals: the sign and size of the change in exchange rates. The input signals were prices, returns and various indicators. Refenes (1995b) showed that neural network predictions on the US dollar-Deutschmark exchange rate were superior to those using classical techniques such as moving average and mean value strategies (in the former case, buying when the shorter moving average rises above the longer moving average and selling when it moves below; in the latter case, buying when the price falls below the mean value and selling when the price rises above the mean value). Schoenberg (1990), Kamijo and Tanigawa (1990) and Baba and Kozaki (1992) have successfully applied neural networks to the prediction of share prices. Yet other studies have demonstrated the usefulness of neural networks in the analysis of bond markets, e.g. Kingdon (1995) in predicting a price trend in the gilt futures market 57 per cent of the time and Moody and Utans (1995) in predicting the rating on corporate bonds more effectively than predictions based on linear regression.

There are other nonlinear modelling techniques that have been used in finance, particularly regressions based on polynomials that can account for higher powers (e.g. cubics) and cross-terms. However these techniques still involve a particular functional form and they also require very high-order polynomials in order to approximate models that are not in fact polynomial, thus making them inefficient to estimate and forecast. These problems are avoided with neural networks which, in comparison, are relatively efficient to implement in terms of computational speed and computer memory.

One of the major problems with neural networks, however, is that their results cannot be replicated. This is because the output from a neural network is sensitive to the thresholds set and to the particular training algorithm used. It is also sensitive to the initial values of the weights which are usually selected randomly. Without knowing the precise way in which a neural network has been calibrated, it is possible for two different networks to produce different results with the same input data. So despite the apparent success of neural networks in predicting exchange rates and other security prices, a neural network still remains for many people something of a 'black box' approach to forecasting or a rather sophisticated example of 'data mining'.

## Selected references

Azoff, E.M. (1994), *Neural Network Time Series Forecasting of Financial Markets*, Wiley, Chichester.

Baba, N. and Kozaki, M. (1992), 'An Intelligent Forecasting System of Stock Prices using Neural Networks', *International Joint Conference on Neural Networks*, Baltimore, MA, vol.1, 371–7.

Bae, K. and Cheung, Y-L. (1993), 'International Spillovers and Volatility Asymmetries', Working Paper, City Polytechnic of Hong Kong.

Baumol, W. and Benhabib (1989), 'Chaos: Significance, Mechanism and Economic Application', *Journal of Economic Perspectives*, 3, 77–105.

Black, F. (1986), 'Noise', *Journal of Finance*, 41, 519–43.

Blackburn, K. and Sola, M. (1996), 'Market Fundamentals versus Speculative Bubbles: A New Test Applied to the German Hyperinflation', *International Journal of Finance and Economics*, 1, 303–16.

Blake, D. (1996), 'Efficiency, Risk Aversion and Portfolio Insurance: An Analysis of Financial Asset Portfolios held by Investors in the United Kingdom', *Economic Journal*, 106, 1175–92.

Bollerslev, T. (1986), 'Generalised Autoregressive Conditional Heteroscedasticity', *Journal of Econometrics*, 31, 307–27.

Bollerslev, T., Chou, R.Y. and Kroner, K.F. (1992), 'ARCH Modelling in Finance: A Review of the Theory and Empirical Evidence', *Journal of Econometrics*, 52, 5–59.

Brock, W.A. and Malliaris, A.G. (1989), 'Differential Equations, Stability and Chaos', in *Dynamic Economics*, North Holland, Amsterdam, 297–341.

Day, R. and Huang, W. (1990), 'Bulls, Bears and Market Sheep', *Journal of Economic Behaviour and Organization*, 14, 299–329.

Diba, B. and Grossman, H. (1987), 'On the Inception of Rational Bubbles', *Quarterly Journal of Economics*, 102, 697–700.

Diba, B. and Grossman, H. (1988), 'Explosive Bubbles in Stock Prices?', *American Economic Review*, 78, 520–30.

Dowd, K. (1998), *Beyond Value-at-Risk*, Wiley, Chichester.

Economist Survey (1993), 'Frontiers of Finance', *Economist*, 9 October.

Engle, R.F. (1982), 'Autoregressive Conditional Heteroscedasticity with Estimates of the Variance of UK Inflation', *Econometrica*, 50, 987–1008.

Engle, R., Lilien, D. and Robbins, R. (1987), 'Estimating Time-Varying Risk Premia in the Term Structure: The ARCH-M Model', *Econometrica*, 55, 391–408.

Engle, R. and Ng, V. (1991), 'Measuring and Testing the Impact of News on Volatility', Working Paper, University of Michigan.

Evans, G. (1989), 'Pitfalls in Testing for Explosive Bubbles in Asset Prices', Financial Markets Group Discussion Paper No.65, London School of Economics.

Glosten, L., Jaganathan, R. and Runkle, D. (1993), 'On the Relation Between the Expected Value and the Volatility of the Nominal Excess Return on Stocks', *Journal of Finance*, 48, 1779–1802.

Jackson, P. (1995), 'Risk Measurement and Capital Requirements for Banks', *Bank of England Quarterly Bulletin*, May, 177–84.

Jackson, P., Maude, D. and Perraudin, W. (1997), 'Bank Capital and Value-at-Risk', *Journal of Derivatives*, 4, 73–90.

Kamijo, K-I. and Tanigawa, T. (1990), 'Stock Price Recognition - A Recurrent Neural Network Approach', *International Joint Conference on Neural Networks*, San Diego, CA, vol.1, 215–21.

Kingdon, J. (1995), 'Criteria for Performance in Gilt Futures Pricing', Chapter 18 in Refenes (ed.) (1995a).

Lo, A.W. (1991), 'Long-Term Memory in Stock Market Prices', *Econometrica*, 59, 1279–1313.

Mills, T.C. (1993), *The Econometric Modelling of Financial Time Series*, Cambridge University Press, Cambridge.

Moody, J. and Utans, J. (1995), 'Architecture Selection Strategies for Neural Networks: Application to Corporate Bond Rating Prediction', Chapter 19 in Refenes (ed.) (1995a).

Nelson, D. (1991), 'Conditional Heteroscedasticity in Asset Returns: A New Approach', *Econometrica*, 59, 347–370.

Peters, E. (1996), *Chaos and Order in the Capital Markets*, John Wiley, New York.

Refenes, A-P. (ed.)(1995a), *Neural Networks in the Capital Markets*, Wiley, Chichester.

Refenes, A-P. (1995b), 'Managing Exchange-Rate Prediction Strategies with Neural Networks', Chapter 14 in Refenes (ed.) (1995a).

Schoenburg, E. (1990), 'Stock Price Prediction Using Neural Networks', *Neurocomputing*, 2, 17–27.

Shiller, R. (1989), 'Fashion, Fads and Bubbles in Financial Markets', in *Market Volatility*, MIT Press, Cambridge, MA.

Tata, F. and Vassilicos, C. (1991), 'Is there Chaos in Economic Time Series? A Study of the Stock and Foreign Exchange Markets', Financial Markets Group Discussion Paper No.121, London School of Economics.

Tirole, J. (1982), 'On the Possibility of Speculation Under Rational Expectations', *Econometrica*, 50, 1163–81.

Tirole, J. (1985), 'Asset Bubbles and Overlapping Generations', *Econometrica*, 53, 1071–1100.

Weigend, A., Huberman, B. and Rumelhart, D. (1992), 'Predicting Sunspots and Exchange Rates with Connectionist Networks', in Casdagli, M. and Eubank, S. (eds.) *Nonlinear Modelling and Forecasting*, vol.12, Addison-Wesley, Redwood City, CA., 395–432.

West, K. (1987), 'A Specification Test for Speculative Bubbles', *Quarterly Journal of Economics*, 102, 553–80.

West, K. (1988), 'Bubbles, Fads and Stock Price Volatility Tests', *Journal of Finance*, 43, 639–59.

White, H. (1988), 'Economic Prediction using Neural Networks: The Case of IBM Daily Stock Returns', *Proc. IEEE International Conference on Neural Networks*, vol.2, IEEE, New York, 451–58.

# Index